Letters from the Hittite Kingdom

SBL

Society of Biblical Literature

Writings from the Ancient World

Theodore J. Lewis, General Editor

Associate Editors

Edward Bleiberg
Billie Jean Collins
F. W. Dobbs-Allsopp
Daniel Fleming
Martti Nissinen
Mark S. Smith
Terry Wilfong

Number 15
Letters from the Hittite Kingdom
by Harry A. Hoffner Jr.
Edited by Gary M. Beckman

LETTERS FROM THE HITTITE KINGDOM

by

Harry A. Hoffner Jr.

edited by

Gary M. Beckman

Society of Biblical Literature
Atlanta

LETTERS FROM THE HITTITE KINGDOM

Library of Congress Cataloging-in-Publication Data

Hoffner, Harry A.
Letters from the Hittite Kingdom / by Harry A. Hoffner, Jr. ; edited by Gary M. Beckman.
p. cm. — (Writings from the ancient world / Society of Biblical Literature ; no. 15)
Includes bibliographical references and indexes.
ISBN 978-1-58983-212-1 (paper binding : alk. paper)
1. Hittites—History--Sources. 2. Hittite language—History—Sources. 3. Hittite letters. 4. Letter-writing—Middle East—History. 5. Middle East—History—Sources. I. Beckman, Gary M. II. Title.
DS66.H645 2009
939'.3--dc22

2009004810

Printed in the United States of America on acid-free, recycled paper conforming to ANSI/NISO Z39.48-1992 (R1997) and ISO 9706:1994 standards for paper permanence.

CONTENTS

Series Editor's Foreword		ix
Chronological Table		xi
Abbreviations		xiii
Explanation of Signs		xvii
1. Introduction		1
1.1	Written Correspondence in the Ancient Near East	2
1.1.1	Primary Function	2
1.1.2	History and Linguistic Media	3
1.1.3	Oral Versus Written Correspondence	4
1.1.4	Materials	6
1.1.5	Personnel	7
1.1.6	The Royal Secretary	20
1.1.7	Languages Used in International Correspondence	21
1.1.8	Types of Letters	22
1.1.9	Literary Conventions: Common Features and Regional Variants	25
1.1.10	Late Bronze Age Epistolary Corpora	34
1.2	Written Correspondence in the Hittite Kingdom	35
1.2.1	The Hittite Letter Corpus	35
1.2.2	Epistolary Coverage in the WAW Series	36
1.2.3	Scope of the Present Corpus	37

1.2.4 Order of Presentation of the Letters in This Corpus 38
1.2.5 Transcriptional Conventions 38
1.2.6 Dating 39
1.2.7 Find Spots 41
1.2.8 Outward Appearance 44
1.2.9 Duplicate Copies of Letters 48
1.2.10 Point of Origin of the King's Letters 49
1.2.11 Hittite Terminology for "Letters" 49
1.2.12 How Letters Were Read 50
1.2.13 Scribes of the Letters 52
1.2.14 Messengers 53
1.2.15 The Literary Form of a Hittite Letter 56
1.2.16 Address Formulas 56
1.2.17 Greeting- and Wish-Formulas 59
1.2.18 Date and Location of Sender 61
1.2.19 The Body of a Letter 61
1.2.20 Subjects Discussed in the Letters 63
1.2.21 Short Summaries of Previous Letters 66
1.2.22 Letters Quoted in Historical Texts 67
1.2.23 Quoted Discourse within Epistolary Material Quoted in Historical Texts 69
1.2.24 The Piggyback Letter 72

2. The Letter Corpus 75

2.1 An Old Hittite Letter (1) 75

2.2 Middle Hittite Letters (2–97) 80
2.2.1 MH Letters Found at Ḫattuša (2–6) 80
2.2.2 MH Letters Found at Tapikka-Maşat Höyük (7–85) 91
2.2.3 MH Letters Found at Šapinuwa-Ortaköy (86–91) 252
2.2.4 MH Letters Found at Šarišša-Kuşaklı (92–93) 262
2.2.5 MH Letters Found at El-Amarna in Egypt (94–97) 268

Series Editor's Foreword

Writings from the Ancient World is designed to provide up-todate, readable English translations of writings recovered from the ancient Near East.

The series is intended to serve the interests of general readers, students, and educators who wish to explore the ancient Near Eastern roots of Western civilization or to compare these earliest written expressions of human thought and activity with writings from other parts of the world. It should also be useful to scholars in the humanities or social sciences who need clear, reliable translations of ancient Near Eastern materials for comparative purposes. Specialists in particular areas of the ancient Near East who need access to texts in the scripts and languages of other areas will also find these translations helpful. Given the wide range of materials translated in the series, different volumes will appeal to different interests. However, these translations make available to all readers of English the world's earliest traditions as well as valuable sources of information on daily life, history, religion, and the like in the preclassical world.

The translators of the various volumes in this series are specialists in the particular languages and have based their work on the original sources and the most recent research. In their translations they attempt to convey as much as possible of the original texts in fluent, current English. In the introductions, notes, glossaries, maps, and chronological tables, they aim to provide the essential information for an appreciation of these ancient documents.

The ancient Near East reached from Egypt to Iran and, for the purposes of our volumes, ranged in time from the invention of writing (by 3000 B.C.E.) to the conquests of Alexander the Great (ca. 330 B.C.E.) . The cultures represented within these limits include especially Egyptian, Sumerian, Babylonian, Assyrian, Hittite, Ugaritic, Aramean, Phoenician, and Israelite. It is hoped that Writings from the Ancient World will eventually produce translations from most of the many different genres attested in these cultures: letters (official and private), myths, diplomatic documents, hymns, law collections, monumental inscriptions, tales, and administrative records, to mention but a few.

Significant funding was made available by the Society of Biblical Literature for the preparation of this volume. In addition, those involved in preparing this volume have received financial and clerical assistance from their respective institutions. Were it not for these expressions of confidence in our work, the arduous tasks of preparation, translation, editing, and publication could not have been accomplished or even undertaken. It is the hope of all who have worked with the Writings from the Ancient World series that our translations will open up new horizons and deepen the humanity of all who read these volumes.

Theodore J. Lewis
The Johns Hopkins University

Chronological Table

ca. 1600–1400	Old Kingdom Labarna I to Muwattalli I	Text 1
ca. 1400–1350	Early New Kingdom (“Middle Kingdom”) Tudḫaliya II Arnuwanda I Tudḫaliya III	Texts 7–93
ca. 1350–1200	New Kingdom Šuppiluliuma I Arnuwanda II Muršili II Muwattalli II Muršili III (Urḫi-Teššub) Ḫattušili III (with Queen Puduḫepa) Tudḫaliya IV Kurunta Arnuwanda III Šuppiluliuma II	Texts 98–126

Abbreviations

1. Bibliographic

AA — *Archäologischer Anzeiger*
ABAW — Abhandlungen der Bayrischen Akademie der Wissenschaften
ABoT — Ankara Arkeoloji Müzesinde bulunan Boğazköy Tabletleri
AfO — *Archiv für Orientforschung*
AHw — W. von Soden, *Akkadisches Handwörterbuch.* Wiesbaden: Harrassowitz, 1959–1981.
AJA — *American Journal of Archaeology*
AnAn — *Anatolia Antiqua*
ANET — J. B. Prichard, *Ancient Near Eastern Texts Relating to the Old Testament.* Princeton: Princeton University Press, 1969.
AnSt — *Anatolian Studies*
AOAT — Alter Orient und Altes Testament
AoF — *Altorientalische Forschungen*
ArAn — *Archivum Anatolicum*
ArOr — *Archiv Orientální*
AT — Alalakh Tablets
BA — *Biblical Archaeologist*
BBVO — Berliner Beiträge zum Vorderen Orient
Belleten — *Türk Tarih Kurumu Belleten*
BiOr — *Bibliotheca Orientalis*
BLMJ — Bible Lands Museum, Jerusalem
BMECCJ — *Bulletin of the Middle Eastern Culture Center in Japan*
BMSAES — *British Museum Studies in Ancient Egypt and Sudan*
BSOAS — *Bulletin of the School of Oriental and African Studies*
BZAW — Beihefte zur Zeitschrift für die alttestamentliche Wissenschaft
CAD — A. L. Oppenheim, I. J. Gelb, Thorkild Jacobsen, Erica Reiner, and Martha T. Roth, eds., *The Assyrian Dictionary of the Oriental Institute of the University of Chicago.* Chicago: The Oriental Institute of the University of Chicago, 1956–2005.

CANE	Jack M. Sasson, ed., *Civilizations of the Ancient Near East*. New York: Scribner's Sons, 1995.
CHD	Hans G. Güterbock, Harry A. Hoffner Jr., and Theo van den Hout, eds., *The Hittite Dictionary of the Oriental Institute of the University of Chicago*. Chicago: The Oriental Institute of the University of Chicago 1980–.
CoS	W. W. Hallo and K. L. Younger, eds., *The Context of Scripture* . 3 vols. Leiden: Brill, 1997, 2000, 2004.
DBH	Dresdner Beiträge zur Hethitologie
DMOA	Documenta et Monumenta Orientis Antiqui
DŠ	Hans G. Güterbock, "The Deeds of Suppiluliuma I as Told by His Son, Muršili II," *JCS* 10: 41–68, 75–98, 107–30.
EA	Text numbers of El-Amarna tablets
GrHL	Harry A. Hoffner Jr. and H. Craig Melchert, *A Grammar of the Hittite Language*. LANE 1. Winona Lake, Ind: Eisenbrauns, 2008.
HANE/M	History of the Ancient Near East/Monographs
Ḫatt	Apology of Ḫattušili III as edited in Goetze 1925
HbOr	Handbuch der Orientalistik
HED	Puhvel 1984–
HHCTO	Ünal 1998
HKM	Alp 1991b
HS	*Historische Sprachforschung*
HSM	Harvard Semitic Monographs
HW	Johannes Friedrich, *Hethitisches Wörterbuch*. Heidelberg: Winter, 1957–1966.
HW^2	Johannes Friedrich and Annelies Kammenhuber, *Hethitisches Wörterbuch*. 2., völlig neubearb. Aufl. auf d. Grundlage d. ed. hethit. Texte. Heidelberg: Winter, 1975–.
IBoT 1–4	Istanbul Arkeoloji Müzelerinde bulunan Boğazköy Tabletleri(nden Seçme Metinler) — Istanbul 1944, 1947, 1954, Ankara 1988
IBS	Innbrucker Beiträge zur Sprachwissenschaft – Innsbruck
IF	*Indogermanische Forschungen*
IOS	Israel Oriental Studies
IM	*Istanbuler Mitteilungen*
JANER	*Journal of Ancient Near Eastern Religions*
JAOS	*Journal of the American Oriental Society*
JCS	*Journal of Cuneiform Studies*
JEA	*Journal of Egyptian Archaeology*
JESHO	*Journal of the Economic and Social History of the Orient*

JIES	*Journal of Indo-European Studies*
JKF	*Jahrbuch für kleinasiatische Forschungen*
JNES	*Journal of Near Eastern Studies*
KBo	Keilschrifttexte aus Boghazköi
Konk.	Konkordanz der hethitischen Keilschrifttafeln. Online: http://www.hethport.uni-wuerzburg.de/hetkonk/
KUB	Keilschrifturkunden aus Boghazköi
KuT	Text numbers from excavations at Kuşaklı
L.	L. followed by a number refers to the hieroglyphic sign according to the numbering in Laroche 1960a
LAPO	Littératures Anciennes du Proche-Orient
Lg	*Language*
MDOG	*Mitteilungen der Deutschen Orientgesellschaft zu Berlin*
MIO	*Mitteilungen des Instituts für Orientforschung*
MVAeG	*Mitteilungen der Vorderasiatisch-Aegyptischen Gesellschaft*
NEA	*Near Eastern Archaeology*
OA	*Oriens Antiquus*
OIS	Oriental Institute Seminars
OLZ	*Orientalistische Literaturzeitung*
Or NS	*Orientalia Nova Series*
PAPS	*Proceedings of the American Philosophical Society*
PIHANS	Publications de l'institut historique et archéologique néerlandais de Stamboul
RA	*Revue d'Assyriologie et d'Archéologie Orientale*
RAnt	*Res Antiquae*
RHA	*Revue hittite et asianique*
RHR	*Revue de l'histoire des religions*
RLA	*Reallexikon der Assyriologie*
RSO	*Rivista degli Studi Orientali*
SAA	State Archives of Assyria
SCO	*Studi Classici e Orientali*
SDIOP	Studia et Documenta ad Iura Orientis Antiqui Pertinentia
SMEA	*Studi Micenei ed Egeo-Anatolici*
StBoT	Studien zu den Boğazköy-Texten
StMed	Studia Mediterranea
THeth	Texte der Hethiter
TPS	Transactions of the Philological Society
TTKY	Türk Tarih Kurumu Yayınları
TUAT	Texte aus der Umwelt des Alten Testaments
TVOA	Testi del Vicino Oriente antico
UF	*Ugarit-Forschungen*

VBoT	A. Götze, *Verstreute Boghazköi-Texte*. Marburg, 1930.
WAW	Writings from the Ancient World
WO	*Die Welt des Orients*
ZA	*Zeitschrift für Assyriologie und verwandte Gebiete*
ZABR	*Zeitschrift für Altorientalische und Biblische Rechtsgeschichte*
ZvS	*Zeitschrift für vergleichende Sprachforschung*

2. General

adj.	adjective
adv.	adverb
acc.	accusative
cf.	compare
col.	column
coll.	collated, collation
dat.	dative
DN	divine name
dupl.	duplicate
ed.	edited by, edition
e.g.	for example
eras.	erasure
esp.	especially
etc.	et cetera
f	female personal name
ff.	and following
frag.	fragment
gen.	genitive
GN	geographical name
Hitt.	Hittite
i.e.	that is (id est)
imv.	imperative
inst.	instrumental
km	kilometer(s)
l. e.	left edge
loc.	locative
m	male personal name
MH	Middle Hittite
MS	Middle Hittite script
Mşt.	Maşat tablet
NH	New Hittite
n.	note
no.	number
nom.	nominative
NS	New Hittite script
obv.	obverse
OH	Old Hittite
OS	Old Hitite script
p(p).	page(s)
pl.	plural
PN	personal name
pres.	present
pret.	preterite
pron.	pronoun
PS	postscript
rt.	right(hand)
q.v.	which see
rev.	reverse
sg.	singular
Sum.	Sumerian
s.v.	under the word (sub voce)

Notations such as L 18 b-c/5 in the identification of tablet find spots refer to quadrants on the official excavator's map of the site.

Explanation of Signs

< >	Encloses signs accidentally omitted by the scribe
[ ]	Encloses signs obliterated by damage to the tablet
⸢ ⸣	Encloses partly broken signs
( )	In translation encloses words not in the Hittite but needed in English
!	Superscripted exclamation point marks emended signs
*	Indicates a collated sign
†	Affixed to the HKM numbers of Maşat tablets for which I have personal photos
:	When a colon occurs directly prefixed (with no space intervening) to a transliterated or transcribed Hittite of Luwian word (see, e.g., text 98 [introduction] and texts 84:12; 99:5; and 101:24, 41, 62), it stands for either a single or a pair of marker wedges, which the scribe used to call attention to something unusual about the word, often (but not always) its foreign origin
/	Indicates the end of the line in multi-line transcriptions of Hittite texts outside of the editions
×	SI×SÁ indicates a SÁ sign inscribed within a SI sign
x	In transcriptions x indicates an illegible sign
⸗	Marks clitic boundaries
a-pé-ez-za	Transliterated characters with dashed underlining indicate text written over an erasure (see text 114, line 8, for an example)

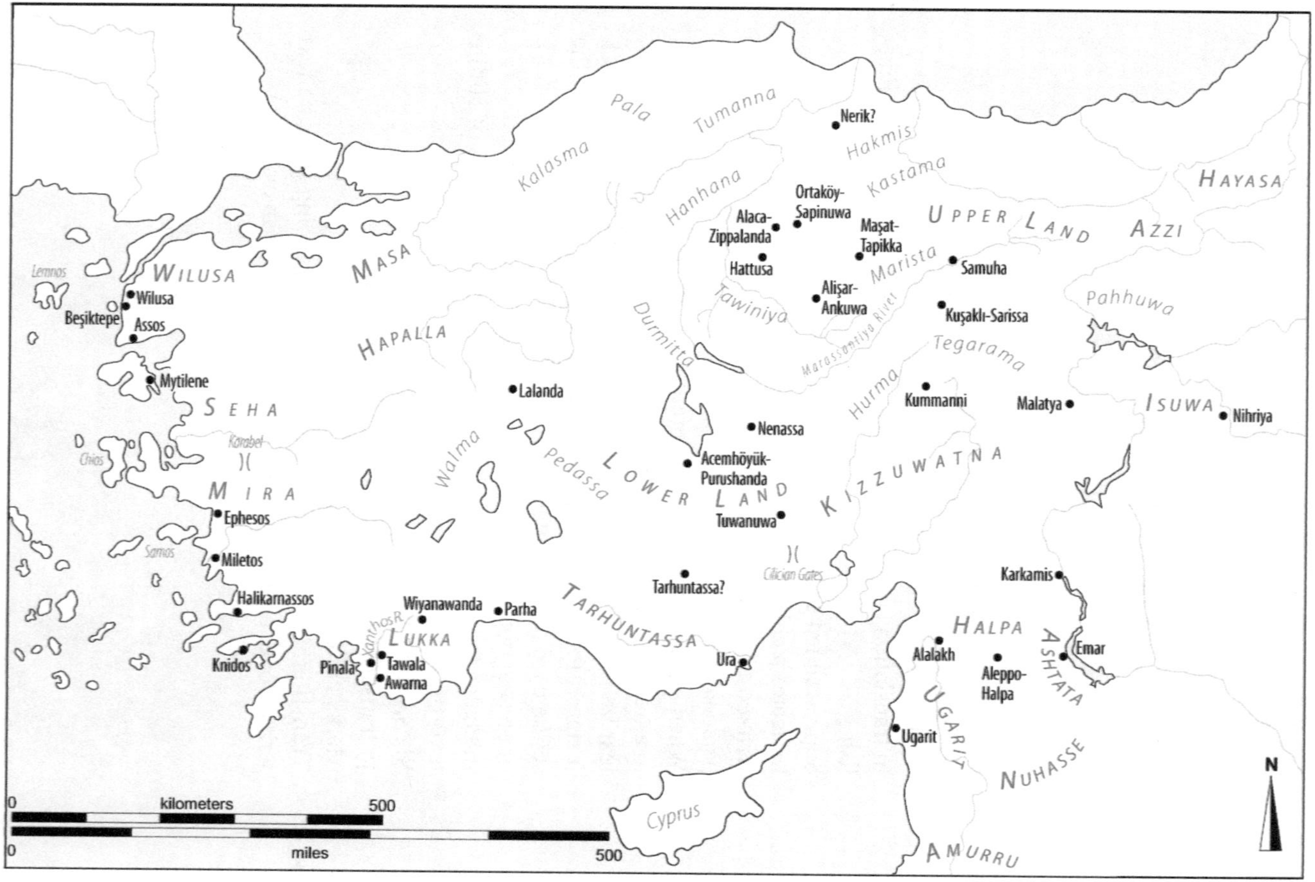

Map of the Hittite Empire. Courtesy of Billie Jean Collins.

1. Introduction

In an age featuring instant communication inexpensively via email and cell phone with people near and far, it is perhaps not immediately comprehensible how much more difficult it was in ancient times to communicate at a distance. Yet such communication was highly prized, as evidenced not only from the abundance of ancient letters found in excavated sites around the Near East, but also from the urgent requests found in ancient documents that a friend or colleague in a distant place keep up regular communication.

Although literacy was by no means as common in those days as it is today, people regularly wrote letters or at least had them written. The texts recovered from the Hittite capital city, Ḫattuša, as well as from the three provincial centers that have yielded an appreciable number of tablets (Tapikka [Maşat Höyük], Šapinuwa [Ortaköy near Çorum], and Šariššа [Kuşaklı]), represent official correspondence carried on in the course of administrating the business of the king. Unfortunately, what private, unofficial letter writing went on has left no examples.

Many people wrote letters or had someone write for them. It is interesting to reflect that of all the common human activities that the ancient Hittites assumed to be pursued also by their gods, writing letters was not one of them.[1] No Hittite mythological narrative records a god or goddess writing a letter. Of course, the equivalent practice of sending an oral message by a messenger is indeed attested. Each god or goddess of any stature had his or her own "vizier" (^{LÚ}SUKKAL), who was available to take his master's (or mistress's) words to a distant target person, and judging from the verbatim repetition of the message at the destination, the mythographers were familiar with and therefore assumed that messengers could memorize messages and repeat them verbatim days later.[2]

1. I am not competent to describe the situation in this regard in ancient Egypt or Mesopotamia. But it is interesting to note that after a fashion deities used written letters to communicate with kings or temple administrators (see §1.1.1).

2. Is it a mere coincidence that only oral communication was practiced by the Hittite

It will be the purpose of this book to acquaint the wider public to the rich epistolary documentation of the ancient Hittite kingdom. The approach will be as follows. First, the subject of letter writing will be explored as it manifests itself in all the major kingdoms of the ancient Near East (Egypt, Syro-Palestine, Anatolia, Assyria, and Babylonia). Secondly, the practice of writing, sending, receiving, and storing of letters in the Hittite kingdom itself will be outlined. This will provide the necessary background for the understanding of the present letter corpus, which forms the third major division.

1.1. Written Correspondence in the Ancient Near East

1.1.1. Primary Function

An epistolary document has been defined as "a written document effecting communication between two or more persons who cannot communicate orally" (Pardee and Sperling 1982, 2). And while circumstances (such as required "social distance") may prevent certain persons from obtaining an audience with their correspondent even within the same city (e.g., a commoner directing a petition to an exalted personage such as a king or governor), most situations required written communication because of the separation of the parties by great distances.

The greatest distances of all were the *metaphysical* ones that separated humans from deities[3] or the living from the deceased. Normally, communication across these boundaries was accomplished through divination. But there is also evidence for a limited use of letters.

---

gods? When we turn our attention to another ancient and familiar literary source, the Hebrew Bible, we find that there too God (i.e., Yahweh) sends his messages orally by means of heavenly messengers called "angels" (actually, the Hebrew and Greek words translated "angel" literally mean "messenger"). And in the very few instances when the "finger of God" writes a short message—the writing of the Decalogue on Mt. Sinai, and the writing of the fate decreed upon Babylonia: *menē teqēl u-pharsîn* "'numbered,' 'weighed,' and 'divided'" in the book of Daniel (5:25), it is because it is a statement of an irrevocable decree. The messages of Yahweh to his people via his prophets did eventually find their way into written form. However, this written form of the oracles was not a means of synchronic communication, but for preservation (i.e., "diachronic" communication). In Hittite texts, the only approximation of evidence for deities writing is also in connection with fate. For the so-called Fate Deities, whose name is ^{d}Gulšeš, are said to "write" (*gulš-*) the fates of mortals.

3. Of course, the distance between humans and deities can also be described as a kind of "social distance."

Letters *from* a god were a means by which a prophet could communicate the words revealed to him in a vision to the ultimate intended receiver, in this case the king (see §1.1.8.3). Mesopotamian letters *to* a god, also called "letter-prayers," were literary compositions studied by scribes; see Hallo 1968; Michalowski 1993, 4–5; Foster 1993, 156–57 (translations of two Old Babylonian letter-prayers), and Hallo in *CANE* 3, 1875–80 (a sample letter-prayer to the god Enki is translated on p. 1876). There is some evidence that letter-prayers were left before the cult statue in a temple. How the gods answered is less certain. One possible method was by "return mail," exemplified by a small group of Old Babylonian Akkadian letters from the goddess Ishtar to the head administrator of her temple in the city of Nerebtum (Ellis 1987). It is not known if this is only a local tradition or a survival of a more general practice.

Letters to a deceased person are attested in Egypt from the Old Kingdom (Sixth Dynasty) to the New Kingdom (see Guilmot 1966; and Wente 1990, 210), while letters to the gods were a more recent development there (see Wente 1990, 210). The letters to the dead were written on bowls of offerings and placed in the tomb. As Lesko notes (*CANE* 3, 1765), "they obviously presuppose a much more common practice that would generally have involved oral or internalized pleas." In one such letter the deceased is asked to punish whatever dead man or woman is distressing the petitioner by doing an injury to her daughter. Such letters promise offerings to the deceased and ask the deceased to intercede on the living correspondent's behalf with various deities. Many such letters are addressed by widowed men or women to their deceased spouses, referring to the husband as "your brother" and the wife as "your sister." Hittite literature contains no composition analogous to either the letters to a god or to a deceased person.

1.1.2. History and Linguistic Media

The exchange of letters on clay tablets and in cuneiform script is attested from the last half of the third millennium until the end of the cuneiform tradition early in the Common Era. This correspondence was carried on in several languages: Sumerian, Akkadian, Ugaritic, Hittite, and Hurrian. In Egypt, correspondence was conducted in all periods of the ancient Egyptian language: Old Egyptian, Middle Egyptian, Late Egyptian, Demotic, and Coptic, as well as in the Aramaic language during the period of Persian rule. In first-millennium Syro-Palestine, letters were sent on ostraca in the Hebrew language.

Aside from the bulk of the surviving examples, which afforded a practical means of communication between persons at a distance, we can mention a much smaller number of letters sent either by or to a deity, others sent to a deceased person, and literary letters used in the training of scribes (see further in §1.1.5.1.7).

1.1.3. Oral Versus Written Correspondence

1.1.3.1. Messenger Gives Oral Gist with No Literacy Required

When sending communications by means of a messenger, there is always the option of sending the message orally. The messenger, depending on the accuracy of his memory, can either deliver it almost verbatim, or only the essential parts. Such a method does not require literacy on the part of either the sender, the recipient, or the messenger. This procedure may have been employed when absolute accuracy was not an issue. Greetings from one family member to another and news items from friends could be delivered in this way, as could requests that were not detailed. See, for example, text 26: 20–21, where the sender Šanda asks the recipient Uzzū to relay his greetings to his supervisor Pulli, and text 69: 3–7, where the addressee is asked to read the sender's greeting aloud to another colleague.

1.1.3.2. When Literacy Was Required

When the message to be conveyed was more detailed or complicated, or when great issues of state were involved, writing was absolutely essential. If the sender was literate, he could either write the message himself, or at least proofread it, once a scribe at his end had written it for him. The messenger could be either literate or not, but at the receiving end either the addressee had to be literate, or he had to employ the services of a literate person to read the letter aloud to him.

1.1.3.3. The Role of Literacy

In ancient times only a minority of the population was literate—mostly, but not by any means exclusively, scribes.[4] Beaulieu writes about the Neo-Babylonian period in Mesopotamia:

4. On literacy in the ancient Near East see Vanstiphout in *CANE* 3, 2181–96 and the literature cited by him on p. 2196. Earlier estimates that in ancient Egypt literate persons comprised only 1 to 5 percent of the population may prove to be too low (Lesko 2001). But it is nonetheless clear that only a small portion of the population could, or needed to, read.

> Cuneiform writing was the preserve of a small caste of professionals. In a letter to his employer the Assyrian king Esarhaddon, the Babylonian scholar Ašaredu the Younger alludes to the restricted diffusion of writing with a touch of wit when he warns him that 'the scribal craft is not heard about in the market place' .... Even kings were rarely literate beyond limited training in reading and writing. Among late Mesopotamian rulers, only the Assyrian king Ashurbanipal and the Babylonian king Nabonidus laid claim to advanced literacy and learning. (2007, 473)

When written communications were sent to the king or queen or other high officials, it was likely that scribes were needed at the receiving end, if not also at the sending one. But one cannot assume illiteracy on the part of high officials. Charpin notes that "[s]ome administrators but also generals were able to read, and, if necessary, to write. Certain letters of poor quality may have been written by their senders without the mediation of a scribe" (2007, 401–2). On their seals some of them bore two titles, one of which was "scribe." And for anyone to imply that they were too poorly educated to be able to read was a genuine affront, to which they took outspoken umbrage (see "How Letters Were Read" in §1.2.12).

1.1.3.4. When an Oral Message Was Preferred

Given the preciseness of writing, why would someone prefer to convey his message orally? One reason that is well attested in the Old Babylonian Mari correspondence is to keep the content secure against interception (Charpin 2007, 411–12). Zimri-Līm's sister wrote to him, revealing the existence of a plot at the court of her husband Sumu-dabi, the Benjaminite king of Samanum, which she hoped to recount in detail at a meeting with Zimri-Līm in person. Only if this could not be arranged, or because the king might consider the situation too urgent for this, would she put the details in writing in a subsequent letter.

Oral messages had the disadvantage that sometimes they were inaccurate or even false. If he did not bring with him a letter of accreditation from the sender of the oral message, there had to be ways to test such a messenger. Šamši-Addu explains the tests that convinced him to trust the message one such envoy brought: "He gave me as evidence a *ḫullum*-ring I had given to the messenger Mutušu. Furthermore, Etellini, a colleague of Mutušu's, was ill at Arrapḫa: he spoke of this man's illness. He gave me these two proofs, and so I had trust in his words" (Charpin 2007, 413).

1.1.4. Materials

1.1.4.1. What Was Written Upon

Letters could be written on various kinds of material, depending upon the demands of the official script and writing system. In lands where the cuneiform system was virtually exclusive, such as was the case during long periods in Mesopotamia, Syria, and Anatolia, the medium of writing was either a clay tablet or (for monumental inscriptions) stone. But even here there is evidence for a parallel system of writing on wax-covered writing boards, whether in the cuneiform script or some other script.[5] In ancient Egypt the materials for writing also depended on the nature and purpose of the written text. Monumental inscriptions were painted on stone in hieroglyphs, while literary and archival materials were written with ink on papyrus or on clay ostraca. In Syria and Palestine during the Bronze Age most non-monumental writing was performed in cuneiform on clay tablets. But, beginning in this period and increasingly during the following Iron Age, it was inked upon ostraca and leather scrolls. Iron Age monumental inscriptions were carved in stone with the local alphabetic script.

In the case of letters, cuneiform script on clay tablets was preferred in the northern regions, and inked text on papyrus or ostraca in Egypt.

Letters almost never exceeded the size of a single tablet (see below in §1.2.8). Reluctance to use more than one tablet encouraged brevity. Charpin quotes a Mari letter in which the sender justifies his brevity on just such grounds (2007, 401).

1.1.4.2. Durability Unnecessary

Communication in written form was often preferred to using an oral message sent by a trusted messenger, especially if accuracy was needed or the recipient needed something in writing with an authenticating seal for legal reasons (see below on EA 32 = *VBoT* 2 [text 94]). But unlike some other kinds of written documents that had enduring value to the extent that they needed to be kept for generations—such as loan and debt vouchers, promissory notes, contracts, deeds, land grants, and tax receipts (or documents declaring tax exemption) on the private level, and treaties and edicts on the palace or municipal level—there was normally no value in retaining ordinary letters for more than a brief period. For this reason they are among the few text genres that were not kept in multiple copies in the palace archives. This is also why they often turn up reused by the ancients themselves as archeo-

5. See Güterbock 1939; Bossert 1952; Archi 1973; and Symington 1991.

logical "fill," and why letters found in a given archeological stratum are all from the final occupation period. The more than 2,500 Old Babylonian letters found at Mari covered a span of twenty-five years (Charpin 2007, 400).

1.1.5. Personnel

1.1.5.1. Scribes (see also below in §1.2.13)

Scribal training was not limited to low-level bureaucrats. Higher officials and members of the extended royal family often identified themselves by titles such as "Chief Wood-Scribe" when they functioned as witnesses to international treaties. Three of the witnesses to the treaty between Tudḫaliya IV and Kurunt(iy)a, king of Tarḫuntašša, were: (1) Šaḫurunuwa, Chief Wood-Scribe; (2) Walwa-ziti, Chief of the Scribes; and (3) Kammaliya, Chief Scribe of the Kitchen Personnel. Over 200 names of persons described as scribes occur to date in Hittite written sources, both cuneiform and hieroglyphic. Of these 200+ names, only one, Lariya, identifies a female scribe (see Herbordt 2005, 104, no. 203). Many fewer names of writing-board scribes (or "wood-scribes") exist than of clay-tablet scribes. Names of the earliest datable Hittite scribes (OH from the reign of Telipinu) are given by van den Hout forthcoming. A list of the names of scribes at Tapikka (Maşat Höyük) is given by Beckman (1995a, 33).

1.1.5.1.1. Family or Social Background. Within the Hittite orbit we may determine as "scribes" those persons bearing the cuneiform title ^{LÚ}DUB.SAR(.GIŠ), or the hieroglyphic one SCRIBA (L. 326),[6] or whose names appear in colophons following the word ŠU ("hand[writing] of"), or who are described in such colophons as "writing" (Akkadogram *IŠṬUR*, Sumerogram IN.SAR, Hittite *aniya-*; van den Hout forthcoming). Of the family and social background of scribes in Mesopotamia, Pearce writes: "Scribes and scholars belonged to the social elite.... Students in the scribal school were male children of members of the upper strata of society. Their fathers were well-to-do merchants, priests, governors, ambassadors, kings, and occasionally scribes" (*CANE* 4, 2265). Was this also true in Ḫatti? We cannot make a blanket statement that no one from a middle- or lower-class family ever rose to scribal status, but it is clear that many members of the elite level of Hittite society employed the title "scribe" (sometimes along with other titles) on

6. Although in cuneiform the term for clay-tablet scribe (^{LÚ}DUB.SAR) is distinguished from writing-board scribe (^{LÚ}DUB.SAR.GIŠ), the hieroglyphic term SCRIBA makes no such differentiation (see van den Hout forthcoming).

their seal impressions (Herbordt 2005). For example, Prince (REX.FILIUS) Šaušga-runtiya bears the title MAGNUS.SCRIBA "Chief Scribe" (Herbordt 2005, 376), and Prince (REX.FILIUS) Arma-nani the title SCRIBA "Scribe." Mizri-muwa (who is not called REX.FILIUS "Prince") nonetheless has two titles: SCRIBA "Scribe" and MAGNUS.PASTOR "Chief Herdsman." It stands to reason that their parents arranged for them to have scribal training as part of their preparation for careers in government, even though in many of these cases the scribal craft was by no means the limit of their eventual offices.

1.1.5.1.2. Training. We know next to nothing of the training of Hittite scribes. There is some indication that their workplace in Ḫattuša (called by the Sumerogram É GIŠ.KIN.TI, Akk. *bīt kiškatti*) may also have served as a place of instruction. A tablet (KBo 19.28) listing personnel active in this workshop was found in the building just south of the Great Temple (Temple I) in the Lower City (called in German the Südareal). But we cannot be sure that its find spot indicates that this area was itself the site of such a workshop. Among the personnel are nineteen clay-tablet scribes and thirty-three writing-board scribes, out of a total of 205 workers in various trades. Colophons to two tablets (KUB 40.2 + KUB 13.9 and KBo 12.41) mention that their scribes were students (GÁB.ZU.ZU) of two men (Zuwā and Mera-muwa), who bear the title EN GIŠ.KIN.TI "Master of the Craft." It is possible that this was a title for instructors in the workshops. On this see Güterbock 1975, 131–32 and van den Hout forthcoming.

1.1.5.1.3. Materials. The materials of a scribe depended upon whether he was a "writing-board scribe" (^{LÚ}DUB.SAR.GIŠ) or a "clay-tablet scribe" (^{LÚ}DUB.SAR); see below "Specialization and Grades" in §1.1.5.1.5. The former required a hinged board covered with wax and a stylus, perhaps a metal one (see Pearce in *CANE* 4, 2266), while the latter required a freshly prepared clay tablet and a reed stylus. The GI É.DUB.BA "tablet stylus" requested by the royal scribe Tarḫunmiya as he travels with the king (HKM 71 [text 73]) was undoubtedly a reed one, since we have clay tablets inscribed by him, and there is no evidence for Hittite scribes serving both as writing-board scribes and clay-tablet scribes.

1.1.5.1.4. Activities. The main function and activity of a scribe was creating and copying written texts. Texts of all types were created on a daily basis. But those of enduring value had to be stored for easy retrieval. Of the various locations in the Hittite capital where significant collections of tablets were found—several on the acropolis, one in the House on the Slope, and a large one in the storage rooms of the main temple in the Lower City—one can see some patterns as to what kinds of texts were kept where (see van den

Hout 2006, 2007a). In all these locations the scribes kept the tablets in a certain order on wooden shelves, sometimes with small clay labels associated with them. The labels may have served also to mark the position of a tablet that was temporarily removed from its spot on the shelf. Furthermore, shelf lists of storage rooms were created, which listed tablets by title in their order on the shelves.

Scribes kept check on older tablets when they had occasion to consult them. If a tablet was determined to be in poor condition, it could be copied over afresh. In this way the tablet collections acquired copies of Old Hittite tablets in the handwriting of the later periods.

Some tablets had to be read aloud. The colophon of a tablet containing a royal prayer to the god Telipinu contains the following: DUB.1.*PU QATI* LÚDUB.SAR=*za* GIM-*an* / *ANA* LUGAL *šer PANI* d*Telipinu* / UD.KAM-*tili arkuwar eššai* "One tablet, complete: When the scribe on the king's behalf makes the prayer-plea daily before (the statue of) the god Telipinu" KUB 24.1 iv 19–21. It is unknown if the king chose a particularly high-ranking scribe—maybe even a member of the royal family—to perform this task, by virtue of his acting as a stand-in for the king. This is the opinion of Pearce in *CANE* 4, 2266. And, of course, if the recipient of a letter was himself illiterate, he would require someone with this ability—often a scribe—to read it aloud to him (see below in §1.2.12).

In one case, a man named Mittanna-muwa, who was "Chief Scribe" (GAL DUB.SAR) during the reign of Muršili II, was commissioned to treat the illness of the prince who in later years became King Ḫattušili III. After he became king, Ḫattušili rewarded Mittanna-muwa and his sons handsomely. Perhaps Mittanna-muwa's knowledge of healing came from reading the various recipes for healing contained in ritual tablets in his collection. The ancient composition that tells his story is CTH 87 (KBo 4.12), available in a German translation in Goetze 1925, 41–45.

1.1.5.1.5. Specialization and Grades. In ancient Mesopotamia there was a special curriculum for the training of scribes in letter writing. Scribes recopied Sumerian letters, the originals of which dated from the Ur III period, and Akkadian letters of all types.

Although in some ancient societies there were specific terms for scribes trained for particular writing duties, in Hittite texts there are only two terms: the regular "scribe" (Sumerian DUB.SAR) and the so-called "wood-scribe" (DUB.SAR.GIŠ), who wrote on wax-covered writing boards. And since our preserved examples of Hittite letters are all clay tablets, our concern here is only with the former type of scribe. It is claimed that no Hittite scribe operated in both specialties (so van den Hout 2002). It is uncertain if a third specialization—inscribing metal tablets—existed. Ḫalwa-ziti, who is identified as the scribe in the colophon to the Bronze Tablet (Otten 1988, 28–29), may have only prepared the text on another medium preparatory to the actual incising of the metal surface by another type of craftsman (stone mason, smith, or seal carver).

Scribes operated in various spheres and could have titles that reflected those spheres of activity: "Military Wood-Scribe" (LÚDUB.SAR.GIŠ KARAŠ), "Storeroom Scribe" (LÚDUB.SAR GIŠ*tuppaš*), and "Scribe of the Stable Area" (hieroglyphic ASINUS_{2A}.DOMUS.SCRIBA).

In both specializations there existed a hierarchy of ranks, at the top of which was the "Chief (GAL or UGULA) of the ...-Scribes." At the bottom were the novice scribes (title: LÚDUB.SAR.TUR, status: (LÚ)GÁB.ZU.ZU). Various intermediate grades may also have existed. An indirect index of these grades is given in the use of generational terms of family relationship (parental, filial, sibling) when addressing a fellow scribe of either superior, inferior, or equal rank ("dear father" [*ABU* DÙG.GA = *YA*], "dear son" [DUMU.DÙG.GA = *YA*], "dear brother" [ŠEŠ.DÙG.GA = *YA*]). It stands to reason that persons rose through the ranks to eventually hold the top rank, but within the Hittite textual evidence we cannot yet actually trace any one historical incumbent through all the levels. Senior rank is also indicated when in a colophon it is written that the scribe inscribed the tablet under the supervision of a second scribe, the latter obviously his senior and his mentor.

1.1.5.1.6. Use in Correspondence. Letters were written in one of two ways: either dictated by the author, or drafted by his scribe. Longer royal letters, especially those for international diplomatic correspondence, were probably always first dictated as notes to a scribe, who then composed the full letter in the appropriate form and style. Such drafts served as skeletons for the definitive text composed by the scribe, who was actually responsible for the drafting. Writing not from dictation but from instructions had several advantages: it eliminated the need to write quickly and allowed the selection of a tablet of a size appropriate to the length of the message.

Once the tablet was inscribed, the scribe would read it over to the author, making whatever corrections were necessary, and then enclose it in an envelope (see §1.2.8.3), which he would seal with the sender's seal. The letter was then ready to be sent to its addressee.

Scribes who wrote out documents of more lasting value—such as legal documents, treaties, land grant texts, royal prayers, myths, and rituals—regularly "signed" their texts in what is called a "colophon" at the end of the document. In the colophon the scribe identified the text by a name, indicated if the composition stretched over more than one tablet, whether it was completed by the present tablet, and sometimes whether or not it was dictated by the king. The scribe might also indicate that the document in question had been checked against an archetype, if it was a recopying of an older tablet. If he had a senior scribal supervisor, the scribe might name this person and his rank (e.g., "under the supervision of PN, Chief of the Scribes"). And finally, he would write his own name, often preceded by the word "hand of…," and sometimes accompanied by his rank or grade (e.g., DUB.SAR TUR "junior scribe"). On the other hand, colophons were not used in letters, and unless the scribe happened to add a personal letter of his own (a "piggyback" letter), he left no evidence of his identity.

Scribes who served to write letters for the king traveled with him. Those who wrote international correspondence had to be capable of translating the king's message into Akkadian, which was the *lingua franca* of international diplomatic correspondence during the Hittite era.

1.1.5.1.7. Training: Model Letters. Scribes were trained to write letters according to an accepted form, in terms of the shape of the document, the order of elements, and the correct wording. There have survived numerous examples of what are called "model letters," that is, non-functional or fictitious letters used in the scribal curriculum. For Egyptian examples, see J. Allen's translations in *CoS* 3.2–5:9–17. For Ugaritic examples, see Pardee's translations of two "practice letters" in *CoS* 3.41–42:115. A possible example of such a Sumerian model letter is that translated by Hallo in *CoS* 3.130:295. Beaulieu (2007, 478) mentions a "fictitious letter of the Old Babylonian king Samsu-iluna, copied in late Babylonian schools."

Since these "model letters" (or "practice letters") look just like real letters and often use existing functioning letters as their basis, it is sometimes impossible to determine if a given example is in fact such a practice tablet (see Wente 1990, 1–2). Wente himself judges several letters in his corpus to be model letters by using historical criteria (a single letter addressed to two persons known not to have lived at the same time) or by the material on which the letter occurs (letter to a pharaoh written on an ostracon!). Other clues for identifying model letters are the existence of multiple copies of the same letter, or the existence on the same papyrus of multiple letters, as is the case with some Egyptian examples (see J. Allen in *CoS* 3.9). The use of multiple letters on the same clay tablet in the Hittite corpus is not comparable and is no indication of the status of these as scribal practice letters. See further below on the piggyback letter (§1.2.24), and the *Sammeltafel* (§1.2.9).

Of this practice in ancient Mesopotamia Michalowski writes:

> The archival letters were used in everyday transactions. Since the scribes had to learn how to compose such texts, practice letters quickly gave birth

> to the literary epistle. This was to happen time and again in literary history; indeed, it is impossible to distinguish between "real" and "imaginary" letters. This is true for Sumerian "literary" letters as well as for classical Greek or Renaissance epistles ... As early as the Old Babylonian period, letters of Ur III scribes and officials from Nippur and Ur were copied and recopied by students as writing and rhetorical exercises ... In addition, revised versions of almost thirty letters between Ur III kings and their high military officers were studied in the schools, as were a few letters from the early rulers of Isin. Not a single Ur III original of this correspondence has survived, and if these texts are copies of authentic texts, then one has to assume that the orthography of the letters had been revised to conform with later standards, as there are no surviving traces of earlier writing habits. Although it is possible that all of these texts were fictitious, it is more probable that *the core of this royal correspondence was based on actual archival texts, but revised*, and that other texts of the same type were written long after the death of the kings of Ur ... We have no way of unraveling the levels of authenticity, and one could argue that any attempt to do so would be technically impossible, as well as theoretically futile (1993, 4, italics mine).

Lucas (1979, 311) writes about Mesopotamian school tablets:

> Common to practically every find are the scattered, frequently-broken remnants of baked clay tablets inscribed with word lists for study and practice writing. A specimen typically will bear on one side a short model sentence (or in some cases a longer literary passage) prepared by a teacher. A more or less crude facsimile will appear on the obverse side, strongly suggestive of some young schoolboy's struggle to master the intricacies of cuneiform writing. The calligraphy varies greatly, from the accomplished hand of an experienced writer to copywork recording a novice's first faltering application of wedged stylus to clay. Besides simple word lists and elementary syllabic exercises, school tablets recovered to date bear geographical place-name lists, syllabaries, mathematical tablets, lists of personal names, magical formulae and religious incantations, collections of wisdom sayings or proverbs, compendia of technical terminology pertaining to various trades and professional specialties, maps, model business contracts, extracts from literary works—in short, a fair representation of all the diverse subjects taught in school.

The only example known to me of a practice letter in the Hittite archives is text 110 (KBo 13.62).[7]

---

7. Giulia Torri (personal communication, August 10, 2008) suggested to me that text 110 (KBo 13.62) was "a kind of school tablet," since it contains a colophon, which real

1.1.5.2. Messengers and Letter Carriers (see also below in §1.2.14)

1.1.5.2.1. Private Messengers and Letter Carriers. In the case of written communications between private individuals in ancient Egypt, Wente observes:

> The external address almost never indicates the place to which a letter was to be sent. In the case of private letters, such an omission, especially when the addressee was not a well-known personality, argues against the existence of a regular postal service for the transmission of private letters. … [M]ost private letters were carried by friends, relatives, or subordinates of the writer, or anyone who happened to be journeying in the direction of the recipient. If there were no professional letter carriers to handle private correspondences, it appears rather unlikely that there were professional village scribes making a living writing letters for illiterate clients. It would seem more likely that when an illiterate person wished to have a letter written, he would seek the services of some family member or acquaintance who knew how to write. At Deir el-Medina, where the degree of literacy was higher than average, the scribes who performed such a role for illiterate inhabitants of the village, were government employees and thus not comparable to the self-employed village scribe whose existence in pharaonic times has been postulated. (1990, 8–9)
>
> As mentioned above, private letters were not transmitted through any sort of organized postal system. The letters themselves indicate that they were carried either by agents, retainers, relatives, or acquaintances of the writer, or by travelers who happened to be going in the right direction …. For the transmission of official letters in the Old Kingdom, some sort of rudimentary postal system may have been developed, one in which the messenger was also empowered to represent the sender in a manner beyond that of a simple postman. At that time temples, unless exempted by royal decree, were required to provide support for these government agents who carried official letters. In the Middle Kingdom these messengers, at least on occasion, served as simple letter carriers. (1990, 10)

---

letters do not have. I independently concluded that the obverse contains the teacher's model text, which was derived from a functional letter. For other speculations about school tablet examples among Hittite texts, see Hoffner 1977b, 79 and 1977a (following Jakob-Rost, on KUB 46.34); and van den Hout 1991, 201 (on a Tiššaruli text). A different type of "school tablet" from Boğazköy is KUB 37.1, about which Güterbock commented: "In KUB XXXVII, finally, Köcher publishes the Akkadian literary texts from the campaigns of 1931–39, which supplement the material known so far (mainly in KBo I and KUB IV) considerably. Nr. 1 is the first 'school tablet' known from Boğazkoy: an Akkadian medical text with Hittite and Luwian glosses, analysed by Köcher himself in *Archiv für Orientforschung* XVI, 47 ff." (1956a, 302).

Letter carriers, or couriers (Akkadian *lāsimu,* Sumerian lú.kaš$_4$), when a message was sent over a long distance, functioned in relays, since a single runner would need to stop and rest at intervals, delaying the delivery (see Charpin 2007, 407).

1.1.5.2.2. Official Envoy-Messengers and Letter Carriers. But when the communications are international and involve heads of state, the "messenger" is something more august.[8] In Hittite texts such a functionary is designated either by the native Hittite term *ḫalugatalla-* or by one of two logograms: DUMU KIN (= Akk. *mār šipri*) or LÚ *ṬĒMI* (Akk. *awīl ṭēmi*). About such messengers (Akkadian *mārē šipri*) Oller comments:

> While in the languages of . . . the ancient Near East there are numerous words designating individuals involved in aspects of communications, it is the Akkadian term *mār šipri* that signifies the scope of the role that a messenger played in this world. "Messenger," "envoy," "ambassador," "diplomat," "agent," "deputy," and even "merchant" are all valid translations of this term in specific instances and contexts; this indicates that *mār šipri* could refer to a simple, lowly courier conveying a message as well as to an envoy or ambassador representing his lord at the court of a foreign potentate. The choice of translation depends on the context, but at the basic level the term refers to an individual who conveys information in a variety of ways, sometimes not only carrying specific messages back and forth but also acting as a spokesperson for the sender as well as information gatherer. Thus the distinction between messenger and diplomat is sometimes blurred. Since along with their messages they often carried goods as "gifts," which in international diplomatic practice was a major means by which foreign trade of the king was carried on, they also can be seen as merchants. Because of these functions, the mār šipri was the major instrument of long-distance communication in all aspects of life (*CANE* 3, 1465–66).

That true diplomatic skills were required of messengers accompanying written international correspondence is shown by examples of ticklish questions asked them by the foreign kings and the adroit answers that they spontaneously gave (see examples cited by Oller, *CANE* 3, 1469).

On the official level, messengers for the king's correspondence were chosen for loyalty, trustworthiness, and speed. Oller also notes:

> When missions were of a personal nature, rulers sent people from their inner circle who often were royal family members. Sometimes individuals were

8. For the carrier of international diplomatic correspondence, see Oller "Messengers and Ambassadors in Ancient Western Asia," *CANE 3,* 1465–73; and Meier 1988.

> picked because they or their families had a special relationship or connection with the recipient's country or court. There are many instances in the El-Amarna correspondence of rulers requesting specific individuals whom they knew and trusted to be sent to them. In diplomatic contexts a messenger who had built a rapport with the recipient could be a valuable asset to the sender. (*CANE* 3, 1466)

Because an international messenger/envoy was extremely trustworthy and often part of the royal sender's inner circle, he could be counted on to witness judicial procedures and resolve disputes between the two courts. In one case the envoy of Kadašman-Enlil, a man named Adad-šar-ilani, helped to resolve a potentially dangerous international dispute when the Babylonian king claimed that a witness had told him that Bentešina of Amurru, a confederate of Ḫattusili III of Ḫatti, had cursed the land of Babylonia. Adad-šar-ilani was called upon to witness Bentešina's denial under oath that he had so cursed Babylonia (see *CoS* 3.31:52 [§11], and English translation of the letter in Beckman 1999a, 132–37).

International messengers also provided an invaluable source of information about the foreign court and its policies, information that might not be acquired from the written communications. It is perhaps unfair to term such information gathering "spying," but it was certainly done unobtrusively. And it is also certain that some of these courts were at pains to keep the foreign messengers under surveillance. Hagenbuchner (1989a, 19 n. 74) mentions that under Hammurabi the messengers who came to his court were guarded.

Correspondence was carried on between parties who spoke different languages or whose cultures differed significantly. The messages were carried by a pair of carriers, one from each side (see below on letters 69 and 94). This practice both aided in the linguistic clarification of the transmissions and in cultural and political explanations that might be needed.

Hagenbuchner posed two questions: At what age could a man become an international messenger? and How many years might he serve in this capacity? Admitting that we have no information to answer the first question, she cites two examples where one can get an approximate duration of service: Maša-muwa's more-than thirty-year[9] tenure (end of the reign of Adad-nirari I [text 104 i 20], all of Šalmaneser I, beginning of the reign of Tukulti-Ninurta I [text 105 obv. 6′]) as envoy to the Assyrian court, and Piriḫnawa's fifteen years during the reign of Ramses II at the Egyptian one (Hagenbuchner

9 Hagenbuchner (1989a, 160) estimates the interval between the two letters as at most forty to forty-five years.

1989a, 19). Owen's proposal that the Maša-muwa attested as a high functionary and a scribe of Carchemish during the reign of Ini-Teššub is the same person as the ambassador to the court of Assyria has not yet been proven (Mora 2004, 441). An impression of the Carchemish scribe Maša-muwa's seal has been found at Korucutepe (Mora 1987, XIIb 1.27).

Since there needed to be a constant monitoring of the health and strength of an international relationship, whether it be of equals in alliance or of suzerain and vassal, it was vital that the flow of messages and messengers between the two parties be constant. Any interruption might signal hostile intent on the part of one of the two parties. Furthermore, the messengers often brought valuable goods in the form of "greeting gifts." The Hittite prince Piḫa-Walwi complained to King Ibiranu of Ugarit: "Why have you not come before His Majesty since you became king in the land of Ugarit? Why have you not sent your messengers? His Majesty is very angry about this matter. So send your messengers to His Majesty quickly and send presents to the king together with presents also for me" (*CoS* 3.32:53).

1.1.5.2.3. Messengers Traveling with the King. Since, when kings traveled—whether on military campaign or on other state trips—needed to be able to send and receive messages, they were regularly accompanied by scribes, messengers, and couriers. In Old Babylonian Mari, we have instances in which large numbers of messengers formed part of the royal entourage: when Zimri-Līm departed with all his army to help the king of Aleppo, he was accompanied by no fewer than one hundred envoys to whom messages were confided (*ša šipirātim*) and sixty-four couriers (*lāsimum*) who transported them (Charpin 2007). This was a major military undertaking. Clearly the numbers would not be so large on an ordinary trip. Yet the district of Saggaratum alone had a total of nineteen messengers and twenty-two couriers. We have no such information about the size of the Hittite king's scribe and messenger entourage when he traveled.

1.1.5.2.4. Risks and Dangers to the Messengers. Messengers who traveled only within the Hittite kingdom and those who traveled between countries faced their quota of dangers and risks. Even traveling within Hittite territory, a messenger might be attacked and killed, either for whatever valuables he carried, or in order to intercept his official correspondence. This risk was even greater for the international messenger, since he carried valuable gifts for the foreign sovereign and his family members, and the messages he carried had greater political value. For details, see Bryce 2003b, 72–74. An ancient Egyptian document called The Satire on the Trades, composed during the Middle Kingdom (ca. 2150–1750 B.C.E.) or earlier, has this to say about international messengers: "The courier goes out to a foreign country, after he has made over his property to his children, being afraid of lions and Asiatics" (translation by Wilson in *ANET* 433).

International messengers could be stopped and detained for lengthy periods or even turned back because they possessed no written authenticating document or credentials (§1.1.8.4).

At times international messengers joined merchant caravans, in order to enjoy a greater measure of security when passing through dangerous regions (Edzard 1980, 415; Bryce 2003b, 72–73). Indeed, merchants themselves sometimes served as international messengers. Often special armed, military escorts were assigned to royal messengers (CAD A, sub *ālik idi*). The pharaoh Amunḥotep III had sent Mane, one of his most senior diplomatic officials, to Mitanni in order to escort King Tušratta's daughter Taduḫepa back to Egypt, where she would become the pharaoh's bride. Burnaburiaš II of Babylonia requested that the pharaoh Akhenaten (Amunḥotep IV) make available his senior official Ḫaya to head the escort which was to convey the betrothed Babylonian princess to her new home in Egypt. And when Ḫaya reached Babylonia, the king was unhappy with the meager escort provided by Akhenaten to accompany the bride to Egypt. He wrote to Akhenaten: "Ḫaya … has but five chariots with him. Are they really going to escort her to you with just five chariots? Should I let her depart from my house under these conditions?"

It was an affront to the reputation of a great kingdom not to be able to provide protection for visiting envoys of another kingdom. The Hittite king Ḫattušili III chided Kadašman-Enlil, the king of Babylonia, on just this matter when he wrote: "In regard to what my brother wrote: 'As to the fact that I stopped my messengers, I stopped my messengers because the Aḫlamū are hostile,' how is it that you stopped your messengers because of the Aḫlamū?! My brother, is perhaps your kingdom a small one? … In my brother's country the horses are more plentiful than straw: should I grant to your messengers 1,000 chariots in order to escort them until Tuttul, and keep the Aḫlamū away?" See the translation of this letter in Beckman 1999a, 132–37. This particular paragraph is translated on p. 134 §6.

Even a military escort, if it was not strong enough, might prove insufficient, and there are examples cited of actual attacks on ancient Near Eastern traveling parties.

And if threat to life and limb were not enough, there is the threat of confiscation of goods by border officials or the imposition of ruinous tolls. Bryce writes:

> We have referred to the human as well as the natural hazards which the

> king's messengers frequently had to deal with in the course of their journeys. Rapacious local officials were sometimes not the least of these hazards. Even if they stopped short of confiscating an entire consignment of goods sent by one Great King to another, they might demand payment of taxes on the goods. Foreign envoys were presumably spared such demands when they were accompanied on their journeys by representatives of the king to whom the local officials were subject. And on occasions an overlord received a request from a brother-king to ensure in advance that safe passage and exemption from taxes be granted to merchants passing through his territory (2003b, 73).

Because of the dangers inherent in long-distance travel, it was common to consult omens or take an oracle before sending out messengers. In Old Babylonian Mari a man named Asqudum declared in a letter: "I took the omens for the safety of the messengers: they were not good. I will take them again for them. When the omens are favorable, I shall send them." And king Išme-Dagan of Ekallatum wrote: "When you have this letter brought to me, give strict orders for [its] protection during the journey. Take omens for the safety of the carriers of the letter, or have thirty of your servants escort them to the river and [then] return to you."

1.1.5.2.5. Physical Conditions for Rapid Travel. Security was not the only consideration affecting the speed of travel. The nature of the terrain traversed, the condition of the roads, and the prevailing weather affected the amount of time required for travel.

A Neo-Assyrian letter to Tiglath-pileser III from Dūrī-Aššur, governor of the province of Tušḫān, tells how spies that he had sent across the border into Šubria for reconnaissance work turned back because of the heavy snowfall. "There is much snow," wrote the governor, "I have dispatched spies (into the enemy land), but they have turned back, saying, 'Where should we go?' But as soon as the snow is less, they will set out (again), enter the enemy land, and bring back reports" (Janowski and Wilhelm 2006, 124).

Travel in winter within Anatolia was extremely slow and hazardous, and was avoided when possible. In a letter from the Hittite king to three officials at Tapikka (HKM 17 [text 22], lines 9–12), the king refers to a mission on which he sent one of the three the preceding winter. But the presence of ice and snow on the roads was always a reason not to travel (KBo 18.79 [text 117], and §1.2.20.3). This factor was certainly one that encouraged Hittite armies to break off a military campaign and go into winter quarters.

> The roads of the ancient Near East were unpaved (with a very few, small-scale exceptions in the last century of the Neo-Assyrian Empire). Nevertheless, they had to be staked out, leveled, and—at least in the case of those

> intended for wheeled transport—maintained in good repair. Kings, who boasted in their inscriptions of building temples, palaces, canals, and fortifications, seldom mentioned road construction ...; that is because, as is known from infrequent mentions in juridical documents, roadwork was one of the duties of the local populations (Astour in *CANE* 3, 1401).

Hittite officials paid close attention to the condition of the roads in all seasons of the year. According to an Old Hittite law (§56A, English translations in Hoffner 1997f, 226; 1997g, 68, 193; and 2000, 112), among the projects of public—and in view of the above quote, local-area—labor were the building of roads and (ironically, when mentioned together with road-building!) the collection of ice/snow. The heritage of the Old Assyrian trade with Anatolia also insured that there were good roads for international travel.

Messengers carrying correspondence would keep to good routes, the same as those used by merchant caravans and armies on campaign. Itineraries of merchant caravans are known from Mesopotamia, but nothing of this type is yet known from Hittite texts. Instead, for travel within Anatolia scholars try to reconstruct itineraries from oracular inquiries about prospective military campaigns (see Franz-Szabó 1976–1980, and literature cited there, especially Ünal 1978), and (less reliably) from the sequence of stops on cult journeys of the Hittite king or his representative. Routes between Anatolia and Egypt, Assyria, and Babylonia are discussed in Hagenbuchner 1989a, 27–28.

Nowhere does one find a complete description of the long itinerary between Aššur and the cities of Cappadocia, but several tablets list, in sequential order, places on different segments of the route (or routes). The problem consists in piecing the segments together, establishing whether they belong to the outbound or inbound leg of the journey, and locating as many of the places as possible. Students of the geographical aspect of the Cappadocian tablets have sometimes tried to string all places that occur in those texts along one single route, but the evidence contradicts this approach.

Astour offers his solution to the reconstruction of these routes in *CANE* 3, 1409–10.

1.1.5.3. Correspondents

1.1.5.3.1. Identity of the Correspondents. In private, non-governmental correspondence, anyone might send or receive a letter. In official correspondence, letters are attested to and from kings, queens, princes, generals, and various grades of bureaucrats.

1.1.5.3.2. Relative Social Status of Correspondents. ROYALTY. Letters to or from kings, queens, princes, and princesses could cross international borders. Not just Hittite kings, but also their queens and children wrote and received letters from foreign courts. There was a kind of royal club, to which members of royal families in the Amarna Age belonged. And members of this club kept in regular contact with each other, sending greetings and gifts. Members addressed each other as "brother" and "sister" (see Jakob 2006). Tadmor first described the group of Middle Eastern "Great Kings" in the Amarna Age (Ḫatti, Egypt, Assyria, Babylonia) as a "club" (1979, 3), and Bryce (2003b, 76, 108) calls them a "club of royal brothers."

OFFICIALDOM, INCLUDING SCRIBES. Officials not only wrote to each other on the business of the state, but also on private matters. In the piggyback letters in the present corpus it can be seen how thoroughly the officials availed themselves of the royal post to see to the welfare of their real estate and families in remote places of the realm.

PRIVATE CITIZENS. Although letters between private citizens clearly existed (see examples from Egypt in Wente 1990), the Hittite documentation, limited as it is to clay tablets from the royal administration, reveals no examples. All recovered Hittite letters are official in nature.

CORRESPONDENCE BETWEEN FAMILY MEMBERS. The convention of using terms of familial relationship ("father," "mother," "son," etc.) for strictly collegial relationships obscures what may be examples of actual blood-relationships in the Hittite letter corpus.

1.1.6. The Royal Secretary

About the "royal secretary" in the Old Babylonian Mari correspondence Charpin (2007, 409) has written:

> In the case of administrative correspondence, letter-carriers would not normally be admitted to the royal presence but left their letters "at the door of the palace." It was only in case of urgency that they would have direct access to the sovereign. Hence the great importance of the royal secretary, who read the correspondence to his master. Among such officials the best known is Šu-nuḫra-Ḫalu, secretary to Zimri-Lim .... Correspondents would often attach to their letter to the king another addressed to Šu-nuḫra-Ḫalu [*see the Hittite piggyback letters in §1.2.24*], in which they copied or summarized the first. In this way the royal secretary would know in advance the content of the message he was to read and could draw the king's attention to specific points; the letter he received would often conclude with the announcement that a gift was on its way. A letter to Šu-nuḫra-Ḫalu from Ibal-Addu shows that messages sent to Zimri-Lim had first to be heard by his secretary, even when delivered orally and not in tablet form: "Behold, I have sent you a complete report by Ladin-Addu. Pay close attention to his report and bring

> him before the king." It is notable that certain correspondents implicitly accuse Šu-nuḫra-Ḫalu of having "censored" parts of certain letters they had sent to the sovereign. The general Yasim-Dagan, for example, threatened to come and read his letter to the king in person. Others would flatter the powerful royal secretary: "When I found myself at Mari, with my lord, and you were my friend and you fought by my side, I saw your power. Everything you said before my lord was agreed; nothing happened without your consent."

The royal scribe Ḫattušili, known to us in the present corpus in text 55 and elsewhere, seems to have enjoyed powers approaching those of the Old Babylonian royal secretary Šu-nuḫra-Ḫalu.

1.1.7. Languages Used in International Correspondence

Domestic correspondence was always conducted in the native language. But in international correspondence the favored language was Akkadian. Thus we find international correspondence conducted in Akkadian in Egypt, Syria-Palestine, and central Anatolia. The limited evidence for international correspondence involving western Anatolian states (specifically, Arzawa) shows a preference for the use of the Hittite language, even when corresponding with Egypt (see text 94, lines 24–25).

Outgoing international correspondence might be first drafted in the local language and subsequently translated into Akkadian. This accounts for Hittite drafts of letters to be sent to foreign courts (e.g., text 98). Contrary to earlier speculation, incoming international correspondence in Akkadian was not translated into the local language in writing before it was read to the king. Instead, incoming letters in the Ugaritic language from Ḫatti and Egypt found at Ugarit are evidence that in these foreign courts there were scribes capable of drafting letters in Ugaritic (Niehr 2006, 265).

1.1.8. Types of Letters

1.1.8.1. International Diplomatic Correspondence

This category comprised letters between the heads of state—that is, kings—or their ministers and in some cases between queens or princes. When the two kingdoms were of equal status, the correspondence dealt with such subjects as the exchange of luxury items between the courts, the arrangement of royal marriages, state visits, and the security of caravans carrying messengers and goods between the two countries. When the two kingdoms were of unequal status, such as Ḫatti and Ugarit, the correspondence could concern in addition the payment of tribute and the settlement of border disputes. Examples of Mesopotamian, Syro-Palestinian, and Egyptian diplomatic correspondence in translation can be found in *CoS* 3, and the Amarna letters in Moran 1992. Hittite diplomatic correspondence in translation may be found in Beckman 1999a.

1.1.8.2. Administrative Correspondence

Non-international correspondence was of two types: official and private. Official correspondence could be between the kings and their officials or between the officials themselves. Most examples of recovered correspondence from the ancient Near East are of the official variety. The best sources for a selection of such letters in translation are *CoS* (for English translations) and TUAT (for German). Some Egyptian letters of this type can be found in Wente 1990.

Subjects of the official correspondence included reports from officials about matters connected with their responsibilities. Border officials reported reconnaissance. An example from Twelfth Dynasty Egypt follows:

> Another dispatch brought to him from the retainer Ameny, who is in the fortress "Repeller of the Medjay" (Faras fort?), as one fortress sends a communication to another fortress. It is a communication to the lord, l.p.h., to the effect that the warrior of the city of Hieraconpolis, Senu's son Heru's son Renoker, and the warrior of the city of Tjebu, Rensi's son Senwosret's son Senwosret, came to report to me, your humble servant, in Year 3, fourth month of the second season, day 2, at breakfast time on business of the soldier, Khusobek's son Mentuhotep's son Khusobek ... , who is substituting for the marine of the Ruler's Crew in the troop of Meha (near Abu Simbel), saying, "The frontier patrol that set out to patrol the desert margin extending near(?) the fortress 'Repeller of the Medjay' in Year 3, third month of the second season, last day, has returned to report to me saying, 'We found the track of thirty-two men and three donkeys, that they had trod [...]: [...] the frontier patrol [...] my places:' so [he] said. [...] command to(?) the troop [...] on the desert margin. I, your humble servant, have written [about this to ..., as one fortress sends a communication to another] fortress. It is a communication [about] this. [All business affairs of the King's Establishment], l.p.h., are prosperous [and flourishing]. (Wente 1990, 71–72)

A Ramesside letter from an official on the southern border of Egypt reports to an overseer of cattle, who was presumably located at Thebes, and is concerned with the delivery of cattle from Nubia, the source of long-horned cattle that figure prominently in depictions of the Feast of Opet in the Luxor temple (Wente 1990, 112, 119–20).

Hebrew letters from Arad and Lachish report on cross-border raids in the eastern Negev from Moabites, Ammonites, and Arameans based in Edom (Lindenberger 1994, 100). Israelite Arad was a fortress on the southern border. As such it was not only a guard and watch point against enemies, but was a fortified supply depot. Staple foods were stockpiled and sent on demand to Judean army units stationed throughout the region. It also served as a troop transit point (Lindenberger 1994, 100).

A letter from an official on the northeastern frontier of Ugarit reported to his king that "the border with the kingdom of Carchemish is holding solid" (RS 34.148 in *CoS* 3.45W:105).

A Neo-Assyrian letter from Sin-aḫḫē-riba to King Sargon II includes the following about news from the border official Aššur-reṣuwa concerning Nabû-le'i, the governor of Birate:

> This was the report of Aššur-reṣuwa. Nabû-le'i the governor of Birate has written to me: "I have written to the guards of the forts along the border concerning the news of the Urartian king and they (tell me this): 'His troops have been utterly defeated on his expedition against the Cimmerians. Three of his magnates along with their troops have been killed; he himself has escaped and entered his country, but his army has not yet arrived (back).'" This was the report of Nabû-le'i. The (king) of Muṣaṣir and his brother and son have gone to greet the Urartian king, and the messenger of the (king) of Hubuškia has also gone to greet him. All the guards of the forts along the border have sent me similar reports. They have brought me from Tabal a letter from Nabû-le'i, the major-domo of Ahatabiša. I am herewith forwarding it to the king, my lord. (Parpola 1987, 32)

Officials and city governors in border areas were well stationed to send spies and scouts over the border into enemy territory to collect information about the enemy's intentions. In a letter to the Neo-Assyrian king Sargon II, Nasḫira-Bēl, the governor of Amidi (modern Diyarbakir), reports about the preparations for war by king Argišti II of Urartu, based upon information collected by spies sent across the border (Radner in Janowski and Wilhelm 2006, 136–37).

1.1.8.3. Letters to or from Gods

A special type of official correspondence between officials and the ruler is that which concerns communication from the gods. Ancients received communications from their gods in at least two ways: via divination (omens and oracles), and through prophetic visions. Letters in which officials reported to the king the course of oracular or divinatory inquiries and the authoritative interpretations of such figure in almost all known text corpora from the ancient Near East. For examples in the Hittite corpus see texts 3 and 50. When a prophet received an oracle from his god by dream, vision, or other means, he often communicated it in person to the sovereign, if audience was granted. When this was impossible, he would send it by letter. An example of the latter is mentioned by Charpin: "An explicit mention of dictation comes from the city of Andarig, south of Jebel Sinjar, where a prophet of the god Šamaš asks the Mari representative to provide a scribe so that he may dictate to him a letter from his god to the king Zimri-Lim" (2007, 401 with n. 4).

1.1.8.4. Letters Guaranteeing the Bearer Safe Conduct

One such letter drafted by the king of Mittanni was sent along with his messenger through Syria and Canaan to his destination in Egypt (EA 30).[10] What is mentioned in text 30 of the present corpus is not the same thing: it is merely a reference to a second letter that was sent by the same messenger in the same trip. As Liverani (2001, 73) adds,

> The courier's "diplomatic passport" is of no use against brigands, but it can at least prevent him from being held up by the local kinglets. Of course, if he is carrying a politically sensitive message across the territory of a "third" great king, he can be intercepted: Kamose intercepted a Hyksos messenger to Kush, and Tukulti-Ninurta intercepted a Babylonian merchant-messenger who was probably traveling to Ḫatti. In both cases the content of the letter signified hostile intent to the "third" great king, whose discovery of it provoked major political reactions.

In a letter from Kadašman-Enlil of Babylon to Ḫattušili III of Ḫatti, he attributed the failure of his messengers to reach Ḫatti to the refusal of Assyrian authorities to grant them passage, as well as to the habit of the Aḫlamu people of harassing his messengers. Ḫattušili found both excuses weak and reproached the Babylonian king (see translation in *CoS* 3.31:52 [§§6–9]).

10. English translation in Oppenheim 1967, 134 and Moran 1992, 100, both of whom call it a "passport." See also discussion in Oller, "Messengers and Ambassadors" in *CANE* 3, 1467 with text box (who also cites an earlier example from Old Babylonian Mari); Liverani 2001, 73; and Bryce 2003b, 73–74. Hagenbuchner's (1989a, 10) term for such a letter is "Begleitschreiben."

1.1.8.5. Intercepted Enemy Correspondence

A few letters in the Old Babylonian Mari palace archives are addressed to kings other than the king of Mari. These seem to be letters intercepted by Mari border officials and submitted to the king for whatever strategic information they might contain (Charpin 2007, 408). No such letters have been found in Hittite archives.

1.1.9. Literary Conventions: Common Features and Regional Variants

Common features in letter format and wording include (1) the address line, identifying sender and addressee, and usually the word "say"; (2) greeting formulas, wishing the addressee well (or that the gods may keep him well) and sometimes reporting that all is well with the sender; (3) indications of receipt of a previous message from the addressee; (4) highlighted new information for the addressee, and (5) the use of topic transitional markers. The last feature is sometimes marked both by a visible paragraph marker in the writing (on this visual marker see below in §1.2.8) and by a verbal transition-marker. The latter type is attested in Akkadian language texts by the adverb *šanītam* "next," in Hebrew and Aramaic letters by *wʿt* "and now," and in Hittite letters by *kinuna* "but now." Change of subject, when related to the content of an earlier message received by the sender from the addressee, can also be indicated by the frequently used phrase *(kī) kuit ... ḫatraeš* "concerning/regarding (this) that you wrote."

1.1.9.1. The Address Formula

Egyptian letters to the pharaoh have address formulas and greeting formulas that are much longer and flowery than similar letters from Hittite or Ugaritic officials to their king. Murnane's translation of a letter from the Steward of Memphis, Apy, to the pharaoh (1995, 50–51) illustrates this most clearly:

> The estate servant Apy addresses the Horus, [Mighty] Bull, "Tall-Plumed"; Two Ladies, "Great of Kingship in Karnak"; Horus of Gold, "Who Elevates the Crowns in Upper Egyptian Heliopolis"; the King of Upper and Lower Egypt, who lives on Maat, [the Lord of the Two Lands], NEFERKHEPERU-RE; the Son of Re who lives on Maat, AMENHOTEP IV, long in his lifetime, may he live forever continually (p. 50).

Contrast with the foregoing the simple address formula used by Hittite officials: "Say to His Majesty, my lord!" (e.g., texts 5, 48, 50, 51). The Egyptian form was more flowery because it was actually read to the pharaoh as part of the missive, whereas the opening words on the Hittite letter tablets were *instructions to the scribe*, and were not part of what would be read aloud to him (see §§1.1.9.1; 1.2.16). Nevertheless, other written records of how Hittite officials addressed the king show the same avoidance of language that could be considered flowery or fawning.

In Egyptian letters not addressed to the king, Wente (1990, 9–10) distinguishes the Old and Middle Kingdom practices from the New Kingdom ones:

> With regard to the conventions and formulae employed in letter writing, letters from the Old and Middle Kingdoms generally display a greater consciousness of the relative social status existing between writer and addressee than do New Kingdom correspondences. Adopting a humble attitude toward a superior recipient, the [Old and Middle Kingdom] writer may refer to himself in the salutation as "servant of the estate," while in the body of the letter he uses an expression which I, for sake of clarity, have rendered by "I, your humble servant," although the first person pronoun is not actually present in the Egyptian. The superior recipient in the older letters is referred to either as "lord," or sometimes obliquely as "your scribe," that is, the recipient's secretary, who supposedly would read out the communication to his master. The writer of the letter in such cases does not want to presume that the recipient will have to read the letter himself. A writer who is equal in status to the recipient may politely refer to himself as "your brother" … By the New Kingdom such formal expressions are normally dispensed with in the body of a letter, and first and second person pronouns are used almost exclusively. In the introductory formulae of New Kingdom letters, however, the writer often continues the earlier practice of calling a superior "lord."

About the situation in the Ugaritic letter corpus Pardee wrote: "The address formulae in Ug[aritic] letters reflect in various ways the form of expression appropriate for dictating the letter to the messenger who would have borne the tablet and given the message orally, plausibly sometimes including more details than were present in the brief message inscribed in clay" (*CoS* 3.45A:89 n. 3). The command "say/speak to PN!" (Akkadian *qibī-ma*) is addressed to the messenger, who would read the letter aloud to the addressee.

Charpin (2007, 403) writes:

> The opening formula of an Old-Babylonian letter betrays the oral origins of the transmission of messages; the first lines always consist of two parts: "To X, say: thus speaks Y." Who is addressed by the imperative "speak"? It is generally thought that the formula retains the memory of its oral origins,

> and that it is the messenger who is addressed. Two examples confirm this as they demonstrate how messengers communicated orally their master's message. This is how Išme-Dagan's envoys to Ḫammu-rabi accomplished their mission: "They were asked for news. They therefore delivered their report: 'Thus (speaks] your servant Išme-Dagan (…).'" In the same way, when one of king Šarraya's ministers passes on his message to a neighboring king he says: "Thus (speaks) Šarraya." These examples clearly show that the first part of the address is directed to the messenger.

The same may have been the case in Hittite letters to the king (see §1.2.16).

In Ugaritic letters, as in Hittite ones, the order of mention of writer and addressee has significance, for it usually reflects the relative social status of the correspondents—the superior being mentioned first. Pardee observes:

> The expression of social status may reflect either a familial situation ("mother," "father," "son" …) or one of the other strata of society ("lord," "lady," "servant"); it may reflect equality ("brother"); and it may be mixed … [a man's] social situation, which allows him to have an audience with the Hittite king, … permitted him to address himself to his mother as he would to an inferior. (*CoS* 3.45A:89 n. 3)

It was extremely important to use the correct term for this pseudo-family relationship. To choose the wrong one could be counterproductive, if not outright offensive. Charpin writes:

> Certain texts show that there were clear rules which the ancients took care to observe: according to his hierarchical position, a king would address another as his father, brother, son or servant. One thus sees the nomad chief Ašmad advising king Zimri-Lim at the beginning of his reign, concerning his relations with Aduna-Addu, the powerful king of Ḫanzat: "Aduna-Addu had a tablet brought to me, saying: 'Why does your lord write to me as a father?' This tablet was brought to me by Yattu-Lim. Let my lord question Yattu-Lim. My lord must gain the goodwill of Aduna-Addu, because of the Benjaminites. Aduna-Addu, continually … (gap) … 'Why does Zimri-Lim not address me as a brother?' Now, tone down your address. When you have a tablet taken to Aduna-Addu, write to him as a brother, if you wish him to reject an alliance with the Benjaminites. My lord must gain the goodwill of Aduna-Addu." (2007, 403)

In the Old Babylonian Mari letters, letters addressed to the king begin "'To my lord." When this is followed by the name of the king (e.g., "To my lord Zimri-Līm"), the sender is a foreigner. Hittite letters by officials to the king begin "To His Majesty (^{d}UTU-*ŠI*, literally 'my sun god'), my lord."

1.1.9.2. The Greeting Formula

Outside of the Hittite kingdom and its heavily influenced vassal states like Ugarit, the customary wish for health in letters invokes one or more specific gods by name.

About the situation in Egyptian letters to non-royalty, Wente writes:

> When inferiors write to superiors, greetings and invocations to gods on the addressee's behalf are commonly employed, but very rarely does a superior writer proffer wishes for the well-being of a subordinate ... For the Old and Middle Kingdoms the formulae of invocation tend to be more rigidly phrased than in the New Kingdom, when a freer style was adopted, reflective of a more personal relationship between a person and a god. This was true particularly during the Ramesside period, which was noted for pietistic developments in religion (1990, 10).

Here are a few samples from New Kingdom Egyptian letters:

> "Every day I am calling upon Pre-Harakhti [the Egyptian sun god] when he rises and sets to keep you healthy, to keep you alive, and to keep you vigorous" (Wente 1990, 128 no. 152).

> I am calling upon Pre-Harakhti in his rising and in his setting, upon Amon of Ramesses-mi-amon, ... upon Ptah of Ramesses-mi-amon, ... and (upon) all the gods and goddesses of Pi-Ramessu-mi-amon, ... the great Ka of Pre-Harakhti, to keep you healthy, to keep you alive, to keep you prosperous, and to let me see you in health (Wente 1990, 32 no. 24).

> I am calling upon all the gods of Pi-Ramessu-mi-amon, ... to keep you healthy, to keep you alive, and to keep you prosperous (Wente 1990, 32 no. 25).

> "I am calling upon Ptah the Great, South-of-his-Wall, lord of Ankh[towy], upon Pre-Harakhti in his rising and in his setting, and (upon) all the gods and goddesses of Pi-Ramessu-miamon, ... the great Ka of Pre-Harakhti, to keep you healthy and to keep you alive" (Wente 1990, 33 no. 26).

> "I am calling upon Ptah and all the gods and goddesses of Pi-Ramessu-mi-amon, ... to keep you healthy, to keep you alive, and let me see you in health and fill my embrace with you" (Wente 1990, 34 no. 30).

In Mesopotamia of the Old Babylonian period, letter writers often invoked the sun god Šamaš to keep the addressee alive and well. And when two or three deities were invoked, often Šamaš led the list (e.g., Šamaš and Marduk,

Šamaš, and Ninurta). But these well-wishes only appear in private correspondence, never in letters addressed to kings or sent by them (so Charpin 2007, 403, quoting Dalley 1973, and CAD B, 59–60). For other Akkadian examples involving divine names other than Šamaš, see CAD N/II, 40. See also: *Šamaš aššūmi-ya* MU.ŠÁR *liballiṭ-ka* "may Šamaš keep you alive for 3,600 years for my sake (i.e., in answer to my prayers for you)" (OB letter cited in CAD Š/II, 35 and 201). Other OB variants are: *Marduk rāim-ka aššūmi-ya lilabbir-ka* "May Marduk, who loves you, keep you alive (literally, make you grow old) for my sake" (cited CAD L, 15,); and *imittam u šumēlam bēlī u bēltī ana naṣāri-ka ay īgû* "may my lord and my lady [two deities] not neglect to protect you everywhere (literally, to the right and the left)" (CAD I/J, 119).

Only in Akkadian-language letters from Ugarit and regions heavily influenced by the Hittite kingdom do we find the phrase "keep you *in well-being*": *ilū ana šulmāni* PAP-*ru-ka* "let the gods protect you in well-being" MRS 9 180 RS 17.286: 5 (cited from CAD N/II, 40). This is the Akkadian-language equivalent of the Hittite *aššuli paḫš(anu)-*, so common in letter greetings.

In Ugarit, letter well-wishes may be characterized as follows: "The most typical greetings included the verbs *šlm* (*yšlm lk*, 'may it be well with you,' and *ʾilm tšlmk*, 'may the gods keep you well' [D-stem factitive]) and *nǵr* (= Hebr. *nṣr*, also with 'gods' as subject, 'may they guard you'). Only here [in *CoS* 3.45A:89] in the Ug[aritic] correspondence are the gods qualified as those of Ugarit" (Pardee in *CoS* 3.45A:89 n. 4).

An interesting example is found in an Aramaic letter written by a pious Egyptian Jew to fellow Jews: "The welfare of my brothers may *the gods* [seek after at all times]," on which the translator, Bezalel Porten, commented: "The form ['the gods'] is plural (*ʾlhyʾ*), and it is not clear, here and in other letters by Jews, whether it was understood as a majestic singular, whether a pagan formula was used unthinkingly, or whether a pagan scribe actually wrote the letter" (*CoS* 3.46:117 n. 7).

1.1.9.3. The Prostration Gesture (German Huldigungsformel*)*

In the Amarna and Ugaritic letters to the king, the subject sometimes employs a statement to the effect that he prostrates himself at the feet of the royal majesty a certain number of times (for discussions see Gruber 1980 and Hagenbuchner 1989a, 55–63). The wording of this formula is in its essentials identical, no matter what language is used: Akkadian, Ugaritic, or Hittite. But there are variations in the specific verb used for "fall/prostrate oneself," in the indication of the number of times the prostration is made, and in the manner of prostration, all of which may be social or rank indicators. Not all letters to kings by non-royal persons contain such a formula (see the letter to the king of Ugarit from *Ydn,* possibly a military commander; Singer 1999b, 718–19).

1.1.9.3.1. The Verbs Used. In the Akkadian-language formulation (attested in Amarna, Ugarit, Emar, and Ḫatti), the verb can be *amqut* "I fall" (from *maqātu* 1c in CAD M/I, 242 and Š/III, 315) , *uška*ʾʾ*in* (or *ulka*ʾʾ*in* or *uškên*) "I prostrate myself" (from *šukênu*), its variant *uš*ḫ*a*ḫ*in* (from the quadriliteral root *š*ḫḫ*n*) (CAD Š/III, 218), and (in Emar) an N-stem form of *q/garāru* "to roll on the ground, grovel." There seems to be no significant difference in the meaning of these verbs when used in this formula. Hagenbuchner (1989a, 56 §4.3) claims that the set expression employing *amqut* does not occur together with other introductory formalities, but always in the body of the letter. Yet in KBo 9.82 (text 115) it clearly belongs to the introductory formalities and precedes the beginning of the letter's body.

In Hittite texts, outside of the epistolary context, the Akkadogram *UŠKEN(NŪ)* (from *šukênu*) probably conceals the Hittite verb *aruwai-* "to prostrate oneself," which denotes a gesture of submission to gods and kings. It is used in worship scenes, as well as in scenes of military surrender.

1.1.9.3.2. The Numerical Expression. As for the number, the most usual wording in the Amarna letters is 7-*šu u* 7-*šu* "seven times and again seven times" (i.e., a total of fourteen times). Gruber (1980, 233) correctly notes that Akkadian 2-*šu* 7-*šu*,which lacks the conjunction *u* "and"—as well as Ugaritic *ṯnid šb'id*, which lacks the conjunction *w* "and"—is multiplicative ("two *times* seven times") and is the mathematical equivalent of Akkadian 7-*šu u* 7-*šu* and Ugaritic *šb'(i)d w šb'id*, which contain the "additive" conjunctions Akkadian *u* and Ugaritic *w*.

1.1.9.3.3. Further Qualifications of Manner. The repeated sevenfold prostration is made more specific by the addition "on (my) belly (Akkadian *kabattu, pantu, baṭnu*) and back" (Akkadian *ṣēru, ṣu'ru*), and the writer can also indicate that he is nothing more than "the dust of your feet" (Akkadian *eperu ša šēpē-ka*). In letters from Ḫatti, Ugarit, and Emar, the sender can add to this "from afar" (Akkadian *ištu rūqiš* [CAD R, 415], Ugaritic *mrḥqtm*), perhaps indicating that, although he is not present in person, he bows as he sends the letter off and thus bows at a distance. The use of this phrase may also seek to show that the majesty of the addressed king is so great as to be felt at great distance. This expression is not limited to great kings such as the Egyptian pharaoh or the Hittite emperor, but is even used in an exceedingly flattering letter from a governor of Qadeš to the king of Ugarit (see Niehr and Schwemer 2006, 260–61).

1.1.9.3.4. Political Implications. Morris (2006) has argued that, within the corpus of Syro-Palestinian letters to the pharaoh found at El-Amarna, one can discern a pattern in the form of this formula that reflects the degree of Egyptian military-political control. She writes:

> … the results of a systematic study of the greeting formulas used by Egypt's vassals when addressing the pharaoh can reveal a great deal about the varying degrees of political control within the Egyptian empire. … I will discuss the clustering in social rank that I believe is discernible among the different geographic areas of Egypt's northern empire. Whether these proposed rankings may potentially shed light on the preparation of individual treaties between the Egyptian state and particular vassals is the subject of the concluding section of this article. …
>
> That the rulers of each city-state were allowed a specific range of greeting formulas divvied out according to their perceived rank in the empire cannot confidently be asserted. There are certainly variations in formulas from letter to letter sent by the same vassal, often correlating with the degree of urgency communicated. What is interesting, however, is that each geographic area maintained a generally consistent ranked level of obsequiousness— despite the occasional change of ruler or variation in political fortune. The kings of the northern frontier and those of the coastal lowlands of Canaan, for example, employed mutually exclusive greeting formulas, and one expects that the nature and number of their respective imagined prostrations would in fact be consistent with those performed in reality if the vassal were granted an audience with the king.[11] The rest of the Levant exhibited a less stark division of formulas; yet the cities in the southern hill country, with the exception of Qiltu, utilized consistently higher-status greeting formulas than those used on the Phoenician coast and in northern Canaan. …
>
> Certainly, we know from the Amarna archive that seemingly small matters concerning rank and status, such as greeting formulas or physical position at a ceremony, were taken very, very seriously. For example, in one letter, the Hittite king upbraids Akhenaten roundly for a perceived insult lodged in the greeting formula of a letter that the pharaoh had sent to him.

Morris identifies four geographical "tiers," with the northernmost and the one in the high hills of Palestine showing the least subservient formulas, and

11. Morris also notes that "New Kingdom art is rife with depictions of foreigners in various attitudes of submission. For differing postures that appear linked specifically to status, see, for example, the rulers of Kush and Wawat in the tomb of Huy. In this case, the artist has also carefully differentiated the types of tribute offered by both and makes it clear that it is only the rulers of Wawat who bring their children to court" (2006, 192 n. 13).

the southern coastal one (Philistine plain)—the closest to Egypt—showing the most subservient.

> If the varying levels of obsequiousness expressed in the Amarna letter greetings may be taken as a general indicator of the strength of imperial control in a particular region, Egypt had the cities of Akko, Gezer, Lachish, Yursa, and Ashkelon grasped tightly by the hair. To these rulers, the pharaoh was "their king, their lord, their Sun, their god and the Sun from the sky" (EA 235, 298–300, 331), while they themselves were "the dirt at his feet and the groom of his horses" (EA 320–321, 316, 328) or "the ground upon which he treads" (EA 233–234). Finally, when these rulers prostrated themselves, they did so mostly seven times and seven times, on the stomach and on the back (2006, 190).

The prostration gesture of the author of the letter would be performed by the messenger who brought it: "The messenger-diplomat would have to go through the proper bureaucratic channels to receive an audience with the king. The granting of such a meeting in certain periods (Neo-Assyrian) was a major privilege. At the beginning of such an interview, certain matters of protocol would be observed, including offers of hospitality and prostration as a mark of submission" (Oller in *CANE* 3, 1468).

1.1.9.4. The "All is Well with ..." Reports

Letters from officials to the king regularly include brief formulas, indicating that all is well with those in their charge. Local officials thus generally write that "all is well with the district (or 'in the land/territory')." For examples from Mesopotamia see Oppenheim 1967, 100, 150, and 181. For Hittite examples in the present corpus, see texts 26, 42, 81, 89, 92, 95, 96, 98, and 107, among others. Military commanders, on the other hand, report that "all is well with the troops." A request for such information about the troops is found in our text 111, lines 3–6. These formulas often appear immediately after the address or the well-wishing formulas, but are sometimes used to end the letter.

But in a less functional than ceremonial manner this formula is also used in a letter from a Hittite prince to the vassal king of Ugarit, reporting that all is well at present with the Hittite emperor (see translation in *CoS* 3.32:53).

1.1.9.5. "With Regard to What You Wrote"

All but the shortest of letters concern multiple topics. These are often directly related to a previous letter received from the addressee. As each subject is broached in turn, the letter writer employs a formula *kuit (uttar)* ...

ḫatraeš/ḫatratten/ḫatrānun, which can roughly be translated as "concerning what you/I wrote about …." There then follows the reply or comment on what was written in the previous letter. See examples in texts 4, 5, 8, 9, 12, 13, 14, 15, 16, 22, and *passim.* Especially notable is text 16, in which the king uses the formula five times, and the chief scribe Ḫattušili in his piggy-back letter once more. If the letter writer has nothing important to say about the message he references, but wishes his correspondent to know that it was received and understood, he could write: "I have heard it" (texts 9, lines 3–4; 12, lines 17–23).

Charpin (2007, 404) points out that this practice has a direct bearing on the practice of not keeping copies of outgoing correspondence; just as in today's digital world, e-mail correspondents often request that replies include selected and relevant parts of the e-letter that the sender received. But occasionally, although the addressee would still have a previous letter from the sender, he quotes a small portion of that letter to introduce further comment on the matter (text 9, lines 5–13).

1.1.9.6. Highlighted New Information

When new information is of importance, indeed urgent, it may be verbally highlighted through the use of either an imperative or a jussive form of the verb "know." This is attested from earliest to latest periods of Mesopotamian letter writing (see examples in Oppenheim 1967, 128, 132, 145, 156–57, 161, 180, and 184). Random examples can be cited from Mari (*bēlī lū īde* "may my lord know"; ARM 2 76, 38); from El-Amarna (*u bēli-ni līde* "and may our lord know;" EA 170: 18; *anumma išpur ana bēli-ya u damiq enūma īde* "now I(!) have written to my lord, and it is good that he should know"; EA 147: 70); and Neo-Assyrian letters (*šarru bēlī uda* "the king, my lord, should know"; ABL 482: 9).

It is also attested in Ugaritic letters, where a jussive form of the verb "know" (*yd*ʿ) or a double imperative "know! know!" (*d*ʿ *d*ʿ) is employed (Pardee in *CoS* 3.45A:89 n. 5; 3.45FF:110 n. 175). A Ugaritic example is the emergency report from a city commander to ǴRDN, his master: "BN ḪRNK has come (here), he has defeated the (local) troops, he has pillaged the town, he has even burned our grain on the threshing floors and destroyed the vineyards. Our town is destroyed, and you must know it" (*CoS* 3.45FF:109–10). The double imperative "know! know!" (*d*ʿ *d*ʿ) underscores the dire situation and the urgency of assistance.

The comparable Hittite formula likewise employs the command form "know!" (*šāk*) or "may (Your Majesty) know!" (*šakdu*) (see below in §1.2.19.1).

1.1.9.7. Proofreading and Corrections

Whether dictated or otherwise, once a letter tablet was inscribed, the scribe had to read it back to the author before placing it in its envelope, or dispatching it without envelope. During rereading, the author would occasionally request changes to be made in the text: this is how we must understand those occasions when words (text 13: 5), or even entire lines (text 114: 8), have been erased and rewritten, and the additions in small characters, written between the existing lines and beginning at a point immediately above where they were to be inserted. Examples of above-the-line additions from the present corpus of Hittite letters are found in texts 11: 7 (*-kán)* and 29: 57 (*ḫa-at-ra-a-eš*). The vast majority of cases where the scribe uses the right edge of the tablet to complete a word or phrase are not examples of corrections made after the tablet was completed. But a few that involve lengthy additions certainly were. The best example is found in text 68: 8, where the scribe originally wrote: *na-aš-ša-an A-NA* ANŠE.KUR.RA.ḪI.A *ti-it-ta-nu-ut-tén* "mount them (i.e., the captives) on horses," and then—realizing (or being told by the letter's author) that he has omitted an important preliminary step—added on the edge: ŠU.ḪI.A-*ŠU* GÌR.MEŠ-*ŠU-ya* SIG_5?-*at-tén nam-ma-aš-kán* "secure them hand and foot, then …."

1.1.10. Late Bronze Age Epistolary Corpora

1.1.10.1. El-Amarna Corpus

This collection of official international correpondence from the court of the pharaoh Amunḥotep III and IV is available in a good recent English translation (Moran 1992). The collection contained letters exchanged between the Egyptian pharaohs and the kings of Anatolia, Syria, Palestine, Mittanni, Assyria, and Babylonia. It is roughly contemporary with the Hittite kings Tudḫaliya III and Šuppiluliuma I (ca. 1360–1322 B.C.E.).

1.1.10.2. Ugaritic Corpus

Letters recovered in the excavations at Ras Shamra (ancient Ugarit) include ones written in Akkadian and in the alphabetic script used for the Ugaritic language. The examples of international correspondence were predominantly written in Akkadian.

Important studies of Ugaritic letters in the alphabetic script have been made by Dennis Pardee (1987) and by his student Robert Hawley (2003). Several Ugaritic letters were translated into English in *CoS* 3 by Pardee, and into German by Herbert Niehr (2006).

Since for a considerable stretch in its history the Ugaritic kingdom was a vassal state of the Hittites, it is not surprising that its epistolary corpus shares more formal features with the Hittite corpus than those of Assyria, Babylonia, or Egypt.

1.1.10.3. Egyptian Corpus

Letters exchanged between parties in Egypt itself and written in the Egyptian language were translated by Edward Wente in the present series (1990). English translations of some Egyptian letters can also be found in *CoS* 3. An English translation of a single letter from the Amarna period—from the Steward of Memphis, Apy, to the pharaoh—can be found in Murnane 1995, 50–51.

1.1.10.4. Hittite Corpus

See below in §1.2.1.

1.2. Written Correspondence in the Hittite Kingdom

1.2.1. The Hittite Letter Corpus

The first and only attempt to treat the comprehensive corpus of all known official letters exchanged by the Hittites was Hagenbuchner 1989a, 1989b. This two-volume work contains in its first volume a general discussion of Hittite letter writing: the circumstances of the discovery, findspots, publication, study and storage of the letters, what Hittite texts tell us about letters, scribes, messengers, and the post, the physical appearance of letters, the use or non-use of clay envelopes, the use or non-use of seals, the various greeting formulas used in the letters and various expressions typical of letters, the themes found in Hittite letters and how these are the same or differ from other cuneiform letters written by those more or less contemporary with the Hittites. Volume two is devoted to the transliteration and translation of the letters and to limited commentary. Where a particular letter has been subjected to a good and recent edition, Hagenbuchner refrains from retransliterating and retranslating, but offers additional comments relating to its content and style as well as bibliographical additions to the earllier edition. Certain very important additions to the corpus were published too late for Hagenbuchner to be able to include them, chiefly the almost 100 Middle Hittite letters from Maşat Höyük, published two years later by Alp (1991a), but also the few important Middle Hittite letters from Ortaköy near Çorum (ancient Šapinuwa) and Kuşaklı (ancient Šarišša). When we speak of "Hittite letters," we do not exclude letters sent to or from the Hittite royal court in the Akkadian language. In the land of the Hittites only letters of international diplomacy were written in Akkadian. Of these, we possess a few drafts (e.g., text 98) composed in the Hittite language prior to translating into Akkadian for dispatch to foreign destinations. Letters between Hittite officials, which make up the bulk of the non-diplomatic correspondence, were inevitably written in the Hittite language itself.

There exist also fragments of a few letters in the Luwian language (Houwink ten Cate 1995, 267), but they are too small and poorly preserved to be treated here.

The letters in the present corpus belong to the category of *official* correspondence, although some strictly private and personal transactions were carried out in the piggyback letters of the scribes. *Purely* private and personal letters, if they existed on non-perishable media (e.g., clay tablets), have not come down to us. Hagenbuchner (1989a, 20) speculates that privately employable messengers transported personal correspondence. As mentioned above (§§1.1.3.1; 1.1.5.2.1), however, it is also possible that such letters were carried by friends or family members, who could also convey their personal impressions of the health and doings of the sender.

1.2.2. Epistolary Coverage in the WAW Series

Over the span of its existence (1990-present), the Writings from the Ancient World series has produced three volumes entirely devoted to letters from the ancient Near East: Edward Wente's *Letters From Ancient Egypt*, Piotr Michalowski's *Letters from Early Mesopotamia*, and James M. Lindenberger's *Ancient Aramaic and Hebrew Letters*.

While none of the volumes claimed to present an exhaustive collection of known examples, the accidents of archeological recovery and preservation contributed to a much larger collection in some: many more documents have been preserved and studied in Egypt and Mesopotamia than in Syria, Palestine, or Hittite Anatolia.

As yet, the series has no coverage of the later periods of Mesopotamian (i.e., Old Babylonian, Old Assyrian, and later) epistolary literature, nor any coverage of Ugaritic letters. Some letters emanating from the Hittite kingdom, specifically international diplomatic correspondence, were translated by Gary M. Beckman in his book *Hittite Diplomatic Texts*. Other individual letters found treatment in volumes not specializing in that genre, for example, the letter of Apy to the pharaoh, published in William Murnane's volume, *Texts from the Amarna Period in Egypt*.

The present volume intends to fill a gap in this series' coverage of Hittite epistolary literature in general. Compared with earlier volumes in the series devoted to texts from the Hittite kingdom relating to religious and diplomatic subjects, the present book contains some innovations. Earlier volumes did not attempt to present the Hittite or Akkadian texts themselves, but like the volumes in the series on Egyptian texts were content to give English translations. When the present volume was originally commissioned by the editorial board, it was requested that it contain the Hittite text as well as English translation.

1.2.3. Scope of the Present Corpus

Hagenbuchner's comprehensive corpus of published letters numbers 424 letters and letter fragments. The corpus in this book is considerably smaller.

The present corpus differs from Hagenbuchner's in its purpose. Hagenbuchner's corpus was directed exclusively to specialists in the study of ancient Near Eastern texts, that is, scholars who are capable of and interested in studying badly broken fragments for the purpose of lexical, historical, and cultural research. The present volume, like others in the WAW series, is aimed at an educated general audience, which also includes scholars in the aforementioned category. It intends to present a representative corpus of well-preserved letters in both transliterated original text and connected English translation.

Most Hittite letters exist only in small fragments, whose connected content can hardly be reconstructed. For purposes of the series in which this volume appears it is unwise and unnecessary to include such badly broken fragments.

Some of the larger well-preserved letters of significant historical and diplomatic content (e.g., texts 98, 102, 103, 104, and 105) have already appeared in translation earlier in the present series (Beckman 1999a). But since the editorial mandate of the present volume was to include transliterations of the texts, and since these previously translated letters are of importance for understanding how Hittite letters work, I have chosen to include them here.

For two reasons the Middle Hittite corpus of letters from Maşat, edited by Sedat Alp (1991a, 1991b), is given a disproportionately large representation: it represents the largest single group of exceedingly well-preserved Hittite letters, and its letters were not included in Hagenbuchner's corpus.

But even the Maşat corpus contains several letters that are insufficiently preserved to be included here.

1.2.4. Order of Presentation of the Letters in This Corpus

In Hagenbuchner's large corpus, the letters were organized and arranged according to the rank and station of sender and receiver. No attempt was made to use a diachronic sequence. There are, of course, considerable advantages to this procedure, since it is often difficult to determine the date of a letter except within very large and approximate divisions (see below in §1.2.6 under "Dating"). But our purpose differs from that of Hagenbuchner, in that we limit ourselves to letters that are sufficiently well-preserved to permit connected translation and a context adequate for interpretation. Following this principle has significantly reduced the number of letters suitable for inclusion, which in turn leaves many of Hagenbuchner's organizational categories unrepresented. For this reason it has seemed preferable to us to present the letters in a roughly chronological series, and in the case of the Maşat letters, all of which can be dated within a period of a generation (or fifteen to twnety years, according to Houwink ten Cate 1998, 159), to simply follow the sequence of Alp's edition.

1.2.5. Transcriptional Conventions.

The transcription of Hittite texts requires a more complicated typography than Egyptian, Sumerian, Ugaritic, Aramaic, and Hebrew ones. Hittite sentences written out contain not only Hittite words, but also logograms—i.e., words written in the Sumerian and Akkadian language but intending to evoke in the reader's mind the corresponding Hittite word. In some cases the identity of the Hittite word underlying a Sumerian or Akkadian logogram is unknown. For this and other reasons relating to orthography, it is impossible to produce a written approximation of what the spoken Hittite would have sounded like. But so long as the reader keeps these limitations in mind, there is some value to be had from a standard transcription of the Hittite texts.

In general the conventions used in this book for the writing of Sumerian, Akkadian, and Hittite words are those employed in the *Hittite Dictionary of the Oriental Institute of the University of Chicago* [CHD]. But there are some differences that arise from the nature of this book. In the CHD entire texts are not edited in transliteration. So the following rules describe the text formatting in this book.

In the transliterated text of the letters presented here in full the Hittite words are not italicized, but are presented in lower case roman type. Sumerograms and Sumerian determinatives are written in upper case. Akkadograms appear in upper case italics. This style is slightly modified in other parts of the book, where short excerpts of text or even individual words are cited in the English context. There even the Hittite words are italicized, in order to set them off from the surrounding English text. When Akkadian words are referred to in their own right, not as Akkadograms in Hittite contexts, they are often written in lowercase italics.

1.2.6. Dating

Dating of letters by historical criteria is often impossible. Although royal senders or receivers are indicated by name in the diplomatic correspondence, in the internal correspondence the king and queen are not identified by name. And the fact that high-ranking bureaucrats often have the same name makes it difficult to use prosopography to identify the reign in which a given letter was written. Hagenbuchner (1989a, 106) cites KBo 28.66, KBo 18.59, and KUB 3.80 as rare examples of letters that gives their dates. None of these three letters is included in this corpus.

Letters found at the Hittite capital were all found in the archives that belong to the final archeological stratum. In this case it is often only the ductus that serves as a guide as to whether or not a letter is Middle or New Hittite. For some criteria permitting the identification of Middle Hittite letters found at Ḫattuša see de Martino 2005b and below on text 2.

Letters found outside of the capital are sometimes recovered from datable archeological strata. The many letters from Maşat Höyük belong to the Middle Hittite period, as do the few letters found at Kuşaklı and El-Amarna, while the few found at Alalakh, Ugarit, and Emar (Meskene) are New Hittite (ca. 1350–1200 B.C.E.). For purposes of this volume it is unimportant to date the New Hittite material more precisely, that is, by royal reigns, since the Hittite epistolary conventions do not differ significantly between the reigns of the first and last kings of this 150-year period. A more precise dating would, of course, be useful in order to understand their historical or political allusions.

If, as it seems likely, the tablets from Maşat Höyük all date from a period of a single generation,[12] it is likely that they were written during the reigns

12. On this see now van den Hout 2007b.

of at most two kings, Arnuwanda I and Tudḫaliya "II/III," the father of Šuppiluliuma I. The tablets of HKM 4 and 14 (texts 10 and 19) have parts of the seal impression of an emperor Tudḫaliya on the left corner of the upper edge (see Alp 1991a, pl. 1–2 for photos and figure 2 for a reconstruction of the impression combining traces from both tablets). Tudḫaliya "II/III" is shown to be the father of Šuppiluliuma I on a seal impression of the latter king. He is also thought to be portrayed on the silver fist-shaped rhyton in the Boston Museum of Fine Arts as the king making a libation (Güterbock and Kendall 1995). For historical sources attesting him and his reign see Klengel 1999, 127–34. For further discussion of this subject see Alp 1991a, 109–12; Klinger 1995b; Houwink ten Cate 1998, 159; and de Martino 2005b, 313–18. According to Houwink ten Cate (1998, 161), HKM 46–51 may be among the earliest of the letters in the corpus and belong to the end of the reign of Arnuwanda I. But van den Hout gives cogent reasons to question this early dating (2007b).

De Martino describes the problem as follows:

> It is not an easy task to solve the problem concerning the chronology of Middle Hittite letters. Only two Tapigga letters HKM 4 and 14 reveal the impression of a royal seal. The name of the king on the seal is Tutḫaliya and, along with S. Alp, it would seem quite possible that the king in question is Tutḫaliya III. One criterion regarding the chronological order of the letters is given by the study of the dignitaries who are mentioned. However, it is often difficult to identify them and, furthermore, we do not know how long they lived. What's more, it is also very difficult to establish whether letters which deal with similar subject can actually be put in any sort of chronological sequence within a brief space of time. In fact, theoretically, these letters might refer also to a series of similar cases that happened within a certain amount of distance between them. So for example, if we take the Tapigga letters relative to the sites of Kašaša and Kašepura (HKM 1, 5, 6, 19, 24, 25, 27, 31, 37, 45) which had undergone raids and attacks by the Kaškas, it is not possible to establish if all the letters deal with events that had happened in the same season or in a couple seasons one after the other. Or rather, we do not know if they mention episodes which were repeated in continuation, year after year and, therefore, whether they regard a period that stretched for a longer amount of time (2005b, 313).

And again:

> In conclusion, the Middle Hittite letters appear datable above all from the period of Arnuwanda I and Tutḫaliya III. The presence in the Ḫatti archives of letters from the times of these kings and the absence or scarcity of similar

> documents from earlier periods might be due to the chance factor involved in their discovery. However, it could also be due to the formation of a steady and well organized bureaucratic apparatus (requiring continuous and close contacts between functionaries and dignitaries) under kings Tutḫaliya II, Arnuwanda I and Tutḫaliya III. This correspondence could also imply, therefore, that it was with these three kings that a deep-rooted change in the structures of state organisation had been undertaken (2005b, 318).

1.2.7. Find Spots

1.2.7.1. In Ḫattuša

In the Hittite capital almost half of all letter fragments were found during the Winckler excavations, for which there is information as to the find spot in only a very few cases.[13] But reliable indirect evidence indicates that Winckler recovered the letters from the area of the acropolis (Büyükkale). During the Bittel excavations (1931–1939 and 1952–1977) most of the letters were found on the acropolis, principally in fill used for later Phrygian buildings. But the pattern of the ascertainable findspots—Buildings A, B, C, D, and F—suggests that there existed no special archive for letters as a genre.

Many letter fragments were found on the acropolis in areas unassociated with a specific building. This has raised the question why such documents, several of political importance, were not kept in the archive buildings down to the very end of the Hittite occupation. It is unclear if already during the Hittite occupation of the site letters were discarded instead of being kept in an archive building, or if their present findspots are the result of scattering by occupants of the site in post-Hittite periods. Güterbock (1971, X–XII) noted that of the seventy letters from an area east of Building D that he was then publishing, all were intentionally smashed in antiquity, indicating that for Hittite administrators there was no reason to keep most letters beyond a relatively short period. This fact perplexed even Güterbock, since—according to our way of thinking—correspondence of a political nature should be one of the most important components of the archives of a capital city and should have been kept until the end of the kingdom. Indeed some letters of this character were not intentionally destroyed by the Hittite scribes and have been recovered.

Not all letters found in the ruins of Ḫattuša were found on the royal acropolis proper. One was found on the south slope of the acropolis, another

13. Bittel 1937, 32–33, quoted in Hagenbuchner 1989a, 4 n. 34.

in the House on the Slope, to the west of the acropolis on the way to the main temple in the Lower City. Two more letters were found in the south area of this Temple I, and seven more from the discardings of the early excavation of Temple I itself.

Text 4 (KBo 12.62) is one of the few MH letters found in the House on the Slope (L 18 b–c/5), where otherwise mainly *current* (i.e., late NH) administrative documents were kept (see van den Hout 2007a). One NH text appears to be a practice tablet of a scribe learning to copy letters (text 110).

Since what information is known about the precise find spots of Boğazköy tablets is easily found online at the Hethitologie Portal (http://www.hethport.uni-wuerzburg.de/HPM/hethportlinks.html), there is no need to provide here in print a complete list of tablets found in each of the areas of the city (i.e., the acropolis buildings, Lower City, and the House on the Slope). Information as to the find spot of each text in the present corpus is given in its respective "Sources" paragraph.

1.2.7.2. Elsewhere

Some letters to or from the Hittite capital were found outside of Ḫattuša. The largest corpora of such letters were found in Maşat Höyük[14] and Ortaköy near Çorum.[15] Isolated examples have been found in Šarišša (Kuşaklı),[16] Egypt (El-Amarna),[17] Alalakh,[18] and Emar.[19]

14. See texts 7 through 85. Published in Alp 1991a, 1991b.

15. See texts 86 through 91. The complete corpus has not yet been published, but has been described in several places (Süel 1995; 1998a; 1998b; 2002a; and Ünal 1998). A small group of the tablets, those already in the Çorum Museum prior to the beginning of the Süel excavations, was published by Ünal 1998.

16. See texts 92 and 93.

17. *VBoT* 1 and 2 (our texts 95 and 94) are not strictly speaking "Hittite" letters, inasmuch as neither sender nor receiver was a Hittite. But they are written in the Hittite language, since the king of Arzawa preferred to use this language instead of Akkadian, the language of Amarna Age diplomatic correspondence. The El-Amarna corpus also contains at least one letter in Akkadian between the Hittite and Egyptian kings (EA 41 [text 96], English translation in Moran 1992, 114–15).

18. See texts 125 and 126, and discussions in Friedrich 1939 and Niedorf 2002.

19. See texts 123 and 124.

Find Spots of Maşat Tablets			
Quadrant	Room/Location	No. of items	HKM numbers
G/5	Room 8	48 (40 letters, 8	HKM 2, 3, 4, 7, 8, 9, 13, 16, 17, 18, 27, 34, 43, 44, 48, 49, 51, 52, 54, 55, 57, 58, 61, 62, 63, 65, 66, 68, 69, 70, 72, 74, 75, 76, 79, 81, 83, 94, 95, 96, 100, 102, 103, 105, 107, 109, 111, 114
H/5	Room 9	22 (20 letters, 2	HKM 1, 5, 6, 11, 12, 14, 15, 19, 21, 22, 24, 25, 30, 33, 36, 38, 42, 50, 64, 92, 113, 335
G/5	Portico W of Rooms 8 and 9	26 (22 letters, 4	HKM 10, 23, 26, 28, 29, 31, 32, 39, 40, 41, 46, 47, 53, 67, 71, 73, 77, 80, 84, 87, 88, 93, 97, 99, 106, 110
E/3	Room 33	1 letter	HKM 20

There is no obvious correlation between the findspots of the letters as opposed to the other administrative texts, since there was a smattering of the latter in each of the three loci. The largest concentration of tablets in a single location was that in Room 8.

The Kuşaklı letters [texts 92 and 93] were recovered from Building C. No information has been published on the find spot of the Emar letter, text 123. And text 124 is unprovenienced, since it was recovered from the art market.

1.2.7.3. Secondary Locations of Letter Tablets

1.2.7.3.1. Secondary Cities. Charpin (2007, 410) notes that, when the king of Mari received letters while traveling, his accompanying secretary stored them in a chest and deposited them in the palace archives on their return. This explains why many of the letters received by the king while he was away from the palace were actually recovered at Mari. As a result, in the same find spot both the letter to the king and his reply to it were found. This has a potential bearing on Hittite letters found at Ḫattuša, which may have initially been received while the king was traveling, perhaps at Šapinuwa/ Ortaköy.

There are also Mari letters that claim to have been accompanied by a second letter originally addressed to the sender and now forwarded to the king. Consequently, its eventual find spot would not provide evidence for its original destination.

1.2.7.3.2. Secondary Locations within the Same Ancient City. Hittite scribes themselves may have moved some documents from a location where they were actively consulted to one where they were merely kept in storage for eventual occasional reference. And the Phrygians who occupied the city mound of Ḫattuša after the Hittites used Hittite tablets and tablet fragments as fill in their building projects. This means that the excavators did not find them in the locations where the Hittite scribes originally left them.

1.2.8. Outward Appearance

1.2.8.1. Writing Direction, Axis of Inversion, and the Like

All Hittite tablets are inscribed from left to right and top to bottom of the first side, then flipped on a horizontal axis and written from the new "top" to "bottom" on the reverse. Long texts required larger tablets with two columns to the side. Hittite scribes employed three-columned tablets only for descriptions of festivals and rituals. The column sequence of multi-columned tablets is left-to-right on the front (obverse) and right-to-left on the back (reverse). If the text required only a little more space than afforded by the obverse and reverse, the left edge was used, since the right edge was used for text lines that needed to extend beyond the space on the main surface. At the end of a typical tablet would be the colophon: a few lines of text identifying the tablet's contents (a "title" in some cases), a notation of the number of tablets in the composition and whether or not this was the final tablet, and the name of the scribe. Here is the wording of a typical colophon:

> DUB.1.KAM *MA-AḪ-RU-Ú ŠA* m[*Ma-ad-du*]-*wa-at-ta wa-aš-túl-la*[-*aš*]
> "tablet one—the first—of (the composition called) 'the sin of Madduwatta'"
> KUB 14.1 left edge.

This is a simple colophon, containing information as to the title (or general description of the contents) of the tablet, and its position within a series of tablets. Other, more elaborate colophons, indicated by the words "completed" (Akkadian *QA-TI*) or "not completed" (*Ú-UL QA-TI*) whether there existed a continuation of the series on another tablet, and the names of the scribe and his supervisor:

> DUB.1.KAM *še-er še-e-šu-wa-aš QA-TI* [Š]U ^m*Šak-ka-pí* DUMU ^m*Nu-za* DUMU.DUMU-*ŠÚ ŠÁ* ^m*Ma-u-i-ri* / *PA-NI* ^m*An-gul-li IŠ-ṬUR* "tablet one of (those officials allowed or required) spending the night up (in the acropolis). Completed. The scribal work (literally, 'hand') of Šakkapi, son of Nuza, grandson of Mawiri. He wrote under the supervision of Angulli" KBo 5.11 iv 26-28 (NH).

Letters—at least Hittite ones—typically have no colophon: the information usually found in a colophon either was not needed in a letter or was indicated somewhere other than at the end (e.g., in the initial formulas).

Some letter tablets [texts 40 , 42] begin the text on the upper edge. This is usually a sign that the tablet was inscribed in the MH period.

1.2.8.2. Size, Shape and Dimensions of the Tablets

Hittite letter tablets are not uniform in size or outward appearance. They are rarely large, and never multi-columned in format. Alp gives no data in either HKM or Alp 1991a regarding the measurements of individual tablets. But the centimeter measuring stick is visible in his photographic plates at the back of Alp 1991a, which enables us to know the measurements of the depicted tablets.

HKM #	Text #	Dimensions		Scribe
		Horizontal	Vertical	
10	16	*8 cm*	*11.5 cm*	*Tarḫunmiya*
19	24	*5.6 cm*	*7.2 cm*	*Ḫašammeli*
21	26	8 cm	6.4 cm	Šanda
22	27	5 cm	4.25 cm	Mār-ešrē
26	31	*8 cm*	*9.2 cm*	*Tarḫunmiya*
46	48	6.5 cm	5.5 cm	Adad-bēlī
52	55	*6 cm*	*7.6 cm*	*Tarḫunmiya*
81	80	*6.5 cm*	*7.4 cm*	*Tarḫunmiya*

Tablets with vertical measurement larger than the horizontal are shown above in italics. It will be seen from the table that the scribe Tarḫunmiya always used tablets with larger vertical measurement than horizontal. Only one example each of the tablets of the other scribes were given measurement.

But Ḫašammeli's tablet (HKM 19, text 24) is also taller than wide, while those of Šanda, Mār-ešrē, and Adad-bēlī are wider than tall.

The relative size of the tablet, of course, depended upon the amount of its text. Hittite letter tablets, unlike Assyrian ones from certain periods, were not of standard size. Most Hittite letters did not require more space than a one-columned tablet afforded (see above in §1.1.4.1). Some are extremely small, such as the one-columned pillow-shaped tablets containing only a few lines of greeting formulas (cf. texts 10, 15, 41, 54) which Hagenbuchner (p. 29) compares to postcards. But in international diplomatic correspondence, where many issues needed to be discussed and background information provided, much more space was required. A notable case is the large, one-columned tablet in Hittite, the sender's copy of a communication from Puduḫepa to Ramses II of Egypt (text 98). Another such case, the "Tawagalawa letter" from the Hittite king to the king of Aḫḫiyawa (see text 100), required as many as three two-columned tablets to contain all of the text. But since neither of these two tablets left Ḫattuša, one must pose the question: were they in fact letters? Heinhold-Krahmer, who uses the size of text 100 as part of her argument that it was not a letter at all, but a briefing document for the messenger-representative, would say "no." Admittedly, the Puduḫepa letter too might be claimed as a briefing document. We lack the opening lines of the text in both cases, and with them any possible address or greeting formulas. One small tablet in the present corpus preserves the beginning of the text, yet lacks the opening formalities (text 94). It contains far too little text to make it probable that it was just a note to the messenger (e.g., a briefing document).

1.2.8.3. Envelopes and Sealings

Elsewhere in the ancient Near East, when confidentiality and security of the contents were needed, a clay envelope protected the contents from the eyes of unauthorized persons and was sealed with the seal of the sender, which authenticated the document. On the outside of the clay envelope could be found, at the very least, the name of the addresssee, but often the contents of the letter itself were repeated. This practice is known from Babylonian and Assyrian letters. The Sumerian and Akkadian terms for a tablet envelope are IM.GUR (*imgurru*), IM.ŠÚ (*imšukku*), and *ermum ša ṭuppi*. None of these terms occurs in Hittite texts.

Letters that were never dispatched have been found still in their envelopes (Ziegler 2001, 202). A clay envelope is preserved for only one of the Amarna letters, which is a kind of "passport" to facilitate travel through various check points on the route of the messenger (see Liverani 1998, 50).

Liverani's mention of Amarna letters which do not specify an addressee as providing indirect evidence for the original existence of an enclosing envelope, on which the addressee's name would have appeared, could provide an explanation for the rare example of a Hittite letter with no introductory wording of sender's name, addressee's name or greeting formula (see text 41). Whether this explanation also serves *VBoT* 2 (text 94), the incoming letter to the pharaoh from the Arzawan king, is uncertain.

Hagenbuchner (1989a, 32) regards the short sentence *nu ṬUP-PU ḫe-e-eš* in KBo 18.48 obv. 17, in a broken and therefore incoherent context, as a reference to "opening" a tablet envelope. For full discussion of Hittite letter envelopes see Hagenbuchner 1989a, 32–34.

Supposed evidence for its use with Hittite letters came from the Maşat letter HKM 86 (Alp 1991a, 284–85 with n. 427; accepted without further comment by Beal 1993, 246; de Martino 1996, 91–92; 2005b, 307). The wording of the alleged envelope was published as HKM 86a, and that of its enclosed letter as HKM 86b. As admitted by all, the surviving wording on HKM 86a and 86b is not similar, and there are no seal impressions of the sender on HKM 86a, as was the custom in Mesopotamia. Another letter from the Hittite king to an official at Tapikka-Maşat bears an impression of the royal seal on the tablet itself (text 10 [HKM 4]). Furthermore, since the handwriting on HKM 86a is not the same as on 86b, a different scribe seems to have inscribed it. For these and even more compelling reasons, which they will disclose in their forthcoming treatment of the problem, van den Hout and Karasu have informed me (Sept. 3, 2008) that their examination of the tablet itself has led them to conclude that HKM 86a is not a tablet envelope.

Hagenbuchner posits three possible explanations for the scarcity of recovered tablet envelopes on Hittite sites: (1) clay envelopes were used sparingly, chiefly with confidential messages, i.e., diplomatic correspondence; (2) clay envelopes were commonly used, but after their removal they were used in a kind of recycling to prepare new tablets; and (3) the envelopes normally used were not made of clay, but of perishable material such as cloth, leather, or wood. The third explanation runs afoul of the rare but actual recovery of a clay tablet envelope, and provides an inferior medium for the writing of the names of sender and addressee on the exterior.

Hagenbuchner (1989a, 9) assumes that, if no envelope was used, the messenger had to be unable to write cuneiform, so that he could not alter the wording of the tablet.

1.2.8.4. Paragraph Dividers

In many periods and regions of cuneiform writing one finds cases where a tablet's written content is subdivided into sections by means of horizontal lines (see also §1.2.15). This practice was widespread among tablets found at Hittite archaeological sites, and in all literary genres: documents of historiography, law, mythology, magic rituals, cult liturgy, and oracular divination. Some large single-columned tablets containing letters, especially those drafted in Akkadian (see text 1), contain no marking of subdivisions ("paragraphs") by means of horizontal lines. But most letters drafted in the Hittite language itself do contain these marks, even when they are quite short (for example, see texts 7, 10, 15, 18–20, 25, and 31). Hagenbuchner (1989a, 31 n. 11) notes that in the Amarna letters one can observe how some writers use these dividers liberally (Tushratta, for example) and others quite sparingly (Rib-Hadda of Byblos). The sections so demarcated in Hittite letters *do* seem in most cases to contain information related to a subject distinct from what precedes or follows. They can therefore be regarded as equivalent to paragraphs. For verbal clues to the beginning of new subjects in a letter see below in §1.2.15 and §1.2.19.1.

1.2.9. Duplicate Copies of Letters

Ordinary private lettters only existed in a single copy, that which was sent to the addressee (see Lindenberger's comment about Hebrew and Aramaic letters [1994, 9]). For this reason the presence of multiple copies of a letter can be an indication that it was not a functional letter, but a model letter used in scribal training (see §1.1.5.1.7). But at least in the capital, duplicate copies of outgoing letters for the sender's archives were made of important state correspondence.[20] This may even have been the case in the provincial centers as well; see texts 48–54 found at Maşat, but addressed to the king. These letters found at Maşat are unlike the preliminary drafts of diplomatic correspondence (or briefing documents) found at Ḫattuša (e.g., Puduḫepa's letter to Ramses II [text 98] or Ḫattušili III's letter to the king of Aḫḫiyawa [text 101]), which were intended to be translated into Akkadian or at least augmented with the introductory courtesy phrases prior to being sent to foreign destinations. So unless all the Maşat letters addressed to the king belong to the very last days of the settlement and were never sent at all (the view of Alp, Bryce, Freu and Mazoyer[21]), they are indeed copies kept for refer-

20. Examples cited in Hagenbuchner 1989a, 9 n. 17, e.g., CTH 178 (to Assyria).

21. Bryce (2003b, 173) claims that the provincial officials in Tapikka never kept copies of tablets they had dispatched to the king. For him, the above-mentioned letters

ence by the officials at Tapikka. The same must also be true of text 88, from Uḫḫa-muwa to the king, found at Ortaköy, unless it was sent from another center and intended for the king while the latter was temporarily resident in Šapinuwa. Hagenbuchner also mentions a few cases of duplicates of letters found at Boğazköy. The draft of text 105 was kept in at least three copies. And that not all of these were just chance finds of *discarded* drafts is clear from the fact that at least one was on a tablet with drafts of other outgoing correspondence to Assyrian rulers (KUB 23.92). Such a tablet containing multiple documents, all of related content, is what Hittitologists call a *Sammeltafel.* For a thorough discussion of such tablets, see Mascheroni 1988. This *Sammeltafel* must have been kept for reference as part of the "Aššur dossier," for officials advising the king on future correspondence with the Assyrian rulers (van den Hout 2002, 873–73).

1.2.10. Point of Origin of the King's Letters

Many of the letters found at Maşat were sent by the king. But was he always at Ḫattuša when he sent them? Since we know that Šapinuwa was a royal residence for use during part of the year, it is quite probable that some of the letters from the king came from there. In fact, some scholars have argued that the royal scribe Tarḫunmiya served the king in Šapinuwa.[22] Whether or not he remained permanently in Šapinuwa or always accompanied the king in his travels, we have no knowledge. Other scribes write from Ḫattuša to Tapikka, asking colleagues there to look after their houses (texts 32: 23–35; 55: 25–30; 63: 35–36), which indicates that they were in Tapikka for part of the year and elsewhere with the king the rest of the time.

1.2.11. Hittite Terminology for "Letters"

The Hittites had no specific word for "letter," but referred to such a document only with the word "(clay) tablet" (*tuppi-*), a Hittite word borrowed

were unsent outgoing correspondence. This was also the view of Alp (1991a, 4) and now voiced as well by Freu (Freu and Mazoyer 2007, 187–88), who believed that Tapikka was destroyed by enemies before they could be dispatched. On this point Freu appears to have changed his mind, for in 1983, 93 he claimed that these could be *either* drafts ("brouillons") of still unsent letters *or* copies of sent ones ("soit … soit"). Van den Hout (2007b, 392–93 n. 31) rejects the view that they were unsent letters.

22. Alp 1991a, 96–98 and Imparati 1997, 203 n. 26.

from Akkadian *ṬUPPU*.[23] Isolated cases exist of the use of other words, such as *ḫatreššar* "sending" or *ḫaluga-* "message." Hagenbuchner (1989a, 8) notes that the noun *ariyašeššar* "oracle" can be used to denote a tablet with the opening formulas of a letter and sent as such, but containing only the description of the results of an oracular inquiry (e.g., KBo 18.140 obv. 3–4). Texts 3 and 50 are examples in the present corpus.

In first-millennium hieroglyphic Luwian (the Aššur letters on lead strips, edited initially by Meriggi 1935–36) the word for "letter" seems to have been *hatura/i-* (see Hawkins 2000, 540–41). And there is limited evidence also for the use of wax-covered writing boards (Sumerogram GIŠ.ḪUR, Akkadogram ^{GIŠ}*LE-U*$_5$,[24] Luwian $^{\text{GIŠ(.ḪUR)}}$*gulzattar*) for correspondence;[25] see Šarpa's reference to sending a letter on a writing board (text 63: 4–6) and the passage cited from KUB 31.68 in §1.2.22 (end).[26] From KBo 18.69 rev. 3′ and 9′ it appears that both types were employed at the same time (Hagenbuchner 1989a, 7).

Within the letters themselves reference to another letter usually employs the phraseology "what I/you/he wrote" (*kuit ḫatrānun, kuit ḫatrāeš*)[27] instead of using a specific noun for the letter.

1.2.12. How Letters Were Read

The formulaic opening words of a Hittite letter instruct someone to "say" (Akkadian *QIBI*=*MA,* i.e., read) the words of the message to the addressee:[28] *ANA* PN … *QIBI*=*MA* "Say (i.e., read aloud) to PN!" This practice might be assumed anyway in lieu of the low rate of literacy in the ancient world

23. Contra Hagenbuchner 1989a, 7, the form *tuppi(y)anza* in the Maşat letters is not a "hethitisierte Form" of *tuppi-*, but merely its ergative case form (*GrHL* §3.8 and following).

24. HZL 103 no. 25 notes that one can also regard this as a "pseudo-Sumerogram," writing it as ^{GIŠ}LE.U$_5$.

25. On this meaning of GIŠ.ḪUR (and Akkadogram ^{GIŠ}*LE'U*) see Güterbock 1939; Bossert 1952; Archi 1973, 210 w. n. 7; Hoffner 1980, 285–86; and Hagenbuchner 1989a, 7. For Luwian *gulzattar* see *CLL* (Melchert 1993) 108 and *HED* K, 243. *HED* fails to observe that GIŠ(.ḪUR) is a determinative in this use, whereas *CLL* rightly identifies and transcribes it.

26. For other occurrences in letters see Hagenbuchner 1989a, 7 n. 7.

27. See Hagenbuchner 1989a, 8, as well as the discussion here in §1.1.9.5.

28. The Hittite phrase is: *ANA* PN *peran ḫalzai-* "to call out (i.e., read aloud) in front of PN" (Hagenbuchner 1989a, 8 with n. 14).

outside of scribal circles. But who was it who was addressed in this opening command? Who read the tablet? The incoming messenger, the addressee's scribe, or someone else? Most scholars assume that it was the bearer of the message who did the reading. He is the obvious first choice: a scribe at the hand of the recipient would be an option, but the messenger who delivered the tablet would always be there.

But when there was a scribe present at the destination, he might very well do the reading, since his voice and native pronunciation would be more familiar to the recipient. In HKM 81 (text 80): 29–30, the sender, Tarḫunmiya, asks Uzzū, the scribe at the destination, to read distinctly (SIG_5-*in*) to his elderly parents, who may also have been hard of hearing.

And it is impossible to insist that the recipient never read the letter for himself. Letter recipients who were literate most likely read their own incoming letters. In an ancient Hebrew letter found at Lachish, a civil servant named Hoshayahu complains bitterly to his superior, Ya'ush, of an insulting letter that Ya'ush had sent him. Hoshayahu writes:

> And now, please explain to your servant the meaning of the letter which you sent to your servant yesterday evening. For your servant has been sick at heart ever since you sent (that letter) to your servant. In it my lord said: 'Don't you know how to read a letter?' As Yahweh lives, no one has ever tried to read *me* a letter! Moreover, whenever any letter comes to me and I have read it, I can repeat it down to the smallest detail. (Pardee 2002, 79)

Clearly, Hoshayahu regarded it as an insult to his competence that he would have to have someone else read to him an official letter!

An interesting theory, which however is shared by almost no one else, is that of Kristensen (1977, 144; see comments by Cunchillos 1989, 242 and 244 n. 13), who maintains that the opening formula "say to PN" had become a mere fiction: that the letter (i.e., tablet) itself had replaced both sender and messenger in the function of conveying its contents to the addressee and was in fact the object addressed by this command.

But in many cases the recipients of Hittite letters did indeed have those letters read to them (the Hittite verb used is *ḫalzai-*; see texts 26: 20–26; 27: 12–16; 30: 20–25; 69: 3–7; and 94: 14–15, as well as the remarks of Hagenbuchner 1989a, 8). In cases where it was appropriate for an incoming letter to be read aloud to its addressee, usually in the case of a royal personage receiving diplomatic correspondence, the messenger served as more than simply a means of reading the written text. Oral messages by the messenger *supplemented* what was written. It is these supplementary messages, not the simple reading aloud of the written ones, that Hagenbuchner (1989a, 8) has in mind when she writes that this practice was restricted to diplomatic correspondence. Confronted by supplementary oral messages not verifiable from the written one, the letter's recipient might have reason not to trust the messenger's version. See text 94: 1–6 and my annotations to that text. Compare the following advice from a Hittite king to a king of Kizzuwatna with whom he was in correspondence:

> Whenever I send you a tablet on which words are written, and there are also words spoken to you by the messenger, if the words spoken by the messenger correspond to those on the tablet, you may trust the messenger. But if the words spoken by the messsenger do not correspond to what is written on the tablet, you must not trust him. (KBo 1.5 iv 32–39, treaty written in Akkadian; ed. Weidner 1923, 108–9; an English translation exists by Beckman 1999a, 24 [§59])[29]

In the case of a messenger carrying a message of the king deliberately falsifying a diplomatic letter, he might be put to death by beheading.[30]

Evidence from Old Babylonian Mari makes it clear that sometimes the messenger was actually instructed by the sender to convey an oral message *intended* to mislead bystanders who were present when the messenger presented the tablet to the addressee and to disguise the actual content of the written message (Charpin 2007, 413): "When my lord sends me a messenger, let my lord send orally this message: 'Let your people be gathered together. Assuredly, I shall be going to Der' (or wherever my lord wishes). Let him send me this message orally, but on the tablet inform me of the true route that my lord will follow."

1.2.13. Scribes of the Letters (see also above in §1.1.5.1)

Unlike in other document types from Hittite sites, where the name of the scribe appears in a colophon at the end, Hittite letters have no colophons. The scribes who wrote the letters are not mentioned, unless the scribe has appended to the letter he wrote for his superior a piggyback letter of his own (see §1.2.24). And since in Hittite letters only rarely is the title or occupation of a person mentioned, it is possible only in a few cases to identify persons

29. Cited in Heinhold-Krahmer 2007b, 41–42.

30. KUB 14.3 (text 101) iv 46–52 ("Tawagalawa letter"). Various possibilities, none of them certain, as to how such a falsification might be determined are explored by Hagenbuchner 1989a, 9.

who are scribes. Mainly this is possible when the scribe of an incoming letter writes a piggyback letter to someone other than the addressee of the first letter, and addresses him, for example, as "dear brother" or "dear father," indicating a colleague (see also §1.1.5.1.5 and §1.2.16). Using this criterion—the address with a familial term—to identify scribes, Hagenbuchner (1989a, 14–15) lists eight names from the Boğazköy letters (Ḫešni, Lupakki, Nananza, Pallā, Šaušga-ziti, Zuwa, GUR.(d)LUGAL-ma, and NU.GIŠ.SAR), one from a letter found at Emar (Mār-Šeruwa), eight from letters found at Maşat (three resident in Maşat: Uzzū, Walwanu, and Adad-bēlī; five writing from Ḫattuša: Tarḫunmiya, Šanda, Šuriḫili, Mār-ešrē, and Ḫašammili), and a large number of others from Boğazköy letters that possibly were scribes.

1.2.14. Messengers (see also above in §1.1.5.2)

Messengers transported the letters. In the Akkadian-language correspondence the messenger is called DUMU KIN (= Akk. *mār šipri*), while Hittite-language texts rarely employ this term, but regularly use LÚ *ṬĒME.* As already noted by Hagenbuchner 1989a, 15 n. 46, in the earliest Hittite texts the LÚ in this construction was a *status constructus* (*awīl/amēl*) and the second noun always in the genitive *ṭēme/i*, as it was in Akkadian ("man of a message").[31] But in the course of time Hittite scribes lost this knowledge and began to view the LÚ as a determinative and to decline the noun *ṬĒMU.* The underlying Hittite word, written out syllabically only rarely,[32] was LÚ*ḫalugatalla-*, a derivative of *ḫaluga-* "message."

Both the Akkadogram in its earliest Hittite understanding (*awīl ṭēmi* "man of a message") and its Hittite equivalent (*ḫalugatalla-*) nicely reflect the difference between this functionary—a real messenger (Akkadian *mār šipri, ša šipirāti*), who presented the text and remained at the destination in order to interpret the letter to its recipient and bring back a reply—and a mere letter carrier (Old Babylonian Akkadian *wābil ṭuppim, lāsimum*), who delivered the tablet(s) and returned immediately (see Charpin 2007, 407). Specialized terms for types of letter carriers/couriers found in Hittite texts are LÚ*PĒTḪALLU* "horseback rider" and LÚKAŠ$_4$.E "runner, courier" (Akkadian *lāsimu*). Although these two terms are by no means rare in Hittite texts, their

31. According to the CAD Ṭ, 96–97 the exact equivalent of the Hittite Akkadogram LÚ *ṬE-MI/E* (**awīl ṭēmim*) is not yet attested in Akkadian texts. A close approximation, however, does exist in *bēl ṭēmi* "bearer of a report."

32. Occurring five times in text 95 (*VBoT* 1), lines 12, 19, 20, 23 [*bis*].

occurrence in letters is rare, and the contexts in which they appear too poorly preserved to enable us to learn anything useful. Possibly ^{LÚ}NÍ.ZU in text 122 is a shorter writing of ^{LÚ}NÍ.ZU ^{LÚ}KAŠ$_4$.E "scout courier."

In the first-millennium hieroglyphic Luwian texts, the word for "messenger" may have been *haturala-*, a derivative in *-(a)la-* from *hatura-* "letter(?)" (Hawkins 2000, 484).

Even those messengers (*ḫalugatalla-*/LÚ.MEŠ *ṬĒME*) entrusted with correspondence within the Hittite heartland (i.e., correspondence between the royal court and its officials in outlying posts, or between those officials themselves), on occasion did more than merely receiving, carrying, and delivering the tablets. But this was certainly the case with those accompanying international diplomatic correspondence.

Messengers entrusted with correspondence with foreign powers clearly had additional duties and powers. In Old Babylonian Mari such messengers were the equivalent of diplomats (Lafont, cited by Charpin 2007).[33] Such messengers (LÚ.MEŠ *ṬEME*) also had to be available to answer truthfully and accurately whatever questions the recipients of the letters might ask about the meaning of the written documents (see Heinhold-Krahmer 2007b, 42).

Obviously, such messengers needed to be bilingual in order to communicate with their foreign hosts and scribes. In some cases, when the messenger's control of the foreign language was minimal, what was employed was a "pidgin" language (Heinhold-Krahmer 2007b, 171). This "pidgin" sometimes even shows itself in the written communications (Bryce 2003b, 233). *VBoT* 1 (text 95) may show evidence of a "pidgin" language in written form, but the details of interpretation are still to my mind unclear.

1.2.14.1. Named Hittite Messengers

Hagenbuchner assembled a list of the names of persons holding this office in Hittite texts:[34]

Foreign origin or destination	**Name of envoy(s)**
To Egypt	Ḫattuša-ziti, Kula-ziti, Nerikkaili, Pikašti,

33. See RS 34.165 (Ugaritica VII, pls. XLIV–XLV = Lackenbacher 1982) obv. 21–29, where a messenger (^{LÚ}DUMU.KIN) seems to use his own judgment as to whether he should present a "tablet of war" or a "tablet of peace" (personal communication of G. Beckman).

34. Hagenbuchner 1989a, 21–22. Only a very few names are given in Pecchioli Daddi's articles in 1982, 110–11, 142–44.

	Reamašši/Reamašya, Tili-Teššub, Zitwalla
To Syria	Alalimi, Ḫilanni, Nerikaili, Piḫašdu/ Piḫaddu, Šauška-muwa, Tiḫi-Teššub, Zuzu
To Ugarit	Aliziti (*rēš šarri*), Arma-ziti, Kukuli, Kunni, Mizra-muwa, GAL-^{d}IŠKUR, PAP-^{d}LUGAL-ma
To Carchemish	Arwašši, Ebina'e, Iltaḫmu, Kurkalli
To Aššur	Maša-muwa, Urapa-^{d}[U]
From Egypt	Iršappa (envoy of Amunḥotep III), Ḫani (envoy of widow of Akhenaten), and 13 envoys of Ramses II (Aniya, Aya, Leya, Manya, Mairiya, Naḫḫa, Pareamaḫu, P/Wariḫnawa, Piyati, Re'anna, Tuttu, Wašmua-rea-naḫta, Zinapa), Kalbaya[35]
From Babylon	Adad-šar-ilī, Ana[-X], Ellil-bēl-nišê
From Aššur	Amurru-ašarēd, Bēl-qarrad, Ṣillī-Aššur
From Ugarit	Aḫaltena, Amutaru, Takuḫli
From Amurru	Zinupi
Other international envoys	Zuwa, Marku[-X], Na-[X], Kuliziya
Domestic envoys	Wandapa-ziti

1.2.14.2. How Did the Messengers Carry the Letters?

Some messengers (especially international carriers) kept the tablets in wicker or wooden chests or cases (^{GIŠ}PISAN, ^{GIŠ}PISAN.DUB, ^{GIŠ}PISAN.KASKAL.LA; Hagenbuchner 1989a, 24 n. 83). The one instance in which the pharaoh Amunḥotep II claimed that an international messenger was intercepted with a tablet around his neck may be a special case (Helck 1962, 479 n. 23). Perhaps the tablet in question was his "passport" (§1.1.8.4, §1.2.8.3).

35. Hagenbuchner lists Kalbaya as an envoy *from* Arzawa (to Egypt), but he appears only in EA 32 = *VBoT* 2 (text 94), a letter replying to EA 31 = *VBoT* 1 (text 95) as the *Egyptian* messenger who accompanies the Arzawan messenger ("So send Kalbaya back to me quickly together with my messenger").

1.2.15. The Literary Form of a Hittite Letter

1.2.15.1. The Normal and Complete Form

In its normal form a Hittite letter opens with an address formula, followed by a greeting formula, followed by the body of the letter. There are no closing formulas. Usually a horizontal line divides each of the three parts. In longer letters with multiple subjects, these "paragraph lines" punctuate the discourse.[36] If there is more than one greeting formula, a paragraph line may keep them separate. In general this procedure is followed also in contemporary letters sent from Ugarit, Qatna (EA 52–55), Tunip (EA 59), and Kāmid al-Lōz (Hagenbuchner 1989a, 31).

1.2.15.2. Omission of Some Components of the Form

The Old Hittite Akkadian letter of Ḫattušili I (no. 1) contains no greeting formula, nor does the letter have a single paragraph marker. Middle Hittite letters from Maşat sometimes lack one or more of these three elements. Letters between equally ranked persons (e.g., those addressing each other as "my dear brother") or from a subordinate to a superior always have greeting (well-wishing) formulas. But those from a superior to an inferior do not. Lacking the greeting formula are the king's letters to his subordinates in Tapikka (Maşat): nos. 7, 8, 9, 10, 11, 12, 13, 14, 15, 16, 17, 18, 19, 20, 21, 22. The king's scribes Šuriḫili, Ḫattušili, Ḫašammili, and Šanda use a greeting formula in their piggyback letters to persons styled as "my dear brother" (nos. 8, 9, 16, 22, and 26), but they do not use a paragraph line to separate address from greeting. On the other hand, the royal scribe Pišeni uses no greeting formula in his piggyback letter to Kaššū and Pulli (no. 23), who are ranked below him and are called "my dear sons" (DUMU.MEŠ DÙG.GA-*YA*), nor does Ḫašammili in his piggyback letter to Uzzū (text 24). The scribe also fails to use a paragraph line to separate two "concerning" sections in text 36 (see n. 163 and Hagenbuchner 1989a).

1.2.16. Address Formulas (see §1.1.9.1)

The opening lines of a typical Hittite letter are written in Akkadian. The sender is identified by the Akkadian phrase *UMMA* PN-*MA* "thus speaks PN," the recipient by the phrase *ANA* PN (plus or minus titles) *QIBĪ-MA* "say to

---

36. On the rare absence of an expected paragraph line to mark a new subject see note 118.

PN." As demonstrated for other epistolary corpora (§§1.1.9.1; 1.1.10.3), so also we assume in Hittite letters the person addressed in the *ANA* PN *QIBĪ-MA* "say/speak to PN" clause is the messenger who delivers the letter, or possibly the scribe who will read it aloud to the recipient. This affects how in this corpus I translate the royal title ᵈUTU-*ŠI*, literally "my sun god." If the title is used when addressing the king, I translate "Your Majesty" (e.g., see texts 16, 24, 48, 49, 50, 51, and 89). If another is addressed, and the king is referred to, I translate "His Majesty." If the king refers to himself with the title, I render it "My Majesty" (e.g., see texts 13: 13; 16: 22; 18: 10; 19: 6). Since the opening words in a letter "say/speak to ᵈUTU-*ŠI*" are addressed not to the king, but to the messenger or scribe, I employ the translation "His Majesty." Likewise, the *UMMA* ᵈUTU-*ŠI* phrase—"thus speaks His Majesty," since these words would be what the messenger or scribe would say to the addressee.

The combination of *UMMA* and *QIBĪ-MA* "thus (says) PN_1 ... say to PN_2" is paralleled by the address formula in an Edomite letter ("a saying of Lumalak: say to Bulbul"), which Lindenberger (1994, 6–7, 118) calls a "double-saying formula." But in the Edomite example the same verbal root (ʾMR) is used for both phrases, whereas in Hittite and Ugaritic letters, both of which use the "double-saying" form, there is no use of a similar verbal root. Since in the Hittite examples Akkadian words are written (*UMMA, QIBĪ-MA*), we do not know if Hittite words might have been pronounced when the letter was read aloud, and if so, what they were. It is quite possible that the scribe pronounced the Akkadian. Evidence that the Akkadian was read out in a letter to the Egyptian pharaoh is found in Amarna. On one occasion the reading aloud of the formula containing Akkadian *ANA* "to" seems to have resulted in an unintentional haplological clipping of the first part of an addressed pharaoh's royal name: *A-NA* ᵐ*A-na-ḫu-u-ri-ya* was read *A-NA* ᵐ*Ḫu-u-ri-ya* (see Freu and Mazoyer 2007, 283, citing Wilhelm and Boese 1987).

The order of these two phrases depends upon the rank or status of each correspondent. In most Hittite letters it is customary to give first the name of him who is of higher rank, regardless of whether he is the sender or recipient. If the two parties are of equal rank, the sender's name precedes the recipient's, as is usual (but not always: see text 8, lines 14–16) in the piggyback letters, where both parties are often scribes. This pattern was not followed in the Old Hittite letter (text 1, lines 1–3) composed in Akkadian, where the name of Ḫattušili's subject (ARAD) precedes the king's own name.

Sometimes the *-MA* fails to appear after the sender's name. Hagenbuchner (1999, 53–54) has described the conditions under which this happens:

in (NH ?) letters from Ḫattuša, the *-MA* is omitted after names ending in that syllable or when the document is merely a draft for an outgoing letter to a foreign ruler; in the MH letters found at Maşat, *-MA* is omitted when the sender's name stands first and aside from his name or title no additional characterization such as "your brother" occurs (see HKM 18: 21; 19: 26; 21: 16; 22: 9; 27: 11; 31: 20); only in letters from the king does the *-MA* occur in these circumstances. For this and other reasons Hagenbuchner considers text 122 to be a letter sent from Tapikka (Maşat) to Ḫattuša.

Likewise, when there is more than one addressee, there are two different patterns of writing the second and following names. In the letters from Ḫattuša, *Ù A-NA* "and to" occurs before the last-named addressee, whereas these words do not occur in the Maşat letters (Hagenbuchner 1989a, 53–54).

Such address lines, including both sender's and addressee's names, are found in all cases, even in the letters of scribes attached to the end of tablets containing the letters of their superiors. The only exception known to me is *VBoT* 2 (text 94), the circumstances of which are quite unusual. First of all, the sending scribe apparently does not know the name of his counterpart at the receiving end. And secondly, the tablet as we have it lacks even the address lines in the principal letter, making it look like some sort of draft or copy of the original letter.

Persons of high rank, whether addressees or writers, often use only their titles. Usually, it is the superior of the corresponding pair who is identified only by rank. The most obvious case is the king, who is superior to all of his subjects and whose actual name never appears in the address formula. But also the ruler of Kizzuwatna called "the Priest" (text 76), the *BEL MADGALTI* (texts 60 and 62), the Chief of the Heralds (UGULA NIMGIR. ÉRIN.MEŠ; text 71), the Chief of the Chariot-Warriors (GAL $^{\text{LÚ.MEŠ}}$KUŠ$_7$; texts 72 and 73), the GAL GEŠTIN "Field Marshall" (text 118), the Chief of the Scribes (GAL DUB.SAR; text 74), and the Chief of the "Wood-Scribes" (GAL DUB.SAR.GIŠ; text 75). When the queen writes to the king, she identifies herself only by title as "the queen" (texts 89 and 107). Rarely, both sender and addressee are identified only by their titles (text 6 = KBo 18.95), in this case the Chief of the Palace Servants to the Chief of the Guard.

As in Mesopotamian and Syro-Palestinian letters, the sender may address a colleague, using terms of familial relationship: DUMU DÙG.GA=*YA* "my dear son (i.e., junior colleague),"[37] *ABI* DÙG.GA=*YA* "my dear father (i.e.,

37. DUMU É.DUB.BA.A in Old Babylonian scribal parlance.

senior colleague)," [38] and ŠEŠ.DÙG.GA=*YA* "my dear brother (i.e., colleague of equal rank and seniority)." This practice suggests relationships in the scribal schools and continuing collegiality in the trade.[39] Since also in Old Babylonian a distinctive writing was used to distinguish such cases from a real father–son relationship (AD.DA.É.DUB.BA.MU vs. AD.DA.MU), so also the addition of DÙG.GA (rendered above as "dear") may have served the same purpose in Ḫatti. The phrase "my dear brother," however, seems to be used also for high-ranking persons who are not scribes but are of equal rank,[40] suggesting that also "my dear son" may denote a lower-ranked colleague and "my dear father/mother" one of higher rank. HKM 2 (text 8 below), line16 and HKM 3 (text 9), lines 14–16 show, however, that a fellow scribe who addressed his colleague as "my dear brother/father" did not use the "dear" element in referring to himself as "your brother." For the same use of familial terminology in first-millennium Hebrew and Aramaic letters, see Lindenberger 1994, 7.

There is evidence to suggest that in the opening lines of a letter the polite forms of terms of relationship, such as "my lord," "my lady," "your servant" were used, and later in the body of the letter the less formal and affectionate ones of family relationships appear (see KBo 18.95 [text 6], where a man begins his letter addressing his correspondent as "my lord, the Chief Margrave" and styles himself as "your servant, the Chief of the Palace Attendants" (lines 1–2), yet two lines later expresses his wish that "all may be well with my dear son" [line 4]).

1.2.17. Greeting- and Wish-Formulas

Following the custom of Egyptian, Syrian, and Mesopotamian epistolography (see §1.1.9.2), Hittite letter writers regularly employed a formula of well-wishing in their letters to persons who were either their social superiors or equals, but not when the letter recipients were inferiors.

In the Hieroglyphic Luwian letters from Aššur the greeting and wish formulas are standard, and correspond to those used in Hittite letters, although the Luwian lexical items are of course different (Hawkins 2000 I/2, 538).

38. AD.DA É.DUB.BA.A in Old Babylonian scribal parlance.
39. So Otten 1956, 181, 189. See Hagenbuchner 1989a, 10–11.
40. Hagenbuchner 1989a, 12–13.

The typical Hittite practice does not invoke specifically named deities, but only "the gods" (DINGIR.MEŠ) in general. The following are standard well-wishes used in Hittite letters:

(1) "May the gods keep you alive" (*nu=tta* DINGIR.MEŠ TI-*an ḫarkandu*): found in KBo 18.95 (text 6), HKM 10 (text 16), 17 (text 22), 27, 29, 36, 52, 53, 56, 57, 64, 67, 71, 73, 80, 81, 82, 84, ABoT 65 (text 81), Güterbock 1979 (text 107), KBo 13.62 (text 110), etc. Of course, minor variants also occur, such as "May the gods keep my brother (= you) alive" (KBo 18.35: 4), and even "May the Thousand Gods (*LI-IM* DINGIR.MEŠ) keep you alive" (see texts 34, 85, and KBo 18.77: 18–19). "The Thousand Gods" is the Hittite term for their entire pantheon (see Singer 1994; Hawkins 1998a; Karasu 2003).

(2) "And may (the gods) lovingly protect you" (*nu=tta aššuli paḫšantaru*): HKM 2, 3, 10, 17, 21, 27, 29, 31, 33, 36, 52, 53, 56, 57, 58, 60, 63, 64, 67, 71, 73, etc. The only letters lacking this expressed wish are those from the king to his subordinates (e.g., nos. 7–43). Even the queen uses it to the king (no. 89). And the reigning king himself uses it in a letter to his mother, the dowager queen (no. 106).

This phrase is not limited to letters, but occurs also in treaties. For example, in the treaty of Tudḫaliya IV with Kurunt(iy)a of Tarḫuntašša there occurs: *tuk=ma kūš* DINGIR.MEŠ *aššuli paḫšantaru nu=kan ANA* ŠU ᵈUTU-*ŠI meḫuntaḫḫut* "But may these gods keep *you* in good health, so that you may grow old in the service of (literally, in the hand of) His Majesty" (iv 14–15).

The exact equivalent is found in the Akkadian and Ugaritic letters from Ugarit. The Akkadian reads DINGIR.MEŠ *ana šulmāni liṣṣurūka* "may the gods keep you in good health" (see CAD Š/III, 244). Akkadian *ana šulmāni* "in good health" corresponds to the literal meaning of Hittite *aššuli* "in goodness" or "in well-being."

There exists also a fuller expression *nu=tta* ŠU.ḪI.A-*uš araḫzanda aššuli ḫarkandu nu=tta paḫšandaru* "May the gods lovingly hold their arms about you and protect you," on which see de Martino and Imparati 2004, 797 with n. 50. This fuller expression associates *aššuli* with holding arms around the protected person, instead of with "may they keep (you)," and therefore may suggest a looser meaning for *aššuli* than "well-being, good health" in this phrase. For that reason, I prefer to render *aššuli* in both variants with the adverb "lovingly," describing the gods' attitude rather than as expressing a goal for the protected person. The divine protective embrace, in its application to the Hittite king himself, is doubtless shown in royal reliefs depicting the king in the embrace of a deity (see, for example, the frequently photographed relief in chamber B of Yazılıkaya: Akurgal 1962, pls. 84–85; Macqueen 1986, 132, pl. 120; and Seeher 2002, 150, pl. 141).

A special greeting formula is that which invokes the god Ea specifically. In HKM 2 (text 8), lines 19–22—also in HKM 3 (text 9), lines 18–20—in addition to the general subject "the gods," the god Ea, "the king of wisdom," is added. This is because one scribe is addressing another. Ea was the patron deity of scribes. In Akkadian his epithet was *bēl nēmeqi* "lord of wisdom," which the Hittite scribes modified to "king of wisdom." The inclusion of Ea, king of wisdom, in the wish formula (see line 19b) is not common in previously known Boğazköy letters. But see *VBoT* 2 = EA 32 (text 94; Tarḫunta-radu to Amunḥotep III), 15–18. This special form of the blessing always seems to be addressed to scribes. See also HKM 3 (text 9): 17–20. There is no other attested example of invoking a particular god or goddess to protect the addressee.

Another pair of standard statements employs the term SIG_5-*in* "well," used similarly to Hebrew *šalôm.* In this pair, writers express their wish that all be well with their addressee, and report that all is similarly well with themselves. That the second type especially can be a mere formality is shown by text 89, where immediately after reporting to the king that "all is well with me," the writer (who is the queen) proceeds to enumerate her physical ailments!

1.2.18. Date and Location of Sender

Unlike modern letters, ancient ones normally indicate neither a date of composition nor a place of origin. Probably, the bearer of the message would provide this information. When letters are dated (as, for example, in the Old Babylonian Mari letters), they show the day of the month, but never the year. This suggests that such dating was not due to the requirements of archiving, as is the case with administrative and legal texts. No Hittite letter bears a date or an indication of its place of origin. Presumably, the king knew where his principal officials were located. But since the king moved around, his location at the time of sending the letter would have to be communicated by the letter carrier.

1.2.19. The Body of a Letter

As mentioned in §1.2.8.4, the scribes of most letters used horizontal lines to set off subdivisions of the main body of the letter, which represent something like our modern paragraphs. But since in many cases the tablet contents were read aloud to the intended recipient, he or she could not see the lines. In this oral presentation of the letter the sender embedded certain words or expressions that indicated his/her transitions. In the Akkadian letters from El-Amarna the favorite word was *šanītam* "next." In the Hittite-language letters other terms or phrases served this function. When a correspondent wished to reply individually to more than one issue raised in the letter he had received from the addressee, he could begin each of those sections with "concerning what you wrote to me" (see §1.1.9.5), and follow by quoting a short part of the message he had received.

1.2.19.1. Phrases and Formulas Recurring in the Body of the Letters

The topic-transition marker "Concerning ..." (*kuit* [or *uddār kue*] *ḫatrāi-*) occurs in the vast majority of the letters treated here, but especially in the king's letters to his officials at Tapikka. Not infrequently he uses it several times in the same letter (twice in letters 8 and 12, and six(!) times in text 16).

The main purpose of letters is to convey and solicit information. This is typified by the somewhat stereotyped inquiries about the health of the addressee that usually form part of the opening formulas: "With me all is well. May it be well with you." But it is also reflected in the phrase "write to me how it is with ..." (see texts 58, lines 33, and 35; 89, lines 13–16; 106, lines 5–7; 108, lines 8–12; and 111, left edge 6).

Important new information for the addressee is usually highlighted by the use of an imperative/jussive form of the verb "know" (*šāk* or *šakdu*). Four typical examples occur in texts 35 (left edge 4), 40 (rev. 5), 48 (left edge 1) and 101 (iii 5–6). An identical feature is found in the Ugaritic letter corpus (see above in §1.1.9.6).

Official letters by superiors to their subordinates often contain rebukes, and at times sarcasm and irony. Two examples from the Maşat corpus are found in HKM 6 and 17 (texts 12 and 22; see already Hoffner in *CoS* 3.18:47 and 3.28:50–51). And for further examples see text 58, line 31 (noted already in CHD Š, 258) and possibly text 73, line 71. For some examples of sarcasm in other Hittite texts see Beckman 1999a, 132–33, and Haas 2006, 41–42. Bryce (2003b, 70–71) cites an example of sarcasm by the Assyrian king Aššur-uballiṭ to the pharaoh Akhenaten. For examples of hyperbole in Maşat letters, see de Martino and Imparati 1995, 104–5. And for a rare complaint by a subordinate to his superior about an insulting letter, see §1.2.12.

A special verbal figure—*uwat duwaddu*—has been interpreted by Alp and Hagenbuchner (most recently, 1999, 55) as a formula of well-wishing. This figure virtually always accompanies a command. Alp's translation is "may (the god's) mercy be upon you," and Hagenbuchner's idea is similar. It occurs six out of nine times in letters from Tapikka (HKM 6, 18, 31, 33, 70, and 84 [texts 12, 23, 37, 39, 72, and 83]), and if one regards VS 28.129 (text 122) as originating in Tapikka, that makes a total of seven out of ten. The remaining two occurrences are found in KUB 31.101 (lines 35 and 37). *uwat duwaddu* always indicates the need for urgent action (HKM 18 left edge 1; HKM 31: 30; HKM 33: 27–28; HKM 70: 13; HKM 84 rev. 12). And its location either in the middle or at the end of the letter and never at the beginning, where the polite courtesy language occurs, shows that it is not (contra Alp 1991a, 71, Marizza 2007a, 98) a greeting formula (*Begrüßungsformel, formula di benedizione*) used with particularly high-ranking persons. The writer of the letter is always someone superior in rank to the addressed person, which hardly fits the pattern of the use of the noun *du(wa)ddu* "mercy!" with which this formula is usually connected. Perhaps therefore the two have nothing in common but similarity of sound to each other. I have usually rendered the forumula "get a move on!" or "quickly now!," because the context usually suggests that the speaker wishes hasty compliance with his wishes.

1.2.19.2. The Style of the Letters

On analogy with modern correspondence, we expect the style of ancient letters to be informal and in some ways less inhibited by traditional forms than the formal documents that form the majority of recovered literature. To a certain extent, we are not dissappointed in this respect by Hittite letters. Yet if we expect also a kind of freedom from the normal rules of grammar observed in the official texts, we will indeed be disappointed. With the exception of letters written in Hittite by foreign scribes (e.g., the Amarna letters 94–95), the normal rules of Hittite grammar are consistently followed. Yet the language of the letters can be quite colorful and vivid. There is humor in the king's sarcastic rebuke of his poorly performing official Kaššū: "Was that enemy perhaps enchanted, that you did not recognize him?" (text 12: 11–14). And one wonders at the stupidity of the official who sent freshly killed birds, undoubtedly without preserving ice, on a 160 km trip from Alalakh to Carchemish (text 125), and thought the king of Carchemish would find them tasty!

1.2.20. Subjects Discussed in the Domestic Correspondence

1.2.20.1. Foreigners Crossing the Borders

Letters from the king to officials in border areas are almost exclusively attested in the Maşat correspondence. As a parallel to reports to the king from Hittite officials in border areas, here is a lengthy quote from such an official to Esarhaddon, king of Assyria:

> As to Your Majesty's giving me the following instructions concerning the guards who are posted in the border fortresses toward Urartu, the land of the Manneans, the Medes, and the land of Ḫubuškiya: "Give them this order (which is) to be strictly executed: 'Do not be negligent in your guard duties!' Also, their attention should be directed to refugees coming from the regions around them in such terms: should a refugee come to you(r posts) from the land of the Manneans, of the Medes, or from the land of Ḫubuškiya, you will hand him over immediately to a messenger of yours and send him on to the crown prince. And if it should happen that he has some information, you will talk it over with the crown prince, a report [should c]ome from you that a Mannean scribe [is to be sent to you] ...; he should write down what he (the refugee) has to say. They should seal (the report) with the cross-shaped stamp seal; Aḫi-dūr-enši, the commander of the troops of the crown prince, should send it to me at once by a swift messenger!" (I report that) right now two refugees have arrived here from the land of the Manneans, one eunuch and one official; I have sent them to the crown prince. They have information. (ABL 434, translated by Oppenheim 1967, 171–72 no. 119)

Foreigners crossing the border into Hittite territory could be coming in peace or to do harm. Either way, the officials and their troops needed to report each passage and its nature. Examples of Kaškaean groups coming to make peace are found in texts 16 (HKM 10), 73 (HKM 71), and 84 (HKM 88). In one instance (text 18 [HKM 13]), Marruwa, a petty ruler (literally "man") of Ḫimmuwa, has made "capitulation" (*ḫaliyatar*), that is, submitted to Hittite control.

1.2.20.2. Enemy Activities

In the Middle Hittite Maşat letters references to enemy troops are almost always expressed without specific identification of their ethnic or national identity. Given the location of Tapikka/Maşat, it is virtually certain that during the reign of Tudḫaliya III the only serious enemy in that area was the Kaška tribes (see my note on HKM 6 [text 12] and HKM 7 [text 13]: 24). Enemy troops entering the area with hostile intent are reported in letters 7, 9, 12, 13, and 14. The sending out of scouts to locate the enemy within Hittite territory is referred to in letters 12 and 13. Reports of marauding enemies in Hittite territory destroying crops and taking plunder—including cattle and captives—occur in letters 10 and 14. A report of a military engagement with the enemy and the number of casualties incurred is found in text 16.

Summarizing the king's instructions is this passage from text 14 (HKM 8): "Because the enemy thus marches into the land at a moment's notice, you should locate him somewhere, you should attack him. But you must be very much on highest alert against the enemy."

1.2.20.3. Weather Conditions

Writers sometimes report on weather or climate conditions, especially if they restrict their ability to fulfill a request of the addressee. For example, heavy snow and ice (*ŠURĪPU*) hindered the unknown sender from complying with a request of his superior (text 117 = KBo 18.79). Earlier in the same letter he entitles one of his paragraphs "(concerning) the matter of sickness" (line 3), which must also have been mentioned in order to explain his inability to comply with some request or commission.

1.2.20.4. Crops, Drought, Food Shortages

The macro-climate of Anatolia during the period of the Hittite Empire (ca. 1500–1200 B.C.E.) was more favorable to crops than that of the following centuries. On this factor, Gorny (1989, 91) could write:

> Although we lack reliable climatic and chronological data for central Anatolia, the available evidence suggests that the Hittite Empire flourished during a climatically favorable period. In fact, the three centuries between 1500 and 1200 B.C.E. (the Late Bronze Age) appear to have been cooler and moister throughout the whole of the ancient Near East .... This was followed by a somewhat drier period that is thought to have lasted from 1200 to about 900 B.C.E.

But in spite of this, throughout Hittite history both textual and archeological evidence attest to the recurrence of food shortages, leading to famines and a high death toll. These shortages were due to local weather conditions, producing crop failures, or to locust plagues, and often led to the importing of large amounts of grain from Syria or Egypt. To protect themselves against these periodic food shortages, the Hittites—from the Old Hittite period onwards—also undertook the storing of large quantities of grain in paved and straw-lined underground silos, called ÉSAG in the cuneiform texts (Hoffner 1974a, 34–37; 2001, 208–9; archeologically see Seeher 2000b; Neef 2001; Fairbairn and Omura 2005). On Hittite famines and "hunger years," see Klengel 1974; del Monte 1975b; Ünal 1977; Bryce 2002a, 72–73, 255–56; and van den Hout 2004a.

The mention of famines in texts 14 (HKM 8), 24 (HKM 19), 29 (HKM 24), 53 (HKM 50), 79 (HKM 80), and 120 (Bo 2810 = Klengel 1974) leaves it unclear if the same year is being referred to, or if there were repeated bad years for the harvest (so correctly de Martino 2005b, 313–14).

In the Tapikka/Maşat letters to and from the king it is clear that the monarch had a vital interest in the condition of the crops and the vineyards. HKM 4 (text 10) reveals the direct concern of the king for viticulture (see comments on text 40) and livestock in the provinces, a fact we would otherwise not have known. It is well known, however, that the material prosperity of the land, as often measured by these two criteria, depended upon the king's proper relationship with the gods who had entrusted the land and its governance to him. The fact that he does not ask about the cereal crops might indicate a date for the letter in early autumn, after their harvest in early summer but when the vineyards had yet to be harvested in the fall. Concern for the cattle and sheep might coincide with the period when they were being brought down from the summer pastures to winter quarters. For the seasonal cycle of agriculture see Hoffner 1974a, 12–51.

Crops might fail through drought or locust attacks. A locust attack (BURU$_5$.ḪI.A) is mentioned in text 24. Such attacks were a regular threat to farming communities all across the Near East in antiquity. Among preventative measures employed by the farmers of Old Babylonian Mari, Lucia Mori mentions the raising of water levels in secondary channels in the hope of creating a barrier, and the beating of the ground by the population and any available livestock to frighten them (2007, 45).

1.2.20.5. Greetings to a Third Party

Occasionally, one correspondent asks the other to pass along his greetings to a third friend (literally, read them aloud from the tablet). Examples in this corpus are limited to the Maşat letters, texts 26: 20; 27: 12–14; 59: 28–29; 69: 3–4. In one case (text 27: 12–14), this request is made in a piggyback letter to the receiving scribe who was going to read the main letter to the same man, Pulli. Examples of this feature can be found in other ancient letter corpora (e.g., in Hebrew and Aramaic letters, Lindenberger 1994, 8 "secondary greeting").

1.2.21. Short Summaries of Previous Letters

Sometimes there are short summaries within letters themselves of a previous letter's contents. Examples of this practice of quoting verbatim parts of incoming messages can be found in letters 7: 4–5; 8: 4–9; 12: 3–10, 17–23; 13: 3–8; 16: 14–41; 114: rev. 1–4. Often also the content of a previous letter is merely paraphrased as indirect discourse or even just alluded to by a single name: 8: 3–4; 14: 3–11; 15: 3–8; 16: 3–6, and in the longer diplomatic correspondence in Akkadian (Mineck in van den Hout, and Hoffner 2006, 276).

1.2.22. Letters Quoted in Historical Texts

In the body of historiographic literature (e.g., annals, treaty prologues) we sometimes encounter reports of letters. Occasionally there is preserved either a brief excerpt from the letter in question or a summary of its content. It might be thought that, when the quoted speech is very short, *ḫatrāi-/ŠAPĀRU* merely means "send (with an oral message)," not "write." There is some evidence for such totally oral messages in Old Babylonian Mari (Charpin 2007, 409). But even in Akkadian texts, the verb *šapāru,* when it is not specifically qualified by the words *ina pîm* "orally," normally refers to a written communication (see CAD Š/I, *šapāru* mng. 2). And this was certainly also true in the use of that Akkadian word as a logogram in Hittite texts. And considering that many of our attested official domestic letters are quite short, consisting of little more than the address and the wish formulas, we should not exclude the possibility that even these short reports actually describe something written, merely eliminating the introductory formulas (address and courtesy phrases). On the excerpts in annals of letters exchanged between commanders of armies on the battlefield see Beal in *CANE* 1, 546.

[ki-iš-ša-an-na-aš-ši EGIR-pa ḫa-at-ra]-a-nu-un ma-aḫ-ḫa-an-wa-at-ta a-aš-šu nu-wa *QA-TAM-MA* i-ya	I wrote back to him as follows: "Do what you think best!" (KUB 14.1 obv. 83).
tu-uk-m[a-wa ki-iš-ša-an ḫ(a-at-ra-a-nu-un)] (17) e-ḫu-wa za-aḫ-ḫi-ya-u-w[a-aš-ta-ti zi-ik-ma-wa za-aḫ-ḫi-ya] (18) *Ú-UL* ú-wa-aš	Then I wrote to you as follows: "Come! Let us fight each other!" But you did not come to meet me in battle! (KUB 34.23 ii 16–18 restored from duplicate KBo 12.27 iii 1–5).
A-NA LÚ.MEŠ URUKam-ma-am-ma[-ma *Ù A-NA* LÚ.MEŠ URU... ki-iš-ša-an] (13) ḫa-at-ra-a-nu-un mPa-az-za-an-na-aš-wa-kán m[Nu-un-nu-ta-aš-ša šu-ma-aš an-da ú-e-er] (14) nu-wa-ra-aš e-ep-tén nu-wa-ra-aš-mu pa-ra-a p[é-eš-tén]	To the men of Kammamma and the men of ... I wrote as follows: "Pazzanna and Nunnuta sought refuge with you. Now arrest them and hand them over to me!" (KUB 14.15 i 12–14).

[am-mu-uk-ma] (14) [(ki-iš-ša-an EGIR-p)a ḫa-a]t-ra-a-nu-un am-mu-uk-wa ú-wa-nu[-un nu-wa-k(án)] (15) [(*A-NA* ZAG KUR-*KA* pé-ra-an) tu]-uz-zi-ya-nu-un nu-wa KUR-*KA* *Ú-UL* GUL-aḫ-ḫu-un (var. wa-al-aḫ-ḫu-un) (16) [nu-wa-ra-at am-mu-uk *IŠ-T*]*U* NAM. RA GU$_4$ UDU *Ú-UL* da-aḫ-ḫu-un (17) [(nu-wa zi-ik) *A-NA* ^{d}UTU-*ŠI* šu]-ul-li-e-et nu-wa ú-et KUR ^{URU}Da-an-ku-wa (18) [GUL-aḫ-ta na-at dan-na-at-ta-(aḫ-)]ta nu DINGIR.MEŠ am-m[(e-e-da)]-az ti-an-du (19) [nu-wa DI-eš-šar am-me-e(-da-az)] ḫa-an-na-an-du

But I wrote back as follows: "I have come and have made camp at your border. I have not attacked your land, nor have I taken your civilian captives (NAM.RA-people[41]), cattle, and sheep. But you have behaved insultingly[42] toward My Majesty, and have proceeded to attack the land of Dankuwa and depopulate it. May the gods take my side and render a judgment in my favor (by battle)!" (KUB 14.17 iii 13–19).

nu GIM-an *I-NA* ^{URU}Ta-pa-aš-pa ar-ḫu-un (6) nu-mu GIŠ.ḪUR *ŠA* ^{m}Ḫé-eš-ni ú-te-er *MA-ḪAR* ^{d}UTU-*ŠI*-wa le-e pa-a-i-š[i] (7) LÚ.MEŠ GAL.ḪI.A-wa am-mu-uk kat-ta ú-wa-ti *A-NA* ^{m}Li-la-u-wa-an-ta-y[a] (8) [G]IŠ.ḪUR ú-te-er nu-wa a-pé-e-da-ni-ya *QA-TAM-MA* ḫa-at-ra-eš (9) ^{m}Ta-at-ta-an-ma LÚ.MEŠ GAL.ḪI.A-ya *MA-ḪAR* ^{d}UTU-*ŠI* le-e pé-e-ḫu-te-ši (10) ma-a-an-ma-wa-ra-aš pé-e-ḫu-te-ši-ma nu-wa i-da-la-u-wa-aḫ-ti

When I arrived in Tapašpa, they brought to me the writing board of Ḫešni (which read): "Don't go to His Majesty! Bring the high officials to me!" They brought the writing board to Lilawanta, (which read): "So to him also you/he wrote in the same way. But don't take Tatta and the high officials to His Majesty! If you take them (there), you will do harm." (KUB 31.68: 5–10).

41. See comments on texts 16 and 42.

42. For the meaning of the verb *šulle-* "to behave insultingly, wantonly" see Melchert 2005a.

43. Del Monte (1993, 80) renders *warpa tiyaweni* as "indirizziamo la (nostra) attenzione." For my translation see CHD *man* b 2′ b', and *-pat* 4 a.

(27) am-mu-uk-ma-kán NAM.RA.MEŠ ku-it pé-ra-an ar-ḫa [par-še-er nu *A-NA* ^{m}LUGAL-^{d}*SIN*-uḫ ki-iš-ša-an ḫa-at-ra-a-nu-un] (28) NAM.RA.MEŠ-wa-mu-kán ku-i-e-eš pé-ra-an ar-ḫa pár-še-er NAM.RA ^{URU}Ḫur-[ša-na-aš-ša-kán NAM.RA ^{URU}Šu-]ru-ta (29) *Ù* NAM.RA.MEŠ ^{URU}At-ta-ri-ma an-da ú-e-er nu-wa-ra-at ku-w[a-pí ...-an-ta-a]t (30) ar-ḫa-wa-ra-at-za šar-ra-an-da-at nu-wa-kán ták-ša-an šar-r[a-an *I-NA* $^{HUR.SAG}$A-ri-]in-[na-a]n-ta (31) še-er NAM.RA.MEŠ ^{URU}Ḫur-ša-na-aš-ša-aš-ma-aš-kán NAM.RA ^{URU}At-[ta-ri-im-ma *Ù*] NAM.RA ^{URU}Šu-ru-da (32) an-da *I-NA* ^{URU}Pu-ra-an-ta-ya-wa-kán ták-ša-an šar-ra-an [še-er] (33) NAM.RA ^{URU}Ḫur-ša-na-aš-ša-ya-wa-aš-ma-aš-kán NAM.RA [^{URU}At-ta-ri-ma] *Ù* NAM.RA ^{URU}Šu-ru-ta an-da ... (36) NAM.RA.Ḫ[.A-wa-mu-kán] ku-it pé-ra-an ar-ḫa pár-še-er nu-wa-aš-ma[-aš-ká]n ḪUR.SAG.MEŠ na-ak-ki-ya-aš (37) EGIR[-pa e-e]p-pir MU.KAM-za-ma-wa-an-na-aš še-er te-e-pa-u-e-e[(š-ša-an-za nu-wa-kán)] ú-wa-at-tén (38) 1-[e-d(a-ni ku)]-e-da-ni-ik-ki wa-ar-pa ti-ya-u-e-ni nu-w[(a-ra-an-kán kat-ta)] ú-wa-te-u-e-ni

(27–33) Because the civilian captives had fled from before me, I wrote as follows to Šarri-Kušuḫ: "The civilian captives who fled from before me—the civilian captives from Ḫuršanašša, those from Šuruta, and those from Attarimma came here, and as soon as they ...-ed, they split up. Half of them are up in Mt. Arinnanda—among them, civilian captives from Ḫuršanašša, Attarima, and Šuruta. The other half is up in Puranta—among them also are civilian captives from Ḫuršanašša, Attarima and Šuruta. ... (36–38) Because the civilian captives have fled from before me and have taken refuge on the steep slopes of the mountains, (and) very little (remains) to us (of) the (present campaigning) year, let us proceed to surround[43] only one of the two groups and lead it back down" (KUB 14.15 iii 27–38, duplicate KUB 14.16 iii 3–5).

1.2.23. Quoted Discourse within Epistolary Material Quoted in Historical Texts

Occasionally one even finds the citation of a previous message within another such citation.

> Around the year 1325 BC the Hittite Great King Suppiluliuma I campaigned in Syria and laid siege to the city of Karkemish in the late summer. Meanwhile, he sent two of his generals to raid Amqa, the Egyptian controlled territory to the south of Karkemish. With this, Suppiluliuma violated a century old Egyptian-Hittite treaty. In Karkemish he then received a letter from the Egyptian queen, informing him of her husband's death and asking him for a son to marry, knowing, as she wrote, that he had many sons. The identity of the Pharaoh and his queen is still a matter of debate, but most scholars tend to identify them as Tutankhamun and Ankhesenamun. After some initial hesitation and the dispatch of embassies to verify the sincerity of the queen's request, Suppiluliuma finally sent his son Zannanza. By the spring or early summer of the following year, it was already too late: adherents of the traditional Amun religion had again seized power and the Hittite prince was killed. Thereupon Suppiluliuma ordered another son, Arnuwanda, to carry out a punitive raid into the same area. Although Arnuwanda returned victorious, by Muršili's own account an epidemic of some kind developed among the thousands of prisoners and deportees whom the Hittites brought with them into Ḫatti-Land (the Hittite kingdom). (van den Hout in Mineck, van den Hout, and Hoffner 2006, 259)

nu *A-NA A-BU-YA* (51) MUNUS.LUGAL ^{URU}Mi-iz-ri tup-pí-ya-az EGIR-pa ki-iš-ša-an (52) ḫa-at-ra-iz-zi ku-wa-at-wa a-pé-ni-iš-ša-an *TAQ-BI* (53) ap-pa-le-eš-kán-zi-wa-mu am-mu-uk-ma-an-wa (54) ku-wa-pí DUMU-*YA* e-eš-ta am-mu-uk-ma-an-wa am-me-el (iv 1) [*R*]*A-MA-NI-YA* am-me-el-la KUR-e-aš te-ep-nu-mar (2) ta-me-ta-ni KUR-e ḫa-at-ra-nu-un (3) nu-wa-mu-kán pa-ra-a *Ú-UL* i-ya-aš-ḫa-at-ta (4) nu-wa-mu e-ni-eš-ša-an im-ma *TAQ-BI* am-me-el-wa (5) ^{LÚ}*MU-DI-YA* ku-iš e-eš-ta nu-wa-ra-aš-mu-kán BA.ÚŠ (6) DUMU-*YA*-wa-mu NU.GÁL ARAD-*YA*-ma-wa nu-u-ma-an da-aḫ-ḫi (7) nu-wa-ra-an-za-an ^{LÚ}*MU-DI-YA* i-ya-mi

The Queen of Egypt wrote back to my father on a tablet as follows: "Why did you say *'Maybe they are laying a trap for* me'? If I had a son, would I have written about my own and my country's shame to a foreign land? You did not believe me and have even spoken to me in that way! He who was my husband has died. I do not have a son. I will never take one of my subjects and make him my husband. I have written to no other country: only to you I have written. They say you have many sons. So give me one of your sons. To me he will be a husband, but in Egypt he will be king" (KBo 5.6 iii 50–54, iv 1–12; excerpt from the Deeds of Šuppiluliuma I, ed. Güterbock 1956b, 96).

(8) nu-wa da-me-e-da-ni-ya KUR-e *Ú-UL* ku-e-da-ni-ik-ki (9) *AŠ-PUR* nu-wa tu-uk *AŠ-PUR* DUMU. MEŠ-*KA*-wa-at-ta (10) me-ek-ka$_4$-uš me-mi-iš-kán-zi nu-wa-mu 1-*EN* (11) DUMU-*KA* pa-a-i nu-wa-ra-aš am-mu-uk LÚ*MU-DI-YA* (12) *I-NA* KUR URUMi<-iz>-ri-ma-wa<-ra>-aš LUGAL-uš

nu ma-aḫ-ḫa-a[n …] (12) nam-ma *A-NA* LU[GAL KUR URUMi-it-ta-an-ni …] (13) nu-uš-ši ki-iš-š[a-an … ḫa-at-ra-a-eš] (14) ka-ru-ú-wa ú-w[a-nu-un …] (15) URUKar-ga-miš-ša-an UR[(U-an)] (16) wa-al-aḫ-ḫu-un tu-uk-m[a-wa ki-iš-ša-an ḫ(a-at-ra-a-nu-un)] (17) e-ḫu-wa za-aḫ-ḫi-ya-u-w[a-aš-ta-ti zi-ik-ma-wa za-aḫ-ḫi-ya] (18) *Ú-UL* ú-wa-aš ki-nu-n[(a-wa nam-ma) …] (19) nu-wa-at-ták-kán KUR-e iš-[(tar-na pé-di) …] (20) nu-wa e-ḫu nu-wa za-aḫ-ḫi-[(ya-u-wa-aš-ta-ti) …]

And when my father …-ed …, then to the king of Mittanni he sent a message and *wrote him ... as follows*: "I came previously. … I attacked the city of Carchemish. And to you I *wrote as follows*: *'Come! Let us fight each other!'* But you did not come to fight me. And now … again. And … in the midst of your land. So come, let us fight each other!" (KUB 34.23 ii 11–20 with restorations from the dup. KBo 12.27 iii 1–5 DŠ fragment 26)

See also the letter of Ḫattušili III to the king of Aḫḫiyawa, KUB 14.3 i 47–56 (text 101, §§4–5).

Not all written communications quoted in texts are introduced by the verb *ḫatrai-* (*ŠAPĀRU*) "to send, write." Some can be identified as written communication by contextual considerations, such as this one introduced by *watarnaḫḫ-* "to remonstrate," but referred back to with *ḫatrai-*:

LÚ-ni-li-iš-ši wa-tar-na-aḫ-ḫu-un šu-ul-li-ya-at-wa-mu-kán nu-wa-za zi-ik LUGAL.GAL am-mu-uk-ma-wa-kán 1-*EN ḪAL-ṢÍ* ku-in da-li-ya-at nu-wa-za *ŠA* 1-*EN*

I remonstrated with him (i.e., Urḫi-Teššub) in a manly way, (writing as follows): "You have treated me with disrespect! While you are a Great King, I am nevertheless the

ḪAL-ṢÍ LUGAL-uš nu-wa e-ḫu nu-wa-an-na-aš ^{d}*IŠTAR* ^{URU}Ša-mu-ḫa ^{d}U ^{URU}Ne-ri-ik-ka_4-ya ḫa-an-né-eš-šar ḫa-an-na-an-zi nu *A-NA* ^{m}Úr-ḫi-^{d}U-up ku-wa-pí e-ni-iš-ša-an ḫa-at-re-eš-ke-nu-un…

king of the one province which you left to me. So come! (The deities) Šawuška of Šamuḫa and Teššup of Nerik will judge our case (by the ordeal of battle)!" That is how I wrote to Urḫi-Teššub (Apology of Ḫattušili III, iii 68–73 in the edition of Otten 1981, 22–23).

1.2.24. The Piggyback Letter

Royal scribes[44] often hitched a ride for their own personal letters on the letters they wrote for their royal patrons. These have been called "postscripts" (or "PS"),[45] but a true PS is an afterthought addition to a letter by the author to the same person addressed in the main body of the letter. They have also been called "second letters" (Otten 1956; Hagenbuchner 1989a, 3 ["Zweitbrief"]) and "supplementary letters" ("Nachtragsbriefe") by Kammenhuber and Alp. In some cases there is more than one (nos. 22 and 32 contain two additional letters). In both cases, the first and second piggyback letters share either the same sender or addressee. I choose to call them "piggyback letters," since they hitch a ride on the primary letter, whose sender is a more important person than the writer of the "piggyback letter."

44. Bryce claims that others than scribes were involved:

It was common practice for officials in His Majesty's service to append to royal dispatches messages addressed to their friends and colleagues. Generally one, sometimes two, messages were so attached. The Tapikka archive contains numerous examples of the practice, with informal communications passing between high-ranking functionaries (as in the example above) as well as between lower-level scribes. It was a very useful way of conveying information and requests, often of a personal and sometimes of a trivial, mundane nature, between officials employed in different locations in the royal administration. An appended message dealing with a private domestic matter sometimes gives an unintentional touch of pathos to an official dispatch concerned with matters of serious import. But the frequency of the practice suggests that it was carried out with the king's knowledge or was at least condoned by him, rather like permitting embassy staff today to send personal mail in the diplomatic pouch" (2003b, 174–75).

45. E.g., Güterbock 1979.

It is fairly common in the piggyback scribal letters for the sender to inquire about the well-being of his correspondent, about conditions in the distant destination (especially if that happens to be the sender's home, or if he has relatives there), and to make requests. The requested items vary. Sometimes it is an ox that was promised to the sender by someone at the destination (texts 27b and 37b). In the two just-cited cases Mār-ešrē may have done favors for Pulli and Ḫimmuili at the court in Ḫattuša, and was promised a gift in return. In these letters he is attempting to collect. But other items occur as well (texts 36 and 56). Ḫimmuili's request of a chariot and horses through Ḫattušili (HKM 27 [text 32]), may also involve exchange of personal favors (so Marizza 2007a, 121).

2. The Letter Corpus

2.1. An Old Hittite Letter (1)

1. Salvini 1994
Ḫattušili I to King Tuniya (= Tunip-Teššub) of Tikunani

Text, Copy, and **Edition**: Salvini 1994; 1996, 107–16; Durand and Charpin 2006. **English translation**: Collins 1998, 16. **Historical discussion:** Salvini 1996; Bryce 1998, 82–87; Klengel 1999, 38–39, 45, 52 (discussion of source [A2]); Klinger 2001b, 202; Miller 2001; de Martino 2002, 80–81, 84–85; Freu, Mazoyer, and Klock-Fontanille 2007, 90–91; Collins 2007, 30 with n. 36. **Comments** on other aspects of the text: Collins 1998, 16 (lion metaphor); Klinger 2003, 240 (paleography of Akkadian texts composed by Hittites); Durand and Charpin 2006, 219–27.

This tablet comes from a private collection, and therefore its provenience cannot be verified. Its paleography and ductus (see the sign tables in Salvini 1994, 70–77 and the discussion in Klinger 2003, 240) are consistent with a date in the reign of Ḫattušili I, although it appears to have been written by a Syrian scribe of that period (Archi 2003, 8 with n. 33). The scribe does not use paragraph lines to set off parts of the letter, as do later Hittite scribes; I have formatted the transliteration and translation so as to reveal what I consider to be his main sections, yet without separating each section with a visible horizontal line.

This letter is from a Hittite king, identified only by the title Labarna, to his vassal Tunip-Teššub (in this letter referred to with the shortened form of the name Tuniya), ruler of Tikunani. Based on the historical references in the letter, this "Labarna" is clearly Ḫattušili I, also known as Labarna II. Tunip-Teššub was one of a number of Hurrian rulers of kingdoms in northern Mesopotamia at this time. Contrary to the opinion held until recently, the Hurrians were by no means newcomers to northern Mesopotamia, but can be attested there as early as the fourth millennium B.C.E.

Of the unique value of this text Miller has written (2001, 410):

> The letter is the first epistolary document authored by Ḫattušili ever discovered, indeed the first from the Old Kingdom, and the only document of any nature that deals with Ḫattušili's campaigns which is contemporary with the events it relates. Most other texts concerning his campaigns consist of later copies—in most cases upwards of 300 years later—of legends, annals or historical references which had entered into the literary corpus of the Hittites. Hence, it is important, contemporary confirmation of the historicity of elements in Hittite legend and "history" in general and the campaigns of Ḫattušili in particular.

The precise location of Tikunani is still debated (see de Martino 2002, 80 n. 26), but this territory probably lay east of the upper Euphrates, not far from the country of Niḫriya, which is also mentioned in this letter (line 17; see Miller 2001, 410–23, map in fig. 1 and de Martino 2002, 80–81).

Ḫattušili, having failed in an earlier attempt to secure control of the main routes of communication between Anatolia and Syria—failing initially to win either against Uršum, Aleppo, Ḫaššum, or Ḫaḫḫum—decided to take a more indirect route, further to the north and east. In the area east of the Upper Euphrates he was able to secure an ally in Tuniya, king of Tikunani (see de Martino 2002, 80–81). In the language of this letter—"You are my servant. Protect me! And I will protect you (as) my servant. The city of Tikunani is my city. You are my servant, and your country is my country. I will surely protect you" (lines 4–7)—Tuniya is already Ḫattušili's vassal. But, as Miller has argued (2001, 424), given the distance of Tikunani from Ḫatti's easternmost border under Ḫattušili and the fact that the intervening kingdom of Ḫaḫḫum has not yet been brought under Hittite control, it is more likely that in this letter the Hittite king is persuading Tuniya to *act like* a Hittite vassal, and is offering him inducement through promises of shares in the booty.

Ḫaḫḫum, about which the Hittite king writes in this letter, is one of the Hurrian cities whose destruction Ḫattušili recounts in his annals during his military foray across the Ceyhan River (trans. Beckman in Chavalas 2006, 221).

The present letter was sent to urge Tuniya to coordinate with Ḫattušili's own troop movements in the raiding of important provincial centers in Syria. This he did, recruiting into his army bands (Akkadian *ṣābū*) of *ḫapirū* mercenaries (Freu, Mazoyer, and Klock-Fontanille 2007, 91), each band consisting of ten men comprising an overseer (UGULA, Hurrian *emantuḫlu* "leader of a ten-man group") and nine underlings (see also Edzard in *RLA* 10, 432 "Personenliste"). There is a remarkable similarity between these ten-man *ṣābū* bands and the ten-person economic units of NAM.RA personnel known from Hittite Anatolia.

These raids are outlined in Ḫattušili's own annals, which have come down to us only in much later Akkadian and Hittite copies from the New Kingdom (edition of the Hittite version by de Martino 2003, 21–79, and of the Akkadian version by Devecchi 2005; translations by Kümmel 1985; Bernabé and Álvarez-Pedrosa 2000 and Beckman in Chavalas 2006, 219–22). See especially the narrative of the king's fifth year of campaigning, where the king of Tikuna is mentioned in KBo 10.2 iii 25, p. 70, line 132 in de Martino's edition, the paragraph numbered §18 (A iii 25–28) by Beckman. Beckman reads the city name as *Timana*, not correcting the text to *Ti-ku*$^{!}$*-na*, as it should be in view of the Akkadian version (KBo 10.1 rev. 16): ^{URU}*It*$^{!}$-*ku-na-ya* (see de Martino 2003, 70 n. 207 and Devecchi 2005, 54–55 n. 171, both dependent on the full discussion of Miller 2001, 40, who argues for an initial metathesis *tik* > *itk*). Exhaustive bibliography on the annals of Ḫattušili I through 2003 is given in de Martino 2003, 22–24.

As is also known from New Hittite copies of other firsthand compositions of Ḫattušili I, such as his Political Testament (editions by Sommer and Falkenstein 1938; Klock-Fontanille 1996; English translation by Beckman in Hallo and Younger 2000, 79–81), in which his conniving wife is called a "snake" (Sum. MUŠ), and the Siege of Uršum (translation in Beckman 1995b), in which he savages his own troops with insults often involving animal metaphors—his personal language was filled with vivid, unforgettable animal metaphors (Hoffner 1980, 296–302). In this letter we find the dog (10), the bull (33–34), the lion (33–34) and the fox (35–36), all used to characterize individuals or peoples. The bull, a symbol of the Storm God of Ḫatti, personifies courage and strength. The lion, to which Ḫattušili compares himself in battle in his annals (Hoffner 1980, 297), personifies ferocity and savageness. The dog (line 10) is the scavenger-predator, who devours what it finds, in this case the faithful vassal who joins his lord in devouring the goods of the defeated foe. The fox is the clever enemy, as in Telipinu's application of this metaphor to Hurrian invaders in the Old Kingdom (see translation in Hallo and Younger 1997, 195 §14).[1] On the lion and fox metaphors in the letter KBo 1.14 see Giorgieri 2001 and Mora and Giorgieri 2004, 57, 66, 71. On bird metaphors and similes in the diplomatic correspondence of a later Hittite king see van den Hout 1993 (falcon and chick). On animals in Hittite literature see Collins 2002b.

(1) a-na Tu-ni-ya ARAD-di-ya (2) qí-bí-ma (3) um-ma la-ba-ar-na LUGAL.GAL-ma	(1–3) Say to Tuniya, my servant: Thus speaks Labarna, the Great King:

(4) ARAD-di at-ta ú-ṣur-an-ni (5) ù a-na-ku ARAD-di <lu>-ú-ṣur-ka (6) ^{URU}Ti$_4$-ku-na-an URU-lì ù at-ta (7) ARAD-di ù KUR-at-ka KUR-ti lu-ú-ṣur-ka

(4–7) You are my servant. Protect me! And I will protect you (as) my servant. The city of Tikunani is my city, you are my servant, and your country is my country. I will surely protect you.

(8) KASKAL-ti-ya pí-te-et ù it-ti (9) LÚ ^{URU}Ḫa-ḫi-ya-ú lu-ú <a->i-la-at (10) ŠE.BA-šu ki-ma UR.GI$_4$ a-ku-ul-šu (11) GU$_4$.ḪI.A ša ta-la-qè lu-ú ku-ú (12) U$_8$.UDU.ḪI.A ša ta-la-qè-ma lu-ú ku-ú-ma (13) a-na mu-ḫi-šu lu-ú a-i-la-at (14) a-na-ku iš-tu an-na-nu-um (15) ù at-ta iš-tu a-nu-um-ma-nu

(8–15) My campaign has begun (lit. my road is open). So you should be a man with respect to the man of Ḫaḫḫum. Devour his food rations like a dog! The oxen which you take shall be your own. The sheep and goats which you take shall be your own. Be a man with respect to him! I from this side, and you from that side.

(16) AN.BAR-zi-lu-ú ù UR.MAḪ (17) ša iš-tu ^{URU}Ni-iḫ-ri-ya ú-te-ru (18) eš-me i-na-an-na šu-bi-lam (19) ù ḫa-ši-iḫ-ta-ka ma-la ḫa-aš-ḫa-tú (20) šu-up-ra-am-ma lu-ú-ša$^{!}$-bi-la-kum (21) lu-ú * KÙ.BABBAR lu-ú ANŠE.KUR.RA (22) ù ARAD-di kab-ti ARAD-di x x (23) lu-ú-ša-bi-la-ak-kum

(16–18) Now send me the iron and the lion which I heard they brought back from the city of Niḫriya! (19–20) And whatever you want/need, as much as you want/need, write me about it, and I will send them to you. (21) Whether it be silver or horses (that you want/need). (22–23) And—my important servant, my … servant—I will send it to you.

(24) i-nu-ma i-na ^{URU}Za-al-pa-ar (25) a-la-kam-ma ^{m}Bu-ul-li-ṭá-di (26) ù ARAD-ka šu-up-ra-aš-šu-nu-ti (27) šum-ma qa<-ar>-ni i-su i-ba-aš-ši-ma (28) šu-bi-lam (29) ù za-ap-pí ANŠE.KUR.RA (30) lu-ú pé-ṣú-ti lu-ú ṣa-al-mu-ti (31) šu-bi<-la>-aš-šu-nu-ti ù a-wa-ti (32) ša-ra-ti ša i-dá-bu-ub (33) la ta-ša-mi qa<-ar>-ni ri-mi ú-ṣur (34) ù ši-pa-aṭ UR.MAḪ ú-ṣur (35) ši-pa-aṭ še-la-bi-i la ta-aṣ-ba-at (36) ša ša-ra-ti

(24–26) When I come to Zalpa(r), send Bulliṭ-adi and your servant to me. (27–31) If there is some horn (and?) *isu*, send (it/them) to me. If (there are) horse hairs, white or black, send them to me. (31) And do not listen to those lying words which he says. (33–34) Keep to the bull's horns and the lion's side, (35) and don't take the side of the fox. (36) The fox who does these lying things, he acted like the

i-te-né-pu-uš (37) ki-ma ^{URU}Za-al-pa-ar-ma (38) e-pu-šu ù ša-tu_4 qa-tam-ma (39) e-pu-uš	Zalparans acted.
i-mi-tum ù «ù» šu-mi-lum (40) a-wa-ti la te-eš-te-né-mi (41) a-wa-ti-ya ú-ṣur	(39–40) Stop listening to words on the right or left. Listen carefully to my words.

Commentary

Lines **1–3** contain the address formulas. This letter is addressed to Tuniya, the ruler of the small state of Tikunani, who is the vassal (ARAD "servant," lines 4, 5, 7) of Ḫattušili I.

Lines **4–7** state clearly the relationship between Ḫattušili and Tuniya. Tuniya's country is Ḫattušili's, and Tuniya is Ḫattušili's servant. But Ḫattušili's country is not Tuniya's, nor is Ḫattušili Tuniya's servant. Although the obligations are unequal, the arrangement involves mutual protection, which is the main subject of the letter.

Ḫattušili has begun a military campaign (line 8), which involves attacking the city of Ḫaḫḫum (lines 8–15). Ḫattušili requires Tuniya's assistance in making a coordinated attack (lines 14–15). Tuniya is to be allowed booty in the form of grain, oxen, sheep, and goats.

8 KASKAL-*ti-ya pí-te-et* see further examples in CAD P, *padānu* 1b and *petû* 2e.

8–13 This section correponds to what Liverani refers to as "the spoken aspect of war," more specifically the exhortation of the king/commander to his forces:

> More features of the spoken aspect of war are attested on the occasion of the battle itself. The first is the exhortation of the king to his soldiers to prepare their armour and weapons and to be in readiness for the combat. Here is Tuthmosis III before the battle of Megiddo: 'Prepare yourselves, make ready your weapons, for one will engage with that wretched foe in the morning'; and here is Shalmaneser I before the battle of Nihriya: 'Put on your armour, mount your chariots! The Hittite king is coming in battle array'. The second is the reciprocal reviling by the two armies or their champions—thus repeating in a baser way the content of the formal challenge. (2001, 113)

13 *lū a-i-la-at* stands here for *lū awilat*, attested at Mari also in the sense "act like a (brave) man" in the same sense as *hitḥazzĕqû vihyû lĕ'anāšîm* 1 Sam

4:9 "Take courage, and be men, O Philistines."

16–23 Tuniya is asked to send on to Ḫattušili iron and a lion statue[2] that was brought to Tikunani from Niḫriya (lines 16–18), and horn or horse hair (lines 27–31). In return he is invited to request whatever he wishes from Ḫattuša (lines 19–23). In Ḫattušili's annals, where we read of the booty taken from Ḫaḫḫum, it is said that the king of Tikunani sent gifts to Ḫattušili. De Martino is probably right to see in this gift-sending Tunip-Teššub's indication of his subordination to Ḫattušili (2002, 85). Niḫriya elsewhere figures in Hittite history towards its end, in connection with Assyro-Hittite relations (see Singer 1985; Freu 2007).

24–26 "When I come to Zalpa(r)" (line 24) appears to initiate another subject. This Zalpa(r) is to be kept apart from the well-known Anatolian city of Zalpa/Zalpuwa, located in the north near the Black Sea coast. It was located in North Syria not far from Birecek (see del Monte and Tischler 1978, 491–92, and 1992, 191). Its destruction by Ḫattušili is mentioned in his annals (KBo 10.1 9–14). Tuniya must send a man named Bulliṭ-adi, accompanied by one of Tuniya's officers ("your servant"), to Ḫattuša. Bulliṭ-adi is seen as a notorious liar by the Hittite king (lines 31–33), which suggests that he is a captured enemy of the Hittites being sent under guard to the capital.

35–36 As an animal metaphor for human character in ancient Near Eastern texts, the fox exemplifies hostility and treachery (Haas 2006, 303–4). The fox as an animal metaphor is applied to hostile Hurrians also in the Old Hittite Telipinu Proclamation (English translation by van den Hout in *CoS* 1.76:195 [§14]).

In the final section of the letter (lines 39–41) Tuniya is warned to comply to the letter with all of Ḫattušili's requests: "Do not deviate to the right or left."

2.2. Middle Hittite Letters (2–97)

2.2.1. MH Letters Found at Ḫattuša (2–6)

Letters can be dated by various criteria (see §1.2.6). In the case of Hittite letters found in the capital and tentatively dated to the Middle Hittite (i.e., early New Kingdom) period, the evidence for this dating is mostly of the last-named type. A thorough investigation by de Martino (2005b) has identified a small but not inconsiderable corpus of Middle Hittite letters from Ḫattuša itself. Among them the following are some of the better preserved.

2. KUB 31.79
River Traffic on the Euphrates

Text: Bo 6049 + Bo 7036. **Find spot**: Unknown. **Copy**: KUB 31.79. **Edition**: Lebrun 1976, 217–18 (edition of lines 1–20); Hagenbuchner 1989b, 136–41 (no. 90; edition of the entire text). **Translation**: Garstang and Gurney 1959, 33–34 (translation of 4–20 and discussion of the geographical aspects). **Discussion**: Cornelius 1958, 373–74; Hoffner 1972, 33 (on the dating of the text by linguistic criteria); Forlanini 1997, 408 n. 41 (geography); Hagenbuchner-Dresel 2002, 47–48 (on the bread sizes/weights in lines 6–18); Wilhelm 2002 (on the localization of Šamuḫa); Gurney 2003 (on the geography); de Martino 2005b, 302.

The tablet shows the MH script, and is characterized by MH spelling conventions, on which see Hoffner 1972, 33. Hagenbuchner (1989b, 138–39) is undecided whether to assign a MH date to this letter, although she admits that it makes the impression of a document older than standard NH letters. The online "Konk." dates it as Middle Hittite with no indication of doubt. De Martino (2005b, 302) writes: "The mention of Šamuḫa and Arziya could be a clue for dating this letter to the time of Tutḫaliya III. As a matter of fact, we learn from the Deeds of Suppiluliuma I (DŠ 10) that at the time of Tutḫaliya III Šamuḫa acted as a royal residence. Furthermore, the site of Arziya is also mentioned in fragment 3 of the Deeds of Suppiluliuma I, even though it is in a very fragmentary passage." The unknown author, an official in a remote province, writes to his "lord" in Ḫattuša, where this tablet was found. The "lord" could be either a high official under the king or even the king himself.

Since the first twenty preserved lines deal with shipments of foodstuffs by boat along a river from Pa/itteyariga to Šamuḫa, it is probable that the letter's author was charged with supervising the shipments by riverboat. This letter makes it likely that both Šamuḫa and Pitteyariga were towns on a river, either the Upper Euphrates itself, one of its tributaries (the Murad Su?), or the upper Kızılırmak. The text tells us that there was not much depth to this river (lines 7–8); and since the text tells us that two shipments (line 4) were required to transport what from the quantities described must have weighed about 1350 kg, it is likely that small flat-bottomed boats were used, thus not requiring that this stretch of the unidentified river be "navigable" in the usual sense of the word.

What is transported is called *ḫalkueššar* (line 4). This noun has nothing to do with the noun *ḫalki-* "grain," although Garstang and Gurney rendered it here as "food supplies." Hagenbuchner's translation "the harvest" has no basis, despite the fact that grain *products* form part of the shipment. Other examples of *ḫalkueššar* include breads, cheese, fats, and vessels, showing that *ḫalkueššar* is not limited to plant products (*HED* H, 39–40). Its Akkadogram is *MELQĒTU* "revenue, income" (CAD M/II ,13). Lebrun's translation "l'approvisionnement" ("supplies, provisions") comes closer to the word's actual meaning. The word denotes "provisions or supplies for cultic use" (see *HED* H, 39), which is appropriate, since Šamuḫa was a major Hittite cult center.

From line 21 to the end of the letter another subject is taken up. On the difficulty of sorting out who is being quoted in rev. 21–26, and where the quote within a quote (beginning in line 23) ends, see Hagenbuchner 1989a, 37.[3] The addressee of this letter (he who is called "my lord" in line 21) had written to the sender, describing the latest development in an ongoing situation involving Zidašdu and Kurunt(iy)a-ziti. The former has written to this "lord," outlining intended actions of the two men. The two will jointly *šiya-* [something]—the direct object being lost in the break. The untranslated verb could mean "to seal." Then (*namma*) Kurunta-ziti will [...] (intransitive verb), and will "open(?) it," the "it" presumably referring back to whatever object was "sealed." The "lord" has reason to believe that one or both of the two has failed to do what was promised, resulting in a failure (*waštul* "sin"). The "lord" orders the author of this letter to summon the two and investigate the matter (lines 24–25). If Kurunta-ziti was the guilty party, he must be punished (line 26). The letter's author explains that he attempted to summon Zidašdu for the investigation, but he failed to appear (lines 27–28). The rest of the letter (lines 29–35) is too badly broken to interpret.

(2) [...... ḫa-at-r]a-a-nu-un ki-nu-n[a ...] (3) [.........] LÍL[4] ^{GIŠ}ša-ma-ma-na-aš x[...]	(2) I wrote ... But now ... (3) ... meadow *š.*-wood ...
(4) [ma-a-aḫ-ḫa-an[5] ^{GIŠ}]MÁ.ḪI.A ^{URU}Pít-te-ya-ri-ga-za ḫal-ku-eš-šar ^{URU}Ša-mu-u-[ḫa] (5) [*I-NA* 1$^?$+]1$^?$-*ŠU*[6] pé-e-te-er[7] nu ḫa-an-te-ez-zi KAŠKAL-ši ki-iš-ša-an (6) [.... 4 *ME.* 50 NINDA.ÉR]IN.MEŠ 10-ti-li-iš 6 *ME.* NINDA.ÉRIN.MEŠ ^{URU}Ka$_4$-aš-ka$_4$[8] 15 (or 16) *PA.* ZÍD.DA ZÍ[Z$^?$][9] (7) [o o o]x nu wa-a-tar	(4) When ships transported provisions from Pitteyariga to Šamuḫa in two$^?$ trips, (5) on the first trip (they carried) the following: (6) ... 450 soldier-rations each made from a tenth (of some unit of dry measure), 600 soldier-rations of Kaška type from 15 (or 16) *PARISU* of wheat flour, ... (7) And

te-pu ku-it e-eš-ta nu-uš-ša-an *A-NA* ^{GIŠ}MÁ[.TUR.ḪI.A?][10] (8) [...... a]-pád-da da-i-e-er ki-nu-na-aš-ša-an ú-i-te-e-ni ne-e-a-[a]t (9) [...... ^{GIŠ}M]Á.ḪI.A ^{URU}Pít-te-ya-ri-ga nam-ma da-iš-te-i-e-er (10) [...... -a]n *A-NA* ^{GIŠ}MÁ.ḪI.A ki-iš-ša-an da-i-e-er (11) [80[11] *PA.* ZÍZ 1?+]1 *ME.* 20 *PA.* ŠE nu ŠU.NIGIN-ma? *I-NA* 2 KAŠKAL-*NI* 1 *ME.* 30 *PA.* ZÍZ (12) [2 *ME.* 20 *PA.*] ŠE 1 *LI-IM* 50 NINDA.ÉRIN.MEŠ	since there was little water (in the river?), they put those things also on *small* boats .... (8) But now the (situation) has changed? with respect? to? the water(-level), (9) and ... they have loaded the ships again of/in Pitteyariga. (10) And they put ... as follows on the ships: (11) 80 *PARISU* of wheat, 220 *PARISU* of barley, so that the total in the two/second? trip(s) (is) 130 *PARISU* of wheat, (12) 220? *PARISU* of barley, 1,050 soldier-rations.
(13) [ḫa-an-t]e-ez-zi pal-ši-ya ^{GIŠ}MÁ.TUR ^{URU}Ar-zi-ya-za da-iš-te-ya-an-zi (14) n[u-uš-š]a-an ki-iš-ša-an ti-ya-an-zi 50 *PA.* ŠE 6 *ME.* NINDA.ÉRIN.ME[Š ...] (15) [... ŠU.NIG]IN.GAL ki-iš-ša-an ^{GIŠ}MÁ.ḪI.A ku-it ka-[......] (16) ^{URU}Ša-mu-u-ḫa pé-e-ḫu-te-er 1 *LI-IM* 6 *ME.* 50 [NINDA.ÉRIN. MEŠ ...] (17) ŠÀ.BA 4 *ME.* 50 NINDA.ÉRIN.MEŠ 10-ti-li-iš 1 *ME.* 30 *PA.* ZÍZ [...] (18) [x-x-]x 3 *ME. PA.* ZÍZ ŠE [-ya?]	(13) For the first trip they load a small boat from Arziya, (14) and put the following on it: 50 *PARISU* of barley, 600 "soldier-rations," (15) ... the grand total is as follows: that which the boats brought ... (16) to Šamuḫa: 1,650 "soldier-rations," (17) including 450 soldier-rations each measuring a tenth (of ...), 130 *PARISU*-measures of wheat, (18) ... and 300 *PARISU*-measures of wheat and barley.
(19) [ki-nu-na] ^{GIŠ}MÁ.ḪI.A ^{URU}Pít-t[e-ya]-ri-ga nam-ma x[...] (20) [na-]aš-[t]a? a-pí-ya da-iš-te-ya-an-zi	(19) But now the ships have returned again to Pitteyariga. (20) There they will load them (again).
(21) nam-ma-ma-mu ku-it am-me-el *BE-LÍ-YA ŠA* ^{m}Zi-da-[aš-du ḫa-at-ra-a-iš] (22) ^{m}Zi-da-aš-du-uš-wa-mu ki-iš-ša-an ḫa-at-ra[-a-it ...-wa-...] (23) ták-ša-an ši-ya-a-u-e-ni nam-ma-wa $^{\text{m.d}}$LAMMA-LÚ-iš [...] (24) [nu-wa]-ra-at ḫa-a-ši nu-wa ^{m}Zi-da-aš-du-un $^{\text{m.d}}$LAMMA[-LÚ-ya? ...]	(21) Furthermore, because my lord has written to me of (the affair of) Zidašdu, (22) "Zidašdu wrote to me as follows: (23) 'We will ... ... together. Then Kurunt(iy)a-ziti will ... (24) and will *open* it.' So summon? Zidašdu and Kurunt(iy)a-ziti. (25) And if it has resulted in a

(25) nu-wa-ra-at-ša-an ma-a-an *A-NA* $^{m.d}$LAMMA-LÚ wa-aš-túl kat-ta [a$^?$-aš$^?$-zi] (26) nu-wa-ra-an-kán ḫa-ap-ti nam-ma-wa-ra-an za-a-aḫ (nu erased) […]	failure on the part of Kurunt(iy)a-ziti, (26) *hold* him *accountable*,[12] and beat him!"
(27) [nu] *A-NA* ^{m}Zi-da-aš-du ḫa-at-ra-a-nu-un u-un-ni-ya-wa nu-wa-aš-ma-aš zi[-…] (28) [ud$^?$-d]a-ni-i an-da tar-na-aḫ-ḫi a-pa-a-ša-mu kat-ti-mi *Ú-UL* u-un-ni-iš (29) [… $^{U]RU?}$Ku-uš-pí-iš-ša [… ku-it]-ma-an-kán am-mu-uk-ma ut-tar (30) […]x ar-ḫa x[-…]x-mu $^{m.d}$LAMMA-LÚ-iš ^{m}Ta-aš-ku-wa-an-ni-iš (31) […] x x [… ^{m}PN-]x-iš ARAD-*YA* ^{m}Ḫi-il-la-an-ni-iš (32) […]	(27) Therefore I wrote to Zidašdu: "Drive here! I will *involve* you (pl.) in the affair of *zi-*…" (28) But he did not drive here to me. (29) … the city Kušpišša … while I/me the word (30) … to me Kurunt(iy)a-ziti (and) Taškuwanni (31) … my servant, Ḫilanni (32) …
(33) [… ^{m}]Zi-da-aš-du-uš-ma-wa (34) […] ḫa-at-ra-u-e[n] (35) […] x x x[…]	(33–35) … "Zidašdu … we wrote …

3. KBo 15.28
Three-Plus Augurs to the Queen

Text: 225/g. **Find spot:** Bk. D: Büyükkale m/12, right on top of the layer of brick rubble. **Copy:** KBo 15.28. **Edition**: Hagenbuchner 1989b, 81–84 (no. 49), 178 (no. 130); Archi 1975, 135–36. **Discussion:** Otten 1955, 17; Klinger 1995a, 101; Haas 1996, 77–78; Houwink ten Cate 1998, 176–77 (on rev. 5–22); van den Hout 2001a, 427–28, 431–32; Forlanini 2002, 260–61. On the dating see de Martino 2005b, 295.

(1) *A-NA* MUNUS.LUGAL *BE-EL-TI$_4$-NI QÍ-B[Í]-M[A]* (2) *UM-MA* ^{m}A-wa-u-wa-a ^{m}NU.GIŠ.SAR $^{m.d}$U-SIG$_5$ (3) *Ù* $^{LÚ.MEŠ}$MUŠEN.DÙ ARAD.MEŠ-*KA-MA*	(1) Say to the Queen, our lady: (2–3) Thus speak Awawa, NU.^{GIŠ}KIRI$_6$, ^{d}U-SIG$_5$, and the augurs, your servants:

(*In three badly broken paragraphs [obv. 4–15, rev. 1′–4′] the writer gives to the queen a detailed description of the behavior of observed oracle birds, mentioning details of the locale where they were observed: specifically, the city of Ḫaitta and the Zuliya and Imralla Rivers.*)

3b. KBo 15.28
Piggyback Letter from NU.^{GIŠ}KIRI$_6$ to Tumnī, Tumna-ziti, and Tuttuwaili

(rev. 5) *UM-MA* ^{m}NU.^{GIŠ}KIRI$_6$ *A-NA* ^{m}Tum-ni-i ^{m}Tum-na-LÚ (rev. 6) *Ù A-NA* ^{m}Tu-ut-tu-wa-DINGIR-*LIM* (rev. 7) DUMU.MEŠ DÙG.GA-*YA QÍ-BÍ-MA*	(rev. 5–7) Thus speaks NU.^{GIŠ}KIRI$_6$: Say to Tumnī, Tumna-ziti, and Tuttuwaili, my dear sons:
(rev. 8) ka-a-aš-ma *I-NA* É.GAL-*LIM* ku-it am-me-el (rev. 9) pár-na-aš ut-tar ḫa-at-ra-a-nu-un nu-mu DUMU. MEŠ DÙG.GA-*YA* (rev. 10) ḫu-iš-nu-ut-tén na-at *I-NA* É.GAL-*LIM* (rev. 11) me-mi-iš-tén nu *I*[-*NA* É.]GAL-*LIM* ma-aḫ-ḫa-an (rev. 12) da-ra-an-zi [nu-mu DUMU.MEŠ DÙG.]GA-*YA* (rev. 13) ḫa-at-r[a-at-tén]	(rev. 8) Since I have just written about the status (lit., the word) of my house to the palace, (rev. 9) rescue me, O my dear sons! (rev. 10) And tell it to the palace! (rev. 11–13) And, my dear sons, write to me how they are talking in the palace!

Commentary

I follow de Martino and others in identifying ^{m}NU.^{GIŠ}KIRI$_6$. with the man by this name who is a scribe in the Middle Kingdom.

On the geography referred to in the badly broken paragraphs (obv. 4–15, rev. 1′–4′), which I did not attempt to translate, Forlanini writes:

> A mere 50 km down the valley of the Sulusaray, the Çekerek/Zuliya river makes a wide curve northwards; at this point the river passes its closest to Ḫattuša. In the letter KBo 15.28 written to the queen by three augurs, it refers to the flight of oracle birds from Ḫaitta 'down the river Zuliya [*INA* ^{ÍD}*Zuliaš*=*šan katta*, line 5] and further on (it refers) to other observations in connection with the river Imralla(ya). The itineraries of the 16 festivals show that Ḫaitta was located a day's journey from Ḫattuša at the foot of Mt.

Puškurunuwa, from which it is possible to ascend to Ḫarranašši . . . while the village of Imralla, which bears the (Luwian) name of the other river, was only a stopover place from Ḫattuša on the road that led by a three days' trip to Ankuwa (= Alişar).[13]

4. KBo 12.62
[...] to [...]

Text: 524/t. **Find spot:** House on the Slope: L/18 b-c/5, from the under-edge of a gravel layer over scree. On the findspot of KBo 12.62, see §1.2.7.1. **Edition**: Hagenbuchner 1989b, 120–23 (no. 78). **Discussion:** Kümmel 1967, 159; Oettinger 1976, 83; Beckman 1991, 213; de Martino 1991, 7–8; Reichardt 1998, 133; Boley 2000, 287; van den Hout 2001b, 179 with n. 59; Goedegebuure 2003, 190; de Martino 2005b, 294–95 (on the dating as MH).

(*Beginning of the tablet broken away.*)	
(2′) [mZi-i-t]i-iš x - x ka-ru-ú ku-it ki-[x x x] (3′) [... *A-N*]*A*? ÉRIN. MEŠ.ḪI.A pé-ra-an ar-ḫa nu-u-ma-a[n x x x] (4′) [nu-mu-ka]n? *BE-LÍ-YA* mZi-i-ti-in EGIR-pa [pa-ra-a] (5′) [na-a-]i? nu-mu aš-šu-ul ḫu-u-da-a-ak ú-d[a?-ú]	(2′–5′) Since Ziti previously/already ..., I? do not wish to ... from in front of the troops. O my lord, send Ziti back to me.[14] And may he bring me (your?) greeting promptly.
(6′) [zi-ik-m]a-mu ku-it *ŠA* fKu-pa-a-pa DAM mDu-u[d-d]u-mi (7′) [EGIR-pa ḫa-a]t-ra-a-eš fKu-pa-a-pa-aš ma-a-aḫ-ḫa-an *I*?[-*N*]*A* URUU-da (8′) [i-da-a-lu u]t-tar i-e-ez-zi (9′) [x x x]-pí[15]	(6′–9′) Concerning what you wrote me back about Kupapa, the wife of Duddumi: *Here* on *the tablet*?[16] (which you sent to me)is how Kupapa is perpetrating evil in the city of Uda.
(10′) [nu m]a-a-aḫ-ḫa-an tup-pí u-uḫ-ḫu-un nu-za [a]m-mu-uk ma-a-aḫ-ḫa-an (11′) ki-iš-ḫa-at nu DINGIR.MEŠ mDu-ud-du-mi-in-pát (or: -n[a]) *QA-DU* DAM-*ŠU* (12′) [DUM]U.MEŠ-*ŠU QA-TAM-MA* ḫar-ni-in-kán-du	(10′) As for how I reacted as I read the tablet—(11′–12′) well, may the gods in the same way destroy this same Duddumi together with his wife and children!

(13′) [na-a]š!?-ta[17] ka-a-ša an-du-uḫ-še-eš ta-a-wa-na[18] ši-pa-an-da-an-da-at (14′) [nu?] SIG_5-in i-an-te-eš-ša a-pé-ni-iš-šu-wa-an-da (15′) [*Ú-UL*] ša-ak-kán-ta *Ú-UL* ú-wa-an-da ud-da-a-ar (16′) [iš?-šu?-]u-wa-an da-i-e-er a-pé-ni-iš-šu-wa-an (17′) […]a-ap-pa-ya *Ú-UL* me-mi-an (18′) […] kat-ta-ma *Ú-UL* NUMUN-an […]	(13′–18′) People have offered *properly*.[19] Yet even those who have acted properly have begun to do such things that were (previously) unknown (and) unseen! Such is the …, and again/back not said? … accordingly no seed …
(Breaks with lower edge quite near)	

Commentary

Only one side of the tablet is preserved, which the copyist (Otten) guessed was the reverse. An indeterminate number of lines were in the missing beginning of this side.

6–9 On these lines see Hagenbuchner and Reichardt 1998, 133 (and my n. 61). See also Hagenbuchner 1989a, 151 on the use of indirect speech here instead of a direct quote.[20]

13–16 On Neu's collation, which he claimed showed that one must read *ta-a-wa-al* see nn. 63 and 64. Problematic, and therefore uncertain, is my understanding of the participle *ianteš* (line 14) as active, rather than passive. Participles of transitive verbs in Hittite are normally passive (*GrHL* §§21.1–2, 10–11), but there are well-known exceptions; see *GrHL* §25.39: "Participles of transitive verbs used generically [i.e., 'detransitives'] can be either active (*šekkant-* 'knowing', *ištamaššant-* 'hearing [ear]', *uwant-* 'seeing [eye]', *adant-* 'having eaten', *akuwant-* 'having drunk', *wišuriyant-* 'the strangleress') or passive. One even finds the very same verbs used in both ways: *šekkant-* both 'knowing (spirit)' and 'known (person).'" To these examples I would hesitantly add this one. Since active participles of such transitive verbs elsewhere are not construed with direct objects, I do not consider SIG_5-*in* (line 14) as such, but as a modifying adverb: "those who have acted properly."

5. KBo 18.14
To the King from Pazzu

Text: 300/e. **Find spot**: Bk. A: s/12 in destruction layer (on the findspots, see §1.2.7.1). **Copy**: KBo 18.14. **Edition**: Hagenbuchner 1989b, 50–51. **Date:** The script and language are possibly Middle Hittite (Konk.). The man Pazzu lived during the reigns of Tudḫaliya III, Šuppiluliuma I, and the early years of Muršili II. Mašḫuiluwa's letter to Muršili II (KBo 18.15 [text 103]) mentions Pazzu as an old man who is ill. **Discussion:** Otten 1969, 25 n. 4; Heinhold-Krahmer 1977, 183; Klinger 1995a, 102; Klengel 1999, 175 [A23.4]; de Martino 2005b, 296, 299; Marizza 2007a, 60–62.

(1) *A-NA* dUTU-*ŠI* EN-*Y*[*A QÍ-BÍ-MA*] (2) *UM-MA* mPa-az-zu AR[AD-*KA-MA*]	(1) Say to His Majesty, my lord: (2) Thus speaks your servant Pazzu:
(3) ka-a-ša-kán ŠÀ KUR-*TI* (4) ḫu-u-ma-an SIG$_5$[-in]	(3–4) All is well (here) in (this) land.
(5) dUTU-*ŠI*-mu ku-it EN-*YA* [kiš-an] (6) *TÀŠ-PUR* mDu-wa-a-an-wa-kán *(Breaks off)*	(5–6) Concerning what my lord wrote to me, saying: "Tuwā …" (*Breaks off*)
(rev. 1′) […] (rev. 2′) nu ḫa-an-da-an[-…] (rev. 3′) mPí-it-ta-ni-pí-x[…] (rev. 4′) nu-uš-ši DUMU-*ŠU* ar-ḫa da-a-i[-e-er][21] (rev. 5′) 10 LÚla-aḫ-ḫi-ya-la-an ú[-wa-te-ez-zi] (rev. 6′) 20 LÚla-aḫ-ḫi-ya-la-an-ma (rev. 7′) *Ú-UL* ú-wa-te-ez-[zi] (rev. 8′) ki-nu-na mDu-wa-a[- an?] (rev. 9′) ku-it iš-tar-ak-[ta][22] (rev. 10′) ma-aḫ-ḫa-an-ma-k[án] (rev. 11′) ḫa-at-tu-le[-eš-zi] (rev. 12′) nu un-na-i […]	(rev. 1′) … (rev. 2′) And *truly* … (rev. 3′) Pittanipi-… (rev. 4′) and stole his son away from him. (rev. 5′) He will lead ten travelers (or persons on a military campaign), (rev. 6′–7′) but he will not lead 20 travelers (or persons on a military campaign). (rev. 8′) Because now Duwa has become ill, (rev. 10′–11′) as soon as he recovers, (rev. 12′) he will drive here and …
(l. e. 1) [dUTU-*ŠI*-ma-mu] ku-it EN-*YA* (l. e. 2) [kiš-an *TÀŠ-PUR*] LÚpít-ti-an-za-wa-kán (l. e. 3) […-]i?-li EGIR-an (l. e. 4) [… ar-ḫa] na-a-i (l. e. 5) [… d]ḫa-an-ta-še-pu-uš (l. e. 6) […]- i	(l. e. 1–6) Now concerning what Your Majesty, my lord, wrote to me, saying: "A fugitive … behind …; so send out … *ḫantašepa*-deities …

Commentary

About the dating of this letter de Martino (2005b, 296) has written:

> KBo XVIII 14: the sender of this letter sent to the king is Pazzu. Another person by the name Duwa (obv. 6, rev. 8′) is also mentioned. Pazzu appears also in the letter KBo XVIII 15, sent to the sovereign by Mašḫuiluwa, most probably the same person who became king of Mira during the time of Muršili II. This hypothesis identifying Pazzu in KBo XVIII 14 as the same one in KBo XVIII 15 has encouraged some scholars, like S. Heinhold-Krahmer, A. Hagenbuchner and H. Klengel, to also date KBo XVIII 14 from the time of Muršili II. On the other hand, KBo XVIII 14 has already been considered to be a Middle Hittite letter by J. Klinger and S. Košak (see also CHD). This dating is based not only upon the ductus, but also upon the mention in KBo XVIII 14 of Duwa. As a matter of fact, a dignitary with this name bearing the title of GAL DUMU.MEŠ É.GAL is mentioned in Arnuwanda I'[s] land donation KBo V 7 rev. 51.

And again (2005b, 317):

> [The] letter KBo XVIII 14 was sent by Pazzu. In the letter Duwa is also mentioned. … Duwa appears also in the land donation of Arnuwanda I KBo V 7. Pazzu, on the other hand, is also present in KBo XVIII 15, datable to a time not before Šuppiluliuma I, since this letter was sent by someone called Mašḫuiluwa who, as has previously been written, could be the person who became king of Mira at the time of Muršili II.
>
> In my opinion, we can hypothesise that Duwa in KBo V 7 is the same as the one in KBo XVIII 14, as is also the case with Pazzu of KBo XVIII 14 who could be the very same person mentioned in KBo XVIII 15.
>
> In fact, we might suppose here that Duwa was at the peak of his career during the time of Arnuwanda I (compare KBo V 7) whilst during the time of Tu[d]ḫaliya III he was still alive but already old and infirm, as would show the letter KBo XVIII 14 where (rev. 8′–12′) an illness suffered by this dignitary is mentioned. The old age and death of Duwa during the reign of Tu[d]ḫaliya III could explain the absence of his name in the Maşat archive. Under Tu[d]ḫaliya III the name of Pazzu in KBo XVIII 14 makes an appearance. During the time of Šuppiluliuma I, when Mašḫuiluwa wrote KBo XVIII 15, Pazzu was also old and infirm as would indicate the following passage: "(lines 4–7) [illness] has struck Pazzu and his father's gods have begun to torment him."

See also KBo 18.15 (text 103).

6. KBo 18.95
To the Chief of the Guard from the Chief of the Palace Servants

Text: 2218/c (online Konk. photo). **Find spot:** Bk. E: casemate or wall sleeve (*Mauerkasten*) in g 14. **Copy:** KBo 18.95. **Date:** MH? (Konk.). **Edition:** Hagenbuchner 1989b, 156–57 (no. 102), 194–95 (no. 148). **Discussion:** Starke 1996, 155–56; Marizza 2007a, 25, 62–64.

A rare case in which both sender and addressee are identified only by their titles (see §1.2.16, p. 58).

(1) [*A-N*]*A BE-LÍ* GAL *ME-ŠE-DI BE-LÍ-YA Q*[*Í-BI-MA*] (2) [*U*]*M-MA* GAL DUMU.MEŠ É.GAL ARAD-*KA-MA* (3) *MA-ḪAR* MUNUS.LUGAL *BE-EL-TI*$_4$*-YA* ḫu-u-ma-a[n SIG$_5$-in e-eš-du *MA-ḪAR*] (4) DUMU DÙG.GA-*YA* ḫu-u-ma-an SIG$_5$-in e-[eš-du nu-ut-ta DINGIR.MEŠ TI-an] (5) [ḫ]ar-kán-du nu-ut-ta aš-šu-ú-li [pa-aḫ-ša-an-da-ru]	(1) Say to the lord, the Chief of the Guards, my lord: (2) thus speaks the Chief of the Palace Servants, your servant: (3) May all be well with the Queen, my lady. (4) May all be well with my dear son. (4–5) And may the gods keep you alive, and lovingly protect you.
(About 10 lines to the bottom of the obverse and the first 10 lines of the reverse are broken away. A second letter may begin at this point, since lines 3′–4′ contain a wish for health and protection for addressees.)	
(1′) [...] x x [......] (2′) [... ^{m}x-p]í-te-eš-šu-u-p[a$^{?}$]-an-na [DINGI]R.M[EŠ pa$^{?}$-aḫ-ša-an-da-ru nu-uš-ma-aš] (3′) [Z]I-aš[23] ḫa-ad-du-la-a-tar ZI-aš la-a-lu-u[k$^{?}$-ki-ma-an pí-an-du] (4′) [nu-u]š-ma-aš ŠU.ḪI.A-uš a-ra-aḫ-za-an-t[a aš-šu-ú-li ḫar-kán-du]	(1′–2′) May the gods *keep* X and x-pí-Teššup. (3′) And may they give you health of soul and brightness of soul, (4′) and may they lovingly hold their arms (protectively) around you.
(Lines 5′–9′ are too fragmentary for connected translation.)	

Commentary

The name in line 2′, [^{m}x-*p*]*i-Teššupann*=*a*, could be restored either as Tuppi-Teššub or Tulpi-Teššub. The absence of the divine determinative before a syllabically written DN in the second component of a PN is normal. The accusative case, however, is unattested in an address formula. The restoration of the verb *paḫš-* "to keep" is merely a guess, in order to fit with an accusative object. For the concept behind ZI-*aš lalukkima-* see CHD L–N, 28–30. This illumination/brightness in the soul is something requested for the king and queen in prayers.

2.2.2. MH Letters Found at Tapikka-Maşat Höyük (7–85)

I accept the identification of this site with ancient Tapikka, for which see Alp 1977 and del Monte 1992, 160 with literature cited there. Yakar (1980, 90–94) rejected the identifcation with ancient Tapikka and favored an identification with ancient Šapinuwa (now claimed for Ortaköy). For further discussion of the problem see Houwink ten Cate 1992, 133–37.

The letters from Maşat Höyük often reflect the tenuous military situation on the northeastern frontier of the Hittite kingdom during the so-called Middle Hittite period. Constituting the chief military threat were the Kaška people. Text 14 gives a fairly good idea of the scope of most of the military operations of the enemy. They were razzias, raids on villages, rather than large-scale pitched battles. One sees here too the typical size of the losses: 30 oxen and 10 men (text 14, line 10). What was most troublesome to the Hittite king and his officials was the frustrating situation that these enemies could appear at a moment's notice, do damage, and then escape (text 12, lines 3–14). The damage done to the crops was perhaps more serious than the small numbers of lost animals (see texts 14, 22, 24, 26, 30, 50, 53, 69), because this attacked the future food supply not only of Tapikka itself, but of the capital city, which received supplies from towns like Tapikka located in the Hittite "bread basket."

The Maşat letters also provide us with a picture of the personnel and structure of a Hittite provincial capital over the period of a single generation.

2.2.2.1. Akkadian Names in the Tapikka-Maşat Letters

The following Akkadian names were borne by persons residing among the Hittites in this correspondence: Adad-bēlī ("[the god] Adad is my lord"), Ilī-kakkab ("my god is a star"?), Ilum-bēlī ("the god is my lord"), Mār-ešrē (= DUMU.UD.20.KAM, "son of [i.e., born on] day twenty"), Tāḫaz-ili ("battle of [my] god"), and Ilī-tukultī ("my god is my trust").[24] Contra Alp 1991a, 94, the personal name Šuriḫili is most likely not linguistically native Anatolian, but Akkadian *Šūriḫ-ilī*, meaning either "hasten, O my god!" or "destroy, O

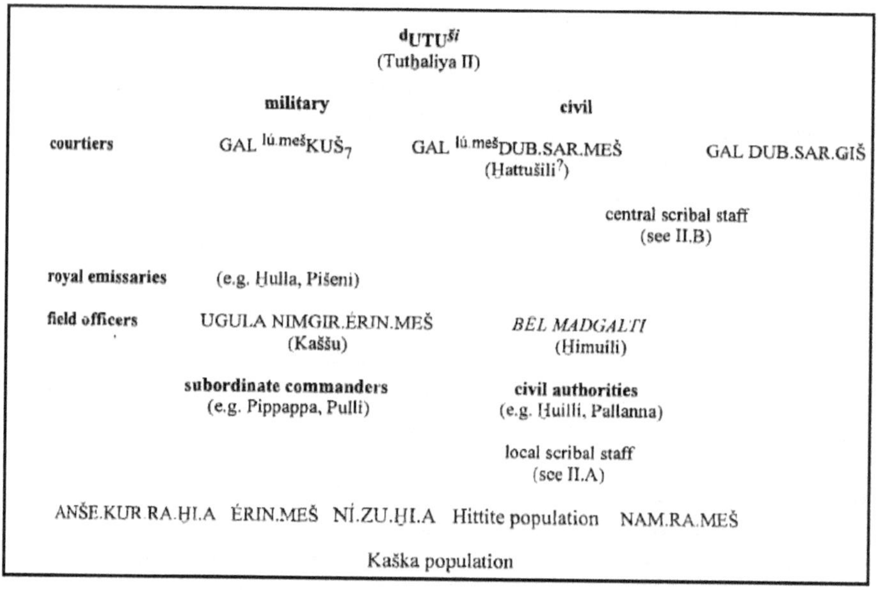

Fig. 1. Administrative hierarchy as reflected in the Maşat Texts.
From Beckman 1995a, 33.

my god!" (a Š-stem imperative of either *arāḫu* A or B). Despite the examples of final DINGIR-*LIM* as a mere rebus for Anatolian *-ili* in the Maşat name Ḫimmuili, Šuriḫili is more likely an Akkadian name of a scribe, on the order of Mār-ešrē. Beckman (1983b) considers these to be native Mesopotamians, not native Anatolians with Akkadian names (*noms de plume*).

2.2.2.2. Names of Persons Figuring in the Tapikka-Maşat Letters.

The following named individuals figure in the Tapikka letters.

Adad-bēlī. Alp 1991a, 52–53. His name is written as $^{m.d}$U-*BE-LÍ* and $^{m.d}$IŠKUR-*BE-LÍ*. Since Hittite names with a possessive pronoun "my" are not known, and the nominative case of the name $^{m.d}$IŠKUR-*BE-LÍ-iš* (HKM 66 [rev.] 34) shows a final vowel *-i-* of the stem, this name must have been pronounced as Akkadian. The name does not occur in texts from Ḫattuša itself. Adad-bēlī was a scribe, but also had duties in regard to harvesting grasses for fodder (text 69: rev. 39–42), and was requested to send foodstuffs to Ḫattuša (text 68).

Ḫašammili. Alp 1991a, 57. Mentioned five times in four letters. All references to a Ḫašammili in the Maşat letters (HKM 17, 19, 30, and 36) refer to a scribe serving the king, usually if not always operating out of Ḫattuša itself.

Ḫattušili. Alp 1991a, 58–59; Marizza 2007a, 119–27. The scribe Ḫattušili is mentioned seven times in seven letters. He is—after Kaššū and Ḫimmuili—the third most frequently mentioned person in the Tapikka correspondence. He appears also in ABoT 65 (text 81). Ḫattušili, the author of the first piggyback letter (text 32, line 11), is one of the Maşat officials discussed by Klinger 1995a, 88–89. He may appear anonymously with the title GAL DUB.SAR "Great/Chief Scribe" in KBo 18.54 (text 111; first proposed by Beckman 1995a, 25; see most recently Marizza 2007a, 110, 119 n. 5). His own position as chief of the scribes may account for how heated he becomes when he argues to Ḫimmuili in HKM 52 (text 55): 10–18 that scribes should not have to render *šaḫḫan* and *luzzi*. His activities in the capital apparently did not allow him to travel to Tapikka (Marizza 2007a, 120), although Tarḫuntišša, writing from somewhere other than Ḫattuša or Tapikka (ABoT 65 [text 81]) notes that Ḫattušili had been there, but was forced to return to Ḫattuša because he had contracted a fever.

Ḫi(m)muili. Alp 1991a, 59–62; Klinger 1995a, 86–87. Next to Kaššū, it is Ḫimmuili to whom the king sends the most letters. He is mentioned thirty-two times in twenty-two letters. He is not the same Ḫimmuili who occurs twice in text 60 (HKM 57); see Alp 1991a, 62. A third Ḫimmuili, a man from Kamamma, is included in the list of hostages in HKM 102 obv. 8. The name Ḫimmuili ("man from Ḫimmuwa") was a popular one borne by several men mentioned in Hittite texts. As Alp notes (1991a, 62), it is quite possible that the Ḫimmuili who figures so prominently in the Maşat letters is the same man who occurs in the Deeds of Šuppiluliuma as a general. From the replies of the king to Ḫimmuili it is clear that he sent many letters to the king, although none of them was found at Maşat (Alp 1991a, 59). According to texts 32 (HKM 27) left edge 1–4; 55 (HKM 52) rev. 40–46; 67 (HKM 64) rev. 25–26; and 36 (HKM 30) rev. 21, Ḫimmuili had several messengers at his disposal, including his personal messenger named Šanda (^{m}AMAR.UTU-*aš*, HKM 56 [text 59]: 13–15).

Ḫimmuili bore the title *BĒL MADGALTI* (= Hittite *auriyaš išḫa-*), which designates the "margrave," or provincial governor (see HKM 27 [text 32] and 36 [text 35], and the list HKM 111 rev. 16). Detailed descriptions of all his duties can be found in the MH "instructions" (Hittite *išḫiul,* Italian *vincolo,* German *Dienstanweisungen*) document CTH 261, edited by Pecchioli Daddi 2003a, and translated into English first by Goetze 1969 and most recently by McMahon in Hallo and Younger 1997, 221–25. See Bryce 2002a, 16–17, 116–17; and Alp 1991a, 60 for further secondary literature through 1982. He is usually addressed in the letters not by this full title, but as "lord" (*BĒLU*) or "first lord" (*BĒLU MAḪRÛ*). But in at least one case he is addressed (without name) only by that title (HKM 27 [text 32], see Alp 1991a, 317). Ḫimmuili was superior in rank to the high-ranking official resident in Ḫattuša named Ḫattušili (HKM 10 [text 16]: 42–52), since his name precedes the latter's in the address formula in HKM 10 (Alp 1991a, 60). Ḫimmuili often used Ḫattušili as his middleman in the procurement of horses and chariots for his command (HKM 27 [text 32]: 13–16).

Foremost among his duties was the securing of the borders against hostile or unauthorized entry (see HKM 26 [text 31], 27 [text 32], 30 [text 36], 31 [text 37], 36 [not edited here], and 52 [text 55]). In this respect his duties overlap with those of Kaššū, who bears the title "Chief of the Army Inspectors" (UGULA NIMGIR.ÉRIN.MEŠ).

Other functions performed by Ḫimmuili in these letters are:

- supervision and securing of the imposts called *šaḫḫan* and *luzzi* (HKM 52 [text 55])
- oversight of the sowing and cultivation of state lands (HKM 54 [text 57] and 55 [text 58])
- maintenance of the state vineyards (HKM 31 [text 37]) and livestock (HKM 31 [text 37] and 54 [text 57])
- judging legal cases (HKM 52 [text 55] and 57 [text 60])

Ḫuilli. Alp 1991a, 63. Mentioned seven times in seven letters: HKM 55 (text 58), 56 (text 59), 57 (text 60), 60, 75, 84, and 85. In HKM 56 (text 59) Ḫimmuili writes—according to Alp, from Ḫattuša—to his colleague Ḫuilli in Tapikka, giving him the position of preference (superiority) in the address form, and adding a wish for his welfare (lines 5–6), which is customary when writing to a superior. This relationship to a superior does not, however, keep Ḫimmuili from complaining bitterly about Ḫuilli's failures.

Ḫulla. Alp 1991a, 64. Mentioned eight times in five letters: HKM 17 (text 22), 25 (text 30), 61 (text 64), 62 (text 65), and 66 (text 69). Ḫulla operates out of Tapikka. In HKM 17 his name stands first in the group of three Tapikkan officials addressed by the king, the other two being Kaššū and Zilapiya. This might indicate that Ḫulla was at least Kaššū's equal in rank. In the same letter he is singled out (lines 9–12) as one whom the king sent out at the head of a troop detachment, and who was successful in the mission. He appears to be addressed alone again in lines 24–27, again indicating his importance in relationship to the other two. In HKM 25 (text 30) the king addresses him together with Tatta, whose name precedes his. Again his duties are military with the added responsibility to guard the crops. In HKM 61 Ḫulla himself writes a letter to his subordinate Taḫazzili, sending him on a mission to search for the son of Kammammanda, who has been captured by the Kaškaeans. In HKM 62 Ḫulla writes to Ḫimmuili. Since both of these men operated at times out of Tapikka, the question is, which one is in Tapikka at this time and which one writes from somewhere else? Since the piggyback letter HKM 62 "b" was sent by Tarḫunmiya, a scribe who operated mainly from Ḫattuša, it may be Ḫulla who writes from the outside to Ḫimmuili in Tapikka. Again Ḫulla's name precedes, indicating that he considers himself Ḫimmuili's superior. In HKM 66 Ḫulla writes to Adad-bēlī, with his own name preceding the latter's, yet addressing him as an equal ("dear brother").

Kaššū. Alp 1991a, 70–75. Kaššū was the "Chief of the Army Inspectors" (UGULA NIMGIR.ÉRIN.MEŠ), responsible for all the troops in the province and resident at Tapikka. The king sent more letters to Kaššū than to any other official at Hittite Tapikka. He is mentioned in thirty-four of the letters. KBo 18.54 (text 111) in Middle Hittite ductus and language from a certain Kaššû, who *might* be this same man, was edited by Pecchioli Daddi 1978–1979. Many letters are addressed to him alone, but a smaller number are addressed to him together with Zilapiya, Ḫulla, Pulli, Pipappa, or Pišeni. In most cases where he is addressed with others his name stands first, indicating a superior rank. Only Ḫulla and Pišeni appear to have ranked above him. As the primary addressee, Kaššû received letters from the following persons: the king, "the Priest," the "Chief of the Scribes," the "Chief of the Chariot Warriors," Piyamatarḫu, and Šaḫurunuwa. He received piggyback letters from Ḫašammili and Pišeni. His many letters to the king are attested by the frequent quotes from them contained in the king's replies (texts 7, 8, 9, 12, 13, 14, and 16).

His duties (see Alp 1991a, 70–75 and Marizza 2007a, 95) included:

- defending the land, livestock, and crops from attacks by enemies (mainly Kaška)
- sending out scouts to determine the location of marauding enemy groups (HKM 6: 17–23 [text 12], HKM 7: 3–8 [text 13]) and attacking them, and thus keeping the enemy bottled up in his own land (HKM 3: 7–10 [text 9])
- retrieving fugitives (see for example HKM 9 [text 15])
- keeping the king informed of the status of all military operations in his area (e.g., HKM 6: 3–10 [text 12], HKM 8: 3–11 [text 14])
- keeping the king informed of the condition of the vines, crops, cattle, and sheep (HKM 4 [text 10])
- receiving and deploying troops and equipment dispatched to him from the king (HKM 1: 8–10 [text 7] and HKM 2: 4–9 [text 8])
- transferring resources from one district in his area to another, including livestock (HKM 5 [text 11])

- ◦ taking necessary defensive measures mentioned in the Instructions for the Commanders of the Border Garrisons (CTH 261, ed. Pecchioli Daddi 2003a), such as bringing livestock within the city walls at night or during times when the enemy was observed in the area.

In many of the king's letters to Kaššū, these detailed measures are simply referred to in general terms by the words "let the land be (or more simply, 'be') on the highest level of alert against the enemy" (e.g., HKM 3 [text 9]: 11–13; HKM 6 [text 12]: 15–16, 25–l. e. 1; HKM 7 [text 13]: 26; 8 [text 14]: 18–19; HKM 22 [text 27]: 6–7, etc.). The temporary nature of the alert is shown by: "Be very much on your guard toward the enemy, while the (reinforcing) troops are on their way (lit. are coming afterwards/behind)" (HKM 22 [text 27]: 6–8).

Mār-ešrē. Alp 1991a, 78–79. He is mentioned six times in six letters. He writes mainly from Ḫattuša, but may accompany the king to other "palaces" from where he could also write.

Pallā(n)na. Alp 1991a, 83–84. He is mentioned three times in three letters.

Pi(p)pa(p)pa. Alp 1991a, 86–87. He is mentioned four times in four letters.

Pišeni. Alp 1991a, 87.

Piyama-Tarḫu(nta). Alp 1991a, 88–89.

Pizzumaki. Alp 1991a, 89.

Pulli. Alp 1991a, 89–90. He is mentioned eight times in six letters: HKM 18 (text 23), 19, 21, 22, 65, and 76. In HKM 18, the opening lines of the main letter from the king are lost, but either Kaššū or Pulli or both are addressees. Yet the singular "you" forms in what survives of the letter suggest that perhaps only one of them was addressed. The duties are military, which would fit what we know of Kaššū. In the piggyback letter of Pišeni to the two men, he instructs them both to be active in overseeing the harvesting of seed grain and storing it in underground silos.

Šaḫurunuwa. Alp 1991a, 90–91. Mentioned two times in two letters.

Šanda. Alp 1991a, 91. Mentioned two times in two letters.

Šaparta. Alp 1991a, 92. Mentioned five times in two letters.

Šarla-LAMMA. Alp 1991a, 92. Mentioned once in text 50.

Šarpa. Alp 1991a, 92. Mentioned four times in four letters.

Šuriḫili. Alp 1991a, 94. Mentioned two times in two letters. Šuriḫili is the king's scribe in Ḫattuša, while Uzzū is the scribe of Kaššū in Maşat.

Taḫa(z)ili. Alp 1991a, 94. Mentioned four times in four letters.

Tarḫumimma. Alp 1991a, 95–96. Mentioned three times in three letters.

Tarḫumuwa. Alp 1991a, 96. Mentioned two times in text 60: 15, 34.

Tarḫunmiya. Alp 1991a; de Martino and Imparati 1995, 111–12; Houwink ten Cate 1998, 158, 162–65, 170, 172–75; van den Hout 2003a; and Bryce 2003b, 177–78. This person Tarḫunmiya figures very prominently in the Tapikka letters (see HKM 27 [text 32], 29 [text 34], 52 [text 55], 56 [text 59], 60 [text 63], 62 [text 65], 65 [text 68], 71 [text 73], and 81 [text 80]), both as a party to disputes about taxes due on his house in Tapikka, and as an influential scribe with a very elegant handwriting (on the handwriting of Tarḫunmiya see Alp 1991a, 98).

Tarḫunmiya was born in Tapikka, but worked in Ḫattuša during the period of these letters, where he served as the representative of the provincial administration.

Uzzū. Alp 1991a, 104. He is one of the most frequently mentioned persons in the letters from Maşat Höyük—mentioned eighteen times in seventeen letters: HKM 2, 3, 17, 19, 22, 30, 31, 33, 39, 53, 71, 73, 77, 80, 81, 95.

Zilapiya. Alp 1991a, 106–7. He is mentioned eight times in seven letters: HKM 15, 16, 17, 43, 45, 68, and 75.

2.2.2.3. The Texts

7. HKM 1†
From the King to Kaššū

Text: Mşt. 75/12. **Find spot:** Maşat H/5 Room 9. **Copy**: HKM 1. **Edition**: Alp 1991a, 120–21. **Translation**: Hoffner 2002b, 45. **Discussion**: Beal 1992, 314; Goedegebuure 2003, 200; *GrHL* §29.6 (for lines 8–13) and §21.11 (for lines 11–13).

(1) *UM-MA* dUTU-*ŠI-MA* (2) *A-NA* mKa-aš-šu-ú (3) *QÍ-BÍ-MA*	(1) Thus speaks His Majesty: (2–3) Say to Kaššū:
(4) *ŠA* LÚ.KÚR-[m]u [k]u-it (5) uttar ḫa-at-⌜ra-a⌝-[e]š (6) LÚ.KÚR-wa URU[UGa-ša-š]a-an (7) ḫar-zi	(4–5) Concerning the matter of the enemy about which you wrote to me, saying: (6–7) "The enemy holds the city Kašaša"
(8) nu-kán ka-a-aš-ma (9) ANŠE.KUR.⌜RA⌝.ḪI.A (10) pa-ra-a ne-eḫ-ḫu-un (11) nu-za *PA-NI* LÚ.KÚR (12) me-ek-ki pa-aḫ-ḫa-aš-ša-nu-an-za (13) e-eš	(8–10) I have just dispatched chariotry. (11–13) So be on the highest level of alert against the enemy.

Commentary

The sections beginning with the words "Concerning the matter of …" (lines 4–7) confirm to the addressee the receipt of his previous letter, which dealt with the referenced matter (§1.1.9.5). In this case the letter received by the king from Kaššū was a report on enemy activities in his area, specifically the capture and occupation of the city Kašaša. The "enemy" referred to anonymously in the Tapikka letters is thought to have been the non-sedentary tribal people called the Kaška. When the sender has no substantial comment to make on the matter about which his correspondent has just written him he may simply refer to the subject matter and add "I have heard it" (*na-at AŠ-ME*). See HKM 3 (text 9), line 4.

6 The restoration of the city name URU[*Ga-ša-š*]*a-an* is merely Alp's guess. Kašaša is mentioned alongside Taḫazzimuna in text 30: 5–6, and its vineyards are mentioned in text 35: 8–12, and 40: 13–16. In text 50 it figures as a halting place for the king while on a campaign against the Kaška(?), and subsequently a place where Šarla-LAMMA performs augury. It lay not far from Tapikka/Maşat in the Upper Yeşilırmak Valley.

11–13 For the "so" force of the conjunction *nu* see *GrHL* §29.6. About *pa-aḫ-ḫa-aš-ša-nu-an-za* Alp comments (1991a, 302) that it implies taking protective measures (*Schutzmaßnahmen*). My wording "highest level" interprets *mekki* (see my remakrs on pp. 95–96).

8. HKM 2†
From the King to Kaššū

Text: Mşt. 75/44. **Find spot:** G/5 Room 9. **Edition**: Alp 1991a, 120–23, 302–3. **Translation**: Hoffner 2002b, 45. **Discussion**: Goedegebuure 2003, 208; *GrHL* §28.69 (lines 12–13).

(1) *UM-MA* dUTU-*ŠI-MA* (2) *A-NA* mKa-aš-šu-ú (3) *QÍ-BÍ-MA*	(1–3) Thus speaks His Majesty: Say to Kaššū:
(4) *ŠA* ANŠE.KUR.RA.ḪI.A-mu (5) ku-it ut-tar ḫa-at-ra-a-eš (6) na-aš-ta ka-a-aš-ma (7) ANŠE.KUR. RA.ḪI.A ka-ru-ú (8) pa-ra-a ne-eḫ-ḫu-un (9) na-an-za-kán me-na-aḫ-ḫa-an-da a-ú	(4–9) Concerning the matter of chariotry about which you wrote to me: Be advised that I have already dispatched chariotry. So be on the lookout for it.

(10) *ŠA* ŠEŠ mḪi-mu-DINGIR-*LIM*-ma (11) ku-it ut-tar ḫa-at-ra-a-eš (12) na-an-kán ka-a-ša (13) pa-ra-a ne-eḫ-ḫi	(10–13) Concerning the matter of Ḫimmuili's brother about which you wrote: I am dispatching him right now.

Commentary

The term translated "chariotry" (line 4), literally "horses," refers to charioteers together with their vehicles and steeds. Kaššû has requested additional troops in his district, specifying charioteers. The king assures him that the contingent has been dispatched and is on its way.

Lines **1–9** were cited by Bryce 2003b, 172 to illustrate how letters from the king to his officials were free of the elegant circumlocutions of polite diplomatic discourse and were "terse" and "straight-to-the-point." Other letters in this corpus in which the king announces the sending of troops are: texts 7; 8: 1–9; 23: 17–20; 24: 1–25; 27: 1–8; 36: 1–10; and 35: 1–9 (see Beal 1992, 314 [lines 1–9] with n. 1198).

Note that *menaḫḫanda au*(*š*)- with *-kan*/*-ašta*, but without *-za* means "see someone/-thing coming" (CHD sub *menaḫḫanda* 4a), whereas with added *-za* (as in line 9) it means "wait for." This latter usage is probably also found in: [...] NINDA.ÉRIN.MEŠ-*ŠU* ZÍD.DA [DUR]U$_5$$^{?!}$ *me-na-ah-ha-an-da a-uš-du* "let [...] wait for his/its soldier-breads of [moist] flour" KBo 16.24 + KBo 16.25 i 43 (dupl., KBo 50.257), where *nu-za-ta* stands for *nu* + -z(a) + *-šta*.

10–13 Concerning the matter of Ḫimmuili's brother see also text 66 (lines 12–26).

8b. HKM 2
Piggyback Letter of Šuriḫili to Uzzū

(14) *A-NA* mUz-zu-u ŠEŠ.DÙG.G[A]-*YA* (15) *QÍ-BÍ-MA UM-MA* mŠu-ri-ḫi-DINGIR-*LIM* (16) ŠEŠ-*KA-MA* (17) kat-ti-mi SIG$_5$-in tu-uk-ka$_4$ (18) *MA-ḪAR* ŠEŠ.DÙG.GA-*YA* ḫu-u-ma-an (19) SIG$_5$-in e-eš-tu nu-ut-ta <DINGIR.MEŠ> dÉ.A-aš (20) ḫa-at-ta-an-na-aš	(14–16) Say to Uzzū, my dear brother: Thus speaks Šuriḫili, your brother: With me all is well. (17) May all be well also with you, dear brother. (19–22) May the gods, including Ea, the king of wisdom, lovingly protect you, the wife, and (your son?) Tazzukuli. (l.e. 1) Here

LUGAL-u[š] (21) DAM m[T]a-az-zu-ku-li-n[a]25 (22) aš-šu-li pa-aḫ-ša-an-ta-ru (l. e. 1) ⸢ka⸣-a-ya *I-NA* É-*K*[*A*] (l. e. 2) [ḫ]u-u-ma-an SIG_5-in (l. e. 3) na-aš-ta ŠEŠ.DÙG.GA «ḪI»-*YA*26 (l. e. 4) [l]e-e ku-wa-at-ka_4 (l. e. 5) la-aḫ-la-aḫ-ḫi-i[š-k]e-ši	too in your house all is well. So stop worrying, my dear brother.

Commentary

The piggyback letter is by the king's scribe. For a brief account of Šuriḫili see in §2.2.2.2.

Wishes (or prayers) that the gods may protect the correspondent are common in this correspondence. See §1.1.9.2 and §1.2.17 for a discussion of the standard types, as well as the special wish-form used by scribes to each other (here in lines 18–22). For "your brother" see §1.2.16.

l. e. 1–2 Since Šuriḫili is with the king, Uzzū's "house," which Šuriḫili writes is "here," could be either in Ḫattuša or in the king's alternate residence in Šapinuwa; on the point of origin of the king's letters see §1.2.10. See also HKM 3 [text 9] l. e. 1–3.

9. HKM 3
From the King to Kaššū

Text: Mşt. 75/40. **Find spot:** G/5 Room 8. **Copy**: HKM 3. **Edition**: Alp 1991a, 122–25 (no. 3), 303–4. **Translation**: Hoffner 2002b, 46. **Discussion**: Hoffner 2007, 392 (lines 7–10); Boley 2000, 174a (lines 5–10); CHD Š, 137 -*šan* B 1 b 26′ (lines 8–10); *GrHL* §29.40 (on clitic -*a* in dÉ.A-*aš-ša* in line 18).

(1) *UM-MA* dUTU-*ŠI-MA* (2) *A-NA* mKa-aš-šu-ú *QÍ-BÍ-MA*	(1–2) Thus speaks His Majesty: Say to Kaššū:
(3) *ŠA* LÚ.KÚR-mu ku-it ut-tar (4) ḫa-at-ra-a-eš na-at *AŠ-ME*	(3–4) Concerning the matter of the enemy about which you wrote me: I have heard it (read to me).
(5) nu-ut-ta ka-a-aš-ma (6) ka-ru-ú ku-it ḫa-at-ra-a-nu-un (7) a-pé-el ku-iš KUR-e ÉRIN.MEŠ (8) na-aš-	(5–6) Concerning what I have already written you: (7) "Let the troops which are in his land (8) not

kán nam-ma (9) ar-ḫa le-e ú-iz-zi (10) a-pí-ya-aš e-eš-tu (11) nu KUR-e *PA-NI* LÚ.KÚR me-ek-ki (12) pa-aḫ-ḫa-aš-ša-nu-wa-an (13) e-eš-tu	come out again. (10) Let them remain there." (11–13) So let the land be on the highest level of alert against the enemy.

Commentary

7 The genitive pronoun *apel* "his" refers to the "enemy" of line 3. The Hittite king wants the enemy's troops bottled up in their own land.

7–11 Since the scribe (or the king while dictating) did not use the quotative particle -*wa* to indicate clauses that represent quoted speech, there is no formal way to determine where the quote of the king's previous instruction ends. But my sense is that the *nu* in line 11 has the attested sense of "so, therefore" (*GrHL* §29.6), and introduces the king's added remarks.

10 The clause *apiya=aš ēštu* is asyndetic, and highlights the fact that it is stating the same wish as the preceding negative clause, using a positive formulation (see *GrHL* §29.49).

9b. HKM 3
Piggyback Letter to Uzzū from Šuriḫili

(14) *A-NA* mUz-zu-u ŠEŠ.DÙG. GA-*YA* (15) *QÍ-BÍ-MA UM-MA* mŠu-ri-ḫi-DINGIR-*LIM* (16) ŠEŠ-*KA-MA*	(14–16) Say to Uzzū, my dear brother: Thus speaks Šuriḫili, your brother:
(17) kat-ti-it-ti <ḫu-u-ma-an?> SIG_5-in e-eš-du (18) nu-ut-ta DINGIR. MEŠ dÉ.A-aš-ša (19) ḫa-at-ta-an-na-aš LUGAL-uš (20) aš-šu-li pa-aḫ-ša-an-ta-ru	(17–20) May <all?> be well with you, and may the gods, including Ea, the King of Wisdom, lovingly protect you.
(21) ka-a-ša *I-NA* É-*K*[*A*] (22) *Ù*!27 *MA-ḪAR* DAM-*KA* ḫu-u-ma-a[n] (23) SIG_5-in na-aš-ta ŠEŠ.DÙG. GA-*YA* (l. e. 1) la-aḫ-la-aḫ-ḫi-iš-ke-zi [le-e ku-wa-at-ka_4] (l. e. 2) ŠEŠ. DÙG.GA-*YA*-ya-mu EGIR-pa (l. e. 3) aš-šu-ul ḫa-at-ra-a-i	(21–23, l. e. 1–3) At present all is well in your house and with your wife. So stop worrying, my dear brother. And send me back (your) greeting, my dear brother.

Commentary

From this piggyback letter and HKM 2 (text 8 above) l. e. 1–5 we learn that Uzzū, the scribe in Tapikka-Maşat, had a house and perhaps a family (Alp 1991a, 104). Šuruḫili reassures him of their safety and well-being. On Ea see above in §1.2.17 and in text 8b. For the meaning "greeting" of *aššul* in l. e. 3 and elsewhere see Alp 1991a, 303–4.

17–20 contains the standard well-wishes (see §1.2.17). But there is no statement of how "it is well with me."

l. e. 1. The negtive *lē* together with the imperfective *-ške-* stem of the verb expresses the meaning of an inhibitive ("stop ...-ing," *GrHL* §24.10).

10. HKM 4
From the King to Kaššū

Text: Mşt. 75/39. **Find spot:** G/5 Room 8. **Photos**: Alp 1991a, pl. 2 (photo of the royal seal impression). **Copy**: HKM 4. **Edition**: Alp 1991a, 124–27 (no. 4). **Translation**: Hoffner 2002b, 46. **Discussion**: Houwink ten Cate 1998, 161 (on the royal seal impression of Arnuwanda I together with his queen Sata(n)du-Heba(t)); Klengel 1999, 128 (equates this queen with Taduḫepa, the wife of Tudḫaliya II/III = Tašmi-Šarruma); Goedegebuure 2003, 61–62, 183.

(1) *UM-MA* ᵈUTU-*ŠI-MA* (2) [*A*]-*NA* ᵐKa-aš-šu-ú (3) *QÍ-BÍ-MA*	(1–3) Thus speaks His Majesty: Say to Kaššū:
(4) a-pé-e-[d]a-[n]i KUR-e (5) *Š*[*A* GE]ŠTIN *ŠA* GU$_4$.[Ḫ]I.A UDU.Ḫ[I].A (6) ut-tar ku-[i]t (7) ma-aḫ-ḫa-an nu-[m]u (8) li-li-wa-aḫ-ḫu-u-an-z[i] (9) ḫa-at-ra-a-i	(4–9) Write to me soon concerning the condition of the vines, the cattle, and the sheep in that land (where you are).

Commentary

Apparently, Tapikka's region was an area of vineyards and good grazing land. An economic map of the Hittite kingdom has yet to be drawn up. It would be interesting to see where the most wheat, barley, fruit trees, vineyards, and so on, were to be found. For more on vineyards see text 37 (HKM 31), a letter from the king to Ḫimmuili about the vineyards of Kašaša.

On the king's concern for the condition of crops and vineyards see above, §1.2.20.4.

The word *liliwaḫḫuwanzi,* formally an infinitive, in MH correspondence serves as an adverb meaning "soon, quickly."

11. HKM 5
From the King to Kaššū

Text: Mşt. 75/21. **Find spot:** H/5 Room 9. **Copy**: HKM 5. **Edition**: Alp 1991a, 126–27, 304. **Translation**: Hoffner 2002b, 46. **Discussion**: Beal 1992, 60 n. 215, 316, 401 n. 1510; Goedegebuure 2003, 199.

(1) [*UM-MA*] ^{d}UTU-*ŠI-MA* (2) [*A-NA*] ^{m}Ka-aš-šu-ú *QÍ-BÍ-MA*	(1–2) Thus speaks His Majesty: Say to Kaššū:
(3) [*Š*]*A* ^{URU}Ga-ši-pu-u-ra ku-it (4) GU$_4$.ḪI.A da-at-t[a] na-an-ša-an (5) *ŠA* ^{m}E[N-t]a-ra-u-wa ma-ni-ya-aḫ-ḫi-ya (6) iš-ḫu-wa-a-it-ta	(3–6) Regarding the fact that you took the cattle of Kašipura[28] and distributed[29] them in the district of EN-tarawa:
(7) ki-nu-na-kán *ŠA* ^{m}EN-ta-ra-u-wa (8) ma-ni-ya-aḫ-ḫi-ya-az ÉRIN.MEŠ an-na-al-li-in (9) ÉRIN.MEŠ wa-ar-ra-aš$^{?}$-ša[30] (10) le-e n[i]-ni-ik-ši (11) nu-uš-ša-an a-pu-u-un (12) GU$_4$.[Ḫ]I.A EGIR-an e-ep-du (13) na-aš-kán KIN-az le-e (14) ša-me-e-ez-zi	(7–10) At this point in time you must not levy veteran troops and auxiliary troops out of the district of EN-tarawa. (11–12) Let him gather the aforementioned cattle, (13–14) and let him (i.e., EN-tarawa) not be deprived of the work.

Commentary

This letter reveals that Kaššū in his official capacity as UGULA NIMGIR ÉRIN.MEŠ[31] was authorized to move royal livestock from one administrative district under his oversight to another (see Kaššū above in §2.2.2.2), in this case, from Kašepura, whose governor's name is not given here, to the unnamed district governed by EN-tarawa. The livestock was moved to the district of EN-tarawa in order to be used for a certain work project (KIN, line 13). Among the available pool of laborers on this project were two classes of (former) soldiers: "veteran troops" (*annalli-*, i.e., those having served for a long time and now retired but still subject to levy) and "auxiliary troops" (i.e., reserves subject to call-up). Because of the importance of this project, at this point in time (*kinuna*, line 7) Kaššū is commanded not to levy any of these men from EN-tarawa's district for military duty, which apparently at any other time he would have had the right to do. Unfortunately, from this letter we know neither the location of EN-tarawa's district nor the nature of the work project. The livestock could have been used for agricultural activities or for hauling building materials for fortification or other construction work.

Lines **3–6** are treated in CHD Š, 134 (*-šan* B 1 b 12′ a').

Lines **11–14** are treated in CHD S, 151 (-šan B 2 i 2′ b').

13 I take *šamēzzi* with *-kan* and an expressed ablative as CHD *ša(m)men-* mng. 2 a, which is usually translated "forfeit," but can easily mean "lose" or "be deprived of." EN-tarawa would be deprived of the work by virtue of insufficient resources, if the cattle were not returned to him.

12. HKM 6
From the King to Kaššū

Text: Mşt. 75/16. **Find spot:** H/5 Room 9. **Edition**: Alp 1991a, 126–29, 304–5. **Translation**: Hoffner 2002b, 47. **Discussion**: Yoshida 1991, 363; Beal 1992, 267, 315, 403; de Martino and Imparati 1995, 105 (on hyperbolic expression in lines 11–14) [reprinted in 2004, 637]; Hoffner 2002c, 66; Goedegebuure 2003, 142, 199, 218, 329–30; Hoffner 2007, 390 (lines 9–10). Lines 9–14 are edited in CHD Š, 26. Lines 18–22 are edited in CHD Š, 205 (*šapašalli-*).

Again Kaššū reports military matters to the king. He says that the enemy has "pressed" (*tamaš-*) two cities (line 6), which probably means attacking them.[32] If they were walled cities, which we do not know, it could mean he surrounded and besieged them, although the "enemy" in question is probably the Kaška people (on whom see von Schuler 1965; cf. text 13 line 24) who are less likely to have had siege equipment at their disposal, and lines 7–10 indicate that the main body of enemy troops was ever on the move.

But although this same letter reveals that Kaššū had "scouts" (line 19) at his disposal to track moving contingents, he failed to discover where the marauding enemy was headed next. This lapse angered the king, who then resorted to sarcasm, asking whether Kaššū thinks he was dealing with an enchanted foe!

Beal (1992, 266–75) has devoted a thorough discussion to the terms for scouts (or "spies"). The two that occur in the Maşat letters are syllabically written LÚ*šapašalli-* and the logogram LÚNÍ.ZU (also used in the laws for "thief"). Beal treats the two terms separately and gives in detail what can be determined of the functions of each, and admits in the end (1992, 274) that since the two terms are never used together, and the tasks of the two overlap considerably, it is impossible to eliminate the possibility that the second is merely the logogram covering the first. In another text we are given the Hattic (or Luwian?) equivalent for the logogram, namely LÚ*kīluḫ* KBo 5.11 i 19 (Soysal 2004, 288).

For what these letters tell us about the role of scouts see above in the introduction.

(1) *UM-MA* dUTU-*ŠI-MA* (2) *A-NA* mKa-aš-šu-ú *QÍ-BÍ-MA*	(1–2) Thus speaks His Majesty: Say to Kaššū:
(3) ki-iš-ša-an-mu[33] ku-it ḫa-at-ra-a-eš (4) ka-a-ša-wa LÚ.KÚR ú-it (5) nu-wa-za-kán URUḪa-pa-ra-an i-ni-iš-ša-an (6) ta-ma-aš-ta URUKa-ši-pu-ra-an-ma-wa-kán (7) ke-e-ez ta-ma-aš-ta a-pa-a-aš-ma[34]-wa-kán (8) iš-tar-na ar-ḫa ú-it (9) nam-ma-ma-wa<-ra>-aš ku-wa-pí pa-it (10) nu-wa!-ra-at!(text incorrectly -aš[35]) *Ú-UL I-DI*	(3–10) Concerning what you wrote me, saying: "The enemy has come. He pressed the city Ḫapara *on that side* (of me) and the city Kašepura on this side. But he himself passed through, and I don't know where he went"—
(11) nu a-pa-a-aš LÚ.KÚR (12) al-wa-an-za-aḫ-ḫa-an-za im-ma (13) e-eš-ta na-an *Ú-UL* (14) ša-a-ak-ta«-aš»	(11–14) So—was that enemy enchanted, that you did not recognize him?
(15) nu-za *PA-NI* LÚ.KÚR me-ek-ki (16) pa-aḫ-ḫa-aš-nu-an-za e-eš	(15–16) (From now on) be on the highest state of alert against the enemy.
(17) ki-iš-ša-an-ma-mu ku-it (18) ḫa-at-ra-a-eš ka-a-ša-wa (19) LÚ.MEŠša-pa-ša-al-li-e-eš (20) *AŠ-PUR* nu-wa URUMa-la-az-z[i]-an (21) URUTág-ga-aš-ta-an-na (22) ša-pa[36]-ši-ya-ar[37] (23) na-at *AŠ-ME* nu SIG$_5$-in	(17) Concerning what you wrote me, saying: (18–20) "I have just sent out scouts, (20–22) and they have scouted out the cities Malazziya and Takkašta." (23) I have heard it. Fine.

(24) ú-wa-at du-wa-ad-du (25) *PA-NI* LÚ.KÚR-za me-ek-ki (l. e. 1) pa-aḫ-ḫa-aš-nu-an-za e-eš	(24–25, l. e. 1) Now get with it! Be on highest alert against the enemy!

Commentary

5–7 As for the apparent contrasting of *iniššan* and *kēz*, the former does have a spatial usage ("out there") alongside its modal one ("thus"): "I wanted to set out (with my army), *nu=mu eniššan kuit* LÚ.MEŠ URU*Taggašta šenaḫḫa peran teškanzi* "but because the men of Takkašta were setting a trap/ambush out there (*eniššan*) before me, (I didn't go)" KBo 5.8 i 16–17 (annals of Muršili II). Nothing in the immediately preceding lines describes actions of the men of Takkašta to which the "thus" meaning could be referring. Also in [*nu=m*]*u eniššan kuit* [m*M*]*uttin* LÚ URU*Ḫalimana* [*me*]*naḫḫanda uiyer* "[and] because from out there (*eniššan*) they sent [to] meet [me] Mutti, the man of Ḫalimana" KBo 4.4 iv 50–51 (annals of Muršili II) *eniššan* is not likely to be the modal use, which is virtually always describing an utterance. Similarly, GIM-*an=ma=mu=kan* m*Urḫiteššupaš eniššan* / *ŠA* DINGIR-*LIM aššulan aušta* "but when Urḫi-Teššup saw the favor of the deity toward me *eniššan*" Ḫatt iii 54–55 has nothing in the preceding context to which a "thus" can be referring. While it is not easy to prove a local adverbial meaning of *iniššan* similar to *edez* or *kez*, it is incontestable that the modal meaning "thus" cannot cover all of the word's uses. The fragmentary passage KUB 27.67 iv 28–29, in which [K]Á-*az iniššan* and *kēz* appear in close proximity, perhaps in contrast, comes closest to the pairing in this letter.

14 On *ša-ak-ta*‹‹*-aš*›› see CHD Š, 22.

24 For *uwat duwaddu* see above in §1.2.19.1.

13. HKM 7
From the King to Kaššū

Text: Mşt. 75/70. **Find spot:** G/5 Room 8. **Copy:** HKM 7. **Edition**: Alp 1991a, 128–31, 305. **Translation**: Hoffner 2002b, 47. **Discussion**: de Martino and Imparati 1995, 113 (reprinted in 2004, 645) (on line 23); Goedegebuure 2003, 196.

(1) [*U*]*M*-[*M*]*A* dUTU-*ŠI-MA A-NA* mKa-aš-šu-ú (2) [*Q*]*Í-BÍ-MA*	(1–2) Thus speaks His Majesty: Say to Kaššū:

(3) ki-iš-ša-an-mu ku-it ḫa-at-ra-a-eš (4) ka-a-ša-wa LÚ.MEŠša-pa-ša-al-li-e-eš (5) pí-i-e-nu-un[38] nu-wa pa-a-er URUTág-ga-aš-t[a-an] (6) URUÚ-ku-du-i-p[u]-na-an-na ša-pa-ši-ya-u-a[n[39] da-a-ir] (7) nu-wa-ra-at la-at-ta-ri-ya-an-ti-⸢aš?⸣ [o o]x […] (8) ⸢ÍD?⸣-ša-wa kat-ta ⸢ḫu⸣-it-⸢ti⸣-ya-an ḫar-zi	(3–8) Concerning what you wrote me, saying: "I have just sent out scouts, and they have proceeded to scout out Takkašta and Ukudui-puna…, but he has 'drawn down' to his/its river."
(9) nu-uš-ša-an a-pé-e-[d]a-ni ud-da-ni-i (10) ú-e-ra-an-za-pát e-eš nu LÚ.MEŠša-pa-ša-al-li-u[š] (11) pí-i-e-ya nu SIG$_5$-in ša-pa-ši-ya-an-du nu-x-[…] (12) ka-a-aš-ma-at-ta ka-ru-ú-ya (13) ku-it ḫa-at-ra-a-nu-un dUTU-*ŠI* (14) a-pé-e-[d]a-ni KASKAL-ši EGIR-an (15) ar-ḫa ḫu-[i]t-t[i-ya]x[…]	(9–15) Be called/summoned to that matter.[40] Send forth scouts, and let them scout thoroughly, and … And concerning what I, My Majesty, have written you previously, draw out behind that road.
(16) ka-a-š[a …] (17) *A-N*[*A*?] x x […] (18) n[u?] x[ ] x x […] (19) x [ ] x [ ] x […] (20) nu x x [o] x x […] (21) ú-wa-mi ÉRIN.MEŠ.ḪI.A-ma an-da (22) ka-ru-ú ta-ru-up-pa-an-da […]	(16–22) … I will come … Troops already assembled …
(23) t[u]-ga-az mKa-aš-šu-ú-un *I-DI* (24) ma-aḫ-ḫa-an na-aš-ta *A-NA*[41] LÚ.MEŠ URUGa-aš-ga (25) kat-ta-an ar-ḫa an-ku *ŠU-PUR* (26) na-at pé-ra-an pa-aḫ-ḫa-aš-nu-wa-an-[te-eš a-ša-an-du]	(23–26) Just as I authorize (lit. recognize) you, Kaššū, send out (the scouts) to (observe) the Kaška, and let them (i.e., the scouts) be protected from (the Kaška).

Commentary

The signs *Tág-ga-aš-ta* in 5 are all written over an erasure. Some other city name was first written here. Lines 7 and 8 are untranslatable by me. The main verb of line 7 is missing in the break, and the noun *lattariyanti-* is otherwise unknown to me. Alp read the first signs in line 8 as *a-pa-ša*, but his copy of the second sign in HKM is either BA, MA or the second half of the ÍD ("river") sign. Spellings of the pronoun *apa-* "that (one)" with the BA sign are exclusively Old Hittite, making such a reading here unlikely. ÍD-*ša* would either be **ḫapaš=a*, with the Old Hittite(!) topicalizing particle attached to the nom. or gen. sg. of "river," or **ḫapa=šša* "to his/its river" (allative). But OH *kāša* has obviously yielded to *kāšma* (line 12), showing that the *-a* allomorph of the particle *-a/-ma* has already been lost in this speaker's dialect, surviving only as a vestige in *kinuna* and on the accented pronouns *ziga, ammuga, tuga, šumāša*. For this reason the allative interpretation seems more likely than the former. The allative might be still alive in MH texts, although in restricted use (URU-*ya* KUB 23.77a rev. 52, *parna=šša* KBo 8.35 i 14, *tuliya* ibid. ii 9). In the Maşat letters it might occur in the forms *šardiya* (HKM 65 [text 68]: 10) and *tuzziya* (HKM 35 [text 41]: 6), in addition to here. But essentially it too is a feature of OH, not MH or NH. None of this yields a convincing translation. The four signs following *a-ba-ša* (or ÍD-*ša*) appear to have been written over an erasure.

In line 15 the photo does not support Alp's reading *-té*]*n*. Nor would I expect a 2 pl. verb form, when the king is addressing only Kaššū.

In the morphology section of CHD *šakk-* the occurrence of *I-DI* in line 23 of this letter is accidentally attributed to both *šakḫi* "I know" and *šakki* "he knows." Contra CHD Š, 31 (sub *šakk-* mng. 7 a), I follow the view that the form *I-DI* represents a first (not third) singular form, as also understood by de Martino and Imparati 1995, 113.

In line 25 *kattan arḫa ŠUPUR* is comparable to *kattan arḫa ḫatrait* in KUB 14.1 obv. 69, where "sent secretly to" fits the context. See also: *našma=naš=kan* LÚ *ṬĒMU=ma kuiški kattan / arḫa uiyazzi nu=nnaš* ḪUL-*lun memian / kuinki ḫatraizzi n=an eppweni* [*UL*] "Or (if) someone sends a messenger to us secretly and proposes an evil action to us, and (if) we do [not] seize him" KUB 31.44 ii 8–10.

In line 26 I take *peran*, although its dative-locative referent *-šmaš* (or *ANA* LÚ.MEŠ URUGašga) is unexpressed, as the *peran* that in NH regularly governs something that is a threat or danger (illness, death, famine, enemies): see CHD P, *peran* 10 c, and *GrHL* §20.23 (where the example *kašti peran akkiš* should be changed to simple *kašti peran* "because of hunger").

14. HKM 8
From the King to Kaššū

Text: Mşt. 75/74. **Find spot:** G/5 Room 8. **Copy:** HKM 8. **Edition**: Alp 1991a, 130–33, 305–6. **Translation**: del Monte 1992, 65 (lines 3–11);

Hoffner 2002b, 47. **Discussion**: Beal 1998, 85; Francia 1996, §3.3.6 (lines 12–14); van den Hout 2004a, 89; Hoffner 2002c, 66 (on lines 18–19).

(1) *UM-MA* [dUT]U-*ŠI-MA* (2) *A-NA* mKa-aš-šu-ú *QÍ-BÍ-MA*	(1–2) Thus speaks His Majesty: Say to Kaššū:
(3) ud-da-a-ar-mu ku-e ḫa-at-ra-a-eš (4) LÚ.KÚR ma-aḫ-ḫ[a]-an ḫal-ki-uš (5) dam-me-[i]š-[ḫ]i-iš-ke-ez-zi (6) URUKap-p[u]-ši-ya ma-aḫ-ḫa-an (7) *ŠA* É MUNUS.LUGAL wa-al-aḫ-ta (8) nu *ŠA* É MUNUS.LUGAL 1 GU_4 ḫa-ap-pu-ut-ri [da-a-ir[42]] (9) *ŠA* LÚ.MEŠMAŠ.EN.KAK-ya (10) 30 GU_4.ḪI.A 10 LÚ.MEŠ-ya pé-ḫu-te-er (11) na-at *AŠ-ME*	(3) Concerning the matters about which you wrote to me: (4–5) how the enemy is damaging the crops, (6–7) how in Kappušiya he has attacked (the property) of the House of the Queen, (8) how they have taken? one team of oxen belonging to the House of the Queen, (9–10) and how they have led away captive 30 oxen and 10 men of the serfs (lit. poor people)—(11) (all this) I have heard.
(12) na-aš-ta LÚ.KÚR *QA-TAM-MA* (13) ku-it KUR-e an-da (14) lam-mar lam-mar i-at-ta-r[i] (15) ma-a-na-an ḫa-an-da-a-ši (16) ku-wa-pí-ki ma-a-na-an (17) wa-al-aḫ-ši (18) *A-NA PA-NI* LÚ.KÚR-ma-az (19) m[e-e]k-ki pa-aḫ-ḫa-aš-nu-an-za e-eš	(12–14) Because the enemy thus marches into the land at a moment's notice,[43] (15) you should locate him somewhere, (16–17) you should attack him. (18) But you must be very much on highest alert against the enemy.

Commentary

The city Kappušiya is in the upper Yeşilırmak Valley according to HKM 17 (see also HKM 99: 17). It is to date unmentioned in Boğazköy texts. If the "poor" (line 9) can own oxen, they are obviously not truly destitute persons, but dependent and relatively small farmers, i. e., "serfs." This picture is confirmed by other texts (KUB 8.75+ l. e., left "col." 1–3; KUB 39.52 + KUB 9.15 iii 17–23). The translation "serfs" is from del Monte 1992: 65 ("Hörigen").

This letter gives a pretty good idea of the scope of most of the military operations of the enemy. They were razzias, raids on villages, rather than large-scale pitched battles. One sees here too the typical size of the losses: thirty oxen and ten men. The capture of humans by the Kaška is noted in the prayer of King Arnuwanda and Queen Ašmunikal, where they say: "[the Kaška people] would take your divine servants and maids and turn them into their own servants and maids ... from some of them [i.e., the lands] the priests, the priestesses, the holy priests, the anointed, the musicians, and the singers had gone ... they divided up the priests, the holy priests, the priestesses ... and they made them their servants" (Singer 2002, 41–42). What was most troublesome to the Hittite king and his officials was the frustrating situation that these enemies could appear at a moment's notice, do damage, and then escape. The damage done to the crops was perhaps more serious than the small numbers of lost animals, because this attacked the future food supply not only of Tapikka itself, but of the capital city Ḫattuša, which may well have received supplies from towns like Tapikka in the Hittite "bread basket."

Lines **15–16** contain examples of the plene-written variant of the speaker-optative particle man (CHD L–N, *man* a 1′; *GrHL* §23.11).

15. HKM 9
From the King to Kaššū

Text: Mşt. 75/41. **Find spot**: G/5 Room 8. **Copy**: HKM 9. **Edition**: Alp 1991a, 132–33, 306. **Translation**: Hoffner 2002b, 48. **Discussion**: Imparati 2003, 235.

(1) *UM-MA* dUTU-*ŠI-MA* (2) *A-NA* mKa-aš-šu-ú *QÍ-BÍ-MA*	(1–2) Thus speaks His Majesty: Say to Kaššū:
(3) 13 LÚ.MEŠpít-te-an-du-uš-kán (4) ku-it pa-ra-a na44-it-ta (5) na-aš ú-wa-te-er	(3–5) Concerning the fact that you dispatched (to me) 13 (apprehended) fugitives: They have brought them here.
(6) *ŠA* ANŠE.KUR.RA.ḪI.A-ma-mu (7) ku-it ut-tar ḫa-at-ra-a-eš (8) na-at *AŠ-ME*	(6–8) I received your message to me about the horse troops.

Commentary

The purpose of this extremely short letter is merely to acknowledge the arrival of persons and messages sent by Kaššū to the king. The king gives no new instructions or tasks.

Here we see another of Kaššū's common duties: apprehending fugitives and sending them under guard to the capital (see §2.2.2.2). The Hittite term *pitteyant-* merely denotes someone fleeing. These men could be fugitive slaves fleeing their Hittite masters. If so, then they are being returned to the king for him to decide how to return them to their masters. For the Hittite laws dealing with fugitive slaves, some who even fled to foreign lands, see Laws §§22–24 in Hoffner 1997g, 31–33. But it is also possible that these are fugitives from neighboring states or from the Kaškaeans. In this case, one might translate *pitteyanduš* in line 3 as "refugees" (see §1.2.20.1).

Although the text is cryptic, it is likely that the "horses" (ANŠE.KUR.RA.ḪI.A, line 6) Kaššū has asked about are teams of chariot horses and their drivers, that is, "horse troops."

16. HKM 10
From the King to Kaššū

Text: Mşt. 75/112. **Find spot:** G/5 Portico. **Photo:** Alp 1991a, pl. 8 (handwriting of Tarḫunmiya). **Measurments** (from the photo)**:** 8 cm wide × 11.5 cm tall (see §1.2.8.2). **Copy:** HKM 10. **Edition**: Alp 1991a, 132–37, 307–9; Giorgadze 2005. **Translation**: Hoffner 2002b, 48. **Discussion**: Lühr 2001, 340–41; Hoffner 2002c, 67 n. 35; Francia 1996, §3.3.9 (lines 10–11); Bryce 2003b, 174 (on the piggyback letter in lines 42–52). Hoffner 2007, 392 (lines 8, 20–21) *GrHL* §16.108 (line 40), §18.25 (lines 23–32), §22.24 (lines 45–46), §28.57 (lines 34–35), §29.7 (lines 3–6), §30.37 (lines 24–28).

This long letter—one of the longest in the Maşat corpus—contains both a lengthy letter from the king and a piggyback letter to Ḫimmuili. As Marizza observes (2007a, 115), this shows that, although Ḫimmuili's duties often took him to the outer periphery of the region, the official "home" of both Kaššū and Ḫimmuili was Tapikka, for they received this letter to both of them there. In the first letter (lines 1–41) the king replies to Kaššū's earlier letters, and makes five comments. From the nature of each successive quote from Kaššū it appears that these matters may have reached the king not in a single letter, but in five successive ones. And since Kaššū's recorded questions seem to overlap, indicating that he repeated the same concerns and questions in several of the letters, this leads to the king's exasperated remark in lines 30–32.

1) Piḫinakki's relocation and settlement of the city Lišipra (lines 3–13);

2) the report that two named Kaška leaders have already made peace (lines 14–16);

3) the request for instructions about handling the many Kaška men coming to make peace (lines 17–22);

4) Kaššū's tendency to wear the king out with queries about matters that he should already know how to handle (lines 23–32; the king's patience with Kaššū is wearing thin);

5) Kaššū's success in a small military engagement (only sixteen casualties) against the enemy in the land of Išḫupitta (lines 33–41).

The king acknowledges without comment the second and fifth (last) messages, making comments only on the first, third, and fourth. He expresses approval at the first message about Lišipra, and gives the requested instructions about the Kaška men coming in large numbers to make peace. But he becomes angry at the persistent Kaššū's fourth message.

Alp (1991a, 22–23) locates Lišipra to the north of Tapikka-Maşat in the region of Išḫupitta, and therefore exposed to the Kaška enemy. He maintains (1991a, 22) that it was a preexisting village/town, whose residents were in danger of attack and were consequently removed and replaced by new families, which makes no sense. I would prefer, with Giorgadze (2005, 374), to see Lišipra as a city whose previous inhabitants had been carried off by the (Kaška?) enemy, and which now the Hittite king wished to repopulate with a group of 300 "families" of NAM.RA available to him from among his captives in earlier encounters with Kaškaeans. Both Alp (1991a, 119) and Giorgadze agree that the uniform size of these NAM.RA "families" was approximately ten persons, making the entire population of the "village/town" about three thousand. The new population was what other texts call *arnuwala-* (Sumerogram NAM.RA.MEŠ). The verb used here (*arnu-*) for relocating them to a new area requiring their services accords with the term designating their class (*arnuwala-*). That term occurs in the Maşat corpus of letters in HKM 24 (text 29): 39 in broken context. For this class of persons in general see Alp 1950–1951; Goetze 1957, 106; Bryce 2002a, 105–7; Hoffner 2002c; and Klengel 2006: 8–9. For the place of the NAM.RA.MEŠ in the administrative hierarchy at Maşat see fig. 1 on p. 92 (§2.2.2).

(1) *UM-MA* dUTU-*ŠI-MA* (2) *A-NA* mGa-aš-šu-ú *QÍ-BÍ-MA*	(1–2) Thus speaks His Majesty: Say to Kaššū:
(3) *ŠA* mPí-ḫi-na-ak-ki-mu ku-i[t] ut-tar (4) ḫa-at-ra-a-eš mPí-ḫi-na-ak-ki-iš-za ma-aḫ-ḫa-an (5) URULi-ši-ip-[r]a-an e-eš-ke-e[t-t]a-ri (6) nu-wa-za ka-ru-ú 30 É-*TUM* a-še-ša-an [ḫ]ar-zi	(3–6) Concerning what you wrote me about how Piḫinakki is (re)settling Lišipra: "He has already settled 30 'families'.[45]

(7) ^{m}Pí-ḫi-na-ak-ki-iš-ma-wa-mu ki-i[š-š]a-an (8) me-mi-iš-ta ^{URU}Li-ši-ip-ra-wa ku-in a-še-eš-ḫi (9) nu-wa-ra-an-za im-ma 300 É-*TUM* ar-nu-mi (10) nam-ma-wa-kán LÚ.MEŠ SIG$_5$ *MA-ḪAR* ^{d}UTU-*ŠI* (11) pa-ra-a ne-eḫ-ḫi ap-pé-ez-zi-ya-az-ma-wa (12) URU-an ar-nu-me-ni na-at *AŠ-ME* nu SIG$_5$-in (13) nu a-pa-a-at ut-tar i-ya-pát	(7–13) "Piḫinakki himself said to me: 'I intend[46] to relocate (*arnu-*) three hundred families to Lišipra which I am resettling (*ašeš-*).[47] Then I will send the (captured Kaškaean?) officers before Your Majesty. Eventually we will relocate (*arnu-*) the (entire) city.'" I received that message. Excellent! Do that very thing.
(14) *ŠA* ^{m}Pí-ḫa-ap-zu-up-pí-ma-mu ku-it (15) *ŠA* ^{m}Ka-aš-ka-nu-ya ut-tar ḫa-at-ra-a-eš (16) ka-ru-ú-wa ták-šu-la-a-er na-at *AŠ-ME*	(14–16) Concerning the matter of the (Kaška leaders) Piḫapzuppi and Kaškanu about which you wrote me: "They have already made peace (with us)," I received that message (too).
(17) ki-iš-ša-an-ma-mu ku-it ḫa-at-ra-a-eš (18) ka-a-ša-wa LÚ.MEŠ ^{URU}Ga-aš-ga ták-šu-la-an-ni (19) me-ek-ki i-ya-an-da-ri nu-wa-mu ma-aḫ-ḫa-an (20) ^{d}UTU-*ŠI* ḫa-at-ra-a-ši nu LÚ.MEŠ ^{URU}Ga-aš-ga (21) ku-i-e-eš ták-šu-li i-ya-an-da-ri (22) na-aš-kán *MA-ḪAR* ^{d}UTU-*ŠI* pa-ra-a na-iš-ke	(17–22) Concerning what you wrote me: "Kaška men are coming here in large numbers to make peace. What instructions does Your Majesty have for me?"[48]— Keep sending to My Majesty the Kaškaean men who are coming to make peace.
(23) ki-iš-š[a-a]n-ma-mu ku-it ḫa-at-ra-a-eš (24) ku-it-ma-an-wa-mu ^{d}UTU-*ŠI* (25) ki-i *ŠA* LÚ.MEŠ ^{URU}Ga-aš-ga ták-šu-la-aš (26) ut-tar ḫa-at-ra-a-ši am-mu-ug-ga-wa (27) me-mi-an *I-NA* KUR ^{URU}Iš-ḫu-pí-it-t[a] (28) ḫu-uš-ke-mi nu ka-ru-ú (29) ku-it DINGIR.MEŠ [i]m$^{?}$-ma-an-x[…] (30) zi-ga-mu-uš-ša-an [p]a-r[a]-a$^{?}$ (31) za-ap-pa-nu-uš-ke-ši nu-mu [*Q*]*A-TAM-M*[*A*] (32) ḫa-at-re-eš-ke-ši	(23–32) Concerning what you wrote me: "Until you, Your Majesty, write me about this matter of the Kaškaean men coming to make peace I will be awaiting word in the land of Išḫupitta." Just because the gods already …, should you keep wearing me out with queries,[49] and keep writing me the same things?

(33) ki-iš-ša-an-ma-mu ku-it ḫa-at-ra-a-eš (34) ma-aḫ-ḫa-an-wa-kán am-mu-uk (35) *I-NA* KUR URUIš-ḫu-pí-it-ta a-ar-ḫu-un (36) EGIR-an-ma-wa LÚ.KÚR URUZi-ik-kat-ta-an (37) wa-al-aḫ-ta nu-wa 40 GU_4.ḪI.A 100 UDU.ḪI.A (38) pé-en-né-eš nu-wa-ra-an-kán ar-ḫa (39) pé-eš-ši-ya-nu-un *ŠA* LÚ.KÚR-ya-wa-kán (40) ap-pa-an-te-et ku-na-an-ti-it (41) 16? LÚ.MEŠ pé-eš-ši-ya-nu-un na-at *AŠ-ME*	(33–41) Concerning what you wrote me: "When I arrived in the land of Išḫupitta, behind me the enemy attacked Zikkatta, and led away forty cattle and one hundred sheep. I expelled him (lit. threw him out). And sixteen men of the enemy—including[50] captives and killed—I felled (lit. caused to fall)."[51] I received that message (too).

Commentary

5 *eške-* in mid., see Neu 1968, 27; *HED* E, 296; and *HW*^{2} s.v. for forms. Alp 1991a, 135, 307 opts for an intransitive interpretation "make a stop-over, stay" ("sich aufhalten"), without explaining the accusative of the city Lišipra. Alp's translation is accepted also by Giorgadze 2005, 375. I prefer to see this as an example of the transitive use of the middle with *-za*; see Neu 1968, 28 (number 2) and 31 n. 20, where anterior literature is cited, including Goetze 1927, 106; and for further examples in the Maşat letters see Hoffner forthcoming, §140. It appears likely from this text that *eške-*, as the imperfective (i.e., *-ške-* form) of the stem *eš-*, is very close in meaning to the *-ške-* forms of the reduplicated stem *ašaš-/ašeš-* "to settle." The imperfective form describes the overall, extended process of settlement (lines 4–5), while the non-imperfective form (*ašeš-*) describes one part or stage (the first tenth) of the process (line 6). The action of transfer (or relocation) itself is expressed by *arnu-*.

9 "in all"—Alp's translation of *im-ma* here as "ganz und gar" (1991a, 135), immediately preceding the number, makes excellent sense.

10–11 If we follow Giorgadze's view that what is described here is the transfer of NAM.RA groups ("families") from one location to another, and the NAM.RA captives are Kaškaeans, then the LÚ.MEŠ SIG_5 could be the captured military officers of the Kaškaeans (Freu and Mazoyer 2007, 184). Because of their rank, they serve either as hostages (elsewhere called in Hittite *šulleš*; for further comment, see below on HKM 14 [text 19]) or as persons competent to "make peace" by taking oaths in the presence of the king, to whom they are being sent in this passage. On the competency of Kaška "leaders" to make peace by taking oaths, see de Roos 2005, 54 and literature cited there in n. 38. In a sense, they are—as Alp wished to render the term LÚ.MEŠ SIG_5—"notables" (German *Angesehene*) among the inhabitants of Lišipra. The German translation "Angesehene(r)" is defended by Alp (1991a, 307), and accepted without comment by Giorgadze (2005, 375). The term also occurs in HKM 13 (text 18): 9 and HKM 65 (text 68): 15, where it clearly indicates military officials.

14–15 For other personal names of Kaška people and their linguistic analysis, see von Schuler 1965, 89–94, 100–107.

17–22 The delegations of Kaškaeans seeking peace are compared by Beckman (1995a, 26 n. 47) with that led by Ašḫapala in KBo 16.50 (CTH 270; Otten 1960).

22–32 For translation and comment on these lines see CHD P, 117 (*parā* 1 eee). I prefer to take the final two clauses as rhetorical questions. For the syntax of rhetorical questions in Hittite see Hoffner 1995a, 89–90 and *GrHL* §27.3.

34–41 Translated and commented upon linguistically in CHD P, 321 (*peš(š)iya/e-* mngs. 7 and 8). We may assume that this report of Kaššū's to the king was one of many of this type, indicating one of his principal duties: the expulsion of raiding parties of Kaška men. Captured and killed enemy warriors totalled 16, suggesting a relatively small-scale engagement. The enemy had previously captured forty cattle and one hundred sheep from the town of Zikkatta. Klinger (1995b, 106–7) uses this passage to illustrate that not all of the land of Išḫupitta was at this time under Hittite control.

16b. HKM 10
Piggyback Letter to Ḫimmuili from the Chief Scribe Ḫattušili

(42) *A-NA* ᵐḪi-mu-DINGIR-*LIM* ŠEŠ.DÙG.GA-*YA* *QÍ-BÍ-MA* (43) *UM-MA* ᵐ ᴳᴵŠ GIDRU-DIN≈GIR-*LIM* ŠEŠ-*KA-MA* (44) kat-ti-ti ḫu-u-ma-an SIG_5-in e-eš-du (45) nu-ut-ta DINGIR.MEŠ TI-an ḫar-kán-du (46) nu-ut-ta aš-šu-li pa-aḫ-ša-an-da-ru	(42) Say to Ḫimmuili, my dear brother: (43) Thus speaks Ḫattušili, your brother: (44) May all be well with you. (45) May the gods keep you alive, (46) and lovingly protect you.

(47) tu-el-mu ku-it *ŠA* LÚ.MEŠan-da-ti-ya-a[t-t]al-la[-aš?] (48) ut-tar ḫa-at-ra-a-eš nu ka-a-ša am-mu-uk (49) ḫar-mi na-at *I-NA* É.GAL-*LIM* (50) me-ma-aḫ-ḫi nu-uš-ma-aš an-tu-uḫ-ša-aš (51) pa-iz-zi na-aš *MA-ḪAR* dUTU-*ŠI* (52) ú-wa-te-ez-zi	(47–52) Concerning the matter of your opponents in court, about which you wrote me, I have (your tablet), and will inform the palace of it. A person will go to them and conduct them to His Majesty.

Commentary

42–46 That this Ḫimmuili is Kaššū's colleague at Tapikka, the *BEL MADGALTI*, is the view of both Alp (1991a, 61) and Bryce, and is supported by the fact that in the order of names in lines 42–43 Ḫimmuili's precedes as the superior, and he receives the polite formula of well-wishing (lines 44–46), normally used when addressing a superior (see §1.2.17). This constitutes an exception to the rule that piggyback letters are normally addressed either to the recipient of the main letter (in this case Kaššū) or to his scribe. Since Kaššū's regular scribe seems to have been Uzzū (see HKM 2 [text 8] and 3 [text 9]), it is more likely that the king's scribe Ḫattušili here sends along a message to Kaššū's colleague, Ḫimmuili. The scribe would probably not do this if Ḫimmuili were Kaššū's superior, since in that case he would merit his own separate tablet. But since, as we have seen, he ranked below Kaššū, the scribal letter to him can be a kind of footnote to the king's letter to his superior. The "my dear brother" terminology, usually employed by scribes, is no obstacle to the addressee being Ḫimmuili the *BEL MADGALTI*, since high officials could also possess scribal training and competence and use the title "scribe" in addition to their other title(s).

45–46 For this use of the imperative of the *ḫar*(*k*)- construction see *GrHL* §22.24.

47–52 Bryce (2003b, 174) follows Alp in taking the term in line 47, *andatiyattalla-*, as synonymous with *antiyant-* "live-in son-in-law," although he translates it as singular in spite of the obvious plural determinative LÚ.MEŠ.[52] The word *antiyant-* is a technical term denoting a young man whose family is too poor to afford the usual bridal gift presented to the family of the bride. Consequently, the bride's family pays this gift to him, and in return he goes to live with them instead of the bride going to live with his family. See Hittite laws §36 (translated in Hoffner 1997f, 222). In the present letter more than one such person is involved (contra Bryce 2003b, 97), and both (or all) of them are to be brought before the king, perhaps to adjudicate a dispute between them. From passages such as KBo 10.2 ii 50–51 and KUB 14.16 ii 15–16 (AM 42) it appears that the verbal complex *anda tiya-* can mean "to enter into (a conflict with someone)." Therefore, *tuel* LÚ.MEŠ*andatiyattalla*[*š*] doesn't mean "your live-in sons-in-law," but "your opponents in court." The presence of *tuel* "your" does not (contra Alp 1991a, 309) indicate that LÚ.MEŠ*a.* must be a term for blood relationship ("Verwandtschaftsbezeichnung").[53] Another analysis that would point in the same direction is that the word in this letter is a faulty spelling of LÚ*ḫantitiyattalla-* "accuser, plaintiff, opponent-at-law."

In either of the latter two scenarios, the persons referred to would be bringing charges or claims against Ḫimmuili. This passage shows provincial officials involved in legal disputes in royal courts (Beckman 1995a, 27 n. 42). But the "palace" (É.GAL) Ḫattušili refers to here is not Ḫattuša, but a regional administrative center to which Tapikka was subject (see Imparati 2002, 95). Most think that this was Šapinuwa. The administrative-governmental structure of the kingdom was three-tiered: (1) central government at Ḫattuša, (2) regional governmental centers, and (3) local urban centers. Šapinuwa was in the second tier while Tapikka was in the third.

17. HKM 12
From the King to Kaššū

Text: Mşt. 75/23. **Find spot**: H/5 Room 9. **Copy**: HKM 12. **Edition**: Alp 1991a, 136–39 (no. 12). **Translation**: Hoffner 2002b, 49. **Discussion**: Alp 1991a, 98, 309.

(1) *UM-MA* dUTU-*ŠI*[-*MA*] (2) *A-NA* mGa-<aš>-šu-ú (3) *QÍ-BÍ-MA*	(1–3) Thus speaks His Majesty: Say to Kaššū:
(4) mTar-ḫu-mi-ya-a[n] (5) [LÚ]DUB.SAR e-e[p] (6) [n]a-an *M*[*A-ḪAR* dUTU-*ŠI* …] *(Breaks off)*	(4–6) Apprehend Tarḫunmiya, the scribe, and send him before My Majesty. …
(rev. 1′) [o o] x x […] (2′) [o] É?-ri d[a-…] (3′) [n]a!-an *MA-ḪAR* d[UTU-*ŠI*] (4′) lam-mar (5′) ú-wa!-da-a[n-du]	(rev. 1′–5′) … in the house? … and let them conduct him immediately before My Majesty.

Commentary

What remains of this short letter appears to be an arrest warrant for the scribe Tarḫunmiya, who is to be seized and escorted to the capital. Alp's restoration of the plural form *e-e[p-ten]* is unnecessary, since only Kaššū is addressed. See further in the sketch of Tarḫunmiya above in §2.2.2.2. For an example of *ep-* meaning only "apprehend (and question)," not "seize" or "arrest," see HKM 19 (text 24): 19.

18. HKM 13
From the King to Kaššū

Text: Mşt. 75/45. **Find spot:** G/5 Room 8. **Copy**: HKM 13. **Edition**: Alp 1991a, 138–39, 309; CHD L–N, 388 (*namma* 6a). **Translation**: Hoffner 2002b, 49. **Discussion**: Klinger 1995b, 107–8; Goedegebuure 2003, 221; Freu and Mazoyer 2007, 183–84; *GrHL* §16.46 (on lines 3–4), §18.25 (on lines 4–5).

(1) *UM-MA* dUTU-*ŠI-MA A-NA* mGa-aš-šu-ú (2) *QÍ-BÍ-MA*	(1–2) Thus speaks His Majesty: Say to Kaššū:
(3) ki-i-mu ku-it *ŠA* mMar-ru-ú-wa[54] (4) LÚ URUḪi-im-mu-wa ḫa-li-ya-tar ḫa-at-ra-a-eš (5) pa-ra-a-wa-ra-an-kán ne-eḫ-ḫu-un (6) na-an-mu tup-pí-ya-az ḫa-at-ra-a-eš (7) pa-ra-a-wa-ra-an-kán ne-eḫ-ḫu-un (8) ki-nu-na-aš nam-ma *Ú-UL* ú-it (9) ki-nu-n[a-a]n *A-NA* LÚ.SIG$_5$ pé-ra-an (10) ḫu-i-nu-ut na-an *MA-ḪAR* dUTU-*ŠI* (11) li-li-wa-aḫ-ḫu-wa-an-zi![55] (12) ú-wa-te-ed-du	(3–12) This capitulation (to the enemy) by Marruwa, the ruler of Ḫimmuwa, about which you wrote me, (adding): "I have dispatched him (to you)." On a tablet you wrote to me about him: "I have dispatched him (to you)," but as of now he has not come. Now put him in the charge of an officer, and have him conduct him quickly before My Majesty.
(13) ma-a-an *Ú-UL*-ma nu-za a-pé-e-el (14) wa-aš-túl zi-ik da-a-at-ti	(13–14) Otherwise, you take upon yourself his 'sin.'

Commentary

The king writes to Kaššū about Marruwa, who is described as the "man (i.e., ruler) of Ḫimmuwa," a Hittite city. The king attaches great importance to winning over clan and tribal chiefs of the Kaškaeans who wish to make peace. Accords comparable to those ratified by Arnuwanda I were certainly negotiated by his successor. This Marruwa, also called "man of Kakkaduwa" (text 19), had capitulated (*ḫaliya-*) to the Kaškaeans. Since Ḫimmuwa is one of the cities that had fallen into the hands of the Kaškaeans according to the prayer of Arnuwanda I and Ašmunikal (Singer 2002, 42), it was probably at that time that Marruwa defected to the Kaškaeans. We do not know how long he remained in alliance with the Kaškaeans before he eventually fell into the hands of the Hittite military. His capture need not imply that Ḫimmuwa itself had been recovered (so correctly Klinger 1995b, 108). After his capture, Kaššū delayed in sending him before the king for punishment. The king may have suspected that Kaššū was seeking to retain Marruwa and add him to the pool of hostages captured from the Kaškaeans, in hopes that he and his Tapikka associates might receive a bribe in return for releasing him. See further in the comments on text 19.

In any event, in text 19 the king threatens Kaššū with the most severe consequences (blinding), if he does not now send Marruwa to him immediately. Since this punishment is described as being due to Kaššū's taking upon himself the consequences of Marruwa's "sin," it is clear that blinding was the usual punishment for traitors. The name Marruwa is borne by at least one other Hittite (KUB 13.35 iii 13, 19, 20; Laroche 1966, 115 no. 768). On this Marruwa, Marizza (2007a, 95 n. 20) refers to Forlanini 1983, 16–17 n. 12.

9–10 The same duty of LÚ.MEŠ SIG$_5$ in conducting someone to the king is seen again in text 68 (HKM 65): 11–19.

13–14 On such threats by the king see Marizza 2007a, 97 with n. 29.

19. HKM 14
From the King to Kaššū

Text: Mşt. 75/10. **Find spot**: H/5 Room 9. **Copy**: HKM 14. **Edition**: Alp 1991a, 138–41, 309–10. **Translation**: Hoffner 2002b, 49. **Discussion**: Hoffner 2002c, 68 n. 40; Houwink ten Cate 1998, 161; Siegelová 2002 (on blinding as punishment); Arıkan 2006, 145 (on blind persons).

This tablet bears the seal impression of a king Tudḫaliya, most likely Tudḫaliya III (see Alp 1991a, 48, 138–41, 309–10; and Freu and Mazoyer 2007, 160).

(1) *UM-MA* dUTU-*ŠI-MA* (2) *A-NA* mGa-aš-šu-ú *QÍ-BÍ-MA*	(1–2) Thus speaks His Majesty: Say to Kaššū:

(3) ma-a-aḫ-ḫa-an-ta ka-a-aš (4) tup-pí-an-za an-da (5) ú-e-mi-ya-az-zi (6) nu *MA-ḪAR* ^{d}UTU-*ŠI* (7) li-li-wa-aḫ-ḫu-wa-an-zi u-un-ni (8) ^{m}Mar-ru![56]-wa-an-na (9) LÚ ^{URU}Ga-gad-du-wa (10) ú-wa-te ma-a-an *Ú-UL*-ma (11) nu-uš-ma-aš-ša-an (12) ú-wa-an-zi (13) a-pí-ya pé-e-di (14) ta-šu-wa-aḫ-ḫa-an-zi	(3–14) As soon as this[57] tablet reaches you (sg.), drive quickly to My Majesty, and bring with you Marruwa, the man of Kakattuwa. Otherwise they will proceed to blind you (pl.) in that place (where you are)!

Commentary

It is probable that this Marruwa, who is called "the ruler (literally, 'man') of Kakattuwa" (cf. this same title in HKM 103 obv. 8) is the same man as the "ruler of ^{URU}Ḫimmuwa" who was mentioned in text 18. A possible reason for threatening Kaššū and his associates is suggested in my comments on that text.

Although text 19 is addressed to Kaššū alone, the threat of blinding is made to "you" plural (Hittite -*šmaš*), just as it is again in text 21, where the letter is addressed to Kaššū and Zilapiya. Either the king's scribe was used to using this formula of threat in letters with more than one addressee and mistakenly used it with Kaššū, or it was assumed in both letters that Zilapiya was complicit.[58]

Bryce aptly comments about this and other examples of threats in the king's letters: "His Majesty could hardly have made more emphatic the necessity of obeying his orders without hesitation or delay. And, indeed, the rarity in the Hittite world of death and particularly mutilation as forms of punishment, at least for free persons, highlights the gravity of the crisis now confronting the kingdom" (2003b, 180).

Blinding was a punishment reserved for the most serious offences, usually treason.[59] Deliberately disobeying a direct order of the king would certainly qualify as treason, as would complicity with a culprit or fugitive.

Otten (1979, 276) noted that blinding as a punishment is extremely rare in NH documents, but common in MH ones. But this may be due to the less common reference in NH texts to the punishment for treason.

HKM 102, edited initially by Del Monte (1995, 103–11), is a list of Kaška men captured in battle and held for ransom by their people/familes. Siegelová (2002, 735–36) has rightly noted that these cannot be just ordinary Kaška soldiers, but must be persons of high rank. It should be added that they are referred to as "man of (place name)," just as Marrruwa is in lines 8–9 of this letter. It would appear then that we have in this letter the first recovered example of how individuals were added one by one to the pool of hostages listed in HKM 102. Since HKM 102 was found at Tapikka, we have to assume that hostages could be kept in the province where they were captured. But since the risk of rescue raids by the Kaška would have been very real, under certain circumstances the more important hostages would be removed from the Kaška zone itself and transferred to the capital. There is, therefore, a definite possibility that the reference in HKM 10 (text 16): 10, in close connection with the transfer of Kaškaean NAM.RA-groups to Lišipra, to sending LÚ.MEŠ SIG_5 to Ḫattuša refers to Kaškaean leaders held as hostages. Each hostage in the list HKM 102 has a price set for his ransom, and usually a notation as to whether or not he was sighted (*uškezzi*) or blinded (IGI.NU.GÁL = *tašuwant-/tašuwaḫḫant-*). As I previously pointed out (Hoffner 2002c, 2004), a good parallel found in the Bible is Samson, the famous champion of Israel, captured by the Philistines, probably kept for ransom, blinded as a rebel against the Philistine overlordship, and used while awaiting ransom as a mill worker (see comments below on HKM 58 [text 61] and HKM 59 [text 62]) and entertainer. The threat to blind Kaššū himself, not only because failure to obey a direct order of the king would be tantamount to treason, but also because he was put in charge of a Kaškaean hostage, who might also have been blinded like those in HKM 102, would be an example of the king's irony.

10–14 Edited and commented upon in CHD P, 340 (*peda-* A f 1′ on the expression *apiya pedi*).

20. HKM 15†
From the King to Kaššū and Zilapiya

Text: Mşt. 75/11. **Find spot:** H/5 Room 9. **Copy**: HKM 15. **Edition**: Alp 1991a, 140–41 (no. 15). **Translation**: Hoffner 2002b, 50; Bryce 2003b, 180. **Discussion**: Imparati 1997, 203 n. 30 (reprinted in 2004, 653 n. 30); *GrHL* §25.14 (lines 10–13); §25.35 (lines 12–13), §28.49 (lines 8–9); Hoffner 2007, 392 (lines 8–9).

(1) *UM-MA* ᵈUTU-*ŠI-MA* (2) *A-NA* ᵐGa-aš-šu-ú (3) ᵐZi-la-pí-ya *QÍ-BÍ-MA*	(1–3) Thus speaks His Majesty: Say to Kaššū (and) Zilapiya:

(4) ma-aḫ-ḫa-an-ša-ma-aš ka-a-aš (5) tup-pí-an-za an-da ú-e-mi-ez-zi (6) nu ÉRIN.MEŠ an-da (7) da-ru-up-pa-an-te-et (8) ANŠE.KUR.RA.ḪI.A-ya-aš-ma-aš-kán (9) ku-iš an-da (10) na-an *MA-ḪAR* (11) dUTU-*ŠI* *I-NA* UD.3.KAM (12) li-li-wa-aḫ-ḫu-u-an-zi (13) ar-nu-ut-tén	(4–13) As soon as this tablet reaches you, quickly—within three days—transfer into the presence of My Majesty the assembled troops and the chariotry which is with them.

Commentary

From the order of addressees in this and the following two letters—Ḫulla, Kaššū, and Zilapiya—it would appear that Zilapiya served under (Ḫulla and) Kaššū. From the contents of the three letters it appears that, like Kaššū, Zilapiya had military duties, but also some connection with grain supply (HKM 17).

The grammar of line 6 appears to be corrupt, as *taruppantet* is the instrumental of a participle, and the clause lacks a main verb.

Line **11** informs us that it will require three days for the recipients to gather the requested troops and march them to where the king was at this time. Assuming that the trip itself requires three days, Imparati (1997, 203 n. 30; 2002, 95 n. 14) notes that, since in HKM 20: 10–12 it takes only two days to reach Šapinuwa from Tapikka, the king must have been somewhere else—perhaps Ḫattuša—when HKM 15 was written. See also van den Hout 2007b, 397 on the short distances between points mentioned in the Maşat letters.

21. HKM 16: 1-15†
From the King to Kaššū and Zilapiya

Text: Mşt. 75/69. **Find spot:** G/5 Room 8. **Copy:** HKM 16. **Edition**: Alp 1991a, 141–42. **Translation**: Hoffner 2002b, 50; Bryce 2003b, 180. **Discussion**: Alp 1991a, 106; CHD Š, sub -*šan* B 2 d' 13′ (p. 141).

(1) *UM-MA* dUTU-*ŠI-M*[*A*] (2) *A-NA* mKa-aš-šu-ú (3) *Ù A-NA* mZi-la-pí-[ya] (4) *QÍ-BÍ-MA*	(1–4) Thus speaks His Majesty: Say to Kaššū and Zilapiya:

(5) ma-aḫ-ḫ[a-a]n-ša-ma-aš (6) ka-a-aš tup-pí-an-za (7) an-da ú-e-mi-ez-zi (8) nu *MA-ḪAR* ^{d}UTU-*ŠI* (9) li-la-aḫ-ḫu-u-an-zi (10) u-un-ni-iš-tén	(5–10) As soon as this tablet reaches you (pl.), drive quickly to the presence of My Majesty.
(11) ma-a-an *Ú-UL*-ma (12) nu-uš-ma-aš-ša-an (13) ú-wa-an-zi (14) a-pí-ya pé-di (15) ta-šu-wa-aḫ-ḫa-an-zi	(11–15) Otherwise, they will proceed to blind you (pl.) in that place (where you are).

Commentary

For the threat of blinding see the comment above on text 19 (HKM 14).

22. HKM 17†
From the King to Ḫulla, Kaššū, and Zilapiya

Text: Mşt. 75/47. **Find spot:** G/5 Room 8. **Copy:** HKM 17. **Edition**: Alp 1991a, 142–47, 310. **Discussion:** Klinger 1995a, 92; Freu and Mazoyer 2007, 180; *GrHL* §15.11 (lines 5–6); §16.74 (line 10), §25.11 (lines 16–17), §28.129 (lines 13–15).

Klinger (1995a, 92) has made a convincing case for the identity of the Ḫulla who occurs in five Maşat letters, always without title, with the person by this name in the MH land grant text KBo 5.7 rev. 52, bearing the title GAL $^{LÚ.MEŠ}$KUŠ$_{7}$ ZAG-*az* "Chief Charioteer on the Right." This same man also appears in another MH letter sent to Ḫattuša (KBo 18.69 rev. 8′).[60] In the present letter the king shows his concern for several matters. He is quite displeased that the movements of his officials are so successfully monitored by the enemy that they are able to strike in his officials' absence (lines 4–12). As usual, in his rebuke of Ḫulla he employs heavy sarcasm (lines 9–12).[61]

(1) *UM-MA* ^{d}[UT]U-*ŠI-MA A-NA* ^{m}Ḫu-ul-la (2) ^{m}Ka-aš-šu-ú *Ù A-NA* ^{m}Zi-la-pí-ya (3) *QÍ-BÍ-MA*	(1–3) Thus speaks His Majesty: Say to Ḫulla, Kaššū, and Zilapiya:
(4) k[i]-iš-ša-an-[m]u ku-it ḫa-at-ra-a-at-tén (5) ku-it-ma-an-wa-za ú-e-eš[62] ^{URU}Ḫa-at-tu-ši (6) e-šu-en	(4–8) Concerning what you (pl.) wrote me: "While we were in Ḫattuša, the Kaškaean men heard,

LÚ.MEŠ [U]RUKa$_4$-aš-ka$_4$-ma-wa iš-ta-ma-aš-ša-an-[zi] (7) nu-wa GU$_4$.ḪI.A EGIR-pa pé-en-ni-ya-an-zi (8) KASKAL.ḪI.A-ya-wa-za ap-pí-iš-kán-zi	and they drove away cattle. They even began to take control of the roads."[63]
(9) na-aš-ta tu-uk mḪu-ul-la-an ku-wa-pí (10) gi-im-ma-an-ti pa-ra-a ne-eḫ-ḫu-un (11) nu-ut-ta a-pí-ya *Ú-UL* iš-ta-ma-aš-še-er (12) nu-ut-ta ki-nu-un-pát iš-ta-ma-aš-še-er	(9–12) When I sent you (sg.), Ḫulla, out (last) winter, (the enemies) didn't hear of you *then*. (How is it that) it is only *now* that they have heard of you?
(13) nu-mu ka-a-aš-ma šu-me-eš-pát ku-it ḫa-[a]t-[r]a-a-at-tén (14) mPí-iz-zu-ma-ki-iš-wa-an-na-aš ki-iš-ša-an (15) me-mi-iš-ta LÚ.KÚR-wa URUMa-re-eš-ta (16) pa-iz-zi nu-wa-kán k[a-a-š]a mPí-pí-ta-ḫi-in (17) ša-[p]a-a-ši-ya-u-an-z[i pa-r]a-a ne-eḫ-ḫu-un (18) TÙR.ḪI.A[64]-ya-wa ku-i-[e-eš URU]Ma-re[-eš-t]a (19) ma-an-ni-in-ku-wa-a?[-an-te-eš[65]] a-pu-u-uš-ša (20) wa-al-ḫu-u-wa-ni nu [SIG$_5$]-in (21) nu i-ya-at-tén *QA-TAM-MA* (22) ma-a-an ḫal-ki-iš-ša ḫa-an-da-a-an e-eš-zi (23) nu-za ÉRIN.MEŠ.ḪI.A da-a-ú	(13–23) Concerning what you yourselves (pl.) have now written to me: "Pizzumaki told us: 'The enemy is on his way to Marišta. And I (i.e., Pizzumaki?) have sent Pipitaḫi out to do reconnaissance.' So we will attack the sheepfolds which are in the vicinity of Marišta." Fine. Do as you (pl.) have said. (22) And if the grain crop is ready, let the troops take it.
(24) ki-iš-ša-an-ma-mu ku-it (25) ḫa-at-ra-a-eš URU?-an-wa ma-aḫ-ḫa-an d[a-a?-u?-e?-ni?] (26) nu-wa URUKa-pa-pa-aḫ-šu-wa-an-ma (27) wa-al-ḫu-u-wa-ni	(24–27) Concerning what you (sg., perhaps Ḫulla line 9) wrote me: "How shall we? take the city?[66] Or is it Kapapaḫšuwa that we should attack?"
(28) URUKa-pa-pa-aḫ-šu-wa-aš me-ek-ki ku-it (29) [pa-aḫ-ḫa-aš-n]u-wa-an-za nu-mu-kán *ŠA* URUKa-pa-pa-aḫ-šu-wa (30) […] *Ú-UL* ZAG-an ke-e-ez-za-aš-ši-kán KUR-e (31) [… ta-m]a?-aš-ša-an ḫar-kán-zi nu-ut-ta ši-na-ḫa ti!-	(28–32) Since Kapapaḫšuwa is well protected, so that the capture? of Kapapaḫšuwa is not likely to succeed for me, they will keep the territory enclosed? on this side of it, and lie in ambush against you (sg.). . . .

ya[!]-an ḫar-k[án-zi] (32) [… A.ŠÀ ku[?]-]e[?]-ri-ya-aš-ša	
(33) [… URUTá]g-ga-aš-ta-za im-ma ku-it-ki (34) [… A.Š]À [k]u-e-ri an-da wa-al-aḫ-ši (35) [nu-ut-ta …] ZAG-ni-eš-zi nu mar-ri ‹‹-aš›› le67-e ku-it-ki i-ya-ši (36) […] na-aš-ši ku-it NU.GÁL ku-iš-ki	(33–36) From the direction of Takkašta you (sg.) should attack whatever … and the cultivated land, and it will succeed for you. So do not do anything rash! Because of the … there is no one for him.

Commentary

4–8 are cited by Beckman (1995a, 26) to show how officials from Tapikka frequently traveled to Ḫattuša. The mention of Kaškaeans taking control of the roads probably refers to the increased danger in traveling back and forth to Ḫattuša, because of enemy ambushes.

In line **13** and following, because of the difficulty of establishing the boundary of a quote within a quote, we can only use the distinction between "I" and "we" to assume that Pizzumaki's words end with line 17, and line 18 begins what the addressees themselves say to the king. He approves of their plan: after Pipitahi's reconnaissance of the area of Marišta is completed, they will attack the sheepfolds there (lines 13–21). But the king instructs them to harvest the crops before they can be damaged or stolen by the enemy (lines 22–23). For other indications of how troops used sheepfolds as places of shelter from which attacks could be launched see HKM 36 (text 35).

In lines **24–36**, much of which is destroyed, the king advises one of the three (perhaps Ḫulla, note the singular "you" forms in 31, 34, and 35) on military strategy in reply to their request "How [shall we[?]] take the city? Or is it Kapapaḫšuwa that we should attack?" Among other matters he warns him against possible ambushes (*ši-na-ḫa*, line 31). Perhaps in view of the singular forms just noted one should restore *d*[*a-aḫ-ḫi*] "shall [I] t[ake]" in line 25.

28 On the *n*[*u*] that Alp mistakenly read at the beginning of this line see comments in CHD P, 9–10 (*paḫšanu-* 3c).

22b. HKM 17
Piggyback Letter to Ḫulla, Kaššū, and Zilapiya from Ḫašammili

(37) [*A-NA* mḪu-ul-la mKa-aš-š]u-	(37–40) Say to Ḫulla, Kaššū, (and)

ú mZi-la-pí-ya (38) [*QÍ-BÍ-MA UM-MA* mḪ]a-ša-am-mi-li ARAD-*KU-NU-MA* (39) [kat-ta-an-ša-ma-aš ḫu-u-ma-an] SIG$_5$-in e-eš-du (40) [nu-uš-ma-aš DINGIR.MEŠ p]a-aḫ-ša-an-da-ru	Zilapiya: Thus speaks Ḫašammili, your servant: May all be well with you (pl.), and may the gods protect you (pl.).
(41) [… k]a-ru-ú tar-na-at-ta-at (42) [… k]a-ru-ú wa-aš-ša-an ḫar-kán-zi (43) [… D]ÙG.GA-*YA* az!-za-ki-it-tén[68] (44) […] x x	(41–44) … was already released. … are already dressed. … my dear brother, keep eating (pl.), and …
(45) […] x x x […] x ut-tar x-x-ši?-ya (46) […] x x […] x x (47) [… ma-a]ḫ-ḫ[a-a]n[…] x [… ḫa-a]t-ra-a-mi (48) […] x […] (49) […] k[u]-i[t …] (50) [… nu-m]u ḫa-at-ra-a-i […] x-kán (51) x-x-e ku-it-ma-an ku-it […] (52) [k]u-it-ma-an *A-NA* x.MEŠ-*YA* am-m[u-uk …] (53) k[e!-]e-«e-»-ez ḫa-at-ra-a-mi	(*Lines 45–53 are too broken for translation.*)

22c. HKM 17
Piggyback Letter to Uzzū from Ḫašammili

(l. e. 1) *A-NA* mUz-zu-u [*QÍ-BÍ-MA UM-MA* mḪa-ša-am-mi-li] (l. e. 2) [ŠE]Š-*KA-MA* DINGIR.MEŠ-t[a TI-an ḫar-kán-du nu-ut-ta aš-šu-li pa-aḫ-ša-an-da-ru …] (l. e. 3) EGIR-an ti-ya nu-uš-ši-iš-š[a-an ma-a-an? … p]a-ra-a *Ú-UL* a[p?-pí?-]i[š-ká]n-zi (l. e. 4) nu-mu ḫa-at-ra-a-i da-at-tén-ma-aš-ši-kán le-e ku-it-ma-an ku-it-k[i ḫa-at-ra-a-mi] (l. e. 5) nu-ut-ta ma-aḫ-ḫa-an ḫa-at-ra-a-mi na-at *QA-TAM-MA* (l. e. 6)[69] pí-pa-at-ti	(l. e.) Say to Uzzū: Thus speaks Ḫašammili, your brother: May the gods keep you alive and lovingly protect you. Get busy with the …, and write me if the … are not …-ing the…. But don't take (*this verb is pl.*) anything from him until *I write* something. And you must *pi(p)pa-* it just as I instruct you in writing.

Commentary

There are two piggyback letters on this tablet. The first is from the king's scribe Ḫašammili to the three officials. Its contents, other than the respectful greeting formulas, are unfortunately mostly broken away. The second letter is from the same scribe to his Tapikkan counterpart Uzzū. Although it too has the customary well-wishes (l. e. 2), its tone is more abrupt ("get busy," "write me," "don't take" and "you must … it just as I instruct you in writing") and shows that the two men are equals and can dispense with groveling compliments.

23. HKM 18†
From the King to Kaššū and Pulli

Text: Mşt. 75/61. **Find spot:** G/5 Room 8. **Copy:** HKM 18. **Edition**: Alp 1991a, 146–49, 310–13. **Translation**: Hoffner 2002b, 51. **Discussion**: Beal 1998, 85; Melchert 1999 (on *tukanzi*); Hoffner 2001, 209; Francia 1996, §2.4.1 (rev. 23–27); Goedegebuure 2003, 63, 183, 208; Rieken 2004, 538 (on ÉRIN.MEŠ ^{GIŠ}*za-al-ta-i-ya-aš-ša* rev. 24′); Cotticelli-Kurras 2007, 184 (rev. 27 *ḫa-aš-ke-et*); Klengel 2006, 11 (referring to edge 4–5).

(1) *U*[*M-MA* ^{d}UTU-*ŠI*]-*MA* (2) *A*[-*NA* ^{m}Ka-aš-šu-ú *Ù* ^{m}Pu-ul-li] *Q*[*Í*-[*B*]*Í-MA*	(1–2) Thus speaks His Majesty: Say to Kaššū and Pulli:
(3) […]x (4) [….] (5) […] ^{m}Da-a-ḫa-zi-DINGIR-*LIM* (6) [… ^{m}x-x-]*na*-DINGIR-*LIM* (7) i$^{?}$-x[…] x me-mi-iš-ta	*(Lines 3–11 are too badly broken for translation)*
(8) nu x […] x me-mi-[i]š$^{!}$<-ta> (9) *I-N*[*A* …]x-iš (10) *ŠA* […] (11) *A-NA* […]-x	
(12) nu-wa x […] (13) nu-wa-aš-m[a-aš … ^{d}]UTU-*ŠI* (14) *ŠA* ^{É}tar-n[u-i …]x-ḫa$^{!}$[70] (15) ar-ḫa e-ep-zi (16) na-aš-kán *MA-ḪAR*$^{!}$ ^{d}UTU-*ŠI* pa-ra-a na-i	(12–16) … (16) And send (sg.) them before My Majesty.

(17) *ŠA* ÉRIN.MEŠ-ma-mu ku-it ut-tar ḫa-at-ra-a-eš (18) nu-mu ka-a kat-ti-mi ÉRIN.MEŠ KUR UGU (19) ÉRIN.MEŠ KUR ^{URU}Iš-ḫu-u-pí-it-ta ku-iš-ki (20) na-an-da up-pa-aḫ-ḫi	(17–20) Concerning the matter of troops about which you (sg.) wrote me: I have some troops of the Upper Land (and?) of the land of Išḫupitta here with me. I will send them to you (sg.).

Commentary

1–2 Since the "you" forms in the king's letter are singular, it is possible that only one addressee should be restored in this opening. But if so, should it be Kaššū or Pulli? One of these men wrote requesting troops. The king replies that he will send some troops from the Upper Land ("and" or "namely") from Išḫupitta.

23b. HKM 18: 21-28, l. e. 1–5
Piggyback Letter from Pišeni to Kaššū and Pulli

Discussion: Hoffner 2001, 209.

(21) *UM-MA* ^{m}Pí-še-ni[71] *A-NA* ^{m}Ka-aš-šu-ú (22) ^{m}Pu-ul-li DUMU.MEŠ DÙG.GA-*YA QÍ-BÍ-MA*	(21–22) Thus speaks Pišeni: Say to Kaššū and Pulli, my dear sons:
(23) ka-a-aš-ma ÉRIN.MEŠ ^{URU}Iš-ḫu-u-pí-it-ta (24) ÉRIN.MEŠ ^{GIŠ}za-al-ta-i-ya-aš-ša ku-in (25) ḫal-ki-in tu-kán-zi ḫar-k[án-z]i (26) ki-nu-na a-pé-e-da-ni ḫal-ki-i (27) ^{d}UTU-*ŠI* še-er me-ek-ki ḫa-aš-ke-et (28) *QA-TAM-MA*[72] ḫ[a-a]t-ra-a-at-tén (l. e. 1) nu ú-wa-at du-wa-ad-du (l. e. 2) ḫal-ki-iš-ma-<aš-ma->aš[73] a-pí-ya a-ni-ya-an-za (l. e. 3) ku-it[74] nu EGIR-an ti-ya-at-tén (l. e. 4) na-an an-da ep-tén na-an-kán ÉSAG.ḪI.A (l. e. 5) an-da iš-ḫu-u-it-tén nu *A-NA* ^{d}U[TU-*ŠI* ḫa-at-ra-a-at-tén]	(23–28, l. e. 1–5) The grain which the troops of Išḫupitta and *zaltayaš* hold for *cultivation*?, now His Majesty was very *irritated*? about that grain. Send…. And quickly now. Because grain has been sown/cultivated there[75] for them (or: for you pl.), get busy: gather it (i.e., the crops produced from having sown seed) in and store it (i.e., the newly produced grain) in underground silos. Then write to His Majesty.

Commentary

21–22 Pišeni addresses Kaššū and Pulli as "dear sons," which could indicate actual blood relationship, but could also be scribal terminology for younger and perhaps subordinate colleagues. His piggyback letter, difficult as it is in places, is of greater interest to us than what is preserved of the king's letter, which however it definitely builds upon. The king has mentioned sending troops of Išḫupitta.

23–28 l. e. 1–5 Pišeni follows up with instructions regarding grain that these troops have. It is still unclear what the terms *tukanzi* (line 25) and *ḫašket* ("was very irritated[?]" line 27) mean here. *HW*[2] 424 considers *ḫa-aš-ke-et* an error for *ḫa-at-re-eš-ke-et*, which cannot be explained by merely assuming the leaving out of two signs. On the other hand, *ḫašket* could be a form of the verb *ḫaššike-* "be satiated, fed up" or it could be an imperfective of *ḫanna-* "reach a decision." Between the two I favor the former, since it is hard to see how the latter would fit with the use of *mekki* "very, quite." On the possible interpretations of *ḫašket* see the suggestions by Alp (1991a, 313) and Cotticelli-Kurras (2007, 184). Melchert (1999) has argued plausibly that *tuk*(*kan*)*zi* means "cultivation." This would mean the grain is to be used as seed grain, not for immediate consumption. The grain in question is to be put into underground silos (ÉSAG.ḪI.A) for storage until such time as it is needed.[76] It is quite possible that the king expressed his own concern in a broken-away part of the main letter. But his scribe Pišeni reinforces it here. If the verb "write" is correctly restored in l. e. 5, it refers to the need to record and send to the capital information as to the total volume of grain in each of the silos. Houwink ten Cate (1998, 162–63) includes this passage among many in the Maşat letters that—he believes—allude to present or potential food shortages.

l. e. 1 For *uwat duwaddu* see above in §1.2.19.1.

24. HKM 19†
From the King to Kaššū and Pulli

Text: Mşt. 75/15. **Find spot:** H/5 Room 9. **Photo:** Alp 1991a, Tafel XIII. **Dimensions** (taken from the photo; see §1.2.8.2): 5.6 cm wide × 7.2 cm tall. **Copy:** HKM 19. **Edition**: Alp 1991a, 148–51, 313–14. **Discussion**: van den Hout 2004a, 88–89 (with photo); Marizza 2007a, 95–96, 139, 144, 154, 157, 167.

(1) [*U*]*M-MA* ^{d}UTU-*ŠI-MA* (2) *A-NA* ^{m}Ka-aš-šu-ú (3) *Ù A-NA* ^{m}Pu-ul-li *QÍ-BÍ-MA*	(1–3) Thus speaks His Majesty: Say to Kaššū and to Pulli:
(4) ki-iš-ša-an-mu ku-it (5) ḫa-at-ra-a-eš ka-a-ša-wa-aš-ša-an (6) ḫal-ki$^{HI.A}$-aš[77] ka-ru-ú a-ra-an-te-eš (7) *I-NA* ^{URU}Ka$_4$-aš-ka$_4$-[m]a-wa ḫal-ki$^{HI.A}$-uš (8) BURU$_5$.ḪI.A e-ez-za-aš-ta	(4–8) Concerning what you (sg.) wrote to me, saying: "The crops are already ripe, but in the Kaškaean territories a plague of locusts has devoured the crops."
(9) nu-wa-aš-ma-aš-kán *ŠA* ^{URU}Ga-ši-pu-u-ra (10) ḫal-ki$^{HI.A}$-aš zi-ig-ga-an-zi (11) ÉRIN.MEŠ.ḪI.A-ma-wa-kán ANŠE.KUR.RA.ḪI.A (12) an-da NU.GÁL ^{d}UTU-*ŠI*-ma-wa (13) ^{m}Kal-lu-un ^{LÚ}*BE-EL* ANŠE.KUR.RA (14) wa-tar-na-aḫ-ta ANŠE.KUR.RA.ḪI.A-wa-kán (15) pa-ra-a na-i ki-nu-na-wa (16) ANŠE.KUR.RA.ḪI.A na-ú-i (17) ku-iš-ki ú-iz-zi	(9–17) "As a result (Kaškaean people) are setting upon the (Hittite) crops in the region of Kašepura. There are no troops and chariotry here. Your Majesty instructed Kallu, the (Royal) Stable Master, 'Dispatch chariotry (to Kašepura),' but as of now no chariotry has come."
(18) nu ka-a-ša ^{d}UTU-*ŠI* (19) ^{m}Kal-lu-un e-ep-pu-un (20) nu ki-iš-ša-an me-mi-iš-ta (21) 20 *ṢÍ-IM-DU*[78] ANŠE.KUR.RA.ḪI.A-wa-kán (22) [k]a-ru-ú pa-ra-a ne-eḫ-ḫu-un	(18–22) I, My Majesty, have just apprehended Kallu, and he told me: "I already dispatched twenty teams (i.e., pairs of horses) of chariotry."
(23) ka-a-aš-ma-kán ^{m}Pa-a-ḫi-na-ak-ke-en-na (24) EGIR-an-da pa-ra-a ne-eḫ-ḫi (25) na-aš ú-iz-zi	(23–25) I have just dispatched Paḫinakke too after (them), and he is coming.

Commentary

The king replies to a letter from either Kaššū or Pulli, who reports with alarm that Kaškaeans—whose own crops have been devastated by a locust attack—are stealing Hittite crops in Kašepura, and requests troops to control the looting. This shows that Kaškaeans did not confine their activities to herding, but that some actually cultivated fields and crops (see von Schuler 1965, 77). The original letter also complained that no troops had arrived from Kallu, whom the king had originally ordered to send them. The king confronts Kallu, who insists that he did send the troops. So the king writes back that he has sent a second officer to make sure the troops arrive.

On lines **5–17** see also Beal 1995, 545–46 and CHD Š, 146.

9–10 The *-šmaš* is 3rd pl., not 2nd, as Alp and del Monte 1992, 71 take it—"Sie greifen Euer Getreide von K an" (Alp 1980, 43). With a 3rd pl. verb it functions identical to *-za* in the construction *-za dai-/zikke-* "to set upon." So far as I am aware, the Hittites did *not* employ a 2nd plural pronoun to refer politely to their king, as in German "Ihr" and "Euere Majestät."

24b. HKM 19†
Piggyback Letter of Ḫašammeli to Uzzū

(26) [*U*]*M-MA* mḪa-ša-am-me-li (27) [*A-N*]*A* mU-uz-zu-u ŠEŠ.DÙG.GA-*YA* (28) [*QÍ-B*]*Í-MA*	(26–28) Thus speaks Ḫašammili:[79] Say to my dear brother Uzzū:[80]
(29) [tu-]el ku-it (30) [*NA-A*]*P-ŠA-TÙ* a-pí-ya (l. e. 1) nu-uš-ša-an *NA-AP-ŠA-TÙ* (l. e. 2) *A-NA NA-AP-ŠA-TI* an-da e-ep (l. e. 3) na-at-mu up-pí	(29–30) Regarding your labor group there: (l. e. 1–2) combine (one) labor group with (another) labor group, (l. e. 3) and send them to me.

Commentary

Ḫašammili's piggyback letter to Uzzū is unclear, because information necessary to any outside reader is assumed and therefore unstated by the correspondents. We have no information as to the identity of the labor groups (Akk. *NAPŠĀTU*), or why are they being sent from Tapikka to Ḫattuša. Alp (1991a, 57, 314) correctly observes that in MH texts the term *NAPŠĀTU* always refers to slaves. But his understanding of *anda ep-* as "seize" ignores the fact that it stands in a special construction with a local particle (*-šan*), an accusative, and a dat.-loc. noun (*NA-AP-ŠA-TÙ A-NA NA-AP-ŠA-TI*), excluding the translation "seize," and requiring a translation "combine X with Y."

25. HKM 20†
From the King to Kaššū and Pipappa

Text: Mşt. 78/157. **Find spot:** E/3 Room 33. **Copy:** HKM 20. **Edition**: Alp 1991a, 152–53, 314. **Discussion:** Beal 1992, 283, 313, 400, 460; Imparati 1997, 653 n. 30; Imparati 2002, 95 with n. 14 (lines 10–12).

(1) [*U*]*M-MA* dUTU-*ŠI-MA* (2) [*A-NA* mG]a-aš-šu-ú (3) [*Ù* mPí-pa-]ap-pa *QÍ-BÍ-MA*	(1–3) Thus speaks His Majesty: Say to Kaššū and Pipappa:
(4) ma-aḫ-ḫa-an-ša-ma-aš (5) ka-a-aš tup-pí-an-za an-da (6) ú-e-mi-ez-zi nu an-ni-in (7) 1 *LI-IM* 7 *ME.* 60 ÉRIN.MEŠ URUIš-ḫu-pí-it-ta (8) li-li-wa-aḫ-ḫu-u-an-zi (9) ni-ni-ik-tén (10) na-an *MA-ḪAR* dUTU-*ŠI I-*[*N*]*A* UD.2.K[AM URUŠ]a-pí-nu-wa (11) li-li-wa-aḫ-ḫu-u-an-zi (12) ú-wa-te-et-tén	(4–6) As soon as this tablet reaches you (*pl.*), (6–9) quickly mobilize (*pl.*) that 1,760[81]-man troop of Išḫupitta (10–12) and lead (*pl.*) it quickly to My Majesty in Šapinuwa within two days.

Commentary

When he dispatched this letter, the king was in Šapinuwa (line 10). The time limit of two days for the march from Tapikka to Šapinuwa is appropriate, given the actual known distance between the two sites (see Imparati 2002, 95 with n. 14). It is furthermore clear from excavations at Šapinuwa that it was a royal residence. The 1,760 troops of Išḫupitta might be the troops that Kallu sent to Tapikka according to text 24.

26. HKM 21†
From the King to Pulli

Text: Mşt. 75/20. **Find spot:** H/5 Room 9. **Photo:** Alp 1991a, pl. 11 (showing the scribe Šanda's handwriting). **Dimensions** (from the photo; see §1.2.8.2): 8 cm wide × 6.4 cm tall. **Copy:** HKM 21. **Edition**: Alp 1991a, 152–55, 314–15. **Discussion**: Beal 1992, 317, 462; Lühr 2001, 340; Goedegebuure 2003, 200; van den Hout 2004a, 89.

(1) *UM-MA* dUTU-*ŠI-MA* (2) *A-NA* mPu-ul-li *QÍ-BÍ-MA*	(1–2) Thus speaks His Majesty: Say to Pulli:
(3) *ŠA* ÉRIN.MEŠ-mu ku-it ut-tar (4) ḫa-at-ra-a-eš ar-ḫa ku-iš (5) [t]ar[82]-na-an ḫar-zi a-pé-e-ya (6) [ku-]iš še-er EGIR!-an[83]-mu	(3–7) Concerning what you (sg.) wrote me about 'troops': "One group has left, and the other one is up there," the number (of workers)

kap-pu-u-wa-ar[84] (7) [ku-]it ḫa-at-ra-a-eš na-at *AŠ-ME*	which you wrote to me I have heard it.
(8) [*Š*]*A* LÚ.KÚR-ya-mu ku-it ut-tar (9) [ḫ]a-at-ra-a-e[š] a-pé-e-da-ni (10) [*P*]*A-NI* LÚ.KÚR me-ek-ki (11) pa-aḫ-ḫa-aš-ša-nu-wa-an-za e-eš (12) [k]a-a-ša-za ku-[i]t-ma-an (13) [o] x[85] ar-ḫa a-ri-ya-mi	(8–9) Concerning what you wrote me about the enemy: (9–11) Be very much on your guard toward that enemy, (12–13) while I am about to make oracular inquiries (whether and how to proceed against him).[86]
(14) [ḫal]-ki$^{HI.A}$[87]-uš-ša-k[á]n ar-ḫa (15) [ḫ]u-u-da-a-ak wa-ar-aš	(14–15) Reap the crops immediately.

Commentary

Pulli, an officer resident in Tapikka, one of whose principal duties seems to have been oversight of the harvests, has written to the king, reporting his limited troop strength, which takes into account that part of the troops he once had has left and the other part is "up there" (*apēya … šer*). Since "up" usually means in a walled city, and "there" (i.e., where you are) in Pulli's mouth should refer to his addressee's location, perhaps this part of the troops had been transferred back to Ḫattuša. Pulli also sent a number to the king, perhaps the number of troops (or workers) remaining in Tapikka or the number he will need in order to be safe from the enemy. The king replies that Pulli is to take every measure available to protect his post from the enemy while the king by means of oracular inquiries devises a strategy to protect him. In the meantime Pulli is to harvest the crops, which would be the enemy's main target. Since the term ÉRIN.MEŠ (usually translated "troop(s)") does not always have a primarily military reference, Pulli may be referring to groups of harvesters assigned to him by the king.

26b. HKM 21†
Piggyback Letter of Šanda to Uzzū

(16) *UM-MA* ᵐŠa-an-d[a] *A-NA* ᵐUz-zu-u (17) ŠEŠ DÙG.GA-*YA* *QÍ*-[*B*]*Í-MA* kat-ti-mi SIG_5-in (18) *Ù MA-ḪAR* ŠEŠ DÙG.GA-[*Y*]*A* ḫu-u-ma-an SIG_5-in e-eš-du	(16–19) Thus speaks Šanda:[88] Say to my dear brother Uzzū:[89] All is well with me. May all be well with my dear brother. May the gods protect you.

(19) nu-ut-ta DINGIR.MEŠ pa-aḫ-ša-an-da-ru	
(20) am-me-el-kán aš-šu-ul *PA-NI* mPu-ul-li (21) ḫal-za-i nam-ma-at-ta ki-iš-ša-an (22) [t]e-mi tu-el-wa [k]u-e tup-paḪI.A (23) pé-da-an-zi nu-wa-ra-at-kán (24) am-mu-uk ḫal-zi-iš-ša-aḫ-ḫi (25) nam-ma-wa-at-ta EGIR-pa (26) a[r-ḫ]a w[a-r]i-iš-ša-aḫ-ḫi	(20–21) Read my greetings aloud to Pulli. (21) In addition I promise you (sg.): (22–24) "I read aloud (to the king) your (sg.) tablets that they bring (here), (25–26) and I help you (sg.) in every possible way."

Commentary

The king's scribe Šanda writes from Ḫattuša to Pulli's scribe Uzzū, in which he assures him that he not only reads aloud to the king all correspondence incoming from Uzzū at Tapikka, but that he does everything possible to see that action is taken on their contents. He also asks Uzzū to give greetings to his supervisor Pulli.

27. HKM 22†
From the King to Pulli

Text: Mşt. 75/14. **Find spot:** H/5 Room 9. **Photo:** Alp 1991a, pl. XII (showing handwriting of Mar-ešrē). **Measurements** (taken from the photo; see §1.2.8.2): 5 cm wide × 4.25 cm tall. **Copy:** HKM 22. **Edition**: Alp 1991a, 154–57, 315. **Discussion**: Lühr 2001, 337.

(1) *UM-MA* dUTU-*ŠI-MA* (2) *A-NA* mPu-ul-li (3) *QÍ-BÍ-MA*	(1–3) Thus speaks His Majesty: Say to Pulli:
(4) *ŠA* ÉRIN.MEŠ-mu ku-it ut-tar (5) ḫa-at-ra-a-eš na-at *AŠ-ME*	(4–5) I have heard what you wrote me about the troops.
(6) nu-za *PA-NI* LÚ.KÚR pa-aḫ-ḫa-aš-nu-an-za (7) e-eš ku-it-ma-an (8) ÉRIN.MEŠ EGIR-an-da ú-ez-zi	(6–8) Be very much on your guard toward the enemy, while the troops are on their way (lit. are coming afterwards/behind).

Commentary

6–7 Edited with comments in CHD P, 9 (*paḫšanu-* 3 c) and 295 (*peran* 1 c 1′ a’).

27b. HKM 22†
Piggyback Letter of Mār-ešrē to Uzzū

(9) 90 *UM-MA* ^{m}DUMU.UD.20. KAM (10) *A-NA* ^{m}Uz-zu-u (11) ŠEŠ. DÙG.GA-*YA QÍ-BÍ-MA*	(9–11) Thus speaks Mār-ešrē: Say to Uzzū, my dear brother:
(12) *PA-NI* ^{m}Pu-ul-li-i-kán (13) am-me-el aš-šu-ul (14) ḫal-za-i GU$_4$-ya-wa-mu (15) ku-in te-et (16) nu-wa-ra-an-mu up-pí	(12–14) Read my greetings aloud to Pullī (and say): (14–16) “Send me the ox that you promised me.”

Commentary

See *GrHL* §1.36 (on the name Mār-ešrē). On the relative clause in 14–15 see Lühr 2001, 337.

12–16 It is not quite clear if Mār-ešrē expects the courier who delivers this tablet in Tapikka to bring the ox with him on his return to Ḫattuša, or if other arrangements had already been agreed upon between the two parties. The brevity of this message implies it is only a reminder of a debt that needs repaying. For such requests in scribal letters see the introduction (§1.2.20). For another request by Mār-ešrē to Ḫimmuili for an ox promised by him see text 37b: 25–30.

28. HKM 23†
From the King to Pišeni and Kaššū

Text: Mşt. 75/116. **Find spot:** G/5 Portico. **Copy:** HKM 23. **Edition**: Alp 1991a, 156–59.

(1) *UM-MA* ^{d}UTU-*ŠI-MA A-NA* ^{m}Pí-še-ni (2) *Ù A-NA* ^{m}Ka-aš-šu-ú *QÍ-BÍ-MA*	(1–2) Thus speaks His Majesty: Say to Pišeni and Kaššū:

(3) *A*-[*N*]*A* [L]Ú.MEŠ ^{URU}Ga-aš-[g]a ku-e-da-aš (4) x x [o] x x [^{m}A]t-ti-ú-na (5) LÚ.M[EŠ …] x x [a]r-ḫa LÚ.MEŠ ^{URU}Ku-ru-pa-aš-ši-ya (6) ḫa-at-[…] nu-uš-kán ka-a-ša (7) ka[-a? pa-r]a-a ne-eḫ-ḫi (8) nu-u[š-ma-aš pé-ḫu]-da-an-zi	(3–8) To what Kaška men … … Atiuna, the men of … the men of Kurupaššiya away. I am about to dispatch them (from) here, and they will lead? you?.
(9) […-]x-kán ku-i-uš (10) […-]x-iš *A-NA* UDU.ḪI.A da-an-na (11) […] ú-wa-te-et (12) [……] ḫa-at-ra-a-eš ku-it (13) […] *AŠ*?-*M*[*E*?] (14) [… … … … … … … … …] (15) [… … … … … …] (16) [… … … …]	(9–16) … what …-s … you/he? brought … to take sheep … (12) … what you wrote (13) … I heard … (14–16) …
(17) […]x [z]i-[i]k ^{m}Ka-[aš-šu-uš?] (18) […] x x x […]	(17–18) … … … you, Kaššū, … …
Reverse (only traces in line 1–7)	
(rev. 8) x x[…] (rev. 9) ḫu-u-ma-an[-…] (rev. 10) [K]UR-e wa[…] (rev. 11) im-ma m[a?- …]	(rev. 8–11) … every …the land … indeed(?) …
(rev. 12) ^{URU}Ga-aš-g[a?] x […] x […] (rev. 13) na-aš x x x […] (rev. 14) ma-an-x-x x […] (rev. 15) e-ep-pé-er URU?-an x x […] (rev. 16) [n]a?-an na-ak-ki-i x x[…] (rev. 17) e-eš-ta ki-nu-na-za-kán pa-r[a-a …] (rev. 18) im-ma wa-ar-ši-an-za […]	(rev. 12–18) The Kaška … and them(?) … they seized. The city(?) … severe … it was. But now …[91] indeed soothed(?) …

Commentary

1–2 On the use of the Akkadogram *Ù* here representing Hittite *-a/-ya* "and" see *GrHL* §29.2 with n. 4.

29. HKM 24
From the King to Pišeni

Text: Mşt. 75/18. **Find spot:** H/5 Room 9. **Copy:** HKM 24. **Edition**: Alp 1991a, 158–63, 315–16. **Discussion**: Houwink ten Cate 1998, 162 (on mention of food shortage in 4–10; see also text 47 = HKM 45); Hoffner 2002c, 67; Imparati 2002, 94–95; 2003, 235; van den Hout 2004a, 90; Rieken 2004, 538 (on ÉRIN.MEŠ *zalta-*); Akdoğan 2007, 6 (quotes lines 49–59 from CHD P, 23).

(1) *UM-MA* ^{d}UTU[*-ŠI-M*]*A A-NA* ^{m}Pí-še-ni *Q*[*Í*]*-BÍ-MA*	(1) Thus speaks His Majesty: Say to Pišeni:
(2) 2 $^{\text{LÚ.MEŠ}}$pí[t-t]i-ya-an-du-uš-kán ku-i-uš (3) pa-ra-a [n]a-it-ta na-aš ú-wa-te-er	(2–3) They have brought here the two fugitives that you dispatched.
(4) ki-iš-š[a-an]-ma-mu ku-i[t ḫ]a-at-ra-a-eš (5) ÉRIN.MEŠ ^{GIŠ}za-[al]-ta-ya-[aš-wa k]u-iš (6) ^{URU}Ka-še[-pu-u-]ra [pa-it[92] nam?-m]a?-aš-ši-iš-ša-an (7) ka-aš-ti [a?-r]a-a-an[93] [ki-i]š-ša-an me-mi-iš-kán-zi (8) ma-aḫ-ḫa-an[94] L[Ú.MEŠ] ^{URU}Ga-aš-g[a ú-wa-an-]zi (9) nu-wa-k[án pa-r]a-a EG[IR-an-da pa-i]-wa-ni (10) nu-w[a-ru-uš-ká]n ša-ra-a [ar-n]u[-m]e-ni[95]	(4–10) Regarding the following which you wrote me: "The *zaltayaš*-troops who went to Kašepura, … in a famine, are saying the following: 'When the Kaška-men come, should we go ⸢out after⸣ (them) and bring them up (here)?'"
(11) […]x ^{m}Ták-ša-aš ku-it u-un-ni-iš (12) [nu-uš-ša-an][96] ÉRIN.MEŠ ^{URU}Ka-še-pu-u-ra (13) [*Ù* ÉRIN.MEŠ[97] ^{URU}M]a-ri-iš-ta pé-ḫu-te-ed-du (14) [nu-za pa-id-du *ŠA*] É.GAL-*LIM* ḫal-ki-in tu-kán-zi (15) [da-ad-du ma-a-a]n-za-kán ša-ra-a ú-it (16) [… ki-nu]-un-pát ÉRIN.MEŠ ^{URU}Ka-še-pu-u-ra-a[z] (17) [pé-ḫu-te-ez-z]i ma-a-an ta-ma-in ku-in-k[i] (18) [pé-ḫu-t]e-ez-[z]i nu-uš-ši-kán ḫal-ki-in (19) [tu-kán-zi pé-]da-ú	(11–19) (His Majesty answers:) Because Takša drove here, let him lead the troops of Kašepura and the troops of Marišta. Let him proceed to take grain of the palace for cultivation?. If he has come up, right now he will lead troops ⸢from⸣ Kašepura. If he leads any other (troops), let him ⸢take⸣ grain for them for cultivation?.
(20) [nam-ma-an-ši-kán] EGIR-an iš-kal-[li] (21) [na-an ú-wa-a]n-zi *I-NA* (22) [BURU$_{14}$ EGIR-pa iš-ḫu-u-w]a-an-zi	(20–22) Then break/tear (open?) behind …, and they will proceed to replenish it in the harvest season.

Commentary

On the dating of this letter de Martino observes: “Pišeni is, together with Kaššū, the receiver of letter HKM 23 (where Atiuna is also mentioned; …). Furthermore, he is the receiver of letter HKM 24 and is mentioned in letter HKM 25 sent by the king to Tatta and Ḫulla. Therefore, Pišeni is a contemporary, more or less, of Tarḫumimma, Kaššū and Ḫulla” (2005b, 316).

2–3 On the ambiguity of the term “fugitive” without adequate context see above in comments on HKM 9 (text 15).

8–10 It is also possible to interpret lines 8–10 as a statement rather than a question, as does CHD Š, 211 (*šarā* B 1 a 5′).

21–22 “Replenish” here and below in line 52 renders what is literally “pour back.”

29b. HKM 24
Second Letter from the King to […]

(23) [*UM-MA* dUTU-*ŠI-M*]*A A-NA* m[… *QÍ-BÍ-MA*] (24) […]	(23–24) Thus speaks His Majesty: Say to …
(25) […]x ku-it ḫa-at-r[a-a-eš] (26) [… -i]t ki-iš-ša-a[n ḫa-at]-ra […] (27) [… URU.DIDLI.ḪI.A? -]uš ar-nu-ši (28) [URUTa-ḫa-zi-mu-na-]an URUḪa-pa-ra-an (29) [URUTa-pí-ga-a]n-na nu-wa-kán (30) […]x *A-NA* URUKa-še[-p]u-[u-ra] (31) […-i]t nu-wa-mu-kán ÉRIN.MEŠ [UKU.UŠ] (32) [ú-wa-te]-ez-zi *Ú-UL* te-ek-[ku]-uš-ša-[nu-zi] *Ú-UL* (33) […….-l]i-in-wa-kán ša-ra-a (34) [……. -]kán ÉRIN.MEŠ GIŠza-al-ta (35) […(-?)d]a-aḫ-ḫ[i] x x x […]	(25–35) Regarding the following which you wrote to me: “The… cities you are transferring, (28) namely, Taḫazzimuna, Ḫapara and Tapikka. (29) You/He …-ed … to Kašepura, (31) and he will not lead heavily armed troops to me. (32) He will not show. (33) … up … I will take? … *zalta(ya)*-troops.”
(36) […]x dUTU-*ŠI* ka-ru-ú-i-l[i-i]t (37) [… a-p]u-u-uš [k]u-i-uš 3 URU[.ḪI.A] (38) [URUTa-ḫa-zi-mu-na]-an URU[Ḫ]a-pa-ra-an [URUTa]-pí-ga-[an] (39) […]x NAM.	(36–41) … My Majesty with former … those three cities which … Taḫazzimuna, Ḫapara, Tapikka, … the civilian captives of … (*Rest of paragraph too broken to translate.*)

RA URUWa[…]x-un-ga […] (40) […]-wa? URUTa[98]-pa-a [… URUUr?-ša-pí-k]án?-nu?-ú? ša-ra-a (41) [… K]UR-e e-ša-an[-…]	
(42) […]x *Ú-UL I-NA* KUR […] (43) […-]ut? *IŠ-TU* ÉRIN.MEŠ [KUR UGU]-*TIM* (44) x[…] ú?-ga-az *IŠ-TU* ÉR[IN.MEŠ URUU]r?-ša-pí-kán?-nu-wa-ya (45) URUŠ[a-n]a-[aḫ-ḫu-it]-ta ku-ez-zi[99] [ša?-r]a-a (46) da-a-i na-an-k[án š]a-ra-a tar-n[a]	(42–46) … not in the land of … with troops of the Upper Land … with troops of Uršapikannuwa and Šanaḫuitta … *set* up?, and let them go up.
(47) nam-ma-[k]án KUR-e a[n-d]a ka-aš-za ú-it (48) nu a-pu-u-un ÉRIN.MEŠ URUMa-re-eš-t[a] pé-ḫu-te (49) nu-za pa-id-du *Š[A]* É.GAL-*LIM* ḫal-[k]i-in tu-kán-zi (50) da-ad-du na-an-z[a-k]án URU-ri ša-ra-a pé-ḫu-te-ed-du (51) nam-ma-an-ši-kán EGI[R]-an iš-kal-li (52) na-an ú-wa-an-du *I-NA* BURU$_{14}$ EGIR-pa iš-ḫu-u-an-du	(47) Furthermore, a famine has come into the land; (48) so lead that troop of[100] Marišta (that is with you). (49) Let it proceed to take the grain for cultivation (i.e., seed grain)[101] of the palace (50) and conduct it up to the (capital) city for themselves. (51) Then … it for him behind it,[102] (52) and let them proceed to replenish it in the harvest season.
(53) nam-ma a-pu-u-un ÉRIN.MEŠ URUKa-še-pu-u-ra EGIR-an-pát (54) ti-ya nu-za NINDAtu-u-ma-ti-in ša-ra-a me-ek-ki (55) ḫa-an-da-a-id-du *ŠA* MU-za-kán an-ku (56) NINDAtu-u-ma-ti-in ša-ra-a ḫa-an-da-a-id-du	(53) Furthermore station those troops behind (i.e., in the outskirts of) Kašepura.[103] (54) Let them prepare (i.e., store up?) for themselves much *tumati*-bread.[104] (55–56) Let them prepare for themselves *even* a year's supply of *tumati*-bread.
(57) ki-iš-ša-an-ma-mu [ku-i]t ḫa-at-ra-a-eš NAM.RA.MEŠ URUKa-al-za-na-wa (58) URUMa-ri-iš-t[a] ku-in ma-ši-wa (59) pé-eḫ-ḫi nu-wa-ra-a[n]-t[a-k]án[105] ḫa-at-ra-a-m[i] n[a-an?/-at?] (60) te-ek[-ku-ša]-nu-ut	(57) Concerning what you wrote to me, as follows: (57–58) "I will report to you however many civilian captives of Kalzana and Marišta I give, (59) and you should make it known …."

(l.e. 1) [.......]x-[t]i-eš ši-ya-an-te-eš (l.e. 2) [....... ḫu-lu-]ga-an-ni-eš ki-it-t[a ...] (l.e. 3) [.......] a-pé-ni-iš-šu-wa-an pa-a-i[...]	*(Too badly broken to translate.)*

Commentary

47–50 Edited in CHD P, 23 (*pai-* A 1 c 3′, serial use) and *GrHL* §28.71 (line 50). The word *apūn* "that" refers to a troop that is with the addressed person (on this use of the distal demonstrative see *GrHL* §7.1 "you-*deixis*").

49–59 For these lines see Akdoğan 2007, 6, quoting CHD L–N, 23.

57–60 The king quotes Pišeni as promising to tell the king how many civilian captives (NAM.RA-persons of Kalzana and Marišta) he is able to give to the king (HKM 24). Presumably this means they would be transferred out of Pišeni's district and moved by the king to wherever their services were needed (see Hoffner 2002c, 67).

30. HKM 25†
From the King to Tatta and Ḫulla

Text: Mşt. 75/13. **Find spot:** H/5 Room 9. **Copy:** HKM 25. **Edition**: Alp 1991a, 164–65. **Discussion**: Puhvel 1993, 37; Klinger 1995a, 92; Houwink ten Cate 1998, 164; van den Hout 2004a, 89.

(1) *UM-MA* ᵈUTU-*ŠI-MA* (2) *A-NA* ᵐTa-at-ta (3) *Ù A-NA* ᵐḪu-ul-la *QÍ-BÍ-MA*	(1–3) Thus speaks His Majesty: Say to Tatta and Ḫulla:
(4) ka-a-ša-mu ᵐPí-še-ni-iš (5) ᵁᴿᵁKa-še-pu-u-ra-az ḫa-at-ra-ạ-[it] (6) LÚ.KÚR-wa pa-an-ga-ri-it (7) iš-pa-an-da-az ku-wa-pí 6 *M*[*E* LÚ.KÚR] (8) ku-wa-pí-ma 4 *ME*. LÚ.KÚR i-a[t-ta-ri] (9) nu-wa-kán ḫal-ki-uš (10) ar-ḫa wa-ar-aš-ke-ez-zi	(4–10) Pišeni has just written me from (the town of) Kašepura: "The enemy is moving *en masse* at night—sometimes six hundred, sometimes four hundred of the enemy—and is reaping (our) crops."
(11) [nu-u]š-ma-aš ma-aḫ-ḫa-an ka-a-aš (12) tup-pí-an-za an-da	(11–19) As soon as this tablet reaches you, go to Kašepura. If the crops.

ú-e-m[i-e]z-z[i] (13) nu *I-NA* URUKa-še-pu-u-ra (14) ḫu-it-ti-ya-at-tén (15) nu-uš-ša-an ma-a-an (16) ḫal-ki-e-eš a-ra-an-te-eš (17) na-aš-kán ar-ḫa wa-ar-aš-tén (18) na-aš-kán *A-NA* KISLAḪ pa-ra-a (19) ar-nu-ut-tén	have ripened,[106] reap them and transport them to the threshing floor.
(20) na-aš LÚ.KÚR le-e (21) dam-me-iš-ḫa-a-iz-zi	(20–21) Do not let the enemy damage them.
(22) ka-a-aš-ma-aš-ma-aš tup-pí mPí-še[-ni-ya-aš] (23) up-pa-aḫ-ḫu-un-pát (24) nu-uš-ma-ša-at-kán (25) [p]é-ra-an ḫal-zi-[an-du]	(22–25) I have sent you herewith the tablet of Pišeni. Have it read aloud in your presence.

Commentary

On the dating of this letter to the reign of Arnuwanda I (ca. 1400–1360 B.C.E.; historical sketches in Bryce 1998, 154–67; Klengel 1999, 116–25) see above on text 29.

1–3 On the use of the Akkadogram *Ù* here representing Hittite *-a/-ya* "and" see *GrHL* §29.2 with n. 4.

7 For *iš-pa-an-da-az* "by night" as an ablative of "kind of time" see *GrHL* §16.96.

7–8 It is difficult to decide whether *kuwapi* ... *kuwapi=ma* refers to local or temporal distribution. Alp opted for the local, translating "an einer Stelle ... an anderer Stelle" (1991a, 165). My rendering "sometimes ... sometimes" reflects my preference for the temporal distribution in this instance. For obligatory imperfective verbs (e.g., *-ške-* stems) with temporal distributive adverbs, except notably in the case of the medio-passive verb *iya-* (note *i-a[t-ta-ri]* in line 8), see *GrHL* §24.12. It is intriguing, but at present unclear, why the enemy's numbers are either six hundred or four hundred, and never some other number. For the numerical regression see *GrHL* §9.65.

31. HKM 26†
From the King to Ḫimmuili

Text: Mşt. 75/115. **Find spot:** G/5 Portico. **Photo:** Alp 1991a, pl. 9 (showing handwriting of Tarḫunmiya). **Measurements** (taken from the photo; see

§1.2.8.2): 8 cm wide × 9.2 cm tall. **Edition**: Alp 1991a, 164–67, 316. **Discussion**: Beal 1992, 142 with n. 512; CHD s.v. *parai-* B (analyzed as "verbal subst."); Pecchioli Daddi 2003b (on the KUŠ$_7$ KÙ.SIG$_{17}$); van den Hout, fothcoming in a festschrift.

(1) [*UM-MA*] ^{d}[UT]U-*ŠI*-[*M*]*A* (2) [*A-N*]*A* ^{m}Ḫi-mu-DINGIR-*LIM QÍ-B*[*Í-MA*]	(1–2) Thus speaks His Majesty: Say to Ḫimmuili:
(3) *Š*[*A*] LÚ.KÚR ku-it ut-tar (4) ḫa-at-ra-a-eš LÚ.KÚR ma-aḫ-ḫa-a[n] (5) 30 *ṢÍ-IM-DÌ* ANŠE.KUR.RA.ḪI.A (6) ^{URU}Pa-na-a-ta ši-na-a[ḫ]-ḫ[a da-a-iš]	(3–6) Concerning what you wrote about the enemy, how the enemy set a trap for thirty teams of chariotry (from/at?) Panāta,
(7) nu ^{LÚ}KUŠ$_7$ KÙ.GI ku-it (8) ku*-ra*-an-na-aš wa-ḫa-an-na š[a-an-aḫ-ta] (9) EGIR-an-ma-an-kán LÚ.KÚR ku-e[n-ta] (10) na-at *AŠ-ME*	(7–10) and that the Gold Chariot-Warrior sought to make a circuit of the *perimeter*, but the enemy killed him from behind—I have heard it (all).
(11) *ŠA* ÉRIN.MEŠ-ma-mu ku-it ANŠE.KUR.RA[.ḪI.A] (12) ut-tar ḫa-at-ra-a-eš (13) nu ka-a-ša ÉRIN.MEŠ.ḪI.A ANŠE.[KUR.RA.ḪI.A] (14) an-da a-ra-an-zi (15) [… É]RIN.MEŠ ANŠE.[KUR.RA.ḪI.A] (16) […] x [ ] x [ ]	(11–16) Concerning what you wrote me about the infantry and horse troops: "The infantry and horse troops have just arrived, and? the infantry and horse troops …"

Commentary

7 As is well known, very high-ranking persons in these texts are often referred to only by the rank that they at present alone hold,[107] so that there can be no confusion as to who is being referred to (especially the king, the queen, the *BEL MADGALTI*, etc.). Since the rank of Gold Charioteer was such a high rank, we are not given the man's name here. Since elsewhere multiple contemporaneous Gold Charioteers ($^{\text{LÚ.MEŠ}}$KUŠ$_7$ KÙ.SIG$_{17}$) are mentioned (Ḫatt ii 60; KUB 13.35 i 6), and even in later NH there appears a "Chief of the Gold Charioteers" (UGULA $^{\text{LÚ.MEŠ}}$KUŠ$_7$ KÙ.SIG$_{17}$; see Pecchioli Daddi 1982, 127), the reason the title-holder could remain nameless in this text without confusion is that there was only one such ranked person in the administrative district of Tapikka (or perhaps on the Kaška front at this time). Elsewhere, in administrative lists, names of the holders of this rank appear (see the list of holders of this rank in Pecchioli Daddi 1982, 126). We even know the name of one such person from this period at Tapikka: Tarpa-Kurunt(iy)a (^{m}*Tar-pa*-^{d}LAMMA-*aš* ^{LÚ}KUŠ$_7$ KÙ.SIG$_{17}$, HKM 100: 22). For a study of high office holders whose titles contain the attribute "Gold," including the Chief Charioteer, see Pecchioli Daddi 2003b.

8 Alp restored [*pa-aḫ-ḫa-aš-ta*] at the end of line 8, whereas the CHD P, sub *parai-* B (p. 134) preferred [LÚ-*aš e-eš-ta*]. But collations of line 8 have yielded different readings of the line.[108] The first word begins not with *pa*, but *ku*, as can be seen both from Alp's published photo (Alp 1991a, Tafel 9) and my personal photo. The trace after *wa-ḫa-an-na* is a sign beginning with parallel horizontals, perfectly compatible with *i*[*š*] or *š*[*a*]. As for the word *kurannaš,* van den Hout reminds me that in the MH *BEL MADGALTI* instructions the *kuranna-* (sometimes in the plural accus. *kurannuš*) denotes a peripheral area, outside the gates of the walled city, which must be searched after an enemy has left the area. Van den Hout suggested to me that he would read this line as *nu* ^{LÚ}KUŠ$_7$ KÙ.GI *ku-it ku-ra-an-na-aš wa-ḫa-an-na-i*[*š*] "And that the Gold Chariot Warrior began to turn into the perimeter area," taking *waḫannaiš* as the imperfective stem in *-anna/i-*, used here to express an inceptive aspect. Subsequently, the possibility of reading *š*[*a-*. . .] at the end of the line occurred to me. And Craig Melchert suggested to me a solution which I have adopted here: to read *š*[*a-an-aḫ-ta*] (or even *š*[*a-an-ḫa-an ḫar-ta*]) together with the infinitive *wa-ḫa-an-na.* The advantage of this reading over *wa-ḫa-an-na-i*[*š*] is that an *-anna/i-* imperfective stem of this verb is unattested elsewhere, while the infinitive *waḫanna* in combination with a finite verb such as *šanḫ-* is well known. The rest of the interpretation is my own. For *šanḫ-* and the infinitive, meaning "seek to do" see CHD Š, sub *šanḫ-* 4–5. The verb *weḫ-/waḫ-* occurs often with a dative-locative (sometimes in the plural, as here) to denote traveling through a region in a circuitous manner, for example, *ma-a-an a-ru-ni na-aš-ma* ḪUR.SAG.MEŠ *wa-ḫa-an-na pa-a-an-za na-aš-ma-za I-NA* KUR LÚ.KÚR *za-aḫ-ḫi-ya pa-a-an-za* "If you have gone to make a circuit through the mountains, or if you have gone to battle in the enemy land" KUB 24.1 i 9–10. When construed without local particle and with an accusative of place, *weḫ-/waḫ-* only has the sense of "pass/roam/circle *through*," or "encircle," not "turn into" (see [*nu*] KUR.KUR.MEŠ *ḫu-u-ma-an-da ú-e-ḫe-eš-ke-ez-z*[*i na-aš-kán*] / [(^{URU}*Ú*-)] *ra-ga* URU-*ri a-ar-aš* "he circled/roamed through all the lands, [and] he arrived at the city of Uruk" KUB 8.57 i 10–11). Also with the dative-locative and *anda,* but without local particle: [^{m}*K*]*e-eš-ši-iš* ITU.3.KAM-*aš*

ḪUR.SAG.MEŠ-*aš an-da ú-e-ḫa-at-ta* "Keššī circled about/roamed in the mountains for three months" KUB 33.121 ii 15; *ma-a-an I-NA* UD.3.KAM (var. UD.5.KAM) *n[a-a]š-ma I-N[A* UD.4.KAM] / URU*Ḫa-at-tu-ša-an Ú-UL ú-*⸢*e*⸣*[(-ḫ)i-i(š-ke-ez-zi)]* "If he does not patrol Ḫattuša either in three (var. five) or [four days]" KBo 13.58 iii 7–8 (restored from KBo 10.5 iii 2–3); *an-dur-za-ma* É.MEŠ DINGIR.MEŠ LÚ.MEŠ É.DINGIR-*LIM* GE$_6$-*an ḫu-u-ma-an-da-an / ú-e-ḫe-eš-kán-du nu-uš-ma-aš* Ù-*aš le-e e-eš-zi* "But all night long let the temple guards patrol the inside of the temples, and let there be no sleeping for them" KUB 13.4 iii 10–11; "turning into," on the other hand, usually requires a dative-locative and a local particle. A local particle is also used with the medio-passive and intransitive *weḫ-* "turn back": *na-aš a-ku le-e-ya-aš-kán ú-e-eḫ-ta-ri* "Let him be put to death; let him not return (i.e., be pardoned)" KUB 13.4 iii 20.

9 I have understood EGIR-*an* "(from) behind" here to refer to the ambush (*šinaḫḫa-*) mentioned in introducing this subject in lines 3–6. According to this interpretation, the Gold Chariot Warrior is singled out from the total of thirty chariots making the circuit of the perimeter after they thought the enemy had left, because he was the principal (or perhaps even the only) casuality of the ambush. The EGIR-*an* would then indicate that they were attacked from in hiding (i.e., "from behind"). An alternate interpretation of EGIR-*an* "afterwards"—that is, the Gold Chariot Warrior sought to turn into the *kurannaš* area, but afterwards the enemy killed him—seems awkward, since the Gold Chariot Warrior was killed *while* either starting to turn into the *kurannaš* or trying to make a circuit of the *kurannaš* area. "Afterwards" would seem to point to a greater time interval than the context allows.

32. HKM 27
From the King to Ḫimmuili

Text: Mşt. 75/43. **Edition**: Alp 1991a, 166–69, 317. **Discussion**: Goedegebuure 2002–2003, 20; 2003, 84; van den Hout 2003a (on Tarḫunmiya); Bryce 2003b, 177–78 (on Tarḫunmiya). The first piggyback letter (lines 11–16) was treated in CHD *parā* 1 e 1′; the second (lines 21–22) in *paḫš-* 1 a 2′. For Ḫattušili, the author of the first piggyback letter (line 11), see above in §2.2.2.2.

(1) *UM-MA* dUTU-*ŠI-MA* (2) *A-NA* mḪi-mu-DINGIR-*LIM QÍ-BÍ-MA*	(1–2) Thus speaks His Majesty: Say to Ḫimmuili:

(3) [*Š*]*A* LÚ.KÚR ku-it ut-tar (4) ḫa-at-ra-a-eš LÚ.KÚR-za-kán (5) ma-aḫ-ḫa-an ^{URU}Ka-ša-ša-an (6) ^{URU}Ta-ḫa-az-zi-mu-na-an-na (7) zi-ik-ke-ez-zi[109] na-at *AŠ-ME*	(3–7) I have received what you wrote about the enemy, how the enemy is undertaking/planning something[110] against the cities of Kašaša and Taḫazzimuna.
(8) na-aš-ta a-pa-a-aš LÚ.KÚR ku-wa-pí (9) na-iš-ke-et-ta-ri (10) nu-mu ḫa-at-re-eš-ke	(8–10) Keep me informed as to where that enemy is heading.

Commentary

The “how” (Hittite *maḫḫan*) in line 5, and in other subordinate clauses governed by a main clause whose verb denotes either conveying or receiving information, is the marker for indirect speech. In contrast to clauses with the quote marker *-wa/-war-*, the *maḫḫan* clause gives only the gist of what was said, not the very words. On the other hand, the “where” (Hittite *kuwapi*) in line 8 requests information from Ḫimmuili about the direction in which the enemy is moving.

32b. HKM 27b
Piggyback Letter from Ḫattušili to Ḫimmuili

(11) *UM-MA* ^{mGIŠ}GIDRU-DINGIR-*LIM* (12) *A-NA* ^{m}Ḫi-mu-DINGIR-*LIM* ŠEŠ.DÙG.GA-*YA QÍ-BÍ-MA*	(11–12) Thus speaks Ḫattušili: Say to Ḫimmuili, my dear brother:
(13) *ŠA* ^{GIŠ}GIGIR-mu ku-it (14) *ŠA* ANŠE.KUR.RA.ḪI.A-ya ut-tar ḫa-at-ra-a-eš (15) nu ka-a-ša EGIR-an ti-ya-mi (16) na-at-kán pa-ra-a ar-nu-mi	(13–16) Regarding the matter of a chariot and horses about which you wrote to me: I am tending to it now and will carry it out.

Commentary

On Ḫimmuili’s request see above in §1.2.20.

32c. HKM 27c
Piggyback Letter to Ḫimmuili from Tarḫunmiya

(17) *A-NA BE-LÍ* ^{LÚ}*BE-EL MA-AD* <*-GAL*>*-TI* (18) *BE-LÍ-YA MAḪ-RI-YA Q̣Í-BÍ-MA* (19) *UM-MA* ^{m}Tar-ḫu-un-mi-ya *AR*-[*D*]*E*$_4$*-KA-MA* (20) kat-ti-ti ḫu-u-ma-an SIG$_5$-in e-eš-du (21) nu-ut-ta DINGIR.MEŠ TI-an ḫar-kán-du (22) nu-ut-ta pa-aḫ-ša-an-da-ru	(17–22) Say to my lord (Ḫimmuili?), the District Governor, my lord, my superior: Thus speaks Tarḫunmiya, your servant: May all be well with you. May the gods keep you alive and protect you.
(23) *BE-LU*-mu aš-šu-ul ḫa-at-re-eš-ke (24) nam-ma-aš-ša-an *A-NA* É-*YA* (25) IGI.ḪI.A-wa ḫar-ak (l. e. 1) *ŠA BE-LÍ*-ma ku-i-e-eš (l. e. 2) LÚ.MEŠ *ṬE*$_4$*-MI* i-ya-an-da-ri (l. e. 3) na-aš-kán am-mu-uk (l. e. 4) pa-ra-a na-iš-ke-mi	(23–25) Lord, keep writing me greetings and keep your eyes on my house (there in Tapikka). I will send on the messengers of (my) lord who come (here).

Commentary

The elaborate use of hierarchical terms emphasizing Ḫimmuili's exalted status (*BE-LÍ-YA MAḪ-RI-YA* "my lord, my superior") and Tarḫunmiya's lowly one (*AR*-[*D*]*E*$_4$*-KA* "your servant") is striking, and undoubtedly plays a role in Tarḫunmiya's attempt to secure the governor's favor and interest in giving him justice and relief from the unfair imposts (*šaḫḫan* and *luzzi*), about which we learn in HKM 52 (text 55). The repetition of the possessive pronoun "my" in *BE-LÍ-YA MAḪ-RI-YA* shows clearly (*pace* Hagenbuchner 1989b, 161) that *MAḪ-RI-YA* "my superior" is used nominally, not as an attributive adjective modifying "my lord."

33. HKM 28
From the King to [Ḫimmuili?]

Text: Mşt. 75/107. **Find spot:** G/5 Portico. **Copy:** HKM 28. **Edition**: Alp 1991a, 168–71 (transliteration and translation), 317 (commentary).

(1′) [x-]aḫ[… … … … … … … … … … … … … … … … … … … …] (2′) x [… …] (3′) nu-za É?[… … … … … … … … … … … …]	

33b. HKM 28
Piggyback Letter from Ḫattušili to Ḫimmuili

(4′) [*U*]*M-MA* mGIŠGIDRU-DIN≈GI[R-*LIM A-NA* mḪi-mu-DINGIR-*LIM*] (5′) ŠEŠ.DÙG.GA-*YA QÍ-B*[*Í-MA*] (6′) kat-ti-ti ḫu-u-ma-an S[IG$_5$-in e-eš-du] (7′) nu-ut-ta DINGIR.MEŠ TI-an ḫ[ar-kán-du] (8′) nu-ut-ta aš-šu-li pa[-aḫ-ša-an-da-ri]	(4′–8′) Thus speaks Ḫattušili: Say to Ḫimmuili, my dear brother: May all be well with you. May the gods keep you alive. May they lovingly protect you.
(9′) ŠEŠ.DÙG.GA-*YA*-mu k[u-it] (10′) *ŠA* ANŠE.KUR.RA.M[EŠ] (11′) ut-tar ḫa-at[-ra-a-eš] (12′) nu-mu k[a-a-ša? … … …] (13′) nu x [… … … … … … … …] (*14′–15′ only traces*)	(9′–13′) Concerning the matter of the horses that you, my dear brother, wrote to me: … (to?) me …
(l. e. 1) nam-ma-a[š-ša-an … … … … … … …] (l. e. 2) TÚGNÍG.LÁ[M.MEŠ … … … … … … …] (l. e. 3) pa-ra-a [… … … … … … … … … … …] (l. e. 4) *Ú-UL* x[… … … … … … … … … … … …]	(*l. e. 1–4 and the rest of the tablet too broken for connected translation.*[111])

Commentary

4 On this Ḫattušili, in addition to Alp's summary (1991a, 58–59), see Klinger 1995a, 88–89.

9–13 This may be another reference to Ḫimmuili's request of a chariot and horses that Ḫattušili mentioned in HKM 27 (text 32): 13–16.

34. HKM 29
From the King to [...]

Text: Mşt. 75/101. **Find spot:** G/5 Portico. **Copy:** HKM 29. **Edition**: Alp 1991a, 170–73 (no. 29). **Discussion**: van den Hout 2003a (on Tarḫunmiya).

(1′) [… … … … EG]IR-pa [… … … … … … … … … … …] (2′) [… … … … …] a-pé-e [… … … … … … … … … … … … …] (3′) [… … … …] a-ru-e-eš-kán-[zi … … … … … … …] (4′) [… … … a]m-mu-uk-pát ar-k[u-wa-ar i-ya-mi] (5′) [… … … k]u-it ku-it i-ya-an-[… … … … … … …] (6′) [… … …] ḫu-u-ma-an EGIR-an am-mu-u[k … …] (7′) [… … …] ú-wa-mi ḫu-u-ma-an pé-ra-a[n … … …] (8′) [EGIR-p]a a-pé-el ut-tar ša-ak-ti [… … … …] (9′) […-z]i ḫu-u-ma-an a-pé-e-da-ni u[d-da-ni-i] (10′) [pa-r]a-a pu-nu-uš-ta-ri	(1′–10′) … back … … they … they repeatedly bow. … I alone will make a reply. … whatever …… everything afterwards I … I will come. Everything before … you know his/its matter … Everything will be investigated in that matter.

Commentary

The beginning of the tablet is broken away, leaving us ignorant of the identity of sender and receiver of the primary letter. *pu-nu-uš-ta-ri* (10′) is the only known example of a medio-passive form of *punušš-* "to inquire."

34b. HKM 29
Piggyback Letter to Ḫimmuili from Tarḫunmiya

(11) [*A-N*]*A BE-LÍ* mḪi-im-mu-DINGIR-*LIM MA-AḪ-RI-YA* [*QÍ-BÍ-MA*] (12) [*U*]*M-MA* m.dIŠKUR-mi-ya DUMU-*KA-MA* [*M*]*A-ḪAR* E[N-*YA* ḫu-u-ma-an] (13) [SI]G_5-in e-eš-du nu-ut-ta *LI*[-*IM* DINGIR.MEŠ TI-an ḫar-kán-du] (14) [nu-ut-]	(11–14) Say to lord Ḫimmuili, my superior: Thus speaks Tarḫunmiya, your son: My all be well with my lord! May the Thousand Gods keep you alive and lovingly protect you.

t[a aš-šu-l]i pa-aḫ-š[a-an-da-ru]	
(15) [*ŠA*$^{?}$ … ku-i]t ut-tar [ḫa-at-ra-a-eš] (16) […] x […]	(15–16) Concerning what matter you wrote to me: …

35. HKM 36
From the King to […]

Text: Mşt. 75/8. **Find spot:** H/5 Room 9. **Copy:** HKM 36. **Edition**: Alp 1991a, 182–87 (no. 36). **Discussion**: Beal 1992, 428 n. 1599, 430 n. 1606, 519 n. 1915; Goedegebuure 2003, 85–86 (on *apūš* in lines 3–9); del Monte 1992, 72 (mistakenly written as "HKM 34"; comments on lines 29–36).

(1) [*UM-MA* ^{d}UTU-*ŠI-MA*] (2) [*A-NA* ^{m}… *QÍ-B*]*Í-MA*	(1–2) Thus speaks His Majesty: Say to …:
(3) *ŠA* [x x x ku-it] ut-tar ḫa-at-ra-a-eš (4) *A-NA* TÙR.ḪI.A-wa kat-t[a-a]n a-ra-an-ta-ri (5) nu-w[a]-mu-kán ÉRI[N].MEŠ pa-ra-a na-i (6) na-aš-ta ka-a-[š]a ÉRIN.MEŠ pa-an-ga-ri-i-it (7) pa-ra-a ne-e[ḫ-ḫu-u]n nu a-pu-u-uš TÙR.ḪI.A (8) an-da SIG$_5$[-in a-u]š$^{?}$-tén[112] na-at-kán (9) SIG$_5$-in aš-nu-w[a-an-ta-ru][113]	(3–9) Concerning the matter of … which you wrote: "They (i.e., the Kaškaeans?) have taken up positions next to the sheepfolds! Dispatch troops to me!" I have just dispatched troops in large numbers. So *watch* those sheepfolds carefully, and provide for them well!
(10) *ŠA* ÉRIN.MEŠ $^{\text{UR[U}}$Iš-ḫu-p]í-it-ta-ma-mu ku-it (11) ut-tar ḫa-at-[ra-a-eš n]u-wa-kán an-da (12) ^{LÚ}EN *MA-AD*[*-GAL-TI* ^{LÚ}UGUL]A[114] *LI-IM*-ya NU GÁL (13) na-aš-ta k[a-a-aš-]ma a-pé-e-da-ni KUR-e (14) ^{LÚ}E[N *MA-AD-GAL-T*]*I* p[a-r]a-a ne-eḫ-ḫ[u]-un (15) x [x ^{LÚ}UGULA *L*]*I-IM* ar-ḫa ti-it-ta<<-ta>>-nu-wa-an-zi (16) x […] x wa-tar-na-aḫ-ḫa-an-zi (17) x […] x	(10–17) Concerning the matter of the troops of the town Išḫupitta which you wrote to me, saying: "There is neither a district governor nor an UGULA *LIM* there." I have dispatched a district governor to that district (lit., 'land'). They will depose$^{?}$ an$^{?}$ UGULA *LIM*. … they will order/direct ….

(18) *Š[A* …-ma-m]u (19) k[u-it ut-tar ḫa-at-ra-a-eš šu-u]l?-le-e-eš-wa (20) ÉRIN.M[EŠ … URUTa?-pí?-i]g?-ga[115] (21) t[u-…]x (22) nu-w[a? … LÚ.MEŠ] IG[I].NU.GÁL (22a) […]-x-zi	(18–22a) Concerning the matter of … which you wrote to me: "hostages(?), troops … of Tapikka, …. And … blind men …"
(23) nu […] (24) LÚ.M[EŠ …] x x […] x (25) na-an […-]it […]-an-zi (26) nam-ma […-]x-ra-[…]x-wa-kán-zi (27) zi-ga-za ki-nu-u[n … IGI.N]U.[G]ÁL (28) 6 GU$_4$.ḪI.A d[a?-…]	(23–26) … (27–28) Now you must … blind men (and) six oxen …
(29) *ŠA* ÉRIN.MEŠ URUIš-ḫu-u-pí-it-ta-ma-mu (30) ku-it ut-tar ḫa-at-ra-a-e[š] (31) 300 ÉRIN.MEŠ-wa-kán da[-aḫ-]ḫ[u-u]n (32) nu-wa-r[a-a]n-kán *I-NA* URUKa-ši-p[u-ra] (33) ša-ra-a tar-na-aḫ-ḫu-un ku-u-un-ma-wa [ÉRIN.MEŠ …] (34) nam-ma ÉRI[N.ME]Š ša-ra-am-ni-it da-aḫ-ḫu-un (35) nu-wa-ra-an-kán *I-NA* URUI[-š]a-aš-pa-ra-a (or: URUI[-š]a-aš pa-ra-a) (36) ne-eḫ-ḫu-un [n]a-at *A[Š-M]E* nu SIG$_5$-in	(29–36) Concerning the matter of the troops of the town Išḫupitta which you wrote to me, saying: "I took three hundred troops and left them up in Kašepura. But I kept(?) this troop?. Then I took troops together with (their) bread allotment? and sent them to the city of Išašparā."[116] I have received your message. Fine.
Uninscribed space of about 4–5 lines.	

Commentary

3–9 The break in line 3 could be filled by "the enemy" or "the sheepfolds." No situation of sheep breaking out of their folds would require an urgent request for troops from the king! So it is clear that the mention of the sheepfolds has nothing to do with restoring escaped sheep to their folds. Positioning the Hittite defenders inside the folds would conceal their presence from the approach of the enemies and would allow them effectively to repulse any Kaškaean attempt to raid the folds for sheep. If, as I have suggested below (in note 157), the TÙR.ḪI.A is a dative-locative governed by immediately following *anda*, then the pronoun *apūš* "those" must refer back to the nearest preceding referent, which would be the troops sent by the king.

Beal's (1992, 428, 519 n. 1915) translation of lines 16–17 ("They will commission an UGULA *LIM* for installation there") is impossible, since *arḫa tittanu-* means not "install" but "remove from office" (German *absetzen* [*HW*b 225], see Otten 1988 I 8 for an example).

18–22 If my conjectural restoration [LÚ.MEŠ*šu-u*]*l-le-e-eš* is correct, then the mention of "blinded men" later in the paragraph fits what we know about the blinding of dangerous POWs held as hostages (see Hoffner 2002c; 2003b, 86, HKM 102, and the literature on that text). On the word LÚ/DUMU*šulla/i-* "hostage" see the full discussion in von Schuler 1965, 113–14. The verbs most commonly used with the word are "to seize" (*ep-*) and "to give" (*pai-*). According to Melchert 2005a, n. 10, "Three examples of the dative-locative singular *šullanni* definitely belong to a homonymous noun *šullatar* 'hostage-hood' and are irrelevant to our inquiry: KUB 19.39 iii 10, KBo 14.4 i 14, and ABoT 60 obv. 9 (text 49). Likewise the examples *šullānun* at KBo 5.8 ii 2 and *šulla*[*i*] at KUB 19.49 i 68 belong to a separate verb *šullā(i)-* 'impose hostages upon; give as a hostage.'" On the LÚ.MEŠ*LĪṬŪTI* as "hostages" (abbreviated LÚ(.MEŠ)*LI.*) in Hittite see already Sommer 1932, 234 and CAD L, 223. The only other example of the nom. pl. of this word in the Maşat letter corpus (HKM 89: 19) has non-plene spelling *šu-ul-le-eš*. But KBo 16.27 (MH/MS) has the same spelling as in this letter: *šu-ul-le-e-eš*.

35b: HKM 36: 37–l. e. 4
Piggyback Letter to a superior (Ḫimmuili?) from Ḫašammili

Discussion: de Martino and Imparati 1995: 108 (relating the affair of the slave woman in this letter to HKM 30 (text 36); Houwink ten Cate 1998, 163 (the affair of the slave woman).

(37) *A-*[*NA BE-L*]*Í MAḪ-RI-YA A-BI* DÙG.G[A-*Y*]*A* (38) [*QÍ-BÍ-MA*] *UM-MA* mḪa-ša-am-mi-i-[l]i DUMU-*KA-MA* (39) [*MA-ḪA*]*R A-BI* DÙG.GA-*YA* ḫu-u-ma-an (40) S[I]G$_5$-[i]n e-eš-du nu *BE-LÍ* DINGIR.MEŠ (41) TI-an ḫar-kán-du nu *BE-LU* pa-aḫ-ša-an-ta-ru	(37–41) Say to the lord, my superior, my dear father: Thus speaks Ḫašammili, your son: May all be well with my dear father, and may the gods keep (my) lord alive and protect (my) lord!

(42) *ŠA* GÉME-*YA*-at-ta ku-e-da-ni (43) ud-da-ni-i wa-tar-na-aḫ-ḫi-iš-ke-nu-un (44) tu-el-ma-an-kán ma-aḫ-ḫa-an (45) ma-ni-ya-aḫ-ḫa-an-te-eš *IŠ-TU* ZÍD.D[A] (46) ar-ḫa da-ya-er na-an-ša-an [...] (47) *I-NA* URUTa-ḫa-az-[z]i-mu-na[] (48) EGIR-pa pé-e-ḫu-t[e]-er	(42–48) Concerning what I informed you about my female slave: how your agents stole her away together with[117] the flour (she had milled), and led her back to Taḫazzimuna.
(49) na-aš ma-a-an še-p[í-i]t-ta x [...] (50) ma-a-an an-da [i-y]a-mi [...] (51) nu-u[š- ...] (*About 6 lines missing in the break at the end of the reverse.*) (l. e. 1) nu-ut-ta DINGIR.MEŠ aš-šu-li pa-aḫ-ša-an-da-ru ŠEŠ DÙG.GA-*YA*-mu (l. e. 2) aš-šu-ul ḫa-at-re-eš-ke na-aš-ta *Ú-UL* la-aḫ-la-aḫ-ḫi-i[š-ke-ši] (l. e. 3) ka-a-ša-za URUḪa-at-tu-ši *MA-ḪAR* LÚ.MEŠ*TAP-PÍ-NI* nu ŠEŠ DÙG.GA-*YA* (l. e. 4) *QA-TAM-MA* ša-a-ak	(49–51) ... (l. e. 1–4) ... May the gods lovingly protect you! My dear brother, keep sending me (your) greetings! And stop worrying! I am presently in Ḫattuša with our colleagues. I want you to know this, my dear brother.

Commentary

There is a descrepancy between line 37 in this letter, where the addressee is called "my dear *father*" and l. e. 1 and 3, where the addressee is called "my dear *brother*." It may be possible that in the missing last six lines of the reverse another person is introduced as the primary addressee.

The piggyback letter was interpreted by de Martino (1995, 108–9), as follows:

> In the postscript in question, Ḫašamili, after the greeting formula, describes to the addressee a situation about which he has informed him on other occasions, concerning a female slave belonging to Ḫašamili himself. She, who had with her some flour that was most probably stolen, had been captured by Ḫimuili's administrators (*maniyaḫḫanteš*) and taken back by them to the locality of Taḫazzimuna. There then follow some lines containing many gaps, in which it seems that grain is mentioned, but it is not clear if this is connected with the preceding topic. The other letter as well (HBM 30) was

> sent by the king to Ḫimuili and another person whose name is missing because of a gap in the text. In the postscript Ḫašamili himself addresses Uzzu as his brother, and thus equal in rank to him. We learn from the passage that Uzzu, after having written repeatedly to Ḫašamili on the subject of the latter's slave, now gives no more news of her. It is possible that Uzzu kept the woman, either as compensation for the theft she had committed or because someone had entrusted her to him to await judgement, perhaps since he was a scribe in Maşat and worked next to Ḫimuili. In fact Ḫimuili seems to have been *BEL MADGALTI*, and we know that this official was responsible also for the administration of justice. Ḫasamili requests that the slave be returned to him by means of his messenger; he specifies that he wants her back "in good condition" (SIG_5), that is integral/intact, stating thereby that he is willing to make restitution with triple whatever she took or stole. This recalls §§ 95 and 99 of the Hittite Laws, which provide that a master could make restitution for damages resulting from a crime committed by one of his slaves, thereby avoiding the slave's mutilation. In our letter this is alluded to in the request to have the slave back intact. The physical wholeness of a slave, in fact, was a guarantee of his or her efficiency in work and thus constituted an advantage for the master.

De Martino and Imparati (1995, 108) think that the person addressed in this piggyback letter (HKM 36b [text 35]) is Ḫimmuili, and that the female slave affair here described is the same as in the piggyback letter HKM 30b (text 36) . Houwink ten Cate (1998, 163) seems to agree.

De Martino and Imparati also understand *maniyaḫḫanteš* as "administrators," although the participle of a transitive verb (such as *maniyaḫḫ-* "to govern" certainly is) should be passive. For this reason I prefer to regard ^{LÚ}*maniyaḫḫatalla-* as the correct term for "administrator," and follow Freydank and von Schuler (cited in CHD L–N, 169 sub *maniyaḫḫant-*) in taking ^{LÚ}*maniyaḫḫant-* as "subject; subordinate," in this case the underling agents of Ḫimmuili.

If the maidservant mentioned in this letter is indeed the same as that in letter HKM 30b (text 36), then she certainly has stolen something, as de Martino and Imparati assume. But from letter HKM 30b (text 36) lines 18–25 and l. e. 1–4 one can hardly assume without great difficulty that the person from whom she has stolen was Ḫimmuili, and that Ḫimmuili's agents took her either as compensation for the theft or to hold her for trial. See my discussion there.

l. e. 3–4 are edited in CHD Š, 29. I do not agree that the translation "we are in Ḫattuša ..." is an option here, since there is only one sender of this letter.

36. HKM 30
From the King to Ḫimmuili and [...]

Text: Mşt. 75/25. **Find spot:** H/5 Room 9. **Copy:** HKM 30. **Edition**: Alp 1991a, 172–75 (no. 30).

(1) *U*[*M-M*]*A* dUTU-*ŠI-MA* (2) [*A-N*]*A* mḪi-mu-DINGIR-*LIM* *QÍ*-[*BÍ-MA*] (3) […]-x x x […]	(1–3) Thus speaks His Majesty: Say to Ḫimmuili: …:
(4) *ŠA* LÚ.KÚR-mu ku-it ut-tar (5) ḫa-at-ra-a-eš nu-za *PA-NI* LÚ. KÚR (6) me-ek-ki pa-aḫ-ḫa-aš-nu-an-za e-eš (7) *ŠA* ANŠE.KUR. RA-ma-mu ku-it ut-t[ar] (8) ḫa-at-ra-a-eš nu-mu ka-a (9) ANŠE.KUR. RA.MEŠ ku-iš-ki kat-ta-an (10) na-an-da up-pa-aḫ-ḫi	(4–10) Concerning what you wrote to me about the enemy: Be very much on your guard against the enemy![118] Concerning what you wrote to me about chariotry: Some chariotry is here with me.[119] I will send them to you.

Commentary

The use of *ka-a* ("here") in this context might suggest that the king was not in Ḫattuša when he sent this letter. He only had limited chariotry available there. But he would send what was needed.

36b. HKM 30
Piggyback Letter to Uzzū from Ḫašammili

Discussion: de Martino and Imparati 1995, 108 (relating the affair of the slave woman in this letter to HKM 36b (text 35b); Houwink ten Cate 1998, 163 (the affair of the female slave).

(11) *A-NA* mUz-zu-u ŠEŠ-*YA* (12) *QÍ-BÍ-MA* (13) *UM-MA* mḪa-ša-am-me-li (14) ŠEŠ-*KA-MA*	(11–14) Say to Uzzū, my brother: Thus speaks Ḫašammili, your brother:
(15) *ŠA* GÉME-*YA*-mu u[t]-t[ar] ḫa-a[t]-re-eš-ke-eš (16) ki-nu-na-mu na[m-ma] *Ú-UL* (17) ku-it-ki ḫ[a-a]t-ra-a-ši	(15–17) You were writing to me about my female slave, but now you no longer write anything:

(18) ki-nu-na-m[u] G[ÉME-*Y*]*A* ar-ḫa up-pí (19) ma-an-m[a-an x-]x x[-x-]x?-ši?[120] (20) nu GÉME[121]-*Y*[*A* ḫ]a-ap-pa-la?[-aš]-š[a-at-]ti?[122] (21) *A-NA* LÚ *ṬE*$_4$*-MI* SIG$_5$ pa-i (22) na-at-mu kat-ti-mi ú-da-ú? (23) [k]a-a-ša-za GÉME ku-it (24) [ku-i]t da-a-an da-ya-<an-> na[123] (25) ḫar-zi (l. e. 1) na-aš-ta a-pa[-a]-at-ta (l. e. 2) 3-*ŠU* da-a na-at-mu u[p-pí] (l. e. 3) ma-a-an da-ma-iš ku-iš-k[i LÚ *ṬE*$_4$*-MI*?] (l. e. 4) ú-iz-zi [...]	(18–25) Now send off my female slave to me! You must not ... or injure my female slave![124] Give the goods to a messenger, and let him bring them to me. (For) whatever this female slave has taken and stolen (from you), (l. e. 1–4) take threefold that amount also (as compensation), but send it (i.e., the rest of my goods) to me whenever some other messenger comes (my way).

Commentary

19–20 It appears that Ḫašammili's female slave and some goods of his were where Uzzū lives. This female slave then stole from Uzzū (or his household), so that the threefold compensation is due to him. He has informed Ḫašammili, who now tells him not only to retrieve his own stolen property from the woman, but also to deduct from his own goods the threefold compensation for theft. But Uzzū must send the slave woman and the rest of Ḫašammili's goods (SIG$_5$) back to him. If Alp's restorations of 19–20 are correct, Uzzū must not allow anyone else to detain or harm her. Threefold compensation for theft fits the picture obtained from the laws on theft in the Hittite law corpus. But there were other ratios in special circumstances: see the "twofold restitution" mentioned in Beckman 1999a, 13, §7.

21–22 In line 21 Alp and de Martino and Imparati 1995 take SIG$_5$ as adverbial "in good condition" ("intact") and supply the unexpressed object "her" (i.e., the slave woman). But this view encounters insurmountable difficulties in the following clause. There the direct object *-at* (neuter) cannot (contra Alp 1991a, 175) refer to the female slave: the Hittite noun underlying GÉME is common gender and always takes a common gender resumptive pronoun. Alp's German "sie" could mean "them," but the context shows that he intends the meaning "her." Nor would one use the verb *uda-* "to bring (objects)" with a human direct object, unless the person had to be carried. CHD *pai-* B j 12′ takes SIG$_5$ to be a greeting (*aššul*) instead of "goods" (*aššū*). But the proper way to ask for another's greeting is ŠEŠ.DÙG.GA-*YA-ya-mu* EGIR-*pa aš-šu-ul ḫa-at-ra-a-i* " Dear brother, send back your greeting to me!" HKM 3 (text 9) l.e. 2–3. The least difficult option is to understand SIG_5 as the direct object, but representing the neuter plural noun *aššū* "goods," which is properly continued with *-at* in the following clause.

l. e. 1–2 *-ašta* is still in active use in these letters. And its use with *da-* "to take" in older texts is well established (cf. e.g., [*na-a*]*t-ta-aš-ta ku-it-ki ku-e-da-ni-ik-ka da-aḫ-ḫu-un* "I did not (ever) take anything from anyone" KUB 31.4: 4 + KBo 3.41: 3 (OH/NS).

l. e. 3 For the word order of *kuiški* when modifying an attributive adjective plus head noun, see *GrHL* §§18.35–18.36.

l. e. 4 There is no following lacuna to accommodate a continuation of this sentence. The *mān* "whenever" (CHD *mān* 5c) clause must be an asyndetic postposed temporal clause, dependent upon the preceding main clause (see *GrHL* §29.55 and §30.37).

37. HKM 31
From the King to Ḫimmuili

Text: Mşt. 75/104. **Find spot:** G/5 Portico. **Copy:** HKM 31. **Edition**: Alp 1991a, 174–77 (no. 31). **Discussion**: Beal 1992, 431 n. 1610; Hoffner 2002a, 167.

(1) *UM-MA* ᵈUTU-*ŠI-MA* (2) *A-NA* ᵐḪi-im-mu-DINGIR-*LIM QÍ-BÍ-MA*	(1–2) Thus speaks His Majesty: Say to Ḫimmuili:
(3) *ŠA* ÉRIN.MEŠ GIBIL-mu ku-it (4) ut-tar ḫa-at-ra-a-eš (5) 100 ÉRIN.MEŠ GIBIL-wa-kán (6) *I-NA* ᵁᴿᵁGa-ši-pu-ra ša-ra-a (7) tar-na-aḫ-ḫu-un na-at *AŠ-ME*	(3–7) I have taken note of what you wrote me about new troops, (saying:) "I have left up in the city Kašepura one hundred new troops."
(8) *ŠA* ᵁᴿᵁGa-ša-ša-ma-mu (9) ku-it *ŠA* ᴳᴵᔆGEŠTIN ut-tar (10) ḫa-at-ra-a-eš nu EGIR-an ti-ya (11) na-aš tuḫ-ša-an-du na-at le-e (12) dam-mi-iš-ḫa-an-da-ri	(8–12) Concerning the matter of the vineyards of (the city) Kašaša about which you wrote to me: See to it that they are harvested. Let them not be damaged.
(13) *ŠA* É ᵈUTU-*ŠI*-ma-mu (14) ku-it ᴸᵁma-ni-ya-aḫ-ḫi-ya-aš (15) EN-aš ut-tar ḫa-at-ra-a-eš (16) ka-a-wa	(13–19) Concerning the matter of the district lord of the house of My Majesty about which you wrote.

NU.GÁL ku-iš-ki (17) na-at ku-e-da-ni pé-di (18) nu-uš-ma-aš ḫa-at-ra-a-i (19) na-at-kán kat-ta-an-da ú-ni-an-du	me, (saying:) "There is none here." Write to them (the district lords) in the place where they are, and let them drive down (to you).

Commentary

3–7 On ÉRIN.MEŠ GIBIL see also HKM 43: 3 and discussion in Alp 1991a, 304 and 317 and Beal 1992. Alp believes that in the opposition ÉRIN. MEŠ GIBIL vs. ÉRIN.MEŠ *annalli-* the latter are seasoned veterans and the former new, inexperienced troops, "Truppen des jungen Jahrganges." On 5–7 see CHD Š, 219.

Compare the numbers given with ÉRIN.MEŠ: 9,000 (AM 158), 5,000 (AM 158), 3,000 (AM 188), 1,760 (HKM 20: 7), 1,400 (KBo 3.22: 70), 700 (KUB 36.99 i 2), 600 (HKM 25, DŠ frag. 28, AM 74 [both NH]), 400 (HKM 25), 300 (HKM 36, 41), 200 (KUB 14.1 rev. 51), 150 (KUB 26.41+ rev. 1), 100 (KBo 22.2 rev. 6, HKM 31, Bronze Tablet iii 35, 37), 30 (CTH 15A, HKM 33), 20 (CTH 15A, HKM 86b), 10 (HKM 33). The numbers are all multiples of ten. An apparent exception: 9 ÉRIN.MEŠ *ŠU-TI* (DŠ frag. 13) may refer to nine tribal groups. Note too that even numbers of enemy troops are always multiples of 10: 600 and 400 (HKM 25: 4–10). These figures may be deliberately rounded for enemy troops, but together with the Hittite military rank UGULA.10 they indicate ten as a basic unit of troop strength.

13–19 This translation follows CHD L–N, 168 sub *maniyaḫḫai-* 3a. To the two passages cited there add now *maniyaḫḫiaš išḫān kuin BEL=ŠU iezi* KBo 32.14 iii 13–14, ed. Neu 1996. In KUB 24.13 iii 21–22 the district lord immediately follows [LÚ]*ḪAZZIYANNI* in a listing of high officials.

37b. HKM 31
Piggyback Letter of Mār-ešrē to Uzzū

(20) *UM-MA* [m]*MA-RE-EŠ-RE-E* (21) *A-NA* [m]Uz-zu-u ŠEŠ.DÙG.GA-*YA* (22) *QÍ-BÍ-MA* kat-ti-ti ḫu-u-ma-an SIG_5-in (23) e-eš-du nu-ut-ta DINGIR.MEŠ (24) aš-šu-li pa-aḫ-ša-an-da-[r]u	(20–24) Thus speaks Mār-ešrē: Say to Uzzū, my dear brother: May all be well with you. And may the gods lovingly protect you.

(25) mḪi-im-mu-DINGIR-*LIM*-iš-mu 1 GU_4 (26) te-et nu-uš-ši ŠEŠ. DÙG.GA-*YA* (27) EGIR-an ti-ya na-an-kán (28) pa-ra-a ar-nu-ut (29) na-an-mu up-pí (30) ú-wa-at du-wa-ad-du	(25–30) Ḫimmuili promised me an ox. See to it, my brother. Expedite it and send it to me. Quickly!

Commentary

25–26 For further examples of *te-* "to promise" in the Maşat letter corpus see HKM 21 (text 26): 21–22; HKM 22 (text 27): 12–16, and HKM 63 (text 66): 12–16. For such requests in scribal letters see the introduction (§1.2.20). For an identical request by Mār-ešrē to Uzzū see text 27.

30 For *uwat duwaddu* see above in §1.2.19.1.

38. HKM 32
From the King to Ḫimmuili

Text: Mşt. 75/117. **Find spot:** G/5 Portico. **Copy**: HKM 32. **Edition**: Alp 1991a, 176–77 (no. 32).

(1) *UM-MA* dUTU-*ŠI-M*[*A*] (2) *A-NA* mḪi-im-mu-DINGIR-*L*[*IM QÍ-BÍ-MA*]	(1–2) Thus speaks His Majesty: Say to Ḫimmuili:
(3) ud-da-a-ar-mu k[u-e] (4) ḫa-at-ra-a-eš n[a-at *AŠ-ME*]	(3–4) I have heard the words that you wrote to me.
(5) ki-iš-ša-an-m[a-mu ku-it u]t-t[ar] (6) ḫa-at-ra-a-eš š[u?- (7) [*I*-]*NA* KUR URUx[(8) [pa?-r]i-an x [(9) […]x an-da x - x [	(5–9) Concerning the following matter about which you wrote to me … in the land of …
[*Reverse broken away.*]	
(upper edge 1) […] x x x [(2) [ḫ]a-[a]t-ra-a-ši […]	

39. HKM 33
From [...] to [...]

Text: Mşt. 75/19. **Find spot:** H/5 Room 9. **Copy:** HKM 33. **Edition**: Alp 1991a, 176–81 (no. 33). **Discussion**: Beal 1992, 110, 286.

(First 21 lines either broken away or too badly broken for treatment.)	
(22) [...] *A-BI* <DÙG.>GA-*YA* (23) [...-ḫ]a?-aš?-da (24) [Ú.ḪI.A-y]a wa-ar-aš-tén (25) [...] É.GAL.ḪI.A ḫu-u-ma-an-[te-eš] (26) [...]x.MEŠ pa-aḫ-ḫa-aš-nu-an[-te-eš] (27) [a-š]a-a[n]-du ú-wa-at (28) [d]u-wa-ad-du	(22–28) ... my dear father ... Harvest (*pl.*) the grasses too! Let all of the palaces and ... be protected/guarded. Get a move on!
(29) *I-NA* URUAn-zi-li-y[a ... ...] (30) ša-ra-a 30 ÉRIN.MEŠ ḫa-pí-ri-i[n u-i-ya-at-tén[125]]	(29–30) Send up to the city Anziliya thirty *ḫapiri- work-gangs*.[126]
(31) [*Š*]*A* 10 ÉRIN.MEŠ-ma URUAn-zi-l[i-ya-aš ku-i-uš] (32) URUTa-pí-ig-ga p[é-eḫ-ḫu-un] (33) nu Ú.ḪI.A wa-a[r-a]š-du	(31–33) Let some of the ten *work-gangs* from the city Anziliya that I deployed to Tapikka harvest the grasses.

Commentary

25 Mention here of "all the palaces" seems to suggest that different "palaces" (i.e., administrative offices) were involved in the various letters (so Imparati 1997, 653).

The *ḫapiri*-"troops" appear to be foreign mercenaries or men otherwise recruited from the *ḫapiri*-peoples. In this case their duties are agricultural (harvesting) rather than military (see n. 171). For this reason a translation of ÉRIN.MEŠ as "Soldaten" (so *HW*2 H 250) is inappropriate here. On this class of social outsiders, which appears throughout the Levant during the Late Bronze Age, there have been many studies (for example: Greenberg 1955; Loretz 1984; Salvini 1996; Lemche 1995, 1207–8; Naaman 2000; von Dassow in Chavalas 2006, 201–2; and Rainey 2008. On the *ḫapiri*-gods among the Hittites see van Gessel 1998–2001, 91–92, and *HW*2 H, 249–50. There seem to be two different accounts of the etymology of this word. While most scholars identify the word in the Hittite texts with the word widely attested in Akkadian, Egyptian, and West Semitic sources containing the triconsonantal root *ʿpr*, Haas (1999) has proposed a Hurrian etymology *ḫav- + -iri.*[127]

27–28 For *uwat duwaddu* see above in §1.2.19.1.

33 Re the “grasses” see text 200, line 35.

39b. HKM 33
Piggyback Letter of Mar-ešrē to Uzzū

(34) [*UM-MA*] ^{m}[M]a-re-eš-re-e *A-NA* ^{m}Uz-zu-u (35) [*QÍ-BÍ-MA*] *MA-ḪAR* ŠEŠ DÙG.GA-*YA* (36) [*Ù M*]*A-ḪA*[*R*] NIN DÙG.GA-*YA* (37) [ḫu-u-ma-an S]IG$_5$-in e-eš-du (38) [nu-uš-ma-aš DINGIR.M]EŠ aš-šu-li (39) [pa-aḫ-ša-an-d]a-ru	(34–39) Thus speaks Mar-ešrē: Say to Uzzū: May all be well with my dear brother and my dear sister! And may the gods lovingly protect you!
(40) [… tar-pí-i]š an-na-ri-i[š] (41) […] x […]	
(Rest of the letter broken away. Mere traces on the left edge.)	

Commentary

35–36 On *MAḪAR … U MAḪAR* see *GrHL* §29.2 (n. 5).

40. HKM 34
From the King to Zardumanni, […], and […]

Text: Mşt. 75/68. **Find spot:** G/5 Room 8. **Copy:** HKM 34. **Edition**: Alp 1991a, 180–83 (no. 34).

The king writes here to three officials in Tapikka. Only the first man’s name, Zardumanni, is fully legible. According to Alp (1991a, 105–6), he is the same person referred to elsewhere under the different writings Zartummani (HKM 68 [text 71]) and Zaldumanni (HKM 60 [text 63]). Marizza (2007a, 169) identifies him with the man from Išmerika mentioned in KUB 23.68 rev. 20 (CTH 133), a treaty composed in the reign of Arnuwanda I.

Royal concern for the vineyards and grapes is expressed also in other letters from Maşat (texts 10, 37, and 42). For Hittite viticulture and the use of its products see Hoffner 1974a, 39 and 113, and Gorny 1995. For the archeobotanical data from the ancient Near East see Miller 1997.

The last sentence (lines 13–16) appears incomplete, but in fact it is a type of sentence familiar not only elsewhere in Hittite (CHD L–N *mān* 7 e and *GrHL* §30.31), but in other ancient Near Eastern languages as well (for Akkadian see CAD Š/III, 276 [*šumma* a 2′]; for biblical Hebrew see Gesenius, Kautsch, and Cowley 1910, §149 and HALOT אִם *ʾim* mng. 4). See also n. 124. The suppressed (and implied) apodosis is "you will face a horrible punishment," that is, the unmentionable. The effect of this suppression of the apodosis is to transform the conditional clause into an imperative of the reverse: "keep your eyes on the harvesting of the grapes!" For examples where the threat is expressed, see text 41 (*ú-wa-ši ḫar-ak-ši* "you will surely be put to death") and text 19 (*nu-uš-ma-aš-ša-an ú-wa-an-zi a-pí-ya pé-e-di ta-šu-wa-aḫ-ḫa-an-zi* "they will surely blind you in that place"). The word *lūwan* (line 10) is unattested elsewhere. For Alp's comments see Alp 1991a,320. From its context here it could mean "a report."[128]

Upper Edge	
(1) [*UM-MA* dUTU-*Š*]*I-MA* (2) [*A-NA* mZa-]a[r-d]u-ma-an-ni (3) [m]x-x-[p]al?-la (4) [*Ù* m]x-du-uš-ši-ya *QÍ-BÍ-MA*	(1–4) Thus speaks His Majesty: Say to Zardumanni, x-x-palla and x-duššiya:
(5) [ma]-aḫ-ḫa-an-ša-ma-aš ka-a-aš (6) [t]up-pí-an-za an-da (7) ú-e-mi-ya-zi	(5–7) As soon as this tablet reaches you (pl.),
(8) nu *ŠA* É dUTU-*ŠI* (9) GIŠGEŠTIN x? túḫ-ša-at-t[én][129] (10) nam-ma lu-u-wa-an (11) *A-NA* dUTU-*ŠI* (12) ḫa-at-ra-a-at-tén	(8–12) harvest the grapes of His Majesty's estate. Then write/send a *report*? to His Majesty.
(13) zi-ga-aš-ša-an […] (14) mZa-a[r-du-ma-an-ni] (15) m[a-a-an *A-NA* GIŠGEŠTIN túḫ-ša-an-na] (16) IGI.ḪI.A-wa (17) *Ú-U*[*L*] ḫa[r]-ši	(13–17) But you, … Zardumanni, if you do not keep your eyes on the harvesting of the grapes, (may the gods curse you)!

41. HKM 35
From [the King(?)] to Pipappa

Text: Mşt. 75/9. **Find spot:** H/5 Room 9. **Copy:** HKM 35. **Edition**: Alp 1991a, 182–83 (no. 35). **Discussion:** Beal 1992, 38–39; Hoffner 2007, 395 (lines 8–9).

(1) zi-ga-kán (2) mPí-pa-ap-pa-aš (3) ÉRIN.MEŠ UKU.UŠ pa-ri-ya-an (4) li-li-wa-aḫ-ḫu-u-wa-an-zi (5) ú-wa-te (6) na-an-kán tu-uz-zi-ya (7) an-da ú-wa-te (8) ma-a-an *Ú-UL*-ma (9) ú-wa-ši ḫar-ak-ši	(1–9) As for you, Pipappa—bring the regular troops across here quickly, and incorporate them into the army! If you don't, you will surely be put to death.

Commentary

Alp (1991a, 182 n. 129) thinks that in spite of the lack of the usual introductory matter, this is a short letter from the king. That would make this text unique. Alternatively, it might be a short memorandum used to compose a regular outgoing letter, which was sent off to Pipappa. But the former supposition is the more likely one. For another explanation of the lack of opening formulas, see above in §1.2.8.3.

This text forms a part of Beal's discussion of the UKU.UŠ troops, which he considers part of the Hittite standing army. Here a group of them, stationed near the addressee Pipappa, were to be brought to a staging area and merged with a larger group making up "the army" (*tuzzi-*).

There are two possible locations for the clause boundary in lines 8–9. Although it could be after *uwaši* ("but if you don't come"), I would assume it is before *uwaši* ("but if you don't [i.e., bring them]"), making the final clause a serial construction (*GrHL* §24.38 and §24.42). In this case, the serial construction adds a certainty to the future prospect: hence, my translation "will *surely* be ...." In either case the final clause shows asyndeton (see Hoffner 2007, 395).

42. HKM 37
From the King to [...]

Text: Mşt. 73/79. **Find spot:** H/2 Room 26. **Copy**: HKM 37. **Edition**:

Alp 1991a: 186–89 (no. 37). **Discussion:** Alp 1991a, 322 (on *parā au(š)-* "abwarten").

(1) *UM-MA* dUTU-*ŠI-MA A-NA* [… *QÍ-BÍ-MA*]	(1) Thus speaks His Majesty: Say to …:
(2) *ŠA* LÚ.KÚR-mu ku-it ut[-tar ḫa-at-ra-a-eš LÚ.KÚR-wa KUR-ya] (3) an-da pa-an-ga-ri-it [i-ya-at-ta-ri na-at *AŠ-ME*]	(2–3) I have heard the matter concerning the enemy about which you wrote to me, saying: "The enemy is invading the territory in large numbers."
(4) *ŠA* ÉRIN.MEŠ-ma-mu ku-it u[t-tar] (5) ḫa-at-ra-a-eš ke-e-da-ni[-wa …] (6) UD.3.KAM pa-ra-a u-uḫ-ḫi nam-m[a-wa-ra-aš ḫu-u-da-a-ak] (7) ú-wa-te-mi nu ma-a-a[n ÉRIN.MEŠ] (8) li-li-wa-aḫ-ḫu-u-an-z[i] *Ú-UL* ú[-wa-te-ši] (9) ap-pé-ez-zi-ya-an ma-a-a[n] ku-it x[…]	(4) Concerning the matter of troops about which you wrote to me, saying: (5) "In this … I will *wait*? for three days, (6) then I will promptly bring him/them?."—(7–9) If you do not bring ... troops quickly, if afterwards ……
(10) ma-a-na-an ki-nu-un *Ú-UL* ú-wa-te-ši (11) na-an-kán nam-ma KUR*-az ar-ri*-x-x[(-)x?] (12) ku-wa-at ú-wa-te-ši	(10) If you do not bring them now, (11–12) why do you bring them then from the land ……?
(13) *ŠA* GIŠKIRI$_6$.GEŠTIN URUG[a]-ša-ša-ma-mu ku-i[t] (14) ut-tar ḫa-at-ra-a-eš [tú]ḫ-šu-wa-an-zi-wa-ra-aš-ša[-an] (15) ka-ru-ú a-r[a-an-te-]eš ma-a-an-wa-kán (16) an-tu-uḫ-ša-a-[tar pa-ra-a ḫ]u-u-da-a-ak na-it-ti	(13) Concerning what you wrote me about the vineyards of Kašaša: (14) "They are already ripe for harvesting. (15–16) If only you would promptly dispatch workers!"
(17) x - x […] G[I]ŠK[I]RI$_6$.GEŠTIN.ḪI.A (18) [túḫ-ša-an-zi na-at *AŠ-ME* *ŠA* …]x-[m]u (19) [ku-it ut-tar ḫa-at-r]a-a-eš (20) […] (21) […]-e	(17) "The …-s are harvesting the vineyards." (18–19) Yes, I have heard that. Concerning what you wrote me about … (20–21) …

Commentary

The unknown addressee had earlier requested from the king workers for harvesting the vineyards of Kašaša. The workers are called "people" (*antuḫšatar*), a common designation for easily moved fieldworkers (something like, if not identical with, NAM.RA-groups). In the *Deeds of Šuppiluliuma*, fragment 13, Šuppiluliuma I defeated a Kaškaean group, and after building fortifications to protect previously occupied but now empty settlements, he brought groups of workers (*antuḫšatar*) to settle in those towns (see Güterbock 1956b, 65). Harvesting royal vineyards was one of various duties that could be imposed by the crown, not just upon NAM.RA-groups, but on free citizens liable to taxes and corvée (*šaḫḫan* and *luzzi*); cf. the metal workers' obligation in Hittite law §56 in Hoffner 1997g, 68, 193.

The NAM.RA-people (Hittite *arnuwalaš*) are kept distinct in Hittite texts from slaves, who are referred to with the Sumerian terms ÌR "male slave" and GÉME "female slave." The Sumerian word nam-ra denotes "booty" including "captives, prisoners of war" (Akkadian *šallatu*). Since the earliest days of Hittitology it has been known that the NAM.RA.MEŠ were groups of persons seized in battle from defeated opponents and who could be settled by the king in any area in need of agricultural exploitation. In his 1933 book *Kleinasien,* Albrecht Goetze described the NAM.RA as follows: "They belong to specific lands, settlements or temples, that they may not leave. If—discontented with their lot—they ever cross over into a foreign land, diplomatic exchanges immediately arise concerning their extradition. They form a good portion of the spoils of war and as such are transplanted from one land to another in order to settle newly founded villages or in order to put stretches of waste land under cultivation."

The provincial governors (or "margraves," *BĒLĒ MADGALTI*) in the MH period were authorized to settle NAM.RA groups in areas denuded by the Kaškaeans and in need of agricultural exploitation to feed the empire. The governors were responsible for the registration of the king's share in individual villages and overseeing the administration, irrigation, and cultivation of crown land in their districts. The governor had to ensure that the king's share of the fields was sown and reaped within the terms of *luzzi* and that those required to provide draught animals supplied them on time. He was also authorized to resettle civilian captives (NAM.RA) in his province, provide them with agricultural land, and establish their *šaḫḫan* and *luzzi* obligations, as well as to apprehend fugitives and dispatch them to the king.[130]

Agricultural workforces were partly recruited out of the realm of the palace in the form of required services, and partly as members of individual household groups, including both family members and moveable NAM.RA-groups, that is, prisoners of war, the latter in units of ten persons. The texts from Tapikka/Maşat, which reflect a reorganization and reconstitution of territories whose infrastructure had been disturbed by Kaškaean incursions, mention work units of up to twenty-two persons under the supervision of a DUGUD-officer and provided with barley rations of two *sūtu* per person. This amount corresponds precisely to the daily wage (*kuššan*) for a male agricultural worker set in §158a of the Hittite law corpus: "If a (free) man in the harvest season hires himself out for wages, to bind sheaves, load (them on) wagons, deposit (them in) barns, and clear the threshing floors, his wages for three months shall be 1,500 liters of barley."[131]

Along with the NAM.RA-groups, there were other groups settling empty lands and performing agricultural service for the crown. Among these were those called *arzanant-*.

> Deriving from the word *arzana-* ... by way of a posited intermediate stage, the hypothetical denominative verb **arzanai-* "to provide with food and lodging" is the participle *arzanant-*, which describes members of a class of mobile persons at the disposal of the crown. These persons were settled on crown lands, provided with livestock, seed and winter food supply, and were expected to cultivate crown lands in return for support and an unspecified proportion of the crop. Members of this class, often further described as *arzanant-* "supported, provided with food and lodging," were more commonly designated by either the Sumerogram NAM.RA or its Hittite equivalent *arnuwala-*. (Hoffner 1974b, 117 with nn. 18 and 19)

On the food support of the *arzanant-* NAM.RA-people see also Hoffner 1993b, 203–4. Pecchioli Daddi (2003b, n. 61) points out that in KUB 51.23 obv. 11 the Chief Gold Charioteer (^{LÚ}KUŠ$_7$ KÙ.SIG$_{17}$) has at his disposal forty-six NAM.RA.

4–12 The king reminds the official to whom he writes that the latter had promised to lead troops (ÉRIN.MEŠ, line 4) somewhere that the king wished them. The official claimed that he would need three days to be ready for this task. But the king urges haste, noting that they are needed very quickly (*lilaḫḫuwanzi*, line 8). The singular pronoun object (lines 10, 11) which I render "them" probably refers to the troops, the word for which (ÉRIN.MEŠ) is singular.

11–12 My photo shows a clear KUR, not the GAM that Alp's note claims; no emendation "KUR$^!$" is necessary. After KUR-*az* a reading *ar-ḫa* would be semantically plausible, but the sign after *ar-* in the photo has too many verticals for *ḫa*. I would be inclined to read either *ri* or *ú*, although I cannot yet solve the line. The next sign is written over a depression, perhaps an erasure. It is more or less as Alp copied it in HKM: either NA$_4$ (which makes no sense to me here) or two signs *ni-w*[*a-*...]. Interogative *kuwat* "why?" occurs either clause initial or (as here) immediately before the finite verb (see *GrHL* §27.12).

13–18 is a report of ongoing harvest of grapes in the royal vineyards and a plea for more laborers.

I take *mān* in line 15, therefore, as the optative man "Oh that … would," despite its plene writing. Such plene-written optative *man*s exist. See CHD *man*.

42b. HKM 37
Piggyback Letter of […] to […]

Discussion: Alp 1991a, 56 (sub PN "Ḫašš[a?]").

(Beginning of the piggyback letter is lost in the break at the beginning of the reverse.)	
(rev. 1′) […. aš-šu-]ul ḫa-at-re-eš-ke (rev. 2′) […] du-uš-ki-iš-ke-mi	(rev. 1′) … Keep sending your greetings. (rev. 2′) … I am rejoicing.
(rev. 3′) ^{m}Ḫa-aš-š[a-x-x-]ti-ya-kán kat-ta-an (rev. 4′) ḫu-u-ma-an SIG$_5$-in nu ŠE[Š D]ÙG.[G]A-*YA* (rev. 5′) a-pé-ni-iš-ša-an ša-a-ak (rev. 6′) na-aš-ta le-e ku-wa-at-ka$_4$ (rev. 7′) la-<aḫ>-la-aḫ-ḫi-iš-ke-ši	(rev. 3′) All is well with Ḫašša-x-x-ti too. (rev. 4′–5′) You should know this, my dear brother. (rev. 6′) And please do not worry at all.

Commentary

3 Alp (1991a, 56) restores this line ^{m}*Ḫa-aš-š[a É-]ti-ya-kán* ("O Ḫašša! With your family …") so that a man named either Ḫašša or Ḫaššana is addressed and told that his family in Ḫattuša is safe and well. The copy shows more space available than needed for Alp's restoration. I have preferred to take ^{m}*Ḫa-aš-š[a-x-x-]ti-ya* as one long personal name. A vocatival form at this point seems to me unnecessary. This information was for the person to whom this piggyback letter was intended. Were it not for the personal name wedge at the beginning of the line, one could make a case for a common noun here: *ḫašša[nni=]ti=ya=kan kattan* "with your family too."

43. HKM 38
From the King to […]

Text: Mşt. 75/17. **Find spot:** H/5 Room 9. **Copy:** HKM 38. **Edition:** Alp

1991a, 188–91 (no. 38). **Translation**: Imparati and de Martino 2004, 181 (lines 3–7).

(1) *UM-M*[*A* dUTU-*Š*]*I-MA* (2) *A-NA* m[... *Q*]*I-BI-MA*	(1–2) Thus speaks His Majesty: Say to ...:
(3) ma-an-za É[RIN.MEŠ] EGIR-an (4) ka-ru-ú p[a-a]ḫ-ḫa-aš-nu-ut (5) an-tu-uḫ-ša-ša-kán ut-tar (6) ki-iš-ša-ri-i an-da (7) ka-ru-ú da-iš	(3–7) If you had already protected the troops behind yourself, they would have already put into (their) hand the matter of the persons!
(8) *MA-ḪAR* dUTU-*ŠI* (9) [li-l]i-wa-aḫ-ḫu-u-an-zi (10) [u-u]n-ni ka-a-ša ut-tar (11) ku-it-ki nu-un-na-ša-at (12) ú-wa-u-e-ni ar-ḫa (13) ták-[š]a-an a-ri-ya-u-e-ni	(8–13) Drive quickly to My Majesty. There is a problem, and we must proceed to work it out jointly by oracle.

Commentary

3–7 I take the man particles here as expressing a contrary-to-fact condition and its unrealized outcome (*GrHL* §23.16). A different interpretation—taking both clauses as speaker-optatives—was proposed by Imparati and de Martino (2004, 793–94), who refer to CHD L–N *man*, itself based on Hoffner 1982a. Their translation fails to translate the particle *-za*, which I take to represent the pronoun "yourself" on which EGIR-*an* "behind" depends. For the latest grammatical treatment of "speaker optative" *man* see *GrHL* §23.11. The same complex—the reflexive particle *-za*, EGIR-*an* and the verb *paḫšanu-*/*paḫḫašnu-*, is found in KBo 19.42 rev.? 7–8: [dUTU?-*Š*]*I-ma-za* EGIR-*an pa-aḫ-ša-nu-wa-a*[*n ḫar-ak*] (8) [...-]KA *pa-aḫ-ḫa-aš-nu-an ḫar-ak* "But keep [His Maj]esty protected behind yourself, and keep your [...] protected."

7 Contra de Martino and Imparati, *daiš* (line 7) cannot be second-person singular ("avessi"), which would require *daitta* or *dait* (see *GrHL* §13.15). It must be third-person. I have therefore taken *da-iš* here as 3rd sg., as Alp (1991a) also did. But I take the referent to be the grammatically singular collective noun behind ÉRIN.MEŠ "troops." Hence, my translation "they."

12 *uwaweni* cannot (as Alp thinks) be a form of *au*(*š*)- "to see," but is the verb *uwa-* ("to come"), used as a serial verb in the sense of "to proceed to (do *something*)" (*GrHL* §§24.31–24.42). The attested forms of "we will see" are *ú-me-e-ni*, *a-ú-ma-ni*, and *a-ú(-um)-me-ni*. See *GrHL* §13.22; *HED* A, 234–44; and Kammenhuber, *HW*2 I, 577.

44. HKM 39
From […] to […]

Text: Mşt. 75/100. **Find spot:** G/5 Portico. **Copy**: HKM 39. **Edition**: Alp 1991a, 190–91 (no. 39).

(First 5 or 6 lines of tablet broken away.)	
(1) […] x ku-i-e-[…] (2) […] x […] ma-a-an (3) x x x (4) na-aš-ša-an k[u]-e-[da-ni] (5) [u]d-da-ni-i ḫa-at-r[a-a-it] (6) nu ANŠE.<KUR.RA.ḪI>.A m[e-e]k-ki (7) ḫu-u-it-ti-ya-an (8) e-eš-du	(1–8) … Let many horses be drawn up for the matter about which he/you sent.
(9) *A-NA* ANŠE.KUR.RA.ḪI.A-ya (10) [*I*]*Š-TU* 2 *ŠA-A-TI* ŠE [… pí-ya-an-du]	(9–10) And for the horses let them give barley, with two seahs …

44b. HKM 39
Piggyback Letter of Ḫimmuili to Uzzu.

Although many letters *to* Ḫi(m)muili were found at Maşat Höyük, this piggyback letter is one of only two letters in which this Ḫimmuili functions as the *sender*. The other is HKM 56 (text 59).

(11) *UM-MA* mḪi-im-m[u-i-l]i (12) *A-NA* mU-uz-z[u-u *QÍ-B*]*Í-MA*	(11–12) Thus speaks Ḫimmuili: Say to Uzzū:
(13) ka-a-ša x[…] (14) LÚ URUGa-aš-ga […] x (15) me-mi-iš-ta […]-ma-wa-za-k[án] (16) ú-iz-zi […-]zi (17) […]… (l.e. 1) […-]x-an (l.e. 2) […]-an-na-ri-kán (l.e. 3) [… pa-aḫ-ḫa-aš-nu-an-te-e]š a-ša-an-d[u]	*(Rest of the letter too fragmentary for translation. Mention in line 14 of a Kaškaean man.)*

45. HKM 43
[…] to […]

Text: Mşt. 75/73. **Find spot:** G/5 Room 8. **Copy:** HKM 43. **Edition**: Alp 1991a, 194–97 (no. 43). **Discussion**: Alp 1991a, 88 (on Pittaruru), 99 (on

Taruli), 107 (on Zilapiya); Beal 1992, 128–29; Goedegebuure 2003, 195 and 313 (obv. 1–7); Marizza 2007a, 157 (Pittaruru), 163 (Tarul[i]), 169 (Zilapiya).

Alp writes about Zilapiya: "In HKM 43 obv. 2′ Zilapiya appears in connection with the new troops and perhaps with the deportation of population groups of hostile, Kaška villages. but since the beginning of the letter is not preserved, and the letter is for the most part fragmentary, many details remain unclear" (1991a, 107; my translation of the German).

A Hattic derivation of the PN Taruli may be possible on the basis of the Hattic words listed by Soysal 2004, 760–61.

(First 8 to 10 lines broken away.)	
(1′) na-[aš-]ta mTa-ru-l[i?]-y[a]-aš?[132] (2′) tu-uz-zi-in mZi-la-pí-ya-aš-ša (3′) ÉRIN.MEŠ GIBIL ma-aḫ-ḫa-an ša-ra-a ú-wa-te-er (4′) KUR-ya-kán ku-i-e-eš an-da URU.DIDLI.ḪI.A (5′) ar-nu-ma-an-zi! ta-ra-a-an-te-eš	(1′–5′) How could they have brought up the army of Taruli(ya) and the new troops of Zilapiya? The cities in the territory which were promised to be relocated,
(6′) nu a-pu-u-uš URU.DIDLI.ḪI.A ka-ru-ú (7′) ar-nu-er na-aš-ta a-pa-a-at ut-tar (8′) ka-ru-ú aš-nu-er na-aš-ta ma-a-an (9′) tu-uz-zi-in š[a]-r[a]-a […] (10′) ú-wa-te-er nu […]	(6′–10′) they have already relocated those cities. They have already finished that assignment. And when they have brought the army up to …, then ….
(11′) ma-a-an a-pu-u-u[š URU.DIDLI.ḪI.A] (12′) ar-nu-ut-te-ni [ÉRIN.ME]Š x x- […] x […] (13′) [š]a-[r]a-a ma-aḫ-ḫa-an ú-wa-te <-te>-ni	(11′–13′) If? you relocate those cities, as soon as (or: when) you bring up infantry and chariotry?,
(14′) [nu] k[i-i]š-ša-an-ma tar-te-ni (15′) […-]ni *A-NA* URU.DIDLI.ḪI.A (16′) […-u?-]e?-ni (17′) […] mPí-it-ta-ru-ru-ya (18′) […] x na-at ku-wa-pí (18′a) […]	(14′) you must speak as follows: (15′–16′) We will … to/for the cities. *(17′–18a′ too badly broken for translation.)*
(19′) […]x a-pé-e-da-aš URU.DIDLI.ḪI.A-aš (20′) […] na-at ú-iz-	*(19′–24′ too badly broken for translation.)*

zi ap-pé-ez-zi-an (21′) [… -]x-ša-ri ú-wa-an-zi (22′) [….Ḫ]I?.A? [k]u-wa-pí i-da-a-lu i-ya-an-zi (23′) […-]x-ni? ú-wa-te<-te>-ni x[…] (24′) […] x x x x […]	

Commentary

1 The traces in HKM and on my photo can support Alp's reading ᵐ*Ta-ru-l*[*i*-, but not the following -e]š?-x. But they could also support ᵐ*Ta-ru-*⌈*uz*⌉-*z*[*i*-…].

1–3 Both Alp (1991a, 195) and Beal (1992, 128–29) mistook *Tarul*[*i*-…] and Zilapiya as the grammatical subjects of "they brought up." The grammar does not permit that interpretation.

3 The "new troops" of line 3 are probably inexperienced (or "green," to use the colloquialism employed by Beal 1992, 128–29, in referring to them). Line 3 is edited in CHD Š, 220–21.

18a Quite possibly there was afinal verb on the left side of the line immediately before the paragraph stroke.

46. HKM 44
From […] to […]

Text: Mşt. 75/86. **Find spot:** G/5 Room 8. **Copy**: HKM 44. **Edition**: Alp 1991a: 196–97 (no. 44). **Discussion**: Alp 1991a: 78 (Marakui), 323–24 (discussion of evidence for the Hittite reading of the logogram *KARTAPPU*); Klinger 1995a: 100 (Marakui); Hoffner 2002a: 167 (on temporal EGIR-*an* in line 7); Marizza 2007a: 150 (Marakui).

Since the imperative verb in line 8 is plural, this letter must have had more than one addressee. The identity of the sender is unknown. Klinger (1995a: 100) excludes Alp's identification of this Marakui with the man mentioned in a land grant text datable to the reign of Alluwamna, on the grounds that the separation in time from the Maşat text is too great.

(First half of the letter is broken away.)	
(lower edge 1) […] x x […] (2) [a]n-	(lower edge 1) … Since I have just

da-ma-kán ka-a-[aš$^{?}$-ma$^{?}$[133]] (rev. 3) ^{m}Ma-ra-ku-in (rev. 4) ku-it ^{LÚ}*QAR-TAP*<*-PU*> (rev. 5) pa-ra-a ne-eḫ-ḫu-un (rev. 6) na-aš a-pí-ya e-eš-d[u] (rev. 7) na-an-za EGIR-an SIG$_5$-i[n] (rev. 8) wa-tar-na-aḫ-tén (rev. 9) pa-aḫ-ḫa-aš-nu-ma-aš-ši-k[án] (rev. 10) ki-iš-ri-i an-da [ÉRIN.MEŠ] (rev. 11) [S]IG$_5$-in da-i[š-tén]	dispatched (to you) Marakui, the charioteer, let him stay there (with you). And afterwards give him detailed instructions. But place securely in his hands troops$^{?}$ for his protection.

47. HKM 45
From [...] to [...]

Text: Mşt. 76/1. **Find spot:** G/5 Room 8. **Copy**: HKM 45. **Edition**: Alp 1991a: 198–201 (no. 45). **Discussion**: On the food shortage (line 19) see also text 29 (= HKM 24) and Houwink ten Cate 1998, 162; del Monte 1992: 27 (Ḫapara), 71 (Kašepura), 152 (Taḫazzimuna; according to Forlanini, Taḫazzimuna = Dazmana near Turhal).

(2) [...] pu-nu-u[š ...] nam-ma-z[a-k]án [...] (3) [... na]-aš pa-ri-ya-an x [...] (4) [... ^{URU}Ta-ḫa-a]z-zi-mu-na-an ^{URU}Ḫa-pa-ra-an [...] (5) [... a]r-nu-ud-du nam-ma-ya-ká[n] (6) [...] x x x x KUR-e an-da (7) [...] x x ar-nu-ud-du	(2–7) ... ask ... Then ... ... Let him relocate[134] the town Tahazzimuna, the town Ḫapara, and ... And then ... let him relocate ... in the land.
(8) [... S]IG$_5$-in e-ep-du nam-ma-aš al-[...] (9) [...-]ya-id-du ud-da-na-a-aš-ma k[u-iš EN-aš] (10) [...] *A-NA PA-NI* LÚ.MEŠ KUR-*TI* ga-a[š-za] (11) [...] KUR-e an-da du-ud-du-uš-k[i ...]	(8–11) Let ... hold ... well. Then let him ... But he who is master of affairs .... In the presence of the men of the land a food shortage ... administer$^{?}$ ... in the land.
(12) [...]x-x-x-x-ma ḫal-la-e$^{?}$-ni x x [...] (13) [...-]uš ku-iš x-x-ak-k[i-...] (14) [^{m}Z]i-la-pí-ya-aš ka-a-aš-ma-a[t$^{?}$-ta$^{?}$ ...] (15) a-pu-u-un ... [...]	*(12–15 Too broken for translation.)*

(16) [ÉR]IN.MEŠ-ya-kán da-at-tén na-an-kán [*I-NA* URU...] (17) ša-ra-a tar-na-ad-du nu U[RU...] (18) pa-aḫ-ḫa-aš-nu-ud-d[u ...]	(16–18) Take (pl.) troops, and let them[135] escort? him up .... Let them guard ....
[*About 3 lines' space uninscribed*]	
(19) nam-ma-[k]án KUR-e ga-aš-za ku-i[t ...] (20) URUKa-še-pu-u-ra še-er na[-an URU...] (21) pé-ḫu-te-ed-du nu-za pa-id-d[u ḫal-ki-in] (22) tu-kán-zi da-a-ú na-a[n-za-kán URU-ri ša-ra-a] (23) pé-e-da-ú nu-uš-ši-kán NIN[DAtu-u-ma-ti-in] (24) [me-e]k-ki ḫa-an-d[a-i]d-d[u] (25) [k]a-a-ša UD?-m[a? ...] (26) [...] nam-ma *A-NA* [...] (27) [GIŠa]r-mi-iz-z[i ...] (28) [... a]r?-[mi?-iz?-zi? ...] (l. e. 1) [K]UR?-e? ga-aš-za ÉRIN.MEŠ ANŠE.K[UR.RA.MEŠ ...] (l. e. 2) *I-NA* [U]RU[K]a-ši-pu-u-r[a ...] (l. e. 3) [...]x ku-iš x[...]	(19–24) Furthermore, because there is a food shortage in the land, up in the city Kašepura, let them[180] conduct him .... And let them proceed to take seed? grain?, and carry it up to the city, and let them prepare much *tumati*-bread for it. (25–26) ... (27) ... bridge (28) ... bridge ... (l. e. 1) ... in the territory a food shortage, troops and horses ... (l. e. 2) in Kašepura ... (l. e. 3) ... who ...
(Rest of the tablet too broken for connected translation.)	

Commentary

Although the broken condition of the tablet prevents connected translation of most of the letter, individual words (some without context) indicate an interesting content: a bridge (*armizzi*, lines 27–28) and a food shortage (lines 10, 19, l. e. 1). On the mentions of or allusions to food shortages see §1.2.20.4.

16–24 The translation in Alp 1991a is faulty. The singular verbs here all refer to the ÉRIN.MEŠ ("troop"), which covers a grammatically singular Hittite noun. See n. 135. My translation "escort(?)" is tentative, since the verb *tarna-* has a wide range of possible English translations. Basically, it means either "cause to go" or "allow to go." A different verb, *pehute-* "lead, conduct," is used in line 21.

21–22 contains a serial construction *paiddu ... dau*. For this construction see *GrHL* §24.31 and following.

2.2.2.4. Letters to the King (48–54)

On the implications of the presence in Tapikka of these outgoing letters to the king see §1.2.9.

48. HKM 46
To the King from Adad-bēlī

Text: Mşt. 75/113. **Find spot:** G/5 Portico. **Photo:** Alp 1991a: pl. 10 (showing the handwriting of Adad-bēlī). **Dimensions** (taken from the photo; see §1.2.8.2): 6.5 cm wide × 5.5 cm tall. **Copy**: HKM 46. **Edition**: Alp 1991a: 200–203, 324 (no. 46). **Translation**: del Monte 1992: 56–57 (lines 3–12). **Discussion**: Hoffner 1979 (on the meaning of *latti-* = *ŠUTU* "tribe, tribal troop"); Alp 1991a: 15 (on the GN Išteruwa), 32 (on Mt. Šakaddunuwa and the Zuliya River), 47 (on the GN Zišpa), 52 (on Adad-bēlī), 324 (discussion of *latti-* = *ŠUTU* "tribal troop," as determined by Hoffner, but also the long-distance scouts mentioned in line 19); Goedegebuure 2002–2003: 20; 2003: 84 (lines 8–17); Francia 1996: §3.3.6 (lines 8–12); del Monte 1992 *passim* (on the toponyms); Forlanini 2002: 259, 267–68; Bryce 2003b: 180 (on lines 3–7).

Forlanini explains the enemy incursion described here geographically and strategically, as follows:

> The letter of Adad-beli, HBM 46, shows one of these incursions [of the Kaškaeans]. The writer— announcing to the king that the enemy has crossed the border at two points, Išteruwa and Zišpa—thinks he might enter the region of Mt. Šaktunuwa, and that, if he should decide to return, he could penetrate the province. Therefore, in order to be sure that he can keep the herds outside the shelter of the walls of Tapikka, he decides to send scouts into Mt. Ḫapidduini. It is possible to attempt a reconstruction of these events on a map. The two enemy contingents would have passed through the mountains to the north of the province near the two mentioned localities, of which Zišpa has a very clear name, which in Hattic signifies "on the mountain." From there they didn't turn back into the province, but instead headed to the southeast to penetrate the massif of Šaktunuwa, going in the direction of the Upper Land. At this point a turn towards the west would have brought them to a position for a direct attack on Tapikka, and only the scouts posted on Mt. Ḫapidduini would have been able to give the alarm in time to allow the livestock to be brought into the shelter of the city walls" (author's translation of Forlanini's Italian).

All this is, of course, assuming that the initial movement of two distinct Kaškaean "tribes" (*latti-* = Akk. *ŠUTU*, see Hoffner 1979) was intended to be hostile. Certainly Adad-bēlī saw it had that potential, fearing damage to the KUR and theft of Hittite livestock. But given the fact that the Kaškaean groups were sedentary pastoral communities practicing transhumance, meaning that they lived in lower elevation settlements in winter, moving with their herds to mountain campsites in the summer (Singer 2007, 169, and Yakar 2000, 300–301), it is quite possible that the two "tribes" moving through the mountains (Šaktunuwa and Ḫapidduini) at Išteruwa and Zišpa were leading their flocks to summer pasture sites. Considering the large numbers of people involved in such movements, it is not impossible that Hittites in the plains below considered them a military threat. If this was the case, then the scout sent out to monitor their movements would have reported back to Adad-bēlī that there was no threat.

(1) *A-NA* dUTU-*ŠI BE-LÍ-YA QÍ-BÍ-MA* (2) *UM-MA* m.dU-*BE-LÍ* ARAD-*KA-MA*	(1–2) Say to His Majesty, my lord: Thus speaks Adad-bēlī, your servan*t*:
(3) ka-a-ša-kán LÚ.KÚR pa-an-ga-ri-it (4) 2 *AŠ-RA* za-a-i[š] nu-kán 1-iš (5) la-at-ti-iš *I-NA* URUIš-te-ru-wa (6) za-a-iš 1-iš-ma-kán la-at-ti-iš (7) *I-NA* URUZi-iš-pa za-iš	(3–7) The enemy (probably Kaška troops) has crossed (the frontier) in large numbers in two places. One tribal troop crossed at the city Išteruwa; another tribal troop crossed at the city Zišpa.
(8) na-aš-kán ma-a-an *I-NA* KUR ḪUR.SAGŠa-kad-du-nu-wa (9) pa-re-e-an pa-iz-zi (10) ma-a-an EGIR-pa ku-wa-at-ga (11) wa-aḫ-nu-zi na-aš-kán KUR-ya (12) an-da ú-iz-zi nu-uš-ši EGIR-an (13) na-ú-i ku-it-ki (14) te-ek-ku-uš-ši-ya-iz-zi	(8–14) Whether he has gone over (to) the land of Mt. Šakaddunuwa,[136] or perhaps has turned back and come into the territory, no trace of him has shown up yet.[137]
(15) ma-an-kán dUTU-*ŠI BE-LÍ-YA BE-LU* (16) ku-in-ki pa-ra-a na-it-ti (17) ma-an[!138] KUR-i[139] LÚ.KÚR *Ú-UL* dam-mi-iš-ḫa-iz-zi	(15–17) If Your Majesty, my lord, were to send some lord, the enemy would not damage the countryside.
(18) am-mu-ga-kán (19) *ŠA* KASKAL GÍD.DA LÚ.MEŠNÍ.ZU-*TIM* (20) ḪUR.SAGḪa-píd-du-i-ni an-da (21) ša-ša-	(18–27) For my part, I am sending long-distance scouts[140] to pass the night in the Ḫapidduini Moun-

an-na pé-e-i-iš-ke-mi (22) nu-mu ma-aḫ-ḫa-an me-mi-an (23) EGIR-pa ú-da-an-zi ḪUR.SAG-aš-wa (24) *ŠA* LÚ.KÚR ud-da-na-za pár-ku-iš (25) nu-kán URUTa-pí-ig-ga-za (26) GU_4.ḪI.A UDU.ḪI.A kat-ta *QA-TAM-MA* (27) tar-ši-ik-ki-mi (l. e. 1) nu dUTU-*ŠI BE-LÍ-YA* (l. e. 2) *QA-TAM-MA* [š]a-a-ak	tains.[141] As soon as they bring me back word: "The mountain is clear of any trace of the enemy," I will resume letting the cattle and sheep down out of Tapikka. (l. e. 1–2) Your Majesty, my lord, should know this.

Commentary

On the possible dating of HKM 46–51 to the end of the reign of Arnuwanda I, see above in §1.2.5.

12–14 That is, he has left no trail of evidence about himself. Goedegebuure prefers to see in the dative-locative *-ši* a reference to the mountain. She translates: "nothing yet shows up behind it (the mountain)" (2002–2003, 84). For intransitive *tekkuššiye-* (here *tekkuššiyai-*) see Oettinger 1979, 355.[142]

18 "For my part" reflects the presence of the contrastive clitic -a on *ammuga*. See *GrHL* §29.23 and following.

24 My "any trace" renders *uddanaza* "from the matter/thing."

25–27 I understand *QATAMMA* (= Hitt. *apeniššan*, usually "likewise") here to mean "as before," hence my translation "will resume." The cattle were withdrawn into the walled cities when there was an enemy threat in the vicinity (Beal 1992, 272, and 1995), and then after he had left and the area was inspected to assure it was safe, the livestock would be let out of the city. See the explicit instructions given to the provincial governor: "When the scouts see any sign of the enemy, they will send a message immediately. Let them (then) close up the cities; they are not to let out the fieldworkers, cattle, sheep, horses, (or) donkeys. ... But in the morning, the scouts (come out) from the city. They must inspect the *kuranna*-s (see above on text 31 with note on line 8) thoroughly [...] and take (their) posts. They may then let the workers, cattle, sheep, horses, and donkeys down out of the city" (translation by McMahon in Hallo and Younger 1997; edition in Pecchioli Daddi 2003a, 82–85, 90–91). In this letter it is the mountain, instead of the *kuranna*-s, that must be clear of the enemy before the workers and livestock can be let out. The imperfective verb forms[143] *pé-e-i-iš-ki-mi* and *tar-ši-ik-ki-mi* reflect the fact that the commander will be doing this often, whenever an enemy appears and subsequently disappears from the vicinity.

49. ABoT 60
To the King from Kaššū?

Text: AnAr 9133. **Find spot:** unexcavated piece that came to the Ankara museum, undoubtedly in originating in Maşat. **Copy**: ABoT 60. **Dating:** Hoffner 1972. **Edition**: Laroche 1960b; Hagenbuchner 1989b, 76–79. **Discussion**: von Schuler 1965, 43, 75, 81, 93, 97, 98; de Martino 2005b, 307; Sidel'tsev 2007, 622.

The sender, perhaps Kaššū, relays to the king a message from Nerikkaili of Tapḫallu to the effect that he is short of all critical resources for defense against the enemy. This enemy is not called "Kaška," but he refers to Kaškaean fugitives who used to join him and fight alongside the Hittite troops as no longer coming. The enemy has assembled a huge number of fighters (7,000; lines 10–12), and yet they are not referred to as "tribes" (*ŠUTI*$^{HI.A}$ or *latti-*), as is often customary when the enemy is the Kaška. Like the Kaška, this enemy invades and carries off livestock and personnel (in this case, oxherds and shepherds, whose skills were made good use of by the semi-nomadic Kaška), see lines 12–14.

Von Schuler (1965, 43) considers the enemy in this text to be the Kaškaeans, and even suggests that their leader may have been Piggattalli, who is known from other texts in which he led large numbers of Kaškaean troops against the Hittites.

In lines 15–18 the enemy's own thoughts are relayed. He is concerned that the Hittites may build (or complete what has already been begun?) a fortress to guard the main routes in that area. If the fortress is built, the Hittites themselves will have free passage along those routes, but the enemy will not. Since this is a quote within a quote, it is impossible on the basis of the presence or absence of the quotative particle *-wa* to know when the enemy's words end and Nerikkaili's continue. Line 19 could be either the enemy's or Nerikkaili's. In line 20, the sender's words to the king resume. The king needs to know—and he can see from the words of the enemy just quoted—how strategic this location is for the Hittites to control. It is the enemy's "granary?" (*arziyan*). For that very reason he is invading in large numbers, but the sender is short of horse troops. When the enemy invaded, it would be vital to the defending Hittites that they also have good horse troops. The complaint in rev. 5–7 that Kaškaean fugitives no longer come and join the Hittite forces is particularly meaningful in this context, since they might have provided both badly needed horses and horsemanship skills.

(1′) […-]an-te-eš (2′) […] (3′) a-pád-d[a-an … …] me-mi-an (4′) ka-ru-ú *ṬUP-PA*ḪI.A ḫa-a[t]-ra-a-nu-un (5′) nu-kán ma-a-aḫ-ḫa-an a-pé-e *ṬUP-PA*ḪI.A (6′) *MA-ḪAR* dUTU-*ŠI* *BE-LÍ-YA* pa-ra-a ne-eḫ-ḫu-un	(1′–2′) … … … for that reason … (3′–4′) I already sent the … message (on) tablets. (5′) And as soon as I dispatched those tablets (6′) to Your Majesty, my lord,
(7′) ša-li-ka-aš-ma-mu ka-ru-wa-ri-wa-ar (8′) mNi-ri-ik-ka$_4$-i-li-iš LÚ URUTa-ap-ḫa[-al-lu nu-mu] (9′) me-mi-an ú-da-aš ku-it-wa šu-ul-la-an-ni ḫar-mi (10′) LÚ.KÚR-wa ku-iš *I-NA* URUTa-ri-it-ta-ra-a (11′) ka-ru-ú an-da a-ar-aš nu-wa-ra-aš (12′) 7 *LI-IM* ar-ḫa-wa LÚ.MEŠSIPA.GU$_4$ LÚ.MEŠSIPA.UDU (13′) *Ú-UL* da-li-iš-ke-ez-zi *IŠ-TU* GU$_4$-wa (14′) ka-ši-iš-ke-ez-zi (15′) nu-wa ki-iš-ša-an me-mi-iš-ke-ez-zi (16′) ma-a-an-wa ku-u-un BÀD-an ú-e-da-an-zi (17′) nu-wa-aš-ma-aš KASKAL.ḪI.A *Ú-UL* EGIR-pa ḫi-iš-wa-an-da-ri (18′) an!-za-aš-ma-wa-ra-at-kán iš-tap-pa-an-da-ri (19′) nu-wa ma-aḫ-ḫa-an i-ya-u-e-ni	(7′) Early the following morning Nerikkaili, the man from Tapḫallu, awoke me (8′) and brought me the message: (9′) "What do I have in the way of hostages? (10′–12′) The enemy who has already invaded Tarittarā numbers 7,000! (12′) He isn't leaving behind oxherds (or) shepherds. (13′–14′) He is *supplying himself* with cattle. (15′) And he is saying: (16′) 'If they build this fortress, (17′) will not the roads lie open to them? (18′) But to us they will be closed. (19′) So what shall we do?'"
(20′) nu dUTU-*ŠI BE-LÍ-YA* ša-a-ak pé-e-da-an (21′) me-ek-ki na-ak-ki *A-NA* LÚ KÚR-ya-at![144] (22′) ar-zi-ya-an nu-mu ka-a-š[a …] (23′) kat-ta pa-an-ga-ri-it ú-iz-z[i …] (24′) […-]BIḪI.A[…]ta-an-x[…] (25′) [n]am-ma ANŠE.KUR.RA.ḪI.A-ma-mu […] (26′) [k]i-ša-ri	(20′–21′) Your Majesty, my lord, should know: The place is very important: (21′–22′) it is the enemy's granary! (Therefore,) he is already coming down to me in large numbers. … … furthermore, I am short of horse troops.
(rev. 1) [ki-nu-un m]D[a-]a-[t]i-i-li[-iš] (rev. 2) *I-N*[*A* UR]UŠa-pí-nu-wa EGIR-an […] (rev. 3) nu-mu-kán dUTU-*ŠI BE-LÍ-YA* ARAD.MEŠ-*KA*? (rev. 4) li-li-wa-aḫ-ḫu-wa-an-zi na-i	(rev. 1–4) Now Tatili … behind the town Šapinuwa. So Your Majesty, my lord, send me quickly your servants!

(5) LÚ.MEŠ ^{URU}Ka$_4$-aš-ga-ya-mu-uš-ša-an ku-i-e-eš (6) an-da i-ya-an-ta-at nu-mu nam-ma (7) kat-ta-an *UL* ku-iš-ki ú-iz-zi	(5–7) None of the Kaškaean men who used to come in to me comes with me anymore.
(8) an?-ni?-[m]a-mu ka-a-ša x x x (9) kat-ta NU.GÁL ku-iš-[ki m].^{d}*SÎN*-EN LÚ.GÉŠPU?? (10) ku-iš NU.GÁL nu-za ḫa-an-za-an *Ú-UL* ku-e-da-ni-ki (11) x x x x e-ep-zi	(8–11)… there is no one with me … *SÎN*-EN, the ^{LÚ}GÉŠPU, who is not present, gives support to no one.

Commentary

obv. 5–9 is edited in CHD sub *šalik(i)-* 2. As rightly claimed by Melchert 2005a n. 10, *šullanni* here is a form of the word *šullatar* that means "hostages." If, however, it should prove to be the homonym *šullatar* "arrogance, presumption?" identified by Melchert (perhaps even by extension "aggravation"), the sentence could be paraphrased "As if I didn't have enough (to deal with) …" (so, according to a suggestion by Beckman, personal communication).

obv. 16–18 Puhvel (*HED* E/I, 472) takes the clitic pronoun *-šmaš* in line 17 as "to you (pl.)." But the unnamed enemy is describing how the completion of the Hittite fortress will have the opposite effect on the opposing forces, "them" (*-šmaš*) and "us" (*anzaš*). Therefore, I have construed the first clause as a negative rhetorical question (see Hoffner 1995a, 89–90).

obv. 18 Twice Hagenbuchner (1989a, 151 nn. 13–14) mistakenly cites this line as containing a clause-initial verb to which clitics are attached. On *nu* ^{d}UTU-*ŠI BE-LÍ-YA ša-a-ak* in

obv. 20 See Hagenbuchner 1989a, 99 §4.1.

obv. 20–21 is edited in CHD sub *nakki-* A 1 e, *peda-* A e 8′ d', *šak(k)-* 3 b, and *GrHL* §15.9. As noted in the cited treatments, one could also translate: "The place is very difficult to reach."

rev. 3–4 For *lilaḫḫuwanzi* as infinitive of manner see *GrHL* §25.35.

rev. 5–7 are edited in CHD sub *-šan* B 2 f 1′.

50. HKM 47
To the King from Šarla-LAMMA

Text: Mşt. 75/110. **Find spot:** G/5 Portico. **Copy:** HKM 47. **Edition:** Alp

1991a, 202–7, 324–25 (no. 47). **Discussion:** van den Hout 2001a, 429–30; 2007b, 392.

On the possible dating of HKM 46–51 to the end of the reign of Arnuwanda I, see above in §1.2.5.

Although addressed by Šarla-LAMMA to the king, this letter represents a report of the activities of several augurs (§1.2.11), as can be seen by the "we" verb forms. Beckman has observed:

> Local authorities within Anatolia were no more than the surrogates of the Great King, exercising little in the way of independent initiative. Rather, their role was to provide the monarch with the information needed to issue his orders, which they then dutifully carried out. This is most definitely the picture painted in the Maşat letters, where the Hittite king intervenes directly in many affairs, concerning himself above all with troop movements. Interestingly, three letters from Tapikka deal with the performance of oracles, and in addition a fragmentary oracle report was found in the archive. Such material is also known from Emar and Alalakh, suggesting that divination was an integral part of Hittite administration on the provincial level as well as in the capital. (1995a: 24 with nn. 25-30)

Šarla-LAMMA reports that his group was repeatedly frustrated by the observed birds, which did not give an unambiguous answer to the queries that they posed. The somewhat obscure expression *appa tittanu(ške)-* in lines 6, 9, and 11,[145] used in one text (KUB 23.16 iii 6′) of repulsing or repelling an invading army, must according to the context mean something like "refused to give (us) an answer" (so also van den Hout 2001a, 429). When the first inquiries in Šipišaši, Pišatenitišša, and the land of Malazziya failed, the augurs tried other locations, hoping to find one that was propitious and would yield a result. But in Panāta and Kašaša they met only with failure. The king had intended to march from Kašaša to Takkašta, but tarried in Kašaša, until the augurs could give him the information he sought which was essential for his expedition. Finally, the augurs returned to Tapikka, where they had success (expressed by *arḫa uškenu-*), and from where they send this report both of the upshot of the oracle's decision, namely that the king will be successful against Takkašta, and (almost like an appendix) a detailed description of the course of the oracular investigation, so that the king's own specialists can see how the final decision was reached. The oracle's decision, which is relayed here, is phrased in the third person "(the king) will …," in contrast to the augurs' own words to the king in the body of the letter, which are "you" forms. This shows that the intention is to reflect the actual wording of the questions that the augurs had posed to the oracle for a “yes/no” reply: “Will His Majesty (successfully) attack Takkašta?” and “Will he reap (its) crops?”

(1) *A-NA* ^{d}UTU-*ŠI BE-LÍ-YA QÍ-B*[*Í-MA*] (2) *UM-MA* ^{m}Šar-la-^{d}LAMMA ARAD-*KA-M*[*A*]	(1–2) Say to His Majesty, my lord: Thus speaks your servant Šarla-LAMMA:
(3) ^{URU}Ši-pí-ša-ši-in ^{URU}Pí-ša-te-ni-ti-iš-š[a-an$^{?}$] (4) KUR ^{URU}Ma-la-az-zi-ya ku-it uš-ga-u-en nu-u[n$^{?}$-na$^{?}$-aš$^{?}$][146] (5) [MUŠE]N$^{?}$ ar-ḫa *Ú-UL* ku-iš-ki ḫu-u-ul-la-i (6) MUŠEN.ḪI.A-ma-an-na-aš EGIR-pa ti-it-ta-nu-uš-kán-zi	(3–6) Regarding the fact that we were making oracular observations (of birds) in the towns Šipišaši, Pišatenitišša, and the land of Malazziya: no bird$^{?}$ was actually defeating us, but the birds were *refusing to give us an answer*.
(7) nu-[z]a ^{d}UTU-*ŠI* ku-it *BE-LÍ-YA* ^{URU}Ka-a-ša-<ša$^{?}$> e-eš-ta (8) ú-e-eš-na-aš ^{URU}Pa-na-da e-šu-ú-en ma-aḫ-ḫa-an-ma ^{d}UTU-*ŠI* (9) *BE-LÍ-YA* ḫu-u-i-it-ti-ya-at nu-un-na-aš MUŠEN ku-it EGIR-pa ti-it-ta-nu-ut (10) nu EGIR-pa ^{URU}Ka-a-ša-ša u-un-nu-me-en nu-un-na-aš ^{URU}Ka-a-ša-ša-ya (11) [MUŠ]EN.ḪI.A EGIR-pa ti-it-nu-uš-ke-wa-an da-e-er	(7–11) Since you, Your Majesty, my lord, were in Kašaša, we situated ourselves in Panāta. But when you, Your Majesty, my lord, marched$^{?}$, since the bird *refused to give* us *an answer*, we drove back to Kašaša, and the birds began *refusing to give* us *an answer* (in?) Kašaša as well.
(12) nu EGIR-pa ^{URU}Ta-pí-ig-ga u-un-nu-me-en na-aš-ta ka-a-ša (13) ^{URU}Ta-pí-ig-ga-az-za$^{?}$ ar-ḫa uš-ke-nu-mi<-en$^{?}$>[147] nu ^{d}UTU-*ŠI BE-LÍ-YA* (14) *QA-TAM-MA* ša-a-ak	(12–14) Then we came back to Tapikka and from (the base of) Tapikka have now carried out the auguries! So let Your Majesty, my lord, be informed!
(15) [nu-]un-na-aš *ŠA* ^{URU}Tág-ga-aš-ta im-ma ut-tar a-wa$^{!}$-an kat-ta (16) [a-]ú$^{!}$-me$^{!}$-en$^{!}$ [n]u$^{?}$-un-na-š[a$^{?}$]-at ḫa$^{?}$-an$^{?}$-da$^{?}$-i-it-ta-at (17) [LÍL$^{?}$-r]i-ma-kán an-da ki-iš-ša-an me-mi-ya-u-en (18) [nu ú-iz-z]i ^{d}UTU-*ŠI* ^{URU}Tág-ga-aš-ta-an wa-al-aḫ-zi ḫal-ki-iš-ša-kán (19) [a]r-[ḫ]a wa-ar-aš-zi	(15–19) We thoroughly investigated by augury the matter of (Your Majesty’s planned attack on) the town Takkašta, and we obtained an answer. Regarding the campaign we said (i.e., predicted?) as follows: “His Majesty will (successfully) attack Takkašta and reap its crops as well.”

The remainder of the letter contains a detailed and highly technical description of the course of the oracular investigation.

Commentary

15 On Takkašta in this context see Marizza 2007a, 59 n. 44.

16 On *ḫandaittat* here see van den Hout 2001a, 438.

17 Alp restored [URU-*r*]*i*. No restoration suggested in *HED* M, 131. Since the space in the lacuna is insufficient for [*ud-da-a-a*]*r*, I would prefer either [LÍL-*r*]*i* (as given in my text) or [*gi-im-r*]*i* "for (i.e., regarding) the campaign."

18–19 As I have restored them, these lines contain what is called a "serial construction" in Hittite, on which see *GrHL* §24.31 and following.

51. HKM 48
To the King from Mariya and Ḫapiri

Text: Mşt. 75/62. **Find spot:** G/5 Room 8. **Copy**: HKM 48. **Edition**: Alp 1991a, 206–11 (no. 48); Hoffner 1997b. **Discussion**: van den Hout 2001a, 424 n. 2, 438 n. 74, 439 with n. 77; Collins 2003, 73, 78 n. 21 (on the identification of the *kūrala*-); Marizza 2007a, 138, 150 (on the PNs); van den Hout 2007b (on the relationship of the group HKM 47, 48, 51, and 78 to the Maşat corpus as a whole).

On the possible dating of HKM 46–51 to the end of the reign of Arnuwanda I, see above in §1.2.6.

Royal hunts are known all over the ancient Near East—from Egypt, Syria, Mesopotamia, and the Aegean—and among the Hittites from as early as King Anitta (see in general Hoffner 1974a, 124–26; 1980, 326–27; Collins 2002a, 249–50, 327–29; Hoffner 2003a, 98–99, 102, and especially Hawkins 2006 on Tudḫaliya as a hunter). Ḫattušili III wrote to congratulate Kadašman-Enlil II on his hunting prowess (KUB 3.72 + KBo 1.10 rev. 49–50, translated in Oppenheim 1967, 145; Beckman 1999a, 143; and Mineck in Chavalas 2006, 279, cited in Archi 1988, 30 n. 31). On the royal hunt as a kind of "war game," see Liverani 2001, 89–90.

The Anitta Text (Neu 1974; Hoffner 1997d; Carruba 2001) even provides evidence for the establishment of a royal wild animal park. But this text provides the first evidence for the stocking of such a park through the efforts of persons other than the king himself in his hunting expeditions. Soysal (2006, 568) believes that additional textual evidence may have been found: on the basis of a short passage in text 110—*nu ḫuwetar mašiwan ú-m[i-e-ni] / n–at uwami ANA BĒLTI*=*YA ḫ[atrāmi*?] "I will certainly wr[ite?] to my lady how much wildlife[148] [we] see (in the land)" KBo 13.62 obv. 18–19—he asks the question: "Is this perhaps another safari report in a Hittite letter like HKM 48?"

Two officials, Mariya and Ḫapiri, address this letter to the king. Ḫapiri's name suggests that his background may have been as a member of the foreign group called the ÉRIN.MEŠ *ḫapiriyaš*, which some think is the Hittite equivalent of the Akkadian writing *ḫapirū* (consonantal spelling *'pr*), on which see comments on text 39. There is no connection (*pace* Alp 1991a, 56) with the PN Ḫappi, which has a geminate *p*. Ḫapiri, as Alp correctly observes, is both an augur and a bird collector. On this dual role, see now Bawanypeck 2005.

The king has commissioned Ḫapiri to go on a trip to collect different kinds of birds and wild animals for him (lines 7–8). And the majority of his letter concerns details of the quest for these creatures the king has asked for, and questions about where the king wished him to search for them. He reports some success in finding birds (lines 9–10), but failure to date in finding and catching alive a lion, a leopard, a *šarmiya-* and a *kūrala-*. He asks in which direction he should seek for the birds (lines 14–23), and whether the requested *kūrala-* animal should be sought in the dense forest or in an area (a meadow?) called a *šekkuni-* (lines 24–27).

Although the end of his letter concerns an augury that he performed in order to assure the king that one of his sons, who must has been stationed in Ḫapiri's area, near the town Palḫiša (line 28), will be safe from contracting the fever that has been raging in that area (lines 28–33), the letter itself should not be assigned to the category of oracle letters (*Orakelbriefe*; see van den Hout, 2001, 424 n. 2, 438 n. 74).

Without definitive contexts for *kūrala-*, its identification has to remain provisional. We still cannot even be sure it is a quadruped, and not a bird (as Alp speculated). Collins has proposed that *kūrala-* designated the "hart," or "male red deer," defending this identification primarily on etymological constructs. But premature identifications based solely upon etymology often have proven false. If Collins' supposition should prove to be correct, Ḫapiri would have been seeking specifically the horned member of the species (*kūrala-*), rather than a female red deer.

(1) *A-NA* ^{d}UTU-*ŠI BE-LÍ-NI* (2) *QÍ-BÍ-MA UM-MA* ^{m}Ma-ri-ya (3) *Ù* ^{m}Ḫa-pí-ri ARAD.MEŠ-*KA-MA*	(1–3) Say to His Majesty, our lord. Thus speak Mariya and Ḫapiri, your servants:
(4) ^{d}UTU-*ŠI*-m[u] ku-it *BE-LÍ-YA* (5) am-mu-uk ^{m}Ḫa-pí-ri-in (6) ki-iš-ša-an wa-a-tar-na-aḫ-ta (7) ke-e-da-ni-wa-za-kán KASKAL-ši MUŠEN.ḪI.A (8) an-da da-a-an e-ep	(4–8) Concerning the fact that you, Your Majesty, my lord, commanded me, Ḫapiri, as follows: "On this trip collect birds,"
(9) nu-un-na-aš-kán MUŠEN.ḪI.A an-da (10) aš-šu-li ta-ru-up-pé-er	(9–10) (People) kindly collected birds for us.
(11) nu-un-na-aš-kán UR.MAḪ pár-ša-na-aš (12) šar-mi-ya-aš ku-ú-[r]a-la-aš-ša (13) an-da *Ú-UL* ap-pa-an-te-eš	(11–13) (But) a lion, a leopard, a *šarmiya-*, and a *kūrala*-animal have not been captured for us.
(14) nu-un-na-aš-za-kán ^{d}UTU-*ŠI* ku-it (15) *BE-LÍ-NI* ^{URU}Ti-wa-li-ya-za (16) ^{URU}Pal-ḫi-iš-na-za ar-ḫ[a-ya-a]n (17) z[i!-i]k-ke!-e-eš[149]	(14–17) And because you, Your Majesty, our lord, *initiated*? (the matter) with us (*-naš*) separately, from the towns Tiwaliya (and) Palḫišna,
(18) nu-kán ke-e MUŠEN.ḪI.A (19) ku-e-da-ni KASKAL-ši an-da (20) ša-an-ḫu-e-ni (21) nu-un-na-ša-an ^{d}UTU-*ŠI* (22) *BE-LÍ-NI* EGIR-pa ḫu-u-da-a-ak (23) ḫa-at-ra-a-i	(18–23) write us back immediately (and tell us) in which direction (literally: on which road) we should seek these birds.
(24) ku-ú-ra-l[a-an ma-a-an *Ú-U*]*L* (25) še-ek-ku-ni-[ya an-da ša-a]n-ḫu-e-ni (26) na-an ^{GIŠ}T[IR-ni an-da ša-a]n-ḫu-e-ni (27) nu-un-na[-ša-an ḫu-u-da-a-ak ḫa-at-ra-]a-i	(24–27) Write us immediately if we should seek a *kūrala*-animal not in the *meadow*?, but in the forest.
(28) ^{URU}Pal-[ḫi-iš-na-za a-ap?]-pa-an (29) ta-pa-aš-[ši-iš …-z]i? (30) nu ak-k[i-iš-kat-ta-ri]	(28–30) In the *neighborhood* of the town of Palḫišna a fever *rages*. And people are dying.
(31) *A-NA* DUMU-ma [še-er MUŠE]N? (32) la-aḫ-la-aḫ-ḫi-[ma-	(31–33) But for the sake of the (king's) son I observed "birds of

aš …] u-uḫ-ḫu-un (33) nu MUŠEN.ḪI.A SI[G_5-an-te-eš]	agitation" …, and the birds were of favorable import.

Commentary

2–3 see *GrHL* §29.2 (on use of *Ù*).

11 On the *šarmiya-* animal see CHD Š, 278.

14–17 Previously (*GrHL* §12.42 citing Hoffner 1997b) I read line 17 ⸢*Ú-UL*⸣ *te-e-eš*, and translated the lines: "And because Your Majesty, our lord, didn't give us separate instructions (for operating) from the towns of Tiwaliya and Palḫišna." For the GN Tiwaliya, see Forlanini 1980, 75–76.

25 Probably a noun in the dative-locative case, not a Luwian pres. pl. 1 verb in *-uni* (regarded as unclear by van den Hout 2006, 230 n. 65).

31–32 The DUMU is a Hittite prince. DUMU = DUMU.LUGAL, as regularly abbreviated in the festival texts. Bryce comments: "… some of the younger members of the royal family were relegated for a time to the provinces, presumably to broaden their range of experience in preparation for the roles they would later be called on to play in the service of their kingdom. While in the provinces, young royals no doubt remained under the watchful eye of officials charged with their safety and security. We have two letters from Tapikka [HKM 48: 31–32; HKM 49: 4–5] in which officials apparently assigned this responsibility reported to His Majesty that all was well with his son (in one case) and his daughters (in the other). He was assured that he need have no concern about them" (2003b, 175). As we shall see below, however, the sentence in lines in HKM 49: 4–5 is not a report that the daughters are well, but a greeting and well-wishing to the princesses, who are with the king, and about whose prospective well-being an oracle was taken. Although the mention of birds earlier in this letter (line 18) may have nothing to do with augury, this last paragraph does indeed refer to the practice. On HKM 48: 31–33 see briefly van den Hout 2001a, 424 n. 2, and 439.

52. HKM 49
To the King from Four Men

Text: Mşt. 75/84. **Find spot:** G/5 Room 8. **Copy:** HKM 49. **Edition**: Alp 1991a: 210–11, 430 (no. 49). **Discussion**: van den Hout 2001a, 430; de Martino 2005b.

On the dating of HKM 46–51, see above in §1.2.4 and §1.2.6. On Atiuna and ABoT 65, see also Klinger 1995a, 88, and de Martino 2005b, 317 (§3.5).

(1) [*A-N*]*A* ^{d}UTU-*ŠI BE-LÍ-NI QÍ-BÍ-MA* (2) [*U*]*M-M*[*A*] ^{m}Du-ud-du-ši/wa$^{?}$ ^{m}A-ti-un$^{?}$-na$^{??}$ (3) ^{m}A[l]-x *Ù* $^{m.d}$I[M-ḫ]u-mi-im-ma (4) *MA-ḪAR* DUMU.MUNUS.MEŠ ḫu-u-ma-an-da-aš (5) ḫu-u-ma-an SIG$_5$-in [e-eš-tu]	(1–5) Say to His Majesty, our lord: Thus speak Dudduši, Atiuna$^{?}$, Al-…, and Tarḫumimma: May all be well with all the princesses.[150]
(6) k[a]-[a[-š]a me-e-na<-aš> MUŠEN.ḪI.A m[a$^{?}$]-a[ḫ$^{?}$-ḫa-an …] (7) ḫu-u-ma-an-te-e[š] x x […] (8) x-x-x tar.-u-a[n …] (9) x x x […] (10) […] (11) […] x […] (12) [k]a-a-ša x […]	(6–12) I have just … the migratory birds … all …
(13) x x x x […] (14) x x x x […] (15) [x]x x x x […] (16) wa-ra-e-eš x […] (17) ÚŠ-an pa-a-an-[…]	(13–17) … plague$^{?}$ …
(18) ka-a-ša me-e-na[-aš$^{?}$ MUŠEN. ḪI.A] (19) ma-aḫ-ḫa-an a-ú-e-e[r …] (20) na-aš ka-a-ša *A-NA* ^{d}U[TU-]*ŠI* (21) *BE-LÍ-NI* ḫa-at-ra-a-u-en	(18–21) As soon as they observed (the oracular behavior of) the migratory birds, we have herewith reported them to Your Majesty, our lord.

Commentary

On the basis of the apparent wish that all be well with the royal princesses in lines 4–5, and its appearance in a very similar letter from Kuşaklı/Šariššа (KuT 50), de Martino has concluded: The coincidence between the content of KuT 50 and the content of HKM 49 as well as the presence in both letters of the same greeting to the "daughters," which is not found in other Middle Hittite letters, encourage me to believe that these two tablets are contemporary and both concern oracle enquiries for daughters of the royal couple, maybe during a moment in which they were suffering from health problems or it was feared they would have suffered from such problems" (2005b, 313).

The *me-e-na<-aš>* MUŠEN.ḪI.A in line 6, and the *me-e-na*[*-aš*$^{?}$ MUŠEN.ḪI.A] in line 18 are the same birds of oracular value treated in CHD sub *meya(n)ni-* b, although this passage is not treated there. See the genitive form *me-e-na-aš* KUB 27.1 i 22 cited in the CHD list of spellings, which argues for a stem *mēna-*, not *mēni-* as posited there. I understand the term to mean literally "birds of the (seasonal) cycle," that is, migratory birds. In other passages where the oracular behavior of *meyan(iy)aš* MUŠEN.ḪI.A is recorded, this is interpreted as showing whether or not there is a significant threat to the king or his family.

The use three times of the adverb *kāša* (lines 6, 18, 20) is to stress the urgency of the situation and the promptness of the three officials' response to the possible threat. On the force of *kāša* in Hittite to stress temporal immediacy see Hoffner 1968; and *GrHL* §§24.27–24.29.

53. HKM 50
To the King from Atiuna

Text: Mşt. 75/2. **Find spot:** H/5: Room 9. **Copy**: HKM 50. **Edition**: Alp 1991a, 212–15 (no. 50). **Discussion:** Beal 1992: 178 n. 654, 183–84; Houwink ten Cate 1998, 162 (lines 3–7).

On the possible dating of HKM 46–51 to the end of the reign of Arnuwanda I, see above in §1.2.5. The restoration of the scribe's name in line 2 is assured by ABoT 65 (text 81) rev. 8′.

The restorations of the beginning of the lines are for the most part uncertain, especially since it is difficult to determine the distance to the original left edge of the tablet. If one works on the basis of the most likely restoration, that in line 1, there was space to the left for 6 signs of average width before the *LÍ* sign. Yet this means that in line 7 much more would be needed to fill that space than the obvious restoration [*BE-LÍ-YA*]. Alp's restored [*antu-uḫ-ša-an-n*]*a-aš* in line 3 would have sufficient space. But the trace does not look like -*n*]*a*-, and the form as it stands is a genitive, not the required nominative. Despite Alp's and Houwink ten Cate's preference for a noun denoting the whole populace here, therefore, it is more likely that a proper name stood in this line. If this is not a single individual, it is of course possible that it is the nominative of a city or region name.[151] If the latter were the case, then one could think of restoring a number at the beginning of line 5, since space requires something before *antuḫšeš* "people."

(1) [*A-NA* ᵈUTU-*ŠI BE-L*]*Í-YA QÍ-*	(1–2) Say to His Majesty, my lord: Thus

BÍ-MA (2) [*UM-MA* mA-ti-u]n?-na ARAD-*KA-MA*	speaks your servant Atiuna:
(3) [URU?x-x-x-]x-aš ma-aḫ-ḫa-an ta-pa-aš-ša-za (4) [EGIR?-an? ki-i]t[152]-ta-at ḫi-in-ga-na-za-ma-kán (5) [x-x an-tu-u]ḫ-še-eš ḫu-iš-šu-er (6) [ḫa?-ad?-du?-le?-še?-]e-er na-at *A-NA* dUTU-*ŠI* (7) [*BE-LÍ-YA* x-x] ḫa-at-ra-a-nu-un	(3–7) I *previously*? reported to Your Majesty, my lord, how the town/region? … was *harrassed* by a fever, and (so many) people survived the plague (and) *regained health.*
(8) […-r]i?-uš-ma-za-kán ku-i-uš an-da (9) […-a]t-kán ka-a-ša EGIR-pa ša-ra-a (10) [x - x URUAn?-z]i?-li<-ya?> i-ya-an-da-ri (11) [nu dUTU-*ŠI B*]*E-LÍ-YA QA-TAM-MA* ša-a-ak	(8–11) The …-s which … are about to go back up to *Anziliya*?. Your Majesty, my lord, should take note accordingly.
(12) [m x - x - m]u?-u-wa-al-la-aš-ša-aš-ma-aš-kán ku-iš (13) [*I-NA* URUḪu-p]í-iš-na LÚma-ri-ya-an-ni-iš (14) [x x x x -]e an-da e-eš-ta nam-ma-aš-ši-kán (15) [x x x x] x ARAD.MEŠ-*ŠU* ANŠE.KUR.RA.ḪI.A-*ŠU* (16) [ku?-in? pé-]ḫu-da-an-zi na-aš-kán EGIR-pa (17) […] x-x-x ša-ra-a ú-it (18) [… dUT]U-*ŠI* (19) [… …] (20) […-d]a?	(12–20) … x-x-*muwallašša* who was the *mariyanni*-officer for you (pl., or: 'for them') in Ḫupišna …, whom? they further (*namma)* are conducting his servants and his troops to him, he? came back up to … And … Your Majesty …
(21) [… da]m-mi-iš-ḫa-a-an (22) […]x.ḪI.A (23) [… -p]í (24) [… … ud?]-da-na-az (25) [… a]r-ta-ri (26) […] x ar-ḫa (*eras.*) (27) […-z]i	(21–27) … damaged? … stands …
(28) [ma-a-an(-)… dUTU-*ŠI B*]*E-LÍ-YA* ÉRIN.MEŠ ANŠE.KUR.RA.ḪI.A (29) […-]x-ma-an URUAn-zi-li-ya-an (30) [… ḫa]l?-ki-uš LÚ.KÚR *Ú-UL* (31) [dam?-mi?-iš?-ḫa?-iz?-z]i KUR-ya *Ú-UL* (32) [dam?-mi?-iš?-ḫa?-iz?-z]i	(28–32) If Your Majesty, my lord, will send infantry and chariotry …, the enemy will not damage Anzila and its crops. And the countryside he will not damage.

Commentary

3–7 This passage was cited by Houwink ten Cate 1998, 162, as evidence for a plague and famine during this period (1375–1355, according to his chronology), which was reflected also in other documents dated to the reign of Tudḫaliya "II/III."

12 I analyze this sequence of signs as a long PN in the nominative ^{m}x-x-*mūwallaššaš* + -*šmaš* ("for you" [pl.]) + -*kan*. The PN in the nominative agrees with the relative *kuiš* "who" in line 12, and is resumed by the dative -*ši* "to him" in line 14.

31–32 The concern, expressed in other letters from Tapikka (e.g., HKM 46 [text 48]), that the enemy not "damage the KUR" could refer to the district or territory (KUR), or to the countryside as opposed to the cities. On the Hittite conception of city versus countryside see Beckman 1999b. Del Monte writes:

> Narratives of war deeds of Hittite kings eventuate ordinarily in the devastation of conquered towns and their countryside, the deportation of part of the populace and the move to Anatolia of livestock and precious booty, while the countryside was rearranged in order to meet the economic needs of wealth accumulation of the new country lords. The extent of the devastation was in inverse relationship to the value of the conquered town; in a way, the Arzawian cities of Western Anatolia and even more the wealthy Syrian cities were given in general a milder treatment in comparison with the ferocity in laying waste the Kaskean settlements in the Pontus region. Here the local population was as a rule expelled and wiped out, the countryside peopled anew and fortified towns built or rebuilt. In any case the objective of a military expedition was by no means mere plunder and booty, but the reorganization of the conquered land for the benefit of the ruling Hittite elite. (2005, 21)

In this article, del Monte regularly translates a city name "and its KUR" as "with its countryside." It is the devastation of their own countryside—the fields and orchards outside the city walls—that the Hittites themselves were concerned about in these letters to and from Tapikka. But the distinction could be a minor one. For most administrative districts were small enough to consist of only one substantial city and its surrounding country.

54. HKM 51
To the King from Kašturraḫšeli

Text: Mşt. 75/76. **Find spot:** G/5 Room 8. **Copy**: HKM 51. **Edition**: Alp 1991a, 214–15 (no. 51).

The reference to "Mşt. 75/76" (HKM 51) in Lühr 2001, 339 n. 12 is a typo for Mşt. 75/56 (HKM 58), not this text. On the possible dating of HKM 46–51 to the end of the reign of Arnuwanda I, see above in §1.2.5.

This is a strange letter in two ways: it lacks the customary address and salutation, although addressed to the king himself, and it commands the king in a manner quite unusual in the mouth of a subject who is not even identified with a rank. Van den Hout notes these irregularities and uses them as evidence that the letter is not an integral part of the network of Tapikkan correspondence. He qualifies this, however, by the remark "These may be cases of inexperienced writers, cf. D. Charpin, CRAIBL 2004, 502, for a Neo-Assyrian parallel" (van den Hout 2007b, 392 n. 29).

The expression "man of GN" is ambiguous, since it can simply mean a person hailing from a place or can represent a rank similar to a petty ruler (a usage attested already in Old Babylonian texts from Mari, cf. *AHw* 90 [*awīlum* B 2 a]).

Alp (1991a, 70) understands this letter as a plea by Kašturraḫšeli that the king treat the elders kindly, because Pittalaḫšuwa has shown itself to be a Kaškaean city friendly to Ḫatti.

The elders of a city or district are fully empowered to make decisions for the land regarding war and peace. When Hittite armies approached a hostile land, it was the elders who came out to negotiate terms of surrender. The "elders of Pittalaḫšuwa" (line 9), who are at this time in the presence of the king, may have traveled a long way, since Alp localizes Pittalaḫšuwa north of the upper Yeşilirmak valley (1991a, 8, 31). In view of the vacillation in the spellings of the notable north Anatolian city Zalpa/Zalpuwa, this territory may be the same as Pittalaḫša, which is likewise in Kaškaean territory.

The elders of a political-territorial unit are, of course, its official representatives. In some cases, when a territory is menaced by an approaching Hittite army, it sends ambassadors to plead for mercy, in which case they are usually either very old people or women, calculated to elicit the Hittite king's pity.

I have arranged the text below so as to make it easier to see the three main sections of the message (lines 1, 2–5, 6–11). But this was not the ancient scribe's intention, since there are no paragraph lines on the tablet to separate these parts.

(1) *UM-MA* ᵐGa-aš-tu-ur-ra-aḫ-še-li	Thus speaks Kašturraḫšeli:
(2) ᵁᴿᵁGa-al-za-na LÚ.KÚR (3) ᵐTi-ip-pu-u-ur-ru-u-iš (4) LÚ ᵁᴿᵁPí-it-ta-la-aḫ-šu-wa (5) ú-wa-te-et	Tippurrui, the "man" of Pittalaḫšuwa, has brought here the enemy (who is) from the city Kalzana.
(6) nu *MA-ḪAR* ᵈUTU-*ŠI BE-LÍ-YA* (7) ku-i-e-eš (8) LÚ.MEŠ ŠU.GI (9) ᵁᴿᵁPí-it-ta-la<-aḫ-šu-wa> (10) na-aš ᵈUTU-*ŠI BE-LÍ-YA* (11) pa-aḫ-ḫa-aš-nu-ut	Your Majesty, my lord, guard/protect the elders of Pittalaḫšuwa who are in my lord's presence.

2.2.2.5. Letters between Officials at Tapikka-Maşat (55–85)

55. HKM 52
From Ḫattušili to Ḫimmuili

Text: Mşt. 75/57. **Find spot:** G/5 Room 8. **Photo:** Alp 1991a, pl. 6 (obverse only; showing the handwriting of Tarḫunmiya). **Dimensions** (taken from the photo; see §1.2.8.2): 6 cm wide and 7.6 cm tall. **Copy**: HKM 52. **Edition**: Alp 1990, 107–13 and 1991a, 214–17, 332–33. **Discussion**: Beal 1992, 41 and 43 w. n. 171 (on the UKU.UŠ troops employed as gendarmes); Beckman 1995a, 27 (lines 10–18); Imparati 1997; Houwink ten Cate 1998, 173–74; Lühr 2001, 335–36 n. 7c–e; Imparati 2002, 93; Hoffner 2007, 390 (lines 38–39); Marizza 2007a. On lines 25–28 see CHD *per* 1 a 3′. On lines 30–31 see CHD *peran* 1 c 2′ i'. Beal 1992, 43 (on lines 10–39). Lines 13–16 are edited in CHD Š, 6 (*šaḫḫan* b).

The principal sender, Ḫattušili, was a well-known and prominent scribe of the Middle Hittite period (see Alp 1991a, 58–59; Klinger 1995a, 88–90; Imparati 1997, 649; 2002, 93), operating out of the capital city Ḫattuša, and with powers approaching those of the "royal secretary" of Old Babylonian Mari (see §1.1.6).

It is unclear where Ḫattušili and Tarḫunmiya were at the time the letter was written, although it was certainly in a place where there was a palace, that is, a regional administrative center (Imparati 1997, 655). Ḫattušili's words of warning to Ḫimmuili in lines 17–18 that he will report Ḫimmuili to the "palace," if he doesn't remedy the situation in Tapikka, has force if the one reported to was the king himself, perhaps on his next visit to that palace. Imparati has plausibly proposed that the palace nearest to Tapikka and exercising oversight over Tapikka was in Šapinuwa (Ortaköy), where excavations have shown that the king had a residence and a huge archive of official documents:

> At this point, it would seem plausible also to hypothesize that in most of the above-mentioned cases reference is made to the same Palace, situated in an administrative district not far from that of Tapikka, but of greater prominence. The administration of Tapikka would presumably have consulted this Palace on issues of greater importance; there would therefore have been no need for geographical specifications to indicate it. Occasionally the king would stay in this Palace for a period of time, for various reasons (military, religious, administrative), and see to various affairs involving neighbouring districts, to whose governors he must at times have sent letters. For their own part, these governors would take advantage of the fact that the king was in their area to inform him of various matters and consult him with a view to resolving various issues.... Now, given that we know that Šapinuwa was a more important district than that of Tapikka's whose administration appears in certain respects to have been under the jurisdiction, or at least within the sphere of influence, of Šapinuwa, to me it seems possible that in our letter HKM 52 (and perhaps also in others where the term É.GAL appears) reference is made to the Palace situated in this centre. The existence of a Palace here has been known about for some time, and is confirmed by excavations presently being carried out there. (Imparati 1997, 653–54)

(1) *UM-MA* ^{mGIŠ}GIDRU-DINGIR-*LIM A-NA* ^{m}Ḫi-mu-DINGIR-*LIM* (2) ŠEŠ.DÙG.GA-*YA QÍ-BÍ-MA* (3) kat-ti-ti ḫu-u-ma-an SIG$_5$-in e-eš-du (4) nu-ut-ta DINGIR.MEŠ TI-an ḫar-kán-du (5) nu-ut-ta aš-šu-li pa-aḫ-ša-an-da-ru	(1–5) Thus speaks Ḫattušili: Say to Ḫimmuili, my dear brother: May all be well with you; may the gods keep you alive and lovingly protect you.
(6) ŠEŠ.DÙG.GA-*YA*-mu ku-e tu-el ud-da-a-ar (7) ḫa-at-re-eš-ke-ši na-at *I-NA* É.GAL-*LIM* (8) *Ú-UL* am-mu-uk-pát me-mi-iš-ke-mi (9) nu-ut-ta EGIR-pa ar-ku-wa-ar iš-ša-a[ḫ]-ḫi	(6–9) My brother, the affairs of yours that you keep writing about, do I for my part not speak about them in the palace and send you a reply?
(10) tu-ga-kán a-pí-ya ma-ni-ya-aḫ-ḫi-ya an-da (11) *ŠA* ^{LÚ}DUB.SAR 1 É-*TUM*-pát nu-ut-ták-kán	(10–18) There in your administrative district, there is only one 'House of the Scribe.' Others are oppressing

[UR]U?-i (12) an-d[a] ta-ma-e-eš dam-mi-iš-ki-iš-kán-zi[153] (13) *A-NA* LÚ.MEŠDUB.SAR.MEŠ ša-aḫ-ḫa-an lu-uz-zi (14) a-pí-ya-ma-at ku-wa-at iš-ša-i (15) ki-nu-na-aš-ša-an IGI.ḪI.A-wa ḫar-ak (16) na-an le-e dam-mi-iš-ḫi-iš-kán-zi (17) ma-a-an *Ú-UL*-ma na-at ú-wa-mi (18) *I-NA* É.GAL-*LIM* me-ma-aḫ-ḫi	(it/him) in your town. Are *šaḫḫan* and *luzzi* (incumbent) upon scribes? Why does he perform it there? Now keep (your) eyes (on the matter). Let them stop oppressing him. Otherwise, I will proceed to report it to the palace.

Commentary

9 Decision on the meaning of this line is heavily influenced by how one understands the noun *arkuwar*. Alp (1991a, 332) followed Friedrich (*HW* 31), Kammenhuber (*HW*2), and others in deciding for the meaning "petition, plea" (German *Bitte*). If so, this line would constitute a kind of apology by Ḫattušili to Ḫimmuili. The translation "I will make a plea/defense back to you" as an apology makes no sense here. The order of names in lines 1–2 indicate that Ḫimmuili is not Ḫattušili's superior, but either his equal (so Imparati 1997, 649) or his subordinate. Ḫattušili seems upset in the letter and is hardly inclined to apologize. In lines 17–18 he even threatens him (see above). Marizza (2007a, 114) is justified in characterizing Ḫattušili's language to Ḫimmuili and his reminder that it is he who alone can bring matters to the attention of the palace on Himuili's behalf, as "blackmail" (*l'arma di ricatto*). The only way to salvage the translation "plea" here would be to understand it as voicing a complaint and pleading with the addressee to rectify it. Certainly there are Hittite *arkuwar* prayers of this type in which complaints are brought to the gods, who are urged to rectify the situation. D'Alfonso (2005b, 126) recognizes this two-sided aspect of *arkuwai-/arkuwar iya-* and proposes a translation "presentare una lamentela" (present a complaint) as a means of covering both a charge and a defense.

My view—which is influenced by widespread occurrences of both this noun and the related verb form, as well as by the tenor of Ḫattušili's other words in this letter—is that the basic meaning of the word is "reply," from which other nuances ("defence, argument," and even a complaint or plea in the form of a prayer) can be derived. The noun *arkuwar* fundamentally means "reply, response," from which the more common technical usage "plea, defense (against a charge)" developed. The more basic and non-technical meaning fits better here. See also another quote from Ḫimmuili in HKM

63, where again a "reply to my words" makes best sense. That the combination *arkuwar iya-* was felt as a tight unity is shown by the word order *UL arkuwar iya-* (HKM 57: 26) for the negation instead of *arkuwar UL iya-*.

10–18 For this section, as well as for 34–39, and other similar sources the words of Imparati in *CANE* 1, 562 are directly relevant:

> Law 55 describes a scene that must have occurred more than once: a group of citizens petitioning the king for relief from an intolerable economic situation. A Middle Hittite letter from an official in the capital city to another official in the outlying city of Tapikka [HKM 52] and a similar New Hittite one from Emar (modern Meskene) attest to the necessity of bringing petitions for relief from the state imposts of land taxes and corvée (Hittite *šaḫḫan* and *luzzi*) to the personal attention and adjudication of the king. In both cases the petitioner claimed that if the officials would only inquire in the old records they would learn that his family had never before paid this tax on the property in question.

Cases such as these demonstrate that tax records were kept, not only in the capital, but also in the provincial administrative centers. Furthermore, as Marizza stresses (2007a, 114), this letter attests to a supervisory capacity of the *BEL MADGALTI* over those who perform the tax gathering (in this case, the "men of the district" and "men of the town," which function is not reflected in the official Instructions for the Provincial Governors (CTH 261), edited by Pecchioli Daddi 2003a.

The fact that the matter in question has been protracted for some time is confirmed by references to it in other letters from Maşat (texts 32, 63, and 79) and by the use in this specific document of various verbs in the iterative ("are oppressing," "stop oppressing" in lines 12 and 16).

Imparati writes:

> The statement at 1. 10 f., that 'there within your (= Ḫimuili's) district *(maniyaḫḫiya a[nd]a)* (there is) only one scribe's house', may suggest that the place in question was not specifically Tarḫunmiya's dwelling or patrimonial and/or family complex, but possibly an administrative centre where he worked; however, this does not exclude that when he was in Tapikka he also resided there. Note, by way of comparison, the administrative centre described as the "house of the scribes on wood" (É LÚ.MEŠDUB.SAR.GIŠ) in KUB XXV 31 + 1142/z Obv. 10. A public institution would also be suggested by Tarḫunmiya"s request to place a man UKU.UŠ (Rev. 30–31) in front of the "house," this presumably meaning a watchman/gendarme. It seems to me that the interpretation of this "house" as a public place is further supported by Ḫattušili's threat to take the matter up in the Palace and

> the weighty intervention of Šarpa, the high dignitary of Šapinuwa, in favour of Tarḫunmiya's 'house', an intervention which constitutes the reason for the "principal" letter HKM 60. In Lower Edge 18 - Rev. 20 Šarpa even announces that, when he goes before the king, he will bring with him two persons who are guilty in relation to Tarḫunmiya. The request for royal intervention in the matter shows the gravity and importance of the issue and is more in keeping with a situation that in some way affected also the interests of the central administration, rather than with a private affair. (1997, 657)

One wonders in view of Imparati's interpretation here, if the "houses" of the persons mentioned in law §50, in front of which an *eyan*-tree/pole erected/displayed exempts them from *šaḫḫan* and *luzzi,* are not also in some sense public, rather than private.

The word order in *ŠA* LÚDUB.SAR 1 É-*TUM-pát* is both unusual and interesting. The numeral "1" interrupts the genitive + head noun sequence, and the *-pat* is placed at the end of the long sequence, rather than on its first component, as Hart's rule about *-pat* seems to have entailed (Hart 1971, 102–3; see *GrHL* §28.118). Since the *-pat* "only" modifies the word "one," according to my earlier formulation of the rule regarding *-pat*'s position within the clause (Hoffner 1973, 104–7), it might have been expected to be attached to that numeral here, which it clearly is not in this instance. But neither does the present sequence fit Hart's rule, according to which one would expect **ŠA* LÚDUB.SAR-*pat* 1 É-*TUM*. What this unusual case seems to indicate is that here the entire sequence *ŠA* LÚDUB.SAR 1 É-*TUM* is regarded as an indivisible logogram, to which the Hittite particle can only be affixed at the end. This in turn allows us to attribute the numeral interrupting the genitive + head noun sequence to *Akkadian* syntax, not Hittite.

55b. HKM 52
Piggyback Letter of Tarḫunmiya to Ḫimmuili

This is an example of a typical type of letter, attested from all regions of the ancient Near East: a letter to an official's superior, protesting and appealing what is regarded as an illegal or unjust action on the official's part. For a Hebrew letter of protest, possibly from the reign of King Josiah, found on an ostracon from Yavneh Yam, see Pardee in *CoS* 3.41:77–78, and possibly the unprovenienced letter translated in *CoS* 3.44:86.

That the scribal circle to which Tarḫunmiya belonged must have been under the control of Ḫattušili is clear from the interest that Ḫattušili shows in the problems of Tarḫunmiya, as well as from the already mentioned difference in rank between the two men (Imparati 1997, 650).

The mention in lines 30–31 of an UKU.UŠ-soldier helps us to understand this functionary as a kind of policeman under the command of the provincial governor (Rosi 1983, 109–29; Beal 1992, 41 and 43 w. n. 171; Marizza 2007a, 116).

(19) *A-NA BE-LÍ* mḪi-mu-DINGIR-*LIM BE-LÍ-YA* (20) [*MA*]*Ḫ-RI-YA QÍ-BÍ-MA* (21) *UM-MA* mTar-ḫu-un-mi-ya DUMU-*KA-MA* (22) *MA-ḪAR BE-LÍ* ḫu-u-[m]a-[a]n SIG_5-[i]n (23) e-eš-du nu-ut-ta DINGIR.MEŠ T[I]-an ḫa[r-k]án-du (24) nu-ut-ta aš-šu-li pa-[a]ḫ-ša-an-[t]a-ru	(19–24) Say to lord Ḫimmuili, my lord and my superior: Thus speaks Tarḫunmiya, your son: May all be well with (my) lord. May the gods keep you alive and lovingly protect you.
(25) *BE-LU*-uš[154]-ša-an *BE-LÍ-YA* (26) am-me-el *A-NA* É-*YA* IGI.ḪI. A-wa ḫar-ak (27) na-at le-e dam-mi-iš-ḫi-iš-kán-zi (28) nam-ma-mu DI.ḪI.A ku-e e-eš-zi (29) na-at *BE-LU BE-LÍ-YA* ḫa-an-ni (30) na-at-kán aš-nu-ut nam-ma-kán *A-NA* É-*YA* (31) LÚUKU.UŠ pé-ra-an ti-it-ta-nu-ut (32) na-aš LÚ.MEŠ KUR-*TI* LÚ.MEŠ URU-*LIM*-ya (33) le-e dam-mi-iš-ḫi-iš-kán-zi	(25–33) O lord, my lord, keep your eyes on my house, and let them not oppress it. Furthermore, O lord, my lord, adjudicate such legal affairs as I have, and resolve them (favorably). Then (next) station a policeman in front of my house, and let the men of the land and the men of the town not oppress them.
(34) nam-ma am-mu-uk a-pí-ya (35) ša-aḫ-ḫa-an lu-uz-zi-ya *Ú-UL* ku-it (36) e-eš-ta ki-nu-na-mu LÚ. MEŠ URU-*LIM* (37) ša-aḫ-ḫa-ni lu-uz-zi-ya ti-it-ta-nu-ú-er (38) nu *BE-LU* LÚ.MEŠ KUR-*TI*-pát pu-nu-uš (39) [m]a-a-an am-mu-uk ša-aḫ-ḫa-an lu-uz-zi iš-ša-aḫ-ḫu-un	(34–39) Furthermore, (previously) no *šaḫḫan* and *luzzi* was ever (incumbent) upon me there. But now the men of the town have imposed *šaḫḫan* and *luzzi* upon me! O lord, just ask those same men of the land if I have ever rendered *šaḫḫan* and *luzzi*.
(40) *BE-LU*-ma ku-i-uš LÚ.MEŠ *ṬE$_4$-MI* u-i-e-eš-ke-ši (41) na-aš-kán am-mu-uk pa-ra-a (42) na-iš-ke-mi *ŠA* ANŠE.KUR.RA GIŠGIGIR-ya-mu (43) ku-it ut-tar ḫa-at-ra-a-eš (44) na-aš-ta [ur-g]i-i-in (45) *I-NA*	(40–46) What messengers you keep sending, O lord, I am sending them on. Concerning the matter of the horse(s) and chariot which you wrote: I will forward the … in the palace.

É.GAL-*LIM* am-mu-uk […] (46) pa-ra-a ar-nu-mi	

Commentary

34–39 are edited in CHD Š, 6. The *ku-it* following the negative in line 35 does not need to be emended to *ku-it*<*-ki*>, since such a use of *kuit* following a negative in just this sense is known elsewhere: *parkunuši=ma=za UL kuit* "but you clean nothing up" KBo 3.1 ii 43–44, ed. CHD P, 173.

44 I have rendered the last sentence according to its probable meaning (see HKM 27: 11–16 and CHD *parā* 1 e 1′ and 3 a), but I cannot decide the broken word(s) at the end of line 44. [*ur-*]*gi-i-in* hardly makes sense. *urki-* means "trace, track," and when written plene is *ūrki-*, not **urkī-*. I cannot check Alp's copy, because my photo does not include the edge, where this line stands, and Alp's photo (1991a, Tafel 6) shows only the obverse. If in spite of my just voiced objection the word is indeed *urki-* "trail, track," it might have a meaning something like the modern jargon: "I will forward (it) on the 'paper trail' (*urgi-*) in the palace," taking the accusative [*ur*?*-g*]*i*?*-i-in* as "accusative of the way."

56. HKM 53
From Ḫattušili to Uzzū

Text: Mşt. 75/94. **Find spot:** G/5 Portico. **Copy:** HKM 53. **Edition**: Alp 1991a, 218–19, 335 (no. 53).

(1) [*UM-M*]*A* mGIŠGI[DRU-DINGIR-*LIM*] (2) [*A-N*]*A* mUz-z[u-u *QÍ-BÍ-M*]*A*	(1–2) Thus speaks Ḫattušili: Say to Uzzū:
(3) *ŠA* mḪi-mu-DIN[GIR-*LIM* …] x ḫal-ki-e-eš (4) nam-ma-ya ku-i?-[e?-eš? …] x *Ú-NU-TE*MEŠ (5) *ŠA* mḪi-mu-DINGIR-*LIM* [a-p]é-e-da-ni KUR-ya (6) nu ar-ḫa ku-it ḫar-ni-in-kán (7) [x-x-x-y]a? ku-it na-at tup-pí-az (8) [ḫa-at-ra-a-i n]a-at-mu up-pí (9) [… -z]i? tap?-tap?-pa-ša-kán pa-ra-a-na (9a?) […]	(3–9) The crops … of Ḫimmuili, and furthermore the utensils which belong to Ḫimmuili are in that territory. Write on a tablet what has been destroyed and what …, and send it to me! …, but the cage? … …

Commentary

5 It is unclear to what previous geographical name the *apedani* KUR refers. Perhaps a toponym stood in one of the text breaks that precede.

9 Alp read [... *l*]*um*?-*pa-ša* and suggested a connection with *lu(m)pašti-*. My reading would appeal to the word (GIŠ)*taptappa-* "cage(?)" occurring in Muršili II's plague prayer (KUB14.8 rev. 22): MUŠEN-*iš-za-kán* GIŠ*tap-ta-ap-pa-an* EGIR-*pa e-ep-zi na-an* GIŠ*tap-ta-ap-pa-aš ḫu-*[*iš-nu-zi*] "the bird takes refuge in (his) cage(?), and the cage(?) saves its life." The word also occurs written GIŠ*tap-tap-pa-an* (KUB 6.45+ iii 40) and without the GIŠ determinative in KBo 39.33 iii 2. So long as the following word *parāna* is unexplained, it is impossible to know whether *taptappaš* is nom. sg. or not. Ḫattušili's concern in this short letter is for items of value that were destroyed (line 6), including utensils belonging to Ḫimmuili (lines 4–5). That they were valuable is indicated by his desire to have a list drawn up and forwarded to him. There are mentions in inventory texts of several *taptappa-* ("cages?") made of gold (KUB 42.40 rev. 6′) and of silver (KUB 42.68 rev. rt. col. 8′), edited by Siegelová 1986, 508–11.

56b. HKM 53
Piggyback Letter from Mār-ešrē to Uzzū

(10) [*UM-MA* mDUMU-]UD.20.KAM *A-NA* mUz-zu-u (11) [ŠEŠ.DÙG.GA-*Y*]*A QÍ-BÍ-MA*	(10–11) Thus speaks Mar-ešrē: Say to Uzzū, my dear brother:
(12) [*MA-ḪAR* ŠEŠ.D]ÙG.GA-*YA* ḫu-u-ma-an (13) [SIG_5-in] e-eš-du nu-ut-ta DINGIR.MEŠ (14) [TI-a]n ḫar-kán-du nu-ut-ta (15) [aš-šu-l]i pa-aḫ-ša-an-da-ru	(12–15) May all be well with my dear brother! And may the gods keep you alive and lovingly protect you!
(16) [k]a-a-ša U[RU?x-x-]na-ri-ta-az (17) [LÚ.ME]Š ŠU.G[I ḫu-u]-ma-an-te-eš ú-e-er (18) [... ŠE]Š-*YA* (19) [...] ḫu-u-ma-an SIG_5-in	(16–19) All the elders have just come from URU?...-narita. So do not worry, my brother! ... everything is fine?."
(20) ŠEŠ DÙG.GA[-*YA* ku-w]a-a-pí-ya (21) KUŠÉ[.MÁ.UR]U_7 ú-e-mi-iš-ke-ši (22) nu-m[u x-x	(20–23) My dear brother, (if) you can find quivers anywhere?, send ... weapons and good quivers? to me!

a-p]í-ya ^{GIŠ}TUKUL (23) ^{KUŠ}[*IŠ-PA-TE*^{MEŠ} SI]G$_5$-ya up-pí	

Commentary

16–19 Mention of elders of a city (see Klengel 1965) arriving suggest either that they have come to make a peace treaty—which could easily be considered good news (“everything is fine”)—or are arriving for a trial of some sort requiring elders as judges (see their function in the laws §71; Hoffner 1997g, 79–80; Bryce 2002a, 85). Given the social context of Tapikka as a provincial quasi-military governmental center, perhaps the former interpretation is preferable. Yet, if these elders are Kaškaeans, it forces a reassessment of the view of von Schuler (1965, 72) that the egalitarian nature of Kaškaean society excluded elders. Unfortunately, since most of the city name ([^{URU}…]-*narita*) is broken away, we cannot use that to aid us in deciding of the elders were Kaškaean or not.

20–23 Bryce (2003b, 176), referring to lines 20–23, apparently misunderstood Alp’s translation of ^{KUŠ}É[.MÁ.UR]U$_7$ “quivers” with German *Köcher* (p. 219) and thought Mar-ešrē was asking for cooks(!) to be sent to him.

57. HKM 54
From Kaššū to Ḫimmuili

Text: Mşt. 75/53. **Find spot:** G/5 Room 8. **Copy:** HKM 54. **Edition**: Alp 1991a, 220–21 (no. 54. **Translation**: Klinger 2001a, 67. **Discussion**: Houwink ten Cate 1998, 167; Hoffner 2001, 204 with n. 20; Ofitsch 2001, 329–30; Goedegebuure 2003, 99; Imparati 2003, 235–36.

This letter shows how Ḫimmuili, faced with the problem of a lack of seed grain, goes up the hierarchical chain of authority to Kaššū for help, but Kaššū warns him that an authority higher than himself, namely the area “palace” (perhaps at Šapinuwa) will be unhappy with the management of the resources in that area. The four towns named in lines 8–11 belonged to the district under Ḫimmuili’s supervision. A matter of concern to the palace would be Ḫimmuili’s use (wthout permission) of cattle of Kašepura (lines 18–24), which belonged to the state.

(1) *UM-MA* ^{m}Ka-aš-šu-ú (2) *A-NA* ^{m}Ḫi-mu-i-DINGIR-*LIM* (3) *QÍ-BÍ-*MA	(1–3) Thus speaks Kaššū: Say to Ḫimmuili:
(4) *ŠA* NUMUN.ḪI.A-mu ut-tar ku-it (5) ḫa-at-ra-a-eš NUMUN. ḪI.A-wa (6) $^{\text{A.ŠÀ}}$te-ri-ip-pí-ya-aš (7) NU.GÁL	(4–7) Concerning what you wrote me about seed: "There is no seed for the plowed fields."
(8) nu ^{URU}Ta-pí-ig-ga (9) ^{URU}An-zi-li-ya (10) ^{URU}Ḫa-ri-ya (11) *Ù A-NA* ^{URU}Ḫa-ni-in-ka$_4$-u-wa-ya (12) ŠE-*AM Ù* ZÍZ-ya (13) [k]u-e an-ni-ya-an (14) e-eš-ta ma-an *Ú-UL* (15) a-pé-e-ez da-a-at-ta (16) ma-an a-pé-e $^{\text{A.ŠÀ}}$te-ri-ip-[p]í (17) a-ni-i-er	(8–17) Shouldn't you have taken from there[155] the barley and wheat which was intended for sowing (for) Tapikka, Anziliya, Ḫariya, and also Ḫaninkawa? Then they could have sown those plowed fields.
(18) *ŠA* ^{URU}Ka-ši-pu-u-ra GU$_4$. ḪI.A (19) ku-e $^{\text{A.ŠÀ}}$te-ri-ip-pí (20) $^{\text{A.Š[À]}}$te-ri-ip-pí-ya-at (21) nu-ut-ta ú-wa-an-zi (22) a-pé-e-d[a-n]i ud-da-ni-i (23) *IŠ-T*[*U*] É$^{?}$.[GA]L$^{?}$-*LIM Ú-UL* (24) pu-nu-u[š-š]a-a[n-]zi	(18–24) Regarding the fields that you plowed with[156] the cattle of Kašipūra, will it not result in their questioning you on that matter from the (regional) palace?
(25) ki-nu-na a-pé-e-ez da-a (26) nu a-pé-e NUMUN.ḪI.A an-ni-ya (27) LÚ.MEŠ *ṬE$_4$-MI-IA*-mu le-e (28) kar-aš-ke-ši	(25–28) Now take from there and sow those seeds. And don't withhold (literally, 'cut off') my messengers from me.

Commentary

8–11 The placement of the *A-NA* in line 11 instead of before ^{URU}Ta-pí-ig-ga in line 8 is strange. But the form ^{URU}Ta-pí-ig-ga can be taken as a dative-locative ("for") without any explicit Akkadian preposition. *Ù …-ya* in line 11 seems redundant, but no more so than standard English "and … as well" or "and also … ."

18–24 On this passage see Hoffner 2001, 204. One would expect GU$_4$. ḪI.A-*it* here. The A.ŠÀ in line 20 is probably a determinative on the verb *terippiya-*. See HKM 55: 7. Alp (1991a, 406–7) lists this verb under *terip*(*p*)-. Such a verb indeed exists. But all forms of the verb *terippiya-* in Maşat are preceded by the determinative A.ŠÀ, which cannot be the direct object. The verb *terippiya-* is probably a denominative ("to make as a plowed field"). Alternate translation: "The plowed fields of the cattle of the town Kašepura, they are plowed fields ($^{A.ŠÀ}$*terippi=at*)."

21–24 On the role of the regional palaces (É.GAL) in supervising agriculture see Imparati 1997, 651, and 2002, 94. The verb *uwanzi* is part of a serial construction (*GrHL* §24.31 and following). The *-ta* is the direct object of *punuššanzi*. The sentence in lines 21–24, which I take as a rhetorical question (see Hoffner 1995a, 89–90) like lines 8–15, Klinger (2001a, 67) takes as a statement: "Es wird dazu kommen, daß man dich in jener Angelegenheit durch den Palast nicht verhört."

27 As correctly noted by Beckman (personal communication), this is equivalent to colloquial English "Keep me posted." But it may also refer to the unwelcome practice of detaining royal messengers, so that they do not return quickly to the king with the replies. See text 58, lines 29–35.

58. HKM 55
From Kaššū to Ḫimmuili

Text: Mşt. 75/66. **Find spot:** G/5 Room 8. **Copy:** HKM 55. **Edition**: Alp 1991a, 222–25 (no. 55). **Discussion:** Beckman 1995a, 24 with n. 24; Houwink ten Cate 1998, 167; van den Hout 2001b, 175; Ofitsch 2001, 330.

(1) [*U*]*M-MA* ^{m}Ga-aš-šu-ú *A-NA* ^{m}Ḫi-mu-DI[NGIR-*LIM*] (2) [*Q*]*Í-BÍ-MA*	(1–2) Thus speaks Kaššū: Say to Ḫimmuili:
(3) ka-a-ša-mu ^{m}Pu-ul-li-iš (4) ^{URU}Ka-a-ši-pu-ra-az ḫa-at-ra-a-it (5) $^{A.ŠÀ}$te-ri-ip-pí-wa ku-e (6) ^{URU}Da-a-pí-ik-ka$_4$ ^{URU}Ta-ḫ[a]-ša-ra-ya (7) $^{A.ŠÀ}$te-<-ri>-ip-pí-ya-an nu-wa NUMUN (8) ^{m}Ḫi-mu-DINGIR-*LIM*-iš *Ú-UL* pa-a-i (9) nu-wa NUMUN N[U.G]ÁL	(3–9) Pulli has just written me from Kašepura: "As for the (plowed) fields of Tapikka and Taḫašara which were plowed, Ḫimmuili doesn't give seed (for them). There is no seed."
(10) nu-mu zi-ik ku-e ^{m}Ḫi-mu-DINGIR-*LIM*-iš (11) NUMUN.ḪI.A me-ma-at-ta ke-e$^{!}$-wa[157] (12) ^{URU}Da-a-pí-ik-ka$_4$ a-ni-ya-an-	(10–17) Where did those seeds go, about which you spoke to me, Ḫimmuili, (saying): "These are sown in Tapikka, these in Anziliya,

da (13) ke-e-ma-wa URUAn-zi-li-ya (14) ke-e-ma-wa URU[Ḫ]a-a-ri-ya (15) ke-e-ma-wa URUḪa-a-ni-ik-ka4-wa (16) nu a-pé-e NUMUN.ḪI.A ku-wa-pí (17) pa-it[158]	these in Ḫariya, and these in Ḫanikkawa"?[159]
(18) […] x x [… mḪi-m]u-DINGIR-*LIM*-i[š] (19) […] x x […] x x x (20) […] x x ma-aḫ-[ḫ]a-an (21) *Ú-UL* nu-un-tar-nu-ši na-at (22) *Ú-UL* a-ni-ya-ši	(18–22) … Ḫimmuili … when you do not hasten, you will not sow it.
(23) nu-un-na-aš *ŠA BE-LU*MEŠ*-TI* (24) ma-aḫ-ḫa-an NUMUN.ḪI.A me-na-aḫ-ḫa-an-da (25) nu-un-tar-nu-ši nu *ŠA BE-LU*MEŠ*-TI* (26) NUMUN.ḪI.A an-ni-eš-ke-ši (27) *ŠA* É.GAL-*LIM*-ma-az NUMUN.ḪI.A (28) a-ni-ya-u-wa-an-zi *Ú-UL* mi-ma-at-ti	(23–28) When you expedite the lords' sowing for us, you will keep sowing the lords' seeds. But you say "no" to the sowing of seeds of the palace.
(29) LÚ.MEŠ *ṬE*4*-MI-YA*-mu ku-wa-at *Ú-UL* (30) u-i-eš-ke-et-ta-ni[160] tu-e-el (31) ARAD.MEŠ t[a]-ri-ya-an-zi[161] LÚ.MEŠ *ṬE*4*-MI* (32) *Ú-UL ŠA BE-LÍ-NI* KUR-ya (33) *ŠA BE-LÍ-NI* ma-an-kán ku-it (34) ma-aḫ-ḫa-an an-da ma-an-mu (35) ḫu-u-ma-an ḫa-at-re-eš-ke-ši	(29–35) Why are you (pl.) not sending my messengers (back) to me? Are your servants too tired (to do so)? Do the(se) messengers not belong to our lord? Even the land (itself) belongs to our lord. If only you (sg.) would keep writing me everything about how it is there!
(36) [z]i-ga-za mḪu-i-il-li-iš (37) [*M*]*A*-[*Ḫ*]*AR* dUTU-*ŠI* ku-it e-eš-ta (38) nu-wa-mu LÚ?[162]-na-at-ta-aš *MA-ḪAR* dU[TU-*ŠI*] (39) [t]e-et ka-a-ša-kán KUR-ya […] (40) […] e-eš-ta na-at-kán pa-ra-a n[a-i] (l. e. 1) [t]u-uk dUTU-*Š*[*I*] *BE-LÍ-YA* ša-<ak?>-[d]u?[163] (l. e. 2) S[IG5-]in i[-e-e]t *Ú-UL*-t[a] *A-NA* ÉRIN?.[MEŠ?] (l. e. 3) […]-x SIG5-i[n] i-e-et	(36–40, l. e. 1–3) Because you, Ḫuilli, were with His Majesty, did you speak of me … before His Majesty? … was in the land. Send it out. May His Majesty, My Lord, know about you! He treated (you) well. Didn't he treat you well in regard to the work gangs …?

Commentary

Although this letter is formally addressed only to Ḫimmuili, there is a brief section that is addressed to Ḫuilli (lines 36–40). The bulk of the letter to his colleague Ḫimmuili (lines 10–35), whom he addresses as a subordinate, is a dressing-down, in part due to a bad report Kaššū received from Pulli (lines 3–9). The letter is replete with suspicion, rivalry, and veiled threats. These men really did not get along!

Kaššū's letter begins with a complaint that Ḫimmuili is mismanaging the supply of seed grain (3–17), and a hint that Ḫimmuili had previously lied to him about the availability of seed, or perhaps had purloined it for other purposes in the meantime.

11 I emend the last word in the line (*ki-nu-wa*) to *ke-e*[!]*-wa* (or *ki-u*[!]*-wa* with an u glide). There is no reason to expect a *kinu*(*n*)*=wa* "now" here.

18–28 Kaššū goes on to imply that by doing favors for the wealthy "lords" and their fields, Ḫimmuili is failing in his prior duty to the crown lands.

20–21 Beckman (personal communication) suggests hendiadys may be operating here: "when you do not quickly sow."

23 Contra Alp 1991a, 222, I read *nu-un-na-aš ŠA BE-LU*^{MEŠ}*-TI* … NUMUN.ḪI.A here.

27–28 If my interpretation of *-z*(*a*) … *UL memma-* as "say 'no'" (CHD *mema-* 12 b) is correct, it is the earliest (MH) example yet attested of this expression. All examples cited in the CHD are NH. Note that several of them use the geminated m spelling of *me*(*m*)*ma-* "to say."

29–35 The complaint is that Ḫimmuili is detaining messengers sent to him from Kaššū. This was a serious matter, since the messengers were not Kaššū's own servants, but the king's. As Beckman noted (1995a, 24), this paragraph shows how bad personal relations were between Kaššū and Ḫimmuili. My translation reflects an understanding of the verb *t*/*dariyanzi* different from Beckman's, but otherwise agrees with his interpretation.

31 For the collated reading *ta-ri-ya-an-zi* here see CHD Š, 258, where the sarcasm is also noted.

33 The *ma-an* is merely anticipating the *ma-an* in line 34 and need not be translated in the first clause. Literally: "If only—how it is there—if only you would keep writing …" Interrupted thoughts in the wording are usually a sign that the letter was not drafted by a scribe from preliminary notes, but was either dictated directly or—if the writer is himself a scribe—composed as it was being written.

38 Alp's LÚ-*na-at-ta-aš* is an impossible form. What he translates is LÚ-*na-an-na-aš*. I have no photo to check the signs.

59. HKM 56
To Ḫuilli from Ḫimmuili

Text: Mşt. 75/42. **Find spot:** G/5 room 8. **Copy**: HKM 56. **Edition**: Alp 1991a, 224–27, 335–36 (no. 56). **Discussion**: Goedegebuure 2003, 182–83 (on the non-anaphoric use with a second-person reference ["from your place"] of *apez* in 8).

Ḫimmuili writes—according to Alp, from Ḫattuša—to his colleague Ḫuilli in Tapikka, giving him the position of preference (superiority) in the address form, and adding a wish for his welfare (lines 5–6), which is customary when writing to a superior. This relationship to a superior does not, however, keep Ḫimmuili from complaining bitterly because Ḫuilli did not send a greeting along with Ḫimmuili's messenger Šanda when the latter returned from him. He also issues a request (perhaps already requested previously and still not sent) for quivers and good quality weapons (lines 13–19).

(1) *A-NA* ^{m}Ḫu-il-li (2) ŠEŠ.DÙG.GA-*YA QÍ-BÍ-MA* (3) *UM-MA* ^{m}Ḫi-im-mu-DINGIR-*LIM* (4) *A-ḪU-KA-MA*	(1–4) Say to my dear brother Ḫuilli: Thus speaks Ḫimmuili, your brother:
(5) DINGIR.MEŠ-ta TI-an ḫar-kán-du (6) nu-ut-ta pa-aḫ-ša-an-ta-ru	(5–6) May the gods keep you alive and protect you!
(7) am-me-el [k]u-it LÚ *ṬE*$_4$*-MU* (8) a-pé-ez ú-it ŠEŠ.DÙG.GA-*YA*-ma-mu (9) aš-šu-ul ku-wa-at *Ú-UL* (10) ḫa-at-ra-a-eš	(7–10) Why, my dear brother, did you not send your greeting to me, when my messenger came (back) from you?
(11) nu-ud-du-za-kán ka-a-ša (12) ša-an-za	(11–12) I am angry with you!
(13) ki-nu-na ka-a-ša (14) am-me-el LÚ *ṬE*$_4$*-MU* (15) ^{m}AMAR.UTU-aš ú-iz-zi (16) nu-mu ŠEŠ$^{!}$.DÙG.GA-*YA* (17) ^{KUŠ}*IŠ-PA-TE*^{MEŠ} (18) ^{GIŠ}TUKUL SIG$_5$-ya (19) up-pí	(13–19) Now my messenger Šanda is about to come (again to you); so send me quivers and good weapons, my dear brother!

Commentary

For the *-d/tu* allomorph of *-ta* "(to) you," see *GrHL* §1.69 and §§5.14–15.

59b. HKM 56
Piggyback Letter from Tarḫunmiya to Walwa-ziti

(20) *UM-MA* $^{\text{m.d}}$U-mi-ya (21) *A-NA* ^{m}Wa-al-wa-NU[164] DUMU DÙG. GA-*YA* (22) *QÍ-BÍ-MA*	(20–22) Thus speaks Tarḫunmiya: Say to Walwa-ziti, my dear son:
(23) kat-ti-ti ḫu-u-ma-an SIG$_5$-in (24) e-eš-du nu-ut-ta <DINGIR. MEŠ> aš-šu-li (25) pa-aḫ-ša-an-ta-ru	(23–25) May all be well with you, and may <the gods> lovingly protect you!
(26) DUMU DÙG.GA-*YA*-mu aš-šu-ul (27) ku-wa-at *Ú-UL* ḫa-at-re-eš-ke-ši (28) am-me-el-kán aš-šu-ul *PA-NI* (29) ^{m}Pí-ip-pa-pa ḫal-za-i	(26–29) My dear son, why are you not sending your greeting to me? Read my greetings aloud to Pippapa!

60. HKM 57
From Ilali and Kašilti to the Provincial Governor and Ḫuilli

Text: Mşt. 75/60. **Find spot:** G/5 Room 8. **Copy:** HKM 57. **Edition**: Alp 1991a, 226–29 (no. 57). **Discussion:** de Martino and Imparati 1995, 109–10; Hoffner 1997g, 187; Francia 2002, §2.4.1 (lines 6–8); Goedegebuure 2003, 210; Imparati 2003, 238; Taggar-Cohen 2006, 156–57, 216–17 (on the DUMU SANGA).

It is somewhat unusual for a letter to multiple recipients to have also more than one sender. Yet that is the case here. But that one of these—probably the first-named, Ilali—is actually formulating the letter and occasionally lapses into the singular "I," can be seen in line 22.

The letter concerns a pending case against two offenders, Ḫimmuili and Tarḫumuwa, two men of Ḫaššarpanda, who are charged with stealing a woman (i.e., a purchased woman) belonging to a slave named Kaštanda. Although Kaštanda is a slave, he has influence and standing, because he is the slave of a "son of a priest." And therefore Ilali and Kašilti intercede with the provincial governor and Ḫuilli to judge the case and recover Kaštanda's woman. Ilali(?) says that he has sent Kaštanda to them along with this letter, so that he can see justice done and receive his woman.

(1) *UM-MA* ^{m}I-la-li (2) *Ù* ^{m}Ka-ši-i[l]-ti (3) *A-NA* ^{LÚ}*BE-EL* *<MA>-AD-GAL-TI* (4) *Ù A-NA* ^{m}Ḫu-i-il-li (5) ŠEŠ.ḪI.A DÙG.GA-*NI QÍ-BÍ-MA*	(1–5) Thus speak Ilali and Kašilti: Say to the Provincial Governor and to Ḫuilli, our dear brothers:
(6) kat-ta-aš-ma-aš ḫu-u-ma-an SIG$_5$-in (7) e-eš-tu nu-uš-ma-aš DINGIR.MEŠ TI-an (8) ḫar-kán-du nu-uš-ma-aš aš-šu-li (9) pa-aḫ-ša-an-da-ru	(6–9) May all be well with you (pl.). May the gods keep you (pl.) alive and lovingly protect you.
(10) ka-a-aš ku-iš ^{m}Ka-aš-ta-an-da-<aš> (11) ARAD LÚ DUMU SANGA ^{URU}Ú-ri-iš-ta (12) e-eš-zi nu-za-kán MUNUS ^{URU}Ga-aš-ša$^{!}$ (13) wa-aš-ta na-an-ši-kán (14) ^{m}Ḫi-im-mu-i-li-iš (15) ^{m}Tar-ḫu-u-mu-u-wa-ša (16) 2 LÚ.MEŠ ^{URU}Ḫa-aš-šar-pa-an-da (17) ar-ḫa da-i-e-er	(10–17) This Kaštanda, who is the slave of a man who is the son of a priest in Urišta, purchased for himself a woman from Kašša. But Ḫimmuili and Tarḫumuwa, two men of Ḫaššarpanda, stole her away from him.
(18) ki-nu-na-kán ka-a-š[a] (19) ^{m}Ka-aš-ta-an-da-an […] (20) ARAD ^{LÚ}DUMU SANGA [^{URU}Ú-ri-iš-ta …] (21) kat-ti-šu-mi pa-ra-a […] (22) ne-eḫ-ḫu-u-un nu-uš-ši […] (23) ḫa-an-ne-eš-šar [ḫ]a-an-n[a-a]t-tén (24) na-an-ká[n] aš-nu-ut[-tén]	(18–24) Now I (Ilali?) have herewith sent to you (pl.) Kaštanda, slave of a man who is the son of a priest in Urišta …. Judge the case for him and satisfy him.
(25) nu ú-iz-zi L[Ú DUMU SANGA] (26) *Ú-UL* ar-k[u-wa-ar i-ya-zi] (27) nu-za-kán šu-ma-aš […] (28) EGIR-pa *Ú-UL* t[e-ez-zi] (29) ARAD-*YA*-wa-m[u] (30) *Ú-UL* ḫa-a[n-n]a[-at-te-ni]	(25–30) Will the son of the priest$^{?}$ not proceed to make a plea$^{?}$.[165] Will he not speak for himself back to you (pl.), saying: "Will you not judge the case of my slave (i.e., Kaštanda)?"

(31) ma-a-an ḫa-an-n[a-at-te-ni-ma?] (32) a-pí-ya [nu] S[IG₅-in ma-a-an *Ú-UL*-ma nu MUNUS-an] (33) e-ep-t[a-n]i n[u?-un-na-aš-kán] (34) mḪi-im-mu-i-li-i[n mTar-ḫu-u-mu-wa-an] (35) ku-u-un-na mKa-aš-t[a-an-da-an] (36) pa-ra-a na-i[š-kat-tén?]	(31–36) If you (pl.) adjudicate there, fine. But if not, then you (pl.) should take the woman into custody, and send to us? Ḫimmuili, Tarḫumuwa, and this Kaštanda (so that I may judge them).

Commentary

10–17 Since there are two abductors, probably this is not elopement by a rival suitor (unless the second man is his helper, the *šardiyaš* of law §37), but abducting the woman to use or sell her as a slave. Kaštanda is clearly the injured party, not the offender (contra de Martino and Imparati), and it is difficult to see how they could claim that the final two paragraphs show him to be the offender! On the contrary, lines 18–24 show that the judges are to satisfy Kaštanda as the plaintiff (*na-an-ká*[*n*] *aš-nu-ut*[*-tén*]), illustrating the claim often made that Hittite justice imitated that of the Sun God who defended the just causes of widows and orphans (Singer 2002, 34 §8).

11 The LÚ may be a determinative here. The DUMU SANGA stands for Akkadian *mār šangê* "member of the priestly class."

13 Alp (1991a, 228) and de Martino and Imparati (1995, 109) emend the text to *wa-aš-ta*<*-aš*> "sinned." I follow Beal 1992, 433 in retaining *wa-aš-ta* "purchased." The verb form *wa-aš-ta* is from *waš-* "to buy" which regularly takes *-za* as in line 12. The verb *wašta-* "to sin" on the other hand never takes *-za*, nor does it take an "accusative of reference" to designate the person sinned against.

13–16 De Martino and Imparati failed to recognize that the issue is theft of Kaštanda's legitimate purchase, not only because they wrongly emended *wa-aš-ta* to *wa-aš-ta*<*-aš*>, but also because they misunderstood and mistranslated *da-i-e-er* as "took" (*daīr*, an impossible form given the spelling) instead of "stole" (*dayēr*).

29–30 The verb *ḫanna-* with the acc. of the person merely means judge someone's case. It does not necessarily indicate an adverse ruling (i.e., "condemn"). Since I have shown (see above on line 13) that there is no indication earlier in the document that Kaštanda is being sent as the accused, one who "sinned" (*wa-as-ta*<*-aš*>), the verb here simply means "judge K.'s case." And since it is his woman who has been stolen, I render this verb as "judge the case of" in the sense of "give satisfaction and justice to" Kaštanda. I have rendered the clauses as questions. Syntactically, it is also possible to render them as statements.

The restorations in 31–36 are my own conjecture, attempting to make some sense of the passage. If I am right, Ilali and Kašilti prefer that the governor and Ḫuilli judge Kaštanda's case. But if they cannot or prefer not to, they should send all three parties in the case to Ilali and Kašilti, who will then see to settling the case.

61. HKM 58
From Kikarša to Taḫazzili

Text: Mşt. 75/56. **Find spot:** G/5 Room 8. **Copy:** HKM 58. **Edition**: Alp 1991a, 228–31 (no. 58). **Discussion**: Beckman 1983b, 109 (on the Akkadian PNs); Alp 1991a, 54–55 (Ašduwarae), 336 (commentary); del Monte 1992, 126 (Piššunupašši), 139–40 (Šapinuwa); Hoffner 1997a, 400; 1997g, 175; 2002c, 68–69 with n. 43; Lühr 2001, 339 n. 12 (the reference to "Mşt. 75/76" [HKM 51] is a typographical error for Mşt. 75/56 [HKM 58], this text); Siegelová 2002, 736; Bryce 2003b, 173–74 (n. 15, translation of lines 5–14), 176 (n. 26, translating lines 29–31); Arıkan 2006, 148–49 (transliteration and translation of lines 5–14), 153; Marizza 2007a, 63, 135, 143, 161; Freu and Mazoyer 2007, 171, 187.

The official Kikarša, judging from the order of names in 1–2 perhaps the superior of Taḫazzili, writes to the latter in Tapikka, where Adad-bēlī (addressed in the piggyback letter) was also headquartered. We have no information about Kikarša's and Ilī-tukultī's whereabouts when they sent this letter to Tapikka.

(1) *UM-MA* mKi-kar-ša *A-NA* mTa-ḫa-az-zi-DINGIR-*LIM* (2) ŠEŠ DÙG.GA-*YA* *QÍ-BÍ-MA*	(1–2) Thus speaks Kikarša: Say to Taḫazzili, my dear brother:
(3) *MA-ḪAR* ŠEŠ.DÙG.GA-*YA* ḫu-u-ma-an SIG_5-in e-eš-du (4) nu-ut-ta DINGIR.MEŠ aš-šu-li pa-aḫ-ša-an-da-ru	(3–4) May all be well with my dear brother, and may the gods lovingly protect you.
(5) *ŠA* LÚ.MEŠ IGI.NU.GÁL-mu	(5–14) Concerning the matter of

ku-it ut-tar ḫa-at-ra-a-eš (6) nu-kán LÚ.MEŠ IGI.NU.GÁL.ḪI.A ḫu-u-ma-an-te-eš (7) URUŠa-pí-nu-u-wa ša-ra-a pé-e-ḫu-te-er (8) ka-a-ma 10 LÚ.MEŠ IGI.NU.GÁL.ḪI.A *I-NA* É.ḪI.A NA4ARA$_5$-*R*[*U*] (9) ar-ḫa ta-a-li-e-er na-aš ka-a-ša pu-nu-uš-šu-un (10) nu-mu zi-ik ku-i-e-eš lam-ni-it ḫa-at-ra-a-eš (11) na-aš-ta NU.GÁL ku-iš-ki an-da (12) nu ma-a-an ḫa-at-ra-a-ši nu *I-NA* URUŠa-pí-nu-wa (13) *A-NA* mŠa-ar-pa ḫa-at-ra-a-i (14) LÚ.MEŠ IGI.NU.GÁL ḫu-u-ma-an-du-uš a-pí-ya	the blind men that you wrote me about: They have conducted all of the blind men up to the town Šapinuwa. They have left behind here ten blind men (to work) in the mill houses. I have now inquired about them, and there is no one here by the names you wrote to me. If you (wish to) write, write to Šarpa in Šapinuwa. All the (other) blind men are there."
(15) k[a-a-]ša *ŠA* mAš-du-wa-ar-ra-e ut-tar (16) [d]U[TU-*Š*]*I* [p]a-ra-a-ya ḫa-at-re-eš-ke-mi (17) [n]a-at-mu EGIR-pa *Ú-UL* ku-it-ki (18) [ḫa-at-r]a-a-š[i] mAš-du-wa-ra-a-en ku-in (19) [U]RUPí-iš-šu-nu-pa-aš-ši a-pí-ya ḫar-kán-zi (20) [nu-u]š-ma-aš-ša-an dUTU-*ŠI* ku-it (21) EGIR-pa ma-ni-ya-aḫ-ta na-an EGIR-pa (22) [k]u-wa-at *Ú-UL* pí-iš-te-ni (23) na-an ma-a-an *Ú-UL* pí-iš-te-ni (24) nu-mu ḫa-at-ra-a-i na-at *I-NA* É.GAL-*LIM* ḫa-at-ra-a-mi	(15–24) I keep writing (to) His Majesty on the subject of Ašduwarrae, but you write nothing back to me about it. Since His Majesty handed Ašduwarrae, whom they are holding there in Piššunupašši, over to you (pl.), why don't you give him back? If you do not give him, write to me, and I will write it to the (regional?) palace.

Commentary

5–14 Cited in full and translated in Siegelová 2002, 736. The blind men referred to in this letter and HKM 59 (text 62) were prisoners of war, who had been blinded after their capture, because they had broken their oaths to the Hittite king (so correctly Siegelová 2002, 736). Some of them were held for ransom by their homelands, as we learn from HKM 102, on which see the comments above on HKM 14 (text 19). While awaiting ransom, they were put to use as temporary labor. Why working in the mill houses was selected as the best place for some of them is not entirely clear. Since milling was traditionally the domestic chore of the women of the household (see Hoffner 1974a, 133), this may have been a form of humiliating these enemies of the state. It was also a job that a blind person could perform almost as easily as a sighted person, which was the not the case with many other tasks. For discussion of the subject, see Hoffner 2002c, 2004; Siegelová 2002; Bryce 2003b: 173, and Arıkan 2006, 148–49, 153. Blinded prisoners of war working in the mill houses provides cultural background for the biblical story of the Israelite strong man Samson, whom the Philistines captured, blinded, and put to work in a mill house. See Judg 16:21, and Hoffner 2002c, 2004.

6–7 Edited in CHD Š, 217 (*šarā* B 1 a 36′).

22–23 Edited in Hoffner 1995a, 99.

61b. HKM 58
Piggyback Letter to Adad-bēlī from Ilī-tukultī

(25) *A-NA* m.dU-*BE-LÍ* ŠEŠ.DÙG.GA-*YA QÍ-BÍ-MA* (26) *UM-MA* mDINGIR-*LIM-TU-KU-UL-TI* ŠEŠ-*KA-MA*	(25–26) Say to Adad-bēlī, my dear brother: Thus speaks Ilī-tukultī, your brother:
(27) kat-ti-ti ḫu-u-ma-an SIG_5-in e-eš-du (28) nu-ut-ta DINGIR.MEŠ aš-šu-li pa-aḫ-ša-an-da-ru	(27–28) May all be well with you. May the gods lovingly protect you.
(29) *A-NA* ŠEŠ.DÙG.GA-*YA* aš-šu-ú-ul KASKAL-ši KASKAL-ši ḫa-at-re-eš-ke-mi (30) zi-ga-mu tuel aš-šu-ú-ul (31) EGIR-pa *Ú-UL* ku-wa-pí-ik-ki ḫa-at-ra-a-eš	(29–31) I keep writing greetings to my dear brother time after time, but you never write back your greeting.

Commentary

25–26 Note that both scribes—Adad-bēlī and Ilī-tukultī—have Akkadian names (perhaps *noms de plume*). On the debated question if scribal *noms de plume* actually existed in Hittite see Hoffner 1980, 319; Beckman 1983b, 107; Archi 2007, 186; and above in §2.2.2.1.

28 On KASKAL-*ši* KASKAL-*ši* "time after time" see CHD P, 77 (*palša-* 7 d), and *GrHL* §19.10.

29–31 See Bryce 2003b, 176.

62. HKM 59
From Šarpa to the Provincial Governor and to Tarḫuni

Text: Mşt. 76/52. **Find spot:** G/5 Room 8. **Copy**: HKM 59. **Edition**: Alp 1991a, 232–33 (no. 59). **Discussion**: Siegelová 2002, 736–37; Arıkan 2006, 149 (edition of lines 4–14).

(1) [*U*]*M-MA* ^{m}Ša-ar-pa (2) [*A*]-*NA* ^{LÚ}EN *MAD-GAL*$_9$-*TI* (3) [*Ù*] *A-NA* $^{m.d}$U-ni *QÍ-BÍ-MA*	(1–3) Thus speaks Šarpa: Say to (Ḫimmuili?), the Provincial Governor, and to Tarḫuni:
(4) [k]a-a-ša-kán ^{URU}Ša-pí-nu-wa-za (5) [L]Ú.MEŠ IGI.NU.GÁL (6) [*I*]*Š-TU* É ^{NA_4}AR[A$_5$] (7) [p]a-ra-a ḫu-wa-a-er (8) [n]a-at a-pád-da ú-e-er (9) [nu]-uš-ma-aš ma-aḫ-ḫa-an (10) [ka-]a-aš tup-pí-an-za (11) [an-da ú-]⌜e⌝-mi-ya-zi (12) [$^{LÚ.MEŠ}$IGI.NU.GÁL-za p]é-ra-an (13) [ḫu-nu-ut-tén[166] na-aš SI]G$_5$-in (14) [EGIR-pa ú-wa-te-et-t]én	(4–14) Blind men have fled from the mill house in Šapinuwa and have come (to you) there. As soon as this tablet reaches you, take charge of the blind men and conduct them back here safely.
(15) [ma-a-an o o o] LÚ.KÚR-ya (16) [o o o KUR-i]a[167] (17) [o o o o an-d]a ú-iz-zi (18) [nu-za pa-aḫ-ḫa-a]š-nu-wa-an-te-eš[168] (19) [e-eš-tén]	(15–19) If the enemy comes into the land, be very careful.

Commentary

12–14 are translated by Arıkan as "[catch] [the blind men] [al]ive and well and [brin]g [them back]."

See comments on HKM 58 above.

63. HKM 60
From Šarpa to Zaldumanni and Ḫuilli

Text: Mşt. 77/1. **Find spot:** H/5 Room 9. **Copy**: HKM 60. **Edition**: Alp 1991a, 232–35 (no. 60). **Discussion**: de Martino and Imparati 1995, 111;

Imparati 1997, 204; 2002, 96–97; Houwink ten Cate 1998, 174; Francia 2002, §2.4.1 (lines 30–31); Goedegebuure 2003, 255–56; van den Hout 2003a (HKM 60 is translated on p. 152–53); de Martino 2005b, 311.

Zaldumanni is believed to be the same person as Zardumanni. Beckman (1995a, 27 n. 42) writes that this letter shows provincial officials involved in legal disputes in the royal court. Šapinuwa was one of several royal residences ("palaces") outside of the capital. The court there functioned even when the king was not in residence, as quite possibly in this case.

Both the sender, Šarpa, and the aggrieved person, Tarḫunmiya, were in Šapinuwa when this letter was dispatched. Imparati cites in proof that "the sender of the letter, Šarpa, a high dignitary who at the time occupied a political position of considerable importance in Šapinuwa, alluding to certain damages suffered by Tarḫunmiya, referred to what the latter had 'said' to him (*memišta*, Obv. 11 and 21), rather than what had been 'written' to him, as occurs instead in other cases" (Imparati 1997, 204). See also the significant use of *mema-* "speak" in HKM 52 (text 55): 8 and 18.

As already noted, the "house" of Tarḫunmiya needs to be protected against oppression by the undue imposition of imposts (*šaḫḫan* and *luzzi*), whereas the physical property (e.g., a chariot) is guarded against damage incurred by persons who use it (lines 21–26).

(1) [*U*]*M-MA* mŠa-ar-pa (2) *A-NA* mZa-al-du-ma-an-ni (3) *Ù A-NA* mḪu-il-li *QÍ-BÍ-MA*	(1–3) Thus speaks Šarpa: Say to Zaldumanni and Ḫuilli:
(4) ka-a-ša-aš-ma-aš *ŠA* É mTar-ḫu-un-mi-ya (5) ku-it *ŠA* DI.ḪI.A ut-tar (6) *IŠ-T*[*U*] GIŠ.ḪUR ḫa-at-ra-a-nu-un (7) nu-uš-ša-an É mTar-ḫu-un-mi-ya (8) IGI.ḪI.A-wa e-ep-tén nam-ma-aš-ši (9) DI.ḪI.A ḫa-an-ni-iš-tén na-an aš-nu-ut-tén	(4–9) Concerning the legal proceedings about the "house" of Tarḫunmiya which I have recently written to (the two of) you on a wooden tablet: Set your eyes on the "house" of Tarḫunmiya! Judge his legal matters and satisfy him!
(10) ka-a-ša-mu mTar-ḫu-un-mi-ya-aš (11) ki-iš-ša-an-na me-mi-iš-ta (12) mLu-ši-wa-li-iš[169]-wa-mu (13) mYa-ra-ap-pí-ya-aš-ša (14) dam-mi-iš-ḫa-a-an ḫar-kán-zi	(10–14) Tarḫunmiya has just told me the following: "Lušiwali and Yarappiya have done me harm."

(15) na-at a-pí-ya an-da da-iš-tén (16) na-at pu-nu-uš-tén (17) [nam]-ma-aš-mu-kán du-w[a-a-a]n (18) p[a-r]a-a na-iš-tén ku-it-m[a-na-aš] (19) *M*[*A-ḪA*]*R* ^{d}UTU-*ŠI* na-a-i[š-ke-mi nu …] (20) pé-en-na-aḫ-ḫ[i]	(15–20) Set it (i.e., the case) down there and investigate it. Then send them (i.e., Lušiwali and Yarap-piya) on to me until I can send them to His Majesty and drive ….
(21) ki-iš-ša-an-na-mu me-mi-iš-[ta] (22) ^{m}Lu-ši-wa-li-iš-wa-za ^{GIŠ}GIGIR (23) tu-u-ri-ya-az-zi nam-ma-wa-ra-at (24) ar-ḫa [d]u-wa-ar-ni-iz-zi (25) nu-uš-ši a-pa-a-at-ta ^{GIŠ}GIGIR (26) EGIR-pa SIG$_5$-in i-ya-ad-du	(21–26) (Tarḫunmiya) also told me the following: "Lušiwali hitched up a chariot (of mine) and then wrecked it." So let (Lušiwali) repair that chariot for him.

Commentary

7–9 are edited in CHD Š, 70 (*šakui-* 1 d 2′ d').

8 There seems to be some distinction between IGI.ḪI.A-*wa ḫar(k)-* "keep your eyes (on) …" (lines 36–37) and IGI.ḪI.A-*wa ēp-* "set your eyes (on) …" (line 8), *ḫar(k)-* "hold" being stative and *ēp-*"grasp, seize" inchoative/ingressive in aspect.

23–24 The two verbs in the present tense are to be taken as indicating past tense, probably influenced by the analytic perfect form in line 14.

63b: HKM 60
Piggyback Letter to Pallanna from Šarpa

(27) *A-NA* ^{m}Pal-la-an-na *A-BI* DÙG.GA-*YA* (28) *Ù A-NA* ^{f}Ma-an-ni-i (29) NIN DÙG.GA-*YA QÍ-BÍ-MA* (30) kat-ta-an-ša-ma-aš ḫu-u-ma-an (31) SIG$_5$-in e-eš-du nu-uš-ma-aš (32) *LI-IM*! DINGIR.MEŠ aš-šu-li (33) pa-aḫ-ša-an-da-ru	(27–33) Say to Pallanna, my dear father, and to Manni, my dear sister: May everything be well with you (two). May the Thousand Gods lovingly protect you.
(34) aš-šu-ul-mu ḫa-at-re-eš-kat-tén (35) na[m]-ma-aš-ša-an *A-BI* DÙG.GA-*YA* (36) *A-NA* É-*YA* IGI.ḪI.A-wa (37) ḫar-ak	(34–37) Please return my greetings. And furthermore, dear father, keep your eyes on my house!

Commentary

If the woman Manni mentioned here is the same person who is paired with Pallanna in HKM 81 (text 80), then perhaps they are man and wife. And if so, then Šarpa uses the terms "my dear father" and "my dear sister" in the extended sense of colleagues, while Tarḫunmiya in HKM 81 (text 80) uses "my dear father" and "my dear mother" of the same two people in the literal sense. Otherwise, if both men use the terms in the extended sense, Šarpa does not wish to indicate that Manni was superior to himself ("mother"), but equal in rank ("sister"). For the somewhat unusual expanded well-being formula, using "the Thousand Gods," see §1.2.17.

37 The scribe has placed a single wedge to the left of *ḫar-ak*, and centered that word in the line. The wedge has no linguistic significance.

64. HKM 61
From Ḫulla to Taḫazzili

Text: Mşt. 75/71. **Find spot:** G/5 Room 8. **Copy**: HKM 61. **Edition**: Alp 1991a, 236–37 (no. 61). **Discussion**: del Monte 1992, 149 (Šuppiluliya); Klinger 1995a, 92; Marizza 2007a, 82–83, 85, 142 (persons mentioned).

(1) *UM-MA* ^{m}Ḫu-ul-la (2) *A-NA* ^{m}Ta-ḫa-az-z[i-DINGIR-*LIM*] (3) *QÍ-BÍ-MA*	(1–3) Thus speaks Ḫulla: Say to Taḫazzili:
(4) ka-a-ša DUMU ^{m}Ka[m-ma-am-ma-]an-d[a] (5) L[Ú] ^{URU}Šu-up-pí-l[u-li-y]a (6) LÚ.KÚR e-ep[-ta]	(4–6) The enemy has just captured the son of Kammammanda, the man from Šuppiluliya,
(7) na-an [...] (8) ša-an-ḫ[a-...] (9) URU-ri [...] (10) x [...] (11) le-e x [...]	(7–11) and ...-ed him. So search for him$^{?}$ ... in the town ... do not ...!
(12) nu-uš-ši-x[-... ...] (13) pé-di ni$^{?}$-[ni-ik na-an ... ...] (14) ti-it-t[a-nu-ut ... ...] (15) a-pu-u-un D[UMU-an EGIR-pa] (16) ú-wa-te	(12–16) For him ... remove$^{?}$! And ... station! ... Bring back that son!

65. HKM 62
From Ḫulla to Ḫimmuili

Text: Mşt. 75/78. **Find spot:** G/5 room 8. **Copy**: HKM 62. **Edition**: Alp 1991a, 236–39 (no. 62). **Discussion:** del Monte 1992, 30 (on the GN Ḫariya); Klinger 1995a, 92; Marizza 2007a, 84–85, 115, 140 (Ḫimmuili), 162 (Tarḫunmiya). See discussion on pp. 94–95.

(1) *UM*[-*M*]*A* mḪ[u]-u-[u]l-la[…] (2) *A-NA* mḪi-mu-DIN[GIR-*LI*]*M QÍ-BÍ-MA*	(1–2) Thus speaks Ḫulla, …: Say to Ḫimmuili:
(3) LÚ.MEŠ pít-ti-ya-a[n-du-u]š […] (4) LÚ.MEŠ URUḪa-ri-ya x x[…] (5) ma-ni-ya-aḫ-[ḫ]a-a[n-t]e-e[š] nu-u[š-ma-aš-ša-an] (6) IGI.ḪI.A-wa ḫa[r-a]k k[a-a-ša] (7) ku-e-[d]a-aš an-[t]u-uḫ-ša-a[š …] (8) na-aš-kán pa-ra-a na[-i]	(3–8) The fugitives of … (and?) the men of Ḫariya … (are?) subordinates. Keep your eyes on them! To/For whatever people now …, dispatch them!

Commentary

4 Del Monte (1992, 30) notes how in HKM 111: 24–27 Ḫimmuili is active in the town Ḫariya: “28 *parisu* of emmer (as seed grain): Ḫimmuili, Maruwa, (and) Tiwaziti, the Gold Charioteer, will sow (it) in Ḫariya.”

65b. HKM 62
Piggyback Letter of Tarḫunmiya to Ḫimmuili

(9) *A-NA BE-LÍ* mḪi-mu-DINGIR-*LIM A-BI* [DÙG.GA-*YA*] (10) *QÍ-BÍ-MA UM-MA* mTar-ḫu-u[n-mi-ya] (11) DUMU-*KA-MA*	(9–11) Say to my lord Ḫimmuili, my dear father: Thus speaks Tarḫunmiya, your son:
(12) ka-a-ša DI.ḪI.A mḪu-u-u[l-la-aš?] (13) a[m]-mu-uk-ka$_4$ *A-NA* x x x […] (14) ⸢na-at⸣ pár-ku-e-eš[…] (15) x x k[a-a-š]a x[…]	(12–15) Ḫulla and I …-ed legal cases to/for … they were innocent? …

(*Lines 16-18 preserved only in traces*) (19) nam-ma [… … … … … …] (20) a-p[é-… … … … … …] (21) n[a]-a[š … … … … … … …] (22) nu x x [… … … … … …] (23) a-pí-ya x [… … … … … …]	*(Rest of tablet too broken for translation)*

66. HKM 63
From Piyama-Tarḫunta to Ḫimmuili

Text: Mşt. 75/49. **Find spot:** G/5 Room 8. **Copy**: HKM 63. **Edition**: Alp 1991a, 238–41 (no. 63). **Discussion**: Houwink ten Cate 1998, 165–66; Melchert 1998, 46 (on *arku-* and *arkuwar*, line 10); Lühr 2001, 335 n. 7b.

This letter gives no clue whether it was written from the capital or the principal provincial palace in Tapikka's region, namely Šapinuwa.

(1) *UM-MA* mSUM-dU (2) *A-NA* mḪi-mu-DINGIR-*LIM* ŠEŠ DÙG.GA-*YA* (3) *QÍ-BÍ-MA*	(1–3) Thus speaks Piyama-Tarḫunta: Say to Ḫimmuili, my dear brother:
(4) *MA-ḪAR* ŠEŠ DÙG.GA-*YA* SI[G_5-i]n (5) e-eš-du nu-ut-ta DINGIR.MEŠ (6) aš-šu-li pa-aḫ-ša-an-ta-ru	(4–6) May it be well with my dear brother. May the gods lovingly protect you.
(7) ŠEŠ DÙG.GA-*YA*-mu ku-it ki-iš-ša-an (8) ḫa-at-ra-a-eš ud-da-a-ar-wa ku-e (9) ḫa-at-re-eš-ke-mi nu-wa-mu ud-da-na-a-aš (10) EGIR-pa ar-ku-wa-ar *Ú-UL* (11) ku-iš-ki ú-da-i	(7–11) Concerning what you, my dear brother, wrote me, as follows: "To the matters which I keep writing (to you) no one brings back an answer (i.e., an explanation) to me."
(12) nu tu-el ku-it ŠEŠ-*KA*[170] (13) ú-it na-an *I-NA* É.GAL-*LIM* (14) *Ú-UL* am-mu-uk tar-kum-mi-ya-nu-un (15) nu *IŠ-TU* É.GAL-*LIM* tu-uk (16) GIŠGIGIR te-re-er	(12–16) With regard to the fact that your brother came: did not I announce him in the palace? And they have promised you a chariot from the palace.
(17) nu *BE-LU*MEŠ-*TIM* EGIR-an	(17–26) I supported the lords. They

(18) ti-ya-nu-un na-at-kán (19) pa-ra-a da-i-e-er (20) na-at *A-NA* ^{d}UTU-*ŠI* (21) ú-wa-an-na ḫa-an-da-a-er (22) ŠEŠ-*KA*-ma EGIR-an ar-ḫa (23) ḫu-wa-iš na-aš-za ar-ḫa (24) *I-NA* É-*ŠU* pa-it (25) am-mu-ga-ma-an ma-aḫ-ḫa-an (26) i-ya-nu-un	*proposed* it. They *arranged* for His Majesty to *consider* (literally "see") it. But afterwards your brother fled and went back home to his house. How could I have treated him (better)?[171]

67. HKM 64
To Kaššū from Piyama-Tarḫunta

Text: Mşt. 75/24. **Find spot:** H/5 room 9. **Copy**: HKM 64. **Edition**: Alp 1991a, 240–43 (no. 64). **Discussion**: Houwink ten Cate 1998, 168; many lines and forms cited in Hoffner forthcoming.

(1) *A-NA* ^{m}G[a-aš-šu-ú] (2) ŠEŠ.DÙG.GA-⸢*YA*⸣ [*QÍ-B*]*Í-MA* (3) *UM-MA* ^{m}SUM-^{d}U [Š]EŠ-*KA-MA* (4) DINGIR.MEŠ-⸢ta⸣ TI-an ḫar-kán-du (5) nu-ut-ta pa-aḫ-ša-an-t[a-r]u	(1–5) Say to Kaššū, my dear brother: Thus speaks Piyama-Tarḫunta, your brother: May the gods keep you alive and protect you!
(6) ḫa-x[…]-x [z]i-na-x x […] (7) x-x […-t]u-u-⸢ug?-ga?⸣[…] (8) ⸢x x⸣ [x]x *ṬUP-PA*$^{ḪI.⸢A⸣}$ [o] (9) ANŠE.K[UR.RA a]r-ḫa ḫu-wa-iš	(6–9) … tablets … horse(s) ran away.
(10) ki-nu-[na …-i]š LÚ *ṬE*$_{4}$*-MI* (11) ú-i[t … z]i-ik (12) ma[-…] (13) EGIR[…] (14) [u]t-tar ku-it-ki (15) [š]a-ra-a wa-at-ku-ut-ta (16) na-aš-ta wa-ar-pu-wa-an-zi (17) ar-ḫa wa-al-aḫ-ḫe!-er (18) nu ku-in-na ku-wa-pí-ki (19) a-ra-a-an ḫar-ke-er (20) nu ka-a-aš LÚ *ṬE*$_{4}$*-MI* (21) ta-me-ta-ni pé-di a-ra-an	(10–21) But now …, the messenger, has come, and … you … back/again … some matter has arisen. And they struck them away from surrounding? you. And they have stopped? each of them somewhere. And this messenger … in/to another place.
(22) nu ud-da-na-aš ar-ku-wa-ar (23) ku-it EGIR-pa i-e-er (24) ne-et-ta ka-a-aš-ma (25) *ṬUP-PÍ ŠA* ^{m}Ḫi-	(22–26) And the replies to the word which they have made, (my) messenger has herewith brought them

mu-DINGIR-*LIM* (26) LÚ *ṬE*$_4$-*MI* ú-da-aš	to you (in?) the tablet of Ḫimmuili.
(27) ma-aḫ-ḫa[-an [d]]UTU-*ŠI* an-da (28) [n]u[?] tar[?]-x[-…(-)]na-aš-š[a(-) …] x x (29) LÚ *ṬE*$_4$-*MI*[?]-*K*[*A*[?]-…] (l. e. 1) pa-ra-a ne-eḫ-ḫu-un (l. e. 2) [nu] ŠEŠ DÙG.GA-*I*[*A* …] (l. e. 3) *QA-TAM-M*[*A* š]a-a-ak	(27–29, l. e. 1–3) As soon as His Majesty …-s there, … your messenger … I have dispatched. So be advised accordingly, my dear brother!

68. HKM 65
From Pulli to Adad-bēlī

Text: Mşt. 75/55. **Find spot:** G/5 Room 8. **Copy**: HKM 65. **Edition**: Alp 1991a, 242–45 (no. 65). **Discussion**: Klinger 1995a, 99 (on Pulli); Houwink ten Cate 1998, 162 (lines 22–27); Lühr 2001, 339 n. 12; Hoffner 2002c, 67; Freu and Mazoyer 2007, 171, 186.

(1) *UM-MA* [m]Pu-ul-li (2) *A-NA* [m.d]IŠKUR-*BE-LÍ* DUMU-*YA* (3) *QÍ-BÍ-MA*	(1–3) Thus speaks Pulli: Say to Adad-bēlī, my son:
(4) *I-NA* [URU]Ga-ši-pu-u-ra ku-i-uš (5) 2 LÚ.MEŠ [URU]Ma-la-az-zi-ya (6) [[m]P]í-š[i]-iš-ši-i[ḫ]-li-in (7) [[m]N]a-iš-tu-u-wa-ar-ri-in-na (8) ap-pa-an-te-eš na-aš-ša-an ŠU.ḪI.A-*ŠU* GÌR.MEŠ-*ŠU*-ya SIG$_5$[?]-at-tén nam-ma-aš-ká[n] (9) *A-NA* ANŠE.KUR.RA.ḪI.A ti-it-ta-nu-ut-tén (10) ÉRIN.MEŠ-ya-aš-ma-aš šar-di-ya ti-ya-ad-du	(4–19) As for the two men of Malazziya, Pišiššiḫli and Naištuwarri, who are held captive in Kašepura: secure them hand and foot, then mount them on horses, and let a troop stand by to assist you.
(11) na-aš-kán [URU]Ga-ši-pu-u-ra-az (12) ša-ra-a SIG$_5$-in ar-nu-ut (13) nam-ma-aš [tu]p[?]-pa-an (14) x - x - x.MEŠ ḫar-kán-zi (15) nu-uš-ma-aš-ša-an LÚ.MEŠ SIG$_5$ [m][Š]i-mi-ti-li-in-na LÚ [URU]Ga-	(11–19) Move them up (here) safely from Kašepura. … (17) Let them conduct them quickly here to His Majesty.

w[a-]at-tág-g[a] (16) an-da x - x - x- ia (17) na-aš *MA-ḪAR* ^{d}UTU-*ŠI* (18) li-li-wa-aḫ-ḫ[u]-u-an-[z]i (19) ú-wa-da-an-du	

Commentary

4–19 See also translation in CHD Š, 292 (taking -*šmaš* as pl. "you") but CHD Š, 137 and 293 (taking -*šmaš* as "them"—"let troops accompany them for help"). Because the imperatives in lines 8 and 9 are plural, the "you" plural option is equally possible. In any event, the assistance (*šardiya*) rendered is not to the captives, but to the addressees, by binding the captives, setting them on horses, and accompanying them on the trip as a guard.

4–8 This long relative clause seems to be grammatically confused. The accusative forms (which should properly be nominatives) are influenced by the writer's anticipation of his next clause, in which they will be the direct objects.

68b. HKM 65b
Piggyback Letter from Tarḫunmiya to Adad-bēlī

(20) *U*[*M-M*]*A* $^{m.d}$U-mi-ya *A-NA* $^{m.d}$U-*BE-LÍ* (21) [Š]EŠ.DÙG.GA-*YA* *QÍ-BÍ-MA*	(20–21) Thus speaks Tarḫunmiya: Say to Adad-bēlī, my dear brother:
(22) *A-NA* ^{m}Du-wa-az-zi me-mi (23) na-aš-ta $^{m.d}$U-mi-im-ma-an (24) ^{m}Na-a-ni-in ^{m}Ku-wa-am-mi-in-na pa-ra-a na-i (25) ANŠE-*YA*-wa BULÙG BAPPIR[172] NINDA ḫar-ši[-…[173]].ḪI.A-ya-wa u-un-ni-an-du (26) [Z]ÍD.DA-*YA* ḫar-pa-nu-ut (27) nu-wa-ra-aš-kán pa-ra-a [na-i] (l. e. 1) [n]a-aš-ma-wa zi-ig-g[a]-ma e-ḫ[u] (l. e. 2) x - x .MEŠ me-ma-ú ut-ni-[y]a-kán (l. e. 3) x[- … p]a-r[a-a n[a]-i (l. e. 4) nu-uš-ši x-[o-u]š ú-da-a[n]-d[u]	(22–27, l. e. 1–4) Speak to Tuwazzi. Then send Tarḫumimma, Nāni, and Kuwammi forth (saying): "Have them … my donkey, malt, 'beer bread', (and) thick loaves; and let them drive here …s as well. Pile up flour too. Then dispatch them (i.e., the three men). Or come yourself." Let him/her speak …s. In/to the land dispatch …. Let them bring …s to him/it.

Commentary

25–26 Interpreting the three YA clitics in these lines is a bit problematic. But taking the first one (in line 25 after ANŠE) as Hittite "and, too, as well" is unlikely, since it begins the direct quote. An Akkadian possessive -*YA* "my" is quite possible here. But in the two succeeding clauses the interpretation as a possessive is less persuasive, leading me to take these as the Hittite "too" or "as well."

69. HKM 66
From Ḫulla to Adad-bēlī

Text: Mşt. 75/63. **Find spot:** G/5 Room 8. **Copy**: HKM 66. **Edition**: Alp 1991a, 244–49 (no. 66). **Discussion**: Alp 1991a, 53 (on Adad-bēlī); del Monte 1992 (on the GNs Tapikka, Panāta, and Pašduwaduwa); Klinger 1995a, 92; Beal 1998, 85; Rieken 2004, 540; Marizza 2007a, 84–85 (on the rank and competence of Ḫulla).

Ḫulla, who outranks both the provincial governor (*BĒL MADGALTI*) and the NIMGIR.ÉRIN.MEŠ (see Marizza 2007a, 84–85), asks Adad-bēlī to relay a message to a colleague, whose name is lost in the lacuna, in which he first (lines 3–7) reassures the colleague that certain things are in good order, and then (lines 8–19) gives instructions about the use of chariot horses. Turning to Adad-bēlī himself (lines 20 and following), Ḫulla gives instructions regarding the slave of a certain Šaparta, whom he has ordered to be sent into Kaškaean territory to seek his master's son (lines 20–33). The slave is to take with him three Kaškaean hostages to exchange for Šaparta's son (lines 26–33). There follows (in lines 34–42) a paragraph that is unclear, because of words of obscure meaning and an unknown context of the situation. The sender has need of grasses (Ú.ḪI.A, perhaps medicinal herbs, as per CHD Š, 31, comparing KUB 22.61 i 14–16) and reeds (*zuppari*), but the agricultural workers of Tapikka have ceased to harvest them. He asks Adad-bēlī, who is knowledgeable in these matters, to see to the resumption of the shipments. Unfortunately we do not know to what use Ḫulla would put these reeds. Alp (1991a, 339) surmised that the word I have translated as "reeds" (*zuppari*), which normally means "torches," refers to a kind of kindling wood (Turkish *çıra*), so that the reeds might have served to light fires. But whether we translate "reeds" or "kindling," this is the only example of *zuppari*- in either of those meanings. Freu and Mazoyer (2007, 171) assume that they were to be used as fodder for horses and livestock.

The complaint that the addressee has not written (lines 43–46) is a normal feature of letters, but especially of letters between officials.

(1) *U*[*M-M*]*A* ᵐḪ[u-ul-la *A-NA* ᵐ·ᵈIŠKUR-*BE-LÍ*] (2) [ŠE]Š.DÙG.GA-*YA QÍ-B*[*I-MA*]	(1–2) Thus speaks Ḫulla: Say to my dear brother Adad-bēlī:
(3) am-me-el-kán aš-šu-ul *P*[*A-N*]*I* [ᵐ… ŠEŠ.DÙG.GA-*YA*] (4) *RA-IM-MU-YA* SIG₅-in ⌜ḫal-za-i⌝ (5) ka-a-ša-wa-mu za-ak-[ki?] še-li-uš[174] pád[-da-an-te-eš?] (6) ka-ru-ú SIG₅-a[n]-te-eš nu-wa-kán [le]-e (7) ku-wa-at-ka₄ la-aḫ-la-aḫ-ḫi-ya-š[i]	(3–7) Read my greeting clearly in the presence of my dear brother …, my beloved: "Already at this moment my *doorbolts* (and) … *grain piles* are in good order; so don't you worry one bit!"[175]
(8) zi-ga-wa-kán ᵁᴿᵁ[T]a-pí-[i]k-ka₄-a[z x-t]a? (9) k[at?-t]a? ku-wa-at pé![-en]-[n]a-at-ti (10) nu-wa-mu! ⌜*ŠA*⌝ LÚ.KÚR ⌜ku⌝-w[a]-[p]í-ki ANŠE?.[KUR?.RA?.MEŠ?] x x (11) nu-wa-at-ták-kán a?-pa-a-[t]a/[š]a pé-e-ḫu-[d]a-an-z[i] (12) nu-wa-kán ma-a-an k[at]-ta-ya ku-wa-pí pé-⌜en-na-ti?⌝ (13) nu-w[a] ANŠE.KUR.RA.Ḫ[I.A] tar-pu-li-iš-m[i?] x[-x-x] (14) tu-u-re-eš-ke ANŠE.KUR.RA.ḪI.A ḫa-an-te-ya-ra-⌜ḫa?⌝[-aš?] (15) ku-i-e-eš nu-wa-ra-aš ᵐIm-ra-LÚ-iš ᵐDu-la-a[k]-k[i-i]š (16) tu-u-ri-iš-ke-ed-du nu-wa-kán ma-a-an (17) ú-it nam-ma ku-it-ki a-aš-ša-an (18) nu-wa-ra-[a]t nam-ma ar-ḫa tar-na-an-du (19) nu-wa-ra-[a]t ar-ḫa du-wa-ar-na-an-du	(8–19) "But you (sg.)—why are you (*sg.*) driving … down from Tapikka? Are the chariot troops of the enemy somewhere? (near) me, that they lead you (*sg.*) *thither*? If you (*sg.*) drive down somewhere, hitch the horses up … to their *tarpula/i*-s! Let Imra-ziti (and?) Dulakki[176] hitch up horses that are *ḫanteyaraḫa-…*! And if it has happened that something is again left over, they should let it go again and break it off."[177]
(20) ARAD ᵐŠa-pár-ta-ya-kán ku-in (21) *I-NA* KUR ᵁᴿᵁGa-aš-ga pa-ra-a ne-eḫ-ḫu-un (22) ú-id-du-wa DUMU ᵐŠ[a]-pár-ta an-da (23) ú[-e-]mi-ya-	(20–25) Šaparta's slave whom I sent into the Kaška land, (saying:) "Let him proceed to find Šaparta's son!"[178]—if he has already gone.

ad-du na-aš [m]a-a-an (24) k[a-]ru-ú pa-a-an-za na-an-m[u]-kán (25) du-wa-a-an pa-ra-a na-i	(and returned), send him on to me *later*.
(26) ma-a-na-aš na-a-ú-i-ma pa-iz-zi (27) nu *A-NA* mLu-ul-lu mZu-wa-an-na-ya (28) ḫa-[a]t-ra-a-i nu-uš-ši 3 LÚ.MEŠ URUGa-aš-ga (29) pé-e-di e-[e]p-du a-pa-a-ša pa-id-du (30) nu DUMU mŠa-pár-ta an-da ú-e-mi-ya-ad-du (31) nam-ma-aš ma-aḫ-[ḫ]a-an EGIR-pa pa-iz-zi (32) na-an-mu-kán du-wa-a-an pa-ra-a na-i (33) LÚ.MEŠ *ṬE$_4$-MI*-ma LÚ URUPa-aš-du-u-wa-du-u-wa LÚ URUPa-na-a-ta-ya ú-wa-an-du	(26–33) But if he has not already gone, write to Lullu and Zuwanna. Let them take three Kaška men (to give) in his place (i.e., as hostages), and let him go (to the Kaška land) and find Šaparta's son. Then, when he (the slave or the ransomed son?) returns (to you), send him on to me. But the messengers, the man of Paštuwatuwa and the man of Panāta, should (also) come (here).
(34) zi-ga m.dIŠKUR-*BE-LÍ*-iš GIŠzu-up-pa-ri-ya-aš (35) *ŠA* Ú.ḪI.A-ya ut-tar ša-a-ak-ti (36) ki-nu-na LÚ.MEŠ URUTa-pí-ig-ga (37) nam-ma *Ú-UL* wa-ar-ša-an-zi (38) nu!? *ŠA* mḪi-mu-DINGIR-*LIM* ḫal-ki-uš wa-ar-aš-kán-z[i] (39) ki-nu-na-m[u] zi-ik m.dIŠKUR-*BE-LÍ*-iš (40) mNa-a-[š]a-a[d]-da-aš-ša (41) *A-NA* Ú.ḪI.A wa-ar-šu-[wa-an-zi] (42) EGIR-an ar-ḫa le-e [kar?-aš?-te-]ni	(34–42) You, Adad-bēlī, know all about *reeds*? and grasses. But now the men of Tapikka no longer harvest (them). (Instead) they are harvesting the crops of Ḫimmuili. Now you (sg.), Adad-bēlī,—and also Našadda —you (pl.) must not avoid? harvesting of grasses for me!
(43) ki-iš-ša-an-na-at-ta k[u-it ut-tar] (44) ḫa-at-ra-a-nu-un KUR-e-wa x[…] (45) ku-it ma-a[ḫ-ḫa-a]n [ḫ]ar?-wa[-ši ? …] (46) nu-mu ku-wa-at! *Ú-UL* ḫ[a-at-ra-a-at-t]én	(43–46) And concerning the fact that I wrote to you (sg.) "Report to me the situation in (your) area," why have you (pl.) not written to me?
(47) *A-NA* LÚ x-x-x-x ku-it […] (48) *A-NA* x-x-x ANŠE.KUR.RA.ḪI.A-ya […] (49) x-x-[x-]x am-mu-uk ka-a?[-ša?] (50) […-]wa?[-…] (l. e. 1) nu am-mu-uk du-wa-a-an ḫa-[a]t-re-eš-kat-tén […] (l. e. 2) mTa-ḫa-	(47–50) Because … to the man … and horses/chariotry … I …. (l. e. 1–5) Keep forwarding your letters to me. And although? they have attacked Taḫazzili, a messenger has just come from him (saying)

az-zi-li-in-na ku-i[t] wa-a[l-ḫ]a-[a]n ḫ[ar-ki-ir] (l. e. 3) nu-uš-ši ka-a-ša L[Ú] *ṬE*$_4$-*MI* a-w[a]-an ar-ḫa […] (l. e. 4) ú-it SIG$_5$-an-za-wa-r[a-a]š-ši-kán le-e […] (l. e. 5) ku-wa-at-ka$_4$ la-aḫ-la-aḫ-[ḫ]i-ya-ši	"He is all right." So don't worry about it.

Commentary

5–19 It is somewhat unusual in a letter for such an extended section of the text, which represents the words of the sender and not a quote of a third party, to be marked as direct discourse with the quotative particle *-wa*, as is the case here in lines 5–19. Such a long section is certainly not the wording of the *aššul* ("greeting") referred to in line 3, but it may be part of what Ḫulla wishes Adad-bēlī to relay to the "beloved [brother X]." Otherwise, I see no reason for the extended use of the quotative particle *-wa*. Alp translated *ḫalzai-* here as "read aloud" (German Lies … vor"), which is certainly possible (see my remarks above in §1.1.3.1). But since the verb basically means "call," it might also simply mean "speak" (i.e., "relay").

4 *RA-IM-MU* is a Hittite spelling (found also in a Ḫattušili I letter, KUB 3.61: 4) of Akkadian *ra'īmu*(*m*) "beloved," the feminine of which (*RA-IM-TÙ*) is also attested in Hittite texts (for references see CAD R, 82).

5 The reading of this line—*za-ak-*[*m*]*u*?*-li-uš* (or *za-ak-*[*z*]*i*?*-li-uš*, or *za-ak-*[*ki*] *še-li-uš*, as noted in n. 174—is uncertain. The rare word *šeli-* denotes a place where harvest grain is stored. It is usually thought of as a pile or heap of grain, not a pit like the ÉSAG. But if we were to read *pád*[*-da-an-te-es*(?)] instead of *-pát* […], it would suggest that the *šeli-* was either the Hittite reading of ÉSAG "silo, grain-storage pit" or has a closely allied meaning. Underground silos played an important role in Hittite communal security against years when harvests were bad or when marauding enemies destroyed the crops. On the underground silos excavated at Ḫattuša and other Hittite sites and the term ÉSAG designating them see Hoffner 1974a; Seeher 1998, 2000b, 2001; Neef 2001; Fairbairn and Omura 2005.

11 Alp (1991, 338) reads *a-pa-a-*[*t*]*a*, and regards it as a variant writing of *apadda* "thither."

14 For attestations and comments on the difficult word *ḫanteyara-* see *HW*^{2} H, 192, where no translation is suggested. Alp (1991a, 339) proposes that it denotes a lower quality of horse, destined for the use of lower-ranked persons, in contrast to the *tarpuli-*, which he regards as the better-quality horses for high-ranked officials. Elsewhere this word is rare. As a proper noun it occurs as the name of a mountain. As a common noun or adjective, it occurs in passages where it was thought to modify water. Accordingly, Oettinger (2001, 83–87) suggested a translation "low" (German *niedrig*). Rieken, on the other hand, who regards it as a Luwian word (2004, 7), translates it as "cranial bone" (German *Schädelknochen*). Following Haas (2002), Rieken maintains that in the passages with the fish in water, it is the fish, not the water, that is modified by *ḫantiyara-*, and the "fish in the cranial bone" is a water turtle characterized by its shell. In this passage it describes chariot horses to be used by officials. Haas and Rieken propose the German translation *Stirnmaske* for the noun *ḫanteyaraḫḫa-*, and think these horses wear such a forehead mask such as Assyrian war horses are shown wearing on reliefs.

24–25 For another passage with *duwān* ("further on"), the verbal complex *parā nai-*, a dative-locative of the person to whom something is sent, and *-kan*, see KBo 3.3+ iii 31–33: *ma-a-an DI-NU-ma ku-it-ki* / *šal-le-eš-zi na-at ar-ḫa e-ep-pu-u-wa-an-zi* / *Ú-UL tar-aḫ-te-ni na-at-kán du-wa-a-an* / *MA-ḪAR* ᵈUTU-*ŠI pa-ra-a na-iš-tén* / *na-at* ᵈUTU-*ŠI ar-ḫa e-ep-zi* "But if some legal case is too big (for you), and you (pl.) are not able to resolve it, send it on to His Majesty, and His Majesty will resolve it." Also HKM 60 (text 63): 17–18. Melchert (2008) prefers to understand *duwān* as "later" with present tenses and imperatives, and "lately" with preterites.

33 There are two messengers identified by their towns. And since we know from other texts that exchanges between peoples speaking different languages (in this case, the Kaška and the Hittites) were carried on through the tandem movements of two messengers, one from each language group (see above in §1.1.5.2.2), it is likely that one of these two is a Kaškaean, most likely the "man from Pašduwaduwa," since Panāta seems to have been a Hittite-controlled area, that was even fortified by Šuppiluliuma I as a border outpost (KBo 12.36 i 6). But Pašduwaduwa is not mentioned in other Hittite texts (see del Monte 1992, 123), and is merely assumed by Alp (1991a, 30) to be a Hittite town on the (in my view, mistaken) assumption that both messengers mentioned here are Hittites.

70. HKM 67
From Šaḫurunuwa to Mešeni and Kaššū

Text: Mşt. 75/91. **Find spot:** G/5 Portico. **Copy**: HKM 67. **Edition**: Alp 1991a, 248–51 (no. 67). **Discussion**: Alp 1991a, 80 (Mešeni), 90 (Šaḫurunuwa); Marizza 2007a, 128–30.

(1) *UM-MA* ^{m}Ša-ḫu-ru-nu-wa (2) *A-NA* ^{m}Me-še-ni *Ù A-NA* ^{m}Ka-aš-šu-ú ŠEŠ.MEŠ DÙG.GA-*YA* (3) *QÍ-BÍ-MA MA-ḪAR* ŠE[Š. D]ÙG.G[A-*I*]*A* (4) ḫu-u-ma-an SIG$_5$[-in e-eš-d]u (5) nu-ut-ta DINGIR.MEŠ [TI-an ḫar-kán-du] (6) nu-ut-ta pa[-aḫ-ša-an-da-ru]	(1–6) Thus speaks Šaḫurunuwa: Say to Mešeni and Kaššū, my dear brothers: May all be well with my dear brother (sg.!), and may the gods keep you (sg.!) alive and protect you (sg.)!
(7) ka-a-ša […] (8) ku-i-e-eš […] (9) nu-uš-ma-a[š-ša-an …] (10) na-aš-ká[n …] (11) pa-ra-a […] (rev. 1′) [o] x x [(rev. 2′) [m]a-aḫ-ḫa-a[n …] (rev. 3′) ḫa-at-ra-a-i […] (rev. 4′) *Ú-UL* la-aḫ-[la-aḫ-ḫi-ya-ši]	(7–11, rev. 1′–4′) … who (pl.) … to them … when … he writes … don't worry!
(rev. 5′) ka-a-ša *IŠ-T*[*U* …] (rev. 6′) na-a-ú-i ku-u[š- …] (rev. 7′) ma-an-ta aš-šu-u[l …] (rev. 8′) ḫa-at-ra-a-nu-u[n …] (rev. 9′) ^{m}Ša-ḫu?-ru?-nu?-u?-wa?-a?	(rev. 5′–9′) … … Oh, that I had sent you (sg.) a greeting …! … Šaḫurunuwa …

Commentary

3–6 The fact that singular forms are used in these clauses, although the letter was sent to two men, indicates how easy it was for the scribe unthinkingly to use boilerplate text.

The signs in line 9 were added after the tablet was fully inscribed and the clay had begun to dry. They are only lightly inscribed, and Alp's reading (given in our text) is rather doubtful, despite the fact that Šaḫurunuwa's name appears in line 1 of this text.

71. HKM 68
From the Commander of the Military Heralds to Pallanna and Zardumanni

Text: Mşt. 75/46. **Find spot:** G/5 room 8. **Copy**: HKM 68. **Edition**: Alp 1991a, 250–53 (no. 68). **Discussion**: de Martino and Imparati 1995, 112–13; Klinger 2001a, 67–68; Imparati 2003, 235–36; Bryce 2003b, 176 (with n. 27); Marizza 2007a, 94–95, 140, 145, 154, 169.

According to Alp (1991a, 70–75) and Imparati and de Martino (1995, 112), this unnamed Commander of the Military Heralds is the Kaššū who figures prominently elsewhere in the Maşat letters.

Here we see another type of situation that must have been part of the everyday concern in the Hittite adminsitration. One official accuses another of wrongdoing, and the accused replies and even threatens to call in a team from the king to investigate. In part this is motivated by mutual jealousy and rivalry among the officials. As has been true in all ages, petty people in official positions, jockeying for advancement, will do so by character assasination of their rivals. On this see Beckman 1995a.

(1) *UM-MA* UGULA NIMGIR. ÉRIN.MEŠ (2) *A-NA* ^{m}Pal-la-an-na (3) *Ù A-NA* ^{m}Za-ar-tum-ma-an-ni *QÍ-BÍ-MA*	(1–3) Thus speaks the Commander of the Military Heralds: Say to Pallanna and Zartummanni:
(4) am-mu-uk *Ú-UL* ku-it-ki ku-it (5) dam-mi-iš-ḫa-a-an ḫar-mi *Ú-UL*-ma-kán (6) da-a-an ku-e-da-ni-ki[179] ku-it-ki ḫar-mi (7) *QA-TAM-MA*-ma-mu ku-wa-at dam-mi-iš-ḫi-iš-kán-zi	(4–7) Since I have done no harm or taken anything from anyone, why are they harming me thus?
(8) ki-nu-na ma-aḫ-ḫa-an ^{d}UTU-*ŠI BE-LÍ-YA* (9) an-da ú-e-mi-ya-mi (10) nu *A-NA* ^{d}UTU-*ŠI* me-ma-aḫ-ḫi (11) na-aš-ta an-tu-uḫ-ša-an (12) pa-ra-a ne-ya-an-zi (13) nu ú-wa-an-zi ut-tar a-pí-ya (14) pu-nu-uš-ša-an-zi nam-ma-aš (15) *MA-ḪAR* ^{d}UTU-*ŠI* ú-wa-da-an-zi (16) na-aš ^{d}UTU-*ŠI* a-pa-ši-la (17) pu-nu-uš-zi	(8–17) But now, when I find His Majesty, my lord, I will report (this) to His Majesty. They will send out a person and proceed to investigate the matter at your post (literally, 'there'). Then they will bring them before His Majesty, and His Majesty himself will interrogate them.
(18) *A-NA* ZÍD.DA-ma-mu ku-e-da-ni (19) ap-pí-iš-kán-zi nu ^{m}Ḫi-mu-DINGIR-*LIM* (20) ku-it *A-NA* ^{m}Ka-pí-ya *Ù A-NA* ^{m}Zi-la-pí-ya (21) pa-iš na-at an-da ar-nu-nu-un (22) na-at *A-NA* LÚ.MEŠ ^{URU}Ka-ši-pu-u-ra (23) *AD-DIN* a-pé-da-ni-ma-kán ku-it (24) ZÍD.DA da-aḫ-ḫu-un	(18–24) The flour/meal concerning which I am being indicted, which Ḫimmuili gave to Kapiya and Zilapiya, I brought in (i.e., retrieved) and gave it to the men of Kašipūra. What flour did I take from that one? Concerning the ox belonging to the mausoleum that

(l. e. 1) *ŠA* <É> NA$_4$-ma-mu ku-in GU$_4$ (l. e. 2) ḫa-at-ra-a-eš nu *Ú-UL* ku-it-ki (l. e. 3) ku-it *I-DI* na-at-mu tup-pí-az (l. e. 4) ḫa-at-ra-a-i	you wrote me about: because I know nothing about (the matter), write me about it on a tablet.

Commentary

l. e. 1 The emendation <É> NA$_4$ is needed to make sense out of the passage. Both Alp and Klinger work with the unemended text, although Klinger translates "ox of the stone," while Alp in his translation recognizes that the "Stone House" (the estate of the royal mausoleum) is meant—German *Rind des Stein*(*haus*?)*es*.

72. HKM 70
From Ḫulla, the Commander of Chariot-warriors, to Kaššū

Text: Mşt. 75/51. **Find spot:** G/5 Room 8. **Copy**: HKM 70. **Edition**: Alp 1991a, 252–55 (no. 70). **Translation:** Klinger 2001a, 68. **Discussion**: Klinger 1995a, 92 (with n. 68); Marizza 2007a, 86–87 (on Ḫulla as the unnamed sender).

(1) *UM-MA* GAL $^{\text{LÚ.MEŠ}}$KUŠ$_7$ (2) *A-NA* ^{m}Ka-aš-šu-ú (3) ŠEŠ-*YA QÍ-BÍ-MA*	(1–2) Thus speaks the Commander of the Chariot-warriors: Say to Kaššū, my brother:
(4) ki-i ku-it i-ya-aš (5) na-aš-ta ka-a-ša ÉRIN.MEŠ.ḪI.A (6) pa-ra-a tu-uk-pát (7) e-eš-zi	(4–7) In view of this performance of yours: Herewith the squadron is henceforth yours alone.
(8) ka-a-ša-za pé-ra-an (9) da-me-i-da-ni[180] *A-NA* ÉRIN.MEŠ (10) lam-ni-ya-an-za (11) nu li-li-wa-aḫ-ḫu-u-an-zi (12) u-un-ni (13) ú-wa-at du-wa-ad-du	(8–13) You are herewith named to another military unit. So drive here as quickly as you can (to receive the command from me). Get a move on!

Commentary

8–10 contains a nominal sentence with *-za*, requiring a first or second person subject (*pace* Alp 1991a, 255, *HED* L, 54, and Klinger 2001a, 68).

Since the *kāša* indicates a performative use ("hereby, herewith"), meaning that the transfer to another unit is effected by the very words spoken, it makes better sense to take it as "*You* are herewith named to ...."

Both Alp (1991a) and Klinger (2001a, 68[181]) translated this short letter quite differently, namely, as a reprimand. It obviously is part of the correspondence that is contained in text 73 (HKM 71).

13 For *uwat duwaddu* see §1.2.19.1 above.

73. HKM 71
From Ḫulla, the Commander of Chariot-warriors to Kaššū

Text: Mşt. 75/111. **Find spot:** G/5 Portico. **Copy:** HKM 71. **Edition:** Alp 1991a, 254–57 (no. 71). **Translation:** Klinger 2001a, 68. **Discussion:** Starke 1996, 152–53 (lines 3–23); Houwink ten Cate 1998, 163; Goedegebuure 2003, 191; Marizza 2007a, 86–87.

According to Marizza (2007a), the unnamed sender of HKM 70 and 71 is Ḫulla. He also rightly assumes that Ḫulla and his scribe Tarḫunmiya are not in Ḫattuša when this was written, but on the road. Alp had already suspected the same on the basis of the request for a replacement stylus in Tarḫunmiya's piggyback letter. While there is criticism of Kaššū by his superior in this letter, it also reflects Ḫulla's appreciation of Kaššū's status ("Are you not a lord?"), and seeks to spur him on to accept the responsibilities that accompany his rank. Kaššū should not defer to Ḫulla, when he is perfectly capable and authorized to handle the contracting of peace with the Kaška envoys. Marizza thinks there is sarcasm in lines 9–11.

(1) *UM-MA* GAL $^{LÚ.MEŠ}$KUŠ$_7$ (2) *A-NA* ^{m}Ka-aš-šu-ú *QÍ-BÍ-MA*	(1–2) Thus speaks (Ḫulla), the Commander of the Chariot-warriors: Say to Kaššū:
(3) ki-iš-ša-an-mu ku-it ḫa-at-ra-a-eš (4) *BE-LU* ma-an-wa u-un-na-at-ti kat-ta-an (5) LÚ.MEŠ ^{URU}Ga-aš-ga-wa ki-iš-ša-an (6) me-mi-iš-kán-zi ma-an-wa GA[L] $^{LÚ.MEŠ}$KUŠ$_7$ (7) u-un-na-i nu-wa ták-šu-la-u-e-ni (8) nu-mu a-pa-a-at ma-aḫ-ḫa-an ḫa-at-ri-iš-ke-ši (9) zi-ik-za *Ú-UL*	(3–7) Regarding what you wrote to me, as follows: "Lord, if only you would drive down here! The Kaška men keep saying: 'If only the Commander of the Chariot-warriors would drive here, we would make peace!'" (8–11) You keep writing to me like that! (But) are

BE-LU nam-ma-du-[z]a (10) UGU≈LA NIMGIR.ÉRIN.MEŠ ḫal-zi-iš-ša-an-zi (11) am-mu-ga-za GAL LÚ.MEŠKUŠ$_7$	*you* not a lord (too)? Furthermore, they call you Commander of the Military Heralds, and I am Commander of the Chariot-warriors.
(12) nu-mu-uš-ša-an im-ma ku-it (13) pár-ki-ya-at-ta-at nu-za LÚ.MEŠ *ṬE$_4$-MI-ŠU-NU* (14) ku-it *Ú-UL* ú-e-mi-ya-at	(12–14) Why have you actually deferred? to me? Why have you not met with their envoys?
(15) nu-za zi-ik *Ú-UL BE-LU* GAL (16) nu-mu-uš-ša-an ma-a-an ÉRIN.MEŠ URUGa-ra-aḫ-na (17) ÉRIN.MEŠ URUIš-ḫu-pí-it-ta (18) ÉRIN.MEŠ ḪUR.SAGŠa-ak-du-nu-[w]a (19) *I-NA* URUNi-ni-ša-an-k[u-wa] (20) *Ú-UL* ar-n[u-ši] (21) nu-ut-ta ú-w[a-mi] (22) ma-aḫ-ḫa-an nu-u[t-t]a [...][182] (23) LÚ.MEŠ URUḪa-at-ti ú-wa-an-zi	(15–23) Are you not a great lord? If you don't bring me the troops of Karaḫna, Išḫupitta, and Mt. Šaktunuwa to Ninišankuwa, the men of Ḫatti will see how I come to you and ... you!
(24) ka-a-ša-kán ki-i tup-pí (25) ku-e-da-ni UD-ti pa-ra-a (26) ne-eḫ-ḫu-un na-aš-ta ÉRI[N].MEŠ KUR UGU (27) a-pé-e-da-ni UD-ti (28) ar-ḫa ḫu-it-ti-ya-nu-un (29) nu-mu-uš-ša-an zi-ik-ka$_4$ (30) KARAŠ-pát ḫu-u-da-a-ak (31) ar-nu-ut	(24–31) On the same day that I have dispatched this tablet I have drawn forth the troops of the Upper Land. You too must bring your army to me quickly!

Commentary

4 Starke's translation "Würdest doch du als Herr ... mitfahren" (italics his) is impossible, since *BE-LU* stands before and outside of the clause beginning with *ma-an-wa*, and cannot be apodosis, but can only stand for the true vocative *išḫā*.

8 The position of *maḫḫan* so late in the clause excludes Alp's interpreation as a conjunction ("da du mir ... schreibst"). Starke's interpretation as a (rhetorical) question ("Wie kannst du mir das immer wieder schreiben?!") is also impossible, because interrogative *maḫḫan* would have to be clause initial. Its position immediately after *apāt* shows it is postpositional ("like that").

11 Coming, as it does, immediately after the sentence in line 10, the clause in line 11 could exhibit gapping (on which subject see GrHL §30.14). In that case the verb *ḫal-zi-iš-ša-an-zi* is implied at its end, and the pair of clauses should be translated: "They call you Commander of the Military Heralds, and me Commander of the Chariot-warriors."

12–14 Causal *kuit* regularly occurs in second position, whereas interrogative *kuit* ("why?") is often later in the clause. Here the first example of *kuit* is later than second and must be "why?" The second example is in second position, but can still be "why?" Starke took the first as causal ("da") and the second as interrogative ("warum?").

13 *parkiyattat*. The CHD *park-*, *parkiya-* article needs a few corrections. It seems to me that there is a strong correlation between the active of this verb as transitive and the middle as intransitive, just as Neu (1968, 138) maintained. Because of the almost identical construction in KUB 57.123 (text 113) obv. 7 cited in CHD P, 157 sub 2b, where the writer claims he has done this to the king, I would hesitate to acccept Beal's proposal that here we translate "you have risen to my level." The writer of KUB 57.123 surely isn't claiming to have risen to the king's level. But neither does the middle voice verb *parkiya-* mean "flatter" (German *schmeicheln*), as Alp has it (1991a, 254–55). I believe that a meaning like "to rise to" > "to defer to" (out of respect for a superior) would fit in both letters.

Lines **16–20** are translated in del Monte 1992, 66, 112; lines 29–30 are translated in CHD Š, 142.

73b. HKM 71
Piggyback Letter from Tarḫunmiya to Uzzū

(32) *UM-MA* $^{m.d}$U-mi-ya (33) *A-NA* ^{m}Uz-zu-u ŠEŠ [DÙ]G.G[A-*Y*]*A* (34) *QÍ-BÍ-MA*	(32–34) Thus speaks Tarḫunmiya: Say to Uzzū, my dear brother:
(35) [D]INGIR.MEŠ-ta TI-an ḫar-kán-du (36) nu-ut-[t]a aš-šu-li (37) pa$^{!}$-aḫ-ša-an-ta-ru	(35–37) May the gods keep you alive and lovingly protect you.
(l. e. 1) GI É.DUB.BA-mu-kán ḫar-ak-ta (l. e. 2) nu-mu ŠEŠ DÙG. GA-*YA* GI É.DUB.BA (l. e. 3) up-pí	(l. e. 1–3) My tablet stylus is lost. Dear brother, send me a (new) tablet stylus.

Commentary

l. e. 1–3 proves beyond doubt that Tarḫunmiya was a scribe. The tablet stylus—Sumerian GI (É.)DUB.BA, Akkadian *qan ṭuppi(m)*, the Hittite term is presently unknown—was a valuable implement and could not simply be improvised on the spot by using a random reed or piece of wood. Whether *ḫark-* is to be translated here with "is broken" (so Alp [ist kaputt] and Marizza [è rotto]) or "is lost" is probably impossible to determine. The verb is attested in both meanings, and in either scenario a new one would be needed. Since Tarḫunmiya was obviously the scribe who wrote the present tablet, he must have borrowed a stylus from another scribe in order to write it. Alp (1991a, 340–41) rightly expresses surprise that a scribe like Tarḫunmiya, who normally worked in the capital, would need to write to a colleague in Tapikka for a replacement stylus, and wonders if perhaps Tarḫunmiya was on the road with his master rather than in Ḫattuša. Marizza has now concluded the same about the whereabouts of sender and scribe. This assumption obviates the need to suppose (with Houwink ten Cate 1998, 163) that metal tablet styluses were regularly furnished to the capital from Tapikka.

74. HKM 72
From the Chief of Scribes to Kaššū

Text: Mşt. 75/67. **Find spot:** G/5 Room 8. **Copy**: HKM 72. **Edition**: Alp 1991a, 256–59 (no. 72), with notes on p. 341. **Discussion**: Haas 1995, 517; de Martino 2005b, 298, 311; Marizza 2007a, 96–97.

An unnamed Chief of Scribes writes (from Ḫattuša?) to Kaššū, who judging from the order of salutation is his inferior in rank. Beckman proposed that the unnamed Chief of Scribes was Ḫattušili, and has been followed by Houwink ten Cate (1998, 158) and de Martino. Marizza (2007a, 119 n. 5, and 121–22) is not convinced that this is the case and raises several objections.

(1) *UM-MA* GAL DUB.SAR *A-NA* ᵐGa-aš-šu-ú (2) *QÍ-BÍ-MA*	(1–2) Thus speaks the Chief of Scribes: Say to Kaššū:
(3) ka-a-ša-mu ᵐTar-ḫu-u[n-p]í-ḫa-nu-uš (4) ki-iš-ša-an ḫa-at-ra-a-eš ᴳᴵŠar-mi-iz-[zi-wa] (5) *IŠ-TU* NA_4 ú-e-du-ma-an-zi (6) ka-ru-ú zi-in-	(3–8) Tarḫun-piḫanu has just written to me as follows: "The building of the bridge with stones is already finished, but there is no timber (for

na-an-d[a] (7) GIŠ.ḪI.A-ma-wa NU.GÁL nu-uš-ša-an k[a-a-ša] (8) *A-NA* GIŠ ḫu-uš-ke	the upper structure).” So for time being wait (sg.) on the timber.
(9) na-aš-ta GIŠmu-ur-ta tu-el-ma (10) kar-aš-ša-an-du<-uš?> (11) kar-aš-tén nu *ŠA* KUR-*TIM* x[…] (12) ni-ni-ik-tén	(9–12) Cut down (pl.) *murta*-trees—but (only) your own cut pieces, and muster the …-people of the land,
(13) nu-wa-ra-at pé-da-an-du (14) nu GIŠar-mi-iz-zi ḫu-u-da-a-ak (15) zi-in-na-at-tén	(13–15) and let them transport them (i.e., the timbers)! And finish (pl.) the bridge quickly!
(16) nu-za k[a]-ru-ú *ŠA* d[UT]U?-*Š*[*I*!?]- x-x […] (17) […]x-li-[i]š ku-iš x-x […] (18) […-a]n mWa-al-wa-x[…] (19) [… ÉR]IN.MEŠ e-eš-du (20) […]x an-da e-eš-du (21) [… ḫu-u-m]a-an-te-e[š …] (22) [… … … … … …] (23) [… … … … … …] (24) x-x [… … … … …] (25) x-x [… … … …] (26) mDu-ut-x[…]	*(The next 11 lines are too badly broken for connected translation. A person named Walwa-x[-x] is mentioned in 18, and troops in 19.)*
(27) nu-uš-ma-aš ú?-wa?-an-du (28) wa-ar-pa-an-na im-ma […] (29) ú-e-du-ma-an-zi a[p]-pa-a[n-d]u	(27–29) Let them proceed to finish the …-ing and building (of the bridges).
(30) ÉRIN.MEŠ-ma-aš-ši-kán *ŠA* KUR URUIš-ḫ[u-pí-]i[t-ta] (31) kat-ta-an le-e ku-wa-at-ka$_4$ (32) ḫu<-it>-ti-ya-ši li<-li>-wa-aḫ-ḫu-wa-[an-z]i (33) ú-wa-te	(30–33) But you (sg.) must not in any way *detain*?? work gangs of Išḫuppitta (needed) for it (i.e., for the project?) . Bring (them?) here quickly!

Although there is no double rule at this point, what follows is a piggyback letter to Zū, the scribe of Kaššū.

(34) zi-ik-mu mZu-u-uš ŠEŠ DÙG.GA[-*YA*] (35) GIŠmu-úr-ta-an-za EGIR-pa (36) *BÁ-BI-LA-Ú* ḫa-at-ra-a-i	(34–36) You, Zū, my dear brother, write back to me about the *murta*-wood in Akkadian?!

Commentary

There are many difficulties—grammatical and otherwise—in translating this letter.[183] There is also the question why it was necessary for Kaššū's scribe Zū to use Akkadian in his reply, since the unnamed scribe of this letter was able to write Hittite, albeit with mistakes. Is the scribe's own difficulty with the Hittite language the cause of his many errors and omissions in the present text? Alp had doubts that the *addressee* of this letter, Kaššū, understood Babylonian. But these doubts are irrelevant, since they are based on the assumption that this is the same Kaššū who wrote KBo 18.54, and on the assumption that Güterbock's understanding of KBo 18.54 14–17 and the restorations and translation of KBo 18.54 14–17 given by Beckman (1983b, 110 with n. 59) are correct. Neither of these two assumptions is by any means demonstrable. And furthermore, it is the sender (or perhaps scribe) of this letter who seems to be more comfortable with Akkadian, and the *scribe* of Kaššū, who is supposedly able to write in that language. Kaššū himself is not in the picture.

35 Melchert 2005b, 447, 449 considers *murtan=za* a word with assured Luwian inflection. Van den Hout (2006, 230, 248) agrees, and cites more Luwian forms in Middle Hittite (and middle script) tablets than were recognized by Rieken and Melchert before him.

36 The form *BABILA(Y)U* "Babylonian" shows the Akkadian gentilic suffix: Old Babylonian *-āyum,* OA *-ā'um* (GAG §56 p). On this reference to a MH scribe requesting correspondence in Babylonian, see de Martino 2005b, 298. Alp speculated (p. 341) that the reason for the request of a reply in Akkadian was to keep it confidential.

75. HKM 73
From the Chief Wood Scribe to Kaššū

Text: Mşt. 75/97 + 75/99. **Find spot:** G/5 Portico. **Copy**: HKM 73. **Edition**: Alp 1991a, 260–61 (no. 73). **Discussion**: del Monte 1992, 38 (on URUḪawalta); Marizza 2007a, 95, 98, 119 (n. 5) and 121 (the identity of the unnamed Chief of the Wood Scribes), 163 (table entry on Tarwaški), 167 (table entry on Uzzū).

(1) *UM-MA* GAL DUB.SAR.GIŠ (2) *A-NA* mGa-aš-šu-ú *QÍ-BÍ-MA*	(1–2) Thus speaks the Chief of the Wood-Scribes: Say to Kaššū:

(3) ka-a-ša-mu ᵐTar-wa-aš-ki-iš (4) ki-iš-ša-an me-mi-iš-ta (5) x x x x MUNUS ᵁᴿᵁḪa-u-wa-al-ta (6) [x x x x x x] ú-e-er x-x ḫar-kán-zi[184] (7) [x x x x x x]x-ni-ya (8) […]x (9) […]x-ši	(3–9) Tarwaški has just told me the following: … the woman of the town Ḫawalta … they came … they hold … … …
(10) n[a-a]n ˹a˺-[p]í-ya pu-nu-uš (11) ˹na-at˺ ma-a-an ḫa-an-da (12) MUNUS ᵁᴿᵁḪa-wa-al-ta (13) nu-uš-ma-aš EGIR-pa pa-a-i (14) ma-a-an *Ú-UL*-[m]a (15) nu«-uš-ma-aš» kat-ti-mi up-p[í]	(10–15) Question him/her there (i.e., where you are)! And if it (*-at*) is right—the woman of the town Ḫawalta—give (her) back to them. But if not, send (her) to me.

75b. HKM 73
Piggyback Letter to Uzzū from Mar-ešrē

(16) ˹*A*˺-*NA* ᵐUz-z[u-]˹u˺ [ŠE]Š DÙ[G.]G[A-*YA*] (17) *QÍ-BÍ-MA* *UM-MA* ᵐD[UMU.UD.2]0.K[AM] (18) ŠEŠ-*KA-MA*	(16–18) Say to Uzzū, my dear brother: Thus speaks Mar-ešrē, your brother:
(19) kat-ti-ti ḫu-u-ma-an SIG$_5$-in e-eš-du (20) nu-ut-ta DINGIR.MEŠ TI-an ḫar-kán-du (21) nu-ut-ta ŠU.ḪI.A-uš a-ra-aḫ-za-an-da (22) aš-šu-li ḫar-kán-du (23) nu-ut-ta pa-aḫ-ša-an-da-ru	(19–23) May all be well with you (sg.), and may the gods keep you (sg.) alive, and lovingly hold their arms around you, and protect you.
(24) [ŠE]Š [D]ÙG.GA-*YA*-mu ku-it (25) [*ŠA*? …ut?-tar? ki-iš-ša-an ḫ]a-at-ra-a-eš (26) x-[…]x-x-x-x-na-a[t]-ra (27) am-mu-ug-g[a N]U.GÁL e-eš-zi (28) na-aš-ta am-mu-ga i-da-a-lu (29) ˹a˺-ar-wa-aḫ-ḫa-at	(24–29) Concerning what you, my dear brother, wrote about … as follows: "… … -natra?"— (This) is not in my possession. And I have …-ed badly?.
(30) nu ŠEŠ DÙG.GA-*YA* *QA-TAM-MA* ša-a-ak	(30) My dear brother, you should be aware of this.

Commentary

15 I assume that the scribe wrote *nu-uš-ma-aš* "to them" and then, realizing that the destination was the speaker, added *kat-ti-mi* "to me" without going back and deleting the signs *-uš-ma-aš*.

76. HKM 74
From "The Priest" to Kaššū

Text: Mşt. 75/52. **Find spot:** G/5 room 8. **Copy**: HKM 74. **Edition**: Alp 1991a, 262–63 (no. 74). **Discussion**: Klinger 1995a, 85, 93; Imparati 1997, 652 (n. 19); Imparati 2002, 94–95 (n. 10); Bryce 2003b, 176–77; Imparati 2003; Taggar-Cohen 2006, 227–28.

The sender of this letter, who identifies himself only with the title "the Priest," was in all likelihood a man named Kantuzzili, high priest of Teššub and Ḫebat, who enjoyed in Kizzuwatna a status equivalent to that of an appanage king (see Klinger and Imparati).

An ordinary priest would never refer to himself solely by his office, but would certainly give his name. Petty kings of Hittite dependent states were invested with the title "Priest" and regularly refer to themselves by this title without giving their names.[185] Here subjects of the ruler of Kizzuwatna have fled his domain and settled in Zikkašta. Imparati says they have "passed into the service of Kaššū in Ziggašta." The construction "is/are behind GN" is fairly common in historical texts (annals, etc.), and might refer either to the environs or to a location inside a city but at the opposite end of the walled enclosure from the main (i.e., "front") gate (i.e., "in the rear").[186] Kaššū refuses to give back the refugees to the Kizzuwatnean on his own authority (ZI-*it*), since his district is a primary border district ("watchpoint") where actions relating to lands beyond the border had to be approved by the king. The Kizzuwatnean is miffed at this refusal and writes back that he is in the process of reporting[187] the matter and awaiting support from the Hittite king, and that since his land too is a primary border district, he will also not in the future return any subjects of Kaššū's that enter his land! The Kizzuwatnean ruler bristles with impatience over bureaucratic protocol.

While the twenty persons are described by Kaššū as *NAPŠĀTU* "people," a term that Alp has claimed always means slaves, the Priest himself refers to them as ARAD.MEŠ, which often denotes slaves, but which—when it refers to servants of a high-ranked person—can also mean free subordinates, that is, “agents” or “officials” (as is also the case with West Semitic ʿ*abdu*). It is interesting to see how the Priest deliberately shows how differently Kaššū and he view these men. Taggar-Cohen (2006) calls them “troops attached to the border garrison.” Since NAM.RA work groups are composed of units of ten persons, it may be that these twenty persons are two runaway groups of NAM.RA.

(1) *UM-MA* LÚSANGA (2) *A-NA* mKa-aš-šu-ú *QÍ-BÍ-MA*	(1–2) Thus speaks the Priest: Say to Kaššū:
(3) ki-iš-ša-an-mu ku-it ḫa-at-ra-a-eš (4) *I-NA* URUZi-ig-ga-aš-ta-wa-ša-an (5) tu-el 20 *NA-AP-ŠA-TÙ* EGIR-an (6) nu-wa ḫa-an-te-ez-zi-iš ku-it (7) a-ú-ri-iš nu-wa-ra-aš-ta ZI-it (8) *Ú-UL* pé-eḫ-ḫi nu-wa-ra-aš[…] (9) *I-NA* É.GAL-*LIM* tar-kum-mi-ya-i	(3–9) Concerning what you wrote to me as follows: “Your twenty people are in the environs? of the town Zikkašta. And because (my district) is a primary (lit., first) watchpoint, I will not give them to you on my own authority. Report them to the palace!”
(10) nu-za am-me-el ARAD.MEŠ-*YA*[188] (11) *I-NA* É.GAL-*LIM* tar-kum-mi-e-eš-ki-mi (12) KUR URUKi-iz-zu-wa-at-na-ya (13) ku-it ḫa-an-te-ez-zi-iš (14) a-ú-ri-iš na-aš-ta (15) ma-a-an tu-e-el (16) ARAD.MEŠ-*KA* kat-ta-an-da (17) ú-wa-an-zi na-aš-ta (18) am-mu-uk-ka$_4$ EGIR-pa (19) *Ú-UL* pé-eḫ-ḫi	(10–19) I am now in the process of reporting my (missing) servants to the palace. And because the land of Kizzuwatna is (also) a primary watchpoint, if *your* servants come down here (from Tapikka), neither will *I* give them back to you!

Commentary

9 On the “palace” here Imparati writes:

The term É.GAL often recurs in the letters from Maşat, where it appears to have had the function of a center responsible for the collection and distribution of goods (HKM 24) and for the organization of armaments (HKM 52 and 63). It also functioned as a higher authority whose task it was, for example, to investigate matters concerning the agricultural life of various districts (HKM 54); it was an establishment that was notified of important events and circumstances, evidently in the hope that decisive intervention could be obtained from it (HKM 52, 74, and possibly 77); and it was also,

> presumably, with the aim of receiving its favors (HKM 10 and possibly 63). From such palaces orders were also sent out (HKM 75, 88, and 94 …). (Imparati 2002: 94–95)

Since in lines 12–14 Kizzuwatna here is seen as a dependency, this text must date after the treaty between Tudḫaliya I and Šunaššura (Klinger 1995a, 85–86).

It is difficult to see how Taggar-Cohen arrives at the interpretation of lines 10–19 as follows: "The SANGA-priest affiliated with Kizzuwatna says, in a very diplomatic way, he will not demand them. He says that Kizzuwatna is also a front line, and that if the men had arrived there he would have kept them" (2006, 228).

77. HKM 75
From […] to […]

Text: Mşt. 75/87. **Find spot:** G/5 Room 8. **Copy**: HKM 75. **Edition**: Alp 1991a, 262–65 (no. 75). **Discussion**: del Monte 1992, 53 (re. Išḫupitta); Houwink ten Cate 1998, 168–69; Cotticelli-Kurras 2007, 183 (rev. 28); Marizza 2007a, 94–95, 141, 169.

(1) […] x-x […] (2) […] x […] x x […] (3) SIG$_5$-in e-e[š]-tu [n]u-u[t-ta] (4) DINGIR.MEŠ aš-šu-li [p]a-aḫ-š[a]-a[n-da-ru]	(1–4)… may all be well with you (sg.), and may the gods lovingly protect you.
(5) nu ka-a-ša UGULA NIMGIR. ÉRIN.MEŠ x[…] (6) *ŠA* É.GAL-*LIM* INIM ku-i[n …] (7) ú-da-a-aš nu-kán *A-NA* UGU[LA] NIM[GIR. ÉRIN.MEŠ] (8) ḫu-u-ma-an-za-pát ḫa-[l]u-[k]i-[i]š x-x […]	(5–8) May everyone … to/for the Chief of the Military Heralds what matter of the palace the Chief of the Military Heralds has just brought.
(9) na-aš-ta ka-a-ša *ṬUP-PA*$^{ḪI.A}$ […] (10) ar-ḫa i-ya-u-e-en n[a?-…] (11) up-pa-u-e-en nu-un-na-aš-š[a-an] (12) ḫu-u-ma-an-za ka-ru-ú ta!-ru-up-pí[-at-ta-at]	(9–12) We have just copied out[189] the tablets, and we sent …, and everyone already *assembled* to us.

(13) nu ki-nu-un EGIR-pa ÉRIN.MEŠ (14) ^{URU}Iš-ḫu-pí-it-ta [M]E$^{?}$-[t]en (15) nu zi-ik ^{m}Ka-a-aš-šu-uš (16) ^{m}Zi-la-pí-ya‹-aš› ^{m}Ḫu-il-li-iš (17) nu-un-tar-nu-ut-^{te}tén nu ÉRIN.MEŠ (18) ḫu-u-da-a-ak ni-ni-ik-tén	(13–18) Now *take* again the troops of Išḫupitta. You (sg.), Kaššū, Zilapiya (and) Ḫuilli, be quick about it! Promptly muster the troops!
(19) nu-uš-ma-aš ḫa-an-te-ez-z[i-...] (20) ku-it ka-ru-ú x x x [...] (21) ši-ya-an-da-an tup-pí ú-d[a]-an$^{?}$-[du]	(19–21) And because ... to them/you (pl.) first ... already ..., let them bring sealed ... (and/on?) tablet.
(22) šu-ma-a-ša-kán ša-ra-a x[...] x-x-x [...] (23) ku-it-ki i-ya-at-te-ni [nu] SIG$_5$-i[n i-ya-at-tén] (24) nu ki-nu-un-ma nu-tar-nu-ut-t[én]	(22–24) For you (pl.) up ... you do/make something, you did/made right. And now be quick about it!
(25) nu-un-na-aš-kán ÉRIN.MEŠ ^{URU}[Iš-ḫu-pí-it-ta] (26) ar-nu-ut-tén ma-a-an x-x [...] (27) nu-uš-ma-aš ú-wa-[t]e-ni *A-NA* x [...] (28) ḫa-at-ra-a-<u->-en nu-uš-ma-aš x[...] (29) i-da-a-la-wa-aḫ-ḫa-an-zi	(25–29) Relocate to us the troops of Išḫupitta. If ..., then you will come to them. We wrote to .... They will do harm to you (pl.).

Commentary

11–12 Alp read *ša-ru-up-pí-*[...] and (in my view) misunderstood the verb. Houwink ten Cate correctly identified the verb *taruppiya-*, but restored it as an active *taruppi*[*yat*$^{?}$] "each of us has assembled the tr[oops]." But there is no word for "troops" in this sentence. I have chosen to restore the verb as medio-passive, that is, in English the intransitive "assemble." The passage is, however, admittedly obscure.

17 The *te* sign in *nu-un-tar-nu-ut-*^{te}*tén* is employed as a guide to the reading of the *tén* sign. For other examples in Hittite, see GrHL §§1.21–23.

19–21 I find Alp's free restorations and his readings of traces in this paragraph unconvincing. His reading "let them bring here the words on a sealed tablet" is impossible grammatically. The word "sealed" (the participle *šiyandan*) is common gender, while *tuppi* is neuter, and both words are accusative, not dative-locative. Alp attempts to explain his interpretation on the basis of gender incongruence (p. 310).

78. HKM 79
From EN-tarawa to [...]

Text: Mşt. 75/65. **Find spot:** G/5 Room 8. **Copy**: HKM 79. **Edition**: Alp 1991a, 268–71 (no. 79). **Discussion**: Lühr 2001, 337; Groddek 2004, 217.

(1) [*UM-MA* mEN-t]a-ra-u-wa (2) [*A-NA* …]x DUMU DÙG.GA-*YA* (3) [*QÍ-BÍ-M*]*A*	(1–3) Thus speaks EN-tarawa: Say to …, my dear son:
(4) [x-x-x] DUMU DÙG.GA-*YA* (5) [x x x x x -d]a-ni KUR-ya *Ú-UL* pa-it (6) [x x x-aš-]ša-an am-me-el (7) [ma-n]i-ya-aḫ-ḫa-an-da-aš IGI.ḪI.A-wa <*Ú-UL* ḫar-ta> (8) [KÚR?-*TA*]*M*?-ma ku-iš e-ep-ta (9) [nu-un-]na-aš 35 LÚ.MEŠ (10) [ḫar-ni]-ik-ta	(4–10) …, my dear son, … did not go to that? territory. He did not keep his eyes on my subordinates/subjects. But he who initiated hostilities has destroyed thirty-five men of ours.
(11) [nu k]i-nu-na ma-a-an EGIR-pa (12) [ÉRIN.MEŠ k]u-i-e-eš-ka$_4$ ú-wa-an-zi (13) [na]-aš nam-ma le-e (14) [ku-]wa-at-ka$_4$ ni-ni-ik-ši	(11–14) And now, if any troops? come back, do not mobilize them at all again.

79. HKM 80
From [Tarḫunmiya?] to [Ḫimmuili?]

Text: Mşt. 75/90. **Find spot:** G/5 Portico. **Photo:** Alp 1991a, pl. 7 (showing the handwriting of Tarḫunmiya). **Dimensions** (taken from a photo; see §1.2.8.2): **Copy**: HKM 80. **Edition**: Alp 1991a, 270–73 (no. 80). **Discussion**: Houwink ten Cate 1998, 162 (lines 7–11, apparently taking NINDA*tumatiš* as "food supply"), 172; Imparati 1997; Marizza 2007a, 113 (n. 13, sender and addressee), 121 (n. 14, restoration of rev. 12), 161 (table listing for Šuriḫili), 167 (table listing for Uzzū).

The identification of sender and addressee was first proposed by Alp, and was followed by Imparati, Houwink ten Cate, and Marizza. Imparati reasons that this letter was from Tarḫunmiya to Ḫimmuili, because "in Obv. 5′–6′ it is written: '(My) lord, keep an eye on my house. And they must not damage/oppress it!'. Moreover, the sender of the *postscriptum* of this letter was Ḫattušili, who as we have seen was linked to Tarḫunmiya" (Alp 1991a, 656; see also 207).

(1) […] x […] (2) [*MA-ḪAR BE-L*]*Í* ḫu-u-m[a-an SIG$_5$-in e-eš-du] (3) [nu-ut-t]a DINGIR.MEŠ TI-an ḫar-k[án-du] (4) [nu-ut]-ta aš-šu-li pa-aḫ-ša-an-da-ru	(1–4) … May all be well with (my) lord, and may the gods keep you alive and lovingly protect you.
(5) *BE-LU*-uš-ša-an É-*YA* IGI. ḪI.A-wa ḫar-ak (6) na-at le-e dam-mi-iš-ḫa-it<-ta>-ri	(5–6) Lord, keep your eyes on my "house," so that it may not be "damaged" (with undue *šaḫḫan* and *luzzi*).
(7) ka-a-ša-mu-kán *A-NA* DUMU. MEŠ tu-u-ma-ti-i[š] (8) zi-in-na-at-ta-at nu ka-a-ša (9) *A-NA* ARAD. MEŠ ḫa-at[-ra-a-n]u-un (10) na-aš-kán *BE-LU* […] (11) nu-mu EGIR-a[n ti-ya]	(7–11) My *tumati-* (food supply?) for the *princes*$^?$ has just now run out. I have just written to the servants/ officials; so … them, O lord! And support me!
(12) *BE-LU*-ma x[…] (13) x-x-x […] (rev. 1) NUMUN$^?$ […] (rev. 2) ḫu-[…] (rev. 3) x-[…] (rev. 4) [pa-]ra-a na-x[…] na-at-ši-k[án] (rev. 5) [x] URU. ḪI.A-*ŠU-NU* x-x […]	(12, rev. 1–5) O lord, … seed … their cities …
(rev. 6) [x] na-aš-ta LÚ.MEŠ ŠU.GI k[a$^?$-x-x] (rev. 7) ne-eḫ-ḫu-un nu[-z]a ú-wa-a[n-du-y]a (rev. 8) [KUR-e *PA-N*]*I* LÚ.KÚR pa-aḫ-ḫa-aš-nu-an-du […] (rev. 9) [x] x-x na-aš na-aḫ-mi […] pa-an-ku (rev. 10) [x] x-x pa-ra-a n[e-eḫ-ḫu-un] (rev. 11) [nu-za *P*]*A-NI* LÚ.KÚR pa-aḫ-ḫa-aš-n[u-an-te-e]š e-eš-té[n]	(rev. 6–11) I have sent elders … Let them begin to guard the land against the enemy. … I fear … entire … I have sent out, so protect yourselves against the enemy!

Commentary

5 On *BE-LU-uš-ša-an* see text 55 and n. 199.
6 This interpretation is Imparati's (1997, 656).

7 Houwink ten Cate 1998, 162 takes NINDA*tumatiš* as "food supply." The word DUMU.MEŠ in lines 7 and l.e. 3 could also be translated "princes" (i.e., sons of the king), but there is insufficient context here to exclude the more usual meaning "sons" or "children."

79b. HKM 80
Piggyback Letter of Ḫattušili to Uzzū

(12) [*UM-MA* m.GIŠGIDRU-]DIN≈GIR-*LIM A-NA* mU[z-zu-u] (13) [*Ù A-NA* … *QÍ-B*]*Í-MA* (l.e. 1) […-š]a-an [m]e-mi[- …] (l.e. 2) […] NINDAtu-u-ma-ti-in […] (l.e. 3) [… up-p]í DUMU.MEŠ ga-aš-t[i pé-ra-an] (l.e. 4) [le-e ak-k]án-da-ri […]	Thus speaks Ḫattušili: Say to Uzzū and …: … matter … *tumati-* … send. Do not let the princes die from hunger!

80. HKM 81
To His Father (Pallanna) and Mother from Tarḫunmiya

Text: Mşt. 75/64. **Find spot:** G/5 Room 8. **Photo:** Alp 1991a, pl. 8 (showing the handwriting of Tarḫunmiya). **Dimensions** (taken from a photo; cf. §1.2.8.2): 6.5 cm wide × 7.4 cm tall. **Copy**: HKM 81. **Edition**: Alp 1991a, 272–75 (no. 81). **Translation**: Karasu 2002, 424 (the first letter), and Karasu 2003, 234–35. **Discussion**: Beckman 1983a, 39 (on TI-*an ḫark-*); Cotticelli-Kurras 1992, 125 (on the nominal sentence *nu ku-it ma-aḫ-ḫa-an* in line 23); Imparati 1997, 652–53; 2002, 95 (n. 12); Imparati and de Martino 2004 (translation of obv. 6–7); van den Hout 2003a (on Tarḫunmiya); Karasu 2003, 234–35; Marizza 2007a, 154, 163, 167 (all in tables).

(1) *A-NA BE-LÍ A-BI* DÙG.GA-*YA Ù A-NA BE-*<*EL*>*-TI-YA* [AM]A DÙG.GA-*YA* (2) *QÍ-BÍ-MA* [*U*]*M-MA* mTar-ḫu-u[n-m]i-ya (3) DUMU-*KA-MA*	(1–3) Say to (my) lord (= Pallanna), my dear father, and to my lady, my dear mother: Thus speaks Tarḫunmiya, your son:
(4) *MA-ḪAR BE-LÍ* ḫ[u]-u-ma-an SI[G_5]-in e-eš-du (5) nu-uš-ma-aš	(4–8) May everything be well with (my) lord. May the Thousand Gods

LI-IM DINGIR.MEŠ TI-an ḫa[r-ká]n-du (6) nu-ut-ta ŠU.ḪI.A-uš a-ra-aḫ-za-an-[d]a (7) aš-šu-li ḫar-kán-du nu-ut-t[a] (8) pa-aḫ-[š]a-an-da-ru	(the entire pantheon) keep both of you alive. May they hold their hands lovingly around you (sg.) and protect you (sg.).
(9) nu-ut-ta TI-tar ḫa-ad-du-la-[tar] (10) in-na-ra-u-wa-tar MU.ḪI.A G[ÍD.DA] (11) DINGIR.MEŠ-aš a-ši-ya-u-wa-a[r] (12) DINGIR.MEŠ-aš mi-ú-mar ZI-n[a]-aš (13) du-uš-ga-ra-ta-an-na pé-eš[-kán-du] (14) nu *A-NA* DINGIR.MEŠ ku-it ú-e-e[k-ti?] (15) nu-ut-ta a-pa-a-at pé-eš-kán-du	(9–15) May they keep giving you (sg.) life, health, vigor, longevity, the gods' love, the gods' kindness, and joy of spirit. And may the gods keep giving you (sg.) what you ask from them.
(16) *A-BI* D[ÙG.G]A-*YA*-mu aš-šu-ul (17) [ḫa-at-re-e]š-ke (18) [x x x l]u?-u-wa-an-ma (19) [x x] *IŠ-TU* É.GAL-*LI*[*M*] (20) *I-NA* [URU]Ḫa-an-ḫ[a-na] (21) pí-i-e-er na-[…] (22) ma-aḫ-ḫa-an-ma u-i-[ia?-an?-zi?] (23) nu ku-it ma-aḫ-ḫ[a-an nu-mu] (24) ḫu-u-ma-an ḫa-a[t-re-eš-ke]	(16–24) My dear father, keep sending me)your) greeting. They have sent … from the palace to the town Hanhana. … When … Keep writing me how everything is.

Commentary

Imparati (1997, 652) claims that the terms "father" and "mother" are used here in the extended sense of senior colleagues. Perhaps so. But is it not rather coincidental that a pair of opposite sex are so tenderly addressed? This would seem to point to the literal sense of "father" and "mother," that is, Tarḫunmiya's own parents. See discussion above on HKM 60 (text 63). Alp (1991a, 98) comments that Tarḫunmiya's well-wishes to this couple are among the longest and most beautiful in the entire Hittite letter corpus. For the somewhat unusual expanded well-being formula, using "the Thousand Gods," see §1.2.17.

80b. HKM 81
Piggyback Letter from Tarḫunmiya to Uzzū

(25) [*UM-M*]*A* ^{m}Tar-ḫu-un-mi-ya (26) [*A-N*]*A* ^{m}Uz-zu-u ŠE[Š.DÙ]G. GA-*Y*[*A*] (27) [*QÍ-B*]*Í-MA* DINGIR. MEŠ-ta (28) [aš-šu-l]i pa-aḫ-ša-an-da-[r]u	(25–28) Thus speaks Tarḫunmiya: Say to Uzzū, my dear brother: May the gods lovingly protect you.
(29) ⸢ki⸣-i-kán *ṬUP-PÍ PA-NI* ^{m}Pa-a[l-l]a-an-n[a] *BE-LÍ-YA* (30) ^{MUNUS}*BE-<EL>-TI-I-YA* SIG$_5$-in ḫal-za-i (31) nam-ma-mu EGIR-pa aš-šu-ul (32) ḫa-at-ra-a-an-du	(29–32) Please read this tablet of mine distinctly to Pallanna, my lord (Tarḫunmiya's father), and to my lady (his mother), and then let them send back (their) greetings to me.

Commentary

30 SIG$_5$-*in ḫalzai* "read *distinctly*" may indicate that the writer's parents were elderly and had difficulty in hearing. Previous translations (Alp, and Karasu 2003, 235) have not brought out this important sense of SIG$_5$-*in*. See above in §1.2.12.

81. ABoT 65
From Tarḫuntišša to Pallā

Text: AnAr 9751. **Find spot:** unknown. **Copy**: ABoT 65. **Edition**: Güterbock 1944; Otten 1956, 183–84, 188–89; Rost 1956, 345–50. **Discussion**: Hoffner 1972, 33 (MH dating); Imparati 1974, 60 n. 48); 1985 (on Armaziti); Neu 1976, 324–25; Beckman 1983b, 97 n. 2 (on É DUB.BA.A [rev. 8] as reflecting the presence of a scribal school at Ḫattuša); Beckman 1995a, 27 with n. 41; Hagenbuchner 1989b, 176 (no. 123); 1989a, 12 n. 37 (re É DUB. BA.A), 14 (re. ^{m}Palla), 65 (re SIG$_5$-*in ēšdu*), 83 (SAG.DU-*GA*), 127 (re. private trips), 152 (re. *tapaššet*, obv. 8); Klinger 1995a, 88; Houwink ten Cate 1998, 158, 162, 175–76; Hagenbuchner-Dresel 1999, 54–55 (survey of non-royal persons bearing the name Ḫattušili); de Martino 2005b, 300, 307–8, 311, 317; CHD *man* b 2′ b' (rev. 5–6).

De Martino writes:

> The findspot of the tablet is unknown. However, H. G. Güterbock and S. Alp believed it came from Maşat/Tapikka. The text is dated as Middle Hittite. The sender is Tarḫuntišša and the receiver is Pallā. In the text Ḫattušili is mentioned (obv. 6, 8, rev. 2′, 16′) to be identified, presumably, with the functionary by the same name present in the other Maşat letters. In ABoT 65 two scribes (known also from other Middle Hittite documents) are mentioned: Arma-ziti (obv. 6, 9) could be identified with the scribe of the Arnuwanda treaty with the Kaška people KBo XVI 27 + KBo XL 330, as suggested by J. Klinger, and with the sender (maybe also a scribe) of the post scriptum of the Ortaköy letter Çorum 21-9-90 obv. 18′; Atiuna (rev. 8′, inferior ledge 1, 3) could be the same person as the sender (the name is partially missing) of the Maşat letters HKM 49 and 50. (2005b: 307–8)

The Arma-ziti in obv. 6 may also be the man who is mentioned in HKM 84 (text 83): 16 (so Alp 1991a, 54; see also Imparati 1985).

(obv.1) [*UM-MA*] mTar-ḫu-un-ti-iš-ša (2) [*A-NA* mPa]l-la-a ŠEŠ.DÙG.GA-*YA QÍ-B*[*Í-MA*] (3) ka[t-ti-mi] SIG_5-in tu-ug-ga kat-ta SIG_5-i[n] (4) e-eš-[t]u[190] nu-ut-ta DINGIR.MEŠ TI-an ḫar-kán-du (5) nu SAG.DU-*KÀ* pa-aḫ-ša-an-da-ru	(1–5) Thus speaks Tarḫuntišša: Say to Pallā, my dear brother: It is well with me. May it be well with you too. May the gods keep you alive, and protect your person (lit. "your head").
(6) *A-NA* m.GIŠGIDRU-DINGIR-*LIM* ku-it *Ù A-NA* m.d*SÎN*-LÚ (7) a-aš-šu-ul ḫa-at-ra-a-eš na-at *Ú-UL* ka-a (8) m.GIŠGIDRU-DIN≈GIR-*LIM*-in ta-pa-aš-ši-i-e-et ku-it-ki (9) nu URUḪa-at-tu-ši pé-en-ni-iš m.d*SÎN*-LÚ-in-na (10) *I-NA* É-*ŠU* tar-né-er	(6–10) Since you sent greetings to Ḫattušili and Arma-ziti, (I must tell you) they are not here. Ḫattušili contracted a bit of a fever and drove off to Ḫattuša (for 'medical' treatment). And they let Arma-ziti go home (on leave?).
(11) am-mu-ga a-aš-šu-ul *Ú-UL* ku-it ḫa-a[t-r]a-a-eš (12) [nu] ar-ḫa da-a-la URUMa-ra-aš-š[a-a]n-ti-ya-az (13) [*Ú-U*]*L*? *MA-ḪAR* dUTU-*ŠI* e-šu-un p[a-r]a-a-mu-za (14) [ke-e-d]a-aš ud-da-na-a-aš pí-e-eš-ke-et	(11–14) To me you sent no greetings. But don't be concerned (lit., let it rest)! I was in Maraššantiya, not in the presence of His Majesty. He has been sending[191] me out on these missions.
(15) [o o o o o o o URUḪ]a-at-tu-ši ku-[…]	(15) … in Ḫattuša …

(rev. 1′) ar-nu-x[o o o]x x x[…] (rev. 2′) pé-ra-an kat-ta-an $^{m.GIŠ}$GIDRU-DINGIR-*LIM* x[…] (rev 3′) me-mi-iš-ta ^{m}Pal-la-a-aš-wa-ra-at[…]	(rev. 1′) … Ḫattušili … he said: “Pallā relocated it ….”
(rev. 4′) nu a-pé-e-da-ni ud-da-ni-i ar-ša-ni-e-[eš?] (rev. 5′) ma-am-ma-an-za-kán ku-iš-ki É-er ta-ma-iš ar-nu-ut (rev. 6′) ma-an zi-ik *Ú-UL* ar-ša-ni-e-še (rev. 7′) nu am-mu-uk-ka$_4$ a-pa-a-at ut-tar kat-ta-wa-a-tar ki-ša-at	(rev. 4′–7′) And he became upset about that matter. If someone else had relocated (your) household/family, would you not become upset?[192] So that matter became a grievance to me as well.
(rev. 8′) nu ḫa-an-da-a-an *A-NA* ^{m}A-ti-u-un-na *I-NA* É DUB.BA.A (rev. 9′) ki-iš-ša-an me-ma-aḫ-ḫu-un *A-BU-KA*-wa-mu-uš-ša-an (rev. 10′) EGIR-an-pát ki-it-ta-ri EGIR-an ar-ḫa-wa-ra-aš-mu (rev. 11′) *Ú-UL* nam-ma ne-e-a-ri *Ú-UL*-wa [ta-]me[-d]a-aš? (rev. 12′) ku-it-ki *Ú-UL*-ma-wa-mu a-pa-a-aš ku-it-ki ḫar-zi (rev. 13′) [*Ú-U*]*L*-ma-wa-aš-ša-an *A-NA* 1-*EN* URU-*LIM* ku-wa-pí-ki ḫar-wa-ni (rev. 14′) [nu-]w[a]-mu-[ká]n EGIR-an ki-it-ta-r[i …] (rev. 15′) [EGIR-an a]r-ḫa-wa-ra-aš-mu-za *Ú-U*[*L* nam-ma ne-e-a-ri …] (rev. 16′) [ma-a-an-w]a-kán $^{m.GIŠ}$GIDRU-DINGIR-*LIM*-ma *A-N*[*A*…] (rev. 17′) [o o o]x-ra-da-an-ta-an-na-an[…] (rev. 18′) pa-a-un	(rev. 8′–18′) And I spoke frankly? to Atiunna in the tablet room as follows: “Your ‘father’ keeps after me:[193] he won’t let me alone! Is there nothing for others? Does that one hold nothing for me? Will we *stay*? nowhere in? (any) single town? He will keep after me! … He won’t let me alone! … If Ḫattušili had …, I would have …
(l. e. 1) […]x ki-ša-at nu *A-NA* ^{m}A-ti-u[n-na -…] (l. e. 2) […^{GIŠ}*L*]*E*-?-*E* nam-ma-ad-du-za […] (l. e. 3) […] *A-NA* ^{m}A-ti-u-un-na[…] (l. e. 4)[… ḫa-]at-ra-a-i É ^{m}Ša-[…] (l. e. 5) [… *A-N*]*A* $^{m.GIŠ}$GIDRU-DINGIR-*LIM* ku-wa-p[í …] (l. e. 6) […]x-za-kán x x [………………………….]	(l. e. 1) That matter became a source of irritation to me! And … to Atiunna … writing board … then … to you. … Write … to Atiunna. The house of … When … to Ḫattušili, …

Commentary

obv. 6–10 *tapaššiya-* "to get a fever," being one of the verbs denoting illness like (*ištark*-and *irmaliya-*), takes its logical subject in the accusative as a direct object (see GrHL §16.31). This fact was not realized by Rost 1956, 346 and Hagenbuchner 1989a, 152, both of whom translate "something provoked (erregte/hat aufgeregt) Ḫattušili."

obv. 9–10 Edited in CHD P, 277 (per 1 a 3′). This may be a unique instance of the employment of the non-literal, "collegial" kinship terms outside of the polite greeting formulas in letters. Is Atiunna's "father" here really his literal father, or his superior in the hierarchy?

rev. 3–6 Although CHD L–N, 141 (man b 2′ b') rendered this section literally as: "If someone else had confiscated/appropriated (your) house, would you not be upset?" it seems to me that we have the same use here as in other Maşat letters (see texts 16: 7′–13′; 45: 1′–13; and 47: 5′) with a household (É-*TUM*) and various towns (URU.DIDLI.ḪI.A) as direct objects, in a context suggesting the relocating of households/families from one town to another and settling them (*ašeš-*).

rev. 13 This might be one of the intransitive uses of *ḫar*(*k*)- with the meaning "to be, stay" (Boley 2001).

82. HKM 82:
From Mar-ešrē to [...]

Text: Mşt. 80/58. **Find spot:** Maşat L/15. **Copy**: HKM 82. **Edition**: Alp 1991a, 274–77 (no. 82). **Discussion**: Marizza 2007a, 150 (re. Mar-ešrē);

The beginning of the obverse and the end of the reverse are broken away. Since the first preserved line on the obverse is an address formula, this is a second (or piggyback) letter, not the main one. Mār-ešrē writes—perhaps from Ḫattuša (see above in §1.2.10)—to a younger colleague in Tapikka. Alp (1991a, 79) posits that the "dear daughter" is the wife of the addressee, and that both he and his wife are younger than Mar-ešrē.

(1′) *UM-MA* ᵐDUMU.U[D.2]0.KAM [*A-NA* ᵐ...] (2′) ŠEŠ DÙG.GA-*YA* *QÍ-BÍ-M*[*A*]	(1–2) Thus speaks Mar-ešrē: Say to ..., my dear brother:
(3′) *MA-ḪAR* ŠEŠ DÙG.GA-*YA* *Ù* DUMU.MUNUS DÙG.GA-*YA*	(3–7) May all be well with my dear brother and with my dear daughter.

(4) ḫu-u-ma-an SIG$_5$-in e-eš-du (5) nu-uš-ma-aš DINGIR.MEŠ TI-an (6) ḫar-kán-du nu-uš-ma-aš […] (7) [aš]-šu-li pa-aḫ[-ša-an-da-ru]	And may the gods keep you (pl.) alive, and lovingly protect you (pl.).
(8) [ŠE]Š DÙG.GA-*YA*-mu ku-it [ḫa-at-ra-a-eš …] (9) a[š-š]u-ul *Ú-UL* [… *Ú-UL*$^?$] (10) [ku-w]a-pí-ik-ki […] (11) [ḫa-a]t-ra-a-ši nu-ud-d[u-za-kán] (12) [š]a-[a]n-za ki-nu-n[a-mu tu-el] (13) [aš-šu-ul] ḫ[a]-at-r[e]-e[š-ke …] (14) [o] x x x x x x	(8–14) Concerning the fact that my dear brother wrote … (to?) me … You do not … a greeting … at no time … do you write. I am angry with you. Now start sending your greeting to me! …
(15) […-]x-at-ta (16) [… up-]pí (17) […-]x	

83. HKM 84
From […] to […]

Text: Mşt. 75/103. **Find spot:** G/5 Portico. **Copy**: HKM 84. **Edition**: Alp 1991a, 278–83 (no. 84). **Discussion**: Arıkan 2006, 145.

(1′) [*UM-MA* …] x [*A-NA* …] (2′) [… DÙG$^?$.GA$^?$]-*YA* *QÍ*-[*BI-MA*] (3′) [kat-ti-ti ḫ]u-u-ma-an S[IG$_5$-in e-eš-du] (4′) [nu-ut-ta DINGIR.MEŠ] TI-an ḫ[ar-kán-du] (5′) [nu-ut-ta aš-šu-li pa-aḫ-ša-an-da-r]u	(1′–5′) Thus speaks PN$_1$: Say to PN$_2$, my dear …: May all be well with you. And may the gods keep you alive and lovingly protect you.
(6′) k[a$^{!?}$-a-ša-mu[194] ki-i]š-ša-an ku-i[t ḫa-at-ra-a-eš] (7′) ^{URU}T[a-p]í-ig-ga-az-wa-kán k[at-ta …] (8′) k[i]-nu-na-at-ta ka-a-ša […] (9′) *IŠ-TU* DINGIR-*LIM*-ya i-da-la[-wa-aḫ-ḫa-an-zi] (10′) na-aš-ta ^{URU}Ta-pí-ik-ka$_4$-a[z kat-ta …] (11′) DUMU.MEŠ-[*Y*]*A*-kán kat-ta le-e [tar-na-at-ti] (12′) ma-an-na-aš	(6′–20′) Now concerning what you (sg.?) just wrote me, as follows, "*Get* out of Tapikka. They are now about to *injure* you through … and through (the command of?) a deity. So *get* out of Tapikka, and don't *leave* my sons down there!" If we have grain, then we will make *bread* for you. But if there is no

ḫal-ki-iš nu-u[t-ta …] (13′) i-ya-u-e-ni ma-a-an ḫal-k[i-iš-ma NU.GÁL] (14′) nu-ut-ta n[am-]ma ku-iš[ku-it-ki i-ya-zi] (15′) nu-uš-ši zi-ik mDu-l[a-ak-ki-iš] (16′) mAr-ma-LÚ-iš-ša A[NŠE.KUR.RA.ḪI.A] (17′) le-e pí-iš-kán-te-ni [ma-a-an] (18′) ku-it-ki ki-ša-ri […] (19′) nam-ma-aš-ma-aš ta-šu-w[a-aḫ-ḫa-an-zi] (20′) ka-a-ša-aš-ši *IŠ-TU* […][195]	grain, then who ever again will make anything for you? And you, Dulakki—and also Armaziti—don't give horses to him! If something occurs, …, then they will blind (both of) you. To him by means of ….
(21′) ka-a-ša-mu-kán x[-…] (22′) na-aš-ta 5 GA.K[U_7[196] …] (23′) NINDA GIBIL.ḪI.A-ya *I*[-*NA*? …] (24′) 1 al-la-a-an<-za?> G[A[197]…] (25′) an-da-ya-aš-ši-k[án …] (26′) na-at […] (27′) ku-it [ma-aḫ-ḫa-an nu-mu] (28′) ḫu-u-ma[-an ḫa-at-ra-a-i]	(21′–28′) Now to me … And five (portions of) sweet milk … and freshly baked breads in …, one (portion of) sour milk …, in addition to it …, and it …. Write to me everything (about) how it is.
(29′) ka-a?[-ša? …] (30′) i-x[…]	(29′–30′) … …
(rev. 1′) n[a?-…] (2′) *A-NA* D[UMU] m[Š]a-pár-t[a …] (3′) nu-uš-ši ARAD-*SÚ* […] (4′) na-aš *Ú-UL*-ma [… na-aš ma-a-an ka-ru-ú] (5′) pa-a-an-za EGIR-pa i-[it na-an-mu-kán du-wa-a-an] (6′) pa-ra-a na-i URU[…] (7′) nu-mu a-pa-a-at-ta […] (8′) ka-a-ša-mu mŠa-pár-t[a …]	(rev. 1′–8′) … to the son of Šaparta … and … his slave to him. And he will not … If he has already gone, go back, and send him to me! … and me … it. To me Šaparta …

Commentary

15–17 On this meaning of *lē* plus the imperfective stem of the verb see Hoffner and Melchert 2002 and now also GrHL §24.10. The form *pí-iš-kán-te-ni* in line **17** appears faulty (so Alp 1991a, 343). Instead of emending to *pí-iš-kat*!*-te-ni*, one might see in the unemended form an example of nasalization: *tt* > *nt*. On this phenomenon see Oettinger 1994, especially his examples in §4.2 on p. 319, where the nasalization comes from a nasal in the following syllable: *mulattin* > *mulantin, naḫšarattan* > *naḫšarantan, šalikanzi*> *šalinkanzi*, etc. If so, this argues for reading *kat*, not *kit*$_9$, in such verb forms.

25 On *anda=ya=šši* see Hoffner 1997g, §70 and §149, and 269 sub *anda.*

83b. HKM 84
Piggyback Letter from Ḫuilli to […]

At rev. 9′ a second letter from Ḫuilli to […] begins. It requires urgent action (*ú-wa-at du-wa-ad-du* "Get with it!"). The addressee is to round up whatever grain or other foodstuffs available in his vicinity and bring them to Ḫuilla. The addressee has been requesting (note the imperfective form of the verb *ḫa-at-re-eš-ke-ši*) headwear (TÚGSAG.DU[L]), perhaps of a protective, military type. Ḫuilli promises to provide this. The final sections of the second letter are written on the left edge of the tablet in reverse directions ("a" and "b"). The clauses on left edge "a" are difficult because of the textual breaks. But if the first word in line 2 could be a neuter gender Hittite noun ending in *-ki*, then one could take the *kuit* that follows as the neuter relative pronoun, and this would become the subject of the final sentence: "and let it remain with [*the gods*]!" The restoration of "gods" in both "a" 4 and "b" 1 depends upon the most likely subject of the final clause "[they will protect] you benevolently." And I believe all would agree that this should be "the gods." This solution by no means eliminates all the awkward points in the translation.

(rev. 9′) *UM-MA* mḪu-il-li ⌜*A*?⌝[*-NA* … *QÍ-BÍ-MA*] (rev. 10′) DINGIR.MEŠ-ta TI-an ḫar-kán-du [nu-ut-ta aš-šu-li] (rev. 11′) pa-a[ḫ-š]a-an-da-ru	(rev. 9′–11′) Thus speaks Ḫuilli: Say to …: May the gods keep you alive and may they protect you benevolently!
(rev. 12′) ú-wa-at du-wa-ad-du MUN≈ [US? …] (rev. 13′) URUTa-pí-ik-ka$_4$-az kat-t[a …] (rev. 14′) ma-a-an še-li-iš-ma ku[-iš-ki] (rev. 15′) na-aš-ma ku-it im-ma k[u-it …] (rev. 16′) ANŠE.KUR.RA.ḪI. A zi-ik t[u-u-re-eš-ke na-at-mu du-wa-a-an] (rev. 17′) pé-en-ni *A-NA* TÚGSAG. DU[L] (rev. 18′) ku-it ḫa-at-re-eš-ke-ši nu[-ut-ta] (rev. 19′) [… pé?-d]a?-aḫ-ḫi nu-ut-ta pa[-ra-a …] (rev. 20′) […] i-ya-mi-it-t[a …] (rev. 21′) […]-ši *Ú-UL* […]	(rev. 12′–21′) Get a move on! …… Down from Tapikka …. If some grain heap exists, or whatever …, you hitch up horses and drive it to me! Concerning the fact that you keep writing (to me) for headwear: I will bring … to you, and …. I will make for you … not …

(l. e. "a")	
(l. e. a 1) [tu-el ku-it ma-a]ḫ-ḫa-an nu-mu ḫa-at-ra-a-i (2) [x x x x-]KI-ya-at-ta [ku-i]t wa-tar-[n]a-aḫ-ḫi-iš-ke-nu-un (3) [ḫar?-zi?-at] ku-iš na-at! (text:-an)-ši-kán ar-ḫa da-a (4) [na-at DINGIR?.M]EŠ kat-ta-an e-eš-du	Write me how you are! And the …-*ki* which I have been giving you instructions about—take it away from him who holds? it. And let it remain with *the gods*?!
(l. e. "b")	
(l. e. b 1) [ma-a-an *A-NA* DING]IR.MEŠ ku-it-ki EGIR-an tar-na-at-ti nu-ut-ta aš-š[u-li pa-aḫ-ša-an-da-ri]	If you turn something over to the *gods*, they will lovingly protect you.

Commentary

rev. 12′ For *uwat duwaddu* see above in §1.2.19.1.

84. HKM 88
From […] to […]

Text: Mşt. 75/108. **Find spot:** G/5 Portico. **Copy:** HKM 88. **Edition**: Alp 1991a, 288–89 (no. 88). **Discussion**: Marizza 2007a, 129.

The beginning and end of this letter are broken away, so we have no idea who the sender or addressee were. The sender quotes a report that reached him (the quotative particle *-wa* occurs in lines 1–7) concerning some Kaškaean groups who are about to make peace (line 3), but another one is not willing (line 4). What the writer then goes on to say concerns troop movements (lines 6–11) and the protection of crops (line 16).

(1) [k]a-a-š[a-wa? …] (2) URUTal-ma-l[i-ya …] (3) ták-šu-la-a-an-zi […] (4) *Ú-UL* ták-šu-la-a-iz-z[i …] (5) ḫu-u-ma-an-te[198]-ya-pát ni-ni-i[k]	(1–5) "The … are about to make peace *in* Talmaliya.[199] but the … will not make peace. So muster *troops* in every (area)!"
(6) nu-wa EGIR-an ti-ya nu-w[a	(6–11) "And get busy, lest …

… *Ú-UL*] (7) ma-an-ga nu-wa-kán *A-NA* LÚ.MEŠ […] (8) nam-ma-ya ku-e-da-aš URU.DIDLI.ḪI.A (9) ÉRIN.MEŠ pa-ra-a ḫu-u-da-a-ak ar-n[u-u]t […] (10) nu-uš-ši ka-a-aš-ma *ŠA* É.GAL-*LIM* (11) me-mi-an ḫa-at-ra-a-u-en	somehow! And … for the men …!” Then also into what cities he promptly brought forward troops, we have just sent the message from the palace to him.
(12) an-da-ma-za : ⸢an-na⸣-ra-a [k]u-it (13) ud-da-a-ar šar-li-x[-…] (14) nu-za ᵐŠa-ḫu-ru-nu-wa-aš […] (15) [u]d-da-a-ar ar-ḫa d[a]-a-a[š …] (16) nu ḫal-ki-e-eš ud-da-ni-i […] (17) *Ú-UL* ma-az-za-aš-[t]e-ni x-[…] (18) ku-iš ᵁᴿᵁKa-ra-aḫ-na x x […] (19) an-da e-eš-ta nu ÉRIN. MEŠ […]	(12–19) In addition, concerning the fact that … words/matters … … Šaḫurunuwa took away for himself the words of …. You will not *risk* crops in the matter …. What … was in Karaḫna, the troops …

Commentary

12 :*an-na-ra-a* is mentioned and briefly discussed by van den Hout 2006, 226 with n. 58.

85. HKM 89
From […] to […]

Text: Mşt. 73/78. **Find spot:** H/2 Room 26. **Copy:** HKM 89. **Edition**: Alp 1991a, 288–91 (no. 89). **Discussion**: del Monte 1992, 171 (on ᵁᴿᵁTiwara in line 11); Beal 1998, 86 (citing CHD P on *peran ḫuinu-*); de Martino and Imparati 2004, 797 w. n. 50 (translation of obv. 5–6); Marizza 2007a, 149 (on Luparrui).

Lines 1–2, although partially broken, indicate more than one addressee. Therefore, although the sender resorts to the more usual “you” (sg.) in the well-wishes of lines 3–6, and there seem to be three places where he addresses only one of the recipients (line 23, 24, 27), the -*šmaš* in lines 9 and 12 must be a plural “you,” not an unreferenced “them” (as per Alp’s translation).

(1) [*UM-MA* …] *A-NA* ^{m}[…] (2) [*Ù A-NA* … *QÍ-BÍ-M*]*A*	(1–2) Thus speaks … Say to … and to …:
(3) [kat-ti-ti … ḫu-u-m]a-an S[IG$_5$-in e-e]š-du (4) [nu-ut-ta ... DINGIR. MEŠ TI-a]n [ḫar-ká]n-d[u] (5) [nu-ut-ta ŠU.ḪI.A-uš] a-ra-aḫ-za-an[-da] (6) [aš-šu-li ḫar-kán-d]u nu-ut-ta pa-a[ḫ-š]a-an-da-ru	(3–6) May all be well with you …, and may the gods keep you alive, and lovingly hold their arms about you, and protect you.
(7) [ma-a-an ^{m}Lu-pár-ru-iš a]n-tu-uḫ-še-eš e-ep-ta (8) [na-at *Ú-UL* š]a-ag-ga-aḫ-ḫi (9) [1? an-t]u-uḫ-ša-an-na-aš-ma-aš *Ú-UL* am-mu-uk (10) [pé-ra]-an ḫu-i-nu-nu-un ^{m}Lu-pár-ru-u-i-ša-aš-kán (11) ⸢^{URU}Ti⸣-i-wa-ra-az pa-ra-a na-it-ta (12) an-tu-uḫ-ša-an-na-aš-ma-aš (13) pé-ra-an ḫu-i-nu-ut am-mu-ug-ga (14) *Ú-UL* ku-it-ki ša-ag-ga-aḫ-ḫu-un	(7–14) I do not know if Luparruis seized the people. It wasn't I who put the one? person in your (pl.) charge. Luparrui dispatched them from Tiwara. He put a person also in your (pl.) charge. I knew nothing about it.
(15) [k]i-nu-na a-pé-e an-tu-uḫ-še-eš ar-ḫa tar-n[i-ir] (16) [nu-k]án ^{m}Lu-pár-ru-u-iš pé-ra-an le-e (17) [ku-i-e]n-ki e-ep-zi am-mu-uk-wa (18) [x-]pí?-iš-ki-iš-ke-mi a-pé-e-ma-wa (19) [pa-r]a-a [š]u-ul-le-eš ap-pí-iš-kán-zi (20) […]	(15–20) But now they have released those people. Luparrui should not seize anyone beforehand?, (saying) "I will begin to …, but *they* will seize hostages."
(21) [x x x] LÚ.KÚR-ya x an-da ar-nu-wa-an[-zi] (22) [x x]-ya-aš-ši-kán x an-da (23) [nu-za? pa-a]ḫ-ḫa-aš-nu-wa-an-z[a] e-eš *A-NA* URU.DIDLI.ḪI.A-ya (24) [ḫu-u-ma]-an-da-a-aš ar-ḫa pé-en-ni (25) [x? pa]-aḫ-ḫa-aš-nu-wa-an e-eš-ta	(21–25) They will bring … and the enemy together. … too is in it. So be (sg.) well protected. Drive (sg.) off to all the cities. (It?) was protected.
(26) [nu-m]u ke-e-da-ni <*A-NA*> *ṬUP-PÍ* ar-ku-wa-ar (27) […]… ḫu-u-da-a-ak ḫa-at-ra-a-i	(26–27) And send (sg.) promptly … to me a reply? to this tablet.

4 Alp restored *LI-IM* because space seemed too wide for simple DINGIR.MEŠ. Yet in the only other places where *LI-IM* DINGIR.MEŠ occurs in the well-wishing fomula in the Maşat letters, the addressee is a superior, sometimes addressed as "my lord" (HKM 29 and HKM 48). That is not the case here.

In both **lines 7 and 15** *an-ti-uḫ-še-eš* is acc. pl., as is *a-pé-e* "those," not nominative (see Hoffner forthcoming §57 and §149). See also acc. [*š*]*u-ul-le-eš* in line 19.

9 There is room at the beginning of the line for more than the sign [*an-t*]*u-*. Yet, the clitic pronoun *-šmaš* normally attaches to the first word in the clause. It is possible that the number "1," being a logographic writing and one which closely attaches to the noun *antuḫšan,* would not bear the clitic. Alp analyzed *antuḫšannaš* as a single word, the genitive of *antuḫšatar.* But I can find no other example of the genitive of *antuḫšatar* as a free-standing genitive in Alp's required sense of "(members) of the people group." And here it would have to be functioning as the direct object of *peran ḫuinu-* "to put (someone) under the command of (another)."

18 On the form [x-]*pí?-iš-ki-iš-ke-mi*, see Hoffner forthcoming §79.

25 There is barely space in the copy for one sign before *pa-*. Yet one would like to restore [*na-at*] in order to provide a neuter subject for the predicate *paḫḫašnuwan* "protected."

26 Alp's translation "write the petition (German *die Bitte*) for me on this tablet" does not seem probable. In fact, even with my translation of *arkuwar* as "reply?," the idea of writing it on "this" tablet would be impossible, since it is a dried and hardened clay tablet. Therefore—with some hesitance—I have understood *kedani* <*ANA*> *ṬUPPI* as a reply "*to* this tablet."

2.2.3. MH Letters found at Šapinuwa-Ortaköy (86–91)

Excavations at the township of Ortaköy, 53 km southeast of Çorum, beginning in 1990, have revealed the ruins of the Hittite city of Šapinuwa, the chief administrative center ("palace") and royal residence for the district, to which Tapikka/Maşat Höyük also belonged. A large part of the tablets discovered in the excavations at Šapinuwa led by Mustafa and Aygül Süel is composed of letters. Only three of the letters recovered through the official excavations have been published. To these one can add five letters in the Çorum Museum found at Ortaköy before the beginning of the official excavations, and published by A. Ünal (1998). All these texts are Middle Hittite in language and script (see de Martino 2005b, 309).

86. Or 90/1400
From the King to Kuikuišanduwa

Text: Or 90/1400. **Find spot:** Ortaköy; debris from upper storey of Building A. **Copy:** none. **Edition**: Süel 1992, 491; CHD Š, 135 (sub 14′). **Discussion**: de Martino 2005b, 310; Forlanini 1997, 398 n. 3; Hoffner 1998, 117 (on Hittite names reduplicated in the manner of Kuikuišanduwa); Freu and Mazoyer 2007, 172–73 (on the official Kuikuišanduwa).

The body of this letter is very short. The main verb "do" (*iyatten*, line 9) is plural, meaning that Kuikuišanduwa and other unnamed persons to whom this letter is addressed (*kuedaš*, dative pl.) are to perform a task outlined in a letter that Ḫašwara "has just/herewith (*kāšma*) brought (*udaš*)." The verb *uda-* "to bring," when occurring without a preverb, because it contains the prefix *u-* (versus *pe-*), usually means "bring here" (i.e., to the speaker/writer). But the present context—especially the use of *kāšma* "herewith"—suggests rather that it is a tablet sent along with this short "cover letter" to Šapinuwa, detailing what it is that the king wishes Kuikuišanduwa and his unnamed associates to do. The accompanying tablet concerned Mt. Ḫaluna, but in what regard we cannot tell: it could have been a military-administrative assignment; it could have been a cultic one. Mt. Ḫaluna, mentioned in line 5, is one of a group of mountains associated with the city of Šapinuwa in cult texts found at Ḫattuša (see Forlanini 1997, 398 n. 3). See further in the discussion of Ünal 1998, no. 4 (text 87).

(1) *UM-MA* dUTU-*ŠI-MA* (2) *A-NA* mKu-i-ku-i-ša-an-du-wa (3) ku-e-da-aš *QÍ-BI-MA*	(1–3) Thus speaks His Majesty: Say to Kuikuišanduwa (and) whoever (pl.) (is there):
(4) ka-a-aš-ma mḪa-aš-wa-ra-aš (5) ku-it *ŠA* ḪUR.SAGḪa-lu-na (6) tup-pí ú-da-aš nu-uš-ša-an (7) a-pé-e-da-ni tup-pí-ya (8) ma-aḫ-ḫa-an ki-it-ta-ri (9) nu *QA-TAM-MA* i-ya-at-tén	(4–9) Do (pl.) according to what is written on the tablet concerning Mt. Ḫaluna that Ḫašwara has just brought.

Commentary

3 *kuedaš*—"(and) whoever (pl.) (is there)"—is nowhere else attested in this sense. Normally *kui-* is either interrogative or relative. The context requires it to refer to more than one person (pl.) whose names the letter-writer either does not know or does not wish to specify.

7–8 On Hittite expressions for the location of writing on the surface of a tablet, see CHD Š, 146–47 (sub g 1′) and 148 (sub 8′ b').

87. HHCTO 4
From the King to […], Mušu, and […]

Text: Çorum 21-8-90. **Find spot:** Ortaköy near Çorum, specifics unknown. **Copy:** Ünal 1998, 101. **Edition**: Ünal 1998, 40–43. **Discussion**: de Martino 2005b, 310.

For another Ortaköy tablet concerning Mt. Ḫaluna, see text 86. There may be a connection between the two letters. In both letters the king writes to several persons in Šapinuwa. It is even possible that this tablet's primary addressee (PN$_1$) is Kuikuišanduwa, and that the unnamed others (*kuedaš* "and to some others") in text 86 are Mūšu and […], the second and third addressees in this letter. In text 86 Kuikuišanduwa and some other men are ordered to follow the instructions given to them on a tablet brought to them by Ḫašwara. Here (lines 5–6) PN$_1$ (Kuikuišanduwa?) refers to a previous letter written to the three of them, which could be either the tablet brought to them by Ḫašwara or the cover letter of the king (text 86). In lines 4–9, PN$_1$, speaking for the group, promises to find [the tablet], which may have been mislaid or disregarded (*waštanu-*) by the scribe who received it from Ḫašwara. The remainder of the partially preserved text (lines 10–17) is not clear. The "instruction" (*taparriyaš*) that was disregarded (*waštanuwanza*) may be what the king in text 86 tells them that they should do, namely, what is written on the tablet that Ḫašwara was bringing them.

(1) *UM-MA* ^{d}UTU-*Š[I-MA A-NA* …] (2) ^{m}Mu-ú-šu *Ù* ⌈*A*?⌉[-*NA* ^{m}x x x] (3) *QÍ-BÍ*[-*MA*]	(1–3) Thus speaks His Majesty: Say to PN$_1$, Mūšu, and to PN$_3$:
(4) ki-iš-ša-an-mu x[-… ḫa-at-ra-a-eš] (5) ^{d}UTU-*ŠI*-wa-an-na-aš *Š*[*A* $^{\text{ḪUR.SAG}}$Ḫa-lu-na ku-it ut-tar[200]] (6) ḫa-at-ra-a-eš nu-wa-ra-a[t *NI-IŠ-ME* nu …] (7) ú-e-mi-ya-u-e-ni nu-wa[-ru-uš? pu-nu-uš-šu-	(4–9) This is what PN$_1$? wrote to me: "Concerning the matter of Mt. Ḫaluna about which Your Majesty wrote to us, we have heard it. And we will find …, and we will inquire by whichever scribe

e-ni] (8) *IŠ-TU* DUB.SAR im-ma! ku![-e-da-az ta-pár-ri-ya-aš?] (9) wa-aš-ta-nu-wa-an-za	the instruction? was disregarded.
(10) na-aš *Ú-UL IŠ-TU* DUB[.SAR …] (11) wa-aš-ta-nu-wa-an-za ḪUR.SAGḪ[a?-… …] (12) ku-iš še-er ZAG-na-az ḫar?[-zi? …] (13) URUZi?-im-ma-la!-an-kán k[u?-iš? …] (14) ar-ta nu-uš-ša-an ta-l[a?-…] (15) ku-iš še-er nu-za a-pa-a-at[(-) …] (16) [p]é-e-da-an ḫa-lu-na-a[n? …] (17) [ḫal-z]i?-i[š?]-ša-an-zi […]	(10–17) And it was not disregarded by a scribe of …, but … who above, in Mt. Ḫaluna … holds it in his right hand. He who … the town Zimmala is standing …, and he who is up in …, they call? that ... place *ḫalunan* ….
(Tablet breaks off here.)	

88. StBoT 45: 671–72
To the King from Uḫḫa-muwa (an excerpt)

Find spot: Ortaköy; debris from upper storey of Building A. **Edition**: Süel 2001, 671–72 (without identifying field or museum number!). **Discussion**: de Martino 2005b, 309; Forlanini 2007, 285.

According to Forlanini, the author of this letter, Uḫḫa-muwa, was part of the Hittite intelligence-gathering team (German *Nachrichtendienst*) in the west, keeping tabs on the movements of military units and key political figures. He writes from the city governed by “the Priest” (line 7).

Süel has given us only an excerpt of the letter. She reports that the letter continues with sentences containing the first-person plural verbs *zammuraweni* “we harm,” *paiwani* “we go,” *daiwani* “we place,” and *daweni* “we take.” I am informed by O. Soysal, who saw the tablet, that the surface is almost completely gone in these succeeding lines.

Since the continuation of this letter is apparently unreadable, there is much about its interpretation that must remain unclear. It might be possible that LÚ “man” in the expression LÚ URU*Ma-ra-a-ša* “the man of Maraša” has the specialized meaning that it often has in the Old Babylonian Mari tablets and in the Amarna letters (see CAD A/II, 57 sub *amīlu* 4d), namely “the *(petty) ruler* of Maraša.” This usage is well-attested in OH historical texts (e.g., KBo 3.22 65, 74, 77; KBo 3.27 obv. 28–30) and perhaps also in MH ones such as *nu* m*Attaršiyaš* LÚ URU*Piggaya=ya ANA* dUTU-

ŠI $^{LÚ.MEŠ}$*kurēwaneš kuit* "because Attaršiya and the 'man' of Piggaya are *kurēwaneš*-vassals to His Majesty" KUB 14.1 rev. 89. This usage is particularly likely when no personal name precedes it, as in the just cited example (and see text 18). But this "man of GN" style is also used when referring to hostages (see text 19). And, of course, it just might be that the king only needed to know that this person came from Maraša and not his name.

Uḫḫa-muwa writes concerning matters of grave concern to the Hittite king that have transpired in the city Ḫappuriya. The city name Ḫappuriya occurs in a fragment containing an itinerary of western lands, including Ašuwa, Awina, Lawanta, Maša, Partuwata, and Tumanta (del Monte and Tischler 1978: 82). Earlier, Forlanini 1977, 215–18 suggested a location near İznik. Later (2007) he tentatively proposed that Ḫappuriya was a capital city in the Arzawa region. Süel also reports that in the unpublished Ortaköy letters the following place names occur: Ḫappuriya, Šallapa, Maša, Kuršamma, Attarimma, Kuwaliya, Lalanda, Zaruna, Kummaḫa, and other sites known to be located in southwest Anatolia in Hittite times. Uḫḫa-muwa reminds the king that he has written before about a coalition forming (such is the meaning of the verbal construct *kattan tiya-* in line 5[201]) in Ḫappuriya, involving Kupanda-Kuruntiya and Tarḫunda-radu (also called Tarḫunna-radu in line 9). Now (*kinuna*) a further development has occurred. It appears that a fugitive has arrived from Ḫappuriya and brought further news. It concerns six additional persons, added to the huge alliance forming against the Hittites. These persons are known to us from other published texts. Several of the persons mentioned in this letter—Tarḫun(t)a-radu, Kupanta-Kuruntiya and Uḫḫa-muwa—were contemporaries of Tudḫaliya III (ca. 1360–1344 B.C.E.), the father and predecessor of Šuppiluliuma I. Tarḫunta-radu was the recipient of Letter 95 (*VBoT* 1 = EA 31), sent from the Egyptian pharaoh Amunḥotep III. The Piyama-radu mentioned here has the same name as the famous trouble-maker in the Arzawa lands almost a century later, during the reign of Ḫattušili III (ca. 1267–1237 B.C.E.). For his activities see text 101 (the "Tawagalawa Letter").

(1) *A-NA* ^{d}UTU-*ŠI* <<ku-it>>[202] *BE-LÍ-YA QÍ-BÍ-MA* (2) *UM-MA* ^{m}Uḫ-ḫa-mu-u-wa ARAD-*KA-MA*	(1–2) Say to His Majesty, my lord: Thus speaks Uḫḫa-mūwa, your servant:
(3) *A-NA* ^{d}UTU-*ŠI* ku-it *BE-LÍ-YA ŠA* ^{m}Ku-pa-an-da-^{d}LAMMA-ya (4) *Ù ŠA* ^{m}Tar-ḫu-un-da-ra-du *ŠA* ^{URU}Ḫa-ap-pu-ri-ya (5) kat-ta-an ti-ya-an-na-aš ut-tar ḫa-at-ra-a-nu-un	(3–5) (You may recall) what I earlier wrote to Your Majesty about the joining in alliance of Kupanta-Kuruntiya and Tarḫunta-radu of the town Ḫappuriya.

(6) ki-nu-na-kán ka-a-ša ^{LÚ}pít-ti-ya-an-za LÚ ^{URU}Ma-ra-a-ša (7) [*A-N*]*A* ^{LÚ}ŠANGA ^{URU}Ḫa-ap-pu-ri-ya-az pít-ti-ya-an-ti-li ú-it (8) [nu]-mu ki-iš-ša-an *IQ-BI* ^{m}Ku-pa-an-da-^{d}LAMMA-ya-aš-wa (9) [^{m}Tar]-ḫu-un-na-ra-du-uš DUMU.MEŠ ^{m}Ku-pa-an-da-^{d}LAMMA-ya (10) [^{m}M]a-aš-du-ri-iš ^{m}Pí-ya-ma-a-ra-du-uš ^{m}Ku-pa-an-da-za-al-ma (11) [*ŠA*] ^{URU}Ḫa-ap-pu-ri-ya ḫu-u-ma-an-te-eš an-da a-ra-an-zi (12) [nu]-wa-aš-ma-aš ^{m}Uḫ-ḫa-wa-ra-nu-uš ^{m}Ḫu-u-li-ya-za-al-ma-nu-uš (13) [^{m}]x-li-ša-ni LÚ ^{URU}Pí-da-aš-ša kat-ta-an	(6–13) Well, now a man from the town Maraša has just come as a fugitive from Ḫappuriya to (take refuge with) "the Priest." And he said to me: Kupanta-Kuruntiya, Tarḫunna-radu, and the sons of Kupanta-Kuruntiya (namely) Mašturi, Piyama-radu (and) Kupanta-zalma, of Ḫappuriya, have all come together, and Uḫḫa-waranu, Ḫūliya-zalmanu (and) x-lišani the "man" of Pitašša have sided with them.

89. Or. 90/800
To the King from the Queen

Text: Or. 90/800. **Find spot:** Ortaköy; debris from upper storey of Building A. **Edition:** Süel 2002b, 819–26. **Translation:** Süel 2002a, 158. **Discussion:** de Martino 2005b, 309–10; Marizza 2007a, 170, 172.

This letter was published by Süel (2002a, 158) only in partial translation (lines 1–16) and with an accompanying photo, which is difficult to read and seen at an angle that obscures the top and side edges. But a full treatment (photos, transliteration, Turkish translation and commentary) was provided in Süel 2002b, 819–26.

The opening courtesy well-wishing includes a statement that "everything is well with me" (line 9) in spite of the immediately following words that indicate that the queen is in great physical discomfort! See §1.2.17. Her condition is a long-standing one, since she adds "I am still the same (as before)," which shows too that she has previously kept the king apprised of her ailment.

(1) *A-NA* ^{d}UTU-*ŠI BE-LÍ-YA* (2) *QÍ-*	(1–9) Say to His Majesty, my lord:

BÍ-MA UM-MA MUNUS.LUGAL GÉME-[*KA*] (3) *MA-ḪAR* ^{d}UTU-*ŠI BE-LÍ-YA* (4) ḫu-u-ma-an SIG$_5$-in e-eš-tu (5) nu ^{d}UTU-*ŠI BE-LÍ-YA* DINGIR.MEŠ (6) TI-an ḫar-kán-du (7) nu ^{d}UTU-*ŠI BE-LÍ-YA* (8) pa-aḫ-ša-an-da-ru (9) kat-ti-mi-ya SIG$_5$-in	Thus speaks the Queen, your maidservant: May all be well in the presence of Your Majesty, my lord! May the gods keep Your Majesty, my lord, alive and protect Your Majesty! Everything is well with me.
(10) SAG.DU-*YA*-mu ma-aḫ-ḫa-an (11) iš-ki-ša-ya iš-tar-ak-zi (12) na-at-mu nu-u-a *QA-TAM-MA*	(10–12) I am still the same: my head and back hurt me.
(13) *MA-ḪAR* ^{d}UTU-*ŠI*-ya *BE-LÍ-YA* (14) ku-it ma-aḫ-ḫa-an (15) nu-mu ^{d}UTU-*ŠI BE-LÍ-YA* (16) [aš-š]u-ul ḫa-at-ra-a-i	(13–16) Please write to me how it is also with Your Majesty, my lord. And, Your Majesty, my lord, send (me your) greetings!
About 8 lines uninscribed at the top of the reverse, followed after a dividing line by a piggyback letter to the King from Zūwā	

89b. Or 90/800
Piggyback Letter to the King from Zuwa

In the address formula, Zuwa refers to the king not as "His Majesty" (^{d}UTU-*ŠI*, literally "my Sun God"), but as "the lord, my lord" and in the body of the letter addresses the king simply as "my lord" (rev. 5). Since in the main letter the queen did not wish to give news beyond her own condition, Zuwa supplements by telling the king that all is well with two other persons Zuwa knows would have his interest.

(rev. 1) *A-NA BE-LÍ BE-LÍ-YA* (rev. 2) *QÍ-BÍ-MA UM-MA* ^{m}Zu-u-wa-a (rev. 3) ARAD-*KA-MA MA-ḪAR BE-LÍ-YA* (rev. 4) ḫu-u-ma-an SIG$_5$-in e-eš-tu (rev. 5) nu *BE-LÍ-YA* DINGIR.MEŠ pa-aḫ-ša[-an-d]a-ru	(rev. 1–5) Say to the lord, my lord! Thus speaks Zuwa, your servant: May all be well with my lord, and may the gods keep my lord!
(rev. 6) ka-a-ša *A-NA MA-ḪAR* […] *Ù* (rev. 7) *MA-ḪAR* DUMU.NITA ^{m}Pal-l[a-] (rev. 8) ḫu-u-ma-an SIG$_5$	(rev. 6–8) All is well here with … and with the son of Palla-…

90. HHCTO 1
From […] to […]

Text: Çorum 21-9-90. Find spot: Ortaköy, specific location of origin unknown. **Copy:** HHCTO 1. Edition: Ünal 1998, 17–31. **Discussion:** del Monte 1992, 26–27 and 62 (textual evidence for Ḫanziwa and suggestion by Forlanini that it was at Karamağara); Beal 2002b, 114 (discussion of military strategy in a campaign near Šapinuwa and Ḫanziwa); de Martino 2004, 353; 2005b, 310.

(1′) […] KASKAL.ḪI.A […] (2′) […] KASKAL.ḪI.A x[…] (3′) [k]a-a-ša LÚ.MEŠ x[…] (4′) ak-kán-du-uš ḫal-z[i-…] (5′) x-ša?-an-te-eš li-in-k[i?- …]	(1′–5′) … the roads … the roads … the men of … summon (the spirits of) the dead … … oaths …
(6′) ka-a-ša *ŠA* KIN-ya ku-it me-ḫur ka-ru-ú x […]x nu *ŠA* KIN x[…] (7′) [x ku?-w]a?-at *Ú-UL* pí-i-e-ši ma-a-na-aš ḫu-u-da-a-ak ú-iz-zi ma-a-na-an-ša-an ḫ[u?-…] (8′) [x x]x-nu-ši ú-iz-zi *ŠA* KIN me-ḫur pa-ra-a ku-it ta-meš?-ḫa-zi KIN-ma x[… …] (9′) [x x x le-e?] a-ni-ya-ši nu *ŠA* KIN *A-NA* ÉRIN.MEŠ GU$_4$.ḪI.A-ya me-na-aḫ-ḫa-an-da *ŠU-PUR* (10′) [na-aš] ḫu-u-da-a-ak ú-id-du na-an-ša-an KIN-ti ti-it-ta-nu-ud[-du]	(6′–10′) Concerning the fact that the time for the work/task has now already come? … why do you not send a work crew …? Whether it comes quickly, or the …-s it, you should not? …, because he? will perhaps proceed to *postpone* the work time? But (at?) work (time) … you must not do … But send for work crews and oxen! And let him come quickly and put them to the task.
(11′) [ka-a-ša-y]a ku-it mar-ša-aš-tar-ra-aš ut-tar ki-ša-at nu LÚ ^{d}IŠKUR ku-it MUNUS ŠU.GI-ya (12′) [ap?-pa?-an] ḫar-kán-zi nu an-ni-iš-kán-zi nu *I-NA* ^{URU}Ḫa-an-zi-wa le-e an-ni-iš-kán-zi (13′) [*I*?-*NA*? Í]D? ^{URU}Ḫa-an-zi-wa-ya-za-kán an-da le-e wa-ar-pí-iš-kán-zi (14′) [*I-NA* ^{URU}x-x-š]a?-ma-a-ša-aš-ša-an še-er an-ni-iš-kán-du nam-ma-za-kán a-pí-ya-pát (15′) [x	(11′–17′) Concerning the fact that an act of sacrilege has now occurred, and they have apprehended? (as guilty parties) a Man-of-the-Storm-God[203] and an Old Woman.[204] They will begin to perform (a purification ritual). But let them not begin to perform (the ritual) in the town Ḫanziwa. Let them not bathe in the river of the town Ḫanziwa. Let them rather perform (the ritual) up

wa-]ar-ap-pí-iš-kán-du *I-NA* URUḪa-an-zi-wa-ma le-e an-ni-iš-kán-zi (16′) [n]u? *I-NA* ÍD URUḪa-[a]n-zi-wa-ya-za-kán an-da le-e wa-ar-ap-pí-iš-kán-zi (17′) ú-wa-ad du-wa-ad-du	in X-šamāša,[205] and let them bathe only (*-pat*) there. Let them not perform (the ritual) in Ḫanziwa. And let them not bathe in the river of Ḫanziwa. Get to it!

Commentary

The “roads” (KASKAL.ḪI.A) mentioned in the fragmentarily preserved opening paragraph could be “paths” created as part of a ritual to draw away (*ḫuittiya-*) impurity or to attract positively-inclined deities (perhaps the spirits of benevolent deceased mentioned in line 4).

Judging from the apparent concern for work crews (*ŠA* KIN ÉRIN.MEŠ) and oxen, the second paragraph (6′–10′) seems unrelated to what precedes (rituals to summon the dead in 1′–5′) or follows it (a reported act of sacrilege in 11′–17′).

The third paragraph (11′–17′) concerns the reported act of sacrilege. See CHD L–N, 198–99 for examples of what actions constituted *maršaštarri-* “sacrilege, profanement, desecration.” Because the two apprehended persons are of opposite sex, Ünal and de Martino may be right in assuming that their sacrilege involved a sexual offence. To counter the objection that an old woman in menopause would not likely be having sex, de Martino argues that as a cult title in Hittite the term “Old Woman” (MUNUS ŠU.GI) only requires that the person be post-adolescent, i.e., mature. Although evidence for sexual activity by the MUNUS ŠU.GI does not exist in Hittite texts, the Code of Hammurabi §145 indicates that a man whose first wife was a *nadītum* (whose status required that she not bear children) was allowed to take a *šugītum* (MUNUS ŠU.GI “old woman”) as a second wife for the purpose of having children (see CAD Š/III, sub *šugītum*). And even women in menopause can and do have sex, because they do not need to fear a life-threatening pregnancy at their age!

But we should be cautious in assuming that the *only* action qualifying as sacrilege committed by two persons of opposite sex *must* be sexual. They may have contrived to steal one or more valuable sacred objects. Furthermore, bathing is not uncommon as an accompaniment of purification rituals and *need* not refer to the normal requirment that cult personnel, when returning from their homes where they have had sex, bathe before resuming their duties in the temple. So while it is possible (perhaps even *likely*) that their act involved sexual intercourse, it is by no means certain.

What is truly intriguing here is the instruction that the purifying bath not take place in Ḫanziwa, but in another locale. Ünal and de Martino both point out that evidence in KUB 22.51 and KBo 23.27 indicates that Ḫanziwa was probably fairly close to Šapinuwa, where the king's temporary residential center was located. If the river passing by Ḫanziwa continued downstream to Šapinuwa, it is possible that secondary pollution from the materials used to purify in the river was feared. In the laws (§44b, see Hoffner 1997g, 52–53, 189–90) severe penalties are imposed on anyone who discards remnants (*kuptar*) from a purification ritual on another person's property, where they may affect him adversely. The case becomes one of sorcery (*alwanzatar*), must be judged in the king's court, and could result in the death penalty.

90b. HHCTO 1
Piggyback Letter to Purra from Arma-ziti

The second letter (lines 18′ and following) is written by Arma-ziti, perhaps the scribe who took down the main letter from dication. It is addressed to a second party, an older "brother" Purra. All that remains of this letter is the greeting and polite well-wishes. A contemporary Arma-ziti functioned at Tapikka-Maşat, and is mentioned in HKM 84 (text 83) and ABoT 65 (text 81). Could this letter have been sent to Šapinuwa from Tapikka, instead of from Ḫattuša?

(18′) *A-NA* ^{m}Pur-ra ŠEŠ *MAḪ-RI* DÙG.GA-*YA* *QÍ-BÍ-MA* *UM-MA* $^{m.d}$*SÎN*-LÚ ŠEŠ-*KA-MA* (19′) [kat-t]i-ti ḫu-u-ma-an SIG$_5$-in e[-eš-d]u nu-ut-ta DINGIR$^{!}$.MEŠ$^{!}$ TI-an ḫar-kán-du (20′) [nu-u]t[-t]a ŠU$^{!}$.ḪI$^{!}$ <.A> a-ra-aḫ-za-[an-da] a-aš-šu-li ḫar-kán-du nu-ut-ta pa-aḫ-ša-an-da-ru (21′) […] ka-a-[ša] kat-ti-mi ḫu-u-ma-a[n SIG$_5$-in]	(18′–21′) Say to Purra, my dear older brother: Thus speaks Arma-ziti, your brother. May all be well with you, and may the gods keep you alive and hold their hands lovingly around you and protect you! With me all is well now.
(22′) [nu-za-kán] *I*$^{?}$*-NA* ku-e-da-aš É.MEŠ a[r$^{?}$-x-x-x] (*Break*)	(22′) … in what houses …

91. HHCTO 3
From the King to [...]

Text: Çorum 21-6-90. **Find spot:** Ortaköy, specific original location unknown. **Copy:** Ünal 1998, 101. **Edition**: Ünal 1998, 38–40.

(1) *UM-MA* ᵈUTU-*ŠI-MA A-NA* [...]	(1) Thus speaks His Majesty: Say to PN:
(2) ka-a-aš-ma-kán u-zi-ya[...] (3) na-at ki-nu-un ar-nu-an[-du? na-at? ...] (4) ḫa-an-da-a-an-du ú-ug[-ga ...] (5) *A-NA* U_4-*MI* 2 g[i?-pé-eš-šar? ...] (6) nu *I-NA* ᵁᴿᵁŠu-ú?[-...] (7) ᵐx-[x]-x-an-za[...] (8) im[-...]	(2–8) I have just .... Now let them relocate/transfer it/them, and let them determine/prepare them .... And I will .... For the day two ... And in the town Šu-...
(Tablet breaks off here.)	

2.2.4. MH Letters found at Šariššа-Kuşakli (92–93)

92. KuT 50
To the King from Ḫalpa-ziti

Text: Ku 97/25. **Find spot:** Building C. **Copy**: KuT 50. **Edition**: Wilhelm 1998, 181–87 (with photos). **Discussion**: van den Hout 2001a, 430–31; Beal 2002a, 66 (nn. 74 and 76) (on KASKAL-*ši* EGIR-*an* in line 21, and *maštayati* in 13, 15, 19, and 22); Hoffner 2002a, 168 (lines 48–55); Imparati 2003, 860 n. 44 (on the "daughter" mentioned in line 4); de Martino 2005b, 312–13 (see also above on HKM 49 [text 52]); Soysal 2006, 562–63 (on the *marašši*-bird in line 13); Marizza 2007a, VII n. 5, 69–70, 75, 119, 126 (both concerning Ḫattušili in line 10); and the tables on pages 133, 137, 140, 166–67; Mouton 2007, 553 (on lines 5–9).

The queen has written to Ḫalpa-ziti, from wherever he wrote this, reporting a disturbing dream that she had experienced, in which her daughters had suffered a beating. Mouton (2007) believes it was the queen's own dream. In line 7 the scribe has apparently omitted the plural marker, since it is several princesses that are the concern in lines 3 and 41. Mouton (2007) correctly translates the apparent singular form DUMU.MUNUS in line 7 as "les filles." The queen asked Ḫalpa-ziti to use oracles to determine from the gods whether this dream actually portended harm for the princesses. Ḫalpa-ziti did as he was told. In lines 12–23 he reports to the king the oracularly significant movements that he and his collegues observed in "birds of agitation," a special type of birds used by the augurs. This was Ḫalpa-ziti's "first" method of oracular checking. As a second, countercheck, he observed something called "the road/path" (KASKAL = *palša-*).

(1) *A-NA BE-LÍ BE-LÍ-YA QÍ-BÍ-MA* (2) *UM-MA* ᵐḪal-pa-LÚ ARAD-*KA-MA* (3) *MA-ḪAR* DUMU.MUNUS.MEŠ SIG$_5$-in *Ù A-NA MA-ḪAR BE-LÍ-Y*[*A*] (4) SIG$_5$-in e-eš-tu an-za-aš-ša kat-ta ḫu-u-ma-an S[IG$_5$-i]n	(1–4) Say to the lord, my lord: Thus speaks Ḫalpa-ziti, your servant: May it be well with the daughters (princesses?) and with my lord. All is well with us too.
(5) ᵐḪa-an-da-pí-iš-mu DUMU É.GAL me-mi-ya-an (6) ki-iš-ša-an ú-da-aš MUNUS.LUGAL-wa-mu ḫa-at-ra-a-it (7) *A-NA* DUMU. MUNUS<.MEŠ?>-wa za-aš-ḫé-et an-da wa-al-ḫa-an-ni-iš-<kat->ta-at (8) nu-wa-az a-pí-ya ku-it zi-ik nu-wa *IŠ-TU* DINGIR-*LIM* (9) zi-ki-la ar-ḫa a-ri-ya	(5–9) The palace official Ḫandapi brought me word, as follows: "The Queen wrote me. In a dream beatings were being administered to the princess<es> (literally, 'the daughter<s>'). Since you are there, you yourself should investigate (the matter) through oracles."
(10) nu ᵐḪa-ad-du-ši-li-iš DUMU É.GAL am-mu-ug-ga (11) *IŠ-TU* DINGIR-*LIM* ar-ḫa a-ri-ya-u-en nu la-aḫ-la-ḫi-ma-aš (12) ke-e MUŠEN. ḪI.A ti-e-er ḫa-an-te-ez-zi-ya-aš-kán (13) ma-ra-aš-ši-iš.MUŠEN EGIR-an kat-ta ma-aš-ta-ya-ti (14) nu Á.MUŠEN gun.-iš nu-kán a-al-li-ya-aš (15) EGIR-an kat-ta ma-aš-ta-ya-ti nu-za a-ra-aš-ša-an (16) kat-ta-an gun.-an *IK-ŠU-UD* na-at zi-la-wa-an aš-šu-wa-az	(10–16) So the palace official Ḫattušili and I investigated (the matter) through oracles. These "birds of agitation" appeared. ... *(What follows in this and the next two paragraphs is a description by the writer of what birds were seen, and their movements, together with comments as to the oracular significance of each.)*
(17) nu-kán Á.MUŠEN pé-ra-an tu-u-wa aš-šu-wa-az pa-it (18) na-	(17–20) ...

an-za *Ú-UL* ḫa-a-u-en nu da--ma-in Á.MUŠEN (19) gun.-an a-ú-mi-en na-aš-kán pé-ra-an ma-aš-ta-ya-ti (20) nam-ma-az EGIR-pa da-a-aš na-aš-kán pé-ra-an aš-šu-wa-az	
(21) KASKAL-ši EGIR-an nu-kán Á.MUŠEN EGIR-an kat-ta (22) ma-aš-ta-ya-ti nu šu-u-ra-šu-re-eš gun.-eš (23) nu ke-e MUŠEN.ḪI.A la-aḫ-la-ḫi-ma-aš	(21–22) … (23) And these (were) the "birds of agitation."
(24) *A-NA* KASKAL-*NI*-ya ku-it te-e-re-er KASKAL-an-wa-az (25) *IŠ-TU* DINGIR-*LIM* pé-ra-an a-uš-te-en (26) nu-kán ma-a-aḫ-ḫa-an ku-u-un LÚ *ṬE*$_4$-*MI* (27) [pa-r]a-a na-i-ú-en lu-uk-ki-it-ta-ma (28) [KASKAL-a]n *IŠ-TU* DIN≈GIR-*LIM* ú-mi-ni (29) [… m]a-a-aḫ-ḫa-an ki-ša-ri nu *A-NA* É.GAL (30) […] ḫa-at-ra-a-u-e-ni	(24–30) And concerning what they said regarding 'the road': "Observe 'the road' beforehand by means of the deity (i.e., the oracle)!" Tomorrow, after we have dispatched this messenger, we will observe 'the road' by means of the deity, and we will write to the palace … as soon as that happens.
(31) [a]n-da-ma-⌜mu?⌝ [ᵐUp-n]a-al-li-in (32) [k]u-it k[i-iš-š]a-an ḫa-at-ra-a-eš (33) KASKAL-an-wa-az *IŠ-TU* DINGIR-*LIM* pé-ra-an (34) a-uš-te-en nu ma-a-aḫ-ḫa-an ᵐUp-na-al-li-iš (35) *IŠ-TU MA-ḪAR BE-LÍ* u-un-ni-iš (36) lu-uk-ki-it-ta-ma ᵐAl-la-wa-an-ni-iš (37) KAS≈KAL-an a-uš-ta-pát	(31–37) Furthermore, concerning what you wrote me by the hand of? Upnalli: "Observe (pl.) beforehand? 'the road' by means of the deity!" After Upnalli drove here from the presence of the lord, on the following day Allawanni indeed observed 'the road.'
(38) nu ḫa-an-te-ez-zi-ya-aš ḫal-li-aš gun.-iš (39) nu-za-kán UD.1.KAM iš-tar-na tar-nu-mi-ni (40) lu-uk-kat-ta-ma ú-me-e-ni	(38–40) First, a *ḫalliya*-bird was *gun.-iš*; for one day we are leaving off (observing), but tomorrow we will observe.
(41) *A-NA* DUMU.MUNUS.MEŠ-ya la-aḫ-ra-aš (42) MUŠEN.ḪI.A a-ú-me-en nu la-aḫ-ra-aš (43) MU≈ŠEN.ḪI.A ar-ḫa pé-e[š-š]i-er	(41–43) We observed birds of *laḫra-* on behalf of the princesses. The birds of *laḫra-* 'discarded.'

(44) an-da-ma-mu *A-NA* GA[L] KÙ.SIG$_{17}$ (45) ku-it ḫa-at-ra-a-eš na-an ka-an-ka-aḫ-ḫu-un (46) nu 30 GÍN.GÍN.NU KI.LÁ-*ŠU* (47) na-an *A-NA* ^{m}Wa-al-wa-al-li *AD-DIN*	(44–47) Furthermore, concerning the gold cup you wrote me about: I weighed it—it weighs thirty shekels—and I gave it to Walwalli.
(48 nu KÙ.SIG$_{17}$ a-šu-ši-eš ḫi-in-ku-wa-aš (49) *MA-ḪAR BE-LÍ-YA* ku-it e-eš-zi (50) na-at EGIR-pa up-pí na-at ša-ni-ya (51) pé-e-ta za-nu-uz-zi nam-ma-an-ši (52) ku-in a-ni-ya-ta-an *BE-LU* EGIR-an (53) da-it-ti nu-mu ḫa-at-ra-a-i (54) na-at ú-wa-mi *A-NA* ^{m}Wa-al-wa-al-li (55) EGIR-an te-eḫ-ḫi	(48–55) Send back whatever gold presentation *ašuša*-vessels are with my lord! He will refine it to the same quality. Then write to me the job that you, my lord, have assigned to him, and I will certainly assign it to Walwalli.

Commentary

7 The imperfective verb form *wa-al-ḫa-an-ni-iš-<kat->ta-at* (with a double imperfective stem *-anniške-*) certainly refers to several beatings.

93. KuT 49
To the GAL DUMU.MEŠ É.GAL from the *ḪAZANNU*

Text: KuT 49. **Find spot:** Kuşaklı C: Building C, Room 8. **Edition**: Wilhelm 1998, 175–80 (with Photo). **Discussion**: van den Hout 2001a, 430; Imparati 2003, 237; Marizza 2007a, 62.

The sender of the letter, the mayor (^{LÚ}*ḪAZANNU*), speaking on behalf of a group of augurs, writes to his superior, the Chief of the Palace Officials. None of the individuals uses his name. A certain Old Woman, one of whose competences was the consulting and interpreting of the KIN-oracle, had requested that the augurs run a countercheck on the result she had obtained through the KIN-oracle to an important question: What were the prospects for recovery from grave illness by the "son of the priestess"? The Old Woman performed the KIN-oracle consultation four times, and all four turned out unfavorable. The fact that it was done four times indicates how important this issue was and how careful the Old Woman was to ensure a correct interpretation of the oracle. At this point, rather than performing a fifth consultation, she asked that her augur colleagues pose the same question(s) to a bird oracle. They do so, using as a safety check two opposite queries: the first in the positive ("Do we have something to fear?") and the second in the negative ("Do we have nothing to fear?"). The first is answered in the affirmative (*ḫandan=at*, line 14), and the second with silence, implying a reply "On the contrary: we *do* have something to fear."

The augurs are not content to simply give their interpretation. They also give a description of the movements of the birds on which they based their interpretation. This would make it possible for specialists at the other end to verify their interpretation. The three birds observed in the first consultation (15–20) are the *šurašura-*, the *ḫalliya-*, and the *ḫaštapi-*. In the second (25–32) they are the *šurašura-*, the falcon (SUR$_{14}$.DÙ.A), the eagle (*ḫara-*), and the *ālliya-*.

This is the interpretation given by van den Hout (2001a), with which I concur. Wilhelm had previously assumed that *ḫandan–at* (line 14) conveyed no specific answer, and therefore that neither of the two questions was actually interpreted by the letter senders, but that it was left to the recipient and his experts to interpret the details of the described behavior of the birds.

(1) [*A-NA*] *BE-LÍ* GAL DUMU.MEŠ É.GAL *BE-LÍ-YA QÍ-BÍ-MA* (2) [*UM-M*]*A* LÚ*ḪA-ZA-NU-MA*	(1) Say to the lord, the Chief of the Palace Officials, my lord: (2) Thus speaks the mayor:
(3) [fI-]ya-aš-mu MUNUS ŠU.GI ki-iš-ša!-an me-e-mi-iš-ta (4) *A-NA* SAG.DU DUMU MUNUSSANGA-wa u-ur-ki-e-eš (5) i-da-a-la-u-eš-ke-et-ta nu-wa ke-e u-ur-ki-e-eš (6) ki-i-ša-an-da-ti	(3) Iya, the Old Woman, spoke the following to me: (4) "The (oracular) trace turned out bad for the person of the son of the priestess, (5–6) and these traces occurred.
(7) i-da-a-lu-wa da-a-an nu-wa-ra-at-kán «aš» EGIR-pa (8) dḪal-ma-aš-šu-it-ti nu-wa ut-tar ar-ḫa 4-*ŠU* (9) a-ri-ya-nu-un nu-wa-ra-at 4-*ŠU*-pát i-da-a-lu-e-eš-ta (10) nu a-pí-ya-ya ar-ḫa a-ri-ya-an-du	(7) "The (token named) 'bad' was 'taken', and (moved) back to (the location) 'Ḫalmaššuit'. (8) I performed the oracular consultation four times, (9) and all four times it turned out bad. (10) So let them perform a consultation there as well."
(11) nu ú-wa-u-e-en *IŠ-TU* MUŠEN.ḪI.A nam-ma ar-ḫa (12) ki-iš-ša-an a-ri-ya-u-en ki-i-wa fI-ya-aš	(11) So we proceeded[206] to seek an answer to the following question further by (observing) birds: .

(13) ku-it ki-iš-ša-an me-e-mi-iš-ta (14) *A-NA* SAG<.DU> DUMU MUNUS SANGA-wa na-a-ḫu-wa-ni ḫa-an-da-a-na-at	(12–13) "Concerning this which Iya has said: (14) 'Should we fear for the person of the son of the priestess?'"—(14) it is confirmed (i.e., yes, we should fear).
(15) nu šu-u-ra-šu-u-ra-aš^{MUŠEN} gun. ḫal-li-aš gun. (16) nu-kán nam-ma ḫal-li-aš EGIR-an kat-ta (17) ku-uš-ta-ya-ti nu-kán ḫa-aš-ta-pí-iš^{MUŠEN} pé-ra-an (18) ku-uš-ta-ya-ti na-aš-kán EGIR-an kat-ta (19) ku-uš-ta-ya-ti KASKAL-ši EGIR-an ar-ḫa na-aš-ta (20) ḫa-aš-ta-pí-iš^{MUŠEN} EGIR-an kat-ta ku-uš$^{!}$-da-ya-ti (21) nu ḫal-li-aš gun.-iš	*(Here is the record of the movements of the birds, which lead to the interpretation given in line 14 "it is confirmed.")*
(22) nu ú-wa-u-en *A-NA* TI DUMU MUNUS SANGA nam-ma (23) a-ú-mi-en *A-NA* SAG DUMU MUNUS SANGA-wa *Ú-UL* (24) ku-wa-at-ka na-a-ḫu-wa-ni	(22) Then we proceeded to make a further observation (of the birds) with reference to the life (i.e., survival) of the son of the priestess: (23–24) "Should we perhaps have nothing to fear for the person of the son of the priestess?"
(25) nu ḫal-li-aš GUN-iš šu-u-ra-šu-u-ra-aš ḫal-zi-an-za (26) gun. nu-kán SUR$_{14}$.DÙ.A a-ra-ma-an-ti-iš (27) pé-ra-an aš-šu-wa-az nu ḫal-li-aš gun.-iš (28) nu-kán ḫa-ra-aš^{MUŠEN} pé-ra-an aš-šu-wa-az (29) nu-kán a-al-li-ya-aš EGIR-an kat-ta ku-uš-ta-ya-ti	*(Here is the description of the movements of the birds.)*
(30) KASKAL-ši EGIR-an ar-ḫa šu-u-ra-šu-u-ra-aš^{MUŠEN} (31) [g]un.-iš nu-kán ḫa-aš-ta-pí-iš pé-ra-an (32) [a]š-šu-w[a]-az nu ḫal-li-aš gun.-iš	*(Since there is no further answer "It is confirmed" (i.e., we should have no fear), this counter-query is answered by an implied: "On the contrary")*

2.2.5. MH Letters Found at El-Amarna in Egypt (94–97)

Among the many letters found at El-Amarna in Egypt in 1887, which formed the diplomatic correspondence of pharaohs Amunḫotep III and IV with other Middle Eastern kings, two tablets stood out from the rest, most of which were written in what was then the *lingua franca* of international corrspondence, the Akkadian language (see Imparati in Klengel 1999, 379 with n. 210). The cuneiform script of these two tablets was not unusual and could be easily read. But the language itself was unknown. Since the proper names in the tablets could be read, it was clear that the two represented correspondence between the pharaoh and a kingdom named Arzawa. We now know that this kingdom was located in western Asia Minor, but at the time its location was unknown. The importance of these two brief letters far outweighed their small size and relatively routine contents, for as early as 1902, J. A. Knudtzon, the Assyriologist who produced the standard edition of the El-Amarna tablets, provoked the world of scholarship with the publication of an article with the astounding news that he had identified the language of these tablets as the oldest Indo-European language yet known, and apparently spoken by an important kingdom in the ancient Near East (Knudtzon 1902)![207] We know today that the language of these tablets is Hittite, and that the spoken language of the kingdom of Arzawa was not the language used in these tablets, but a closely related language today called Luwian. The location of the kingdom of the Hittites was not discovered until a few years later, when archeological excavations were undertaken in central Turkey near the village of Boğazköy. Knudtzon's bold claim, which was based upon what we now know were correct interpretations of the basic features of the grammar of the texts, was vehemently rejected by the scholarly establishment of his day, in part because of prejudices and preconceptions that excluded out of hand that speakers of the "holy" Indo-European languages could have lived in the "primitive" world of the ancient Near East (there was more than a hint of anti-Semitism involved), and in part on the justifiable ground that these two small tablets simply did not provide the quantity of evidence necessary to sustain this bold thesis. That quantity of evidence was soon to appear with the recovery of thousands of tablets in this language from the newly excavated ancient city of Ḫattuša and with a more definitive "decipherment" in 1915 by the Assyriologist B. Hrozný, which was widely accepted and confirmed Knudtzon's thesis. But by that time it was clear that the language of the "Arzawa Tablets" was not "Arzawan," but "Hittite," the official language of a great empire.

As for the two "Arzawa Letters," their initial contribution having been made, they have receded in importance, their modest content overshadowed by the huge output of culturally and historically more significant Hittite materials from Ḫattuša. Their importance today lies in what they can tell us about the kingdom of Arzawa itself and its dealings with the Egyptian pharaohs. Since today we know that Arzawa lay in the far western part of Asia Minor, it is significant that scribes of the governments there could correspond with powers to the east of them using the cuneiform script, just as we now know that Mycenean (i.e., Aḫḫiyawan) kings could correspond with the Hittite kings using the same cuneiform script (see text 99).

With the improved knowledge of the Hittite language and writing system available today, we can see that, on the one hand, the letter sent to Egypt from Arzawa reflects the authentic script tradition of the Hittite capital. On the other hand, we can detect from the unusual grammar and style of the letter sent to Arzawa from Egypt that the native language of its scribe was not Hittite. Nevertheless, it is impressive that the pharaoh's scribes included at least one who was able to write in Hittite, especially since a roughly contemporary letter sent to the pharaoh from the Hittite capital (EA 41 = text 96) was composed in Akkadian.

94. *VBoT* 2 = EA 32
From the King of Arzawa to the Pharaoh Amunḫotep III

Text: VAT 342. **Find spot:** El-Amarna, Egypt. **Copies**: EA 32; *VBoT* 2. **Edition**: Rost 1956, 328–34; **Translation**: Haas in Moran 1992, 103; Liverani 1998, 406–9; Klinger 2006, 193–94; **Discussion:** Hrozný 1931, 107; Otten 1956, 185; Heinhold-Krahmer 1977, 50–55; Hagenbuchner 1989b, 363–64 (no. 255); Hagenbuchner 1989a, 34; Kühne 1993; Haas 1994, 380 n. 517; Mora 1995, 280; de Martino 1996, 81–82; Starke 1997, 470 n. 31 (continuation of multi-tablet letter); Hawkins 1998b, 10 n. 32; Klengel 1999, 128 [A3], 131; Goren, Finkelstein, and Na'aman 2004, 45–47 (chemical analysis of the clay of the tablet in order to determine possible provenience); de Roos 2005; Klinger 2006, 193–94.

(1) [k]a-a-ša-mu ki-i[208] te-et ᵐKal-ba-ya-a[š] (2) [k]i-⸢i⸣ me-mi-iš-ta ma-an-wa-an-na-aš (3) [i]š-ḫa-ni-it-ta-ra-a-tar i-ya-u-e-ni	(1–3) Kalbaya (your messenger) has just now said this to me. He quoted (you as saying) this: "We ought to establish a relationship by marriage between ourselves."[209]

(4) [x] ^{m}Kal-ba-ya-an *Ú-UL* ḫa-a-mi (5) ⸢KA×U⸣-ya-at me-mi-iš-ta *A-NA ṬUP-PÍ*-ma-at-ša-an (6) *Ú-UL* ki-it-ta-at	(4–6) But I do not trust Kalbaya (in this matter). He conveyed it orally, but it was not written (lit. placed) on the tablet.[210]
(7) nu ma-a-an ḫa-an-da-a-an am-me-el DUMU.MUNUS-*YA* (8) ša-an-ḫi-iš-ke-ši nu-wa-ta *Ú-UL* im-ma (9) pé-eḫ-ḫi pé-eḫ-ḫi-it-ta	(7–9) If you are really seeking my daughter (in marriage), will I really not give (her) to you? I will give (her) to you![211]
(10) nu-mu-[k]án ^{m}Kal-ba-ya-an EGIR-pa pa-ra-a (11) *IŠ-TU* LÚ *ṬE*$_4$*-MI-YA* li-li-wa-aḫ-ḫu-u-an-zi (12) na-i ku-u-un-na-mu me-mi-an tup-pí-az (13) EGIR-pa ḫa-at-ra-a-i	(10–13) So send Kalbaya back to me quickly together with my messenger, and write back to me on a tablet concerning this matter.

Commentary

VBoT 2 (text 94) and *VBoT* 1 (text 95) do not identify the Egyptian pharaoh by name. But other evidence, both historical and linguistic, indicates a date between the reigns of the Hittite kings Arnuwanda I and Šuppiluliuma I (on the dating see especially Heinhold-Krahmer 1977: 50–55; Haas in Moran 1992, 103; and Houwink ten Cate 1998, 159–60; that is, during the reign of Tudḫaliya "II/III," the father of Šuppiluliuma I and the king who reigned during all or at least most of the period of the Tapikka/Maşat correspondence (see de Martino 1996, 82).

EA 32 (*VBoT* 2) was written prior to EA 31 (*VBoT* 1; so among others, Rost 1956, 329; Heinhold-Krahmer 1977, Klengel 1999, 131; de Martino 1996, de Roos 2005, 43 n. 12; and Klinger 2006), contrary to the claim of Moran 1992, 103 with n. 1. As de Roos notes, it is hard to understand how the sequence could be as Moran claims, since why would the Arzawan scribe in EA 32 (*VBoT* 2) ask his Egyptian counterpart to write him in Hittite, if he had already received EA 31 (*VBoT* 1) written in Hittite? When the Egyptian scribe complies with this request in EA 31, he writes in a very clumsy and faulty Hittite, showing that he was not a very good translator of the pharaoh's Egyptian language.

The present tablet may not be the complete letter. The present consensus is that it is the end of a longer, only partially preserved reply to EA 31 = *VBoT* 1 (e.g., see Haas in Moran 1992, 103). It is the last tablet of a reply from Tarḫunta-radu, king of Arzawa to Amunḥotep III of Egypt. Since it is not the first tablet of the letter, it bears no address formula, and appears anonymous (for another possible explanation see above in §1.2.8).

In terms of the historical situation in Anatolia at this time, it is likely that the rise in international prestige of the kingdom of Arzawa, which occasioned the request by the pharaoh for an Arzawan princess for his harem, is explained by the geo-political situation at that time—described much later in the time of Ḫattušili III, in KBo 6.28. According to this description the enemies of the Hittite kingdom had pressed in on all sides, reducing severely its geographical extent. In particular, the Arzawan kingdom to the southwest had extended its territorial control eastwards as far as the cities Tuwanuwa and Uda, that is, as far east as Cappadocia (de Martino 1996, 82–83).

The pharaoh does not call the Arzawan king "my brother," indicating that he does not consider him a king of equal rank, but rather subordinate.

The Arzawan king assures Amunḥotep that he will soon send him an Arzawan princess to add to his harem (lines 7–9). The Egyptian envoy, a certain Kalbaya, claiming to convey orally the wishes of the pharaoh, has quoted Amunḥotep as desiring to establish a family relationship by an interdynastic marriage.[212] Tarḫunta-radu is suspicious of such oral communication (ll. 4–6), and asks that the pharaoh put the matter in writing next time (ll. 10–13). On the distrust of mere oral messages in matters of grave importance see above in §1.1.3.2, §1.1.4.2, and §1.2.12. This passage shows that the spoken message of Kalbaya was compared with what was written on the tablet. Another possible reason for the uncertainty was suggested by de Roos (2005, 44), who—following Laroche (1966, 84 no. 490) in assuming from a Semitic etymology (*kalbu* "dog," compare the name Caleb occurring in the Hebrew Bible) that Kalbaya was a Syrian—thought that perhaps his attempt to speak Arzawan (or even Hittite) was indecipherable.

The Arzawan king, wishing to prevent the pharaoh from detaining his messenger, asks that he send both envoys (Egyptian and Arzawan) back to him quickly (ll. 10–13). Here we see again how correspondence between parties speaking different languages was carried on by each party using his own messenger, so that the messengers traveled in pairs, one from each correspondent, and it was considered unethical to delay their departure for the return trip (see §1.1.5.2.2).

94b. *VBoT* 2
Piggyback Letter from the Arzawan Scribe to the Scribe in Egypt

(14) ki-i-kán tup-pí ku-iš DUB.SAR-⸢aš⸣? (15) ḫal-za-a-i na-an d⸢É?.A⸣ (16) ḫa-at-ta-an-na-aš LUGAL-uš (17) ḫi-lam-na-aš-ša dUTU-uš (18) aš-šu-ú-li pa-aḫ-ša-an-ta-ru (19) nu-ut-ta ŠU.ḪI.A-uš a-ra-aḫ-za-an-da (20) aš-šu-ú-li ḫar-kán-du	(14–20) May Ea,[213] the king of wisdom, and the Sungod of the Portico[214] lovingly protect the scribe who reads aloud this tablet, and may they lovingly hold their hands around you.
(21) zi-ik-mu DUB.SAR-aš aš-šu-ú-li (22) ḫa-at-ra-a-i nam-ma-za [*Š*]*UM*-an EGIR-an (23) i-ya	(21–23) You, scribe, kindly write to me (as piggybacks in future correspondence from Egypt) and put your name at the end.
(24) DUB.ḪI.A-k[á]n ku-e ú-da-an-zi (25) nu [n]e-eš-[u]m?-ni-li ḫa-at-re-eš-ke	(24–25) Always write in Hittite the tablets that they bring here.[215]

Commentary

In the piggyback letter (ll. 21–25) the Arzawan scribe, who does not give his name, pronounces a blessing upon his colleague in Egypt, and asks him to identify himself in the next letter and to compose all subsequent correspondence to him in Hittite instead of Akkadian. Since there may not have been any scribe in Egypt at this time familiar with the Luwian language, the Arzawan scribe preferred Hittite to the Akkadian option (see Houwink ten Cate 1995, 268). The normal piggyback letter has an address line at the beginning, identifying both the sending scribe and the receiving one, just as does the main letter on the tablet. This letter lacks such an address line, suggesting perhaps that the sending scribe in Arzawa had already identified himself before. Since there might have been multiple scribes in Egypt receiving letters from the Hittite orbit, and the Arzawan scribe wished to assure himself that he knew with whom he was corresponding, in order to be able to exchange favors, he needed to know his name. The exchange of favors between scribes is apparent everywhere in the piggyback letters from Maşat Höyük (see the piggyback letters in texts 32, 36, and 56).

95. *VBoT* 1 = EA 31
From the Pharaoh Nimmuriya (Amunḫotep III) to Tarḫunta-radu, King of Arzawa

Text: Cairo Museum 4741. **Find spot:** El-Amarna. **Copies**: EA 31; *VBoT* 1. **Edition**: Rost 1956, 334–40. **Translation:** Haas in Moran 1992, 101–2; Liverani 1998, 406–9; Bernabé and Álvarez-Pedrosa 2004, 48; Klinger 2006. **Discussion**: Houwink ten Cate 1963; Heinhold-Krahmer 1977, 50–55; Starke 1981b; Hagenbuchner 1989b, 362–63 (no. 254); Freu 1992, 45–50 (historical background of the Arzawa letters); Kempinski 1993, 82–83; Kühne 1993, 422 (review of Haas' translation of the Arzawa letters); Mora 1995, 280; de Martino 1996, 81–83, 93; Hawkins 1998b, 10 nn. 32–33; Liverani 1998, 406–7; Klengel 1999, 128 [A2]; Rieken 1999, 165; Freu 2002, 92; Bryce 2003b, 64; 2003a, 56; and Klinger 2006.

Of the two EA letters between the Arzawan and Egyptian courts only in this second letter do we have preserved the important opening lines with the address formulas. Here we find the names of the two kings: Nimuwareya (one of the throne names of Amunḫotep III) and Tarḫunta-radu. If the two correspondents were of equal rank, it would probably make little difference in which order the names appeared, although one would suspect that the sender would wish his to be first. But what is more significant is that the pharaoh does not address the king of Arzawa as "my brother," the stock term of Amarna correspondence between equals (de Martino 1996, 82). Neither is he given the title "Great King," claimed by the pharaoh, although this absence may be insignificant considering its absence also in Šuppiluliuma I's address formula to the pharaoh in text 96. The fact that the Arzawan court did not have scribes capable of carrying on international correspondence in the diplomatic *lingua franca,* Akkadian, led Kühne (1973, 96) to conclude that the Egyptian-Arzawan correspondence was initiated solely for the purpose of negotiating a royal marriage between the pharaoh and an Arzawan princess. Royal marriages between the Egyptian pharaoh and a Hittite princess are also the subject of Queen Puduḫepa's letter to Ramses II (KUB 21.38 [text 98]). In regard to this proposed marriage and lines 11–16 in particular, Bryce (2003b, 107–8) has written:

> In most cases the highest-ranking daughters, i.e. daughters of the king's chief wife, were reserved for the most important marriage alliances. But personal qualities were also important. In addition to other accomplishments she might have had, a bride intended for a Great King was expected to be a woman of surpassing beauty.... [T]here was at least one opportunity for an

> inspection of the bride before the prenuptial arrangements were finalized. An envoy was sent from her prospective husband's court to complete the arrangements by seeing the bride and anointing her.... So too, when Amenhotep proposed a marriage alliance with the Arzawan king Tarhundaradu, he arranged for an inspection before the anointing: 'Behold, I have sent to you Irshappa, my messenger (with the instruction): "Let us see the daughter whom they will offer to My Majesty in marriage. And he will pour oil on her head."' In actual fact this was one marriage which never took place, not because of any shortcomings on the part of the bride, but because it was overtaken by events, with the restoration of Hittite authority through Anatolia and the consequent loss of Arzawa's short-lived status as the pre-eminent power in the region. Its king was no longer important enough to warrant the privilege of membership in the ranks of the pharaoh's fathers-in-law.

Accompanying this letter were various gifts for the king of Arzawa (lines 15–16, 28–38), a promise of further gifts to come (lines 17–18), and eventually the brideprice itself (lines 22–24).

Lines 26–27 are important for the understanding of the political situation and the purpose of the pharaoh's initiation of this diplomatic relationship with Arzawa. But they are also controversial. Two terms in these lines which describe the condition in the Hittite kingdom cause difficulty: *zinnuk* in line 26, and *igait* in line 27.

Starke's theory assumes that *zinnuk* is an Egyptian (not Hittite or Luwian) word (meaning "what you said") used without translation. This seems unlikely, since the idea of "what you said" is expressed in this and other Egypto-Hittite letters by the Hittite verbs *mema-* and *ḫatrai-* and would not be difficult for an Egyptian scribe to learn. Nevertheless, Starke's assumption of an Egyptian substratum that gives an un-Hittite cast to the vocabulary and syntax here is accepted by Francia 2006, 350 n. 5 and Klinger 2006, 193 n. 70. But not all features of the letter's syntax need be considered "un-Hittite." Note especially the "extraposition" of components to the right of the finite verb (14–15, 18, 28–29), which is attested in good Hittite (see *GrHL* §30.9 and following).

According to Starke (1981b), followed by Liverani (1998), Freu (2002, 92 n. 25), and Bernabé (2004, 48), the meaning of *igait* (line 27) is not that Hatti is in decline, but at peace ("cooled down").[216] Others such as Klengel (1999, 131 n. 208) prefer the earlier interpretation "burst, split apart" in view of the actual historical circumstances.[217]

Bryce (2003a, 56) observes: "[This is a] clear indication that Amenhotep [III] saw Tarhuntaradu as the next Great King of the Anatolian region," that is, that the Hittite kingdom was in decline. The Egyptian goal in this marriage between unequals was the isolation of a weakened Ḫatti. An indication of the power of the kingdom of Arzawa at this time is the fact that by the beginning of the reign of Šuppiluliuma I the major part of the Lower Land extending as far as Tuwanuwa (Tyana) in Cappadocia was firmly under Arzawan control (Heinhold-Krahmer 1977, 40–41, and Starke 1997, 470 n. 30).

For the name of the king of Arzawa, Tarḫunta-radu, see Hess 1993, 156–57.

(1) [*U*]*M-MA* ^{m}Ni-mu-wa-re$^{!}$-ya[218] LUGAL.GAL LUGAL KUR Mi-iz-za-ri (2) [*A-N*]*A* ^{m}Tar-ḫu-un-da-ra-du LUGAL KUR Ar-za-wa *QÍ-BÍ-MA* (3) kat-ti-mi SIG$_5$-in É.ḪI.A-mi DAM.MEŠ-mi DUMU.MEŠ-mi (4) LÚ.MEŠ GAL.GAL-aš ÉRIN.MEŠ-mi ANŠE.KUR.RA.ḪI.A-mi (5) pí-ip-pí-it-mi KUR.KUR.ḪI.A-mi-kán an-da (6) ḫu-u-ma-an SIG$_5$-in	(1–6) Thus speaks Nimuwareya,[219] Great King, king of Egypt: Say to Tarḫunta-radu, the king of Arzawa: With me it is well. With my houses, my wives, my children, my great men, my troops, my chariot-fighters, my property$^{?}$—everything in my lands—all is well.
(7) du-uk-ka$_4$ kat-ta ḫu-u-ma-an SIG$_5$-in e-eš-tu (8) É.ḪI.A-ti DAM.MEŠ-ti DUMU.MEŠ-ti LÚ.MEŠ GAL.GAL-aš (9) ÉRIN.MEŠ-ti ANŠE.KUR.RA.ḪI.A-ti pí-ip-pí-it-ti (10) KUR.ḪI.A-ti ḫu-u-ma-an SIG$_5$-in e-eš-tu	(7–10) With you too may all be well. With your houses, your wives, your children, your great men, your troops, your chariot-fighters, your property$^{?}$—everything in your lands—may all be well.
(11) ka-a-aš-ma-at-ta u-i-e-nu-un ^{m}Ir-ša-ap-pa<-an> (12) ^{LÚ}ḫa-lu-ga-tal-la-an-mi-in a-ú-ma-ni DUMU.MUNUS-*TI*[220] (13) ^{d}UTU-mi ku-in DAM-an-ni ú-wa-da-an-zi (14) nu-uš-ši li-il-ḫu-wa-i Ì-an SAG.DU-ši (15) ka-a-aš-ma-ta up-pa-aḫ-ḫu-un 1 ^{KUŠ}ḫa-la-li-ya[221] KÙ.SIG$_{17}$-aš (16) SIG$_5$-an-ta	(11–16) I have herewith sent to you Iršappa, my messenger (with the instructions): “Let us see the daughter whom they will conduct to My Majesty for marriage. And pour oil on her head.”[222] I have herewith sent to you one set of good-quality leather sacks of gold.[223]
(17) a-ni-ya-at-ta-aš-ma-mu ku-e-da-aš ḫa-at-ra-a-eš (18) up-pí-wa-ra-at-mu ne-et-ta up-pa-aḫ-ḫi EGIR-an-da (19) na-aš-ta ^{LÚ}ḫa-lu-ga-tal-la-at-ti-in am-me-el-la (20) ^{LÚ}ḫa-lu-ga-tal-la-an	(17–21) But as for the ceremonial garments about which you wrote me (saying): “Send it/them here to me!,” I will send them to you, but later. Send back quickly your

EGIR-pa pa-ra-a ḫu-u-da-a-ak (21) na-i na-at ú-wa-an-du	messenger together with my messenger, and let them come.
(22) nu-ut-ta ú-wa-an-zi ú-da-an-zi ku-ša-ta DUMU.MUNUS-*TI* (23) LÚḫa-lu-ga-tal-<la>-aš-mi-iš LÚḫa-lu-ga-tal-la<-aš>-ša (24) ku-iš tu-el ú-it na-aš ag-ga-aš (25) nu-mu an-tu-uḫ-šu-uš <URU>Ga-aš-ga-aš KUR-ya-aš up-pí iš-ta-ma-aš-šu-un (26) zi-in-nu-uk ḫu-u-ma-an-da	(22–26) Then they—my messenger and the messenger from you who came and …-ed—will proceed to bring to you the brideprice for (your) daughter . And send me people of the Kaška land. I have heard that everything is *finished*?,
(27) nu <URU>Ḫa-ad-du-ša-aš-ša KUR-e i-ga-it (28) nu-ut-ta ka-a-aš-ma pí-ip-pé-eš-šar up-pa-ḫu-un aš-šu-l[i] (29) ki-iš-ša-ri-iš-ši mIr-ša-ap-pa LÚḫa-lu-g[a-tal-li-mi] (30) 1-*EN* KUŠḫa-la-li-ya KÙ.SIG$_{17}$ KI.LAL.BI (31) 20 MA.NA KÙ.SIG$_{17}$ 3 GAD.SIG 3 GAD <GÚ.?>È.A S[IG]? (32) 3 GAD ḫu-uz-zi 8 GAD ku-ši-it-ti-in (33) 1 *ME.* GAD-an(coll.) wa-al-ga-an 1 *ME.* GAD ḫa-a[p?]-x[…] (34) 1 *ME.* GAD-aš pu!-tal-li-ya-aš-ša[…] (35) 4 NA4*KU-KU-BU* GAL Ì.DÙG.GA 6 NA4*K*[*U-KU-BU* …] (36) *ŠA* Ì. DÙG. GA 3 GIŠGU.ZA GIŠESI(coll.) šar-pa *BÁ-NA*[*-A* K]Ù(coll.).SIG$_{17}$ GAR. RA (37) 10 GIŠGU.ZA *ŠA* GIŠESI *IŠ-TU* KA×UD AM[.SI] (38) *U-UḪ-ḪU-UZ* 1 *ME.* GIŠESI aš-šu-li	(27–38) And that the land of Ḫattuša is *paralyzed*?. I have herewith sent you a gift as a token of good will, in the charge of my messenger Iršappa: a leather sack? of gold weighing twenty minas, three sheer linen garments, three sheer linen tunics, three linen *ḫuzzi*, eight linen *kušitti*, one hundred *walga*-linen, one hundred linen *ḫappa-*…, one hundred linen *putalliyašša*, four large stone jars of perfumed oil, six small stone jars of perfumed oil, three beautiful ebony *cross-legged* chairs[224] overlaid with gold, ten chairs of ebony inlaid with ivory, one hundred (beams of) ebony as a token of good will.

Commentary

17–18 Since the noun *aniyatt-* is common gender, whereas the resumptive pronouns (*-at* and *-e*) in line 18 are neuter plural, it is clear that a nom.-acc. *aniyatta* is in view. This neuter plural form, unlike the singular common gender *aniyatt-* "work" (see Klinger's translation of this line as "Über welche *Leistungen* du mir geschrieben hast" (2006, 195), means "regalia, expensive ceremonial garments."

33 For the collated reading and interpretation of this line see CHD Š, 315 sub GADšawalga-.225

36–37 The reading GIŠESI *šar-pa BÁ-NA*[-*A* K]Ù.SIG_{17} GAR.RA, also used in CHD Š, 288, is based on Edmund Gordon's collations described in Moran 1992, 103 n. 12.

96. EA 41
From King Šuppiluliuma I to the Egyptian Pharaoh

Text: Cairo Museum 4747. **Copy:** Winckler and Abel 1889, no. 18. **Edition:** Knudtzon 1964, no. 41. **Translation:** Moran 1992; Liverani 1998, 410–11; Schwemer 2006, 190–91. **Discussion**: Ehelolf 1939a (on lines 30–41); Miller 2007 (on the chronology and therefore the identity of the addressed pharaoh).

The recipient of this letter was either Amunḥotep IV (Akhenaten) (so, e.g., Liverani 1998, 410 n. 12; and Miller 2007), Tutankhamun (so Houwink ten Cate 1963), or Smenkhkare (so Wilhelm and Boese, cited by Moran 1992 and Bryce 1990). The form Ḫūriya (line 2) is a shortened form of his full name, resulting perhaps from an unintentional haplological clipping of the first part (see §1.2.16). The Hittite king calls the Egyptian pharaoh "my brother" (ŠEŠ-*ya,* lines 3, etc.), since the two were of equal rank in the world of "great kings."

Šuppiluliuma often refers to his friendly relations with this pharaoh's father (*abû/î-ka*, lines 7, 8, 10, etc.), that is, predecessor, and urges the new pharaoh, who has recently ascended the throne (lines 16–22), to continue these good relations and fulfill any incomplete promises made by his predecessor (lines 14–15). Šuppiluliuma then describes the gifts that the predecessor had promised—statues of gold, silver, and lapis—and asks that these be sent forthwith. In return, he describes gifts of his own to the pharaoh (*ana šulmāni-ka*) that would accompany this letter (lines 39–43): large silver vessels in the shape of various animals (stag, ram, etc.) and two silver disks (*kakkarū*) depicting two *nikiptu*-trees. The exchange of expensive gifts between members of the "club of royal brothers" was a form of international trade (see §1.1.5.3.2).

(1) [um-ma dUTU-ši] m Šu-up-pí-[l]u-li-u-ma LU[G]AL.G[AL] (2) [LUGAL KUR U]RU[Ḫ]a-[a]t-tiKI	(1–3) [Thus speaks His Majesty], Šuppiluliuma, G[reat] King, [king of Ḫat]ti: Say to Ḫūriya, [king] of:

a-na ^{m}Ḫu-u-ri-i-y[a] (3) [LUGAL KUR ^{URU}Mi-]iṣ-ri-i^{KI} ŠEŠ-ya qí-bí[226]-[ma]	Egypt, my brother:
(4) [a-na ya-ši šu]l-mu a-na maḫ-ri-ka lu-ú šul-m[u] (5) [a-na DAM.MEŠ-k]a DUM[U].MEŠ-ka É-ka ÉRIN.MEŠ-ka ^{GIŠ}GIGIR.MEŠ-k[a] (6) [ù i-n]a Š[À]-bi KUR-ka dan-niš lu-ú šul-mu	(4–6) [With me all is] well. With you may all be well (too). [With] your [*wives*], your sons, your household, your troops, your chariots, [and] in your country, may all be very well.
(7) $^{[L]Ú.MEŠ}$DUMU KIN-ri-ya ša a-na a-bi-ka aš-pu-u-ru (8) ù mé-re-eš$_{15}$-ta ša a-bu-ka e-ri-šu [i]-na bé-e-r[i]-ni (9) at-te-ru-tam-ma lu-ú ni-ip-pu-uš-mi ù "[LU]GAL"[227] (10) la-a ak-t[a-l]a mi-nu-me-e ša a-bu-ka id-bu-b[á] (11) "LUGAL"[227] gáb-b[á-am-m]a lu-ú e-pu-uš ù mé-re-eš$_{15}$-ta-ya "LUGAL"[227] (12) [š]a a-na a-bi-ka e-ri-šu a-bu-ka mì-im-ma ú-ul (13) [i]k-la gáb-bá-am-ma lu-ú id-dì-na	(7–13) Neither my messengers, whom I sent to your father, nor the request that your father made, saying, "Let us establish only the most friendly relations between us," did I *indeed* refuse. Whatsoever your father said to me, I *indeed* did absolutely everything. And my own request, *indeed,* that I made to your father, he never refused; he gave me absolutely everything.
(14) un-du a-bu-ka bal-[ṭ]ù šu-bi-la-a-te-e (15) ša ú-še-bi-la ŠEŠ-ya am-mì-ni ták-la-aš-šu-nu-ti	(14–15) Why, my brother, have you held back the shipments (of gifts) that your father was sending to me, when he was alive?
(16) i-na-an-na ŠEŠ-ya a-na ^{GIŠ}GU.ZA ša a-bi-ka (17) [t]e-e-te-li ù ki-me-e a-bu-ka ù a-na-ku (18) šul-ma-na i-na bé-e-ri-ni ḫa-aš-ḫa-a-nu-ma (19) ù i-na-an-na-ma at-ta ù a-na-ku i-na be-ri-ni (20) ka-an-na lu-ú ṭa-a-bá-a-nu ù mé-re-eš$_{15}$-ta <ša>[228] (21) a-na-ku a-na a-bi-ka aq-bu-ú a-na ŠEŠ-ya-ma (22) [a-qab-bi a-ḫu-]uz-za-ta i-na bé-e-ri-ni i ni-ip-pu-uš	(16–22) Now, my brother, [yo]u have ascended the throne of your father, and just as your father and I were desirous of (exchanging) greeting gifts between us, so now too should you and I enjoy good relations with one another. The request (that) I[229] expressed to your father [I shall express] to my brother, too. Let us establish a [mar]riage bond between us.[230]
(23) [mi-im-m]a ša a-na a-bi-ka	(23–28) [You], my [brother], should

e-ri-iš-ta (24) [at-ta ŠE]Š-ya la-a ta-kà-al-la-a-šu (25) [x x x 2 ṣ]a-al-ma-a-ni ša KÙ.SIG$_{17}$ 1-en (26) [li-zi-iz] 1-en li-ši-ib ù 2 ALAN.MEŠ ša MUNUS.MEŠ (27) [ša KÙ.BAB]BAR-ma[231] ù $^{\text{NA4}}$ZA.GÌN ra-bi-ta «ù» a-na (28) [… k]à-an-na-šu-nu ra-bu-ú ŠEŠ-ya [li-še-bi-la][232]	not hold back [anything] that [I asked] of your father. [As to the two st]atues of gold, one [should be standing], one should be seated. And [let] my brother [send me]two [silver] statues of women, and a large (amount of) lapis lazuli for their[233] large stand […].
(29) […] … (31) … ù šum-ma ŠEŠ-ya [ḫa-šiḫ a-na] (32) [na-dá-ni Š]EŠ -ya li-id-dì-i[n]-šu-nu-t[i-ma] (33) [ù šum-m]a ŠEŠ-ya a-na na-a-dá-ni-šu-nu[-ma] (34) [la]-a [ḫ]a-šiḫ ki-me-e ^{GIŠ}GIGIR.MEŠ-ya a-na (35) [na?-š]e? ^{GAD}ḫu-uz-zi$^{!}$ i-gam$^{?}$-ma$^{?}$-ru-ma a-na ŠEŠ-ya (36) ú-tá-a-ar-šu-nu-ti ù mi-nu-um-me-e (37) ša ŠEŠ-ya ḫa-aš-ḫa-ta [š]u-u-up-ra-am-ma (38) lu-še-bíl-ak-ku	(29–38) […] … (31) If my brother [wants to give], let my brother give them. [But] if my brother does not want to give them, when my chariots are *readied*[234] for … linen *ḫuzzi,* I will return them to my brother. Whatever you want, my brother, write to me so I can send it to you.
(39) a-nu-um-ma a-na šul-ma-ni-ka 1 bi-ib-ru (40) KÙ.BABBAR UDU. <A.>LUM[235] 5 MA.NA KI.LÁ. BI 1 bi-ib-ru (41) KÙ.BABBAR UDU.ŠIR pu-u-ḫi-lu[236] 3 MA.NA KI.LÁ.BI (42) 2 [k]à-ak-kà-ru KÙ.BABBAR 10 MA.NA KI.LÁ. BI-ma (43) 2 ^{GIŠ}ni-kip-tum ra-a-bu-tim ul-te-bíl-ak-ku	(39–43) I herewith send you as your greeting gift: one silver vessel in the shape of a stag, five minas its weight; one silver vessel in the shape of a young ram, three minas its weight; two silver disks, ten minas their weight, (and) two large medicinal shrubs.

97. EA 44
To the Pharaoh from Zita, a Hittite Prince

Text: VAT 1656. **Copies:** Winckler and Abel 1889, no. 29; Schroeder 1915, 11, no. 16. **Edition:** Knudtzon 1964, no. 44. **Translation:** Moran 1992, 117; Liverani 1998, 412–13. **Discussion:** see bibliography in Liverani 1998.

The sender's name is a good "Hittite" name (linguistically Luwian, but widely used in the Hittite kingdom), Zida (see Laroche 1966, no. 1552). Identification of this Zida with the brother of Šuppiluliuma I and a general in the Hittite army was first made by Götze in 1926. For more on this man see Hoffner 1995b, 557; Liverani 1998, 410, 412–13; Freu 2002, 89; Imparati 2003, 851; Haas 2006, 89–90, 92; Taggar-Cohen 2006, 225; and Marizza 2007a, 64.

Zida addresses the pharaoh respectfully as his "father," in part because the pharaoh was older, but also because Zida's rank was not king, but prince (DUMU.LUGAL). The letter stresses Zida's faithful and respectful behavior, including the prompt sending back of messengers and the regular sending of gifts and greetings. Finally (lines 25–28) Zida expresses his wish for Egyptian gold and promises to reciprocate with any item from Ḫatti that the pharaoh might desire.

(1) a-na be-lí LUGAL KUR ^{URU}Mi-iṣ-ri[-i] (2) a-bi-ya qí-bí-ma (3) um-ma ^{m}Zi-i[-d]a-a DUMU.LUGAL (4) DUMU-ka-ma	(1–4) Say to the lord, the king of Egypt, my father: Thus speaks Zita, the prince, your son:
(5) a-na ma-ḫar be-lí a-bi-ya (6) gab-ba lu-ú šul-mu	(5–6) May all be well with the lord, my father.
(7) i-na maḫ-ri-i KASKAL a-i-ú-tim (8) DUMU.MEŠ KIN-ri-ka a-na KUR ^{URU}Ḫa-at-ti (9) it-tal-ku ù ki-i-me-e a-na UGU-ḫi-ka (10) it-ta-as-ḫa-ru ù a-na-ku-ma (11) a-na ak-ka-a-ša a--bi-ya (12) [š]ul-ma-na aš-pur ù šu-bé-el-ta (13) [a-n]a UGU-ḫi-ka ul-te-bíl	(7–13) On an earlier embassy of any of your messengers, they came to Ḫatti, and when they went back to you, then it was I who sent greetings to you and had a present brought to you.
(14–17) Broken away.	
(18) … a-nu-um-ma DUMU.MEŠ KIN-ka (19) [iš-tu] KUR ^{URU}Ḫa-at-ti a-na UGU-ḫi-ka (20) […]-sú-nu-ti ù a-na-ku-ma (21) it-ti DUMU.MEŠ KIN-ka at-tu-ya DUMU.MEŠ KIN-ya (22) a-na UGU-ḫi a-bi-ya aš-pur-šu-nu-ti (14) ù šu-bé-el-ta 16 LÚ.MEŠ a-na šul-ma-ni-ka ul-te-bíl-ak-ku	(18–24) Herewith I send on to you your messengers (coming) from Ḫatti, and I also send to my father my own messengers along with your messengers, and I send as your greeting gift a present of six-teen men.

(25) ù a-n[a]-ku [K]Ù.SIG$_{17}$ ḫa-aš-ḫa-ku (26) ù a-bu-[y]a KÙ.SIG$_{17}$ šu-bi-la (27) ù mi-nu-um-me-e be-lí a-bi-ya (28) ḫa-aš-ḫa-tá šu-up-ra-ma ú[-š]e-bal-ak-ku	(25–28) I myself am desirous of gold. My father, send me gold. Whatever you, the lord, my father, are desirous of, write me so that I can send (it) to you.

2.3. New Hittite Letters (98–126)

2.3.1. NH Letters found at Ḫattuša (98–122)

2.3.1.1. NH International Diplomatic Correspondence (98–105)

98. KUB 21.38
From Queen Puduḫepa to Ramses II of Egypt(?)

Text: Bo 2045 + Bo 3975. **Find spot:** Unknown. **Copy**: KUB 21.38. **Edition**: Helck 1963; Stefanini 1964; Edel 1994, 1, 216–23 (no. 105); 2, 270–72. **Translation**: Beckman 1999a, 131–35 (no. 22E). **Discussion**: Hoffner 1982b (rev. 15–16: *šiwariya-* "to withhold"); Hagenbuchner 1989b, 325–27 (no. 222); Polvani 1988, 174; Wouters 1989, 233–34; Symington 1991, 121; Melchert 1993, 14 (*:annān tiššan*), 129 (*:lumpašti-*), *šiwari(ya)-*, and other glossed forms; de Martino and Imparati 1995, 106–7 (Puduḫepa reusing an old rumor, and Ramses' defense against charges that a Babylonian princess given to him in marriage disappeared; and in obv. 17–24 the use of cold as an excuse); Starke 1996, 157–58 (the career of Alalimi, obv. 32); Neu 1997, 152; Trémouille 1997, 37 n. 112; Singer 1998, 537; Klengel 1999, 222 [B7.14], 244 [A19.II.1]; Imparati in Klengel 1999, 381 (on the marriage arrangements); Liverani 2001, 41, 156; Schwemer 2001, 443 n. 3692; van den Hout 2001c, 216; 2006 (glossed Luwian words); Hawkins 2002, 224 (Zuzu as a *KARTAPPU* and eunuch); Bryce 2003b, 114–15; Freu 2004b, 157–63; 2006, 224; de Roos 2006, 20, 22–23; Heinhold-Krahmer 2007b, 201–2.

The first few lines of the tablet are broken away. Since this was apparently a draft from which the official copy to be sent was prepared, it is possible that the formal opening was omitted and the draft began right away with the communications. On the other hand, if there was an opening, the restoration below in line (0) is a likely representation of the text.

(0) [*UM-MA* ᶠPu-du-ḫé-pa MUNUS.LUGAL GAL MUNUS.LUGAL KUR ᵁᴿᵁḪat-ti *A-NA* ᵐRi-a-ma-še-ša LUGAL.GAL LUGAL KUR ᵁᴿᵁMi-iz-ri ŠEŠ-*YA QÍ-BI-MA*]	(0) Thus speaks Puduḫepa, Great Queen, Queen of the land of Ḫatti: Say to Reamašeša, Great King, King of the land of Egypt, my brother:
(1′) [ŠEŠ-*YA*-ma-mu ku-it] kiš?-[an *TÀŠ-PUR*] LÚ.MEŠ *ṬE₄-ME-K*[*A*?]-wa ku-wa-p[í … ú-e-er nu-mu] (2′) [x x EGIR-pa] ú-te-er nu-wa-za du-uš-ku-un na-at[…] (3′) [*A-NA* DA]M? *ŠA* ŠEŠ-*KA* TI-tar šu-wa-ru SAG.DU-i *ŠA* [ŠEŠ-*YA* TI-tar šu-wa-ru *QA-TAM-MA* e-eš-du nu-mu … up?-pí?] (4′) [na-at *IŠ-TU*] NA₄.ZA.GÌN TI-an-te-eš a-ša-an-du nam-ma-mu-ká[n Š]À? KUR.KUR.M[EŠ …] (5′) [TI-tar šu-w]a-ru *A-NA* ŠEŠ-*YA* am-me-el aš-šu-la-an am-me-el ú-nu-w[a-aš-ḫa-an up-pa-aḫ-ḫu-un am-mu-uk SIG₅-in?] (6′) (*eras.*) *A-NA* ŠEŠ-*YA*-ya *QA-TAM-MA* [SIG₅-in? e-eš-du]	(1′–3′) Concerning the fact that you, my brother, wrote to me as follows: "At the time when your messengers came, they brought back to me gifts, and I rejoiced." When I heard that, I rejoiced likewise. The wife of your brother (i.e., Puduḫepa, the wife of Ḫattušili) enjoys full life. May the person of my brother likewise enjoy full life! Send me …, (4′) and may they be set with lapis lazuli! (4′) Furthermore, my lands enjoy full life. <May> your lands likewise <enjoy> full life! (5′) I have sent my greetings and my ornaments to my brother. With me all is well. (6′) May it be well with my brother likewise!
(7′) [Š]EŠ-*YA*-ma-mu ku-it kiš-an *TÀŠ-PUR* NIN-*YA*-wa-mu *IŠ-PUR* DUMU.MUNUS-wa-ta [pé-eḫ-ḫi ši-wa-ri-ya-at-ma-wa-ra-an-mu nu-wa-mu-za] (8′) ki-nu-un TUKU.TUKU-za-ša ku-wa-at-wa-ra-an-mu ki-nu-un *Ú-UL* pé-eš-t[a? DUMU.MUNUS-*YA*-ya i?-wa?-ru?-ya pé-eḫ-ḫi] (9′) na-at-za *Ú-UL* mar-ki-ya-ši ma-la-a-ši-ya-at-za ki-nu-un-ma-an-ta x[… pí-an-na *Ú-UL* tar-aḫ-mi] LÚ.x[…] (10′) É KUR ᵁᴿᵁḪat-ti-za ŠEŠ-*YA* GIM-an ša-ak-ti na-at-za am-mu-uk *Ú-UL* š[a]-a[g-ga-aḫ-ḫi na-at ar-ḫa a]r-nu-	(7′) Concerning the fact that you, my brother, wrote to me as follows: "My sister wrote to me: 'I will give a daughter to you.' But you have withheld her from me. And (8′) now you are even angry with me! Why have you not now given her to me?" (8′) I will give you both my daughter and the *dowry*. (9′) And you will not disapprove of it (i.e., the dowry); you will approve of it. But at the moment I am not able to give her to you.… (10′) As you, my brother, know the house of Ḫatti, (10′) do I not know that it is a house *relocated*

wa-an É-e[r …] (11′) a-aš-ta-ma-kán ku-it na-at-kán mÚr-ḫi-dU-up-aš *A-NA* DINGIR.GAL pé-eš-ta nu m[Úr-ḫi-d]U-up-aš ku-it a-pí-ya (12′) na-an pu-nu-uš ma-a-an kiš-an ma-a-an *Ú-UL* kiš-an am-mu-uk-ma *A-NA* ŠE[Š-*YA*] ku-in DUMU.MUNUS ne-pí-ša-aš KI-aš-š[a] (13′) pé-eḫ-ḫi na-an-kán ku-e-da-ni ḫa-an-da-mi *A-NA* DUMU.MUNUS KUR URUKa-ra-an-du-ni-ya-[aš KUR] URUZu-la-pí KUR URUAš-šur ḫa-an-da-m[i] (14′) a-pé-e-da-ša-an-kán! ku-wa-pí *UL* GAM-an iš-ḫa-[an-n]a? tar-aḫ-mi na-aš du-wa-an-ma pa-ra-a […]	(to Tarḫuntašša)? (11′) And Urḫi-Teššub gave to the Great God what remained (after the rest was relocated). (11′) Since Urḫi-Teššub is there, (12′) ask him if this is so, or not so. (12′) To whom should I compare the daughter of heaven and earth whom I will give to my brother? (13′) Should I compare her to the daughter of Babylonia, of Zulabi, or of Assyria? (14′) While I am not able to *tie*? her to them, up until now she …
(15′) *A-NA* ŠEŠ-*YA*-ma NU.GÁL im-ma ku-it-ki ma-a-an *A-NA* DUMU dUTU na-aš-ma DUMU dU *Ú-UL* ku-it-k[i] e-eš-zi na-aš-ma a-ru-ni *Ú-UL* e-eš-zi (16′) tu-uk-ka$_4$ *Ú-UL* ku-it-ki e-eš-zi ŠEŠ-*YA*-ma am-me-e-da-za NÍG.TUKU-ti ku-it-ki *Ú-UL*-at ŠUM-an iš-ḫa-aš-šar-wa-tar-ra	(15′–16′) Does my brother have nothing at all? Only if the Son of the Sun God, the Son of the Storm God, and the Sea have nothing, do you have nothing! Yet, my brother, you want to enrich yourself at my expense! It (i.e., such behavior) is unworthy of name and lordly status.
(17′) *A-NA* ŠEŠ-*YA*-ma ku-it kiš-an *AŠ-PUR A-NA* DUMU.MUNUS-wa ku-in NAM.RA.MEŠ GU$_4$.MEŠ UDU.ḪI.A pé-eš-ke-mi nu-wa-mu-kán ŠÀ KUR.KUR.MEŠ (18′) [ḫal-]ki-iš NU.GÁL nu-wa-ta ku-e-da-ni me-e-ḫu-ni LÚ.MEŠ *ṬE$_4$-ME* an-da ú-e-mi-ya-<an->zi nu-wa-mu-kán ŠEŠ-*YA* LÚ*PIT-ḪAL-LI* pa-ra-a [na-a-i] (19′) *A-NA* EN.MEŠ KUR-*TI-YA*-wa GIŠ.ḪUR.MEŠ me-na-aḫ-ḫa-an-da ú-da-an-du nu-wa NAM.RA.MEŠ ku-in [GU$_4$].MEŠ UDU.ḪI.A pé-e ḫar-kán-zi (20′) nu-wa-ra-an-kán	(17′–20′) Concerning the fact that I wrote to my brother as follows: “What civilian captives, cattle and sheep should I give (as a dowry) to my daughter? In my lands I do not even have barley. The moment that the messengers reach you, let my brother dispatch a rider to me. Let them bring documents (lit. writing boards?) to the lords of my land, and let them take away the civilian captives, cattle and sheep which are in their charge and accommodate them.” I myself have sent messengers and tablets to them

ar-ḫa da-aš-kán-du nu-wa-ra-an par-na-wi$_5$-iš-kán-du nu a-pé-e-[da-aš am-mu-uk]-pát LÚ.MEŠ *ṬE*$_4$*-ME* DUB.BA.A-ya *AŠ-PUR* BA.ÚŠ?-za-x[…] ta?-an-[…] LÚ.MEŠ *ṬE*$_4$*-ME* an-da ba?-a-er (21′) (eras.) EGIR-pa-ma nu-un-tar-aš LÚ[*PIT*]-*Ḫ*[*AL-LI* … *Ú-UL*] ú-et LÚ *ṬE*$_4$*-MU-YA Ú-UL* ú-et (22′) am-mu-uk-ma a-pád-da-an EGIR-an-da mZu-zu-un LÚ*QAR-TAP-PU* LÚ.SAG [… na?-aš? ka]t-ta iš-ta-an-ta-it (23′) mPí-ḫa-aš-du-uš-ma ku-e-da-ni me-e-ḫu-ni a-ar-aš nu ka-ru-ú ŠE$_{12}$ [ki-ša-at …] NAM.RA.MEŠ pé-di (24′) *Ú-UL* nam-ma ni-ni-in-ku-un ŠEŠ-*YA* LÚ.MEŠ *ṬE*$_4$*-ME-KA* pu-nu-uš m[a-a-an kiš-an ma-a-an *Ú-*]*UL* kiš-an *Ú-UL* INIM-a[š …] (or *Ú-UL* ka-aš[…])	(my local subordinates). … (21′–24′) But your rider did not come back promptly, and my messenger did not come either. Thereupon I sent Zuzu, charioteer and eunuch, but he was delayed. At the moment that Piḫašdu did arrive, it was already winter, and I did not transfer the civilian captives again. My brother, ask your messengers if this is so, or not so. The matter is not …
(25′) ŠEŠ-*YA*-ma-mu ku-it kiš-an *TÀŠ-PUR* DUMU.MUNUS-wa le-e nam-ma za-lu-ga-nu-u[š-ke-ši …] (26′) am-mu-uk-ka$_4$?-aš-kán *Ú-UL* an-da ma-la-a-an-za DUMU.MUNUS-za-kán EGIR-pa i[m-ma …] (27′) ka-ru-ú a-ra-an-za nu-uš-ši-kán x[…]-pát ku-wa-pí a-wa-an a[r-ḫa …] (28′) ma-a-an-ta ma-a-an DUMU?.MUNUS?-pát? *Ú-UL* ku-wa-pí pé-eḫ-ḫu-un [m]a-a-an-ta [NAM.RA.MEŠ GU$_4$.ḪI.A UDU.ḪI.A me-ma-aḫ-ḫu-un] (29′) (eras.) ki-nu-un-ma *Ú-*[*UL* …]x[…] (30′) nu-kán ŠÀ KUR URUKum-man-ni ŠE$_{12}$-u-an-zi GAM-an-da (eras.) ú-w[a-an-zi] (31′) dUTU-*ŠI*-mu TI-an-za e-eš-du ma-a-na-aš-kán ú-e-eḫ-ta-r[i] (32′) ú-it-ma! mA-la-]	(25′–33′) Concerning the fact that you, my brother, wrote to me as follows: "Do not withhold the daughter from me any longer!" … Was she not approved by me? Do I hold back the daughter for myself? Rather, I wish that she had already arrived. When I myself for her … away, … If I had not at any time (sincerely) given my own daughter to you, I would not have promised you the civilian captives, cattle, and sheep?. But now not … And they (the bride and her party) will come down to spend the winter in Kizzuwatna … May His Majesty (that is, Ḫattušili) live for my sake! If (s)he should turn, … But Alalimi, overseer of the cupbearers, came,

li-mi-iš UGULA ^{LÚ}SAGI.A nu tu?-e?-el?-x[…] (33′) nu-uš-ma-aš-kán a-pu-u-uš-ša 1 URU-*LUM* DIB-an-du a-pu-u-uš-ša[…]	and your rider arrived too?. Let some of them (i.e., of the marriage party?) take possession of a single town, while others …
(34′) ŠEŠ-*YA*-ma-mu ku-it kiš-an *TÀŠ-PUR ŠA* DUMU.MUNUS-wa za-lu-ga-nu-m[ar ku-it *Ú-UL* a-a-ra] (35′) *A-NA* NIN-*YA*-wa-ra-at ḫa-at-ra-mi nu ku-uš-ša-an a-ú-me-n[i …] (36′) an-da ta-par-ri-ya-i za-lu-ga-nu-mar-ra am-me-el nu-un-tar-nu-um-mar […] (37′) i!?-ya-an-du DINGIR.MEŠ nu le-pát za-lu-ga-nu-mi nu nu-un-tar-nu-wa-a[l-lu[237] …] (38′) ŠEŠ-*YA*-ma-mu-za NIN-tar na-ak-ki-ya-tar ZI-ni-pát EGIR-pa *Ú*?[-*UL* da-a-aš …] (39′) *UL*[238]-ya-wa ku-it i-ya-u-wa-aš nu-wa-ra-at i-ya nu-kán ḫa-x[- … (-)m]a?-a-an ḫa-at-ra-[mi] (40′) wa-aḫ-nu-mi-an-kán ku-wa-pí na-ak-ki-iš-ma-du!-za [ku-it ku-wa-at-ta?-an?-kán w]a-aḫ-nu-mi	(34′–40′) Concerning the fact that you, my brother, wrote to me as follows: "I write to my sister that withholding the daughter is not right … "Whenever will we see …? Order …! May the gods … turn the withholding into haste for me, so that I not delay! May I hurry! But my brother has not accepted in his own mind my status as a sister and my dignity, saying: " …, and do what should not (or: cannot) be done!" …… would I not? write …, when I change it? But because I? am? dear to you, why should I change it?
(41′) [ŠE]Š-*YA*-ma-mu ku-it kiš-an *TÀŠ-PUR A-NA* DUMU.MUNUS-wa LÚ.MEŠ [*ṬE*$_4$-*ME-KA* …] me-mi-iš-kán-du (42′) nu *A-NA* ŠEŠ-*YA* ku-u-un me-mi-ya-an a-pád-da-an [ḫa-an-da-aš ḫa-at-ra-a-nu-un … zi-]la-du-wa (eras.) (43′) GIM-an wa-ša-i ku-e-ez [… *A-NA* ŠEŠ]-*YA* a-pád-da-an ḫa-an-da-aš [*AŠ*-]*PUR*	(44′–46′) Concerning the fact that you, my brother, wrote to me as follows: "Your messengers shall speak freely to the daughter." I have thereupon written this word to my brother: "When in the future, conditions are favorable, they will come?." That is why I have written to my brother.
(44′) ma-a-an-ma-an *A-NA* ŠEŠ-*YA* DUMU.MUNUS [….]-an-ta *ŠA* ŠEŠ-*YA* <na-aš-ma *ŠA*> NIN-*ZU* pé-eḫ-ḫu-un (45′) ma-an a-pí-ya-ya ku-it Š[EŠ-*YA* me-mi-iš-ta … nu-wa-mu ku]-in [MUN]US-an	44′–46′) If I had sent? the daughter to my brother precipitously?, or if I had not given you (the gifts appropriate) for my brother <or for> his sister, what would my brother even then have said?

pí-e-er nu-wa-aš-ši iš-ki-ša ku-e-ek-ka$_4$ (46′) e-eš-du nu-wa-ra-at a-pé-e-da-ni-ya […]x-wa-ra-at iš-ḫa-aš-šar-wa-tar	Perhaps: "May the woman whom they gave to me have some support, and may it be generous$^{?}$ for her too! Then it would be lordly behavior."
(47′) MUNUS.LUGAL-aš-za ku-i-e-eš DUMU.MUNUS KUR ^{URU}Ga-ra-an-du-ni-ya-aš [DUMU. MUNUS] KUR ^{URU}A-mur-ri-ya da-aḫ-ḫu-un (48′) na-at-mu *A-NA* LÚ.MEŠ KUR ^{URU}Ḫat-ti pé-ra-an *Ú-UL* im-ma wa-al-li-ya-tar *Ú-UL* ku-it e-eš-ta (49′) na-at (eras.) am-mu-uk i-ya-nu-un nu-za a-ra-aḫ-zé-n[u]$^{?}$-un *ŠA* LUGAL.GAL DUMU. MUNUS *AŠ-ŠUM* MUNUS É.GE$_4$.A da-aḫ-ḫu-un (50′) nu ma-a-an *A-NA* MU[NUS] É.GE$_4$.A ku-wa-pí a-pé-el LÚ *ṬE$_4$-MU* EGIR-an-da mi-iš-ri-wa-an-da ú-wa-an-zi (51′) na-aš-ma-aš-ši *Š[A]* ŠEŠ NIN-*TI* EGIR-an-da ú-ez-zi na-[a]t *Ú-UL* im-ma wa-al-li-ya-tar (52′) nu-mu-kán ŠÀ KUR ^{URU}Ḫat-ti MUNUS-*TUM* NU.GÁL e-eš-ta *Ú-UL*-at *ŠUM*-ni ḫa-an-da-aš i-ya-nu-un	(47′–52′) The daughter of Babylonia and the daughter of Amurru whom I the Queen took for myself —were they not indeed something for me to be proud of before the people of Ḫatti?[239] It was I who did it. I took each daughter of a Great King, though a foreigner, as daughter-in-law. And if at some time his (the royal father's) messengers come in splendor to the daughter-in-law, or one of her brothers or sisters comes to her, are they[240] not also (a source of) praise (for me)? Was there no woman available to me in Ḫatti? Did I not do this out of consideration for renown?
(53′) *A-NA* ŠEŠ-*YA* MUNUS-*TUM* *Ú-UL* im-ma e-eš-ta ŠEŠ-*YA*-ma-at-kán *Ú-UL* am-me-el ŠEŠ-an-ni NIN-ni (54′) na-ak-ki-[y]a-an-ni i-ya-at na-at ma-a-an i-ya-at-ya na-at-kán *A-NA* LUGAL KUR ^{URU}Kar-an-du-ni-ya-aš im-ma (55′) ḫa-an-da-an-z[a] *Ú-UL*-za *ŠA* LUGAL.GAL LUGAL KUR ^{URU}Ḫat-ti LUGAL KALAG.GA DUMU.MUNUS MUNUS-an-ni da-a-aš ma-a-an te-ši LUGAL KUR ^{URU}Kar-an-du-ni-ya-aš-wa$^{!}$ (56′) *Ú-*	(53′–56′) Did my brother have no wife at all? DId not my brother make them (i.e., the marriage arrangements) <out of consideration for> his(!) brotherhood, my sisterhood, and (our$^{?}$) dignity? And when he made them, they were indeed settled in conformity with (the arrangements of) the King of Babylonia. Did he not also take the daughter of the Great King, the King of Ḫatti, the mighty King, for marriage? If you should say: "The

UL LUGAL.G[AL] nu-za ŠEŠ-*YA* KUR URUKar-an-du-ni-ya-aš *Ú-UL I-DE* ku-e-da-ni-ya-at i-li-iš-ni	King of Babylonia is not a Great King," then my brother does not know the rank of Babylonia.
(57′) na-at i-ya-at-ta ku-iš DINGIR-*LUM ŠA* SAG.DU-*YA* nu<-mu> MUNUS.LUGAL GIM-an dUTU URUTÚL-na dU dḪé-bat d*IŠTAR*-ya i-ya-a[t] (58′) nu-mu *IT-TI* ŠEŠ-*KA* ḫa-an-da-it nu-za DUMU.NITA.MEŠ DUMU.MUNUS.MEŠ DÙ-nu-un nu am-me-el : an-na-a-an (over eras.) (59′) ti-iš-ša-a-an LÚ.MEŠ Ḫat-ti me-mi-iš-kán-zi ŠEŠ-*YA*-ya-an ša-a[k]-ti nam-ma-kán ŠÀ É-*TI* ku-wa-pí ú-wa-nu-un (60′) [DU]MU.MUNUS.MEŠ LUGAL ku-i-e-eš ŠÀ É-*TI* ú-e-mi-ya-nu-un nu-mu-[za-ká]n ŠU-i ḫa-a-ši-ir na-aš-za am-mu-uk (61′) [šal-la-nu-n]u-un ka-ru-ú-ma ku-i-e-eš ḫa-aš-ša-an-te-eš [ú-]e-mi-ya-nu-un nu a-pu-u-uš-ša (62′) [šal-la-nu-nu-un] [n]a-aš (eras.) EN.MEŠ KARAŠ.ḪI.A i-ya-n[u-u]n nu am-me-el-la *ŠA* SAG.DU-*YA* DINGIR-*LUM* (63′) [...-]x-ad-du nu *A-NA* ŠEŠ-*YA* ku-in DUMU.MUNUS pé-eḫ-ḫi nu-uš-ši-kán *ŠA* MUNUS.LUGAL an-na-a-an (64′) [ti-iš-ša-a-an] GAM ḫa-ma-an-kán-du nu MUNUS.LUGAL a-pád-da-ya *AQ-BI* ŠEŠ.MEŠ-*ŠU-NU*-wa-aš-ši EGIR-an-da (65′) [ti-ya-an-]zi ma-a-an-ma-at *A-NA* ŠEŠ-*YA UL* ZI-za nu *A-NA* ŠEŠ-*YA* ZI-ni lu-pa-aš-tin DÙ-mi	(57′–65′) (It was?) my personal deity who did it. And when the Sun Goddess of Arinna (together with) the Storm God, Ḫebat, and Šauška made <me> Queen, she joined me with your brother, and I produced sons and daughters, so that the people of Ḫatti often speak of my experience? and capacity for nurture?. You, my brother, know this. Furthermore, when I entered the royal household, the princesses I found in the household also gave birth under my care. I raised them (i.e., their children), and I also raised those whom I found already born. I made them military officers—may my personal deity ...! And may the gods likewise endow the daughter whom I will give to my brother with the Queen's experience? and capacity for nurture?! And I, the Queen, spoke thereby: Her brothers will be concerned for her." If this is not acceptable to my brother, will I do anything displeasing to my brother?
(rev. 1) ŠEŠ-*YA*-ma-mu ku-it kiš-an *TÀŠ-PUR* GIM-an-wa-mu DUMU.	(rev. 1) Concerning the fact that you, my brother, wrote to me as follows:

MUNUS pa-ra-a [p]é-eš-ti nu-wa-ták-kán *A-WA-TE*^{MEŠ} ku-i-e ZI-ni (rev. 2) nu-wa-ra-at-mu ma-a-an ḫa-at-ra-a-ši-ya nu-wa-ra-at-mu a-pí-[y]a *ŠU-PUR* nu a-pa-a-aš me-mi-ya-aš i-wa-ar [ŠE]Š-*YA* (rev. 3) MUNUS.LUGAL ku-it *I-NA* KUR ^{URU}A-mur-ri ú-ez-zi ma-an-ni-in-ku-wa-aḫ-mi-at-ta nu-kán *A-NA* MUNUS.LUGAL (rev. 4) ku-i-e *A-WA-TE*^{MEŠ} ZI-ni na-at *A-NA* ŠEŠ-*YA* a-pé-ez-za ḫa-at-ra-a-mi ŠEŠ-*YA*-ma-at-za *UL* mar-ki-ši ma-la-ši-at-za (rev. 5) GIM-an-na-kán *A-NA* ŠEŠ-*YA* DUMU.MUNUS ÚR-ši a-ri nu-za-k[á]n ke-e INIM.MEŠ MUNUS.LUGAL a-pí-ya-ya (rev. 6) *GAM-RA-TI*	(rev. 1) "When you turn over the daughter to me, then write to me about the matters which might be on your mind and which you might wish to write to me about." (rev. 2) This message is just what one would expect from my brother! (rev. 3) Since the Queen is coming to Amurru, I will be in your vicinity, (rev. 3) and from there I will write to my brother whatever matters are on the Queen's mind. (rev. 4) You, my brother, will not disapprove of them; you will approve of them. (rev. 5) When the daughter arrives for my brother's embrace, these matters of the Queen will be settled.
(rev. 7) ŠEŠ-*YA*-mu ku-it kiš-an *TÀŠ-PUR* NIN-*YA*-wa-mu *IŠ-PUR* DUMU.MUNUS KUR ^{URU}Kar-du-ni-ya-aš-wa ku-iš KUR ^{URU}Mi-iz-ri-i (rev. 8) pí-ya-an-za e-eš-ta nu-wa-aš-ši GIM-an LÚ.MEŠ *ṬE*$_4$*-ME* EGIR-an-da pa-a-er nu-wa-ra-at EGIR-pa *IŠ-TU* É$^{?}$ a-ra-an-ta-at (rev. 9) [nu-mu] ku-u-un me-mi-ya-an LÚ *ṬE*$_4$*-MU* LUGAL KUR ^{URU}Kar-an-du-ni-ya<-aš> $^{m.d}$EN.LÍL-EN.UKÙ.MEŠ me-mi-iš-ta (rev. 10) [am-mu]-uk-ma me-mi-ya-an ku-it *AŠ-MI* ma-a-na-an *A-NA* ŠEŠ-*YA* *Ú-UL* *AŠ-PUR* ki-nu-un-ma-mu-za ŠEŠ-*YA* ku-it mar-ki-ya-at (rev. 11) na-at *Ú-UL* nam-ma i-ya-mi *A-NA* ŠEŠ-*YA* ku-iš ZI-[ni] lu-um-pa-aš-ti-iš am-mu-uk-ma-an *A-NA* ŠEŠ-*YA* *UL* nam-ma i-ya-mi (rev. 12) ma-a-an *Ú-UL* ku-it *I-DE*	(rev. 7) Concerning what you, my brother, wrote to me as follows: "My sister wrote to me: (rev. 7–8) 'When messengers traveled to visit the daughter of Babylonia who had been given to Egypt, they were left standing outside!'" (rev. 9) Enlil-bēl-nišē, messenger of the king of Babylonia, told me this. (rev. 10) Because I heard his information, (rev. 10) should I not have written about it to my brother? (rev. 10) But now that about which my brother has now expressed his disapproval to me (rev. 11) I will not again do. I will not again do to my brother anything that displeases him. (rev. 12) If I do not know something, (rev. 12) I might do such a displeasing thing to my brother. (rev. 12) But because I already know,

nu *A-NA* ŠEŠ-*YA* lu-um-[pa-aš-ti]-in a-pu-u-un DÙ-mi ka-ru-ú-ma ku-it *I-DE* (rev. 13) nu *A-NA* ŠEŠ-*YA* lu-um-pa-aš-ti-in *Ú-UL*-pát i-ya[-mi ki-nu-na]-ya *I-DE* ku-it-za KUR URUMi-iz-ri KUR URUḪa-at-ti-ya (rev. 14) 1-*EN* KUR-*TUM* ki-ša-ri ma-a-an-ma *A-NA* KUR URUMi-iz-ri[-i? …] *Ú-UL* iš-ḫi-ú-ul nu MUNUS.LUGAL a-pád-da-ya *I-DE* (rev. 15) GIM-at am-me-el DUGUD-ni ḫa-an-da-aš i-ya-[ši nu-mu-kán] DINGIR-*LUM* ku-iš ke-e-da-ni pé-di ti-it-ta-nu-ut (rev. 16) nu-mu-kán *Ú-UL* ku-it-ki ši-wa-ri-ya-[zi nu-mu-kán] aš-šu-la-an *Ú-UL* ši-wa-ri-ya-at (rev. 17) nu-mu-za LÚ*ḪA-DA-NU* DUMU[.MUNUS-*YA* ……. da-at-ti]	(rev. 13) I will certainly not do anything displeasing to my brother. (rev. 13) And now I know that Egypt and Ḫatti will become a single country. (rev. 14) Even if for the land of Egypt … is not a treaty, (rev. 14) the Queen knows thereby how you will conclude it out of consideration for my dignity. (rev. 15) The deity who installed me in this place does not deny me anything. (rev. 16) He/She has not denied me *happiness*. (rev. 17) You, as son-in-law, will take my daughter in marriage.
(rev. 18) ŠEŠ-*YA*-ma-za ku-it-ma-an x[-…] (rev. 19) na-ak-ki-ya ḫa-at-ri-iš[-ki-…] (rev. 20) nu-mu-kán a-pu-u-uš-ša x[-…] (rev. 21) nu-mu-kán DUMU.MEŠ-*YA* ku-i-[…] (rev. 22) am-me-el-la-mu-kán […]	(rev. 18–22) While my daughter … to an important … writes … And these to me …… Which of my children … my …

Commentary

obv. 10 Using Singer's restoration and translation (1998, 537–38): "… that the house of the land of Ḫatti is a house transferred" instead of the earlier [… *na-at ar*?-*ḫa*? *wa*?-*a*]*r-nu-wa-an* É-*e*[*r*] "[it is [a bu]rned [down] house."

obv. 12 Starke (apud Heinhold-Krahmer 2007b, 201) suggests that the "daughter of heaven and earth" refers to the daughter of the Hittite royal couple, Ḫattušili III and Puduḫepa, as the pendant of the divine pair Storm God of Heaven and Sun Goddess of Arinna.

obv. 16 Edited in CHD L–N, 411 (*natta* b 2′ a′ 1″).

obv. 39 Edited in CHD L–N, 412 (*natta* b 2′ c′).

obv. 65 Edited in CHD *lumpasti-* a.

rev. 2 on *iwar* ŠEŠ-*YA* Hoffner 1993a, 47 (example 60).

rev. 7–17 is discussed in de Martino and Imparati 1995, 106, where the authors write:

> Certainly, it is possible that Babylonian princesses were always the victims of bad luck. It seems more plausible to us, however, to think that Puduḫepa was reusing an episode from the past, which must have been well known in Near Eastern court circles. Her purpose was to procure an important position in the Egyptian court for her daughter, emphasizing to the Pharaoh the poor reputation he had with other courts as to how foreign princesses taken as brides to Egypt ended up. The fact that Puduḫepa specifies even the name of the Babylonian ambassador [Enlil-bēl-nišē] who would have told her the story is not necessarily a sign of veracity, but the use of real elements can function to give verisimilitude to her tale.

rev. 11–13 Edited in CHD *lumpasti-* a.

99. KUB 26.91
From the King of Aḫḫiyawa to the Hittite King

Text: Bo 1485. **Find spot:** Unknown. **Copy:** KUB 26.91. **Edition**: Sommer 1932, 268–74; Hagenbuchner 1989b, 319–20 (no. 219). **Discussion**: (older discussions listed in CTH 183); Starke 1981a (on *guršawar* "island"); Ünal 1991, 20; de Martino 1996, 30–33; Klengel 1999, 105 [A4?]; Taracha 2001, 419–22; Bachvarova 2002, 32; Gurney 2002, 135; Freu 2004a, 293–99; Miller 2005, 285 n. 5 (on Kammenhuber's correct identification of the sender); F. Starke apud Rutherford 2006, 5 n. 10; Heinhold-Krahmer 2007b, 196 n. 49.

Sommer and Starke have both made considerable conjectural restorations that I do not feel sufficiently confident to assume here. In the following I am heavily indebted to an as-yet-unpublished manuscript of Craig Melchert. What does seem clear is the following. Because of a diplomatic marriage (*ḫamakta* in line 9) between the great grandfather of the king of Aḫḫiyawa, perhaps named Kagamunaš, and an Aššuwan princess, it appears that the king of Aḫḫiyawa claims the right to these islands, perhaps because they were ceded to his ancestor as part of the woman's dowry (*iwāru*). But then the Hittite king Tudḫaliya, the great grandfather of the addressee, conquered Aššuwa (line 9). And from this point on in the letter its damaged state does not permit us to follow the train of thought.

This tablet is probably a translation into Hittite of a communication exchanged between trusted bilingual emissaries at the common border between Aḫḫiyawan and Hittite territory. It is not a translation into Hittite made by a scribe at the court of the Aḫḫiyawan king, but one made by the Hittite emissary and conveyed by him to the court of Ḫattuša and delivered together with his oral recollections of the communication from the Aḫḫiyawan emissary.

This fragmentary text is a letter of an Aḫḫiyawan king to his Hittite counterpart, whom he regards on equal terms as Great King, calling him "my brother" (obv. 1, rev. 14′, 15′). I agree with de Martino (1996) and Taracha (2001, 418–19) that the letter alludes to the events recounted also in the Manapa-Tarḫunta letter KUB 19.5 + KBo 19.79 (text 100): that is, the smiting of [the] land of Lazpa (Lesbos) by Atpā of Millawanda at the instigation of Piyama-radu. This incident involved the *ṢARIPŪTU*-men of Manapa-Tarḫunta and the Hittite king, who claim that they came to the island "across the sea" (line 16) and now accept this change of suzerain. These operations of Millawandan troops on the offshore islands controlled by Manapa-Tarḫunta, Hittite vassal in the Šeḫa River Land, were probably prior to the Alakšandu treaty and took place during the reign of Muwattalli II. The Aḫḫiyawan ruler was aware of these actions and accepted them.

The preserved part of the letter mentions "islands" (*guršawara*) that the king of Aḫḫiyawa claims and that the Hittite king claims that the Storm God gave (*paiš*) to him, that, allowed his armies to conquer. That the addressee, whose words are quoted in lines 5–7, is in fact the Hittite king, is argued by Gurney (2002, 135) on the basis of this very statement that the Storm God—the main Hittite male deity—gave the islands to him.

(obv. 1) [*UM-MA* ^{m}… LUGAL.GAL LUGA]L$^{?}$ KUR ^{URU}Aḫ-ḫi-ya-w[a … *A-NA* ^{m}x-x-x-x LUGAL.GAL LUGAL KUR Ḫat-ti ŠEŠ-*YA QÍ-BÍ-MA*]	(1) Thus speaks PN, Great King, King of the land of Aḫḫiyawa: Say to PN_2, Great King, King of the land of Ḫatti, my brother:
(2) [… *I-NA*] k]u$^{?}$-e-ša-an x[…] (3) […]x-x ku-ru-ur iš-tar-na [ki-ša-at …] (4) [x-x] ki-ša-at nu ak-kán-ta-aš : ar-x[…]	(2) … (3) hostility has broken out. … (4) has occurred. And the … of the dead …
(5) [x-]ra-a-an-ni MU.KAM-ti-mu ŠEŠ-*YA* ḫa-at-ra[-e-eš] ú[-uk-wa-at-ták-kán tu-e-el : gur-ša-wa-ra *Ú-UL* ku-it-ki ar-ḫa da-aḫ-ḫu-un] (6) tu-e-el-wa : gur-ša-wa-ra ku-e	(5) My brother, you wrote to me in the … year (as follows): "I did not take from you any of your islands. (6) Your islands which you call (your) inheritance from the King of

z[i-ik *ŠA* LUGAL KUR [URU]A-aš-šu-wa i-wa-a-ru ḫal-ze-eš-ti nu-wa-ra-at] (7) [d]U ARAD-an-ni am-mu-uk pa-iš LUGAL [KUR]A-a[š-šu-wa-ma *A-NA* LUGAL KUR Aḫ-ḫi-ya-wa a-aš-ši-ya-an-za e-eš-ta] (8) (eras.) [m!]Ka-ga-mu-na-aš-za-kán *A-BA A-BA A-B*[*I-YA*? … a-pa-a-aš-ma-aš-ši-za DUMU. MUNUS-*SÚ*] (9) pé-ra-an ḫa-ma-ak-ta nu-za [m]Tu-ud-ḫ[a-li-ya-aš *A-BA A-BA A-BI-KA* LUGAL KUR A-aš-šu-wa tar-aḫ-ta] (10) na-an-za-an ARAD-na-aḫ-ta nu : ku[r-ša-wa-ra ka-ru-ú *ŠA* LUGAL KUR Aḫ-ḫi-ya-wa e-eš-ta-pát nu *A-NA* ŠEŠ-*YA* a-pád-da-an] (11) še-er ḫa-at-ra-a-nu-un *A-*[*NA* …] (12) *Ù ŠA* LUGAL [KUR]Aḫ-ḫi-y[a-wa …] (13) an-ni-ša-an-ma[…] (14) LUGAL [KUR]A-aš-šu-w[a…] (15) nu-kán d[u-…] (16) *I-NA* KUR [URU][…] (17) me-na-aḫ-ḫa[-an-da …] (18) ke-e-x[…] (19) *A-NA*[…] (Break)	Aššuwa, (7) the Storm God gave them to me as subjects." Now the King of Aššuwa was on good terms with the King of Aḫḫiyawa, (8) so that my great grandfather, Kagamuna, … (8) and had previously married his daughter. (9) Tudḫaliya, your great grandfather, defeated the King of Aššuwa, (10) and made him a subject. The islands? *previously belonged to the King of Aḫḫiyawa.* So I wrote to my brother about that matter. (11) And … and of the king of Aḫḫiyawa … (13) Previously … (14) the king of Aššuwa … (15) … (16) in the land of … (17) opposite … (18) this/these … (19) to …
(rev. 2) [n]am-ma […] (rev. 3) nu ARAD-*Y*[*A* …] (rev. 4) an-da x[…] (rev. 5) EGIR-pa x[…] rev. (6) [ZA]G-aš-ši x[…] (rev. 7) [Ḫ]UL-lu ku[…] (rev. 8) [a]m-me-el an-n[a?-…] (rev. 9) [*I*]*Š-TU* [KUR]Mi-e[l-la-wa-an-da …] (rev. 10) [U]N-ša-an UN.MEŠ[…] (rev. 11) [*I-*]*NA QA-QA-RI-Y*[*A* …]	(rev. 2–11) Then … And my servant ……… back/again … the border … evil … my … from Millawanda … person, people … in my territory …
(rev. 12) am-mu-uk-ma-an-kán[…] (rev. 13) ŠEŠ-*YA* uš-ke nam[-ma …] (rev. 14) [x] ŠEŠ-*YA* ARAD.MEŠ![…]	(rev. 12–14) But I … him/it. My brother, see … Then … my brother, the servants …
(Tablet breaks away here)	

100. KUB 19.5 + KBo 19.79
To King Muwattalli II from
Manapa-Tarḫunta of the Šeḫa River Land

Text: VAT 7454 + Bo 2561 + 1481/u. **Find spot:** Temple I (Lower City). **Copy**: KUB 19.5 + KBo 19.79. **Edition**: Houwink ten Cate 1983–1984, 38–64. **Discussion**: Heinhold-Krahmer 1977, 173–75, 208, 210, 222–23, 309; 1983, 85, 93; 1999, 580; 2004, 37–38; Neu 1983, 287 n. 12 (on m*Kaš-šú-ú-uš*, line 24); Beal 1992, 470; Gurney 1992, 220–21; Starke 1997, 453; Hawkins 1998b, 16 n. 67, 23 n. 137; Klengel 1999, 203 [A5.1]; Easton et al. 2002, 99; Bryce 2003a, 38 n. 14, 71; 2003b, 123, 208; 2006, 182; Altman 2004, 146–47; Freu 2004a, 300–301; de Martino 2005a; 2006, 168–70. ee especially Singer 2008b for the identity of the LÚ.MEŠ *ṢĀRIPŪTI* as "purple-dyers," and their mission to Lazpa.

The Šeḫa River Land was a kingdom belonging to the group of western Anatolian lands called the "Arzawa lands." It occupied one of the river valleys lying north of Milawata or Millawanda (Miletos). The river in question was probably either the Caicos or the Hermos, if not the Maeander (see, e.g., Gurney 1992, 220–21). From the additional text provided by the join we learn that a Hittite army on its way to Wiluša had to pass through the Šeḫa River Land. Given the likely route taken, Wiluša must therefore have been situated north of the Šeḫa River Land in the Troad. Close by Wiluša was one of its dependencies, the offshore island of Lazpa (Lesbos).[241]

Manapa-Tarḫunta had broken his allegiance to Ḫatti in the early days of Muršili II's reign. He had avoided Hittite retaliation by a last-minute capitulation, when a Hittite army under Muršili's command reached his gates and was preparing to take his city by storm. Muršili relented and refrained from action when Manapa-Tarḫunta's mother came out of the city and begged for mercy on her son's behalf. Muršili reaffirmed his status as a Hittite vassal, and after this he appears to have remained loyal. As time passed, however, Manapa-Tarḫunta had become increasingly less effective in the advancement of Hittite interests in his area.

Sometime during the early part of the reign of Muršili's successor Muwattalli, Manapa-Tarḫunta suffered a humiliating defeat at the hands of Piyama-radu (see line 7), who installed Atpā of Millawanda over him in a supervisory capacity.

In the broken lines that begin the preserved part of this fragment of a letter, a Hittite army was led into the area to deal with a threat in Wiluša—either a local rebellion or an attack upon Wiluša attempting to detach it from allegiance to Ḫatti. This is mentioned in the past tense ("brought," line 3). Immediately, Manapa-Tarḫunta makes a statement in the present tense ("[I, howe]ver, am ill. I am seriously ill.[242] Illness (6) has [pro]strated me!," lines 5–6). Because of this change of tense, it is unclear if, as has been suggested, the illness was his excuse for not participating with the Hittite army in the campaign to Wiluša. De Martino (2006, 169) understands the illness as his reason for not being able to repulse the atacks of Piyama-radu and Atpā on the island of Lazpa (= Lesbos). Neither view can truly be proven.

The meaning of the term $^{LÚ.MEŠ}$*ṢARIPŪTI* has been thoroughly discussed by Singer (2008b). He has put forward a convincing case that these are "purple-dyers," and that their mission to Lazpa was to make a presentation of purple-dyed stuffs to the unnamed deity on that island.

(1) [*A-NA* ^{d}UTU-*ŠI* EN-*Y*]*A*? *QÍ-BI-MA U*[*M-M*]*A* ^{m}Ma-na-pa-^{d}U ARAD-*KA-MA*	(1) To His Majesty, my lord, speak! Thus says Manapa-Tarḫunta, your servant!
(2) [ka-a-ša-kán ŠÀ KUR-]*TI* ḫu-u-ma-an SIG$_5$-in	(2) At present all is well in the country.
(3) [^{m}o o o o o o][243] ú-it ÉRIN.MEŠ ^{KUR}Ḫat-ti-ya ú-wa-te-et (4) [na-at o o o]x-an EGIR-pa ^{KUR}Wi$_5$-lu-ša GUL-u-wa-an-zi pa-a-er (5) [am-mu-uk-m]a iš-tar-ak-zi GIG-zi-ma-mu ḪUL-lu GIG-aš-mu (6) [me?-ek?-ki?][244] ta-ma-aš-ša-an ḫar-zi	(3) .... came ... and brought Hittite troops with him. (4) And they ..... went back to the country of Wiluša in order to attack (it). (5) I, however, am ill. I am seriously ill.[245] Illness (6) has prostrated me!
(7) [^{m}Pí-ya-m]a-ra-du-uš-ma-mu GIM-an lu-ri-ya-aḫ-ta nu-mu-kán ^{m}At-pa-a-an (8) [o o o o] UGU[246] ti-it-ta-nu-ut nu ^{KUR}La-az-pa-an GUL-aḫ-ta (9) [o o o ^{LÚ}].^{MEŠ}*ṢA-RI-PU-TI* ku-e-eš ku-e-eš am-mi-el e-še-er (10) [nu-uš-ši-kán ḫ]u-u-ma-an-du-uš-pát an-da ḫa-an-da-er *ŠA* ^{d}UTU-*ŠI*-ya ku-e-eš [ku-e-eš e-še-er] (11) [o o $^{LÚ.MEŠ}$*ṢA-R*]*I-PU-TI* na-at-kán ḫu-u-ma-an-du-uš-pát	(7) When Piyama-radu had humiliated me, set up Atpā (8–9) over? me, and attacked (the country of) Lazpa, (10) all of the purple-dyers without exception who were mine joined with him. And all of the purple-dyers of His Majesty without exception joined with him. (12) And x-x-ḫuḫa, the domestic and table man, who had been (13) put in charge? of the purple-dyers,

an-da ḫa-an-da-er (12) [o o o (-?)] ḫu-ḫa-aš ku-iš LÚAMA.A.TU LÚ <GIŠ>BANŠUR *A-NA* LÚ.MEŠ*ṢE-RI-PU-TE*-kán (13) [an?-da? ú?-e?-]ri?-ya-an-za e-eš-ta nu-kán a-pu-u-uš-ša an-da SI×SÁ-at (14) [m o - o -]x[247]-ḫu-ḫa-aš LÚ.MEŠ*ṢE-RI-PU-TE*-ma *A-NA* mAt-pa-a kiš-ša-an (15) [ar-ku-w]a-ar i-[e-]er an-za-aš-wa-an-na-aš ar-kam-ma-na-al-li-uš? (16) [nu-wa-kán] A.AB.BA p[ár-ra-]an-ta ú-wa-u-en nu-wa-an-na-aš ar-kam-ma-an (17) [píd-da-u-]e-ni nu-wa mŠi-ig-ga-ú-na-aš wa-aš-ta-aš (18) [an-za-aš-ma-w]a *Ú-UL* ku-it?-ki i-[y]a-u-en nu-uš-ma-aš GIM-an (19) [ar-kam-m]a-an ar-ku-wa-a[r] ⌜i-e⌝-er mAt-pa-a-aš-ma-wa<-ra>-aš (20) [*Ú-UL*] ar-nu-ut ma-a-an-wa-ra-[aš a]r-ḫa tar-ni-iš-ta (21) [mPí-ya-ma]-ra-du-uš-ma-[aš-š]i? mŠi-[ig-ga-ú-n]a-an *IŠ-PUR* nu-uš-ši kiš-ša-an (22) [me-mi-iš-]ta tu-uk-wa dU-aš! [pí-i]a-na-it EGIR-pa-wa-ra-aš ku-wa-at (23) [pé-eš-ti] mAt-pa-a-aš-ma GIM-an INIM mP[í-i]a-ma-ra-du *IŠ-ME* (24) [na-aš] EGIR-pa *Ú-UL* pé-eš-ta k[i-n]u-na-kán GIM-an mKaš-šú-ú-uš (25) [ka-a an-da] a?-ar-aš mKu-pa-an-ta-dL[AMMA-aš-m]a *A-NA* mAt-pa-a *IŠ-PUR* (26) [LÚ.MEŠ*ṢA-RI-PU-T*]*I*ḪI.A-wa ku-e-eš *ŠA* dU[TU-*ŠI*] a-pí-ya (27) [nu-wa-ra-aš ar-ḫa] tar-ni! nu LÚ.MEŠ*ṢA-RI-P*[*U-TI ŠA*] DINGIR.MEŠ ku-e-eš *ŠA* dUTU-*ŠI*[-ya] (28) [ku-e-eš e-še-er n]a-aš ḫu-u-ma-a[n-du-uš-pát ar]-ḫa [tar]-na-aš (29) [nu-mu mKu-pa-a]n-ta-

x-x-ḫuḫa made those too meet (with him). (14) However, …-ḫuḫa (and) the purple-dyers addressed a petition (15) to Atpā in the following words: “We are purple-dyers? (to the Hittite king?) (16) and we came across the sea. Let us present (17) (our) purple-dyed stuffs! Šiggauna rebelled,[249] (18) but we did nothing whatsoever!” And when they (19) had made their purple-dyed stuffs (the subject of) a petition, Atpā (20) did not carry them off. He would have let them go home, (21) but Piyama-radu dispatched Šiggauna to him and spoke to him (22) in this manner: “The Storm God presented to you a boon, why should you (now) (23) give them back?” When Atpā in his turn heard the word of Piyama-radu, (24) he did not return them to me. But now, when Kaššū (25) arrived here, Kupanta-LAMMA sent a message to Atpā: (26) “The purple-dyers of His Majesty who are there (with you), (27) let them go home!” And he (Atpā) let the purple-dyers who belong to the gods (i.e., to the temple[s]), and (28) who belong to His Majesty all (of them) without exception go home. (29) And Kupanta-LAMMA wrote to me as follows: (30) “We did what you said to me, (31) ‘Write to Atpā about the purple-dyers!’ To Atpā (32) I did write about the purple-dyers!” (33) … he shall/did …. the basket-weavers. (34) to Kupanta-LAMMA

^{d}[LAMMA-aš kiš-ša-an *IŠ-*]*PUR* (*long eras.*) (30) [nu-wa i-ya-u-en] tu-uk[-wa-mu ku-it *TÁQ*]-*BI* (31) [*A-NA* ^{m}At-pa-a-wa … *ŠU*?-]*PUR A-NA* ^{m}At-pa-a-wa (32) [… *AŠ-PU*]*R* (33) […] ^{LÚ}AD.KID-ta-ra-aš-wa-<ra->aš-kán (34) [… *A-N*]*A* ^{m}Ku-pa-an-ta-^{d}LAMMA (35) […] EN-*YA* x (36) [… EGI]R-pa GUL-ḫu-un	(35) … my lord (36) … I raided again (or: I undertook a counter-raid).
(Breaks off)	

Commentary

22 Šiggauna's word to Atpā in line 22 echo the words of the king of Aḫḫiyawa quoted just above.

101. KUB 14.3
From King Ḫattušili III to the King of Aḫḫiyawa
("Tawagalawa Letter")

Text: VAT 6692. **Find spot:** Unknown. **Photo**: Forrer 1929, Tafel I–II; Sommer 1932, pl. I–II. **Copy**: KUB 14.3. **Edition**: Forrer 1929, 95–232; Sommer 1932, 2–194. **Translation:** Garstang and Gurney 1959, 111–14; Bernabé and Álvarez-Pedrosa 2004, 246–50; Miller 2006, 240–47. **Discussion**: more extensive treatments: Page 1959; Huxley 1960; Macqueen 1968; Bryce 1979; 2003a, 76–78, 82, 85; 2003b, 65, 199–212; Bryce 2003c; Güterbock 1983 (reprinted in Hoffner 1997h, 201–4); Heinhold-Krahmer 1983, 81–97; 1984 (reprinted in Hoffner 1997h, 205–10); 1990 (reprinted in Hoffner 1997h, 211–16); 1992 (reprinted in Hoffner 1997h, 217–22); Singer 1983b; Popko 1984 (dating); Heinhold-Krahmer 1986, 2002, 2004; Ünal 1991; Starke 1997; Parker 1999 (on the text, esp. I 71–74 and II 61–62); Gurney 2002. Shorter notes on the text: Alparslan 2005, 34–37; Bachvarova 2002, 36–37; Bryce 2003c, 65 n. 17; Cohen 2001, 79 n. 35; 2002, 119–20, 126–27; de Martino and Imparati 2001, 352; 2006, 170–71; de Roos 2005, 54–55; Easton et al. 2002, 97, 99–100; Freu 1992, 82–83; 2004a, 307; Goedegebuure 2002, 67–68; Hagenbuchner 1989b, 318–19 (no. 216)); Hajnal 2003, 38 n. 55; Hawkins 1998b, 17 n. 73, 23 n. 136, 28–29 n. 176, 181; Heinhold-Krahmer et al. 1979, 175–

76; 1983, 88; 2001, 192; 2004, 38; Hoffmann 1992, 289–90; Hoffner 2007, 393; Jasink 2003, 274 n. 21; 2005, 211 n. 10 (KUB 14.3 is miswritten as KUB 19.3); Klengel 1999, 206 [B7], 246 [A23]; Mountjoy 1998, 48; Singer 1983b, 212; Starke 1990, 127, 377.

It needs to be said at the outset that the term "Tawagalawa letter," by which this text has long been known, is a misnomer on two counts, as Heinhold-Krahmer (2002, 359–60) and Bryce (2003b, 203) have pointed out. Firstly, although his name occurs a few times in this text, Tawagalawa is a peripheral figure, by no means the main subject, which is Piyama-radu. Secondly, although the text is clearly intended to lay out argumentation to be communicated to the king of Aḫḫiyawa and uses the correct diplomatic forms (such as "my brother"), the layout of the material on the tablet (two columns on each side of a multi-tablet composition) is unprecedented with letters and points rather in the direction of a preparatory draft, or, as Heinhold-Krahmer suggests,[251] a briefing document for the envoy(s) who will go to the court of the king of Aḫḫiyawa and present the Hittite king's case (but see above in §1.2.8). But despite this—to me quite convincing—argument that KUB 14.3 is not, properly speaking, a "letter," it belongs in the present collection as an example of a document type that doubtless on many occasions provided the material and the argumentation for the composing of a lengthy diplomatic letter.

As can be seen from the lengthy bibliography above, this tablet has occasioned more animated discussion than any other single tablet in the Hittite collection. It was first read and discussed by the Assyriologist-Hittitologist Emil Forrer in the 1920s. Forrer was excited by having before him the first contemporaneous documentary testimony to the historical existence of figures from the ancient epic traditions of the Greeks surrounding the Trojan War. He understood Tawagalawa to be a Hittite approximation of the Mycenean Greek name Etewoklewes (Eteocles). His enthusiasm, as well as the generally rudimentary knowledge of Hittite grammar and lexicon in those early days, led him to make many minor mistakes and made it easier for sharp-eyed critics and skeptics—among them especially Ferdinand Sommer—to lampoon his ideas. For decades thereafter Forrer's ideas about Myceneans in Hittite texts were generally ignored. But in the last decades of the twentieth century new evidence and the careful reevaluation of old evidence led a number of leading scholars, among them H. G. Güterbock and O. R. Gurney, to advocate an improved version of them.

The Tablet

This tablet was excavated during the period when Hugo Winckler and Makridi were directing the excavations, and information regarding the findspot of the tablet is unfortunately lacking. The tablet is presently in the holdings of the Vorderasiatisches Museum in Berlin.

The tablet's colophon bears the scribe's annotation "tablet 3, (composition) complete," indicating that the tablet was the third and last of a lengthy text. Its author was a Hittite king of the first half of the thirteenth century. On historical grounds most consider this king to have been Ḫattušili III (ruled ca. 1267–1237), but some (e.g., Ünal 1991 and Gurney 2002) think it was his older brother, Muwattalli II (who ruled ca. 1295–1272). Both the paleography and orthography of the tablet favor a dating in the reign of Ḫattušili III (Hoffner 1982b: 134, 136–37 n. 27; Popko 1984). The text is addressed to an unnamed king of Aḫḫiyawa, a major power at the time in far western Anatolia and the offshore islands, most likely an extension of Mycenean Greece. For a thorough discussion of the identity of the author and addressee see Gurney 2002.

Since the first and second tablets are missing, we lack the crucial opening lines of the text, identifying both sender and addressee. Because this third tablet is in places badly preserved, some more optimistic interpreters have been led to make bold and conjectural restorations. I agree with Miller, who pursued what some might call a "minimalistic" treatment:

> As subsequently discovered join pieces to other edited texts have often shown, the restorations of the modern scholar are often incorrect, misleading, or at the least inaccurate. For this reason only the most obvious restorations will be accepted here and more daring ones avoided where possible.[252]

The Location of Aḫḫiyawa

Today the majority opinion is that the land of Aḫḫiyawa is to be identified with the area of control of the Mycenean Greeks, which included parts of the western coast of Asia Minor. There is still no agreement as to the location of the center of the kingdom of Aḫḫiyawa, whether on mainland Anatolia, on an off-shore island, or in some part of mainland Greece. Nor is there unanimity on the location of some key geographical terms relating to the western coast of Anatolia, especially Wiluša and Taruiša.

The Aḫḫiyawan king who is addressed in this text would appear to be overseas, either in the Greek isles (Rhodes is a favorite suggestion), or—

less likely—in mainland Greece (either Thebes or Mycenae), not visiting his overseas possessions on the coast of Asia Minor itself. The Hittite king cannot, therefore, meet face-to-face with him, since Hittite royalty and military assiduously avoided sea travel.[253] But he can communicate in writing and via the oral elaborations of his messengers.

As for the geographical extent of Anatolian Aḫḫiyawa, Mountjoy (1998) favors what she calls "the southern Interface," which would include coastal points south of Miletus, with the governmental center and the royal palace on Rhodes. Miletos (= Hittite Millawanda), at the north end of this Interface

> seems to have been a thriving port geographically isolated from interior Anatolia. Indeed, although Mursili II raided it . . ., he seems not to have been able to hold it, probably owing to difficulties of communication with the interior. . . . I suggest that . . . [in Muršili II's reign] it was already part of Ahhiyawa, although this cannot be proven from the Hittite texts. By the reign of Hattusili III [the time of the "Tawagalawa letter"] it is clear that Ahhiyawa did control Millawanda/Miletos and that its king was a Great King in contrast to the Kings of Mira and the Seha River Land who have vassal status. People escape by ship to Ahhiyawa, and from it conduct raids on Hittite vassal territory, which also suggests it must be close by. That Tawagalawa, the brother of the Great King, was in Millawanda, but that Atpa governed it also indicates that the seat of government for Ahhiyawa was not in Miletos, but on one of the off-shore islands. The language spoken would presumably have been Luvian. The pivotal points of Ahhiyawa were the harbour at Miletos and the control of the Marmara straits by Trianda/Ialysos, the route used by shipping to and from the Greek Mainland and the Near East, since a detour round Rhodes would have involved sailing through the heavy seas between Karpathos and Rhodes. Trianda/Ialysos may have acted as an emporium for this trade. (1998, 51)

Others disagree with this location for the governmental center,[254] preferring somewhere on mainland Greece .

The Aḫḫiyawan king has scribes at his disposal who are able to write in cuneiform on clay tablets that were sent to the Hittite king (Heinhold-Krahmer 2007b, 192, citing i 55, iii 63, iv 18, and iv 32).

Since the messengers of the king are themselves persons of high rank, sometimes even blood relatives of the king (Singer 1983a, 9–23; and Hagenbuchner 1989a, 17 [with literature]), they were well qualified to elaborate on the wishes of their sovereign. That in the process sometimes the real words and wishes of the sovereign were falsified can be seen from a passage in the current text (iv 32–57, on which see Sommer 1932, 179–88; and Hagenbuchner 1989a, 8–9 with n. 16). See also text 94: 1–6 and n. 29.

Tawagalawa himself, who seems to be a brother of the Aḫḫiyawan king, appears from time to time in the city of Millawanda. It is still uncertain if he was still alive at the time the text was written, but he seems to have ruled over some of the Aḫḫiyawan possessions in Asia Minor. The Lukka Lands mentioned in the text are classical Lycia, and Wiluša is Ilios/Troy.

Piyama-radu was a contemporary of three Hittite kings: Muwattalli II, Muršili III (Urḫi-Teššub), and Ḫattušili III. Nowhere is he given the title "prince" (DUMU.LUGAL), but noble, perhaps royal, birth is presumed by his request for recognition by the Hittite sovereign as a vassal king.[255] He has a brother named Laḫurzi and two sons-in-law (Atpā and Awayana). The latter two men are representatives resident in the city of Millawanda. Sommer and Bryce believe he was a rebellious Hittite dignitary. Forrer, Starke, and Heinhold-Krahmer see him as a western Anatolian vassal prince who was stirring up trouble for the Hittites. Starke thinks he was a scion of the dynasty of Arzawa removed by Muršili II. He is not the same man who is mentioned in a letter to the Hittite king that was found at Ortaköy (text 88 in the present corpus) and dates to the end of the Middle Hittite period.

Throughout the text the unnamed king of Aḫḫiyawa is addressed as "my brother," the standard protocol address among sovereign kings of the time who were of equal rank. A subordinate king would never address a superior one using these words. In fact, in this very text (ii 13–15) the Hittite king refers to the king of Aḫḫiyawa as "my equal" (*ammel annauliš*).

The Contents of the Third Tablet

The preserved text begins in the middle of an episode whose initial course was narrated at the end of the lost second tablet.

Piyama-radu has been raiding the Lukka Lands and other territories, western dependencies of the Hittites. He had been carrying off groups of people, delivering them over to Anatolian representatives of the Aḫḫiyawan government. Bryce (2003a) thinks two groups were involved: one defecting willingly from the Hittite domain, and the other constrained by Piyama-radu, and that both were in the western coastal lands awaiting "transshipment" to mainland Greece.

After Piyama-radu attacked Attarimma,[256] representatives from the Lukka Lands asked Tawagalawa for help, and subsequently the Hittite king as well (i 3–5). The Hittite king went to Millawanda to apprehend Piyama-radu. When he reached Šallapa, he received a message from Piyama-radu, asking to be taken as a Hittite vassal (ARAD "servant") and escorted to the king's presence by the appropriate royal representative for confirmation (i

6–8). But when the Hittite king complied, Piyama-radu rejected the royal representative (the crown prince) and demanded to be confirmed as a king on the spot. When the Hittite king then advanced to Waliwanda, he sent another message, demanding that Piyama-radu vacate the city of Iyalanda (Alinda) and allow the king to recover his subjects there. But when the king reached Iyalanda, he was ambushed by Laḫurzi, Piyama-radu's brother (i 22–31). Piyama-radu escaped from Millawanda by ship, probably to Aḫḫiyawa, and took with him his family and a large number of prisoners from the Hittite king's vassal lands. Piyama-radu left his household in Aḫḫiyawa and used that country as a base from which to raid the Hittite vassal lands. It seems that Millawanda was under Aḫḫiyawan protection. The Hittite king claims that he did not enter Millawanda, but stopped at its border. Whereupon he wrote to Atpā, the ruler of Millawanda and the son-in-law of Piyama-radu, with complaints that Atpā should pass along to the king of Aḫḫiyawa. He suggested that a charioteer named Dabala-Tarḫunda, who had ridden on the same chariot with Tawagalawa as well as with the Hittite king, should go to Aḫḫiyawa and act as a hostage for the safe conduct of Piyama-radu. Lest the reader think that Dabala-Tarḫunta, who is styled a "charioteer" (^{LÚ}*KAR-TAPPU*), would be expected to bring Piyama-radu back on his chariot, and thus be restricted to land travel, thus eliminating the possibility that Aḫḫiyawa was anywhere other than on the Anatolian mainland, Easton and Hawkins have pointed out:

> It is well established that by the late Hittite Empire 'charioteers' served as confidential agents (Singer 1983: 3–25. esp. 9), not simply as "drivers", and in the cited context, contrary to what the unwary may have been led to believe, there is no reference to Dabalatarhunda bringing Piyama-radu from Ahhiyawa by chariot. This may be contrasted with an earlier passage in the same letter, where the Hittite king observes that he sent the crown prince to fetch Piyama-radu from Millawanda with the instructions: "Go, drive over, take him by the hand, mount him in a chariot with you and bring him before me" (i 68–70). Millawanda was on the mainland, but Ahhiyawa was not. (2002, 100)

The fact that Piyama-radu is continually raiding Hittite lands and then escaping to Aḫḫiyawa suggested to Mountjoy that Aḫḫiyawa had to be close to the Anatolian Mainland, that is, on an offshore island (Mountjoy 1998, 48).

In the transliteration given below I have marked with the sign * corrections to the KUB copy based upon either Goetze's own corrections published in KUB XIV or the photo published in Sommer 1932. In footnotes to the present edition, the abbreviation "G." refers to these corrections of Goetze's in the front matter to KUB XIV.

(i 1–15) [257] [nam-m]a$^?$-aš pa-it nu ^{URU}At-ta-ri-im-ma-a[n] ar-ḫa (2) [ḫar-g]a-nu-ut na-an ar-ḫa wa-ar-nu-ut *IŠ-TU* BÀD É.MEŠ LUGAL (3) [nu] *A-NA* ^{m}Ta-wa-ga-la-wa LÚ.MEŠ ^{URU}Lu-uk-ka$_4$-a G[IM-]an ZI-ni (4) [a]r-nu-e-er na-aš ke-e-da-aš KUR-e-aš ú-et ú-uk-ka$_4$[306] *QA-TAM-MA* (5) ZI-ni ar-nu-e-er nu$^!$ ke-e-da-aš KUR-e-aš GAM ú-wa-nu-un (6) nu GIM-an *I-NA* ^{URU}Šal-la-pa ar-ḫu-un nu-m[u U]N-an IGI-an-da (7) u-i-ya-at ARAD-an-ni-wa-mu da-a nu-wa-mu ^{LÚ}tu-uḫ-kán-ti-in (8) u-i-ya nu-wa-mu *IT-TI* ^{d}UTU-*ŠI* ú-wa-te-ez-zi nu-uš-ši (9) ^{LÚ}*TAR-TE-NU* u-i-ya-nu-un i-it-wa-ra-an-za-an-kán *A-NA* ^{GIŠ}GIGIR (10) GAM-an ti-it-ta-nu-ut nu-wa-ra-an u-wa-ti a[-pa-a-š]a$^?$-kán (11) ^{LÚ}*TAR-TE-NU* ka-ri-ya-nu-ut nu-za *Ú-UL* me-m[a-aš] ^{LÚ}*TAR-TE-NU*-ma (12) *Ú-UL A-NA* LUGAL a-ya-wa-la-aš ŠU-an-ma-an ḫa[r-ta$^?$] nu-uš-ši-za EGIR-an (13) *Ú-UL* me-ma-aš na-an *A-NA PA-NI* KUR.KUR.MEŠ te-pa-wa-[a]ḫ-ta$^!$ nu a-pa-a-at nam-ma-pát *IQ-BI* LUGAL-*UT-TA*-wa-mu ka-a pé-di-iš-ši (15) pa-a-i ma-a-an-wa *Ú-UL*-ma nu-wa *Ú-UL* ú-wa-m[i]	**1.** (i 1–15) Next he[258] went (there) and destroyed the town Attarimma, and burned it down including the fortification wall of the royal acropolis.[259] (3–4) As the men of Lukka notified Tawagalawa,[260] so that he came into these lands. (4–5) they likewise notified me,[261] so that I (too) came down into these lands. When I reached the town Šallapa, he (i.e., Piyama-radu[262]) sent a man to meet me, (saying:) "Take me as (your) vassal. Send the crown prince[263] to me, that he may escort me to Your Majesty." (8–10) So I sent to him the crown prince, (saying:) "Go stand him alongside yourself on the chariot, and escort him here." (11–12) But he (i.e., Piyama-radu) snubbed[264] the crown prince, and said "no." (11–15) Yet is not the crown prince the equivalent[265] of the king? (The crown prince) held him by the hand,[266] but he said "no" to him and demeaned[267] him in the presence of the lands. And (as if that were not enough,) he said this in addition: "Give me kingship here on the spot. If you don't, I will not come (to Ḫatti)."
(i 16) GIM-an *I-NA* ^{URU}Wa-li-wa-an-da ar-ḫu-un nu-uš-ši *AŠ-PUR* (17) ma-a-an-wa am-me-el EN-*UT-TA* ša-an-ḫe-eš-ke-ši nu-wa ka-a-ša (18) *I-NA* ^{URU}I-ya-la-an-da ku-it ú-wa-mi nu-wa-kán ŠÀ ^{URU}[I-y]a-la-an-da (19) tu-e-el UN-an le-e	**2.** (i 16–31) When I reached the town Waliwanda,[268] I sent (to Piyama-radu) the following message: "If you are seeking my suzerainty, since I am coming to the town Iyalanda,[269] let me not find a single man of yours in the town

ku-in-ki ú-e-mi-ya-mi [zi-i]k-ka$_4$-wa-za-kán (20) EGIR-pa an-da le-e ku-in-ki tar-na-at-ti ta-pa-r[i-ya-wa]-mu-za-kán (21) le-e an-da ki-iš-ta-ti am-me-el-wa ARAD.MEŠ [ú-ki-la EG]IR?-an? (22) ša-an-aḫ-mi GIM-an-ma *I-NA* ^{URU}I-ya-la-an-d[a ar-ḫu-un] (23) nu-mu LÚ.KÚR 3 *AŠ-RA* za-aḫ-ḫi-ya ti-ya-at nu [2+]1? [ku-it *AŠ-R*]*A*? (24) ar-pu-u-wa-an nu-kán GÌR-it ša-ra-a pa-a-u-u[n nu a-pí-ya] (25) LÚ.KÚR ḫu-ul-li-ya-nu-un nu-kán UN.MEŠ-tar a-pí-y[a? …] (26) ^{m}La-ḫur-zi-<iš->ma-mu a-pé-el ŠEŠ-*ŠU* še-na-aḫ-ḫa [pé-ra-an ti-iš-ke-et?] (27) nu ŠEŠ-*YA* pu-nu-uš-pát ma-a-an *Ú-UL* kiš-an ^{m}L[a?[323]-ḫur-zi-iš-ma-k]án (28) za-aḫ-ḫi-ya an-da *Ú-UL* e-eš-ta am-mu-uk-ka$_4$-an [*I-NA* ŠÀ-*BI*] (29) KUR ^{URU}I-ya-la-an-da *Ú-UL AK-ŠU-UD* a-pé-e[z-…] (30) ša-ku-wa-aš-ša-ri INIM ^{URU}I-ya-la-an-da *Ú-U*[*L*-wa x - x] (31) *I-NA* ^{URU}I-ya-la-an-da pa-a-i-mi	Iyalanda.[270] You must not let anyone go back in, nor *attach yourself* to? (*territory under*) my command. (21) I personally look after my subjects." (22) But when I reached Iyalanda, the enemy (i.e., Piyama-radu) offered battle to me in three places.[271] Because the three? places[272] were rugged (terrain), I made the ascent on foot and defeated the enemy there. And the populace … there.[273] But his[274] brother Laḫurzi was setting[275] an ambush ahead of me. My brother,[276] just ask if it was not so.[277] Was not *Laḫurzi*[278] (himself) a participant in the battle? Did I not find him in the midst of the land Iyalanda? From that … in the *whole* matter Iyalanda: "I will not … go to the city Iyalanda."
(i 32) nu-ut-ta ke-e ku-e INIM.MEŠ *AŠ-PUR* nu GIM-an [ki-ša-at?] (33) nu LUGAL.GAL li-in-ku-un ^{d}U iš-ta-ma-a[š-ke-ed-du DINGIR.MEŠ-ya] (34) iš-ta-ma-aš-kán-du GIM-an ke-e *A-WA-TE*$^{ME[Š}$ ki-ša-at?]	**3.** (i 32–34) I, the Great King, have (hereby[279]) sworn, that these things about which I have written to you happened[280] this way. Let the Storm God hear, (33) and let the (other) gods hear (and bear witness) how these things really were.
(i 35) GIM-an-ma KUR ^{URU}I-ya-la-an-da ar-ḫa [ḫar-ga-nu-nu-un] (36) nu KUR-*TU*$_4$ ku-it ḫu-u-ma-an ar-ḫa ḫar-g[a-nu-nu-un a-pí-ya-ma] (37) ^{URU}At-ri-ya-an 1-*EN ḪAL-ṢU A-NA* ^{URU}[…] (38) ḫa-an-da-aš da-	**4.** (i 35–52) But when I had ravaged the land Iyalanda—since (after all) I had ravaged the entire land, (36) I left there the city Atriya, a single fortress?,[281] for the sake of the city …[282]—I came up again to the city

li-ya-nu-un nu-kán EG[IR?-pa *I-NA* URU…] (39) ša-ra-a ú-wa-nu-un KUR[283] URUI-ya[-la-an-da-za-kán an-da ku-it-ma-an] (40) e-šu-un nu-kán KUR-*TU*$_4$ ḫu-u-ma-a[n …] (41) : ḫa-aš-pa-ḫa *A-NA* NAM.RA[.MEŠ-ma EGIR-an-da *Ú-UL* pa-a-u-un] (42) GIM-an wa-a-tar NU.GÁL e?[-eš-ta …] (43) nu-mu-kán KARAŠ.ḪI.A t[e?-pa-u-wa-za e-eš-ta nu *A-NA* …] (44) EGIR-an-da *Ú-UL* pa-a-u-u[n nu …] (45) ša-ra-a ú-wa-nu-un ma-a-n[a-an …] (46) EGIR-pa-ma-a-na-an *Ú-UL* […] (47) nu-za-kán *I-NA* URUA-ba?-x[-…] (48) nu *I-NA* URUMi-el-la-wa-a[n-da …] (49) an-da-wa-mu-kán e-ḫ[u nu ki]š?-a[n *A-NA* ŠEŠ-*YA*-ya *MA*]-*ḪAR*? ZAG (50) *AŠ-PUR* ke-e-da-ni-y[a-wa-ra-a]n[332] me-mi?-ni *AṢ-BAT* ki-i-wa-mu (51) mPí-ya-ma-ra-d[u-uš KUR-*TU*$_4$ k]u?-it wa-al-aḫ-ḫe-eš-ke-ez-zi (52) nu-wa-ra-at ŠE[Š-*YA I-DE* nu-w]a-ra-at *Ú-UL*-ma *I-DE*	…. (39) While I was[283] in the land of Iyalanda, and I had *destroyed* … the entire land, (41) [I did not go] after the civilian captives. (42) And when the water supply was gone, ……,[284] and my troops were few. So I did not go after …. Instead I came up … If …, … not … him …….[285] … in the town A-ba?-[286]…, … in Millawanda: (49) "Come here to me." Again? to my brother …… the border I sent a message; "I have (sought to) seize him on this[287] account, (50) because Piyama-radu is continually attacking this land of mine. (52) Does my brother know it or not?"
(i 53) GIM-an-ma-mu [LÚ*ṬE-MU ŠA* ŠEŠ-*Y*]*A*? an-da ú-e-mi-ya-at (54) nu-mu *Ú-U*[*L* … ku-in-ki] ú-da-aš *Ú-UL*-ya?-mu up-pé-eš-šar (55) ku-it-ki [up-pé-eš-ta ki-iš-ša-an-m]a *IQ-BI A-NA* mAt-pa-wa *IŠ-PUR* (56) mPí-y[a-ma-ra-du-un-wa-ká]n? *A-NA* LUGAL URUḪa-at-ti ŠU-i da-a-i (57) ú?[- o o o o o o] (eras.)-nu?-un (58) n[u *I-NA* URUMi-el-l]a-wa-an-da pa-a-u-un pa-a-u-un-ma (59) […] x x x […] me-mi-ni ḫa-an-da-aš *A-NA* mPí-ya-ma-ra-du-wa (60) [ku-e]	**5.** (i 53–74, ii 1–8) But when the messenger of my brother met me, he did not bring me any …, nor did he offer to me any gift. (55) But he spoke thus: "(The King of Aḫḫiyawa) has sent a message to Atpā: (56) 'Hand over Piyamaradu to the Hittite king.'" … (58) So I proceeded to the city Millawanda. But I went there for the sake of … word: (59) "Let my brother's subjects hear what I have to say to Piyama-radu." (61) Piyama-radu escaped by ship.[289] (62) And Atpā

A-WA-TE^{MEŠ} me-ma-aḫ-ḫi nu-wa-ra-at ARAD.MEŠ ŠEŠ-*YA*-ya (61) [iš-t]a-ma-aš-ša-an-du nu-kán ^{m}Pí-ya-ma-ra-du-uš ^{GIŠ}MÁ-za (62) [ar-ḫ]a ú-et na-an *A-NA A-WA-TE*^{MEŠ} ku-e-da-aš ḫar-ku-un (63) [na-a]t ^{m}At-pa-aš-ša iš-ta-ma-aš-ke-et ^{m}A-wa-ya-na-aš-ša (64) [iš-]ta-ma-aš-ker nu-uš-ma-ša-aš ^{LÚ}*E-MI-ŠU-NU* ku-it (65) [n]u[288]-wa me-mi-an ku-wa-at ša-an-na-an-zi (66) na-aš li-in-ga-nu-nu-un nu-ut-ta me-mi-an ša-ku-wa-šar (67) me-ma-an-du *Ú-UL*-kán ^{LÚ}*TAR-TE-E-NU* pa-ri-ya-an (68) u-i-ya-nu-un i-it-wa-kán pa-ri-ya-an pé-en-ni (69) nu-wa-ra-an ŠU-an e-ep nu-wa-ra-an-za-an-kán *A-NA* ^{GIŠ}GIGIR (70) G[AM-]an$^?$ ti-it-ta-nu-ut nu-wa-ra-an-mu IGI-an-da ú-wa-ti (71) [*Ú-U*]*L* me-ma-aš ^{m}Ta-wa-ga-la-wa-aš-pát-kán ku-wa-pí LUGAL.GAL (72) [*A-N*]*A*$^?$ ^{URU}Mi-el-la-wa-an-da ta-pu-ša ú-et (73) [DUMU.ŠEŠ-*Y*]*A*$^?$[340]-ma $^{\text{m.d}}$LAMMA-aš ka-a e-eš-ta nu-ut-ta LUGAL.GAL (74) [IGI-an-d]a u-un-né-eš-ta *Ú-UL*-aš šar-ku-uš LUGAL-uš e-eš-ta (ii 1) na-aš *Ú-UL*-ma ⌜:za-ar-ši-ya⌝[…] (2) a-pa-a-aš-mu ku-wa-at *Ú-UL* [x x x] x [x x x x] (3) ma-a-an-ma ki-i me-ma-i [INI]M$^?$ ⌜ku$^?$-na-na$^?$-aš$^?$-wa$^?$⌝ na-aḫ-ḫu-un (4) nu-uš-ši *Ú-UL* DUMU-*YA* ^{LÚ}*TAR-TE-*⌜*NU*$^?$ x$^?$ IGI$^?$-an-da u-i⌝-ya-nu-un (5) na-an ki-i wa-tar-na-aḫ-ḫu-un ⌜i$^?$-it$^?$-wa-aš-ši⌝ (6) li-in-ki nu-wa-ra-an ŠU-an ⌜e$^{??}$-ep$^{??}$⌝ nu-wa-ra-an-mu (7) IGI-

was listening, and Awayana too—they were (both) listening to the charges which I had directed against him.[290] But why—just because he (Piyama-radu?) is their (Atpā's and Awayana's) father-in-law—are they concealing the word? (66) I put them[291] under oath to report the entire matter to you. (67) Is it not so, that I sent over there the crown prince, (saying to him:) (68) "Go, drive over there, take (Piyama-radu) by the hand,[292] have him mount the chariot alongside you, and conduct him to me?" (71) [293] But (Piyama-radu) said "no"! When Tawagalawa himself (representing?)[294] the Great King (of Aḫḫiyawa) crossed into the city Millawanda, (73) *my nephew* [295] Kurunt(iy)a was here, and the Great King (of Ḫatti) drove here to meet you, (Piyama-radu). (74) Yet he (i.e., Kurunt(iy)a?) was not a mighty king![296] (ii 1)And he (Kuruntiya?)[297] … not … safe conduct …. (ii 2) Why did he not come to meet$^?$ me? (3) If (Piyama-radu) says: "I feared a plot to murder me," (4) did I not send to him my own son, the crown prince? (5) Did I not give (my son) these instructions: "Go, assure him with an oath, take his hand, and conduct him to me"? (7) And concerning the supposed plot to kill him because of which he was afraid, (8) is murder a thing permitted in the land of Ḫatti? It most certainly is not.

an-da ú-wa-ti ku-na-an-na-aš-⸢ma?⸣-aš me-mi-ni ku-e-da-ni (8) na-aḫ-ta (x) e-eš-ḫar *I-NA* URUKÙ.BABBAR-*TI* a-a-ra ⸢na?-at!?⸣ *Ú-UL*	
(ii 9) GIM-an-ma-mu LÚ *ṬE$_4$-MU ŠA* ŠEŠ-*YA* m[e]-m[i]-an *IQ-BI* (10) a-pu-u-un-wa UN-an da-a le-e-wa-ra?-an? […] (11) nu ki-i *AQ-BI* ma-a-an-wa-mu am-me-el x x x x x (12) *IQ-BI* na-aš-šu ŠEŠ-*YA* ma-a-an-wa a-pé-el-la x x x (13) me-mi-an *AŠ-MI* ki-nu-na-wa-mu ŠEŠ-*YA* LUGAL.GAL am-me-el (14) an-na-ú-li-iš *IŠ-PUR* nu-wa am-me-el an-na-ú-li-ya-a[š] (15) me-mi-an *Ú-UL* iš-ta-ma-aš-mi nu ú-ki-la x x x x (16) pé-en-na-aḫ-ḫu-un ma-a-an ma-a-an x[…]x (17) ma-an ŠEŠ-*YA* nam-ma *IQ-BI* am-me-[el-wa me-mi-]an *Ú-UL IŠ-MI* (18) *Ú-UL*-wa-ra-aš-mu ka-a-ri t[i-ya-]at x x x EGIR-an *UL* (19) pu-nu-šú-un-ma-an *Ú-UL* ŠEŠ-*YA* ki-i […] ka-a-ri (20) ti-ya-at ú-uk-ma pa-a-u-un-pát nu-kán a?-[p]í-[y]a? ku?-w[a]?-pí? pa-ra-a (21) ti-ya-nu-un nu *A-NA* mAt-pa-a *AQ-B[I* …]x-ya-wa-at?-ta ku-it (22) *IŠ-PUR* i-it-wa-ra-an *A-NA* LUGAL ⸢KUR⸣ UR[UKÙ.BABBAR-ti pé]-⸢e⸣-ḫu-te (23) nu-wa-ra-an ú-wa-ti nu-wa-za-kán [k]a?-[r]u?[-ú? GIM-an … am-m]e?-[e]l? (24) me-mi-an GAB-ši : pa-ši-ḫa-a-it m[a?-…]-za-kán (25) me-mi-an GAB-ši : pa-ši-ḫa-a-ti x[-…] x (26) na-aḫ-mi-wa nu-wa ka-a-ša 1-EN *BE-L[U?*…] (27) na-aš-ma-wa ŠEŠ u-i-ya-mi nu-	**6.** (ii 9–50a) But when the envoy of my brother said to me: "Take that person (Piyama-radu?): don't … him," I said: "If my … had spoken to me, or my brother—if his … word I had heard,…. But now my brother, a Great King, my equal, has written to me. And should I not hear the word of an equal?[298] I myself went there to … If … had …, my brother would have said again: "He didn't hear what I said, nor has he complied with my request—…!" Then would I not have asked my brother this?: "Have you (or: Has he) … complied …?" (20) Now I have set out. And when I arrived there, I said to Atpā: "Because … has sent you? …, (22) 'Proceed to conduct him thence to the king of Ḫatti,' therefore bring him here! And as he previously trampled? on my word, he will trample? on the … word. (25) And if Piyama-radu says this: 'I am afraid,' I will send one lord …, or I will send a brother. And let him[299] remain in his place." But (Piyama-radu) still kept saying: "I can't get rid of my fears," Atpā spoke thus to me: "Your Majesty should give the 'hand'[300] to a 'son'."[301] … he gave … to that one, and that also … (32) If … had done much, I would

w[a-ra-aš … pé-]di-eš-ši (28) ⸢e⸣?-ša-ru a-⸢pa⸣a-aš-ma nu-u-wa-pát me-m[i-iš-ke-et …] (29) [na]-aḫ-ḫe-eš!-ke-mi-wa nu-mu ^{m}At-pa-a […] (30) $^{[d]}$UTU-*ŠI*-wa ŠU-an *A-NA* DUMU.NITA pa-a-i […] (31) [a-p]é-e-da-ni pé-eš-⸢ta⸣nu a-pád-da x[-…] (32) [x-]x ma-a-an me-ek-ki-pát i-ya-at[(-) …]-ya (33) […]x-ši-ya GAM*-an da-li-ya-nu-un […] (34) [li?-in?-g]a-nu-nu-un nu-uš-ši ŠU-an *AD-DIN*? x […] x (35) […]-x te-ḫi nu-wa-ra-at-ta INIM […]-at-ta x x x	have left him …. (34) I made Atpā? swear, and I gave to him the ‘hand’. … “I will put *you on the road*?, and … it to you … a word …..

(Rest of §6 and all of §7 in a very bad state of preservation.) I follow Sommer's line count for the rest of this column, not that of the KUB copy.

(ii 56) nu nam-ma-pát *A-NA* ŠEŠ-*YA* ḫa-an-da-aš *Ú-UL* ma-a[n-ka$_4$ i-ya-nu-un nu ma-a-an] (ii 57) ŠEŠ-*YA* ku-wa-at-ka$_4$ da-ri-[y]a-nu-zi *A-NA* LUGAL KUR *ḪA*[*T-TI*-wa pa?-a?-i?-mi?] (ii 58) nu-wa-mu-kán KASKAL-ši da-a-ú nu ka-a-aš-ma ^{m}Da-ba-l[a-^{d}U-an] (ii 59) ⸢^{LÚ}*KAR-TAP-PU* u-<i->ya⸣-nu-un ^{m}Ta*-ba-la-^{d}U-aš-ma *Ú-UL* k[u-iš-ki] (ii 60) ⸢EGIR-ez-zi-iš⸣ UN-aš DUMU-an-na-aš-mu ^{LÚ}*KAR-TAP-PU A-NA* ^{GIŠ}GIGIR (ii 61) ⸢GAM-an ti-iš-ke-ez⸣-zi *A-NA* ŠEŠ-*YA*-ya-aš-kán *A-NA* ^{m}Ta-wa-ka-la-wa ^{G}[^{IŠ}GIGIR-ni] (ii 62) ⸢GAM-an ti-iš-ke-et⸣ nu *A-NA* ^{m}Pí-ya-ma-ra-du : za-ar-ši-ya-an *Ú*[*-UL AD-DIN*] (ii 63) ⸢: za-ar-ši-ya-aš-ma *I-NA*⸣ KUR *Ḫat-ti* kiš-an ma-a-an NINDA ši-ya-an-ta-a[n*][349] (ii 64) ku-e-da-ni up-pa-an-zi nu-uš-ši-kán ḪUL *UL* ták-[k]i-iš-ša-an-zi (ii 65) : za-ar-ši-	**8.** (ii 56–77, iii 1–6) So once again in consideration for my brother I have taken no action at all. (56) Now if perhaps he protests? to my brother, saying: (57) “*I will go* to the king of Ḫatti. (58) Let him put me on the road,”[302] (58) I have just sent out Dabala-Tarḫunta, the charioteer. (59) And (this) Dabala-Tarḫunta is not some man of low rank: (60) from (my) youth as charioteer he has been mounting the chariot beside me.[303] (61) He used to mount the chariot alongside your brother Tawagalawa too. (62) Have I not offered safe conduct to Piyama-radu? (63) Now safe conduct (works) this way in Ḫatti: (63) If they send …[304] to someone, they may not harm him. (65) But with regard to the safe conduct I transported this (message:) (65) “Come, make your case before me![305] (66) Then I will

ya-ma še!-er ki-i ar-nu-nu-un e-ḫu-wa nu-wa-mu-za ar-ku-w[a-ar] (ii 66) i-ya nu-wa-ták-kán KASKAL-ši te-eḫ-ḫi KASKAL-ši-ma-wa-ták-kán GIM-an te-eḫ-ḫi (ii 67) nu-wa-ra-at *A-NA* ŠEŠ-*YA* ḫa-at-ra-a-mi nu-wa!?-ta ma-a-an ZI-an-za (ii 68) wa-ar-ši-ya-zi e-eš-du-wa ma-a-an-ma-wa-at-ta ZI-an-za-ma (ii 69) *Ú-UL* wa-ar-ši-ya-zi nu-wa ú-it GIM-an EGIR-pa-ya-wa-at-ta (ii 70) *I-NA* KUR ^{URU}Aḫ-ḫi-ya-wa-a am-me-el UN-aš *QA-TAM-MA* pé-ḫu-te-ez-zi (ii 71) ma-a-an-ma-wa *Ú-UL*-ma nu-wa-aš-ši ka-a-aš ^{LÚ}*KAR-TAP-PU* (ii 72) pé-di-ši e-ša-ru ku-it-ma-na-aš ú-iz-zi ku-it-ma-na-aš (ii 73) a-pí-ya EGIR-pa ú-ez-zi ka-a-aš-ma ^{LÚ}*KAR-TAP-PU* ku-iš (ii 74) *ŠA* MUNUS.LUGAL-za ku-it *ŠA* MÁŠ-*TI* ḫar-zi *I-NA* KUR ^{URU}*Ḫat-ti ŠA* MUNUS.LUGAL (ii 75) MÁŠ-*TU*$_4$ me-ek-ki šal-li na-aš-mu *Ú-UL* im-ma ^{LÚ}*ḪA-<TÁ->NU*[352] (ii 76) nu-uš-ši a-pa-a-aš pé-e-di-eš-ši e-ša-ru ku-it-ma-na-aš ú-ez-zi (ii 77) ku-it-ma-na-aš EGIR-pa ú-[ez-zi] (iii 1) ŠEŠ-*YA*-ya-an-za-an ḫa-an-za e-ep na-an tu-e-el [UN-aš] (iii 2) ú-wa-te-ed-du nam-ma-aš-ši [ŠE]Š-*YA* : z[a-ar-]ši-ya-an (iii 3) ki-iš-ša-an a-ša-an-ta-an up-pí [o o o o o] x x x x-wa (iii 4) nam-ma ku-it-ki wa-aš-ta-ti nu-w[a-ták-kán *I-NA* KUR-*KA*] nam-ma (5) an-da tar-na-aḫ-ḫi na-an LÚ?/ŠEŠ? x [x x] x […]-zi (6) na-an KASKAL-ši GIM-an te-ḫi n[a-at ŠEŠ-*YA* ša-ak-d]u

put you on the road. And I will write to my brother, how I will put you on the road. (67) If you are satisfied (with my proposals), let it be (so). (68) But if you are not satisfied, (69) then my man will escort you back into the land of Aḫḫiyawa in the same manner as he came (here with you). (71) Otherwise, let this charioteer remain in his (i.e., Piyama-radu's[306]) place, while he (Piyama-radu) is coming and while he comes back there." (73) Who is this charioteer? Because he has (a wife) of the Queen's family, (74) (since) in Ḫatti the Queen's family is very highly regarded, (75) is he not much more to me than just an in-law?[307] (76) But he shall remain in his (Piyama-radu's) place while (the escort) comes (to me) (77) and comes back (there to Millawanda). (iii 1) And you, my brother, take good care of him.[308] Let one of your men conduct him. (iii 2) Furthermore, my brother, convey to him my guarantee of safe conduct in the following manner: "If? … , and? (iii 3) you don't sin against His Majesty in any way, (iii 4–5) I will let you back into your land again," … … (iii 5–6) I want my brother to know how[309] I shall put him on the road.

(iii 7) ma-a-an-ma ke-e!-ya *Ú-UL* [ḫa-iz-zi] (8) nu ŠEŠ-*YA* ke-e-el x-x x x x-an i-ya (9) NAM.RA.MEŠ-kán me-ek-ki [x-]x-x-ya355 ta-pu-ša (10) ú-et 7 *LI-IM* NAM. RA.MEŠ[-y]a-mu ŠEŠ-*YA* x-x (11) nu am-me-el UN-aš ú-ez-zi nu-za ŠEŠ-*YA* […] (12) *BE-LU*MEŠ pé-ra-an GAM da-a-i GÉŠPU-za-kán ku-it [x x x]x? (13) ta-pu-ša ú-wa-te-et nu ŠEŠ-*YA* […] (14) am-me-el-la UN-aš ar-ta-ru n[u? …] (15) me-ma-i *AŠ-ŠUM MU-NAB-TI*-wa-ka[n] x[… šar?-ra?-aḫ?-ḫu-un?] (16) na-aš a-pí-ya e-eš-du ma-a?-[an-ma-aš ki-i me-ma-i] (17) GÉŠPU-aḫ-ta-w[a]-m[u] n[a-aš-mu EGIR-pa an-da ú-id-du] (18) ma-a-an x […] (19) ar-ḫa ta[r?-…]	**9.** (iii 7–21) But if he doesn't trust? even these (arrangements), then, my brother, make … of this … (9) Many civilian captives … have *escaped* to my land.310 (10) My brother … to me 7,000 civilian captives. (11) My man will come. (11) You, my brother, must put the leaders (lit. lords) on trial?. (12) Because (Piyama-radu) has forcibly *abducted* …. (13) And My brother …. (14) Let my (own) man also be present. And if … says: (15) "*I crossed*? *over*? as a fugitive," (16) let him stay there. But if he says: (17) "He forced me," then let him come back to me. (18) If … … … (*Lines 18–40 too badly broken for translation.*)
(iii 41) [*A-NA* m…]…-DINGIR-*LIM*-ya-at DUMU mŠa-ḫu-r[u-un-nu-]wa-kán (42) [ma-aḫ-ḫa-an ki-ša-at] LÚ*MU-NAB-TUM*-kán *A-NA* ŠEŠ-*YA*[-ya ...] (43) EG[IR-pa an-d]a ú-ed-du ma-a-na-aš *BE-LU* ma-a-na-aš [ARAD-ma] (44) tar-na-na-at LUGAL.GAL-za am-me-el an-na-ú?-[li-i]š (45) kar-ga-ra-an-ti a-pé-e-da-ni a-pa-[a-at x-]x-a-i[t] (46) am-me-el-ši-kán ku-wa-pí LÚ.MEŠ*MU-NAB-T*[*I* par-r]a??-an-da? (47) pa-it nu-kán mŠa-ḫu-ru-nu-wa-aš *A-N*[*A*] DUMU-*ŠU* […] (48) a-pa-a-aš-ma ša-ra-a ti-ya-at na-aš-kán a-pé-e?[-da-ni] (49) an-da pa-it ⸢a-pa-a⸣-aš-ma-za-an-kán E[GI]R-pa a[r?-ḫa?] (50) tar-na-aš ŠEŠ-*YA*-[y]a?-an a-pé-e-da-ni INIM-ni [x-]x-ši (51) ma-a-an[-ma-	**10.** (iii 41–51) … It belongs to x-x-x-ili also. The son of Šaḫurunuwa … Let fugitives311 come … back to my brother: whether he be a lord or a slave. It is allowed. Did the Great King, my equal, *willingly* …? that to that one? When my fugitives crossed over to him, Šaḫurunuwa … to his son, and he arose and went to that one. And that one let him back out. Will my brother too … him for that matter? When one of my subjects takes flight, … you? are? running behind ….

mu-kán] ARAD-*YA* [k]u-i[š]-ki ḫu-u-ya-zi nu-kán? […] EGIR-pa-an-da píd-da-eš-ke?-⌜ši!?⌝	
(iii 52) nam-ma ka-a-ša-aš-ši-ya ki-i-wa me-mi-iš-ke-ez-zi (53) ŠÀ KURMa-a-ša-wa-kán KURKar-ki-ya pár-ra-an-d[a] (54) pa-a-i-mi NAM.RA.MEŠ-ma-wa-za DAM-*YA*!(text: -*SÚ*) DUMU.MEŠ É!?[-*TUM*-ya] (55) ka-a ar-ḫa da-li-ya-mi na-aš GIM-an ka-a-[a]š (56) me-mi-aš DAM-*SÚ* -ši ku-wa-pí DUMU.MEŠ É-*TUM*-ya (57) *ŠA* ŠEŠ-*YA* ŠÀ KUR-*TI* ar-ḫa da-li-ya-zi? (58) na-an-kán tu-el KUR-e-an-za ḫa-an-ti-ya-i[z-z]i (59) a-pa-a-aš-ma KUR-*TI-YA* wa-al-aḫ-ḫe-eš-ke-ez-zi (60) [m]a-a-an-ma-ši-ya-at-kán ⌜: ú?-ša⌝-a-i-ḫa (61) na-aš EGIR-pa *I-NA* KUR-*KA* ú-i[z-]zi (62) ŠEŠ-*YA*-za ma-la-a-ši x-x-x x-x … x x x -eš?	**11.** (iii 52–62) Further, … (Piyama-radu) is saying this:[312] "I will go over into the land of Maša (or) the land of Karkiya, but the civilian captives, my! wife, children and the household I will leave here." So what does this mean?[313] During the time when he leaves behind his wife, children and household in my brother's land, your land is affording him protection.[314] But he is continually raiding my land! And whenever I have prevented him in that, he comes back into your territory. Are you now, my brother, favorably disposed *to this conduct*?
(iii 63) nu-uš-ši ŠEŠ-*YA* a-pa-a-at 1-an ⌜ḫa-at-ra-a-i⌝ (64) ma-a-an<-wa> *Ú-UL* nu-wa ša-ra-a ti-i-y[a] (65) nu-wa *I-NA* KURḪat-ti ar-ḫa i-it (66) EN-*KA*-wa-at-ta EGIR-an kap-pu-u-[wa-i]t (67) [m]a-⌜a-an-ma-wa⌝ *UL* nu-wa *INA* KUR⌜Aḫ-ḫi-ya-wa-a⌝ (68) [a]r-ḫa ⌜e⌝-ḫu nu-wa-at-ta ku-e-da-ni pé-[di] / [GAM?-an?] a-ši-ša-nu-mi (iv 1) […] (iv 2) […]x x x[… t]i-i-ya (iv 3) [… dam-me-]e-da-ni pé-di GAM e-eš [nu-wa-za] *A-NA* LUGAL KURḪa-at-ti (4) [k]u-w[a]-pí ku-ru-ur nu-wa-za da-me-da-za KUR-e-za ku-ru-ur e-eš (5) am-me-ta-za-ma-	**12.** (iii 63–69, iv 1–15) (If not,) now, my brother, write him at least this one thing: (iii 64) "If not, then either, arise and go forth into the land of Ḫatti, (since) your lord has settled his account with you, (67) (or) if not, (then) come into the land of Aḫḫiyawa, and in whatever place I settle you, you must remain there. (iv 1) … (iv 2) Arise … and settle down in another place! (3) So long as you are at enmity with the king of Ḫatti, be at enmity from (some) other country! (5) Don't be at enmity from my country! (6) If your[315]

wa-za-kán KUR-e-za ar-ḫa le-e ku-ru-ur (6) ma-a-an-wa-ši *I-NA* ^{KUR}Kar-ki-ya ^{KUR}Ma-a-[š]a ZI-za (7) nu-wa a-pí-ya i-it LUGAL ^{KUR}Ḫa-at-ti-wa-an-na-aš-kán ú-uk (8) ku-e-da-ni *A-NA* [INI]M ^{URU}Wi$_5$-l[u]-[š]a še-er ku-ru-u[r] (9) e-šu-u-en n[u-wa-m]u a-p[é-e-d]a-ni INIM-ni la-a[k-nu-ut] (iv 10) nu-wa ták-šu-la$^?$-u[-en x-]x-x[-x-an-n]a-aš ku-ru-ur *UL* [a-a-r]a (11) nu-uš-ši a-[pa-a-at *ŠU-PUR* m]a-a-an-ma-[an] ^{URU}Mi-el-la-wa-an-da-ma (12) ar-ḫa d[a-li-ya-ši n]u-kán ARAD.MEŠ-*YA* a-pé-e-da-ni (13) : kar-ga-r[a$^?$-an-ti … a]n-da ⸢píd-da-iš-kán-zi⸣ (14) nu ŠEŠ-*YA* [… *A-N*]*A* ^{KUR}Mi-el-la-wa-an-da (15) IGI[-an-da …-]ya-an ḫar-mi	heart is in the land of Karkiya (or) the land of Maša, then go there! The king of Ḫatti and I—in that matter of Wiluša over which we were at enmity, he has converted me in that matter, and we have made peace; … a war would not be right for us," (11) So send that to him! But if you were to leave Millawanda alone, (12) my servants will willingly$^?$ flee/run to that (one), (14) and, my brother, I have …-ed … to the land of Millawanda
(iv 16) [………] ^{m}Pí-ya-ma-ra-du (17) [………] nu-mu ŠEŠ-*YA* me-mi-ya-ni (18) [………] na-at-mu *ŠU-PUR* (19) nu *Š*[*A* ^{URU}Wi$_5$-lu-ša-pát ku-e-da-ni me-]mi-ni še-er ku-ru-ri-aḫ-ḫu-u-en (20) nu-za-k[án ku-it ták-šu-la-u-en nu n]am-ma ku-it (21) ma-a-a[n ^{LÚ}*TAP-PU* ku-iš-ki *A-NA* ^{LÚ}]*TAP-PÍ-ŠU* pé-ra-an wa-aš-túl (22) tar-na-i [nu ^{LÚ}*TAP-PU* ku-it *A-NA* ^{LÚ}*TAP-P*]*Í-ŠU* pé-ra-an (23) wa-aš-túl ta[r-na-i na-an ar-ḫa] *Ú-UL* pé-eš-ši-ya-iz-zi (24) am-mu-uk-ka$_4$ [ku-it am-me-el wa-aš-tú]l *A-NA* ŠEŠ-*YA* pé-ra-an (25) tar-na-aḫ-ḫu-[un … am-mu-uk] *Ù*$^?$ *A-NA* ŠEŠ-*YA* (26) le-e nam-m[a ku-ru-ur …] x	**13.** (iv 16) … Piyama-radu … And to me, my brother, in the matter (18) … . Send it to me! (19) Over what matter concerning Wiluša we were hostile, (20) because we have made peace, then what more is there? If one partner confesses his error/sin to the other, (22) then because he confesses his error/sin to the partner, (23) he will not reject him. (24) Because therefore I have confessed my error/sin to my brother, (25) let there be no more hostility between me and my brother.

(iv 27) nu ma-a-an ŠEŠ[-*YA* ....]-an da-[......] (28) nu-mu EGIR-pa *ŠU*[-*PUR* ......] (29) *ŠA* ARAD-*YA* ku-wa-[pí ....] (30) ar-ḫa pé-eš-ši-y[a?-.........] (31) na-at UN.MEŠ-an-ni-ma[......]	**14.** *(iv 27–31 Too badly broken for translation.*
(iv 32) ŠEŠ-*YA*-ma-mu ka-ru[-ú ki-iš]-š[a-an *IŠ-PUR* ...] (33) GEŠPÚ-wa-mu up-pé-eš-ta a[m*-mu-uk-ma-za nu-u-wa] (34) TUR-aš e-šu-un ma-a-an x [...] (35) ú-uk *AŠ-PUR Ú-UL*-ma?-x[-...] (36) ma-a-an-mu *QA-TAM-MA* a-x[-...] (37) a-pé-e-ni-šu-u-an-za-kán me[-mi-aš ...] (38) KA×U-za i-ya-at-ta-ri x [...] (39) LÚ ÉRIN.MEŠ šu-ul-li-ya-zi [...] (40) mar-le-eš-ša-an-za nu a-pé-ez [...] (41) me-ma-i am-mu-uk-aš-kán ku-wa[-...] (42) a-pé-e-ni-iš-šu-u-an-za me-mi-aš dU[TU-az? ...] (43) ma-a-an-kán a-pa-a-aš me-mi-aš am-mu-uk [...] (44) GEŠPÚ up-pa-aḫ-ḫu-un ki-nu-na-ma [*ŠA* ŠEŠ-*YA* ku-iš] (45) me-mi-aš KA×U-za ú-et *A-NA* LUGAL.GAL[...] (46) ú-et nu-za a-pa-a-at *DI-NU* pí-an GAM [ti-ya-u-e-ni nu ŠEŠ-*YA*] (47) tu-el ku-in-ki ARAD-*DUM* u-i-ya nu-u[t-ta...] (48) ú-da-aš a-pa-a-aš INIM-aš ḫar-kán-na x-x na-an-kán ka-a ḫa-an-ti [...] (49) SAG.DU-an ku-ra-an-du ma-a-an-ma-a[t-ta tu-el UN-aš INIM-an wa-aḫ-nu]-ut (50) nu-kán a-pu-u-un UN-an SAG.DU-an ku[-ra-an-du-pát SAG.DU-an-m]a (51) ku-in ku-ra-an-zi na-an-kán mar-ri[-ya-an-du ...] (52) nu a-pa-a-at e-eš-ḫar ku-wa-pí	**15.** (iv 32–57, colophon) ... (52) But my brother once wrote to me as follows: ... (33) You have acted aggressively towards me." (33) But at that time, my brother, I was young; (34) if at that time I wrote anything insulting, it was not done deliberately .... If likewise to me ... (37) Such a remark may very well fall from the lips ... a man (of?) the army will be wanton/reckless ... foolish, ... (42) Let such a word be judged? before the Sun God. (43) If that word ... to me ... (44) I sent force. But now what message/matter of my brother has come orally, it came ... to the Great King. (46) Then let us put that case down in front of ourselves. And, my brother, (47) send some servant of yours....... (49) let them cut off his head! And if your man has altered my message to you, let them cut off his head likewise! And the head that they cut off, let them crush it and grind it to powder. And where will that blood flow? ... your servant spoke. And if that word did not come from your mouth, then the servant ... it, ... (55) Did he not determine it for you? If the Great King, my peer, had spoken it, the servant would have ... it. That

pa-iz-z[i …] (53) ARAD-*KA* me-mi-iš-ta nu-kán a-pa-a-aš me-[mi-aš ma-a-an tu-el] (54) KA×U-za *Ú-UL* ú-et na-an-kán ARAD-*DUM* EG[IR?-…] (55) *UL*-an-kán tu-uk SI×SÁ-it ma-a-na-an LU[GAL. GAL am-me-el] (56) an-na-wa-li-iš me-mi-iš-ta ARAD-*DUM*-ma-na-an[-…-t]a (57) a-pa-a-aš-kán INIM-aš 1-an-ki ma-⌜an-qa⌝ ne-pí-š[a-aš …] x	word once…
3 DUB *Q*[*A*?-*TI*]	Tablet 3. Complete.

Commentary

i 1 *Attarimma* (= Telmessos according to Mountjoy 1998).

i 18–22 Translated in CHD L–N, 467 (*nu* A h 5′).

ii 24 HZL, no. 169 reads DUḪ-*ši*- (the same signs) and translates that word "ungehemmt, unumwunden."

iv 32–34 The use of the excuse of youth here and elsewhere is discussed in de Martino and Imparati 1995, 107.

102. KUB 19.55 + KUB 48.90 From King Tudḫaliya IV to Tarkašnawa of Mira ("Milawata Letter")

Text: Bo 3287 + VAT 7477. **Find spot:** Unknown. **Photo**: Forrer 1929, pl. III. **Copy:** KUB 19.55 + KUB 48.90. **Editions**: Forrer 1929, 233–61; Sommer 1932, 198–240; Hoffner 1982b. **Translation:** Beckman 1999a, 144–46 (no. 23A). **Discussion:** Hagenbuchner 1989b, 367 (no. 256); van den Hout 1995, 91; Forlanini 1998, 244; Hawkins 1998b, 19 n. 85; Klengel 1999, 247 [A24], 284 [A25.3] (miswritten as KUB 14.55); Cohen 2001, 79 n. 33; 2002, 110; Liverani 2001, 68; Bachvarova 2002, 241; Lebrun 2002, 170; Bryce 2003a, 80; Hajnal 2003, 27, 38 n. 56; Heinhold-Krahmer 2004, 38–39; Bryce 2006, 183; de Martino 2006, 171.

Hawkins has suggested that this letter's author was Tudḫaliya IV, writing toward the end of his reign (ca. 1215–1210), and that the addressee was Tarkašnawa, the king of Mira. The land of Mira is mentioned already in connection with a military expedition by Šuppiluliuma I (reigned 1344–1322) to Arzawa (Deeds of Šuppiluliuma, fragment 18). During the reign of Šuppiluliuma I, a certain Mašḫuiluwa, a son of a king in the Arzawa territory, driven away by his brothers, came to the court of Šuppiluliuma, who gave him his daughter Muwatti in marriage and installed him as a vassal king. During the reign of Šuppiluliuma's second successor, Muršili II (reigned ca. 1321–1295), Mašḫuiluwa fought in the Hittites' service against SUM-LAMMA, the son of Uḫḫa-ziti, king of Arzawa, over territory in Mira. After the destruction of the kingdom of Arzawa by Muršili II in his fourth regnal year (ca. 1318), Muršili fortified and garrisoned three cities in Mira: Aršani, Šarawa, and Impa. Mašḫuiluwa was installed as king of Mira (including the adjacent territory of Kuwaliya), and a treaty was made with him that has not been preserved. Mira was granted equal status with the other Hittite vassal kingdoms created at this time: the Šeḫa River Land and Ḫapalla. With Hittite approval Mašḫuiluwa adopted his nephew, Kupanta-LAMMA, and designated him as his successor. But in Muršili's twelfth regnal year (ca. 1299) Mašḫuiluwa rebelled and fled to the land of Maša, from where, after a successful military campaign by Muršili, he was extradited. Muršili installed Kupanta-LAMMA as the new king and made a treaty with him that has been preserved. Kupanta-LAMMA was still ruling at the time of Muwattalli II (ca. 1295–1272)'s treaty with Alakšandu of Wiluša. Kupanta-LAMMA supported the unsuccessful encumbent Muršili III (also known as Urḫi-Teššub, reigned ca. 1272–1267) against his eventual successor, Ḫattušili III, which must have led to repercussions against Mira. According to Singer (1983b, 214–15), during the reigns of Tudḫaliya IV (ca. 1237–1209), Arnuwanda III (ca. 1209–1207) and Šuppiluliuma II (ca. 1207–?) the kingdom of Mira-Kuwaliya declined in importance vis-à-vis its neighbor, the Šeḫa River Land. At the time of Tudḫaliya IV's treaty with Kurunt(iy)a of Tarḫuntašša, the king of Mira was Alantalli. He was succeeded at the end of Tudḫaliya's reign by Tarkašnawa (so Hawkins 1998b).

About Mira's geographical location and extent, Hawkins has written:

> Mira has been recognized as the most prominent Arzawa kingdom, probably incorporating the rump of Arzawa itself after Mursili's defeat and dissolution of that kingdom. The reading of the Karabel inscription confirms at a stroke the location of Mira in its vicinity and disproves all other proposed locations. Mira itself is known to have had a common inland frontier with Hatti on the western edge of the Anatolian plateau in the neighbourhood of Afyon. Karabel, being placed on the route northwards from the territory of Ephesos in the Cayster valley to the Hermos valley, shows by its reading

> that Mira extended this far west, in effect to the coast. The probability is that this western extension of Mira represents the rump of the Arzawan state with its capital at Apasa, which is thereby doubtless confirmed in its identification with Ephesos. It is also likely that such a large political entity could only be kept together by good control of communications, so one might postulate that the spine of this kingdom of Mira-Arzawa must have been the Meander valley, the main highway from the plateau to the west. (1998b, 1)

While Mira was located in the Meander Valley, the Šeḫa River Land was to the north, in the Hermos Valley and perhaps including the Caicos Valley further to the north.

The text known as "The Sins of the Šeḫa River Land" (KUB 23.13) dates to the reign of Tudḫaliya IV. It narrates the campaign of a Hittite king against this country. It mentions that Tarḫunta-radu of the Šeḫa River Land is relying on the king of Aḫḫiyawa. Singer (1983b) suggested that Aḫḫiyawa had encouraged a campaign by the king of the Šeḫa River Land, which bordered Aḫḫiyawa, against the Hittites.The Hittite king suppressed that rebellion and deported Tarḫunta-radu and many prisoners to Arinna. Although it does not mention Aḫḫiyawa, the Milawata Letter gives some evidence for Milawanda and western Anatolian history in the reign of Tudḫaliya IV. The join made by Hoffner in 1980 (published in Hoffner 1982b, see below in lines rev. 37′–47′ and the left edge) shows that Millawanda did not become a Hittite vassal after the composition of the Tawagalawa Letter, as used to be believed. Milawanda was the target of raids led both by the Hittite king and by the addressee of this letter, Tarkašnawa, king of Mira. Mira, stretching from Afyon to Ephesos, was still very important for Hittite control in western Anatolia. Apparently, the Hittites never ruled Milawanda. The Milawata Letter suggests that Milawanda remained under Aḫḫiyawan control in the reign of Tudḫaliya IV.

The last important reference to Aḫḫiyawa is in the Šaušga-muwa treaty made by Tudḫaliya IV with the king of Amurru, under which that king had to discontinue trading with Assyria via his country. According to one interpretation, this included interdicting Aḫḫiyawan ships unloading at Amurru ports. In this text the Aḫḫiyawan king is named as a Great King, together with the kings of Egypt, Babylonia, and Assyria, although the tablet shows that the scribe later attempted to erase this designation. Much is made of this deletion, but as important is the inference that Aḫḫiyawa was a coastal country with a flourishing maritime trade.

Most of this text is so badly preserved that it is difficult to describe the flow of the events. The part easiest to understand and by far the most important is in the area of the join piece, interpreted in its main lines by Hoffner

(1985a), and summarized later by Bryce (1985a and 1985b). Although Tarkašnawa's father/predecessor, Alantalli in Hawkins' view, had often been hostile to Hittite interests in numerous ways, including by claiming the city of Arinna in southwestern Anatolia and refusing to give back hostages in his possession from the cities of Utima and Atriya, so that Tudḫaliya deposed him, he nevertheless made his son king of Mira, thereby "making him a brother" (literally, *nu-ud-du-za* ŠEŠ-*aḫ-ḫ*[*u-un*] "And [I] made you my brother" in line 10). Whether this is merely a way of saying "I treated you in a kindly way," or perhaps indicates something like giving Tarkašnawa more privileges than the normal western Anatolian vassal king, is hard to say. But the very fact that the text says that Walmu, king of Wiluša, was the *kulawani*-vassal of *both* the king of Ḫatti and the addressee Tarkašnawa, and that the fixing of the border with Millawanda was done in some sense jointly, so that the Hittite king says "*we* fixed" (GIN-*u-en* = *daiwen/tiyawen*), clearly indicates a position of special privilege. Perhaps Tarkašnawa's position and relation to Walmu was not unlike that of Atpā, the son-in-law of Piyama-radu, whom the latter appointed over Manapa-Tarḫunta, king of the Šeḫa River Land. Piyama-radu remained the *de facto* overlord, as Bryce puts it, but Atpā was the immediate controller. Similarly Tudḫaliya was the *de facto* overlord of both Tarkašnawa and Walmu, but the former was the immediate controller of the latter. For more on the possible ramifications of the term ŠEŠ-*aḫḫ*- see CHD L–N, 431 sub *negnaḫḫ*-. At the end of the letter the Hittite king expressed great confidence in Tarkašnawa as a loyal vassal. On all this, see Bryce 1985a.

Of great importance is the fact that recently their *kulawani*-vassal, the king of Wiluša named Walmu, had been expelled by rebels and fled south for refuge with Tarkašnawa, the king of Mira. A Hittite envoy named Kulana-ziti (some read Kuwatna-ziti) had rescued documents (GIŠ.ḪUR.ḪI.A, rev. 38′) authenticating Walmu's legitimate claim to the throne of Wiluša, and had brought them to Tarkašnawa for his perusal. The Hittite king (probably Tudḫaliya IV) requested Tarkašnawa to send Walmu to him as a first step in restoring him to the throne of Wiluša.

For this edition I have retained the line count of the KUB edition, which differs from Sommer's line count often used in discussions of this text. The reader should be aware of that in using the secondary literature and comparing this treatment.

(1) [*U*]*M-MA* dUTU-[*Š*]*I*-[*M*]*A A-N*[*A* … DUMU-*YA QÍ-BÍ-MA*]	(1) Thus speaks His Majesty: Say to … , my son:

(2) ^{d}UTU-*ŠI*-za DUMU-*YA* UN-an [… ša-ra-a da-aḫ-ḫu-un zi-ik-ka$_4$-mu-za EN-*KA*] (3) ša-ak-ta nu-ut-ták-kán [KUR *ŠA A-BI-KA* pé-eḫ-ḫu-un *A-BU-KA*-ma …] (4) [Z]AG.MEŠ-*YA* i-la-liš-ke-[et …] (5) GIM-an-ma-kán a[r-……..] (6) nu-za *A-BU-KA* GIM-an […] (7) GAM ME-iš ^{d}UTU-*ŠI*-y[a …] (8) nu ^{d}UTU-*ŠI*-ya ku-u-r[u?-ri-ya-aḫ-ḫu-un … ……] (9) nu-ut-ta ^{d}UTU-*ŠI* [… ša-ra-a da-aḫ-ḫu-un] (10) nu-ud-du-za ŠEŠ-aḫ-ḫ[u-un …] (11) nam-ma GAM ^{d}UTU AN-⸢*E*⸣ […] (12) nu-za zi-ik ^{d}UTU-*ŠI* [… ša-ak-ta nu ^{d}UTU-*ŠI* …] (13) EG[I]R-pa a-ru-na-an a[m?-me-el ZAG-an DÙ-nu-un …] (14) [k]u-i-e-eš ḪUL-u-i-eš […] (15) nu nam-ma *A-BU-KA* […] (16) iš-dam-ma-aš-ta x […] (17) *A-NA* LUGAL KUR ^{URU}Ḫat-ti […] (18) ša-an-né-eš-ta-ya x […] (19) *A-BU-KA* pa-ra-a i[m-ma …]	(2) I, My Majesty, have taken you up, my son, a … man, and you have recognized me as overlord. (3) I gave the land of your father to you. But your father … was coveting my border territories. (4–6)… When …, and when your father marched against the city of …, he subdued the city of …, (7) and he …… My Majesty, …… (8) Then I, My Majesty, too opened hostilities and defeated your father. (9–10) But I, My Majesty, took you up, …, my son, and treated you in a brotherly fashion. … (11) Furthermore, under the Sun God of Heaven we swore an oath … (12) You recognized My Majesty as overlord. (13) I, My Majesty, thereby made the sea once more my frontier … (14–15) Whatever evil persons … And furthermore, your father heard … . (16–18) … even concealed … from the King of Ḫatti … (19) Your father ……
(20) ki-nu-un-ma-mu *A-BU-KA*[…] (21) [k]u-it DUMU-*YA* SIG$_5$[316]-tar PAP[-aḫ?-ši? …] (22) [x-x]x-mu-za le?-e? i[-la?-li?-ya?-ši?…] (23) […]x-ku-i da-a[ḫ-…] (24) […] *A-BU-KA* ku-w[a-pí …] (25) […] *A-BU-KA* *A-NA* L[UGAL?-*UT-TI* ……..] (26) […]-ká[n Š]À-[t]a […] (27) [x] ZAG-*YA* RA-an-zi nu[-kán? … le-e] (28) [š]ar-ra-at-ti nu am-mu-uk *A-BU-K*[*A* GIM-an i-ya-at nu-mu … *QA-TAM-MA* le-e] (29) DÙ-ši nu-kán ma-a-an ar-ḫa-x ú-w[a?-…] (30) ^{d}UTU-*ŠI*-ma-ta pé-ra-an UGU-ya [……]	(20–21) But now, although your father ……-ed? me, you, my son, must protect (my) well-being. … (22) You shall not covet? my land … (24) when your father … (25) your father for kingship? … (26) he took? to heart … of? my border territory they will attack, (27) then … you will not transgress the oath. (28) And as your father once treated me, you must not treat me in the same way! (29) And if you … away, … (30) I, My Majesty, will not lend you assistance?.

(31) am-mu-uk-ma *A-BU-KA* ku-it ku-i[t …] (32) ka-a-aš INIM-aš SAG.DU-aš INIM ^{URU}[U-ti-ma *Ù* ^{URU}At-ri-ya …] (33) *Ú-UL* e-eš-ta nu ku-u-un INIM ^{URU}[U-ti-ma *Ù* ^{URU}At-ri-ya…] (34) *A-NA A-BU-KA AŠ-PUR* na-at-kán x[…] (35) DUMU-*YA* wa-aš-ti na-at-kán *A-N*[*A NI-IŠ* DINGIR-*LIM* GAR-ru] (36) (*blank*)	(31) But whatever evil your father committed against me …, (32) this matter is a capital crime.[317] The question of the cities of Utima and Atriya … he was not …. (33) I wrote to your father … concerning this matter of Utima and Atriya, (34) and he did not resolve it. If you do not resolve it, you, my son, will commit an offense. (35) It shall be placed under oath.
(37) *A-BU-KA*-ma am-me-el ḪUL -u*-i* […] (38) *A-NA* ^{d}UD.SIG$_5$? ḪU[L].ḪI.A […] (39) še-ek-k[án-zi?…]	(36–38) But your father … in evil against me … the evil matters for ^{d}UD.SIG$_5$ … (39) they know …
[*A total of fifteen to twenty lines has been lost at the bottom of the obverse and the top of the reverse.*]	
(rev. 1′) [ma]-a*-an DUMU-*YA*-ma me-ma-ti ^{d}UTU-*ŠI*-wa *U*[*L* …] (rev. 2′) [x-]x ku-it BAL-nu-un ma-a-an DUMU-*YA* INIM ^{m}A[-ga-pu-ru-ši-ya … ša-ra-a?] (rev. 3′) [ú?-]it INIM ^{LÚ}*MU-NAB-TI*-ma ^{d}UTU-*ŠI* ku-it-ki […] (rev. 4′) ^{LÚ}*MU-NAB-TUM*-ma EGIR SUM-u-an-zi *UL* a-a-ra […] (rev. 5′) nu* GAM ^{d}IŠKUR?-ma[318] ku-it-ki ti-ya-u-en ^{LÚ}*MU-NAB-TUM*-wa[…] (rev. 6′) *A-BU-KA* ku-it ^{LÚ}SANGA ^{URU}Ta-a-r[a?-………] (rev. 7′) EGIR-an-ta up-pé-eš-ta ar[-………] (rev. 8′) na-an-ši-kán an-da *UL* ta[r-…] (rev. 9′) ma-an ma-a-an ^{m}A-ga-pu-ru-ši-[ya …] (rev. 10′) ^{m}Pí-ya-ma-ra-du-uš ku-wa-p[í …] (rev. 11′) ar-ḫa-wa-za pa-a-i-mi […… …] (rev. 12′) ^{m}A-ga-pu-ru-ši-ya-an[…] (rev. 13′) ma-an DUMU-*YA* ša-a[k-………] (rev. 14′) n[u-u]š-ši	(rev. 1′) But if, my son, you say: “Your Majesty did not … (rev. 2′) How have I risen in revolt?” If, my son, the matter of Agapurušiya has come up, (rev. 3′) I, My Majesty, have somehow … the matter of the fugitive. (rev. 4′) But is it not required to return a fugitive? … (rev. 5′) We have placed something under (the oath of) the Storm God: “We will return a fugitive.” (rev. 6′) Because your father …-ed the priest of the city of Tara-…, (rev. 7′) he sent … later. ……, (rev. 8′) did I not turn? him over to him? (rev. 9′) If Agapurušiya were …. (rev. 10′) At the time when Piyama-radu …… (rev. 11′) “I will go away!” … (rev. 12′) Agapurušiya …… (rev. 13′) If you, my son, knew …, (rev. 14′) I? informed him (thus): “…”

wa-tar-na-a[ḫ-…….] (rev. 15′) [x-]x EGIR […] (rev. 16′) ⸢ša-ku-wa⸣-ša-ri-[it ZI?-it …] (rev. 17′) [I]NIM ^{m}A-ga-p[u-ru-ši-ya …]	(rev. 15′) And him in return … (rev. 16′) wholeheartedly … (rev. 17′) the matter of Agapurušiya …
(Break of about 13 lines)	
(rev. 32′) [nu-u]š-ši x[-…] (rev. 33′) a-pa-a-aš-ma kiš-[…]x-x[…] (rev. 34′) [nu] nam-ma ÉRIN.M[EŠ …-]x pa-it (rev. 35′) na-aš-kán GE$_6$-za GAM?[…] (rev. 36′) [n]u-kán GIM-an EN-*ŠU* me-m[i-…]x x-x-x ḫu-u-wa-a-i[š?] (rev. 37′) [nu-]uš-ma-aš dam-ma-in EN-a[n … i-e-er ^{d}]UTU!-*ŠI*-ma-an *UL* ša-ka$_4$-ḫu-u[n] (rev. 38′) *A-NA* ^{m}Wa-al-mu-ma ku-e GIŠ.ḪU[R.ḪI.A i-ya-nu-un na-at] ^{m}KARAŠ-ZA pé-e ḫar-ta (rev. 39′) na-at ka-a-aš-ma *IT-TI* DUMU-*Y*[*A* kat?-t]a?-an [x-x] ú-da-i na-at a-ú ki-nu-un-ma [D]UMU-*Y*[*A*] (rev. 40′) ku-wa-pí *ŠA* ^{d}UTU-*ŠI* SIG$_5$-tar PAP-aš-ti tu-e-el-za SILI[M-a]n ^{d}UTU-*ŠI* ḫa-a-mi (rev. 41′) nu-mu-kán DUMU-*YA* ^{m}Wa-al-mu-un pa-ra-a na-a-i na-an EGIR-pa *I-NA* ^{KUR}W[i$_5$-]lu-ša (rev. 42′) LUGAL-ez-na-ni ti-iḫ-ḫi na-aš ka-ru-ú GIM-an LU[GAL] ^{KUR}Wi$_5$!-lu-ša e-eš-ta ki-nu-na-aš *QA-TAM-MA* [e-eš-du] (rev. 43′) nu-un-na-ša-aš ka-ru-ú GIM-an ARAD-*DUM* ku-la-wa-ni-eš e-[eš-ta k]i-nu-na-aš *QA*!-*TAM-MA* (rev. 44′) ARAD ku-la-wa-ni-eš e-eš-du	(rev. 32′) … to him … (rev. 33′) But he … (rev. 34′) And furthermore the troops … he went away. (rev. 35′) Then by night he … down. … (rev. 36′) And when his lord …… he fled to …. (rev. 37′) Then they made for themselves another lord. But I, My Majesty, did not recognize him. (rev. 38′) Kulana-ziti retained possession of the writing boards which I made for Walmu, (rev. 39′) and he has now brought them to (you), my son. Examine them! Now, my son, (rev. 40′) as long as you look after the well-being of My Majesty, I, My Majesty, will put my trust in your good will. (rev. 41′) Turn Walmu over to me, my son, so that I may reinstall him in kingship in the land of Wiluša. (rev. 42′) As he was formerly king of the land of Wiluša, he shall now likewise be! (rev. 43′–44′) As he was formerly our *kulawani*-vassal, he shall now likewise be our *kulawani*-vassal!
(rev. 45′) ZAG KUR Mi-la-wa-t[a]-ma-na-aš ^{d}UTU-*ŠI* DUMU-*YA*-ya GIM-an GIN-u-en [x-x-x-x t]u-e-	(rev. 45′–47′) As I, My Majesty, and you, my son, set the border(s) of the land of Milawanda, you must

e[l … le-e] (rev. 46′) kar!-ša-nu-ši ᵈUTU-*ŠI*-za tu-e-e[l] SILIM-an ša-ku-wa-aš-ša-r[i-it ZI-it ḫa-a-mi nu-]ut-ták-k[án] (rev. 47) *A-NA* ZAG ᴷᵁᴿMi-la-wa-ta an-da ku-it *UL* pé-eḫ-[ḫu-un …]x[…]	not neglect/omit your ……… I, My Majesty, will trust . firmly in your good will. And the …… which I did not give to you along with the border territory of the land of Mila-wanda…
(lower edge 1) *A-BU-KA*-⸢za⸣ [x-x-x] ku-iš am-me-el ḪUL SIG$_5$-u-wa i-la-liš-ke-z[i *A-NA* ᵈUTU-*ŠI*-ma] (2) ḪUL-u-wa-aš INIM.MEŠ-aš ku-iš INIM-aš SAG.DU-aš nu-mu a-pa-a-at iš-[… *A-BU-KA*-za-kán] (3) am-me-el ARAD!?-iš[319] wa-li-at nu-za-kán ka-ru-ú ku-wa-pí ᵁᴿᵁTÚL-na-an wa-l[i-at nu-mu me-mi-iš-ta …] (4) ši-wa-ri-ya-[w]i$_5$ GIM-an-ma-mu *A-BU-KA* ᴸᵁ́*LI*<-*ṬÙ-TUM*> ᵁᴿᵁU<-ti-ma> ᵁᴿᵁAt-<ri-ya> NU SUM nu an-[…] (5) nu ᵐKARAŠ-ZA u-i-ya-nu-[un …]	(lower edge 1) Your father ……, who always wished for my mis-fortune,[320] (2) and who was the primary factor in unfortunate affairs for My Majesty, … that to me. (2–3) Your father boasted pos-session of my *subjects*?. (3) And when earlier he boasted possession of the city of Arinna, he said to me: "…… (4) I will retain." (4) But when your father did not give me the hostages of the cities of Utima and Atriya, then I …-ed ……, (5) and I sent Kulana-ziti.
(l. e. 1) [zi-ik-]ka$_4$ INIM ᵁᴿᵁA-wa-ar-na *Ù* ᵁᴿᵁP[í-na …]-kán ᵈUTU-*ŠI* x[…] (l. e. 2) […]x-x-x-te-eš *UL* an-da u-uḫ-ḫu-u[n …] *IŠ-TU* ᴳᴵˢTUKUL ᴳᴵKAK.Ú.[TAG.GA] x (l. e. 3) […]x SIG$_5$-an[-n]i še-er an-da *UL* u-uḫ-ḫu-u[n x x x pa-r]a-a ⸢u⸣-uḫ-ḫu-un[321] INIM ᵁᴿᵁA<-wa-ar-na> ᵁᴿᵁPí<-na> zi-i[k-k]a$_4$? m[e-mi-iš-ta] (l. e. 4) […]x ᴸᵁ́*LI-ṬÙ-TUM* ᵁᴿᵁA-wa-<ar-na> ᵁᴿᵁPí-na pa-a-[i am?-mu?-uk?-w]a-ta ᴸᵁ́*LI-ṬÙ-TUM* ᵁᴿᵁU-ti-ma ᵁᴿᵁAt-ri-ya pa-ra-a [pé-eḫ-ḫi] (l. e. 5) nu-ut-ta ᵈUTU-*ŠI* ᴸᵁ́*LI*<-*ṬÙ-TUM*> [ᵁᴿᵁU-<ti-ma> ᵁᴿᵁAt<-ri-ya> p]a-ra-a-pát *AD-DIN* zi-ik-ma-mu NU S[UM? …] (l. e. 6) na-at *UL* i[m-ma	(l. e. 1) You too … the matter of the cities of Awarna and Pina? … . I, My Majesty, …………… (l. e. 2) Therein I did not see the ……… by means of mace and arrow. …… (l. e. 3) Out of consideration for your well-being I did not look ……. I looked away, (saying:) (l. e. 3) (Of) the matter of Awarna and Pina? you too have said: (l. e. 4–6) "Give me the hostages of Awarna and Pina. And I will give the hostages of the cities of Utima and Atriya over to you." I have given the hostages of Awarna and Pina over to you, but you did not give (your hostages) to me. It is not at all right. And your evil. … evil. …

a-a-ra nu tu]-e-el ḪUL *ŠA* zi-x[… ḪUL […] ḪUL […]	

103. KBo 18.15
To King Muršili II of Ḫatti from Mašḫuiluwa of Mira-Kuwaliya

Text: 520/f. **Find spot**: Bk. C: Büyükkale q/16. Under the Phrygian fortress wall. **Copy:** KBo 18.15. **Edition**: Hagenbuchner 1989b, 367–69 (no. 257). **Translation**: Beckman 1999a, 151–52 (no. 26). **Discussion**: Heinhold-Krahmer 1977, 183; Klinger 1996, 586; Klengel 1999, 175 [A23.9] (miswritten as KUB 18.15); de Martino 2005b, 305; Hoffner 2007, 396; Sidel'tsev 2007, 617.

The sender, Mašḫuiluwa, who here employs no title beyond "your servant," is nevertheless identified with the man who fled his native land in western Anatolia following a palace intrigue directed against him and was given refuge in Ḫatti by Šuppiluliuma I, who also gave him the Hittite princess Muwatti in marriage. Šuppiluliuma I's son, Muršili II, installed him as ruler of the kingdom of Mira-Kuwaliya. If so, then the reference to "my land" in line 18 is to Mira-Kuwaliya. Letters from subjects to the Hittite king do not use the king's name in the address formula. Nevertheless, the addressee of this letter is Muršili II. As with all Hittite letters, this one bears no date or indication of such. But since not long after Muršili II's twelfth regnal year Mašḫuiluwa rebelled and joined forces with É.GAL.PAP against the Hittites (see Bryce 1998, 230–33), this letter must pre-date that time.

Pazzu is introduced without title or other identifying terms, presumably because he was known to the Hittite court. Since his ancestral gods could only be worshiped by him in Ḫattuša, it is clear that he is a Hittite, not a native of Mira-Kuwaliya. Mašḫuiluwa's words in lines 5–6 suggest that Pazzu (and he) attributed Pazzu's illness to the displeasure of his ancestral gods. Since Pazzu had to travel to Ḫattuša to appease his ancestral gods, Mašḫuiluwa uses him as a courier, a source of information about the current state of affairs in Mira. The king is invited to question Pazzu (lines 17–19), but no mention is made of any second, accompanying letter that Pazzu might have delivered to the king from Mašḫuiluwa. As is customary in letters, the sender urges the addressee not to detain his messenger unduly, but to send him back promptly. De Martino assumes that Pazzu's prime of life and career was earlier, during the reigns of Arnuwanda I and Tudḫaliya III, and that his sickness here was because of his old age. See discussion of text 5.

(1) *A-NA* ᵈUTU-*ŠI* (2) [*BE*]-*LÍ-YA QÍ-BÍ-MA* (3) [*U*]*M-MA* ᵐPÍŠ.TUR ARAD-*KA-MA*	(1–3) Say to His Majesty, my lord: This is what your servant Mašḫuiluwa says:
(4) [k]a-a-ša ᵐPa-az-zu-un (5) [iš-tar-a]k-ta (6) nu-[uš-ši] *ŠA A-BI-ŠU* DINGIR.MEŠ.ḪI.A (7) na-ak-ki-iš-kán-ta-at (8) na-an-kán ka-a-aš-ma (9) *ŠA A-BI-ŠU* DINGIR.MEŠ (10) i-ya-wa-an-zi pa-ra-a (11) ne-eḫ-ḫu-un nu-za ma-aḫ-ḫa-an (12) DINGIR.MEŠ i-ya-az-zi (13) zi-in-na-a-i (14) na-an-kán *BE-LÍ-YA* (15) EGIR-pa pa-ra-a (16) ḫu-u-da-a-ak na-a-ú (17) *BE-LÍ-YA*-ya-an (18) *ŠA* KUR-*TI A-WA-TE*ᴹᴱŠ (19) pu-nu-uš-du	(4–5) Pazzu has recently become ill, (6–7) and his ancestral gods have begun to trouble him. (8–11) I have just sent him (back to Ḫatti) to worship his ancestral gods. (11–13) When he finishes worshiping the deities, (14–16) may my lord send him back immediately. (17–19) Let my lord also question him concerning the affairs of the district/territory.

104. KUB 23.102
From King Muwattalli II or Muršili III (Urḫi-Teššub) to King Adad-nirāri I of Assyria

Text: VAT 7499. **Find spot:** Unknown. **Copy**: KUB 23.102. **Edition**: Forrer 1929, 246–47; Hagenbuchner 1989b, 260–64, no. 192); Mora and Giorgieri 2004, 184–94. **Translation**: Beckman 1999a, 146–147 (no. 24A); Wilhelm in Janowski and Wilhelm 2006, 237–38. **Discussion**: Collins 1998, 17 n. 16; Klengel 1999, 204 [A5.4], 220 [A8?], 245 n. 465; Liverani 2001, 36, 42; Bryce 2003b, 83; Mora 2005, 309–10; Roth 2005, 191 with n. 42; de Roos 2005; Klinger in Hornung, Krauss, and Warburton 2006, 321; Freu 2007, 282; Heinhold-Krahmer 2007b, 194.

Part of a Hittite draft of a cool letter to Adad-nirāri I of Assyria. We assume his identity from the mention of the defeat of Wasašatta, which was an achievement of that king (see Wilhelm 1982, 54–55). Of the three Hittite kings whose reigns overlapped his, the best candidate is Muršili III (Urḫi-Teššub; see Hagenbuchner 1989b, 263; Bryce 1998, 283; and Beckman 1999a, 146). But the identity of the letter's author is still not entirely certain. Liverani (2001, 42) still favors identifying the author with the Hittite king Tudḫaliya IV and the addressee as Tukulti-Ninurta I. By conquering the last remaining king of what used to be the great kingdom of Mitanni (here referred to as the land of Ḫurri, the “Hurrian land”), the Assyrian king could rightfully style himself a “Great King,” the technical term for a ruler who controlled a network of smaller vassal states. But in Muršili III’s eyes this still did not entitle him to a position of equivalence with the Great King of Ḫatti. In this draft he brusquely rejects the Assyrian’s overtures and claim to be a true peer. The translation cannot truly capture the emotion conveyed by the syntax of the Hittite text. Bryce (2003b, 83) comments:

> Urhi-Teshub grudgingly accepted that the Assyrian’s military achievements justified his claim to the title of Great King. But this in itself did not give him the right to address the Great King of Ḫatti as his brother. ‘Brotherhood’ implied the existence of close personal links between two royal houses, frequently strengthened by marriage ties, and reflected in the exchanges of envoys and gifts and a commitment to friendship and cooperation. Urhi-Teshub had suffered the humiliation of losing to Assyria the last remnants of Hittite authority over former Mitannian territory east of the Euphrates. But Adad-nirari was being outrageously presumptuous in thinking that his military successes gave him the right to an instant ‘brotherhood’ relationship with the king at whose expense these successes had been won.

(1′) [x-]x *ŠA* ^{m}Wa-ša-š[a-at-ta …] (2′) [x x] *ŠA* KUR ^{URU}Ḫur-ri-ya ⸢me⸣-mi-iš-ke-[ši] (3′) [*IŠ*]-*TU* ^{GIŠ}TUKUL-za zi-ik t[ar]-aḫ-ta (4′) [x-]ya-za tar-aḫ-ta nu-za LUGAL GAL (5′) ki-iš-ta-at ŠEŠ-*UT-TA*-ma *Ù ŠA* $^{\text{ḪUR.SAG}}$Am-ma-na (6′) ú-wa-u-wa-ar ku-it nam-ma me-mi-eš-ke-ši (7′) ku-it-ta-at ŠEŠ-*UT-TA* na-at ku-it-ma (8′) *ŠA* $^{\text{ḪUR.SAG}}$Am-ma-na ú-wa-u-wa-ar (9′) ŠEŠ-tar-ta ku-e-da-ni me-mi-ni ḫa-at-ra-a-mi (10′) ŠEŠ-tar ku-iš ku-e-da-ni ḫa-at-re-eš-ke-ez-zi (11′) nu-kán *Ú-UL* a-aš-ši-ya-an-te-eš ku-i-e-eš (12′) nu 1-aš 1-e-da-ni ŠEŠ-tar ḫa-at-re-eš-ke-ez-zi (13′) [t]u-[u]k-ma ŠEŠ-tar	(1′–19′) You keep speaking about the defeat? of Wašašatta and the conquest? of the land of Ḫurri. You conquered by force of arms. You conquered by …. So you’ve become a “Great King,” have you?[322] But why do you continue to speak about “brotherhood” and about coming to Mt. Ammana? What is it, (this) “brotherhood”? And what is it, (this) “coming to Mt. Ammana”? For what reason should I call you my “brother”? Who calls another his “brother”? Do people who are not on familiar terms with each other call each other “brother”? Why then should I call you “brother”? Were you and

ku-wa-at-ta še-er (14′) [ḫa]-at-ra-a-mi zi-ik-za-kán am-mu-uk-ka$_4$ (15′) 1-e-da-ni AMA-ni ḫa-aš-ša-an-te-eš (16′) [*A-B*]*I A-BA A-BI-YA*-ya GIM-an *A-NA* LUGAL KUR ^{URU}Aš-šur (17′) [ŠEŠ-tar] *Ú-UL* ḫa-at-re-eš-ker zi-ik-ka$_4$-mu (18′) [ú-wa-u-wa]-a[r] LUGAL.GAL-*UT-TA*-ya le-e ḫa-at-re-eš-ke-ši (19′) [*Ú-UL*-mu] ZI-an-za	I born of the same mother? As my grandfather and my father did not call the King of Assyria "brother," you should not keep writing to me (about) "coming" and "Great Kingship." It displeases me.
The remaining six lines of column I and the preserved parts of columns II–IV are too broken for translation.	

Commentary

8 The form *ú-wa-u-wa-ar* here and possibly in line 18 is the verbal substantive of *uwa-* "to come" (*GrHL* §12.43). The verbal substantive of *au(š)-* "to see" is *ú-wa-a-tar,* and its infinitive *ú-wa-an-na* (*GrHL* §13.33).

105. KUB 23.103 and duplicates From King Tudḫaliya IV of Ḫatti to an Assyrian Nobleman Bāba-aḫ-iddina

Texts: A. Bo 2151; B. Bo 3089; C. Bo 718. **Find spots:** A: Temple I. B and C: Unknown. **Copies:** A. KUB 23.103 rev. 8–29; B. KUB 23.92 rev. 9–21; C. KUB 40.77. **Edition**: Otten 1959–1960; Hagenbuchner 1989b, 252–60. **Translation:** Beckman 1999a, 149–50 (no. 24C). **Discussion**: Harrak 1987, 147–48, 214; van den Hout 2002, 873; Mora and Giorgieri 2004, no. 17 and passim.

This Hittite-language draft of a letter to an official who occupied a high position at the courts of Adadnirāri I, Shalmaneser I, and Tukulti-Ninurta I, was combined on a single tablet with drafts of other letters with similar concerns addressed to the Assyrian court. The other letters are fragmentary, and the names of their recipients lost. We can be fairly sure of the identity of the parties in this letter from the analysis of its content. The proposed campaign against the region of Papanḫi, probably located in the mountains of southeastern Anatolia, is to be connected with the claim of Tukulti-Ninurta I to have fought against Papanḫi early in his reign (Otten 1959–1960, 46). He would be the new Assyrian ruler, and the author of these letters Tudḫaliya IV. On all this see Beckman 1999a, 149.

For more on this document and its several copies, see above in §1.2.9.

(A rev. 8) *UM-MA* ^{d}UTU-*ŠI-MA A-NA* ^{m}*BA-BA*-ŠEŠ-SUM *QÍ-BI-MA*	(A rev. 8) Thus speaks His Majesty: Say to Bāba-aḫu-iddina:
(A rev. 9) EN-*KU-NU*-ma-aš-kán ku-it BA.ÚŠ nu-uš-ma-aš DUMU EN-*KU-NU* ku-in ša-ra-a [… (^{LÚ}GURUŠ-tar GIM-an EGIR-pa)] (10) me-mi-er DINGIR-*LUM*-ši ma-aḫ-ḫa-an ŠÀ-er pí-ya-an ḫar-zi *PA-NI A-BI-ŠU*-pá[t x x x x…(-ši ku-i-e-eš)] (11) ^{m}GIŠ.GE$_6$-*AŠ-ŠUR*-aš ^{m}MAR.TU-*A-ŠA-RI-*<*ID*>-ša ka-a na-an-mu a-pu-u-uš me-[mi-… (*A-NA* ^{GIŠ}GU.ZA *A-BI-ŠU*-za-aš-kán)] (12) im-ma-ak-ku e-ša-at nu-uš-ši *Ú-UL A-NA* GUD.AM-pát ma-aḫ-ḫa-[an … (nu ki-i me-mi-iš-ke-ez-zi)] (13) i-ya-mi-ma-an-pát-wa ku-it-ki ma-a-an-wa-mu a-ra-aḫ-zé-nu-uš LU[GAL.MEŠ … (a-)pí-(ya[323]-ya-ma-an-wa-mu ú-wa-an-zi)] (14) ma-an-wa-za *ŠUM*-an ku-it-ki i-ya-mi nu me-ek-ki ku-it-ki a-pé[-[324]… (x *I-NA* ḪUR.SAG-*NI*-pát ku-it na-wi$_5$ pu-u-uḫ-ti)] (15) na-aš pa-iz-zi ku-e-da-ni *A-NA* LÚ.KÚR na-aš *IŠ-TU* INIM DINGIR[-*LIM-ŠU* …(x-ya kat-ta a-ar-nu-wa-an-za e-eš-du)] (16) *A-BU-ŠU*-ši-kán ku-it BA.ÚŠ a-pa-a-aš-ma-za-kán *A-NA* ^{GIŠ}GU.[ZA *A-BI-ŠU* … IGI-zi (pal-ši ku-e-da-ni LÍL-ri pa-iz-zi)] (17) na-aš-kán GEŠPÚ-za ku-e-da-ni 3-*ŠU* me-ek-ki ma-a-	(A rev. 9) Because your lord died—as they have attributed manhood to the son of your lord who has been elevated over you, (10) and as the god has given him heart, even in the time of his father … (11) Those who are here on his behalf?, Ṣillī-Aššur and Amurru-ašarēd, have told me about him, (12) that he has just seated himself upon the throne of his father, and how to him, not even as to a bull, …. And he keeps saying this: (13) "I want to accomplish something! If the foreign kings become hostile to me, they would then come against me, (14) and I could make a certain name for myself." Now very much … And because he has not yet … in the mountains in particular, (15) let the enemy against whom he goes be brought down … at the command of the god. (16) Because his father died, and he has just seated himself upon the throne of his father, the campaign on which he goes for the first time (17) should be one on which he enjoys three- or fourfold numerical superiority. If it is …, or some strong position, (18) then the first time they will … in this manner. (19) But the lands

[…(na-aš-ma-at GEŠPÚ-aḫ-ḫa-an) …] (18) ku-it-ki *AŠ-RU* nu IGI-zi pal-ši a-pé-ni-iš-šu-wa-an […(-na-an-zi)] (19) *A-BU-ŠU*-ma-aš-ši ku-e KUR.KUR.MEŠ *IŠ-TU* ^{GIŠ}TUKUL tar-aḫ-ḫa-an ḫ[ar-ta …] (20) ki-i-pát-mu ku-it KUR ^{URU}Ba-ba-an-ḫi me-mi-iš-kán-zi x […] (21) ḪUR.SAG.MEŠ-ya-wa me-ek-ki ḪUL-u-e-eš nu in-na-ra-[wa-tar …] (22) ku-it-ki nu a-pa-a-aš ki-nu-un-pát ku-it me-mi-iš-ke-ez-zi […] (23) na-at le-e-pát i-ya-an-zi DINGIR.MEŠ a-pé-ni-iš-ša-[an …] (24) ka-ru-ú-ya ku-wa-pí pa-iz-zi nu ma-a-an UN.MEŠ-tar x [x] (25) na-aš-ma-aš ÉRIN.MEŠ KUR-*TI*-pát ku-iš-ki na-at-kán šu-me-e[-eš?] (26) […] UN.MEŠ-tar-ma!-kán šu-me-e-da-az *Ú-UL* ku-i[t-ki x] (27) [ku-it-]ki? i-ya-zi nu-za EN-*KA* ku-e KUR[.KUR.MEŠ x] (28) […]-zi […]-zi nu e-eš-š/t[a- …]	which his father had conquered by force of arms. … (20) Because they keep telling me even this about the land of Papanḫi: (21) "…, and the mountains are very treacherous," then vigor? … something. (22) And because he even now continues to say … (23) They shall not do it. The gods thus … (24) And formerly, wherever he would go—if the population …, or it is some troops of the land, *Remainder too fragmentary for translation.*

Commentary

rev. 8 See Mora and Giorgieri 2004, 42.

rev. 12 "Speaking of the transposition of aspects typical of animal behavior into the human world, there is an interesting comparison using the image of a wild bull ($^{\text{GU}_4}$AM) in a letter in Hittite KUB XXIII 103 13 Rev. 12′, where this animal seems to indicate an impetuous and irrational attitude" (de Martino and Imparati 1995, 104).

2.3.1.2. NH Domestic Correspondence within the Royal Family (106–122)

We saw above that there were exceptional cases where older letters from the Middle Hittite period were kept. But as a general rule, letters formed a part of the broad category that van den Hout calls "category B" of which no duplicates were made and which were not kept for more than a few regnal periods (van den Hout 2002, 869). Thus we may expect that the vast majority of the letters recovered in the excavations at Boğazköy will belong to the latter half of the thirteenth century. Van den Hout mentions as examples of exceptions: "for older letters, except for the ones in Building A just mentioned, cf. KBo 18.51 (cf. J. Klinger, *ZA* 85 (1995) 92 with n. 71), KBo 18.54 (cf. StBoT 38, 170–71), KUB 19.20 + KBo 12.23 (ed. *ZA* 84 (1994) 60–88)" (2002, 870 n. 45).

106. KBo 18.2
From the King to the Queen Mother

Text: 2009/u. **Find spot:** Bk. D: in dumps of previous excavation, I b, p/10. **Copy:** KBo 18.2. **Edition**: Hagenbuchner 1989b, 4, 204–5 (Nos. 2 and 158) with anterior literature. **Discussion**: Güterbock 1979, 144 (obv. 1–2, rev. 4–8).

The addressed queen mother is quite possibly Puduḫepa, the widow of King Ḫattušili III, which would make the sender her son, King Tudḫaliya IV. But the identification is not certain. The order of sender and addressee reflects the fact that, although the queen is his mother, the king outranks her and therefore appears first in the opening line. For the somewhat unusual expanded well-being formula, using "the Thousand Gods," see §1.2.17.

Since there are lines at the end of the obverse and beginning of the reverse that are broken away or illegible, and all the commands in the preserved parts of the reverse are plural, the text on the reverse is probably part of a piggyback letter of the king addressed to those around the queen mother, who are urged to write to her royal son, reporting on her health and well-being (l. e. 1–2). The same request is made in obv. 5–6, where, however, no indication is made that others than the addressee herself is being addressed. Perhaps, then, the king first asks his own mother to write (i.e., dictate a letter) to him about her health, and then in a piggyback letter to those around her he orders that they see to the drafting and sending of such a letter.

The translation of the reverse is adapted from Güterbock 1979, 144.

The threefold repetition of the designation "my lady, my dear mother" is noted by Hagenbuchner (1989a, 81). On "let me know" (*šiggallu* rev. 12) as part of a formula see (Hagenbuchner 1989a, 99 n. 61).

(1) *UM-MA* dUTU-*ŠI-MA* (2) [*A-NA*] MUNUS.LUGAL GAŠAN-*YA* AMA.DÙG.GA-*YA* *QÍ-BI-MA*	(1–2) Thus speaks His Majesty: Say to the Queen(-mother), my lady, my dear mother:

(3) [GAŠAN-*Y*]*A* AMA.DÙG.GA-*YA LI-IM* [DINGIR.MEŠ] (4) [aš-šu-]li pa-aḫ-ša-an-da-r[u]	(3–7) May the Thousand Gods keep my lady, my dear mother, in good health.
(5) [GAŠAN-]*YA* AMA.DÙG.GA-*YA* a[š-šu-ul] (6) [ku-it m]a-aḫ-ḫa-an nu-mu ḫa-[at-ra-a-i?]	(5–6) Write to me how it is with my lady, my dear mother.
(7) [ ] ^{m}Ši-mi-ti-[…]	(7) Šimiti-…
(*Rest of the obverse lost in the break.*)	

106b. KBo 18.2
Piggyback Letter from the King to Several Persons

(Opening lines of the reverse lost in the break.)	
(rev. 2′) [x-x-x-x-x] up-pé-eš-[…] (rev. 3′) [x-x-x-x-]x-šar-ra-aš ^{m}*ŠU*?-*MI*-^{d}A.A[…] (rev. 4′) [o - o -o]x?-x?[325] ti-ya-at-tén na-at-kán pa-r[a-a] (rev. 5′) [ar-[326]]nu-ut-tén na-at-mu up-pé-eš-tén (rev. 6′) [k]a-a-ša-mu Ì.DÙG.GA iš-ki-ya-u-[wa-aš] (rev. 7′) NU.GÁL (rev. 8′) nam-ma-mu ma-a-an up-pa-a-i (rev. 9′) ku-iš-ki ma-a-an-mu *Ú-UL* (rev. 10′) ku-iš-ki up-pa-a-i nu-mu *ṬUP.PA*$^{HI.A}$[327] (rev. 11′) ḫa-at-ra-a-at-tén (rev. 12′) nu ši-ig-gal-lu	(*rev. 1′–3′ are too broken for translation.*) (rev. 4′–7′) … bring (pl.) it out and send (pl.) it to me! At present I have no sweet-smelling oil to anoint myself. (rev. 8′–12′) Furthermore, write (pl.) me letters so that I may know whether someone will send (it) to me or no one will send (it) to me.
(l.e. 1) [*MA-ḪAR* MUNUS.LUGAL AMA.DÙG.GA-*YA* aš-šu-]ul (l.e. 2) [ku-it GIM-an nu-mu EGIR-pa ḫa-at-r]a-at-tén[328]	(l.e. 1–2) Write (pl.) back to me how the well-being of the Queen, my dear mother, is.

Commentary

rev. 8–12 Hagenbuchner (1989a, 152 n. 17) comments on the position of the word “someone” (*kuiški*) after the finite verb in rev. 8. This grammatical feature is treated now in *GrHL* §18.34 and §30.11 (“right-dislocation”), where other examples are cited. Lines 8–12 are also edited in CHD *šakk-* 1 c

3′ a'. For the non-cultic anointing of persons for cosmetic or health reasons see Hoffner 1995c, 111.

107. Güterbock 1979, 142–44
To the King from the Queen

Find spot: Unknown. **Copy**: None. **Edition**: Güterbock 1979, 142–44. **Discussion**: Hagenbuchner 1989b, 7 (no. 4), 161–62 (no. 106). According to Güterbock 1979, this letter (especially the piggyback letter on the reverse) is related to text 106.

It is highly doubtful that one can date this letter as early as prior to Muršili II solely on the basis of a common name like ᵐNÍG.BA-ᵈU and the use of a formulaic *katti=mi* or *katti=ti* (*pace* Hagenbuchner 1989b, 161).

(1) *[A-N]A* ᵈUTU-*ŠI BE-LÍ-YA* (2) *[Q]Í-BÍ-MA* (3) *UM-MA* MUNUS.LUGAL GÉME-*KA-MA* (4) *MA-ḪAR* ᵈUTU-*ŠI BE-LÍ-YA* (5) ḫu-u-ma-an SIG_5-in (6) e-eš-du nu ᵈUTU-*ŠI* (7) *BE-LÍ-YA* DINGIR.MEŠ TI-an (8) ḫar-kán-du nu *A-NA* ᵈUTU-*ŠI* (9) *BE-LÍ-YA* ŠU.ḪI.A-uš (10) a-ra-aḫ-za-an-da aš-šu-li (11) ḫar-kán-du nu ᵈUTU-*ŠI* (12) *BE-LÍ-YA* pa-aḫ-ša-an-ta-ru (13) ka-a-ya kat-ti-mi (14) ḫu-u-ma-an SIG_5-in	(1–2) Say to His Majesty, my lord: (3) Thus speaks the Queen, your maidservant: (4–6) May all be well with Your Majesty, my lord! (6–11) May the gods keep Your Majesty, my lord, alive and lovingly hold their hands around Your Majesty, my lord, (12) and protect Your Majesty, my lord! (13) Here, with me too, all is well.
(15) *A-NA* ᵈUTU-*ŠI* ku-it *BE-LÍ-YA* (16) [k]i-iš-ša-an *AQ-BI* (17) [ma]-a-an-wa a-pa-a-at ut-tar (18) [ki-š]a-ri nu-wa *MA-ḪAR* ᵈUTU-*ŠI* (19) [ú-wa-mi m]a-a-an a-pa-a-at-ma (20) [ut-tar *Ú-UL*] ki-ša-ri (21) [...] an-tu-wa-aḫ-ḫa-aš (22) [...-]x ku-it (23) [...]-iz-zi pé-e-da-aš (24) [...] ni-ni-ik-ta-ri (25) [...] a-pa-a-at ut-tar (26) [...] *Ú-UL* (27) [...] nu ᵈUTU-*ŠI BE-LÍ-YA* (28) [...]x u? ma? aš?	(15) Concerning what I said to Your Majesty, my lord, thus: (17) "If that thing happens, I shall come to Your Majesty. (19) But if that thing does not happen, (21) ... a person (22) ... what/since (23) ...... he carried (24) ... is raised? (25) ... that thing/word (26) ... not (27) ... Then Your Majesty, my lord, (28) ....

107b. Güterbock 1979, 142–44
Piggyback Letter from mNÍG.BA-dU
(= Ari-Teššub or Piyama-Tarḫunta) to [PN]

(29) [*A-NA* o - o L]Ú *ŠAL-ŠI MA-AḪ-RI-YA* (30) [*QÍ-BÍ-MA UM-M*]*A* mNÍG.BA-dU (31) [ARAD-*KA-MA* kat]-ti-ti [ḫ]u-u-ma-an (32) [SIG$_5$-in e-eš-du nu-ut-t]a DINGIR.MEŠ (33) [aš-šu-li pa-aḫ-ša]-an-ta-ru	(29–33) Say to PN, the third, my superior: Thus speaks mNÍG.BA-dU, your servant: May all be well with you, and may the gods lovingly protect you!
(34) [...]x É.GAL-*LIM* (35) [...-]x-at-ta-aš (36) [...] GAL LÚÚ.ḪUB (37) [...-]x-ta (38) [GAL LÚ?]Ú.ḪUB ki-iš-ša-an (39) [*IQ-BI*?] GIŠ*IN-BI*ḪI.A-wa-at-ta (40) Ì.GIŠ?-ya am-mu-uk pé-eḫ-ḫi (41) [Ì.]DÙG.GA-ma-wa GAD-ya am-mu-uk (42) [da-aḫ-]ḫi nu *BE-LU I-NA* x [x x] (43) [...] nu Ì.DÙG.GA x [x] (44) [...] x ku-iš pa-a-i	(34–44) ... palace .... the chief of the deaf men .... The chief of the deaf men spoke thus: "Fruit and sesame oil I shall give you, but the sweet(-smelling) oil and linen cloth I shall take." Now, the lord is? in ..., and who will deliver sweet(-smelling) oil ...?

Commentary

29 For the tentative reading [... L]Ú *ŠAL-ŠI*, which is very uncertain, see Güterbock 1979, 144. I wonder if these are not rather the final signs of a man's name? Hagenbuchner has noted that there is little space in the break for an entire PN, perhaps only two signs after *A-NA*. The man could have been addressed by only his title. Read: [...-]x-*a*/*uḫ*?-*ši*?

For *MAḪRÎ–YA* "my superior" at the end of the sequence of PN plus rank designation see HKM 27: 17 (text 32); HKM 29 rev. 11 (text 34); HKM 36: 37; and HKM 52: 19–20 (text 55).

30 For the PN see Laroche 1966, 980–82, 986–88.

31 Restoration by Hagenbuchner 1989b, 7 (no. 4) 161–62.

108. KBo 18.4
From the King of Išuwa to his Father, the Chief of the Charioteers

Text: 327/r. **Find spot**: Bk. F: Büyükkale d/12. In loose rubble over the north corner of Building F. **Copy**: KBo 18.4. **Edition**: Hagenbuchner 1989b, 181–82, no. 132. **Discussion**: Rosenkranz 1973, 73; Pecchioli Daddi 1977.

A "greeting formula letter," whose late script dates it in the reign of Ḫattušili III or his successors. The anonymous sender is obviously a member of the extended imperial family. The name is not found in van den Hout 1995, nor is the man identified in Hagenbuchner 1989b, nor in the Tudḫaliya IV documents of Klengel 1999, 274–85. Perhaps he was the recipient of the letter KBo 4.14 (not in Hagenbuchner 1989b)[329] sent by Tudḫaliya IV to the king of Išuwa (Bryce 1981, 352 quoting Singer 1985); cf. Beal 1992, 447 with nn. 1665–66.

The anonymous Chief of the Charioteers could be the mGAL-dU (Ura-Tarḫunta) known from a legal deposition text and the so-called Bronze Tablet (see Gurney 1993, 25). But for him to be an older person would date this letter in the reign of Tudḫaliya IV. On the ranks Charioteer (LÚ*KARTAPPU*) and Chief of the Charioteers see Pecchioli Daddi 1977.

Often in Hittite letters the personal name of the sender or addressee is omitted, if his title/office and the context is enough to identify him (Hagenbuchner 1989a, 43–44). Although the address formula "my dear father" shows the addressee to be the senior, the king of Išuwa outranks him: therefore his name appears first (Hagenbuchner 1989a, 46).

(1) [*UM*]-*MA* LUGAL URUI-šu-wa-*MA* (2) [*A-NA*] GAL LÚ*KAR-TAP-PÍ* (3) [*A-BI*] DÙG.GA-*YA* *QÍ-BI-MA*	(1–3) Thus speaks the King of Išuwa: Say to the Chief of the Charioteers, my dear father:
(4) *MA-ḪAR A-BI* DÙG.GA-*YA* (5) ḫu-u-ma-an SIG_5-in e-eš-du (6) nu *A-BI* DÙG.GA-*YA* (7) DIN≈GIR.MEŠ aš-šu-li PAP-an-da-ru	(4–6) May all be well with my dear father, and may the gods lovingly protect my dear father!
(8) *MA-ḪAR* dUTU-*ŠI* (9) *MA-ḪAR* MUNUS.LUGAL aš-šu-ul (10) ku-it GIM-an (11) nu-mu *A-BI* DÙG. GA-*YA* (12) EGIR-pa *ŠU-PUR*	(8–12) May may dear father send back to me a report of how it is with His Majesty and with the Queen.

109. KBo 18.48
From the King to Prince Ḫešni

Text: 59/g + 103/g. **Find spot**: Büyükkale. **Copy**: KBo 18.48. **Edition**: Hagenbuchner 1989b, 7–12 (no. 5); **Discussion**: Tani 2001; Mora and Giorgieri 2004, 99–100; Houwink ten Cate 2006.

Houwink ten Cate, whose interpretation requires a great number of conjectural restorations, has assumed that the sender of this letter was Tudḫaliya IV, who was at the time away from Ḫattuša, and that the letter was sent to Ḫešni, the prince of Carchemish, *in* Ḫattuša.

Mora (2004, 99–100) has pointed out that the letter KBo 18.25(+) presents some analogies to KBo 18.48, in which matters of borders seem to be discussed, the kings of Carchemish and Assyria are mentioned, and fragments of preceding messages are referred to. But above all it is the contemporary citation of Prince Ḫešni and of Taki-Šarruma in RS 17.403, a text from Ugarit in which border questions relative to the kingdom of Ugarit are discussed, that suggests so strongly the possibility of links between KBo 18.25(+) and KBo 18.48.

Heinhold-Krahmer (2002, 373 n. 75), however, reminds us of the rival suggestion of Malbran-Labat for reading the name as *Ḫi-iš-ni-i*-LUGAL-*ma* (=*Ḫišni-Šarruma)* LUGAL KUR ^{URU}*Ka*[*r-ga-miš*].[330]

(1) *UM-MA* ^{d}UTU-*ŠI-MA A-NA* ^{m}Ḫi-iš-ni-i DUMU-*Y*[*A QÍ-BI-MA*]	(1) Thus speaks His Majesty: Say to Ḫešni, my son:
(2) ⌜ka-a-ša⌝ *MA-ḪAR* ^{d}UTU-*ŠI* da-pí-an [SIG$_5$-in]	(2) All is well now with My Majesty.
(3) nu ka-a-aš ku-iš LÚ *ṬE$_4$-MU* ú[-it …] (4) ^{m}Ḫa-aš-du-ú-i-le-en GIM-an […] (5) nu-kán INIM LUGAL ^{KUR}Kar-ga-⌜miš⌝ […] (6) da-pí-an i-wa-ar LUGAL ^{KU}[^{R}…]	(3–4) As soon as this messenger who has come has…-ed Ḫašduili, (5) you should tend to? the entire matter/affair of the king of Carchemish … (6) in the manner of the king of …
(7) nu-kán ka-a-aš-ma *A-NA* LUGAL ^{KUR}K[ar-ga-miš pa-ra-a] (8) ne-ḫu-un nu *A-NA* LUGAL ^{KUR}Aš-š[ur][331] […] (9) ka-a-aš-ma ^{m}Kam-ma-li-ya-aš […]	(7) I have just sent to the king of Carchemish. (8) And I? …-ed? to/for the king of Assyria.[332] (9) Now Kammaliya is/has …

(10) nu-mu ki-i GIM-an ^{m}Ḫa-aš-du[-ú-i-li-iš …] (11) wa-tar-na-aḫ-ḫi-iš-ke-et nu […] (12) GIM-an UDU-un *TA-BAR-RI*! […] (13) LUGAL-i-ya ze-en-na-an [ḫar-ši …] (14) *A-NA* LÚ.MEŠ *ṬE$_4$-ME-YA* (or -ya) zi-[ik …]	(10) Since Ḫašduili has been communicating these things … to? me, (11–12) and when/as you have an extispicy performed on a sheep …, (13) and you have finished for the king too, (14) you?… to my messengers ….
(15) nu LUGAL ^{KUR}Kar-ga-miš *ṬUP-PU* […] (16) nu-za pé-dan$_x$ ḫar-du mar-ki[-ya?-zi?-ma ma?-a?-an?] (17) nu *ṬUP-PU* ḫe-e-eš na-at-kán […] (18) nu-ut-ták-kán GIM-an ZAG-na […] (19) ú-uk i-wa-ar LUGAL ^{KUR}Kar-g[a-miš …] (20) [m]a-a!-an-ma-an-za ka-a e-e[š-ta …] (21) […] x […]-ri-ya *UL*[…]	(15) And the King of Carchemish … a tablet … (16) Let him keep (his) place! *But if he refuses?*. (17) Then open the tablet! And *confirm* it …. (18) And just as … …-s you to the right, (19) I—like the King of Carchemish[333]—… (20) If you had been here, … (21) would not …
(Breaks off)	
(rev. 1′) ma-an-na-ša-a[n? d]u?-u-wa-an ar-ḫa GIN!-at []	(rev. 1′) *He would have gone off away from us.*
(rev. 2′) nu :an-na-ri : an-na-ri na-an-za-⸢an?⸣ ^{KUR}Ak-ka$_4$-d[u ša?-ak?-ta?] (rev. 3′) nu me-ek-ki SIG$_5$-in ma-a-an-ma-an-za LÚ.KÚR-ma ⸢e?⸣[-šu?-un?] (rev. 4′) ^{d}UTU-*ŠI*-ma-an-ši-kán *DI-NU* : an-za-nu-uḫ-ḫa ma-an-za S[IG$_5$-in] (rev. 5′) nu-u-wa-ma-na-aš ku-i[t]-ki nam-ma an-ze-el e-eš-t[a]	(rev. 2′) And *annari*?, *annari*?! The country of Babylonia …-ed[334] him. (rev. 3′) And (this is) very good. If I/you had been an enemy, (rev. 4′) I, ‘My Majesty,’ would have *a.*-ed[335] a legal suit against him, I would be successful.[336] (rev. 5′) He (the enemy?) would still have been in some way ours again.
(rev. 6′) a-pé-da-ni-ya-ma-an-ši-kán [INIM-ni še-er] x-ru-x-ni ú-wa-u-e[n?][337] (rev. 7′) LÚ.KÚR-wa! an-ze-el ku-e INIM.MEŠ ḫa-at-re-eš-ke-zi x[- x -x] (rev. 8′) tu-el LÚ.KÚR-aš! *UL*-pát ku-[i]t-[k]i ar-ḫa BAL-zi (rev. 9′) GEŠTU!-ši-ma-wa ku-iš l[a?-a-k]i? nu-wa-kán INIM LUGAL ^{KUR}Ka[r-ga-miš] (rev. 10′) *UL* BAL-nu-uš-k[i-zi]	(rev. 6′) And on account of that matter we would have come to him in … (place name?), (saying,) (rev. 7′) “Our affairs about which the enemy wrote, (rev. 8′) will your enemy change nothing? (rev. 9′–10′) But will not he who …-s in his ear? change the word of the king of the country of Carchemish?”

(rev. 11′) ki-nu-na-aš-kán EGIR-zi-an : ḫur-la ku-it-ki iš[-…[338]] (rev. 12′) EGIR-pa SUD-u-<e>-ni ki-nu-un-ma-at ^{d}UTU-*ŠI* GIM-an mu-[ta?-a?-mi?] (rev. 13′) LUGAL ^{KUR}Kar-ga-miš-ya-at a-pí-ya *QA-TAM-MA* mu-[ta?-id?-du?] (rev. 14′) [n]a-aš-ma-za-kán an-da še-eš-ḫi na-aš-ták-kán x[…] (rev. 15′) na-an-kán *QA-TAM-MA* x [o-]lu nu *TA-BAR-*[*RI* …] (rev. 16′) nu-mu da-pí-an ^{m}K[am]-ma-li-ya-aš[…]	(rev. 11′) Now to us, after (so long?) some *aggravation*?? [is becoming] k[nown]. (rev. 12′) We pull back (from each other). But, now, just as I, 'My Majesty,' se[t] it (viz. the aggravation) [aside], (rev. 13′) in the same manner also the king of the country of Carchemish, [must] then/there set it [aside]! (rev. 14′) Or you should make a choice in it! … (*Rest of the text too broken for connected translation.*)
(rev. 17′) ^{m}Ḫu-zi-ya-aš-ša ku-e *ṬUP-PA*$^{HI.A}$ […] (rev. 18′) na-at-za ma-a-an ma-la!-ši x[…] (rev. 19′) ke-e-ya-kán EGIR.UD x[…] (rev. 20′) ma-a-an-ma-za mar-ki-ya[-…] (rev. 21′) [o o -]ya LUGAL ^{KUR}Kar-g[a-miš …] (22′) DÙ-an-du na-a[t-…]	(rev. 17′) And what tablets of Ḫuziya … (rev. 18′) if you approve them, … (rev. 19′) and these in the future … (rev. 20′) but if you reject … (rev. 21′) … the king of Carchemish … (rev. 22′) let them make …

Commentary

In lines 8 and 10 the Hittite verb underlying the logogram BAL could as well be *waḫnu-* "to turn, change (something)" as *waggariyanu-* "to cause to rebel" (see Hoffner 1997c).

The form in line 9 shows what would be an incorrect sequence of clitics for an interpretation GEŠTU! *=ši=ma=wa* "but … the ear to him": the correct sequence for that meaning would be GEŠTU-*ma-wa-aš-ši* (see *GrHL* §30.15). The regular order of clitics favors taking *-ši* as either the inflection of the noun (or verb) GEŠTU, or a clitic possessive prounoun "his/her." This consideration guided the present provisional translation.

rev. 11′ I take *ḫurla* to be a neuter (perhaps pl.) noun. In this context one expects a meaning like "aggravation", something that has turned the emperor and the king of Carchemish against each other or made them suspicious of each other. There is a noun in the dative-locative singular in KBo 10.37 iii 36–37 in the sequence of parts of the human speech apparatus: KA×U-*i* … EME<-*i*> … *ḫurli* "mouth … tongue … *ḫurla-*", which suggests that the neuter (plural?) *ḫurla* may refer to hostile words. The pronoun *-at* in lines 12 and 13 refers back to this *ḫurla* "aggravation."

2.3.1.3. NH Domestic Correspondence to or from the Royal Family

110. KBo 13.62
School Tablet Based Upon a Real Letter
from [...] to [the Queen?]

Text: 21/u. **Find spot:** House on the Slope: L/18 – c/5, in the Phrygian area. **Photo:** Konk. **Copy**: KBo 13.62. **Edition**: Hagenbuchner 1989b, 22–25 (no. 15). **Discussion:** Hoffner 1977c, 155 (dating); Catsanicos 1986, 131; Ünal 1989, 506 ("Kritzeleien"); Hagenbuchner 1989a, 34; Oettinger 1989/1990, 90; Haas 1994, 125 n. 97, 218 n. 211; de Martino and Imparati 1995, 103–4; Klengel 1999, 248 [A28]; Korolëv 1999, 288–89; Boley 2000, 149, 296; Torri 2008 (on the function of the House on the Slope).

Giulia Torri and I (in e-mail correspondence August 10–12, 2008) agreed that this tablet is a unique example in the Hittite archives of a scribal training tablet (model letter) that used an existing letter (apparently to the queen) as the text to be copied by the student scribe (for model letters outside of Ḫatti see §1.1.5.1.7).[339] That the text on the obverse had its origin in a real letter is made very likely by the occurrence of a personal name (fAruḫipa) in its body that is unrelated to the sender or addressee names. The tablet's find spot, the House on the Slope, makes this identification all the more plausible, since Torri (2008) has made a good case that this was the location for scribes who were recopying and adapting existing older compositions, and may very likely have been a scribal school.

The text on the obverse was the teacher-scribe's copy from the original, real letter. The text on the back is the student's copy. The handwriting on the obverse is neat and without mistakes; that on the reverse is less skilled and shows mistakes and erasures. The student's signature was apparently attempted in the colophon on the reverse, but subsequently erased together with a few additional lines of his writing. The hierogrlyphic signature, ASINUS$_{2A}$-*tà-la-na,* is that of the teacher.

As for the content of the original, real letter that served as the model, unfortunately, all that remains of the opening two lines of the obverse, which would have contained the name and titles or terms of relationship of the addressee and those of the sender, are parts of the final words.

As for the addressee, in view of the repeated use of *BĒLTI=YA* "my lady" in the body of the text (lines 4, 5, 19) and the great concern shown about her illness, as well as the considerable efforts exerted on her behalf, she was a high-ranking woman, perhaps kin to the sender. It is not excluded that she was the queen. This is the view of Hagenbuchner 1989b and de Martino and Imparati 1995, 103. Not realizing that this was a school tablet, and that the scribe named in hieroglyphs was not the scribe who wrote the original letter, Hagenbuchner dated the letter itself to the time of Ḫattušili III, in part on the basis of reading the damaged name(s) in the colophon as referring to the scribe Ša(w)ušga-ziti (Hagenbuchner 1989b, 22–25; Klengel 1999, 248 [A28] recording this opinion). But on the basis of collation by the online photo, Torri questions the readings, preferring to read the hieroglyphic name as ASINUS$_{2A}$-*tà-la-na*, the scribe Tarkasnatalana whose name is known from hieroglyphic seals at Ḫattuša (Torri 2008, 770–80 with nn. 52–53, citing Herbordt 2005, 274 n. 426 [reference conveyed to Torri by E. Rieken] for the seals).

The sender's name is also broken away except for the final term [...-*K*]*A-MA* "your [...]." One expects here [ARAD-*K*]*A-MA* "your [servant]" or [DUMU-*K*]*A-MA* "your [son]." The remaining context of the letter gives no significant clue as to his identity. He is with the king, since he conveys to the addressee the news that the king is well (line 3). This might suggest that the addressee is a close relative to the king, either the queen or the queen-mother.

In the greeting (or well-wishing) formula the sender uses language more intense and lofty than the usual. But instead of bidding "the Thousand Gods" to keep his lady alive, as in at least one letter to the queen (text 106), he employs the usual formula "May the gods keep my [lady] alive!" (line 5; and see §1.2.17). He has been informed about a fever that has attacked the addressee, and his informant adds that she is eating *maḫḫuella*-bread and fruit (line 9), perhaps a diet thought to be helpful in curing a fever. The writer expresses his profound sadness and sympathy for her in words that are also found in a prayer of the king Muršili II, describing his grief over the death of his beloved wife (lines 10–11; see Hoffner 1983). The deliberate use of such an expression, elsewhere only used with reference to the death of the queen, also suggests a royal identity for the addressee. His tearful cry to the gods on his addressee's behalf uses a rare Luwian term (*iyawan*) found elsewhere in the lofty language of mythology or magic rituals. The content of his tearful cry—"Oh that the gods would step in again! If only they will make [my lady] well again! If only ^{d}Za$^{?}$-x[-...] will [...]!" (lines 13–14)—indicates that this woman has been seriously ill before and recovered after divine intervention.

The sender then promises that together with others ("we" in line 15) he will scour the countryside (*gimra-*) to find something that the queen either has requested or needs. It may have something to do with wild animals (*ḫuetar*), but its identity remains unclear. Soysal (2006) suggested the restoration *ú-m*[*i*$^{??}$-*e-ni*] in line 18, and thought this might be another "safari" to retrieve wild animals, as is attested in HKM 48 (text 51; on which see Hoffner 1997b). But the search may rather have something to do with the queen's illness: something derived from animals that could be used in a magic healing or "purification" ritual.

At this point the obverse breaks off, and there was probably much further text on the bottom of the obverse.

The missing majority of the reverse contained the student scribe's copy. This scribe signs his copy at the bottom in the manner normal for scribes of administrative or literary texts, not in any way appropriate for the scribe of a letter: ŠU ^{m}PN "the hand of PN." There are traces of four lines of cuneiform, all erased. Superimposed on this erased cuneiform is the large hieroglyphic name now read by Torri as the scribe ASINUS$_{2A}$-*tà-la-na* (Tarkasnatalana). This man would have been the teacher-supervisor who probably made the model letter on the obverse of the tablet (so Torri in personal communication). The traces of the apprentice scribe's name in the erased colophon are impossible to reconcile with the name Tarkasnatalana. Hagenbuchner proposed $^{m.d}$INANNA-LÚ$^{!}$-*i*$^{!}$, for which she proposed the reading Šaušga-ziti. As to this erased colophon, it is now too damaged for confident reading. But the arrangement of the traces suggests that it was more than just the scribe's name, but contained at least two additional lines, describing his rank and perhaps his supervisor's name. If so, then it might have indicated that he was an apprentice (or student) scribe (GÁB.ZU.ZU), like other scribes identified in colophons from the House on the Slope (Torri 2008).

As Torri (2008) correctly observes, the earlier theory that the scribe tried twice to write his name in cuneiform, then erased it and substituted a hieroglyphic writing of the same name, would not have been possible if he were the writer of the obverse. The writer of the obverse was no incompetent student-scribe, for his writing is clear, precise, and without erasures. But if, Torri and I suppose, the scribe who wrote the reverse was the student, and the writer of the obverse the teacher Tarkasnatalana, then it is indeed possible that it was the student who made the mistakes in the colophon.

I agree with Torri that we simply do not know the motivation for this strange erasure of the cuneiform colophon and the superposition at a different angle of the hieroglyphic name. As to why a letter was chosen as the model text for the only recovered school tablet, when the House on the Slope contained so many other types of text suitable for exercise, and not many examples of historical-political ones, one would assume that student scribes would have to be trained to copy letters, if their future activities involved drafting real ones. There is abundant evidence for model practice letters in

Egypt and elsewhere. We simply have no other evidence yet that scribes in the House on the Slope were doing this.

(1) [*A-NA* MUNUS.LUGAL *BE-EL-TI*$_4$*-YA QÍ-B*]*I-MA* (2) [*UM-MA* ^{m}… ARAD?/GÉME?-*K*]*A-MA*	(1) Say to the Queen, my lady: (2) Thus speaks PN, your servant:
(3) [*MA-ḪAR* ^{d}UTU-*ŠI*] *BE-LÍ-YA* ḫu-u-ma-an SIG$_5$-in	(3) All is well with His Majesty, my lord.
(4) [*A-NA* MUNUS.LUGAL] *BE-EL-TI*$_4$*-YA* ḫu-u-ma-an SIG$_5$-in [e-eš-du] (5) [nu *BE-EL-TI*$_4$*-Y*]*A* DINGIR.MEŠ TI-an ḫar-kán-du nu *BE-EL-T*[*I*$_4$*-YA*] (6) [GIG-an] nam-ma da-an-du nu-ut-ta : ḫa-at-tu-la-aḫ-ḫa-an-du	(4) May all be well with the Queen, my lady! (5) May the gods keep my lady, alive! (5–6) And may they take the illness <from> my lady again and make you well (again)!
(7) [*BE-EL-TI*$_4$-]*IA*-ma-mu ku-it ki-i : ta-pa-ša-aš ut-tar (8) ḫa-at-ra-a-it ^{f}A-ru-ḫi-pa-ša-at-mu ḫa-at-ra-a-iš (9) nam-ma ^{NINDA}ma-aḫ-ḫu-e-el-la-an ^{GIŠ}*IN-BU*-ya e-ez-za-az-zi (10) nu-mu-kán ZI-*YA* da-an-ku-i da-ga-an-zi-pí (11) kat-ta-an-ta pa-a-an-za a-pé-e-da-ni ud-da-a-ni pé-ra-an (12) [nu]-uš-ša-an *A-NA* DINGIR.MEŠ UGU : i-ya-u-wa-an [ḫal-zi-iḫ-ḫi] (13) [ma?-]an-na DINGIR.MEŠ ti-an-zi nam-ma ma-an-na[*BE-EL-TI*$_4$*-YA*] (14) : ḫa-at-tu-la-aḫ-ḫa-an-zi nam-ma ma-an ^{d}Za-a?[- …-z]i?	(7) But concerning this matter of a fever that my lady wrote me about—(8) (actually) it was Aruḫipa who wrote it to me— (9) "In addition she is eating *maḫḫuella*-bread and fruit": (10–11) on account of that matter (i.e., the serious illness of the addressee) my soul has gone down into the Dark Netherworld (i.e., I am *very sad*). (12) And my *tearful* cry goes up to the gods. (13–14) Oh that the gods would step in again! If only they will make my lady well again! If only ^{d}Za?-x-… will …!"
(15) ú-e-eš-ta![340] ka-a-ša gi-im-ra-a-an an-da [ša-an-ḫu-u-]e-ni (16) nu gi-im-ra-aš me-ek-ki ku-it x x x tar[-] (17) na-an-kán wa-ar-ḫu-u-wa-ya-az ar-ḫa x[…] (18) ar-nu-um-mi-en nu ḫu-u-e-tar ma-ši-wa-an ú-m[i??-e-ni] (19) na-at ú-wa-mi *A-NA BE-EL-TI*$_4$*-YA* ḫ[a?-at-ra-a-mi]	(15) We will now scour? the countryside. (16) And because the countryside is very … (17–18)… and (because) we moved it out/away from the *underbrush*, (18–19) I will certainly *write*? to my lady however much wildlife we see?.

(*Bottom half of the obverse and top half of the reverse are broken away.*)	
(rev. 1′) kat-t[a …] (rev. 2′) nu-uš-ma-aš DINGIR.MEŠ […]	… … (rev. 2′) and may the gods … you (pl.) …
(rev. 3′) ŠU mINANNA-LÚ!-i! (rev. 4′) ŠU mINANNA-LÚ!-i!	(rev. 3′) The hand(writing) of Šauška-ziti. (rev. 4′) The hand(writing) of Šauška-ziti.
(Hieroglyphs reading Sà-uš-ga-VIR)	

Commentary

obv. 7–9 is edited in CHD sub NINDA*maḫḫue(l)la-*.

obv. 15 A possible objection to taking *ú-e-eš-ta* as *weš=šta* and as the first word of the clause is the fact that both *kāša* and *kašma* generally occur as the first accented word in the clause, with only unaccented conjunctions (*nu, ta,* etc.) and their clitics preceding. But as with all rules, there are exceptions to this one as well: dUTU-*ŠI-ma-aš* mNIR.GÁL EN KUR.KUR.HI.A *ka-a-ša* [*ḫal-zi-iḫ-ḫu-un nu-za ki-i*] *a*[*r-ku-wa*]*-ar i-*[*ya-mi*] "[I], My Majesty, Muwattalli, lord of the lands, [have] hereby [summoned] you, and m[ake this] p[lea]" is a virtually certain restoration of KBo 11.1 obv. 11. The presence of the clitic object in *-ma-aš* (for *-ma-šmaš*) guarantees that there is a finite verb to follow, and it can only follow *kāša.* A second example occurs in this same text: *ki-nu-na-at ka-a-ša* dUTU-*ŠI* mNIR.GÁL EGIR-*pa* SIG_5-*aḫ-mi* obv. 32–33 "But now I, My Majesty, Muwattalli hereby make it right again." Here *ki-nu-na* "but now" is an accented word and precedes *kāša* in the clause. See further examples in rev. 10, 13, as well as in KBo 16.42 obv. 7 (where *am-mu-ga ka-a-ša* […] begins a new paragraph and must therefore be the beginning of a clause), KUB 13.31: 5′, HKM 44: 2′–5′ (*an-da-ma-kán ka-a*?[*-ša*] (3) m*Ma-ra-ku-in* (4) *ku-it* LÚ*QAR-DAP*<*-PU*> (5) *pa-ra-a ne-eḫ-ḫu-un*). If the general tendency for *kāša/kāšma* to be the first accented word can admit these exceptions, it can admit others. I see no viable way to take *ú-e-eš-ta* differently here.

obv. 18–19 On these lines, and especially the translation "how much wildlife," see comments on text 51 and note 148.

111. KBo 18.54
To the King from Kaššū

Text: 807/w. **Find spot:** Bk. D: p-q/10-11. **Copy**: KBo 18.54. **Photo**: Bittel and Neve 1966, 13 and online in Konk. **Edition**: Neu 1968, 44–45 (rev. 11′–25′, 15); Melchert 1977, 386 (line 21–l. e. 1); Pecchioli Daddi 1978–1979, 204–10; Hagenbuchner 1989b, 57–63 (no. 40), 130 (no. 84); Marizza 2007a, 101–11. **Discussion**: Neve in Bittel and Neve 1966, 13; Haas 1970, 171 (sub 807/w); Ünal 1977, 461 (on the food shortage mentioned in rev. 3′–7′); Beckman 1983b, 110 (on obv. 14–17); Boysan-Dietrich 1987, 76–79; Beal 1992, 402 n. 1513, 457 n. 1693; Cotticelli-Kurras 1992, 125 (on obv. 3–6); Klinger 1995a, 102; de Martino and Imparati 1995, 114; van den Hout 1995, 229 (on Kaššū and the Maşat provenience of KBo 18.54); 2004a (on the food shortage); Klengel 1999, 127 [A1]; Boley 2000, 365.

Very likely a letter from Tapikka to Ḫattuša and datable in the reign of Šuppiluliuma I or slightly earlier. Konk. thinks it might be a Middle Hittite letter ("mh?").

There are many difficulties to translating this letter. In obv. 7–17 the difficulty is mainly in determining the correct restorations for the text breaks. Our choices generally reflect those of Güterbock and Beckman (1983b, 110), but others are certainly possible.

Kaššū, whose duties are primarily military, shows this by his inclusion of the troops in the request for information about health and well-being (lines 3–6); see above in §1.1.9.4. Apparently, Kaššū had received a tablet with instructions on it from the king, but the tablet was written in Akkadian ("Babylonian"), not Hittite. Since the king would never have dictated a letter in that language, it is clear that some royal scribe wanted to make trouble for Kaššū, whose language skills did not include Babylonian. Although he may have suspected a malicious prank, Kaššū could not afford to take the chance that the letter contained important instructions from the king. So he dispatched to the king Wandapa-ziti with the tablet. As always with these letters, it is rarely clear at which of his royal residences the king was: Ḫattuša, Šapinuwa, or some other palace.

After a long lacuna stretching over the end of the obverse and the beginning of the reverse, Kaššū turns to food shortages (*kašti,* rev. 5) and questions of procedure in storming an enemy city (rev. 9′–26′ l. e. 1). The king has dispatched a man named Tuttu with instructions to storm (*epurai-*) the enemy city. But the instructions specified that the wall not be knocked down (*pippa-*). This would have been in order to preserve the fortifications for the protection of the future Hittite garrison there. Kaššū reports that attempts to storm the city, presumably by using scaling ladders, have failed. He also reports that another method of penetrating the city, perhaps (judging from the adverbs "under" and "out") tunneling under the wall, also failed. He concludes that the only way they will ever successfully penetrate the defenses is by knocking down the wall. From other Hittite descriptions of seige we know that they understood the use of the battering ram (^{GIŠ}GU$_4$.SI.DILI). So perhaps they would use it, if the king gave the permission.

In rev. 20′–26′ and l. e. 1, Kaššū does what any good bureaucrat does: he anticipates his boss's objections and tries to answer them in advance. A good example is found in the Bible in 2 Sam 11: 19–21, where King David's general Joab sends a messenger to report casualties in the taking of an enemy city by siege:

> He instructed the messenger: "When you have finished giving the king this account of the battle, the king's anger may flare up, and he may ask you, 'Why did you get so close to the city to fight? Didn't you know they would shoot arrows from the wall? Who killed Abimelech son of Jerub-besheth? Didn't a woman throw an upper millstone on him from the wall, so that he died in Thebez? Why did you get so close to the wall?' If he asks you this, then say to him, 'Also, your servant Uriah the Hittite is dead.'" (2 Sam 11:19–21, NIV)

So if the king asks Kaššū why one of the other methods would not work, the answer is that the enemy city is surrounded by two walls, an outer and an inner, and Kaššū gives the king their measurements. How does he know these measurements if the enemy is defending the city from those very walls? Perhaps Kaššū only gives a very rough estimate. Or perhaps an earlier attempt to scale the walls failed only after an initial temporary occupation of the top of the walls, at which time one of Kaššū's men was able to record the measurements.

Kaššū also reports that in the process of trying to storm the city, using an instrument called the *epureššar* (rev. 25), the object went into the moat surrounding the city, and for this reason he requests that the king send another (l. e. 3). Just what this instrument was is unclear. Since they have been forbidden to use the battering ram, it is unlikely that it was this. A scaling ladder could be built on the spot. Perhaps a siege tower—an elevated platform for Hittite archers to shoot from into the city?

The meaning of the verb *epurai-* and the significance of the actions on the fortification wall (BÀD) and the subsidiary walls (*EGĀRU*) are problematic. Neu translated *epurai-* as "to storm" (German *erstürmen*). Puhvel (*HED*

E, 282–83) translated it as "to besiege, dam up." Boysan-Dietrich (1987, 76–79) took a different tack, rejecting the idea that a military operation is in view, and preferring a repair or maintenance operation. In her view *epurai-* means "to level, smooth down, plane." What has malfunctioned was not a siege, but a repair job on a city wall. I agree with those who reject this line of interpretation. If the verb *epurai-* means either "to besiege," "to storm" or even "to scale (the city walls)," then the derived noun *epureššar* could in addition to being an action noun, also denote equipment for performing that action. I have conjectured what Tuttu will bring (*udai*) is a replacement for the *epureššar* that "went into the moat" (rev. 25–26).

(1) *A-NA* dUTU-*ŠI* EN-*YA* *QÍ-BÍ-MA* (2) *UM-MA* mKaš-šú-ú ARAD-*KA-MA*	(1–2) Say to His Majesty, my lord: Thus speaks your servant Kaššū:
(3) *MA-ḪAR* dUTU-*ŠI* MUNUS.LUGAL aš-šu-ul (4) ku-it ma-aḫ-ḫa-an ŠÀ ÉRIN.MEŠ ša-ri-ku-wa-ya-kán (5) *Ù* ŠÀ ÉRIN.MEŠ ÙKU.UŠ ḫa-at-tu-la-an-na-za (6) ku-it ma-aḫ-ḫa-an nu-mu EN-*YA* EGIR-pa *ŠU-PUR*	(6) May my lord write back to me (3) how Your Majesty and Queen are, (4) and how the regular troops (5) and the ÙKU.UŠ troops are with respect to their health.
(7) mWa-an-da-pa-LÚ-iš ku-it *MA-ḪAR* EN-*YA* (8) pár-ḫi-iš-na-za u-un-né-eš-ta (9) nu *ṬUP-PU* ku-it *MA-ḪAR* EN-*YA* pé-e ḫar-da (10) na-at ar-ḫa pé-eš-ši-ya-at (11) ar-ḫa-ma-at ku-e-da-ni me-mi-e-ni (12) pé-eš-ši-ya-at na-at *A-NA* EN-*YA* (13) *Ú-UL* ka-ru-ú ḫa-at-ra-a-nu-u[n] (14) *ṬUP-PU*-ma ma-aḫ-ḫa-an x[x x x a-ni-i]a-an e-eš-ta (15) nu-mu LÚDUB.SAR ku-i[š ḫa-at-ra-a-iz-zi] (16) nu-za pa-bi-li<-li> an[-da le-e ḫa-at-ra-a-iz-zi <URU>pa-bi-li-li] (17) *Ú-UL* ša-a[g-ga-aḫ-ḫi] (18) x[…] x […]	(7–8) Regarding the fact that Wandapa-ziti drove hastily to my lord, (9–10) and discarded/disregarded[341] the tablet which he held? from? the presence of my lord: (11–13) the reason why he discarded/disregarded I have not previously explained (lit. written) to my lord. (14–15) Whenever the tablet is inscribed …, let the scribe who writes to me (16) not write in Babylonian: (16–17) I do not understand Babylonian. …
(Rest of obv. and beginning of rev. broken away.)	
(rev. 1′) ku-i[š? …] (2′) nu-mu p[ár?- …]	

(rev. 3′) ka-a-ša-k[án …] (rev. 4′) *Ù A-NA* ÉRIN.MEŠ […] (rev. 5′) ka-a-aš-ti za?[-…] (rev. 6′) *A-NA* GAL DUB.ŠAR.MEŠ […] (rev. 7′) nu-uš-ma-aš ḫal-ki-in […] (rev. 8′) […]	(rev. 3′–8′) … and for the troops … in a food shortage … to the Chief of the Scribes … and to them send? grain …
(rev. 9′) EN-*YA*-ya-kán ku-it mDu-ut[-tu-un …] (rev. 10′) e-pu-ra-wa-an-zi pa-ra-a na-a-[iš] (rev. 11′) BÀD-ma pí-ip-pa-wa-an-zi […] (rev. 12′) *Ú-UL* tar-na-aš nu ka-a-ša (rev. 13′) ma-aḫ-ḫa-an e-pu-re-eš-ga-u-en (rev. 14′) nu-un-na-aš-kán e-pu-ra-wa-an-zi (rev. 15′) *Ú-UL* ḫa-ap?-da-at (or ḫa-ad!-da-at) nu-kán BÀD […]x (rev. 16′) kat-ta-an ar-ḫa ḫa-ad-da-an-né-eš-ke-u-en (or ḫa-ap!-da-an-né-eš-ke-u-en) (rev. 17′) na-at *Ú-UL* ZAG-na-aḫ-ḫu-u-en (rev. 18′) nu ma-a-an BÀD ku-wa-pí ar-ḫa *Ú-UL* pí-ip-pa-an-zi (rev. 19′) e-pu-ra-wa-an-zi-ma-kán *Ú-UL* ḫa-ap-da-ri (or ḫa-ad!-da-ri)	(rev. 9′–19′) And concerning the fact that my lord dispatched Tuttu in order to storm (the enemy city) …, but you did not let the city wall be knocked down: Every time we tried to storm (the town), we did not succeed in storming (it). And every time we tried to *tunnel under* the town wall, we didn't succeed there either. If they do not knock the town wall down, it will be impossible to storm (the town).
(rev. 20′) ma-a-an EN-*YA*-ma ki-iš-ša-an te-ši (rev. 21′) ku-e-ez-za-wa-kán *Ú-UL* ḫa-ap-da-ri (or ḫa-ad!-da-ri) (rev. 22′) nu-kán BÀD ku-it iš-tar-na (rev. 23′) *E-GA-RU*-ma ku-iš 4 še-e-kán (rev. 24′) ku-iš-ma 3 še-e-kán (rev. 25′) ke-e-ez-za-ma-kán e-pu-re-eš-šar-ra (rev. 26′) []1?-e-da-za *A-NA ḪI-RI-TI* (l. e. 1) […]-x pa-it nu-un-na-aš-kán a-pé-ez-za *Ú-UL* ḫa-ap-da-ri (or ḫa-ad!-da-ri)	(rev. 20′–26′, l. e. 1) But if you, my lord, say the following: "Why will it be impossible?" Because inside the town wall one (subsidiary) wall is four *šekan* and another is three *šekan*. But in this direction (or: for this reason) the *epureššar* went into the moat on one? side, and for that reason it was impossible for us.
(l. e. 2) [… k]a-a-aš-ma mDu-ut-tu-uš ku-it ú-ez-zi (l. e. 3) […] ma-aḫ-ḫa-an nu e-pu-re-eš-šar ú-da-i (l. e. 4) [… a-pí]-ya a-ú	(l. e. 2–4) Concerning the fact that Tuttu is on the point of coming, it is like …! He will bring the (replacement?) *epureššar*. Look for him? there!

111b. KBo 18.54
Piggyback Letter to the King from Zarna-ziti

(l. e. 5) [*A-NA* dUTU-*ŠI* E]N-*YA* *QÍ-BI-MA UM-MA* mZa-ar-na-LÚ ARAD-*KA-MA*	(l. e. 5) Say to His Majesty, my lord: thus speaks Zarna-ziti, your servant:
(l. e. 6) [… aš-šu]-ul ku-it ma-aḫ-ḫa-an nu-mu EN-*YA* EGIR-pa *ŠU-PUR*	(l. e. 6) My lord, write back to me how it is with …

Commentary

14–19 For the construction infinitive plus the logical subject in the dative-locative see *GrHL* §25.18 and §25.36.

112. KBo 18.29
To the King from UR.MAḪ-[…]

Text: 398/i. **Find spot:** Büyükkale, Building D, storage room 8. **Copy**: KBo 18.29. **Edition**: Hagenbuchner 1989b, 52–55 (no. 38). **Discussion**: Beal 1992, 294 with n. 1115.

(1) [*A*-]*NA* d[UTU-*ŠI* EN-*YA*] (2) *QÍ-BÍ*-[*MA*] (3) *UM-MA* mU[R. MAḪ-… ARAD-*KA-MA*]	(1–3) Say to His Majesty, my lord: thus speaks mUR.MAḪ-x, your servant:
(4) *A-NA* dUTU-*ŠI* [EN-*YA* …] (5) [ku-i]t *A-WA-AT* […] (6) [ḫa-a]t-re-eš-ke-mi (7) [o o]x-zi-li-na x x-a[n] (8) x[o o]-ši ku-u-un me-mi-an (9) nu-uš-ma-aš ka-a-ša (10) LÚ. MEŠ UR[U?Aš?-š]a?-ra-an-da (11) 6 URU.DIDLI.ḪI.A kat-ta-an (12) pé-eš-kán-zi (13) nu-mu ka-a-ša UD-ti GE$_6$-ti (14) x - x- ma-aš ku-e-ez-za e-ep-mi (15) [K]ARAŠ NU.GÁL (16) […]x-za-kán (17) [KAR]AŠ (18) [x-x-]ra-ta *Ú-UL* (19) [tar]-na-aḫ-ḫi (20) [k]i-nu-na-ma-mu	(4–36) To Your Majesty, my lord, … what matter of … I am writing … you are …-ing … this matter. The men of Aššaranda are betraying six cities to them. And to me day and night … I seize … … There are no troops … troops … I am not releasing. But now, Your Majesty, my lord, send to me 3,000—or (even) 2,000—troops and 40 teams of chariot horses. And I will relocate these cities. … And these men of Aššaranda who … the land … feet

(21) dUTU-*ŠI* EN-*YA* (22) 3 *LI-IM* (23) na-aš-ma 2 *LI-IM* (24) KARAŠ up-pí (25) ANŠE.KUR.RA.MEŠ-ya (26) 40 GIŠ*ṢÍ-IM-DU* (27) nu ke-e URU.DIDLI.ḪI.A (28) ar-nu-mi ki-ú-uš-ša (29) ku-i-e-eš (30) LÚ.MEŠ URUA-aš-ša-r[a-an-da] (31) KUR-e GÌR.ḪI.A[(-)…] (32) kat-ta-a[n …] (33) ti-i[t-…] (34) nu a-x[…] (35) [*B*]*E-LÍ*-x[…] (36) nam-m[a …] (37) *BE-LÍ-I*[*A* (38) x[…]	… … … my lord … (*Rest of the paragraph too broken for connected translation.*)
(l.e. 1) [nu-uš *A-NA*] LÚ.MEŠ SIG$_5$-*TIM* pé-ra-an ḫu-u-[i-nu-ut …]	(l.e. 1) And put them in the charge of officers.
(l.e. 2) [mT]e-mi-it-ti-in-ma *BE-LÍ-YA* […] (3) [ma-n]i-ya-aḫ-ta na-aš *Ú-UL* ú-it[…] (4) [*A*]-*NA BE-LÍ-YA* aḫ-x[ ]up-pí[-…]	(l.e. 2) My lord entrusted Temitta with …, but he didn't come. … to my lord …

Commentary

10–12 are edited in CHD P, 53.

113. KUB 57.123
To the King from Taki-Šarruma

Text: Bo 6632. **Find spot:** Ḫattuša, but precise location unknown. **Copy**: KUB 57.123. **Edition**: Hagenbuchner 1989b, 20–22 (no. 14). **Discussion:** Beal 1993, 246–47; Houwink ten Cate 1996, 64–72; Klengel 1999, 272 n. 555.

(1) [*A-NA* d]UTU-*ŠI* EN-*YA* *QÍ-BI-MA* (2) [*UM*]-*MA* mDa-ki-LUGAL-ma ARAD-*KA-MA*	(1–2) Speak to His Majesty, my lord: Thus speaks Taki-dŠarruma, your servant:
(3) [*MA-Ḫ*]*AR* dUTU-*ŠI* EN-*YA* SILIM-la! ku-it GIM-an nu-mu EGIR-p[a *ŠU-PUR*]	(3) Please send word back to me how Your Majesty, my lord, is!

(4) [o o] *A-N[A* m]Ša-mu-ḫa-LÚ DUB.SAR *INA* URU.BÀD-ni-ya [...] (5) [URU]K[u]m-ma-an-ni-ma-kán ta-pu-uš-ša na-a-i-e[r...] (6) [ḫa-ak-ku-u]n-na-a-i DÙ-zi mŠa-mu-ḫa-LÚ DUB.SAR [...]	(4–6)... to Šamuḫa-ziti, the scribe, in the walled city ... But they sent to the side to the town Kummanni, and ... is making a *ḫakkunnai*-vessel. Šamuḫa-ziti, the scribe, ...
(7) [am]-mu-uk-ma-kán ku-it *A-NA* dUTU-*ŠI* pár-ki-ya-aḫ-[ḫa-ḫa-at?] (8) [o? *A*]-*NA* dUTU-*ŠI* EN-*YA* INIM-an ze-en-na-<an->da-an [...] (9) [o]x-ni-kán pa-ra-an-da na-a-ú-i ku-wa-pí[-ik-ki ...] (10) [o k]a-a-ša ut-tar ŠU-za DIB-mi nu-kán ud-da-[a-ar ...] (11) [GAM?-a]n? u-uḫ-ḫi na-at *I-NA* É.GAL-*LIM* ḫa-at-[ra-a-mi] (12) [o o D]UMU.MUNUS URUKar!-an-du-ni-ya-aš-ša na-a-ú-i [...] (13) [o -o-n]a-aš-kán nu-un-tar-aš kad-da-an-da ú-iz[-zi	(7–13) Because I deferred? (lit., "rose") to Your Majesty, ... to Your Majesty, my lord, a finished word. ... across the ... not yet anywhere ... I will take the matter in hand, and will look the matters over ..., and will write it to the (regional?) palace.... the princess of Babylonia not yet ... will come down quickly.
(14) [UN?.ME]Š-tar-ma *A-NA* É-*ŠU* *Ù A-NA* dUTU-*ŠI* IGI-a[n-da ...]	(14) The populace? ... to his house and to meet Your Majesty ...
(*Scattered traces and then the tablet breaks off.*)	

Commentary

7 For *parkiyaḫḫari*, see notes on text 73. CHD *park-* 2 b, restores the form as *pár-ki-ya-aḫ-[ḫa-ḫa-at?]*. Oettinger (1979, 243) identifies the stem of this form as *parkiyaḫḫ-*, cf. CHD P, 160.

10 For the phrase "take the matter in hand" see Imparati and de Martino 2004, 793.

114. KUB 19.23
To the Queen (Puduḫepa?) from Tudḫaliya (IV?)

Text: Bo 2350. **Find spot:** Ḫattuša, but precise location unknown. **Photo:** Konk. **Copy:** KUB 19.23. **Edition:** Hagenbuchner 1989b, 27–33 (no. 18).

Discussion: Heinhold-Krahmer et al. 1979, 311–14; 2001, 191–92; Ünal 1984, 100 n. 69; Haas 1985, 270; van den Hout 1995, 201–2; Singer 1996, 71 with n. 31; Klengel 1999, 247 [A27]; Jasink 2003, 275; Crasso 2005, #6443, 150 n. 30 (on the mention of the king's illness while in Ankuwa).

This is a late NH letter, as is evident from its orthography (*UL* instead of *Ú-UL*, single writing of normally geminate consonants,[342] abbreviated spellings like *pí.-an* for *peran*, etc.) and ductus (sign shapes, e.g., late LI in line 11).

The lack in the address formulas of the characterizing term "your servant" could point to the sender being a member of the royal family (so Hagenbuchner 1989a, 30). But the equal lack of any characterizing word following the sender's name (e.g., DUMU-*KA-MA* "your son," as well as the lack of a characterization of the queen in familial terms (e.g., AMA-*YA* "my mother"), could be a problem for the view that this is prince Tudḫaliya (IV) writing to his mother Puduḫepa. Nevertheless, other scholars also opt for this latter view, and we will follow it as well.

(1) *A-NA* MUNUS.LUGAL GAŠ[AN-*Y*]*A* *QÍ-BÍ*-[*MA*] (2) *UM-MA* ^{m}Tu-ud-ḫa-li-ya-[*M*]*A*	(1–2) Say to the Queen, my lady: Thus speaks Tudḫaliya:
(3) EN-*YA*-kán ku-in : za-⸢mu⸣-ra-nu-un nu-mu-za [EN-*Y*]*A* ku-e-[da-ni INIM-ni] (4) [p]a-ra-a u-i-iš-ke-et ma-na-an ZI-an ku-wa-pí *UL* wa-[ar-ši-ya-nu-un] (5) *A-NA* EN-*YA* LÚ.MEŠ SIG$_5$-*TIM* *UL* e-še-er nu-ut-ta x[…] (6) a-pád-da-an-ma-za ⸢ku-in⸣ pa-ra-a u-i-ya-at am-mu-uk-ma-an-[… me-mi-iš-ta$^{?}$ ma-an] (7) EN-*YA* ZI-an *UL* wa-ar-ši-ya-nu-wa-an ḫar-ku-un	(3–7) (Regarding) my lord (scil. the emperor) whom I offended—if ever I$^{?}$ did not assuage his anger in the matter for which my lord dispatched me, did not my lord have officers? And to you …. The one whom he dispatched there, should have spoken to me. Would I not have assuaged my lord's anger?
(8) *(Entire line erased)* (9) nu-za *A-NA PA-NI* EN-*YA* ku-it ša-ra-a ḫu-it-ti-ya-an ḫar-ku-[un] (10) [k]i-nu-un-ma-kán ka-ru-ú a-pu-u-un EN-an :za-mu-ra-nu-un […] (11) [GAŠ]AN$^{?}$-*YA* ku-in : ya-aš-ḫa-an-ti-in ŠU-i da-li-ya-at ma-an[…]	(8–13) Although I had *elevated*$^{?}$ myself in the estimation of my lord, I have already offended that lord now. What *grace/kindness*$^{?}$ my lady has left in (her) hand, I would have acted … in such a way. … would not have …. I would have

(12) am-mu-uk a-pé-ni-iš-šu-wa-an i-ya-nu-un ma-an *UL* x[…] (13) ma-an *A-NA* GAŠAN-*YA* : ya-aš-ḫa-an-du-wa-ti ḫa-at-ra-nu-u[n]	written/sent to my *gracious*? lady.
(14) [o-]x-aš pí.-an a-ar-aš-za ^{m}Kap-pa-⸢zu⸣-u-wa-aš *A-NA* LÚ.KÚR x[-…] (15) [GU]L?-aḫ-ta KUR UGU-*TI* u?-ga?-ni? (or: *UL*?-aš?!) ar-ḫa wa-ar-nu-[ut? …] (16) [x x ^{URU}Š]a-mu-ḫa ma-ni-in-ku-wa-an 3 URU-*LUM*-ma x[(17) [x x x x -a]n? (*Obverse breaks off*)	(14–17) And out of … Kappazuwa has struck/attacked the enemy …. He destroyed the Upper Land … by fire. … To Šamuḫa (it is) near. Three cities however … (*Broken*)
(rev. 1′) [nu-mu GAŠAN-*YA* ku-it INIM KUR *ŠA*]*P-LI-TI TÀŠ-PUR* nu-x[(rev. 2′) [...[343]-]ša-wa KUR. ḪI.A *ŠA* IN.NU.D[A? (rev. 3′) […[344]]x la-ap-zi-ma-at ku-wa-pí na-at x[-…] (rev. 4′) [...] (*blank*)	(rev. 1′–4′) Concerning what you, my lady, have written to me regarding the matters in the Lower Land: … lands of straw … but when it burns, …
(rev. 5′) [INIM?] ^{m}Ḫa-an-nu-ut-ti-ma-mu ku-it *TÀŠ-PUR* nu INIM ^{m}Ḫa-an-nu-ut-ti [*AŠ-ME*] (rev. 6′) [^{m}Ḫ]a-an-nu-ut-ti-eš TUR-aš (rev. or DUMU-aš?) *A-NA* EN-*YA* LÍL-ri na-a-wi$_5$ ku-wa-pí-ik[-ki …] (rev. 7′) SIxSÁ-at EN-*YA*-ya-an *(long erasure)* (rev. 8′) nu-kán ku-it *AŠ-RU* pa-iz-zi-ya ku-it-ma-kán *AŠ-RU* nu-u-wa še-er ar[-ḫa] (rev. 9′) i-ya-ad-da-ri nu-za a-pu-u-un me-mi-[y]a-an a-pé-ez-za x *UL* ḫa-a-m[i]	(rev. 5′–9′) I have heard what you have written to me concerning the matter of Ḫannutti. Ḫannutti the Younger (or perhaps: Ḫannutti the Prince) has never before been assigned in the field for my lord …. My lord too …-ed him. For that reason I do not believe that interpretation (of his) of what place (my lord) should go to and what place he should still *bypass*?.
(rev. 10′) ma-an-ma-kán LÚ.MEŠ ^{URU}La-la-an-da-ma ku-i-e-eš URU. DIDLI.ḪI.A a-ar-ru-u?[-ša] (rev. 11′) pa-a-er nu UN.MEŠ-uš mar-ša-an-te-eš an-na-la-za-pát-kán GAM-an píd-da-eš-k[er][345] (rev. 12′) EN-*YA*-pát ku-wa-pí ^{URU}An-ku-wa	(rev. 10′–20′) But if the men of Lalanda —that is, some cities—have defected, (well), the people are treacherous. They have often run off before. When my lord fell ill in Ankuwa, at that time they were already on the point of defecting.

iš-tar-ki-it a-pu-u-uš-ma-kán a-pí-y[a …] (rev. 13′) ka-ru-ú a-ar-ru-ú-ša pa-a-er GIM-an-ma *ŠA* ^{d}UTU-*ŠI* […] (rev. 14′) TI-tar iš-dam-ma-aš-šer na-at-kán nam-ma ar-ru-ša *UL* [pa-a-er] (rev. 15′) ki-nu-un-ma GIM-an *ŠA* EN-*YA* ḫar-ga-an iš-dam-ma-aš-šer […] (rev. 16′) x x nam-ma ar-ru-ú-š[a] ˹pa-a˺-er na-x-x-x […] (rev. 17′) : [ka]r-ša-an-tal-li-uš nu-kán ma-a-an KUR ^{URU}La-la-a[n-da] (rev. 18′) [d]a-pí-an-pát la-ga-a-ri nu-un-na-ša-at GEŠPÚ-u-wa-aš ta[r-aḫ-ḫu-u-wa-aš] (rev. 19′) ma-an-ma-kán KUR.ḪI.A *ŠAP-LI-*<*TI*>-ma la-ga-a-ri nu-un-na-[ša-at ma?-an?] (rev. 20′) *UL* ma-an-ka$_4$ i-ya[-u]-wa-aš	But when they heard that His Majesty would survive, they did not defect after all. But now that they have heard of the death[346] of my lord (Ḫattušili III), they have once again defected. And … *karšantalli*-s. If it is only all of Lalanda which falls, it will be for us (a matter) of overpowering (and) conquering (it). Were the Lower Land to fall, there would be nothing at all for us to do (or: would there be nothing at all for us to do?)
(l. e. 1) […] le-e ku-it-ki GÙB-li x É.MEŠ? (l. e. 2) […]x pa-aḫ-ša-nu-mi (l. e. 3) [… Ú-U]L? im-ma-ma/ku? me-mi-ya-an (4) [x-]x-a-šu? DÙ-ri x x […]	(l. e. 1–4) … nothing untoward … houses … I will protect … … word/thing … happens …

Commentary

On the man Ḫannutti and a much earlier man with the same name see Heinhold-Krahmer 2007a, 369. The Ḫannutti in this text is probably the same man who appears in the witness list of the treaty with Kurunt(iy)a of Tarḫuntašša (see van den Hout 1995, 200–202).

obv. 8–13 Literally *-za šarā ḫuittiya-* means “to pull oneself up.” In the context it contrasts with falling out of favor. It must therefore refer to rising in the estimation of the king, literally “in the presence of” the king.

obv. 13 Melchert (CLL s.v.) suggests that *:yašḫanduwati* may be the dative-locative of a possessive (in -want-) from *:yašḫanti-*, “to the one who possesses y.” I understand the Egyptian queen’s words to Šuppiluliuma I in KBo 5.6 iv 3–4 *nu-wa-mu-kán pa-ra-a Ú-UL i-ya-aš-ḫa-at-ta* to mean “you were not gracious/respectful to me (in that you suspected me of lying).”

obv. 14 The form *a-ra-aš-za* is taken as a miswriting of intended *a-ra-aš-zi* "it flows" in *GrHL* §11.8.

rev. 6–7 CHD sub *nāwi* renders these lines: "Ḫannutti Junior had not yet been researched by oracle for my lord in any way in connection with the campaign(?)" My translation "be assigned to" for the middle verb *ḫandai-* follows the usage documented in Neu 1968, 42 no. 3.

rev. 8–9 The translation "bypass" is based on the similar verbal construction *šer arḫa pai-* (CHD P, 39). The translation in CHD P, sub *pai-* A 2 a is incorrect.

115. KBo 9.82
To the King from Maša

Text: 193/n. **Find spot:** Bk. B: Büyükkale r/13. **Copy**: KBo 9.82. **Edition**: Hagenbuchner 1989b, 149–51 (no. 97). **Discussion:** Otten 1959–1960, 44 n. 43; Forlanini 1990, 112–13; Beal 1992, 350 n. 1329; Klengel 1999, 280 [A15.7]; Boley 2000, 338; Singer 2008a.

This letter dates from the late-thirteenth century. The sender's name, Maša, may be a short form of Maša-muwa, the Hittite envoy to Assyria during the thirteenth century (so Otten 1959–1960, 44 n. 43 and Singer 2008a, 716 n. 24). His unnamed addressee—addressed simply as "my lord"—is unknown. Both Hagenbuchner (1989b, 150) and Singer (2008a, 716) deny that the addressee could be the Hittite king, since the address ^{d}UTU-*ŠI* is not used. Yet that he was a very important person, perhaps a Hittite prince or even viceroy, is indicated by the use of the multiple prostration gesture (line 3; see §1.1.9.3), usually reserved for a king.

(1) *A-NA* EN-*YA* *QÍ-BI-MA* (2) *UM-MA* ^{m}Ma-ša ARAD-*KA-MA*	(1–2) Say to my lord: Thus speaks Maša, your servant:
(3) *AM-QUT A-NA* GAM GÌR.MEŠ EN-*YA* 2-*ŠÚ* 7-*ŠÚ*	(3) I fall at the feet of my lord twice seven times (i.e., fourteen times).
(4) ^{URU}U-da-za-kán ku-wa-pí ar-ḫa i-ya-aḫ-ḫa-at (5) nu *A-NA* EN-*YA* *UL* kiš-an me-ma-aḫ-ḫu-un (6) UN-aš-wa lu-uk-kat-ti EGIR-an-da ú-id-du (7) ku-it-ma-an-wa LÚ.MEŠ ^{KUR}Aš-šur ka-a (8) ki-nu-na-an![347]	(4–16) When I set out from Uda, did I not say to my lord the following? "Let a person come after (us??) tomorrow, while the men of Assyria are here." But now in the morning you set him on the road,

lu-uk-kat-ti KASKAL-aḫ-ta na-aš-kán tu-el UN-aš (9) *UL* ta-ma-aš-ta nu GAL ^{LÚ}DUB.SAR.GIŠ (10) ka-a me-mi-iš-ta ḫa-at-ra-a-i-wa-aš-ši (11) nu-wa-mu UN-aš *I-NA* ^{URU}Ta-pa-ru-ka$_4$ GAM-an (12) i-ya-at-ta-ru an-da-ma-wa-<ra->aš-kán tu-uk (13) [o o]x-kán-za[348] e-eš-du nu EN-*YA* ku-it ku-it (14) [o o o-]x-kán UN-an lu-uk-kat-ti (15) [o o o o o n]a-aš am-mu-uk GAM-an GIN-ru (16) [ ] BAD x[… … … … … …]	and your person did not catch up with them (i.e., the men of Assyria). The Chief of the Wood-scribes here said: "Write to him! Let a person go down to me in Taparuka! Let him be met$^?$ by$^?$ you!" Now whatever you do$^?$, my lord, send to me$^?$ a person in the morning …, and let him come down to me. … … ….
(rev. 1′) [o o o o]x x pa-ra-a x x […] (rev. 2′) [o o]x GAM-an GIN-ri nu-uš-ši x[…] (rev. 3′) [a]m-mu-uk LÚ ^{KUR}Aš-šur SIG$_5$-an-da-an up-pa-aḫ[-ḫi$^?$] (rev. 4′) nu-mu ^{m}GUR-LUGAL DINGIR.MEŠ EGIR-an tar-na-an-du (rev. 5′) ^{d}UTU-*ŠI*-ya-mu ti-an-za e-eš-du (rev. 6′) GIM-an tu-uk LÚ ^{KUR}Aš-šur SIG$_5$-an-da-an (rev. 7′) up-pa-aḫ-ḫi nu-mu-kán UN-an lu-uk-kat-ti (rev. 8′) pa-ra-a na-a-i na-aš-mu GAM-an i-ya-at-ta-ru	(rev. 1′–8′) … … When$^?$ he comes down to me, to him …I will send a *high-ranking*$^?$ Assyrian man, and may the gods turn over to me GUR-LUGAL. And may His Majesty also be on my side. As soon as I send to you the *high-ranking*$^?$ Assyrian man, dispatch to me on the following day a person, and let him come down to me.

Commentary

obv. 3 The formula here, *AM-QUT* … 2-*ŠÚ* 7-*ŠÚ* "I fall twice seven times," accords with the alternate way of writing the numerical expression in the Amarna letters: *AM-QUT* … 7-*ŠU U* 7-*ŠU* "I fall seven times and (again) seven times" in which the numerical value is additive, not multiplicative. See above in §1.1.9.3.2. The 2-*ŠU* here is multiplicative (*GrHL* §9.54 and following), not additive ("two times, seven times," as taken by Singer).

obv. 4–16, rev. 1′–8′ According to Singer, this letter is an attempt to reschedule a missed meeting between a Hittite and an Assyrian representative in a new location (Taparukka), perhaps closer to the Assyrian border.

Singer correctly reads SIG$_5$-*an-da-an* as one word (contra Hagenbuchner), but renders it as an adverb "straight away."

Singer considers GUR.LUGAL (rev. 4) to be the son of Bēl-qarrad (EN-UR.SAG), the Assyrian envoy to the Hittite court during the reign of Ḫattušili III. According to him (2008, 717–18), a diplomatic swap was being arranged, with GUR.LUGAL going from Ḫattuša to Assyria, and a man named DUMU-x-ta-AMAR.UTU going in the opposite direction. Singer admits that this is "a daring reconstruction of the meager evidence" (p. 718) and should be considered only one possible scenario.

116. KBo 2.11
From the King of Arzawa(?) to Ḫattušili III(?)

Text: Bo 13. **Find spot**: Bk. E. **Copy**: KBo 2.11. **Edition**: Hagenbuchner 1989b, 1989, 392–97 (no. 102). **Discussion:** Klengel 1999, 247 [A25]; Liverani 2001, 157; Jasink 2005, 211 n. 9; Heinhold-Krahmer 2007b, 193 (n. 314), 199–200 (exchange of gifts as prestige items).

The badly damaged obverse and the first part of the reverse allow us only to note the mention of lordship, horses, the land of Ḫatti, etc. From rev. 6′ we know that this letter was addressed to the king. Sender and addressee are suggested by Jasink 2005. The sender's duties concern valuable items used in the international exchange of gifts between sovereigns. The sender needs silver and gold to carry out his duties. He is not himself a goldsmith or silversmith, but he clearly supervises such skilled persons. Some of the valuable items he deals with are called "good" (*āššu*, rev. 10′), which may be a technical term for higher grade gold or silver content. The phrase "good gold" (= Egyptian *nbw nfr*) is often used in the letters from Egypt (see Beckman 1999a, 128 no. 22A §9, 129 no. 22B §7, and 130 no. 22C §5).

It is unclear to what language the glossed foreign words *antari-* and *gaši-* in rev. 8′ belong (Melchert 1993, 19, 102), and equally uncertain whether they are an indication that the writer is himself a foreigner. For a summary of opinions on the glossed word *gaši-* see *HED* K, 120. Kammenhuber thought that the Hittite language of the text showed that the writer was not a native speaker, and Hagenbuchner (1989, 395) wondered if the letter could have come to Ḫattuša from Ugarit, or even be a translation out of Akkadian for delivery and reading to the king. Heinhold-Krahmer observes that the writer could have been located in north Syria, southern or western Anatolia (p. 199).

The text mentions a "greeting gift" (Akkadian *ŠULMĀNU*, Hittite *aššul*) of the king of Aḫḫiyawa (rev. 11′). Heinhold-Krahmer (2007b, 199) points out that, while in earlier interchanges with Ḫatti, the king of Aḫḫiyawa apparently was ignorant of the custom of sending a prestige gift to one's foreign royal correspondent along with any message, by the time that KBo 2.11 was written he had learned to do so. But the only way that the time lag would be great enough for this to transpire would be to date KBo 2.11 to Tudḫaliya IV's reign, since the Tawagalawa letter, which attests to this lack of knowledge on the part of Aḫḫiyawa is already a product of the reign of Ḫattušili III. Jasink (2005, 211), on the other hand, dates KBo 2.11 to the reign of Ḫattušili III, and sees in it the same inadequate knowledge of protocol on the part of the Aḫḫiyawan king.

That the writer (according to Jasink, a king of Arzawa) does not hesitate to take action on his own—transfering luxury items from one "greeting gift" to another—shows that he at least is quite familiar with the accepted practices of international exchange of gifts (Heinhold-Krahmer 2007b, 200).

(rev. 6′) [d]UTU-*ŠI*-ma-mu ku-it kiš-an *TÀŠ-PUR* ku-it-wa e-eš-ša-at-ti ku-e-x x x x […] x (rev. 7′) […] ke-e-da-ni pé-di *Ú-UL*-za-kán URUKÙ.BABBAR-ši š[a]-ra-a nu-za KASKAL KURMi-iz-ri-i (rev. 8′) […-m]i nu-za :an-ta-ri-iš : ga-ši-in i-la-liš-ke[-e]z-zi (rev. 9′) [ki-n]u-un-ma-an ka-ru-ú ZAG-an ḫar-mi *I-NA* [ITU/MU-x-]KAM-kán ku-wa-pí-ik-ki (rev. 10′) [a-]aš-šu *Ú-NU-TUM* URUKUBABBAR-za KASKAL-aḫ-[m]i	(rev. 6′) Concerning what you, Your Majesty, wrote to me: "What are you doing? ……" (rev. 7′) … is? in this place. Are you not up in Ḫattuša? I will … the road to Egypt. (rev. 8′) *antari-* is desiring *gaši-*. (rev. 9′) But now I already hold it as a border. Sometime in the x-th month/year (rev. 10′) I will dispatch a good vessel from Ḫattuša.
(rev. 11′) [*A-NA ŠUL-M*]*AN* LUGAL Aḫ-ḫi-ya-wa-a-ma-mu ku-it *TÀŠ-PUR* nu a-pa-a-at ku-it *UL I-DE*$_4$ (rev. 12′) [LÚ *ṬE*$_4$*-MI-Š*]*U* ma-a-an ú-da-aš ku-it-ki ma-a-an *UL* nu-kán ka-a-aš-ma *BI-IB-RU* KÙ. BABBAR (rev. 13′) [*IŠ-TU* KÙ.]SIG$_{17}$ *MAŠ-LU IŠ-TU ŠUL-MAN* KURMi-iz-ri-i ar-ḫa da-aḫ-ḫu-un (rev. 14′) [nu-ut-ta ke-e up-]pa-aḫ-ḫu-un nu-ut-ták-kán ku-it ZAG-na nu	(rev. 11′) Concerning what you wrote me about the "greeting gift" of the King of Aḫḫiyawa: Because I[349] didn't know that—(rev. 12′) whether or not his messenger brought something—I took a silver rhyton (rev. 13′) trimmed in gold away from the "greeting gifts" of (the King of) Egypt and sent these to you. (rev. 14′) Send me whatever you think right. Now there is no (more?)

a-pa-a-at up-pí (rev. 15′) [ki-nu-un-mu KÙ.SI]G_{17} e-eš-zi-pát *UL* ku-it-ki KÙ.BABBAR-ya-mu na-w[i$_5$] (rev. 16′) [ú-da-an ma-a-an-ma]-an-mu KÙ.BABBAR-ma ú-da-an e-eš-ta (rev. 17′) [o o o o o o -ma]-an *UL* a-an-ni-iš-ke-nu-un ki-nu-un-ma-m[u KÙ.BABBAR NU.GÁL]	gold (here) with me. Silver too has not yet been brought to me. But if silver had been brought to me, I would not have worked *so slowly* …. But now there is no silver here with me.
(rev. 18′) [x x x x x x x x x x(-)]pí-ni-iz-zi-iš ú-it na-an ša[-…] (rev. 19′) [x x x x x x x x x]x *IŠ-TU* KASKAL KURMi-iz-ri-i mŠa[-…] (rev. 20′) [x x x x x x x-š]i URUTa-at-ta-aš-ša-za ma-ni-aḫ-ḫu[-un?? …] (rev. 21′) [x x x x x x x x] KASKAL KURMi-iz-ri-i EGIR-pa a-aš-z[i …] (rev. 22′) [x x x x x x x x x x]x x GIM-an-mu[-…] (rev. 23′) […]x x -ni x[…] (*Breaks off.*)	(rev. 18′–23′) From … m…-pinizzi came, and … him. … from the road to Egypt … from Tattašša … … the road to Egypt it remains afterward … when to me …

Commentary

rev. 11′–14′ is edited in CHD Š sub *šakk-* 1 c 3′. Jasink (2005) translates *IŠ-TU ŠUL-MAN* KUR*Mi-iz-ri-i* rather loosely as "of Egyptian provenience," not as "from the greeting gift of Egypt."

117. KBo 18.79
From […] to […]

Text: : 2236/c. **Find spot**: Bk. E. **Copy:** KBo 18.79. **Edition:** Hagenbuchner 1989b, 178–81 (no. 131). **Discussion:** Beal 1993, 248; de Martino and Imparati 1995, 107; van den Hout 1998, 88 n. 54; Boley 2000, 227, 238, 281.

Top of the tablet broken away. Only traces on the first two preserved lines (1′–2′).

(3') INIM GIG *BE-LU-YA*-at-k[án …] (4') ša-an-na-at-ti-ma-at-mu-k[án …] (5') e-eš-ša-at-ti na-an *Ú-U*[*L* …] (6') nu-za-kán ŠÀ-er GÌR-it le-⌜e?!⌝ […] (7') ke-e-ez-za ir-ma!-la-aš ke-e-e[z-zi-ya …] (8') ti-ya-an ḫar-ti e-eš-ša-at-t[i …] (9') *Ú-UL A-NA* ZI-*YA* še-er nu ku-[…] (10') nu-mu *ŠU-PUR* e-eš[-…] (11') [n]a-at *KÁN?-ZU-TAM*[350] e-eš-ša-[i?][351]	(3'–11') The matter of illness. My lord … it.[352] But you are concealing it from me … You are doing … and … not … him. Do? not *trample?* the heart with the foot/feet?. On this side a sick person, on that side …. You have placed … You are making … not for the sake of my life/soul. … So write to me! … and make *it KANZUTAM.*
(12') [mT]u-ud-ḫa-li-ya-an-na ku-it wa?/UD?[…] (13') […]x EGIR-an ḫa-tu-k[i-…] (14') […]-uš nam-ma-an EG[IR…] (15') […]-aḫ-tén ku-it-ták-k[án …] (16') […]x GIG iš[-tar-ak-…] (17') [… ku-i]t?-ma-an GIG[…] (18') […]še-eš!-zi na-a[t …] (19') […-w]a-tar SI×SÁ-ri […] (20') [… n]a-at-ši x[…] (21') […]x x x[…] (22') […]-ma-an te-e[z-…] (23') […] […]	*(12'–23' Too badly broken for translation.)*
(24') [INIM SA]G.DU.MEŠ-ma-mu ku-it *TÀŠ-PUR* SAG.D[U.MEŠ-wa-mu-kán] (25') [wa-ag-g]a-ri nu-wa-mu-kán SAG.DU.MEŠ pa-ra-a [na-a-i] (26') [nu? k]a-a-š[a] 20 SAG.DU.MEŠ ú-e-mi-ya-nu-un […] (27') [ma-a-a]n *I-NA* URUMa-ri-iš-ta ma-a-na-at-kán […] (28') [nu? *Š*]*U-RI-PU* ku-it me-ek-ki ma-a-na-aš ma-a-an *Ú-*[*UL*?? …] (29') [ma-]a-na-at-kán ŠÀ KASKAL-*NI* ḫar-ga-nu-e-er ki-nu-n[a-mu ma-a-an] (30') [ḫ]a-at-ra-ši *ŠU-RI-PU*-wa ku-it-ma-an 10 wa-[ak-šur …] (31') nu-wa-ra-aš-kán *QA-TAM-MA* pa-ra-a na-a-i na-aš[-kán *Ú-UL*	(24'–33') Concerning the matter of slaves (lit. heads) you wrote me about: "I am short of slaves. Send me some slaves." I have just found 20 slaves. If … were in Marišta, he/I?? would have … it. Because there is much snow/ice, if he had not …-ed, they would have destoyed it on the road. But now if you write to me: "While the snow is 10 *wakšur* (deep) …, send them anyway." *I might not send* them. But if you say: "I don't have it … there," and it is only here, then I? will certainly …

pa-ra-a ne-eḫ-ḫi] (32′) ma-a-an me-ma-at-ti-ma«-za»[353] a-pí-ya[354]-wa-ra-at-mu-k[án …] (33′) : wa-ak-ka$_4$-a-ri [n]a-at ka-a-pát nu ka[-a-ša …]	
(34′) ka-a-ša-kán *A-NA* LÚ.MEŠ URUTal-ma-li-y[a …] (35′) SAG.DU-aš e-eš-ta mḪi-ir-ḫi-ra-aš x[…] (36′) na-an e-ep-pu-un na-an ka-a-pát[…]	(34′) To the men of Talmaliya …. … (35′) was the head. Ḫirḫira … (36′) and I seized him, and …-ed him here.
(37′) ka-a-ša ku-u-un-na GI[M …] (38′) nu-kán a-pu-u-un-pát x[…] (39′) […]-x-ta mi[…]	(37′–39′ *Too badly broken for translation.*)

118. KUB 57.1
To the Field Marshall (Nuwanza?) from Ḫutupianza

Text: Bo 1608 + Bo 2154. **Find spot:** Ḫattuša, but precise location unknown. **Copy**: KUB 57.1. **Edition**: Hagenbuchner 1989b, 157–60. **Discussion:** Beal 1992, 352–53 n. 1335; 1993, 248; Klengel 1999, 175 [A23.7]; Marizza 2007b, 162–63.

The transliteration below is a result of combining an old transliteration of the as-yet-unpublished tablet by H. G. Güterbock with the more recent handcopy published in KUB 57.1.

As is often the case in correspondence of this type, the writer addresses his superior only by rank (see above in the Introduction). For the rank of GAL GEŠTIN, frequently serving as generalissimo in the Hittite army (hence my translation "Field Marshall"), see Pecchioli Daddi 1982; Beal 1992; Dinçol 1998b; and Marizza 2007b. Marizza proposes the following historical setting for this letter:

> The GAL GEŠTIN to whom the letter KUB 57.1 obv. 1 (CTH 209) was addressed is almost certainly to be identified with our Nuwanza, whereas the sender Ḫutupiyanza (obv. 2) might be a cousin of Muršili II and the above mentioned governor of Pala. The mention of Pittipara (obv. 13, 15) might be connected to the events of [Muršili's] fifteenth year, when the Hittite king confronted and defeated Pitagatalli and Pittipara. Judging from the text, Pittipara is still alive, and seems to prepare for the clash, since he is gathering

soldiers against Ḫatti (obv. 14-15). Due to the fact that this tablet stems from the archive of Ḫattuša, it may he concluded that Nuwanza was still in the Hittite capital, whereas it is known that at the end of that same year the GAL GEŠTIN was sent to reconquer the lands of Kalašma, Lalḫa and Mituwa. Therefore, we may conclude that Ḫutupiyanza sent this letter shortly before the defeat of the Kaška people led by Pittagatalli and Pittipara, and some time after the arrival of the GAL GEŠTIN to north-western Anatolia. Finally, we may note that Nuwanza—if we accept this identification—is mentioned at the beginning of the letter before Ḫutupiyanza. This implies that his rank was higher than Ḫutupiyanza's. Since it is known that the governor of Pala was a cousin of the Hittite king, it might be suggested that a blood tie existed between Muršili II and Nuwanza, who, as said above, bears also the title of DUMU.LUGAL ["king's son"]. (2007b, 162–63)

(1) [*A*-]*NA* GAL.GEŠTIN EN-*YA* *Q*[*Í-B*]*I-M*[*A*] (2) [*UM*]-*MA* ^{m}Ḫu-tu-pí-an-za ARAD$^{!?}$-*KA*[-*MA*]	(1–2) Say to the Field Marshall, my lord: Thus speaks Ḫutupianza, your servant:
(3) ka-a-ša-kán [ŠÀ KUR-*TI* ḫ]u-u$^{?}$-[ma-an] S[IG$_5$-in]	(3) At present all is well in the land.
(4) [^{m}Pí-]it$^{?}$-ti-p[a-ra x]-x ku-it x x [*TÀŠ*$^{?}$-*PUR*$^{?}$] (5) [o o o o] ⸢x-ni$^{?}$ an-da$^{?}$ pa$^{?}$-a$^{?}$-ir$^{?}$⸣ ku-e-da-ni pé-di (6) [n]u-uš-ma-aš še-ek-kán-te-eš me-ek-ka$_4$-e-eš […] (7) x x -pát$^{?}$ x-x-x-eš$^{?}$ ku-i-e-eš‹‹-ma›› ku-i-e-eš (8) na-aš ḫu-u-ma-an-te-eš-pát ar-ḫa tar-nir (9) na-at ar-ḫa ú-e-er nu ^{m}Ša-la-DINGIR-*LIM*-in (10) ⸢ḫa$^{?}$-an$^{?}$-ni⸣-<eš>-kán-zi nu ka-a-ša *AŠ-PUR* na-an ma-a-an (11) ⸢ar-ḫa⸣ tar-na-an-zi ma-a-an ma-aḫ-ḫa-an (12) ⸢nu *A-NA*⸣ EN-*YA* ḫa-at-ra-a-mi	(4–12) Concerning what you/he wrote$^{?}$ about Pittipara$^{?}$: They *went* into …, in some location. And many well-known persons … to them. But whatever …-s …, they released them all, and they came back home. They are judging$^{?}$ Šalaili. And I am herewith writing, and I will write to my lord whether they release him, or whatever they do.
(13) x x x ^{m}Pí-it-ti-pa-ra-ma ku-it (14) *A-NA* ⸢EN⸣-*YA AŠ-PUR* nu-za LÚ.MEŠ ^{URU}Ga-aš-ga (15) kat[-ta ^{m}Pí-i]t-ti-pa-ra ar-ḫa ḫa-li-iḫ-le-eš-kán-zi (16) [am$^{?}$-mu$^{?}$-u]k-ma-a[t *A*]-*NA* ^{d}UTU-*ŠI* (17) [*Ù A-N*]*A*$^{?}$ EN-*YA* ḫa-at-re-eš-ke-mi (18) [o o o]	(13–19) Concerning what I wrote to my lord about Pittipara: The Kaškaean men are prostrating themselves (before) Pittipara, but I am regularly reporting it to His Majesty and to (you,) my lord. I am hereby writing, and whatever

ka-a-ša *AŠ-PUR* nu-mu ku-in (19) [me-mi-an] ú-da-[an]-zi nu *A-NA* EN-*YA* ḫa-at-ra-a-mi	word they bring to me I will write to (you,) my lord.
(20) [o o o]x DUMU? m[P]í?-ip-pu-ri-it-ta-ya x[(21) [o o o -]kán EN-*YA* wa-at-ku-ut (22) [na-aš *A-NA*] KUR URU.ÍDTa-ḫa-a-ra EGIR-pa (23) [pa-a-it nu?] mPí-i-ga-aš-š[i-]il-ta-aš-ša ar-nu-um-ma[-aš?] (24) [o o o]x *I-NA* URUTa-wa-aš-ti-ya (25) [...] nu?-mu ka-a-ša u-i-e-er (26) [... nu?-]wa-an-na-aš *Š*[*A*? ...] (27) [...]a?-ši nu-wa-an[-na-aš ...] (28) [...-w]a-aš-ta-ti [...] EN-*YA* (29) [...]x-in-ni 1-x-li *ŠU-PUR* (30) [...]x-du na-aš pa-ra-a pé-eš-ta (31) [x *A-NA* dU]TU-*ŠI*-ya *AŠ-PUR*	(20–31) ... the son of Pippuritta(ya) ... my lord fled, and went back to the Taḫara River Land. And Pigaššilta too ... in the town Tawaštiya ... And they have just sent to me: "... our ..., and our ... we ..." My lord, ... send ...! ... he gave them over, and I wrote ... also to His Majesty.
(32) [nu-kán] ma-a-an ÚŠ-an *IŠ-TU* KUR URUḪa-at-ti (33) [ar-ḫa] ta-ru-up-ta-ri nu-za EN-*YA* (34) [*A-NA*] *MA-ḪAR* dUTU-*ŠI* nu-za-kán ku-it-ma-an (35) [...]x ta-me-e-da-ni x-x-x-x (36) [... na-]a-ú-i ti-i-e?-zi x x x x (37) [... EGI]R-an ti-i-ya-ši ke-e?-[ez?] ke-e-ez (38) [na?-an? a-p]í-ya-az l[a]?-aḫ-ḫi-ya-at-te-ni (39) [...] x KUR [URU.Í]DTa-ḫa-ra-a-an-na? (40) [...]-ta nu 2?-e-el[355] KUR-e-[aš] (41) [...]	(32–41) And if the plague is taken away from the land of Ḫatti, and you, my lord, are in the presence of His Majesty, while ... in another ... has not yet entered, you will withdraw ... on this side and that side. And you (*pl.*) will make war on him from that direction. ... (the land of) X and the Taḫara River Land, and of the two lands ...

119. KUB 40.1
To the King from [...]

Text: Bo 4899. **Find spot:** Ḫattuša, but precise location unknown. **Copy:** KUB 40.1. **Edition:** Hagenbuchner 1989b, 68–76 (no. 45). **Discussion:** Beal 1992, 442 n. 1657; Puhvel 1993, 37; Beckman 1995a, 19–20 with n. 2; Hoffner 1997c, 193 (l. e. 1).

Comments and partial treatment of lines 18–32 in Beckman 1995a: "Sometime in the 13th century a high-ranking Hittite official whose name and title have not been preserved wrote to the Great King:"

The obverse (published as "reverse") of this tablet is too broken for a connected translation.

(rev.! 1) [x x x x x x x *A-NA*] ᵈUTU-*ŠI* EN-*YA* *Ú-UL* mar-ri ar-ku-wa-a[r DÙ-mi] (rev.! 2) [x x x x x x x x x-]x x *A-[N]A* ᵈUTU-*ŠI* EN[-*Y*]*A*? *UL* mar-ri […] (rev.! 3) [x x x x x x e-eš-ša-]aḫ-ḫ[i] *Ú-UL* mar-ri ḫa-at-re-eš-ke-mi	(rev.! 1–3) It is not rashly … that I make a reply/defense to Your Majesty, my lord. … to Your Majesty, my lord, not rashly I … make …, (and) not rashly do I write.
(rev.! 4) [x x x x x x x x x-]wa-ḫi-iš-ke-mi me-ek-ki-kán te-eḫ-ḫu-un me-ek-ki (rev.! 5) [x x x x x x x x x] me-ek-ki-mu na-ak-ke-e-eš-ta (rev.! 6) [x x x x x x x x x] ⸢a⸣-ra-a-an ᵈUTU-*ŠI*-za-kán EN-*YA* za-at/la-ḫi? (rev.! 7) [x x x x x x x kiš-šu-w]a?-an-mu ZI-ni a-ra-an kiš-šu-an-mu : ú-wa-al-la? (rev.! 8) [x x x x x x x x x] kiš-šu-wa-an ḫa-at-re-eš-kán-zi *Ú-UL*-[a]t? ÚŠ-tar	(rev.! 4–8) I am …-ing …. Much have I set (out). Much … Much difficulty I had. *Evil slander* has arisen. It *affects* Your Majesty, my lord! … Such (a thing) has arisen in my mind/soul. Such (a thing) … … Such a thing they are writing. Is it not death?
(rev.! 9) [x x x x x x x x x] INIM-an : pa-a-x-ḫa-aḫ-ḫa GÉŠPU-za-an x-an (rev.! 10) [x x x x x x x x x] ᵈUTU-*ŠI* ka-ru-ú *I-DE*	(rev.! 9–10) I … the … word/matter. Violence, … … Your Majesty already knows.
(rev.! 11) [x x x x x x x x x x] ḫu-u-un-ḫu-e-eš-ni kat-ta-an-da ú-wa-nu-un (rev.! 12) [x x x x x x x x x-]x ma-a-an na-an nam-ma IGI.ḪI.A-za u-uḫ-ḫi (rev. !13) [x x x x x x x x ki-i]š-ḫa-ḫa-ri nu-kán GIM-an ke-e-ez-za x - x (rev.! 14) [x x x x x x x x x n]a-at-ši ú-ke-el DU$_{11}$-aḫ-ḫi	(rev.! 11–14) I have come down into the deep waters of … It is like the …. And I will see him/it again with my eyes. I will become … and as on this side … I myself will say it to him.

(rev.! 15) [d]UTU-*ŠI*-ma EN-*YA* [ku-it-m]a-an ke-e-ez-za ZAG-za nu-un-tar-aš a-u-wa-an ⌜ar-ḫa⌝ (rev.! 16) [da?-]a-i : pár-za-aš-š[a … ku?-] ⌜e?⌝-ka$_4$: da-a-ya-al-la me-ḫur-ri$^{ḪI.A}$ ar-ta-ri-y[a?] (rev.! 17) INIM.MEŠ-ma me-ek-k[i…-]x-na-an-da na-at-mu-kán RI-za *AŠ-PUR*-zi[356] *UL*	(rev.! 15–17) But while? Your Majesty, my lord, quickly takes (something) away from this side/border, … times will also be present. but words much …. and he will not send/write it to me RI-*za*
(rev.! 18) [a]m-mu-uk-ma ke-e-da-ni KAŠKAL-ši GIM-an GIM-an na-ak-ke-e-eš-ke-et (rev.! 19) GIM-an-za GIM?-an ki-iš-ḫa-ḫa-at ta-pár-ri-ya-an-[ká]n[357] *UL* ku-e-da-ni-ki pé-di (rev.! 20) wa-aš-da-nu-nu-[u]n DINGIR.MEŠ dUTU-*ŠI*-mu a-u-wa-an a[r-nu??-er (rev.! 21) [t]a-pár-ri-ya-an-ma a-pu-un-pát DIB-un dUTU-*ŠI*-za [EN-*Y*]*A* ku-in ma-a-la-a-ši (rev.! 22) ka-a-aš-ma MU.KAM-za pár-ku-wa-ya-pát tar-na-an-za ke-e-da-ni MU.KAM-ti (rev.! 23) na-ak-ki-ya-tar *Ú-UL* nam-ma ku-iš-ki e-eš-zi	(rev.! 18–23) "However difficult it has been for me on this tour of duty, and whatever has happened to me, I have in no point found fault with the command. (Indeed) the gods of Your Majesty carried? me away (i.e., rescued me?). I have, rather, taken up that very command of which you, Your Majesty, my lord, approve. This year has been begun afresh with a clean slate?: during this year there will be no further difficulty.[358]
(rev.! 24) nu-mu-za am-me-el LÚ.MEŠ a-ru-uš le-e nam-ma pa-ra-a ka-ni-iš-šu-wa-an-zi (rev.! 25) mar-kiš-ke-wa-an-zi-ya-mu-za ma-a-la-wa-an-zi RI-za le-e ḫa-at!-ra!-an-zi (rev.! 26) a-u-wa-an UGU-mu-za le-e dam-m[e-u]m-ma-an wa-tar-na-ḫe-eš-kán-zi da-a-l[i-y]a<-an>-du-m[u …] (rev.! 27) nu-kán GIM-an ta-[p]ár-ri-ya-an *A-NA* dUTU-*ŠI* EGIR-an-da ú-da-aḫ-ḫi (rev.! 28) dUTU URUTÚL-na-ma *A-NA* dUTU-*ŠI* EN-*YA* še-er SIG$_5$-in KIN-zi […] (rev.! 29) wa-aš-da-nu-wa-an-wa *UL* ku-it-ki m[a]-a-an[359] ki-i *ṬUP-PU* PAP-an-	(rev.! 24–31) May my colleagues not seek? any further to call attention to me. May they not write in a timely fashion? seeking disapproval or approval for me. May they not broadcast *untruth* (*dammeum-man*?) about me. May they leave me alone! And when I bring back (the results of) the command to Your Majesty, the Sun Goddess of Arinna will treat (me) graciously for the sake of Your Majesty, my lord, (so that it will be said:) "Nothing has been done which should be considered a crime." Let this tablet be saved, (30) so that on

d[u] (rev.! 30) nu GIM-an dUTU-*ŠI* EN-*YA* x-da[…(-)]ma-a-ya-mi nu-mu-za ke-e-da-ni (rev.! 31) ke-e-ez-za tup-pí-az-za kat-ta [p]u-nu-uš-ša-an-du	the day when I … Your Majesty, my lord, they may interrogate me on the basis of this tablet.
(rev.! 32) ku-u-uš ku-e-eš ke-e-el ZAG.MEŠ-aš *BE-L*[*U*ḪI.A]A mḪa-aš-du-DINGIR-*LIM* mTa-ru-piš-ni-iš (rev.! 33) m.dAMAR.UTU-dLAMMA LÚa-an-tu-GAL nu *A-NA* TI dUTU-*ŠI* še-er me-ek-ki PAP-an-d[a?-ru] (rev.! 34) mTa-ru-up-[p]iš-ni-in-ma-mu-kán dUTU-*ŠI* [E]N-*YA* GIM-an a-ša-an-da pa-ra-a [na-it-ti?] (rev.! 35) GIM-an-ma-aš a-ra-[a]š? nu *QA-TAM-MA*-pát KIN[-z]i? a-pé-e-ni-šu-wa-an-da ḫar-zi (rev.! 36) dUTU-*ŠI*-du-za-kán GIM-an EGIR-pa e[-e]š-ša-ti	(rev.! 32–36) May these (men) who are the lords of the borders—Ḫašduili, Taruppišni, Šanda-Kurunt(iy)a the *antušalli-*, be very protective of the life of Your Majesty! And as Your Majesty, my lord, sent? to me Taruppišni *truly*, and as he is a colleague, so he will work. Such things he has, just as Your Majesty will …
(rev.! 37) *A-NA* dUTU-*ŠI*-ma EN-*YA* *ŠA* mḪa-aš-du-DIN[GIR-*L*]*IM* ku-it ḫa-at-ra-a-mi (rev.! 38) dUTU URUTÚL-na [GAŠ]AN-*YA* uš-ki-du ma-a-an-at x […]x ku-e-da-ni-ki ARAD-*Y*[*A*? …] (rev.! 39) u-uḫ-ḫu-un kiš-šu-wa-an ḫa-an-da-an da-a[t-ti? …-]ka-ri-x[-…] (rev.! 40) ku-u-un ma-ši-ya-an UN-an [*Š*]*A* dUTU-*Š*[*I* …] (rev.! 41) dUTU-*ŠI*-za EN-*YA* ú-uk ARAD-in *U*[*L* …] (rev.! 42) ZI-an *UL* : ši-ú-wa-ri-er x[-…] (rev.! 43) [x]-a-at-ta-ya-wa DÙ-zi p[a-…] (rev.! 44) [dUTU]-*ŠI*-ma-an-kán EN-*YA* pé[-…] (rev.! 45) [x x]x *A-NA* dUTU-*ŠI* ú-[…]	(rev.! 37–39) Concerning what I am writing to Your Majesty, my lord, about Hašduili: May the Sun Goddess of Arinna, my lady, verify (it), if it … to any servant of mine … I saw. Such a thing truly you?} accept. … *(Rest of the paragraph not translatable in a connected fashion.)*
(rev.! 46) […] ku-it INIM DUMU.NI[TA …] (rev.! 47) […] INIM DUMU.NI[TA …] (l. e. 1) [nam]-	(rev.! 46–47, l. e. 1–13) … what matter the son … matter the son … once more I turned back … I carried away …

ma-pát [EG]IR-pa BAL-nu-nu-un (l. e. 2) [x a]r-ḫa ar-nu-nu-un (l. e. 3) [x-]ta-ri na-an-kán LÚ.MEŠDUB<.SAR>-za (l. e. 4) [x-]x-an-du na-aš-za le-e *INA* URUÚ-uš-ša (l. e. 5) [x nu ku]-u-un INIM-a[n *A-NA*] dUTU-*ŠI* *UL* mar-ri *AŠ-PUR*-un (l. e. 6) [x ka?-]r[u?]-ú? a-ú [x-]x […] SIG$_5$-in ku-iš DU$_{11}$-i na-an-k[án] (l. e. 7) […]KA?[…]-wa-ti me-ek-ki GAL ri x (l. e. 8) dUTU<-*ŠI*>-mu at?[-…] (l. e. 9) UGU RA[-…] (l. e. 10) RA-*IṢ*-an […] (l. e. 11) ku-it x […] (l. e. 12) ku-u-un [INIM-an …] (l. e. 13) x […]	let them … it by means of the scribes … let not … in Uššа … I did not write this matter to His Majesty rashly … see! … he who speaks well …

Commentary

obv. 37–38 translated in *GrHL* §23.7.
On line **40**, see CHD L–N, 206b.

120. Bo 2810
From the King to […]

Text: Bo 2810. **Find spot:** Ḫattuša, but precise location unknown. **Edition**: Klengel 1974, 171–73. **Translation**: Otten 1967, 59. **Discussion**: Forrer 1924, 5; Meyer 1925, 530 n. 2; Bilabel and Grohmann 1927, 118; Otten 1967, 59; Hagenbuchner 1989b, 14 (no. 9); Beal 1992, 210 n. 782 (grain ships sent by "an official in Syria" to Ura and Lašti[…]); Starke 1992, 814 (on ii 6); Gurney 1992, 218 (on the location of Ura); Singer 1999b, 717; Jasink 2003, 272 n. 11.

The double paragraph-dividing line at the end, followed by uninscribed space, added to the presence of writing on the reverse, indicate that the tablet contained a second letter.

Since this was an outgoing letter, yet was found in Ḫattuša, either it was never sent (rather unlikely) or it is a draft to be used to prepare the final (perhaps translated) version, which was dispatched (so Hagenbuchner). The double line after line 17 probably divides the main letter from a scribal "piggyback" letter. In his edition Klengel designated the preserved part of this tablet the second column of the obverse, a claim that Hagenbuchner doubts because all known examples of Hittite letters on tablets containing a second letter are single column tablets.

All commentators agree that the sender of this letter was most likely the Hittite king—note "my lands" (line 12). The addressee, to judge from the use of the term "my son" by the letter-writer, was either his real son or an official or minor ruler who was his subordinate. Although it was claimed by Otten (1967, 59) that the addressee was the king of Ugarit, Klengel (1974, 172–73) argued that this situation does not fit the king of Ugarit. That the addressee does control "lands" is clear from lines 2–5, and line 5—again according to Klengel—suggests that the addressee's control vis-à-vis the dominion of the sender should not change. All of this suggests that the addressee was a Hittite prince with governing authority somewhere in Syria, who had access to the coast and had grain and ships at his disposal.

(2) [...] KUR.KUR.MEŠ-kán ḫu-u-m[a-an-ta$^?$ ...] (3) [o o -]ma-za a-pé-e-da-aš ku-e-da-aš KUR. KUR.MEŠ-aš (4) [o o] x DUMU-*YA* a-pé-e KUR.KUR.MEŠ kat-ta ḫar-ak (5) nu-kán le-e ku-it-ki ne-ya-ri	(2–5) ... all the lands .... And in those lands which are ..., retain those lands yourself, my "son"! Let nothing change!
(6) DUMU-*YA*-ma-mu ku-in INIM ^{GIŠ}MÁ *TÀŠ-PUR* (7) ḫal-ki-ya-za-wa 1 *ME*. ^{GIŠ}MÁ šu-wa-an-za ú-et (8) nu-mu DUMU-*YA* ku-wa-at i-ya-at (9) a-pé-ni-eš-šu-wa-an *I-NA* UD.1.KAM-pát-aš-ta (10) ku-wa-at GAM-an e-eš-ta (11) DUMU-*YA* *Ú-UL* ša-ak-ti ku-it-mu-kán (12) ŠÀ KUR.KUR.MEŠ ka-aš-za e-eš-ta (13) ki-nu-un-ma-an-kán DUMU-*YA* pa-ra-a na-a-i (14) na-an *I-NA* ^{URU}Ú-ra na-aš-ma ^{URU}La-aš-ti-x[...] (or $^{URU.DU_6}$Aš-ti-g[ur$^?$-ka$_4$$^?$]) (15) kat-ta iš-ḫu-u-wa-a-an-du (16) ku-e-da-ni URU-ri *A-NA* DUMU-*YA* ZAG-na (17) [na-a]n a-pí-ya kat-ta iš[-ḫu-u-wa-a-an-du]	(6–17) Regarding what you, my son, wrote to me regarding ships: "One hundred ships laden with grain have come (to you)." Why, my son, have you acted this way towards me? Why did it (namely the grain) remain with you even as much as one day? Don't you realize, my son, that there has been a famine in my lands? But now, my son, send it, and have them unload it either in Ura or Lašti-x. Let them unload it in whichever city seems best to (you), my son!

Commentary

7 Singer (1999b, 718 n. 385) had doubts about reading the sign before GIŠMÁ as *ME* "hundred," in part because of the singular form of the participle *šuwanza*. But singular agreement was permissible (*GrHL* §9.18 and 9.22).

121. KUB 23.85
From Queen Puduḫepa to Tattamaru

Text: Bo 864. **Photo:** Konk.). **Find spot:** Ḫattuša, but precise location unknown. **Copy:** KUB 23.85. **Edition:** Hagenbuchner 1989, #212, 13 (no. 7), 15–16 (no. 10). **Discussion:** Beal 1992, 386 n. 1486; van den Hout 1995, 118–19; Klengel 1999, 248 [A31]; Beckman, in Hallo and Younger 1997, 215 sub 1.2 (translation of the proverb in line 7).

The recipient of this letter, Tattamaru, appears as a witness in at least two of three important documents during the reign of Ḫattušili III and his son Tudḫaliya IV. In the earliest of these he is styled merely "prince" (DUMU. LUGAL), but in the last of these (the Bronze Tablet) he has been promoted to "Infantry Commander of the Left Wing" (GAL UKU.UŠ GÙB; see Gurney 1993, 23–24). If he is the same Tattamaru who as "prince" appears in the Šaḫurunuwa document, his brothers' names were Duwatta-nani and Tarḫunta-manawa. Starke (1996, 157) thinks that this Tattamaru held three important offices simultaneously: "Chief Shepherd" (GAL NA.GADA), "Chief of the Heavily-armed Guards" (GAL UKU.UŠ), and "Chief Wood-Tablet-Scribe" (GAL DUB.SAR.GIŠ).

As is clear from the context, Tattamaru is not the Queen's own son-in-law, but that of her sister. He was married to Queen Puduḫepa's niece. The Akkadogram LÚ*ḪATANU* therefore has the somewhat looser meaning of a male who by marriage becomes attached to his wife's family, something like what is denoted by the Hittite term *antiyant-*.

From the meager context it is unclear if the queen wished the in-law relationship with Tattamaru had continued after the death of her niece. Therefore it is also unclear if she agreed or disagreed with the proverb she quotes in line 7. But it does appear that the formerly good relationship had dissolved after the death of the queen's niece.

(3) *UM-MA* MUNUS.LUGAL-ma (4) *A-NA* mTa-at-ta-ma-ru *QÍ-BI-MA*	(3–4) Thus speaks the Queen: Say to Tattamaru:

(5) [z]i-ik-za ^{m}Ta-at-ta-ma-ru-uš DUMU.MUNUS NIN-*YA* DAM-an-ni da-a-an [ḫa]r-t[a] (6) [n]u-ut-ta ^{d}Gul-ša-aš ḪUL-aḫ-da na-aš-ták-kán BA.ÚŠ (7) [kiš-a]n-ma ku-wa-at me-ma-an-zi ak-kán-ta-aš-wa ^{LÚ}*ḪA-TÁ-NU* (8) [: š]u-wa -ru-pát ^{LÚ}*ḪA-TÁ-NU* zi-ik-ma-mu-za ^{LÚ}*ḪA-TÁ-NU* e-eš-ta (9) [am]-m[e-e]l-ma-za : pur-pur-ri-ya-ma-an *Ú-UL* ša-ak-ti (10) [...]x-x *Ú-UL* ku-in-ki ša-ak-ti am-me-el-ma-aš-ma-aš (11) [...]x-x-te LÚ.MEŠ ÉRIN.MEŠ EGIR-zi-iš-ša (12) [...-]x-ma-mu-za ^{LÚ}*ḪA-TÁ-NI-YA* e-eš-ta (13) [...]x-x-x-x-ša UD.1.KAM-ya / (*break*)	(5–13) You, Tattamaru, had taken the daughter of my sister in marriage. But Fate dealt you a grievous blow: she died on you![360] Why do they say: "A male in-law remains nevertheless fully an in-law, even if his wife dies"?[361] You were my male in-law, but you do not recognize my *obligation*.[362] You recognize no one.... But my ... to them/you(pl.). ... troops, and a low-ranked ... You were my in-law ...... and one day ....

122. VS 28.129
From [...] to the GAL $^{LÚ.MEŠ}$UKU.UŠ, Nananza, and Ḫattušili

Text: VAT 13047. **Find spot:** Ḫattuša, but precise location unknown. **Copy:** VS 28 (=NF 12) 129. **Edition**: Hagenbuchner-Dresel 1999, 50–58. **Discussion:** Otten 1956, 182–83; Rost 1956, 348; del Monte 1975a, 4–5; Beal 1992, 389 n. 1470 (on the GAL $^{LÚ.MEŠ}$UKU.UŠ); de Martino 2005b, 308.

The text has been dated to the Middle Kingdom. Hagenbucher defends the hypothesis that the tablet belongs to the Maşat corpus of letters on the basis of formal and content elements. The sender's name is partially damaged and cannot be read with certainty. The addressees are the GAL $^{LÚ.MEŠ}$UKU.UŠ, Nananza, and Ḫattušili, the latter presumably being the same as the one mentioned in ABoT 65 and in the aforementioned texts.

This is the first attestation of the rank "Chief of the UKU.UŠ-troops" prior to the NH period (see Beal 1992, 380). This man is addressed by his title alone. The two named recipients that follow his title are very likely the scribes by those names (so Otten 1956, 183). Hagenbuchner calls attention to the Maşat letter HKM 69, in which three men are addressed, the first one only by his title. Although the writer calls these three persons "dear brothers" (not "dear sons"), the placing of his name ahead of theirs in the salutation, as well as the omission of *-MA* following his own name (see §1.2.16), indicate that he considers himself their superior in rank.

The word "this" in line 6 shows that an unnamed "scout" (^{LÚ}NÍ.ZU = Hittite *šapašalli-*), whose immediate return was desired by the writer, accompanied this letter. He could have served as the courier. A NH text lists the titles of various functionaries with access to the royal acropolis, and among them is a "scout courier" (^{LÚ}NÍ.ZU ^{LÚ}KAŠ$_4$.E), whose Hattic equivalent was ^{LÚ}*kīluḫ* (KBo 5.11 i 19). Its position immediately following ^{LÚ}*lu-u-i-iz-zi-i-il* = ^{LÚ}KAŠ$_4$.E "(ordinary) courier, runner" shows that this compound Sumerogram denotes not a special type of scout (^{LÚ}NÍ.ZU), but a special type of courier (^{LÚ}KAŠ$_4$.E). Scout couriers could have served to transport messages through especially dangerous or rough territories. Most likely therefore ^{LÚ}NÍ.ZU here in line 6 is an abbreviated writing of ^{LÚ}NÍ.ZU ^{LÚ}KAŠ$_4$.E "scout courier."

(1) [*U*]*M-MA* ^{m}MAŠ-x-x (2) *A-NA* GAL $^{\text{LÚ.MEŠ}}$UKU.UŠ (3) ^{m}Na-na-an-za $^{\text{m.GIŠ}}$GIDRU-DINGIR-*LIM* (4) ŠEŠ.MEŠ DÙG.GA-*YA QÍ-BÍ-MA*	(1–4) Thus speaks MAŠ-x-x: Say to the Chief of the UKU.UŠ-troops, to Nananza, (and) to Ḫattušili, my dear brothers:
(5) DINGIR.MEŠ-<eš->ma-aš TI-an ḫar-kán-du	(5) May the gods keep you alive.
(6) [k]u-u-un-mu-kán ^{LÚ}NÍ.ZU (7) [EGI]R$^{?}$-pa$^{?}$ pa-ra-a ḫu-u-ta-ak (8) [n]a-iš-tén nu k[u$^{?}$-it$^{?}$ m]a-aḫ-ḫa-an (9) [*A-W*]*A-TE*^{MEŠ} *I-N*[*A*] É.GAL-*LIM* (10) [nu-mu] EGIR-pa ḫ[a-a]t-[r]a-at-tén (11) [ú-w]a-at du-wa-ad-[d]u	(6–11) Send (pl.) this scout(-courier) back to me promptly! (8–10) Write me how things are in the palace! (11) Get with it!
(12) [ke-]⌜e$^{?}$⌝ tup$^{?}$-p[a$^{\text{ḪI.A}}$ …]	(12) These tablets …
(About 13 lines missing in the break.)	
(rev. 1′) […] x x x (rev. 2′) [… n]am-ma-at še-er (rev. 3′) […-]x-an	(rev. 1′–3′) … … … Furthermore, above …
(rev. 4′) [ki-i-mu] ku-it ^{m}A-ša-[…] (rev. 5′) [INIM *ŠA*] LÚ ^{URU}⌜Ta⌝-an-ku-wa (rev. 6′) [ḫa-at-ra-]a-it URU-an-wa-mu (rev. 7′) [*Ù* $^{\text{m?/URU?}}$]x-at$^{?}$-ti-te-na-an	(rev. 4′–6′) Concerning this that Aša-x-x wrote to me about the affair of the man of (city) Tankuwa: (rev. 6′–9′) "They are oppressing my

(rev. 8') š[a-aḫ-ḫ]a-na-az lu-uz-zi-az (rev. 9') [d]am-mi-iš-ḫi-iš-kán-zi (rev. 10') na-an ku-wa-at dam-mi-iš-ḫi-iš-kán-z[i] (rev. 11') ki-nu-na-kán IGI.ḪI.A-wa e-ep-tén (rev. 12') na<-an> INIM-an šu-um-ma-[aš] (rev. 13') EGIR-pa-an SIG$_5$-ya[-aḫ-ḫa-at-tén]	town, and (the town) …, with *šaḫḫan* and *luzzi* obligations." Why are they oppressing it? (rev. 11') Now keep (pl.) an eye (on him/it) (rev. 12'–13') and you (pl.) rectify his/its situation.

Commentary

obv. 1 For the omission of *-MA* after the sender's name, see §1.2.16.

obv. 11 For *uwat duwaddu* see §1.2.19.1.

rev. 4′–13′ Since city/town names are grammatically common gender, the pronouns "him/it" and "his/its" could refer either to the petitioning man or to his town.

2.3.2. NH Letters found at Emar-Meskene (123–124)

123. SMEA 45-T 1
From the Hittite Emperor to Alziya-muwa in Emar

Text: SMEA 45–T 1 (also known as Msk. 73.1097). **Photo:** Laroche 1982, 54. **Copy**: No copy. **Edition**: Laroche 1982; Hagenbuchner 1989b, 40–44 (no. 23); and Singer 1999a (full edition with use of accompanying letter from king of Carchemish to Alziya-muwa [no. 124]). **Discussion**: Imparati 1983, 264–67; Klengel 1999, 175 [A23.3]; Schwemer 2001, 550, 566 n. 4523; Salvini and Trémouille 2003, 226–30; Cohen 2005; D'Alfonso 2005b; Skaist 2005, 610; Yamada 2006, 225–26.

When the Hittites gained control of the kingdom of Aštata, whose capital city was Emar, they assumed control over all aspects of the internal life of the city (D'Alfonso 2005b), including the judicial. The former kingdom—now province—of Aštata fell within the orbit of the Hittite viceroy of Carchemish.

A man named Zu-Baʿla (about whom see Beckman 1995a, 31, 36; 1996, 138; Singer 1999a, 68; and Taggar-Cohen 2002, 158–59; Skaist 2005) appeals (*arkuwai-*, line 5[363]) to the emperor regarding a judgment against his interests in a local court. The phrase "this (*ka-a-aš*) Zu-Baʿla" here (line

3) in the emperor's letter and in lines 3–4 of text 124 probably refers to the fact that Zu-Baʿla accompanied the messenger(s) who brought both letters. Zu-Baʿla was the son of Šuršu, a diviner, and an the son-in-law and heir of Anda-mali(k) (West Semitic Hadda-malik), who had bequeathed his houses and lands to him in a document (Emar VI, 201) ratified by Ini-Tešub, king of Carchemish, himself (Singer 1999a, 68). The "diviner (LÚAZU) of the gods of Emar" was a priestly title held by Anda-malik and four of his descendants in succession (Yamada 1998). Although Hrozný's original translation of *išḫanittar*(*a*)- as "blood relative" (related to *ešḫar*), supported by Benveniste (1962: 101–2), Kammenhuber (in Oettinger 1981: 388), and Neu (in Serbat, Taillardat, and Lazard 1984: 100), was rejected by Tischler (*HEG* 1: 381–82), Puhvel (*HED* 1–2, 338, 395–96), Košak (1990, 151), Melchert (1994, 111), and Rieken (1999, 284) in favor of a connection with the verb *išḫi*(*ya*)- "to bind," and referring to ties created through marriage, it was claimed that the prosopographical evidence from Emar supported the former view, since Yamada had claimed to have evidence that Anda-mali(k) was the father of Zu-Baʿla (Yamada 1998, cited by Singer 1999a, 68, and see Yamada 2006, 228–29). This claim has now been refuted by evidence from other sources, showing that the father of Zu-baʿla was not Anda-mali(k), but a man named Šuršu (Cohen forthcoming). There is now no reason to doubt that *išḫanittar*(*a*)- means "relative by marriage," with the precise translation determined by situations: father-in-law, mother-in-law, son-in-law, daughter-in-law, etc. In a forthcoming article discussing an unpublished Hittite fragment, I adduce new evidence to support the view that MUNUS *išḫanittar*(*a*)- means "daughter-in-law" (= Sum. MUNUSÉ.GE_4.A = Akkad. *kallātu*). For the use of the derived noun *išḫanittarātar* in another letter, see text 94. Just how this term is to be distinguished from *kaena*- "in-law, relative by marriage" (= Akk. *ḫat*(*a*)*nu*) is unclear at present.

On the chronology see Skaist 1998, 2005; and Cohen and d'Alfonso 2008. Salvini and Trémouille (2003, 228) identify the king in text 123 with Muršili II and propose the years 1312–1311 for the two Hittite letters: text 123 and text 124; Yamada (2006, 229 n. 25) prefers Ḫattušili III, and Cohen and d'Alfonso 2008 Muršili III (Urḫi-Teššub).

Alziya-muwa, a Hittite official residing in Emar, had confiscated Zu-Baʿla's landed property and imposed the Hittite obligations *šaḫḫan* and *luzzi* on him. Yamada (2006, 227) makes the following points:

> First, although the king of Ḫatti held the ultimate rulership of Emar, the king of Carchemish, his viceroy in Syria, was in practice responsible for its control, as he was going to visit Emar to settle the dispute. Second, both kings regarded the deeds of Alziya-muwa as "oppression," in other words, abuse

> of his power. Third, the diviner Zu-Baʿla must have been an important person to the Hittites, since he could appeal directly to the king of Hatti and the Hittite kings endeavored to protect his rights.

Yamada regards Zu-Baʿla as an "Emaro-Hittite," a class of persons who are citizens of Emar, but who perform services in the direct employ of the Hittite overlordship, and thus must be liable to Hittite feudal duties:

> In conclusion, as for the Hittite administration of Emar, it is undoubted that in principle the Hittites adopted a policy of indirect control, that is of relying on the local native political institutions for governing. However, there was another aspect, that is, *partial direct control*. They employed a portion of the Emariote citizens, the Emaro-Hittites, as their local staff through a system by which the Emariotes were given landed property in exchange for their services, such as performance of the *šaḫḫan*-, *luzzi*-, GIŠ.TUKUL-, and *ILKU*-duties (2006, 234).

As for what those services might have been, and how Mesopotamian persons obligated to them might deal with the obligation, Selz (2007, 283) writes:

> The citizens at the upper end of the social ladder had various obligations towards the state. In return for their services, they received either prebend fields or rations. They were termed *awīlum,* the Akkadian word for the "(male) human being", … The members of this class possessed full rights and the state was responsible for their welfare. They formed the backbone of the Babylonian society. They often transferred their duties to other persons; then their so-called *ilku*-service was often performed by a class of people of lower social status, called *muškēnum,* roughly translated as "commoner." They received various payments from the citizens for their services, such as subsistence fields … In later periods silver became the standard for such compensations … The commoners had no formal obligations towards the state, but they had also to look after themselves and possessed lesser rights.

Zu-Baʿla was such a person endowed with lands and obligated to services. But since he was a high religious authority whose services to the Hittite government were important, he was given a special exemption in this case.

(1) *U*[*M-M*]*A* d[UTU]-*ŠI-MA* (2) [*A*]-*NA* mAl-zi-ya-mu-wa *QÍ-BÍ-MA*	(1–2) Thus speaks His Majesty: Say to Alziya-muwa:
(3) ka-a-ša-mu ka-a-aš (4) mZu-ú-ba-a-la-aš LÚAZU (5) LÚ URUAš-ta-ta	(3–16) This Zu-Baʿla, the diviner, the man of Aštata, has now bowed

ar-wa-a-it (6) É-er-wa-mu-kán *ŠA* LÚiš-ḫa-ni-it-ta-ra-aš *ŠA* mAn-da-ma-li (7) GIŠKIRI6.GEŠTIN-ya mAl-zi-ya-mu-wa-aš (8) ar-ḫa da-aš-ke-ez-zi (9) nu-wa-ra-at *A-NA* mPal-lu-ú-wa (10) pé-eš-ke-ez-zi ša-aḫ-ḫa-an-na-wa (11) an-na-az *Ú-UL* ku-it-ki (12) iš-ša-aḫ-ḫu-un ki-nu-un-ma-wa-m[u] (13) ša-aḫ-ḫa-ni lu-uz-zi-ya (14) kat-ta-an ti-i-er (15) nu-wa ša-aḫ-ḫa-an lu-uz-zi-in-n[a] (16) e-eš-ša-aḫ-ḫi	before me (saying): "Alziya-muwa is taking away from me the estate of my relative by marriage, Anda-mali, and the vineyard, and is giving it to Palluwa. As for the *šaḫḫan*-duty, in the past I have not performed (it) at all. But now they have put me under *šaḫḫan* and *luzzi* duties, and I have to perform *šaḫḫan* and *luzzi*."
(17) ki-nu-na-aš-ši-kán a-pa-a-at É-er (18) GIŠKIRI6.GEŠTIN-ya ar-[ḫa] le-e (19) ku-it-ki ta-at-[t]i (20) ma-a-an-ma-at-š[i]-kán ka-ru-ú-ma (21) ar-ḫa ta-at-[t]a (22) na-at-ši EGIR-pa pa-a-[i] (23) ša-aḫ-ḫa-an-na ku-it an-na-az (24) *Ú-UL* ku-it-ki e-eš-ši-iš-ke-et (25) ki-nu-un-ma ša-aḫ-ḫa-an-ni lu-uz-zi (26) ku-wa-at kat-ta-an da-iš-tén (27) ki-nu-un-ma an-na-az ku-it (28) e-eš-ši-iš-ta ki-nu-un-na a-[pa-a-at] (29) e-eš-ša-ad-du (30) ta-ma-i-ma le-e ku-i[t-ki] (31) i-ya-zi [n]a-an le-e (32) ku-iš-ki da[m]-mi-iš-ḫa-iz-zi	(17–32) Now, that house(hold) and vineyard you should in no way take from him! But if you have already taken them from him, give them back to him! As for the *šaḫḫan*, which in the past he did not have to perform at all, why did you (plural) now put him under *šaḫḫan* and *luzzi*? Now, whatever he used to perform in the past, he should now keep performing the same. He should do nothing else, and no one should oppress him.

Commentary

As Pruzsinski (2004, 30) has observed, the the Hittite terms *šaḫḫan* and *luzzi* attested in the texts 123 and 124, in which the diviner is freed from these obligations, probably went beyond military tasks and could have included work squads, as originally proposed by Beckman (1996) for RE 78.

For what is known of the practice of corvée in ancient Mesopotamia, see Stol 1995 and "corvée" in Joannès and Michel 2001, 205.

Although *šaḫḫan* and *luzzi* theoretically involved actual public labor, all but the extremely poor could hire a substitute to serve in their place, or in some cases simply pay the enforcing official. So in effect it was a system of taxation.

5 Some interpreters emend the form *ar-wa-a-it* to *ar-<ku->wa-a-it* on the basis of the form used in text 125, line 5. But I follow Singer, who wrote: "Zu-Baʿla's pleading is expressed with different verbs in the two letters: *ar*(*u*)*wait*, "he prostrated (himself)," in the Ḫattuša letter; *arkuwait*, "he pleaded," in the Carchemish letter. The same altenation has already been noted in two duplicates of a ritual text (Otten-Rüster 1977, 61–62). The semantic conflation of the two near-homophones was facilitated by the circumstance that pleading before the king usually entailed proskynesis (Puhvel 1984, 151). Does this mean that the diviner Zu-Baʿla actually appeared in person before the Great King in Ḫattuša? Although this is not impossible, I assume that the same terminology would be used if his appeal was presented in writing and was read out aloud by a messenger" (1999a, 68). D'Alfonso also opposes the emendation.[364] A notable example of the use of the *aruwai-* ("to do reverence") by persons appearing before the emperor to complain about an injustice and to plead for a reversal, is Laws §55 (see Hoffner 1997g, 66–68) and translation by Hoffner in Roth and Hoffner 1997, 225–26 and *CoS* 2.19:112). As noted above, the use of "this (*ka-a-aš*) Zu-Baʿla" in both letters shows that the petitioner personally accompanied the two letters. It might also imply that he had personally accompanied his petition to Ḫattuša.

6 Following the recent revision of our understanding of *išḫanittar*(*a*)- as "relative by marriage" (inter alia see Rieken 1999, 284), the word in this line is translated by d'Alfonso (2005b, 124) as "parente acquisito." On MUNUS*išḫanittar*(*a*)- "daughter-in-law, bride" in Bo 4952, see Hoffner in a forthcoming festschrift.

124. BLMJ 1143
From the King of Carchemish to Alziya-muwa

Text: BLMJ 1143 (cited also as BLMJ-C37, CM 13: 32, and ETJ 32). **Find spot:** Emar. **Copy:** Westenholz and Ikeda 2000, pl. LXXIV. **Edition**: Singer 1999a, 65–72. **Discussion:** Cohen 2005; Singer and Yamada in Westenholz and Ikeda 2000, 78–80 (no. 32); Bryce 2003b, 178–79; Salvini and Trémouille 2003, 229–30; van den Hout 2004b, 185 §3.2; D'Alfonso 2005a, 20; Skaist 2005, 610; Yamada 2006, 226–27.

(1) [*UM-MA*] LUGAL-*MA* (2) *A-NA* ^{m}Al-zi-ya-m[u-wa *QÍ-BÍ-MA*]	(1–2) Thus speaks the King (of Carchemish): Say to Alziya-muwa:
(3) ka-a-ša ka-a-aš (4) ^{m}Zu-pa-la-a-aš ^{LÚ}AZU (5) *A-NA* ^{d}UTU-*Š*[*I* a]r-ku-wa-i[t] (6) ^{GIŠ}KI[RI$_{6}$. GEŠTIN-w]a-m[u] $^{A.ŠÀ}$<A.>GÀR.ḪI.A (7) ^{m}Al-zi-ya-m[u-w]a-aš (8) ar-[ḫ]a da-a-aš (9) nu-mu ^{d}UTU-*ŠI IQ-BI* (10) le-e-wa-ra-an ku-iš-ki (11) [da]m-me-eš-ḫa-iz-zi (12) […] x x [… $^{A.ŠÀ}$A.G]ÀR.ḪI.A (13) […] x LÍL […] (14) [^{GI}]^{Š}KIRI$_{6}$.GEŠTIN-y[a …] (15) pa-ra-a pa-a-[i ku]-it-ma-an ú-wa-mi (16) na-an-kán [tar-n]a-aḫ-ḫi	(3–16) This Zu-Baʿla, the diviner, has now pleaded with His Majesty (as follows): "Alziya-muwa has taken from me (my) vineyard and lands." His Majesty has told me: "No one should oppress him." … lands, … field … and the vineyard give back to him until I come and release him!"
(17) lu-uz-zi-ya (18) ša-aḫ-ḫa-an le-e [e-eš-š]a-i	(17–18) The *luzzi* and *šaḫḫan* duties he should not perform.
(19) ka-a-ša ma-[ši-wa-an …] (20) *A-NA* DINGIR-*LI*[*M* …] (21) na-an-ši x[-… EGIR-pa pa]-a-i$^{?}$	(19–21) However much … for the god … Return it to him …!

2.3.3. NH Letters Found at Alalakh (125–126)

125. AT 125
From the King of Carchemish to a Hittite Official at Alalakh

Text: ATT 16. **Photo:** Woolley 1939, pl. XVIII 1/2. **Copy**: Wiseman 1953, no. 125. **Edition**: Ehelolf 1939b, 73–75; Friedrich 1939; Rost 1956, 340–42; Hagenbuchner 1989b, 387–88 (no. 298). **Discussion**: Wiseman 1953, 62.

The sender is probably the king of Carchemish, the viceroy of the Hittite emperor. The emperor himself would have used the title "His Majesty" (^{d}UTU-*ŠI*), not simply "the king" (LUGAL; so noted already by Ehelolf 1939b, 73–75). As Hagenbuchner observes, it was not customary for a Syrian prince, even one of the Hittite royal family, to use Hittite instead of Akkadian in correspondence with his subordinates.

Singer (1999a) has remarked that this and the letter to Alziya-muwa (no. 124) are the only two presently known letters emanating from the Carchemish office of the Hittite imperial chancellery, and as such are our only evidence for the ductus and orthography of the Hittite scribes of that court.

The specific type of "birds" that were sent for the king to eat is not specified. Undoubtedly, they were a delicacy, perhaps a type of bird not found in the area of Carchemish, but available around Alalakh. The fact that by the time they reached the king they were spoiled indicates a long trip. Following the most direct natural route (via Elbeyli in Turkey and Azaz and Afrin in Syria) the trip would have covered about 160 km/100 miles. Using the figure of 25–30 km per day's stage,[365] this would mean a trip of about six days. And our text leaves us uninformed as to whether any steps were taken to preserve the meat. Other Hittite texts refer to preserving fruits and even the meat of animals, fishes, and birds by drying them (Hoffner 1974a, 116, 124).[366]

Notice that the king of Carchemish's participation in the cult (lines 21–23) takes precedence over his travel or administrative duties.

(1) *UM-MA* LUGAL-*MA* (2) *A-NA* mPí-ir-wa-an-nu *QÍ-BI-MA*	(1–2) Thus speaks the king: Say to Pirwannu:
(3) DINGIR.MEŠ-eš-da aš-šu-li PAP-ru	(3) May the gods lovingly protect you.
(4) ki-iš-ša-an-mu ku-it ḫa-at-ra-a-eš (5) ka-a-aš-ma-wa MUŠEN.ḪI.A ku-e (6) *A-NA* EN-*YA* up-pa-aḫ-ḫu-un (7) nu-wa-za ma-a-an EN-*YA* (8) a-pé-e MUŠEN.ḪI.A ma-la-a-ši (9) nu-wa-mu EN-*YA* EGIR-pa ḫa-at-ra-a-ú (10) nu-wa up-pé-eš-ke-u-wa-an te-eḫ-ḫi (11) nu-mu MUŠEN. ḪI.A ku-e up-pé-eš-ta (12) na-at ar-ḫa ḫ[ar-]ra-an-te-eš e-š[ir] (13) na-aš e-du-un-na *Ú-UL* (14) u-uḫ-ḫu-un-na-aš *Ú-UL* (15) ma-na-at SIG_5-an-te-eš ma-na-[at *Ú-UL*]	(4–15) Concerning what you wrote to me, saying: "May my lord write back to me whether you liked those birds that I have herewith sent to my lord, and I will begin to send them regularly." The birds that you sent to me were spoiled. So I neither ate them nor did I look at them (to see) if they were good or not.
(16) ki-iš-ša-an-ma-mu ku-it (17) [ḫ]a-a[t-ra-a-e]š ma-a-an-wa E[N-*YA*] (18) [… nu-w]a nu-un-tar-ri[-…] (19) [a-pé-e-da-ni U]D-ti	(16–23) Concerning what you wrote to me, saying: "If my lord …-s, I will hasten … on that day. And send back to me …" I have begun

(20) [nu-wa]-mu [EGIR]-pa *ŠU-PUR* (21) nu-za ka-a-š[a] SISKUR.ḪI.A (22) e-eš-ša-aḫ-ḫi nu-za GIM-an [x-]x (23) SISKUR.ḪI.A i-ya-u-wa-an-zi (24) zi-in-na-aḫ-ḫi nu i-i[a-aḫ-ḫa-ri][367]	to perform sacrifices. When I finish performing the sacrifices, I will make the trip.
Rest uninscribed.	

126. ATT 35
From the King to Tudḫaliya

Text: ATT 35. **Copy**: Niedorf 2002, 526. **Find spot:** Alalakh. **Edition:** Niedorf 2002.

(1) [*UM-MA*] ^{d}UTU-*ŠI-MA* (2) [*A-NA* ^{m}T]u-ud-ḫa-li-ya (3) [*QÍ-B*]*Í-MA*	(1–3) Thus speaks His Majesty: Say to Tudḫaliya:
(4) [tu-e-el aš-š]u-ul ku-it (5) [ma-aḫ-ḫa-an nu-mu EGI]R-pa (6) [ḫa-at-ra-a-i …]	(4–6) Write back to me how it is with you. …
Rest of obv. and beginning of rev. broken away.	

126b. ATT 35
Piggyback Letter from […] to […]

(7) [*A-NA* … ŠEŠ-*YA QÍ-BÍ-MA*] (8) [*UM-MA* … ŠE]Š-*KA*[-*MA*]	(7–8) Say to PN_2, my brother: Thus speaks PN_1, your brother:
(9) [*MA-ḪAR* ŠEŠ-*Y*]*A* aš-šu-ul ku-it (10) [ma-aḫ-ḫa-an] nu-mu ŠEŠ-*YA* EGIR-p[a ḫ]a-at-re-eš-ke	(9–10) Keep writing back to me, my brother, how it is with my brother.
(11) [*A-NA* ŠEŠ-*Y*]*A* aš-šu-ul EGIR-p[a pa?-r]a?-a ḫa-at-re-eš-ke-mi (12) [zi?-ga?-m]u aš-šu-ul *Ú-UL* ku-wa-pí (13) [ḫa-at-ra-a-]eš ŠEŠ-*YA* [x x x] ša[…] (14) […] x […]	(11–14) I keep writing back a greeting to my brother, but you never wrote (your) greeting to me. My brother …

Notes

1. See Epictetus, Diatr 1.3, on human types: "It is because of this kinship with the flesh that those of us who incline toward it become like wolves, faithless and treacherous and hurtful, and others like lions, wild and savage and untamed; but most of us become foxes, that is to say, rascals of the animal kingdom. For what else is a slanderous and malicious man but a fox, or something even more rascally and degraded."

2. Collins 1998, 16 n. 7 suggests the lion referred to here is a living animal.

3. "Den höchsten Schwierigkeitsgrad bei der Erfassung von Briefinhalten stellen zitierte Reden in zerstörtem Kontext dar. Der Briefschreiber bringt sowohl Abschnitte aus eigenen Briefen oder Reden als auch frühere Aussagen des Adressaten in der zitierten Rede. Auch Abschnitte, die die verbalen oder schriftlichen Äußerungen einer dritten Person zum Inhalt haben, werden in der direkten Rede zitiert (z.B. KUB XXXI 79 Rs. 21–26). Auf Grund dieser Zitierweise ist es an manchen Stellen nicht möglich, die Aussage eindeutig auf eine der handelnden Personen zu beziehen, woraus sich natürlich nur ein bedingtes Verständnis des Inhaltes ergibt."

4. Hagenbuchner reads É ("Haus des Sesams").

5. Hagenbuchner restores: [*nu A-NA* ^{GIŠ}]MÁ$^{\text{ḪI!.A}}$ ^{URU}*Pít-te-ya-ri-ga-za ḫal-ku-eš-šar* ^{URU}*Ša-mu-u-*[*ḫa*] [*ku-it Ú-UL*] 1-*ŠU pé-e-te-er*, but by the rules of Hittite grammar the normal position of causal *kuit* is the second accented word of the clause (see *GrHL* §30.41–42). There are exceptions to this rule (cited in *GrHL* §30.43–44), but they are rare, and do not justify violating the norm in a conjectural restoration.

6. Everyone reads 1-*ŠU* without noting that the break occurs right on the left side of the "1," making [x+]1-*ŠU* (i.e., 2-*ŠU* or 3-*ŠU*) equally likely. *HED* H, 39 renders this "ships *once* brought" (italics mine), although "once" in the non-numerical sense of "at some time in the past" is regularly expressed by *karū* or *annaz*, not by 1-*ŠU*.

7. Hittite normally uses two consecutive clauses to express point of origin and point of termination with verbs of transporting, thus avoiding both an ablative and an allative or locative in the same clause. But there are exceptions. For an example with *peda-* "to transport" see KBo 3.22 obv. 39–42 in CHD P *peda-* B 1 a 1′ b′ 5."

8. Two kinds of soldier-rations are contrasted here: 10-*tili-* and ^{URU}*Kaška*. It is likely, even if they also had a different ingredient or shape, that they differed also in size or weight, especially since the first is designated by a number. According to both Güterbock (1967a, 149) and Hagenbuchner-Dresel (2002), 10-*tili-* is an indication of the weight of the loaf. Lebrun translated it "de 10 «sicles»." Hagenbuchner ("das Zehnfache," 1989b, 139 and 2002, 34) takes it as a multiple (ten-fold). But there is also a possibility that 10-*tili-* denotes a fraction, that is, "a tenth (of some unit of volume)"; see Eichner 1992 and *GrHL* §9.44.

9. Lebrun (1976, 217–18) reads 16 PA ZÍD.DA.RA "16 demi mesures de farine," Hagenbuchner-Dresel (1989b and 2002) reads this line 16 PA ZÍD.DA KU_7 "16 PA of sweet flour." The last sign from the copy could be read either AL (i.e., KU_7) or ZÍ[Z]. And even if AL is preferred, the break immediately following leaves the possibility that a longer word was written out onto the edge. ZÍD.DA $DURU_5$ KU_7 "sweet moist flour" is attested KUB 9.27 i 7, but not ZÍD.DA KU_7.

10. For ^{GIŠ}MÁ.TUR see line 13. It is unlikely that the TUR part of this compound logogram would be placed at the beginning of the next line (*pace* Hagenbuchner 1989b, 140).

11. Hagenbuchner 1989b, [1 *ME* 30 PA ZÍZ] 1 *ME* 20 PA ŠE.

12. One would expect here an imperative, as in the next clause (*zāḫ*), although *ḫapti* does not look like an imperative, but a second person singular present indicative. *HED* H, 112 (sub *ḫap-*) does not attempt to translate this passage.

13. "Una cinquantina di chilometri a valle di Sulusaray il Çekerek/Zuliya compie un' ampia curva verso nord; in questo punto il fiume passa per il punto più vicino a Hattusa. Nella lettera KBo XV 28 scritta da tre auguri alla regina si riferisce del volo di uccelli da Haitta "giù al fiume Zuliya" [*INA* ^{ÍD}*Zuliaš=šan katta*, line 5] e più avanti di altre osservazioni in connessione col fiume Imralla(ya); gli itinerari delle feste 16 mostrano che Haitta si trovava a un giorno da Hattusa ai piedi del monte Puskurunuwa, dal quale si poteva scendere a Harranassi …, mentre il villaggio di Imralla, che porta il nome (luvio) dell'altro fiume, era pure a una tappa da Hattusa sulla strada che portava in tre giorni di viaggio ad Ankuwa."

14. It is unclear to me how de Martino concludes about Ziti in this letter: "Zidi is mentioned in the text (rev. 4′–5′): he has to *send a letter to* the sender of KBo XII 62" (de Martino 2005b, 294–95, (italics mine). ^{m}*Zi-i-ti-in* is, after all, accusative here, not nominative. He isn't sending anything: he is being sent.

15. See also Hagenbuchner 1989a, 97: "Eine andere Art der Bestätigung scheint [*ka tup*]*pi* "[Die Ta]fel ist [hier]" (KBo XII 62 Rs. 9′) zu sein."

16. So restored by Hagenbuchner and followed by Reichardt (1998, 133).

17. Or perhaps: [*ut-ta*]*r-ta*: "People have consecrated [*a thing*?] *for you* properly."

18. Neu's collated reading *-al* is not supported by the online photo (Konk.), which to my eye has what the copy reads (*-na*), and cannot be AL.

19. *tāwana* as an adverb, translated by *HW*, 219 as "genau, getreu, unverfälscht(?)," and by Kümmel (1967, 159) as "getreulich."

20. "Oblicherweise wird ein Zitat in der direkten Rede wiedergegeben. In zwei Briefen (Mşt. 75/43 Vs. 3–7; KBo XII 62 Rs. 6′–8′) gibt es aber eine Konstruktion, die anstelle eines Zitates in der direkten Rede den Wortlaut des Ausspruches im Erzählstil wiederholt, also fast eine indirekte Rede verwendet. Jener Abschnitt, der den Wortlaut der Rede wiederholt, wird mit der Konjunktion *maḫḫan* 'wie' eingeleitet (vgl. VIII.1.2)."

21. Hagenbuchner reads *da-a-i-*[*ir*]. But the the 3rd plural preterite ending in MH would certainly have been *-er*, not *-ir* (*GrHL* §§11.6–11.7), and since the stem of the verb "take" is simply *da-*, not *dai-*, there would be no explanation for the *-i-* in this form. The form *da-a-i-*[*e-er*] can only be from the verb *taye/a-* "to steal," which is also used in MH letters for abduction (written *da-i-e-er* in HKM 57 [text 60]).

22. Hagenbuchner restores *-zi/-ta na-aš Ú-UL ú-it*, but there is insufficient space for this. Nor is it necessary in the laconic style of letters.

23. Hagenbuchner reads [TI-*t*]*ar* "life" instead of [Z]I-*aš* "of the soul."

24. Taḫa(z)ili could, of course, be an Anatolian name in *-ili*, but so far we know no GN *Taḫaz(a) to which this suffix could be added.

25. Alp 1991a, 122: *ŠAL-MA* f!?[*T*]*a-az-zu-ku-li-na*. Photo favors reading DAM.

26. Although Alp 1991a assumes the ḪI is a scribal error, it is also possible, even if strange, that it is part of an Akkadian phonetic complement to ŠEŠ.DÙG.GA, if the entire word stood for just *AḪI–YA* "my brother" in Akkadian.

27. Alp 1991a, 124: *ŠAL-MA*.

28. Also mentioned in 6: 6; 19: 9; 24; 25; etc. Forlanini identifies Kaši/epura with Gazziura. See the discussion in Alp 1991a.

29. Literally "scattered."

30. Alp 1991a, 126 reads *wa-ar-ra-i-ša*.

31. That Kaššū held this rank can be derived from HKM 71 (text 73) (see Alp 1991a, 71; Beckman 1995a, 23).

32. The verb *tamašš-* is used in military contexts not only of siege actions, but also of catching an enemy by surprise and defeating him: see KBo 14.3 iii 17–19 (DŠ fragment 14 F), ed. Güterbock 1956b, 67 ("wherever he caught him"); KBo 14.4 i 27–28 (DŠ fragment 18 A), ed. Güterbock 1956b, 80 ("took him by surprise"); KBo 3.4 ii 75–77 (decennial annals of Murs. II) w. dup. KBo 16.1 iv 32′–33′, ed. Goetze 1933: 64–65, cf. also KBo 3.4 ii 78; KBo 3.6 ii 8–10 (Apol. of Hatt. III), ed. Otten 1981: 10–11 ("trieb ich den Feind in die Enge und bekämpfte ihn"). In KBo 14.3 iii 17–19 the verb is even used of catching the mobile and evasive Kaška tribesmen.

33. Alp 1991a, 126 *ki-ša-an-mu*.

34. Alp 1991a, 128 omits *-ma-*.

35. See Francia 2006, 350.

36. Alp 1991a, 128 reads *-ú-*. Collation by photo supports a reading *-pa-*; see CHD Š, 204–5 (*šapašiya-*).

37. For this form see Hoffner forthcoming §12, CHD sub *šapašiya-*, and *GrHL* §11.6 with n. 17.

38. Reading *pí-ya-nu-un* is also possible.

39. For this as an example of a rare and archaic non-imperfective stem in the supine see Hoffner forthcoming §129 and *GrHL* §11.24.

40. Cf. Goetze 1933, 74–75, lines 48–48: "Mit den Leuten von Mira sollen sie sich nicht einlassen."

41. Omitted in Alp 1991a, 130.

42. Or *e-ep-pir* "they have seized."

43. Because the verb *iya-* (mid.) "be in motion, march" does not take its imperfective suffix *-anna/i-* except in the inceptive sense "set out" (*GrHL* §24.4), it lacks it here, even though it is accompanied by the distributive expression *lammar lammar* "at any moment" (*GrHL* §24.12).

44. According to my photo, the last word in line 4 (a clear *na-it-ta* in HKM with no indication of previously erased sign traces) is written over an erasure. The scribe started to write the verb *u-i-e-eš* "you sent," but after writing *u* and the beginning of *i* he stopped, partially erased it, and wrote the synonymous verb *na-it-ta* "you dispatched" on top of the erased signs. Alp's copy should therefore not be taken as evidence for a variant shape of *na* with an extra horizontal. One should delete the last two variant shapes of NA (sign no. 57) in the Maşat sign list given in Alp 1991b, 114.

45. Literally, "30 households."

46. Or perhaps "I am relocating."

47. Although the accusative case of Lišipra and its anaphoric pronoun *-an* (line 9) could be an accusative of respect ("in regard to L."), the sense of the sentence is that he relocated the familes *to* Lišipra. Perhaps this is an accusative of direction (see *GrHL* §16.27, p. 248–49). Alp 1991a, 135 translates "I will carry off 300 families from Lišipra, which I am resettling," which violates the grammar of the text. On "enemy" and "resettling" in such texts see Giorgadze 2005. Note also that *arnu-* is used in this sense also in other Maşat letters (texts 45 and 47), including ABoT 65 (text 81).

48. Literally, "How will Your Majesty write to me?" I take *maḫḫan* as interrogative here. Alp 1991a, 135 differently: "in dem Moment in dem du, die Majestät, mir schreibst."

49. *zappanuškiši* lit. "you are causing me (i.e., my strength) to drip away"; see CHD Š, 137.

50. Or "together with," a comitative use of the instrumental; cf. *GrHL* §16.108.

51. Obviously, since those who were *peššiya*-ed (lit. caused to fall) included "captives" (*appantit* line 40) who were not slain, the "falling" merely means being "put out of action."

52. "He [i.e., Ḫattušili] undertook to use his influence in the court on a matter concerning Ḫimmuili's son-in-law. It seems that Ḫimmuili was seeking some sort of career advancement for his daughter's husband using the good services of his well-connected friend Hattusili" (Bryce 2003b, 174).

53. G. Beckman (private communication) calls my attention to the fact that, since *antiyant*-marriage was only resorted to in order for the bride's father to secure a male heir, once a single such person was acquired, there would be no need or wish for further ones. Hence, the plural here excludes the interpretation as *antiyant-* son-in-law.

54. A subjective genitive for the verbal noun *ḫaliyatar* (*GrHL* §16.46, p. 253). The genitive interrupts the sequence of *kī ... ḫaliyatar* (*GrHL* §18.25, p. 284).

55. Tablet erroneously has *li-li-wa-aḫ-ḫu-wa-an-kán*. CHD L–N *liliwaḫḫ-* emendation of *li-li-wa-aḫ-ḫu-u-an-kán* to the infinitive *li-li-wa-aḫ-ḫu-u-an-zi*! was never intended to express doubt that the tablet actually reads *-kán*, as Alp (1991a, 309) seems to think. The photo indeed confirms the hand copy. The point of the CHD treatment, which is still valid, is that *liliwaḫḫuwan=kan* in the *middle* of a clause(!) makes no sense and must be the result of a scribal (not the copyist's) error. Even if the particle *-kan* in mid-sentence could be justified—unlikely, since it is not affixed to a local expression, as are other rare examples (see Neu 1993 and *GrHL* §28.44)—*liliwaḫḫu(w)an* would have to be a supine without any auxiliary verb *dai-* or *tiya-*. It can hardly be an adverb ("eiligst"), as Alp claimed.

56. Alp read mMar-ú-wa-an-na, but the sign can easily be a variant form of RU.

57. For the use of the proximal demonstrative *kā-* "this" in "linguistic self-reference" see *GrHL* §7.1, page 142, and Goedegebuure 2002–2003, 213–14 (§6.2.4).

58. G. Beckman (personal communication) suggests that my supposition that the king's scribe used this formula often indicates that the king sometimes used the threat of blinding rhetorically. He adds that he does not doubt that some persons were actually blinded, as reports in this same group of letters clearly indicate.

59. See also texts 21 (HKM 16) and 83 (HKM 84). I have written regarding the Hittite use of blinding: "Blinding is not mentioned in the Hittite laws as a punishment for any offence. But a royal decree dating to the Middle Hittite period concerning theft allows that a thief who is a slave may be blinded. Maşat officials are threatened with blinding if they fail to perform the duties imposed upon them by the king. And other Middle Hittite treaty

texts from Boğazköy indicate that failure to blind *rebels* and send them to the king was itself treasonous behavior. In the ritual known as the "Soldiers' Oath," military personnel were warned that *treasonous behavior* such as the *violation of their oaths of loyalty to the king* would result in being blinded by the gods," Hoffner 2002c, 68 with nn. 39–42. See also Siegelová 2002, 737, citing two passages from the Soldiers' Oath; Hoffner 2003b; Hoffner 2004; and Arıkan 2006, 145.

60. De Martino (2005b, 310–11, 316) concurs.

61. For another example of a royal reprimand see text 12 (HKM 6): 11–14 and Beal 1986.

62. The two signs that immediately follow were intended to be erased by the scribe.

63. All of the verbs in this quoted passage are present tense (so-called historical presents, see *GrHL* §22.6–7), often used to describe vividly actions that took place in the past. The form *appiškanzi* "they were keeping under control" is imperfective aspect, on which see Hoffner and Melchert 2002. There may also be an inceptive aspect (*GrHL* §24.18) to the imperfective verb *appiškanzi* in KASKAL.ḪI.A*=ya=wa=za appiškanzi* "they even began to seize control of the roads."

64. Alp 1991a, 144 reads impossibly NÍ$^{!}$.ZU$^{!\text{ḪI.A}}$. NÍ.ZU "thief" never occurs without its LÚ determinative. The Maşat sign TÙR is a variant of HZL no. 34/1 (author's photo).

65. Alp 1991a, 144: *ma-an-ni-in-ku-wa-a*[*-an-te-eš*]. Common gender for the Hittite word underlying TÙR is also required in acc. pl. *a-pu-u-uš* TÙR.ḪI.A in HKM 36: 7, *ku-i-e-eš* in HKM 76: 8, and nom. sg. *ku-iš* in KUB 17.18 iii 21. The usual candidate for this word, *ašawar*, appears to be neuter in [*ku-e k*]*u-e a-ša-u-wa-ar e-eš-ta* KBo 10.2 i 7.

66. The clause at the end of line 25 is unclear. Alp's (1991a, 144) reading, *ma-an-wa ma-aḫ-ḫa-an-d*[*a*], makes no sense. But the form of the next clause, *nu ... -ma,* points to an alternative question (for which see *GrHL* §§27.17–18).

67. Alp 1991a, 144: *mar-ri-in ku*$^{?}$*-e*. A collation performed on October 23, 2007 in Ankara by Gary Beckman revealed what I had suspected: *le-e ku-it-ki i-ya-ši*. However, Beckman saw a clear AŠ wedge following *mar-ri*, which I did not foresee. Since the tablet surface is somewhat abraded at that point, it is possible that the AŠ is the remnant of a more complex sign containing a horizontal, e.g., *-i,* which would yield a precedented writing *mar-ri-i*.

68. Alp 1991a, 144 "*a-za-ki-it-ten.*"

69. A single wedge on the left side of the line marks an indent and indicates that the following word is a continuation of the preceding two words. This was mistakenly taken by CHD P, 269 (morphology of *pippa-*) as a *Glossenkeil* on the word itself. CHD P regards this form as belonging to the verb *pippa-* "to knock down, overturn," but does not translate this passage.

70. Alp's restoration [... *ú*$^{?}$*-nu*$^{?}$*-wa*$^{?}$*-a*]*š*$^{?}$*-ḫa* ("Schmuck") cannot be accepted, because the resumptive pronoun *-aš* "them" in line 16 is common gender, while *unuwašḫa* as it stands would be a neuter noun. Furthermore the trace of the sign before *-ḫa* in line 15 does not seem to be *-a*]*š*-.

71. Or: ^{m}*Kaš-še-ni.*

72. Alp 1991a, 148 reads ARÀḪ*-ten*, taking the form as an imperative verb. The copy shows *-ḫi*, not *-tén.* The solution, which I discovered while collating and photographing the tablet years ago, is to see that the ".A" of ÉSAG.ḪI.A on line 4 of the left edge is written around the edge, so as to appear to be the first sign in line 28. That fact in turn solves the problem of the apparent *A-ḪU-MA* that begins line 28, which should simply be

read as *QA-TAM-MA*.

73. Perhaps *-ma* is not needed here. It could be asyndeton (for which see *GrHL* §29.46–47). If not emended, read *ḫalkiš=šmaš*.

74. For the position of causal *kuit* in this later-than-expected position in the clause see *GrHL* §30.43.

75. For *apiya* "there" in this passage as referencing proximity to the addressee see *GrHL* §7.18.

76. On grain storage in such silos see Seeher 1998, 2000a, 2000b; Neef 2001; and Seeher 2001.

77. For this nom.-acc. pl. ending see *GrHL* §3.16.

78. For Hittite *yugan* "pairs," cf. *GrHL* §9.39.

79. The king's scribe.

80. The scribe of Kaššū and Pulli.

81. In view of the large number and the likelihood in the context that the king is thinking in round numbers, it is improbable that the number is to be read 1,701 with Alp 1991a, 152, followed by Beal 1992, 283. The value "60" for the single vertical wedge is admittedly rare at Boğazköy (for which usually the Akkadogram *ŠU-ŠI* is used), but not unprecedented (two cases that I can think of are 60+20+8 [= 88] in KUB 8.75 l. e. 1, and 60+30 [= 90] in KUB 51.76: 4′), and here virtually certain. See the remark in HZL 271 no. 356 without references.

82. So according to collation, against Alp's [*k*]*u-* (1991a, 152). This new reading invalidates Beal's observation (1992, 317) about the king's interest in any soldier killing an enemy.

83. Reading so eliminates the necessity of taking *-an* as an accusative pron., the object of *ḫatrāeš*.

84. From **kappuwawar*, see *GrHL* §1.138 and Hoffner forthcoming.

85. Alp 1991a, 152 reads [*n*]*a*?*-aš*, which would implausibly break lines 12 and 13 into two clauses.

86. Compare the elaborate oracular inquiries about military strategy contained in KUB 5.1 (CTH 561) and similar texts (Ünal 1973and Beal 1999). In the Bible compare Judg 1:1, 20:18, 23, 1 Sam 14:37, 22:13, 23:2, 4.

87. Collated. Alp 1991a, 152 read Ú!.ḪI.A "grasses".

88. The king's scribe.

89. The scribe of Pulli in Tapikka.

90. Although a piggyback letter begins in line 9, the scribe preceded it with a single (not a double) dividing line (HKM copy confirmed by collation).

91. If 17–18 contain only a single clause, and *waršianza* is indeed the predicate, the presence of *-za* constrains the choice of subject to first or second person ("I/you/we am/are soothed"). Since *warš-*, not *waršiya-*, is the verb "to reap/harvest," this cannot be translated "geerntet" with Alp 1991a, 159.

92. Alp 1991a, 158 restored [*pa-a-ir*], but ÉRIN.MEŠ in MH is grammatically singular (a collective noun).

93. Or read [… *pé-r*]*a-a-an* with Alp 1991a, 158. A plene writing of the final syllable of *peran* is unusual. But cf. the examples cited in CHD *peran* and add perhaps: KUB 31.130 rev. 8′ and KUB 26.85 ii 6′.

94. On the omission of the quotative particle *-wa* here see *GrHL* §28.11.

95. Or: *ša-ra-a* [*tar-n*]*u-*[*m*]*e-ni*.

96. Alp 1991a, 160 restores [*na-aš*].
97. Alp 1991a, 160 restores [*A-NA* ^{URU}*M*]*a-ri-iš-ta*.
98. Collated. Alp 1991a, 162 ^{URU}*Ša*$^{?}$*-pa-a*.
99. For the abl. ending *-zzi* on this form see *GrHL* §1.116.
100. Van den Hout (2004a, 90) prefers "to" (Dutch "*naar*(?)").
101. So Melchert (see above in text 23), followed here also by van den Hout ("dat is gereserveerd voor het zaaien").
102. Left untranslated by van den Hout. Alp: "separate it off behind him" ("trenne sie ihm hinterher ab").
103. So van den Hout. Or: "Support (lit., step behind) those troops in Kašipura," taking EGIR-*an* as preverb with *tiya-*, as this is translated in CHD Š 226 (*šarā* B 3 c).
104. Alp: "provisions." Van den Hout: "rations" (Dutch: "*rantsoen?*")
105. Collated. Alp 1991a, 162 reads *nu-wa-ra-a*[*t-k*]*án*.
106. Analytic present perfect construction with *eš-* suppressed (*GrHL* §22.22).
107. Among these the *tuppanuri* and Chief Scribe at Ugarit (Singer 2006, 244), the eunuchs (LÚ.SAG; Hawkins 2002, 226), the UGULA NIMGIR.ÉRIN.MEŠ (Marizza 2007a: 41–42), the Field Marshall (GAL.GEŠTIN; Marizza 71, 73), the GAL KUŠ_7 "Chief/Great Charioteer" (Marizza 2007a, 85), the GAL DUB.SAR "Chief/Great Scribe" (Marizza 2007a, 110).
108. I thank Prof. Theo van den Hout for calling my attention to these corrections from my own photos in the CHD collection.
109. So HKM 27 and photo. Alp 1991a, 166 has a typographical error: *zi-i-ki-iz-zi*.
110. Lit. "putting himself (on/against)" (*-za=kan zikkezzi*). For further examples and discussion see n. 149 on p. 385.
111. Mention of "fine garments" in left edge 2.
112. There is insufficient space in the break for either Alp's SIG_5[*-in pa-aḫ-ḫa-aš-nu-u*]*t-tén* or Goedegebuure's proposed restoration (2003, 86) SIG_5-[*aḫ-ḫe-eš-ke-et-*]*tén* "keep repairing." Space-wise, a shorter reading SIG_5-[*aḫ-ḫe-eš-k*]*i-tén* would be possible, but I suspect that the adverb SIG_5*-in* "well" was used in both lines. Although Goedegebuure seems not to have tried to translate *anda*, her restoration either requires a preverbial construction *anda* SIG_5*-aḫḫ-* or makes it necessary to interpret *anda* as an adverb "there." The former alternative is very unlikely, since the verb *lazziyaḫḫ-*/SIG_5*-aḫḫ-* shows only one preverb, EGIR-*pa*, which unlike *anda* is not of a local variety. The latter alternative—that *anda* means something like "there"—is impossible to either prove or disprove. On the other hand, SIG_5*-in* "well" regularly breaks the nexus between preverb and finite verb (e.g., *na-an-za* EGIR-*an* SIG_5*-i*[*n*] *wa-tar-na-aḫ-tén* HKM 44: 7–8), so that there is reason to look for a verb other than *lazziyaḫḫ-* to fill the break. A good candidate is *anda auš-* "to look at, watch."
113. With Goedegebuure (2003, 86 with n. 79) *aš-nu-w*[*a-an-ta-ru*] "(and) [let] them [be] well provided for." On the common gender of TÙR in the Maşat letters see note 110.
114. See Beal 1992, 430 for the correction of Alp's reading of line 12.
115. Or perhaps [*zi-i*]*g-ga*.
116. Or: "to the city of Išaš," taking *pa-ra-a* as the preverb in *parā nai-* (so CHD Š, 241 *šarā* b 2′ d').
117. Comitative instrumental (*GrHL* §16.109 and §16.111).
118. Normally, when a new subject is introduced, using the words "concerning

the matter" (genitive + *kuit uttar*) to refer back to a previous letter from the addressee, especially when there is a series of such transitions in a single letter (as in texts 16, 22 and 35), it is preceded by a paragraph line. But here there is none (copy confirmed by photo). See §1.2.15.2.

119. *-mu ... kattan* shows the relatively uncommon use of postpositions/adverbs with a locatival sense governing enclitic personal pronouns (*GrHL* §18.10, cf. also §20.21 on *kattan*). On the position of *kuiški* see *GrHL* §18.35.

120. Alp's restoration is full of uncertainties and problems. My photo doesn't show the right edge of the tablet. The 2nd sg. pres. of *lā-* is attested as *la-a-ši* and DÙ-*ši*, but not as *la-a-iš-ši*. Despite CHD Š, 41, which seems to take the reading *la-*[*a-*]*iš-ši* seriously and compares it with *ša-ki-iš-ši,* I do not regard it as a secure reading of the traces. The verb *ḫapallaššai-* has undoubled *p* and doubled *l*, not vice versa as Alp's reading requires. See KBo 6.4 i 22–23 (Law §IX): *takku* LÚ *ELLUM* SAG.DU=*SU kuiški ḫapallašaizzi*. Yet my photo confirms the spelling here [*ḫ*]*a-ap-pa-la*[-…], which is not yet attested for any other verb.

121. My photo shows that the top vertical stroke in Alp's drawing of the sign could be a *Winkelhaken*, making it GÉME.

122. The different reading of Alp 1991a, 172 is incompatible with both the copy in HKM and my photo.

123. The consonant-geminating *-a/-ya* is required here (*GrHL* §29.1, §29.40).

124. Lines 19 and 20 contain an "if" clause without a following main clause stating the expected dire threat in the following main clause. Such constructions are common in both Hittite and other ancient Near Eastern languages. See below in comments on HKM 34 [text 40]. Positive "if" clauses of this type are equivalent to emphatic prohibitions, as in this instance. Negative ones are equivalent to emphatic positive commands.

125. *HW*² H 250 restores [*naišten*] ("führt").

126. Literally "troops." But both Sumerian ÉRIN.MEŠ and the Akkadian term *ṣābu* which ÉRIN.MEŠ renders denote groups of men used for "public" work, either military or otherwise (see CAD Ṣ, 46). Both Alp (1991a, 179) and Beal (1992, 110, 286) take ÉRIN.MEŠ here as *individual* "soldiers," not as *groups* either of agricultural workers or of troops.

127. Although Haas's theory faces an uphill battle against what has been the uncontested view of the term in Hittite texts, it does have the advantage of explaining the consistent spelling of the word with non-geminate intervocalic *b/p* (i.e., *ḫapiri-* versus **ḫappiri-*), the latter being what one would expect if the consonant in question were voiceless (see *GrHL* §§1.84–1.85).

128. The verb *ḫatrai-* normally is used of sending messages. For sending objects other verbs (e.g., *uppa-*) are used. Although Alp does not interpret *lūwan* as "report" (German *Bericht*), note his description of the sense of the passage: "Jene Beamten werden aufgefordert u. a. *Bericht* über die Weintraubenernte(?) des Palastes abzustatten" (1991a, 105).

129. Alp (1991a, 320) read *túḫ-ša-la-u,* which he took as a noun "grape harvest" (German *Ernte*). This letter is addressed to three men (lines 2–3), of whom Zardumanni seems to be the superior. The last two signs in this word can easily be read *-at-t*[*én*], yielding a plural imperative, matching both the *-šamaš* "you (pl.)" of line 5 and the following clause's *ḫa-at-ra-a-at-tén* "write/send!"

130. For more on this subject see Yakar 2000, 38–39.

131. This paragraph is essentially a summary of Klengel 2006, 8–9.

132. Or perhaps ^{m}Ta-ru-⸢uz⸣-z[i-ya-aš]. Marizza 2007a, 163 and Goedegebuure, following Alp, read ^{m}Ta-ru-l[i$^{?}$-…].

133. Alp's restoration *ka-a-[ša]* is also possible.

134. See text 45 for another example of the relocating of city populations. This verb (*arnu-*) forms the base of the term for movable agricultural labor groups (Sumerogram NAM.RA, Hittite *arnuwala-*).

135. The singular verb refers to the singular noun [ÉR]IN.MEŠ translated "troops." The "him" refers to someone mentioned in the preceding broken context.

136. Turkish Karadağ? See map in Alp 1979, 31.

137. Taking these verbs as historical presents, as suggested to me by Beckman.

138. Goedegebuure (2002–2003, 84) takes the *ma-na* in the copy as correct, and analyzes it as *man=a* (*man* + *-a/-ma*). I have not been able to identify another (pre-NH) example of sentence initial potential *man* taking *-a/-ma* as a clitic.

139. I take this form of *utne* as nom.-acc., because the clear use of such a form (KUR-*i*) is undeniable in KBo 16.47 obv. 17, 18, where it is the object of *parḫzi* and *parḫši* (see CHD under *parḫ-* 3).

140. Literally "scouts of the long road (KASKAL GÍD.DA)." Cf. for this Pecchioli Daddi 2003a, 72–75.

141. Perhaps Turkish Yapraklı Tepe directly north of Maşat.

142. Reference courtesy of H. C. Melchert.

143. For the function of Hittite imperfectives see *GrHL* §§24.6–19.

144. Text has *-aš*, which is the wrong gender to match either *pedan* or *arziyan*.

145. Literally, "make to stand back."

146. Or *nu-u[š$^{?}$-ša-an]*.

147. Or: *ar-ḫa uš-ki-nu-mi<-ni$^{?}$>* "and we are in the process of carrying out oracles," so preferred by Hoffner forthcoming §10.

148. Following Soysal ("Wieviel Getier"), I translate "how much wildlife," rather than "how many (individual) wild animals," because of the spelling of *ḫu-u-e-tar,* which showing the characteristic spelling of the collective (*ḫu-u-i-tar, ḫu-u-e-da-ar, ḫu-i-ta-ar*), contrasts with the "count" plural forms with long vowel in the final syllable: *ḫu-i-ta-a-ar, ḫu-i-da-a-ar, ḫu-u-i-ta-a-ar* (*GrHL* §3.20). The writer is not promising the queen a precise number, only a general estimate—many or few.

149. Compare OH/OS 3rd sg. preterite *zi-ik-ke-e-et,* with plene writing of final syllable. For *-za-kán ... zikke-* with accus., see LÚ.KÚR-*za-kán ma-aḫ-ḫa-an* ^{URU}*Ka-ša-ša-an* ^{URU}*Ta-ḫa-az-zi-mu-na-an-na zi-ik-ke-ez-zi na-at AŠ-ME* "I have heard how the enemy is initiating (something) against/toward the towns K. and T." HKM 27: 4–7 (text 32); ^{d}UTU-*ŠI-wa-du-z[a-ká]n ki-iš-[š]a-an ki-iš-ša-an-na zi-ik-ke-ez-zi* "His Majesty is *initiating*$^{?}$ (something) against you" KBo 5.4 obv. 29 (Targašnalli treaty); ^{m}É.GAL.PAP-*aš-wa-za-kán* BAL *zi-ik-ke-ez-zi* "E.GAL.PAP is *initiating*$^{?}$ a rebellion" KUB 6.41 iii 49; *na-at-za-kán ku-it im-m[a ku-it* ḪUL …] [… *zi-i]k-ke-ez-zi na-at-ši Ú-UL ki-ik-ki-iš-ta-ri* "Whatever [evil …] he *initiates*$^{?}$, it will not happen (i.e., succeed) for him" KUB 58.108 i 3–4. A different meaning is involved when *anda* is added: *nu-za iš-ḫa-mi-iš-ke-ez-zi* ^{d}*IŠTAR-iš nu-za-kán ŠA* A.AB.BA *a-ku-un* ^{NA4}*pa-aš-ši-la-an-na an-da zi-ik-ke-ez-zi* "*IŠTAR* sings, and she puts on herself a seashell and a pebble" KUB 36.12 ii 5–6.

150. Literally, "daughters" or "girls."

151. For an example of the inflected nominative of a GN in Maşat, see ^{URU}*Pišatenitiš* (HKM 47 obv. 3).

152. I see the trace as the wedge-head of a final vertical, thus my -*a*]*t*-, not the end of a horizontal, thus Alp's -*a*]*š*-.

153. The writing *dam-mi-iš-ki-iš-kán-zi* for the expected *dam-mi-iš-ḫi-iš-kán-zi* is explained as the neutralization of the *k/ḫ* distinction when the consonant is in direct contact with a sibilant (*š* or z); see *GrHL* §1.137. For the regular insertion of an *i* vowel between a consonantal stem ending and the -*ške/a*- suffix, see *GrHL* §1.80.

154. *BE-LU-uš* as a nom. sg. does not fit the normal Hittite word for "lord" (*išḫa*-). Perhaps the scribe absent-mindedly simply carried forward the vowel he had just written in -*LU*.

155. Or perhaps both here and in line 25 the *apēz* is partitive: "take some of that."

156. I assume that under the uninflected logogram GU$_4$.ḪI.A was an inflected Hittite instrumental noun. The neuter *ku-e* clearly does not modify common gender GU$_4$.ḪI.A, but rather $^{\text{A.ŠÀ}}$*te-ri-ip-pí*.

157. Tablet has *ki-nu-wa*, which Alp and van den Hout read *ki-nu*<-*na*>-*wa*. If one must emend the text, I would prefer simply emending *nu* to *e*.

158. Collated from photo. Alp (1991a, 222 with n. 259) notes both possibilities and favors *p*[*a-i*]*š*.

159. Neuter plural subjects can take either singular or plural predicates in Hittite. See van den Hout 2001b.

160. For this rhetorical question see Hoffner 1995a example (95).

161. Alp 1991a, 224 reads *š*[*a*$^{?}$-]*ri-ya-an-zi*.

162. So Alp 1991a, 224. Reading of the sign uncertain.

163. So Alp 1991a, 224.

164. Alp: ^{m}*Wa-al-wa-nu*. But Sum. NU = Akk. *awīlum* "man" = Luwian *ziti*-; this name is Walwa-ziti (Laroche 1966, no. 1486).

165. Perhaps meaning he will not attempt to act as a *šardiyaš* for his slave. See laws §37 and §38. Does his reluctance to involve himself in judicial procedures stem from his being a priest?

166. *ḫu-nu-ut-tén* is a by-form of *ḫu-i-nu-ut-tén*. Alp 1991a, 232 (followed by Arıkan) restores [*e-ep-tén*] and no -*za* in the preceding line.

167. Or: [o o *ut-ni-i*]*a*. Alp 1991a, 232 [KUR-*i*]*a* does not fill the available space.

168. Alp's restoration (1991a, 232) [*me-ek-ki pa-aḫ-ḫa-a*]*š*- exceeds the available space and fails to include obligatory -*za*.

169. Alp 1991a reads this name here and in line 22 semi-ideographically as ^{m}UDU-*ši-wa-li-iš*.

170. This may be a logographically written "split genitive" construction (*GrHL* §16.38).

171. This translation assumes *ammuga*=*ma*=*an*. If one analyses *ammuga*=*man* a translation "How might I have acted (otherwise)?" is possible.

172. Alp 1991a, 244 reads incorrectly: ANŠE-ya-*wa-mu* GA-*iš*.

173. Much space here, contra Alp 1991a.

174. The readings *za-ak*[-*m*]*u*$^{?}$-*li-uš-pát* and *za-ak*[-*z*]*i*$^{?}$-*li-uš-pát* are also possible, although no such words are yet attested in Hittite texts.

175. See text 170, lines 31–33.

176. Since the verb "hitch up" is singular, are two persons the subject?

177. Translated "And if anything else came—(is) remaining, they must further let it go" in van den Hout 2003b, 185. If one reads Ú-*it* in line 17, one could translate: "and if together with (comitative inst.) grass anything further remains."

178. Translated by van den Hout (2003b, 186) as "Let the son of Šaparta come—a[r]rive!" But the virtual repetition of this phrase in lines 29–30 shows clearly that "Šaparta's son" is not the subject of *anda wemiya-*"find," but its direct object, as already Alp correctly translated in both lines. The passage *am-mu-uk-ma-an*[*-kán*] (18) ^{URU}*Wi*$_5$*-is-ta-w*[*a-an-da an-da*] *ú-e-mi-ya-nu-un* "But I found him (*-an*) in Wištawanda" KUB 19.9 ii 17–18 shows that the many instances where the case of the verb's object is ambiguous (*-mu, -ta, -šmaš*), the correct interpretation of the pronoun is accusative.

179. *kuedaniki* is a dative of disadvantage together with the local particle *-kan* (*GrHL* §16.68). Note how the two indefinite pronouns *kuedaniki* and *kuitki* break the nexus of the analytic perfect construction *dān ḫarmi.*

180. For the phenomenon of "broken writing" seen in *da-me-i-da-ni* see *GrHL* §1.62.

181. "1–3 So (spricht) der Oberste der Streitwagentruppe: Zu Kaššu, meinem Bruder, sprich: 4–7 Was hast du da mir getan? Siehe, die Truppen sind noch immer draußen bei dir. 8–13 Siehe, sie sind zu den anderen Truppen befohlen. Führe (sie) eilends her. Gnade sei mit Dir."

182. Alp (1991a 256) restores [*pu-nu-uš-šu-wa-an-zi*] conjecturally.

183. The odd placement of the word *tu-el-ma* in line 9 and the abrupt switch from what looks like a 3rd pl. imperative *kar-aš-ša-an-du* to a 2nd pl. one *kar-aš-tén* in 10–11, all suggest that the scribe may have omitted the sign *-uš*. Other clear omissions of signs occur in line 32. I see no justification for the plural *zinnanda* at the end of line 6. I assume that the verb *ni-ni-ik-tén* (12) is used with human objects in the sense of CHD L–N *nini(n)k-* 1, and that those persons transport the timber (-at in line 13). I understand the *-šmaš* of 27 as 3rd pl. used reflexively with *appandu.* The imperative *uwandu* is used as a serial verb with *appandu* ("let them proceed to finish"), and *warpanna* and *wedumanzi* appear to be the infinitives that indicate the undertakings to be completed. The Akkadogram *BÁ-BI-LA-Ú* in line 26 lacks the normal URU ("city") determinative. There is no reason for the particle *-war-* in line 13.

184. The signs *ḫar-kán-zi,* written on the edge with uninscribed space before them, could belong to line 7.

185. Imparati 2003, 234.

186. In the Detailed Annals of Muršili (KUB 19.37 iii 36–40, 42–44) the king speaks of temples that were "behind" the cities of Kappēri and Ḫurna, which he spared together with their cult personnel when he captured those cities. What is meant by "behind" a city has always been somewhat of a riddle (see preliminary thoughts in CHD Š 140 (EGIR-*an* = "rear, interior"). In some few cases a speaker may refer to something "behind the city" to indicate the opposite side from his own perspective. But there are numerous examples of this expression in Hittite texts where there is no obvious perspective indicated. Failing that explanation, what might the front or back of a city be? If a city has a front, it might be where the main gate was located. This would mean that "behind" (or "in the rear of") the city would be inside the walls but at the opposite end of the enclosure from the main gate. This might fit the expected location of a temple. But a position on the opposite side from the main gate does not satisfy all contexts either. It is interesting, therefore, to see that in Old Babylonian Mari *ina warkat dūrim* "behind the city wall" is further explained as *ina ṣērim* "in the open country" (see CAD A/II, 275 rt. col.). This would imply the perspective of someone inside the city. If this perspective is used, then some examples of "behind the city X" might mean outside the city walls but in the near periphery, i.e., "in the vicinity of (the city)."

187. This is how I understand the imperfective verbal form, which Imparati calls an "iterative" and claims that it means the Kizzuwatnean has been reporting such matters regularly to the palace. For the *-ške-* imperfective suffix and its uses see *GrHL*, chapter 24.

188. *ammel ... tuel* (line 15) "my … your," a pair of contrastive independent genitive pronouns (*GrHL* §18.4).

189. Alp: "removed(?)" (*entfernt*[*?*]).

190. Rost 345 read *-d*]*u*.

191. Rost 346 mistakenly regarded *pé-e-eš-ke-et* as a form of *pai-* "to give," rather than of *peye/a-* "to send" (CHD P, 261).

192. See the treatments of this passage in CHD L–N 141 (*man* b 2′ b') and *GrHL* §§26.10, 30.54.

193. For the translation "keeps after me" for EGIR-*an=pat kittari* see CHD L–N, 312 (sub *-mu* c 2′ a'), and (on its occurrence in KUB 14.1 obv. 1–2) CHD P, 144 (*parḫ-* 1 a 2′).

194. There are problems with Alp's restoration *t*[*u-el-mu ŠA ... ki-i*]*š-ša-an ku-i*[*t ḫa-at-ra-a-eš*]. The word usually taken to be *kuit* "concerning what" should precede *kiššan* and stand in the "second position" in the clause according to the rules of Hittite grammar. Furthermore the sequence is usually *kuit kiššan (ḫatrai-)*, not *kiššan kuit (ḫatrai-)*. See examples in texts 12: 3, 13; 13: 3; etc. If what precedes *kiššan* in this clause were either an unaccented word (e.g., a conjunction plus clitics) or a short interjection, not counted in the following clause, then there would be no problem. But Alp's restoration satisfies neither of these conditions. Still, in the following passage *kuit* occurs in the third position: *nu=mu kāšma šumeš=pat kuit ḫatrātten* "concerning what you yourselves have just written to me" HKM 17: 13–15 (MH/MS), ed. Alp 1991a, 142–43.

195. Alp's restoration [DINGIR-*LIM i-da-la-wa-aḫ-ḫa-an-zi*] would violate normal grammar, in that the verb *idalawaḫḫ-* takes an accusative object, not a dative (*-ši*).

196. Or 5 GA.K[IN.AG …].

197. See Taracha 2000, 28–29, where *allanza menuwaš* = GA *EMṢI* "sour milk."

198. For this form as a dat.-loc. sg. in *-e* see *GrHL* §3.24.

199. Or "[The …-s] of Talmaliya are about to make peace."

200. Or: *tup-pí* "tablet."

201. See for example Muršili II's use of it in his annals, where he records his brief prayer: "O Sungoddess of Arinna, my lady! Join with me (*-mu ... kattan tiya*) and strike down the enemy lands for me!" (KBo 3.4 i 25–26), and Ḫattušili III's in his Apology (ii 66–68). Forlanini renders it in the Šapinuwa letter as "arrival."

202. The inappropriate insertion of *ku-it* here was due to the scribe's thinking ahead to what he would write correctly in line 3.

203. A kind of priest.

204. A kind of priestess or exorcist.

205. One might be tempted to restore [*I-NA* URU*Gur*?*-š*]*a*?*-ma-a-ša*, if this city were known to be closer to Šapinuwa. But Forlanini (cited in RGTC VI/2) locates Guršamašša far to the southwest, near Kütahya.

206. An example of the construction with the serial verb *uwa-* "proceed to" (see *GrHL* §§24.31–24.42).

207. For more on Knudtzon's decipherment, which—contrary to what is often claimed—he never disclaimed in the face of criticism, see Singer 2005.

208. So in the published handcopies. Rost (1956, 331), after examining the original tablet, favored a reading *ut-tar.*

209. Optative *man* (see treatment in CHD *man* a 1′ a' 2" and *GrHL* §23.11).

210. See CHD L–N, 93 (*-ma* b 1′) and above in §1.2.12.

211. See CHD *pai-* B a 2′.

212. On the divided opinion as to the meaning of the words *išḫanittar(a)-* and *išḫanittarātar* see below on text 123.

213. Haas in Moran 1992, 103 renders this god's name as "Nabu." But the signs are clearly ᵈÉ.A, and this title "king of wisdom," a Hittite adaptation of Akkadian *bēl nēmeqi,* not only fits Ea perfectly, but is actually attested also in text 9 (line 19), a letter found at Maşat Höyük.

214. For this hypostasis of the solar deity see the comprehensive references in van Gessel 1998–2001, 870.

215. See CHD ᵁᴿᵁ*nišili* b.

216. La terra di Hatti è gelata"—"Per questa traduzione letterale cf. De Martino, *op. cit.,* p. 83 nota 360 [de Martino 1996]; oppure metaforicamente «è ostile». In passato si vedeva qui una notizia sul collasso di Hatti (cf. ad esempio Kühne, AOAT 17, pp. 96–99; Heinhold-Krahmer, *op. cit.,* pp. 52–53); o al contrario, dopo il già citato intervento di Starke, ad una notizia di segno pacifico (cf. Kempinski, *Kutscher Volume,* pp. 82–83). Credo si alluda solo all'impraticabilità della strada: il Faraone prende atto della motivazione (o scusa) addotta dal re di Arzawa" (Liverani 1998, 409 with n. 9). See also Freu 2002, 92 ("le pays de Hatti étant «gelé» (igait), c'est à dire pacifié").

217. Klengel also writes (1999, 131–32): "In Z.27 wird auf eine schwierige Situation im 'Land Ḫattuša' hingewiesen, die für die Zeit Tutḫalijas II. verfügbaren Quellen, insbesondere die 'Taten Suppiluliumas' (DŠ, [B7]), könnten diesen Eindruck des Pharao bestätigen. Vielleicht darf die beabsichtigte dynastische Verbindung Ägyptens mit Arzawa im Bestreben des Pharao nach einem kleinasiatischen Gegengewicht gegenüber Ḫatti begründet sein, das zuletzt zur Zeit des Tutḫalija I. auch auf Syrien übergegriffen hatte, welches seit Beginn des 18. ägyptischen Dynastie das besondere Interesse ägyptischer Machtpolitik gefunden hatte."

218. This reading follows Albright 1937, 195 n. 1 and the collation of Edmund Gordon cited in Moran 1992, 102 n. 1.

219. This writing represents the royal name of Amunḥotep III, *nb mꜣʿt rʿ,* which means "The sun god (Re) is the lord of truth."

220. Not DUMU.MUNUS–*ti* "(look) on your (–*ti*) daughter," as incorrectly translated in CHD L–N, 468 (*nu* A h 8′ a'). The verb *au(š)-* always takes a direct object (acc.), never an indirect one (dat.-loc.).

221. Edmund Gordon's collation found that this word is not *zu-ḫa-la-li-ya* (so Haas in Moran 1992, 102), but ᴷᵁŠ*ḫa-la-li-ya.* See also line 30.

222. Translated differently in CHD L–N, 59 (*lilḫuwai-* a), and 468 (*nu* A h 8′ a'), where no direct quote is assumed in these two clauses.

223. Contrary to all previous translations (Haas in Moran 1992, 101–2; Liverani 1998, 408; Bernabé and Álvarez-Pedrosa 2004, 48; and Klinger 2006, 195), the adjective SIG_5-*an-ta,* being nom.-acc. neut. pl., must modify 1 ᴷᵁŠ*ḫa-la-li-ya,* not the genitive KÙ.SIG_{17}-*aš* "of gold." This means that the numeral "1" refers to a collection or set (see *GrHL* §9.26–37). This example is therefore irrelevant to Starke's study (1982) of Egyptian "good gold." The concept of "good gold," however, is well attested in correspondence with Egypt (see above in comments on text 116).

224. Klinger translates this "with cushions" (*mit Sitzkissen*). CHD Š 288 renders *šarpa*: "cross-legged(?) chairs" and explains: "Our understanding of this word derives from Forlanini's (*Hethitica* 7: 76–77) suggestion equating Mt. Šarpa with the hierogl. DEUS.MONS.THRONUS of the Emirgazi altars and seeing the THRONUS sign as one of the cross-legged chairs often depicted in Hittite art, sometimes covered with a cloth or drape."

225. ""Photos of the lower edge on which line 33 is written confirm Knudtzon's reading. After GAD there is an unmistakable AN followed by a small space, the size of a usual word space, in which the remains of what seems to have been a vertical wedge is visible. This results in a reading 1 ME GAD-*an wa-al-ga-an. walgan* is probably the sg. nom.–acc. neut. part. of the v. *walg*- q.v."

226. Rainey (personal communication): -*bi*-.

227. Gordon saw traces of two further signs after -*ya* at the end of line 11, which Moran (p. 115) speculated could be "LUGAL," which he interpreted as a rebus writing for *ša/urru(mma)* "indeed," following Kühne (AOAT 17, 101 n. 500).

228. Restoration necessary because of the subjunctive *aqbû.*

229. Moran: "*a-na-ku:* virtually certain (Gordon)."

230. So E. I. Gordon and Rainey (personal communication). Moran prefers a shorter restoration: "5. 22 [a-qab-bi] *us-sà-ta (usātu):* favoring *aqabbi* is the enclitic -*ma,* 'my brother, *too.*' Gordon also restored *a-ḫu*]-*uz-za-ta,* "let's make a marriage between us," bur a break of five signs seems excluded. Whether a proposal of marriage would be made so laconically may also be doubted."

231. Rainey (personal communication) omits -*ma.*

232. Moran prefers the imperative form "[šu-bi-la], at the end of line 28."

233. Moran "a large stand," omitting to translate the pronoun -*šunu* "their."

234. Moran*:* "The reading *i*-gam-ma-*ru-ma* is very questionable. Gordon read GADA *ḫu-uz-ḫu-še.*"

235. Moran reads: LU.LIM$_4$ "stag."

236. For other variants of this DAG+KISIM$_5$ (or E$^!$+KISIM$_5$)-framed sign at Boğazköy see HZL nos. 189, 190, 232, 278-285. Rainey (personal communication) reads UDU.ŠIR. BE *pu-u-ḫi-lu* instead of Moran's UDU.DAG+KISIM$_5$×IR(?).

237. So read by CHD L–N sub *nuntarnu*-. Or perhaps: *nu-un-tar-nu-wa-a*[*n-du*] "let them (i.e., my messengers?) hurry."

238. The *UL* sign is written out in the left margin, as though the result of a scribal afterthought.

239. See Hoffner 1995a, example 29.

240. Or "Is it …?" See also line 48.

241. See further Bryce 2002b, 191.

242. On this phrase see Garrett 1990, 270 n. 14.

243. Houwink ten Cate restores the name Kaššū in this break, but we cannot be sure.

244. Houwink ten Cate restores: [*kat-ta*].

245. On this phrase see Garrett 1990, 270 n. 14.

246. Houwink ten Cate 39: [*pí-ra-an* U]GU.

247. The trace is just one or two final verticals, but the final one is not broken, so as to permit Houwink ten Cate's -*a*$^?$- reading. Perhaps É?

248. Houwink ten Cate: "he set Atpas $^{(8)}$ [again]st me(?) (lit., he brought Atpas [u]p [before] me)."

249. Literally "sinned" (*wašta-*).

250. Or: "The basket-weaver [...-ed] them," taking the *-aš* as a late accusative plural.

251. Her aptly-chosen German descriptive terms were *ein Bravourstück diplomatischer Kunst* and *ein Argumentationskonzept für den Gesandten.*

252. Translation from the German of Miller 2006, 242.

253. The sole exception occurred during the final decade of the Hittite kingdom, when Hittite-manned ships fought and won a sea battle off the coast of Cyprus (translation of the text in Güterbock 1967b and Hoffner 1997e).

254. E.g., Taracha 2001, 418 n. 2, criticizing Mountjoy's proposal.

255. This is the argument of Starke (1997, 453).

256. According to Hawkins and Mountjoy, Attarimma = Telmessos. There are objections to this identification by Taracha (2001, 418 n. 1).

257. Although for convenience sake we number sections from 1, it is clear from the colophon that this tablet represents the third tablet of a long letter. So what begins this tablet is by no means the beginning of the letter.

258. Sommer (1932) restored [^{m}*Gul-l*]*a*$^{?}$*-aš*. Forrer had read [$^{m.d}$]LAMMA-*aš*. If we accept Sommer's restoration and also date this letter to the reign of Ḫattušili III, the events are probably too late to identify this man with the Gullaš who is mentioned in the Annals of Muršili II. We assume that the $^{m.d}$LAMMA-*aš* (*Kuruntiyaš*) mentioned later in this letter is the adopted son of Ḫattušili III who was made the ruler of Tarḫuntašša. But whether or not his name occurs in this line depends entirely on the accuracy of Forrer's reading of the traces. Sommer 1932, 20, insisted that the original and his photo could not be so read. Without making an issue of it, Miller seems to have read [*nam-m*]*a*$^{?}$*-aš* (i.e., *namma–aš*, with a clitic pronominal subject, since he translates "[Furthermo]re, he went ..." (German: "[Ferne]r, er zog los ...," 2006, 242). Since this sentence continues the narrative from the end of tablet two, there is really no need for a personal name here.

259. Literally, "the king's houses."

260. According to Heinhold-Krahmer 1986, Tawagalawa was the previous king of Aḫḫiyawa. According to Güterbock, Singer, Bryce, and others, he was the brother of the present king of Aḫḫiyawa.

261. *ú-uk-ka*$_4$ is dative-locative here, in accordance with late Hittite usage (see *GrHL* §5.8 and §5.10).

262. So correctly Singer 1983b. Earlier interpreters had thought this was Tawagalawa.

263. Hittite *tuḫ(u)kantiš* is the Hittite reading of the Akkdogram *TARTENU* (Gurney 1983; Heinhold-Krahmer 1991–1992, 143–44 with n. 59). Both words refer to the crown prince. According to Bryce (1998, 321), the person requested may have been Nerikkaili, the son of Ḫattušili III. But Bryce 2003b, 203, 212 n. 11 seems uncertain about the equivalence of *tuḫkanti-* and *TARTENU*, for he writes "an official called the *tartenu*" (p. 203) and "the distinction, if any, between *tuhukanti* and *tartenu* is uncertain" (p. 212 n. 11). For the translation of Akkadian *tarde(n)nu* as "crown prince" in Boğazköy, Ugarit, and Nuzi see AHw 1329a; CAD T, 225–28; Wilhelm 1970; and Gurney 1983. The related term *tardennūtu* "status of the crown prince" (Hitt. *tuḫukantaḫit-*) occurs in CTH 63 (Klengel 1963; Beckman 1999a, 171 §5 ["as their crown prince"]).

264. Literally "silenced" (*kariyanut*). Miller: "interrupted" (German *unterbrach*).

265. Hitt. *ayawalaš*. Miller: "equal" (German *ebenbürtig*). On *ayawala-* see most recently Goedegebuure 2002, 67–68.

266. Analyzing grammatically as ŠU-*an*=*ma*=*an*. The analysis ŠU-*an*=*man* "my hand," taking *-ma-an* as a form of the possessive pronoun (Sommer 1932: 2–3; de Martino and Imparati 2004, 796–97), is impossible, since that form of the possessive died out at the end of the Old Hittite period. For the same construction of a double accusative, but with the verb *epp-* "to seize" instead of *ḫar-* "to hold," see i 69. The reference is to a gesture of protection and patronage. The translation of Bernabé and Álvarez-Pedrosa 2004, 246 and n. 67, does not distinguish which of the two men—Piyama-radu or Nerikkaili—is the subject of this sentence. Miller also fails to identify the acting person explicitly, although the action itself speaks for the crown prince. Miller's translation: "he would have gi[ven] (him) the hand, but ..." assumes that *-ma-an* is the potential particle *-man*. This intepretation of *-ma-an* is possible, but the verb cannot be "give," since the first sign of the verb is a clear *ḫa*[*r-*...] "to have, hold."

267. The offence appears to be grave. And since demeaning (*tepnu-*) an ordinary "official" in the presence of foreign powers would be trivial compared to the demeaning of the potential successor to the imperial throne, the equivalence of the two terms *tuḫkanti-* and *TARTENU* becomes more likely. Just how important it was to preserve the dignity of the sovereign in the eyes of foreign lands can be seen from at least two passages in Hittite texts: the exchange of letters between Šuppiluliuma I and the Egyptian pharaoh (text 96) and between Queen Puduḫepa and Ramses II of Egypt (text 98), and the description of the effrontery of the surrounding nations to Muršili II upon his accession to the throne, which became a *casus belli*: *a-ra-aḫ-zé-na-aš-wa-mu-za* KUR.KUR ... / TUR-*la-an ḫal-ze-eš-šer nu-wa-mu-za te-ep-nu-uš-ker* "The surrounding enemy lands were calling me 'a child,' and were demeaning me" KBo 3.4 i 23–24, ed. AM 20–21.

268. Freu (1980: 245–46, 266) places it in Isauria. Gurney sought to identify it with Alabanda in Caria.

269. From this context a place in rugged (mountainous) terrain on the eastern approaches of Milawanda. Freu (1980: 306–8) proposed Alinda, 60 km east of Miletus, which Bryce (1998, 322, and 2003b, 203) accepts.

270. i 18-22 is translated in CHD L–N, 467 (*nu* A h 5′).

271. For other examples of x *AŠRA* "in x *places*" see CHD P 343 (*peda-* A j 1′ a' 1′′ a'').

272. The sign trace after *nu* cannot be *-za*, as Sommer 1932 transcribes it, since in a "to be" clause the occurrence *-za* would require a first or second person subject (*GrHL* §28.32), which is clearly not possible here. And since the form [*AŠ-R*]*A* instead of [*AŠ-R*]*U* also favors a plural (see 3 *AŠ-RA* in line 23), I prefer the above reading.

273. Sommer read: *a-pé-e*[*z AṢ-BAT*], but *-za* + ablative + *epp-* is not attested in the meaning "von ... wegnehmen." Miller's "ih[r] ("its"), referring to the populace (*Bevölkerung*), suggests he read *a-pé*[*-el*].

274. I agree with Forrer, Singer, Guterbock and others, that this was Piyama-radu's brother. According to Sommer (1932), Tawagalawa's brother.

275. Or: *da-iš* "set (an ambush)."

276. The king of Aḫḫiyawa is being addressed here. "*My* brother" (ŠEŠ-*YA*) indicates a political equal, another Great King (Goetze 1957, 88, 97–98, and Szabó 1972–1975).

277. Strong affirmations of veracity characterize some categories of Hittite texts, normally letters, but occasionally annalistic historical texts such as the Annals of Muršili II. See for example, CHD *punušš-* on the imv. sg. 2 forms. And see KUB 21.38 obv. 11–12, 24 (text 102), HKM 52: 38–39 (text 55), and HKM 73: 10–15 (text 75).

278. Miller (2006) prefers this reading

279. For "hereby" one might have expected *kāša* or *kāšma* (see *GrHL* §24.27–29), but the context seems to require this translation.

280. [*ki-ša-an-ta-at*] was restored by Sommer (1932), although a neuter plural/collective subject should take a singular predicate in Hittite (*GrHL* §15.16). But, instead of the preterite singular [*ki-ša-at*], one could also restore in 32 and 34 either [*a-ša-an*] or [*a-ša-an-te-eš*], neuter singular or common gender plural depending on the gender of INIM.MEŠ and *A-WA-TE*MEŠ (neuter plural/collective *uddār* or common gender plural *memiyaneš*?). The difference would be "how these things *happened*" versus "how these things *were*."

281. One needs to read *ú-wa-nu-un* KUR URU*I-ya*[*-la-an-da-za-kán an-da ku-it-ma-an*] in line 39. In the photo the *nu* ŠÀ is unclear and just might be KUR.

282. Or "district" (Neu 1996, 132–34). Cf. Hatt. iii 69–70, where however Otten 1981, 23 (following Goetze 1925, 29) renders it "Feste, Festung."

283. Forrer, followed by Sommer, restored Millawanda here, and this restoration has been followed by Bernabé (2004, 247). Gurney apud Bryce (1985a, 18) suggested Iyalanda, reasoning that "while the Hittite king claims to have destroyed the whole land of Iyalanda, with the object of crushing the rebels, the city itself remained intact and was apparently used by the king as his base of operations." Miller takes no position.

284. Sommer's restoration here makes little sense and is only his guess. The two clauses following the water giving out seem to be reasons why he decided not to pursue the NAM.RA.

285. Sommer: "I woutd not have [had to] hold him ac[countable(?)]." I don't see how his restored Hittite can mean this. The restoration of the end of line 46 is uncertain.

286. Identification with Appawiya (Sommer 1932; del Monte and Tischler 1978) is geographically impossible (see Hawkins 1998b, 23 n. 136). Miller read: URU*A-ma*[-…].

287. See Parker 1999, 65.

288. See Miller 2006, 243 n. 29.

289. So almost all interpreters, most recently Bryce 2003b, 204, and Miller 2006, 243. Güterbock (1990) insisted it be translated "came away from the ship." Grammatically, the issue is whether the ablative case of "ship" is to be taken as "from" or (instrumental) "by." But since no ship has been mentioned from which Piyama-radu could have been waiting, the majority view must be considered more likely. The one matter that might favor Güterbock's view is that m*Atpašš=a* "Atpā *too*" (line 63, Miller "*auch* Atpa, *auch* Awajana…") suggests that these two men *in addition to* Piyama-radu himself heard the charges.

290. *HED* H, 151 (differently: "the words to which I treated [lit. held] him").

291. Atpā, Awayana, and *perhaps* (if Güterbock was right) also Piyama-radu.

292. Seen as a significant gesture by Imparati and de Martino 2004, 788.

293. For i 71–74 see Parker 1999, 63–64.

294. Miller simply translates "as the Great King" (German *als Großkönig*).

295. So read by Miller (2006, 243 n. 30), although he admits that the space seems insufficient for the restoration.

296. The title "prominent?/high? king" (Hitt. *šarkuš* LUGAL-*uš*; Akkad. *šar kiššari*) was used by Hittite emperors, first attested in use by Tudḫaliya IV. A clay bulla with the impression of the royal seal of Kurunt(iy)a "Great King" without a genealogy was found in 1986 in the Upper City at Ḫattuša in a context with Šuppiluliuma II seal bullae.

This probably accompanied a shipment of some kind from Tarḫuntašša, where Kurunt(iy)a claimed to be "Great King." See his rock relief published in Dinçol 1998a. Since at the time the Tawagalawa Letter was written, during the reign of Ḫattušili III, this Kuruntiya was only a prince, and had not yet declared himself an independent Great King in Tarḫuntašša, it would be unthinkable that his uncle Ḫattušili III would give him that title! Therefore we should probably render this line not as a rhetorical question, but as a negative claim: in contrast to the Great King Ḫattušili III, who is waiting for the extradition of Piyama-radu, Kuruntiya—though formerly treated better—was certainly not a Great King (this seems to be the interpretation of Gurney 2002, 134–36). Miller and others take the subject of this clause (the "he") to be Tawagalawa.

297. According to the rules of Hittite grammar, if the aš here is "he" (nom. sg.), then the verb must be intransitive, not therefore a verb such as "offered safe-conduct." Otherwise, the aš would have to be "them" (acc.).

298. Aḫḫiyawa was one of a small number of great powers that could be considered equals to Ḫatti, among them Egypt and Assyria. Cf. CTH 105.

299. The Hittite who was sent as a hostage.

300. As previously, referring to the crown prince? Or in general just meaning a hostage as a pledge? On the significance of the gesture of taking by the hand and giving the hand to a subordinate ruler as part of investiture see Imparati and de Martino 2004, 787–802.

301. That is, perhaps "to me." Atpā was a son-in-law of Piyama-radu and the *de facto* ruler of Milawanda. If Piyama-radu himself would not go to meet the Hittite king, would Ḫattušili accept Atpā in his stead, perhaps only as Piyama-radu's representative, just as Ḫattušili's son and crown prince was *his* proper representative?

302. Sommer thought "putting him on the road" meant advancing his career, but it may merely refer to giving him the promised safe passage.

303. Singer 1983b, 210 n. 24 calls attention to the fact that in Ḫattušili III's record of his childhood and adolescent years (Hatt. i 12) he mentions he learned to be a chariot driver (*ŠA* ^{KUŠ}KIR$_4$.TAB.ANŠE).

304. KUB shows a trace of a single horizontal following *ši-ya-an-ta*, while Sommer thought he saw -*y*[*a*] on the photo. The CHD editors thought the trace in the photo looked more like -*a*[*n*]. There is an unusually wide space between NINDA and *šiyanta.* Either "bread (and) *šiyanta*" or "sealed bread." Is this material merely a sign of hospitality, i.e., as a host gives food, so the Hittite king shows by the food that he is the man's host and protector? Or is it something the man is to take with him on the trip as his "passport"?

305. "Come! Make an explanation/justification to me! And I will set you on your way" (Melchert 1998, 46).

306. There are too many places in these lines where the subject is clearly third person for us simply to emend every one. But it is clear from context that all these "he" and "his" forms were intended to refer to Piyama-radu, who is being addressed.

307. The emendation <-*TÁ*> is Sommer's and makes good sense, but the reading has nevertheless been questioned by Pecchioli Daddi 1977, who proposed ^{LÚ}*A-BU* instead of *ḪA-NU.* The published photo—to my eye—shows *ḪA-NU.*

308. *HED* H, 92 ("You, my brother, welcome him!"); Miller: "concern yourself for him." My translation of *ḫanza epp-* (and *ḫanza ḫar-*), which I have used in my publications for years now, assumes a calque to the Akkadian idiom *rēšam kullum* "to take care of."

309. Miller's translation takes no account of the GIM-*an* ("how") of indirect speech.

310. Miller apparently reads [*A-NA*] KUR-*YA* "to my land."

311. Since the marked plural "fugitives" ([LÚ.MEŠ]*MU-NAB-T*[*I*]) in iii 46 takes a singular verb "went" (*pa-it*, iii 47), the singular verb "let him come" (*ú-ed-du*) here does not require that the Akkadogram [LÚ]*MU-NAB-TUM* (not marked with LÚ.MEŠ as a plural) be a singular ("*a*/*the* fugitive"). The sense, however, is the same either way: "A fugitive may come" = "Fugitives may come."

312. Miller (p. 245 with n. 36) paraphrases this grammatically obscure sentence as: "Furthermore, he is also now accustomed to saying this."

313. Literally: "So how (is) it—this word?"

314. See *HED* H, 90–91 ("will sustain him").

315. Text: his.

316. What looks like SIG_5-*u*- is merely this scribe's way of writing the SIG_5 sign (see Hoffner 1982b).

317. Literally, "a word/matter of the head/person."

318. So Beckman, assuming this to be equivalent to *NIŠ* DINGIR-*LIM* GAM-*an*. It is possible also to read: GAM-*an im-ma*.

319. The damaged sign, which I have read ARAD[!?], looks like AN, but "my heaven" (*ammel* AN-*iš*) makes no sense here.

320. For the reading SIG_5-*u-wa*, see Hoffner 1982b, 133

321. So, following Beckman's translation "I looked away."

322. Taking this line as a rhetorical question with Beckman 2006, 281.

323. Hagenbuchner 1989b reads *A*[-*BI*]-*YA-ya*.

324. Hagenbuchner 1989b reads *a-ša*[-.

325. Hagenbuchner 1989b reads [EGIR-*a*]*n-mu* against the traces in the copy.

326. Or read [*ar-n*]*u-ut-tén* with Güterbock.

327. Hagenbuchner 1989b, 204–5 reads *nu-mu ap-pa-tar.*

328. Restored by Hagenbuchner 1989b, following KUB 57.123: 3′, KBo 18.4: 8′–10′.

329. CTH 123, called a "treaty" in CTH and not listed in Hagenbuchner.

330. "Unter diesem Aspekt wäre die von F. Malbran-Labat (in: M. Yon, M. Sznycer et P. Bordreuil (ed.), *Le pays d'Ugarit,* 1995, 37–38) anhand von RS 17.403 aufgezeigte Möglichkeit, daß dort (2.2) ein bislang unbekannter König von Karkemiš genannt sein könnte, trotz der von I. Singer (BiOr 54, 1997, 420) geäußerten Bedenken weiterhin erwägenswert. Zu hypothetisch wäre es wohl, wegen der Nennung eines Muršili (2.6 *Mu-ur-zi-i-li*), den beide Forscher für Muršili II. halten, bei der in Z. 2 genannten Person an jenen König von Karkemiš aus dem 9. Jahr der Muršili-Annalen (siehe oben Anm. 65) zu denken. Es wäre dann statt der von Singer (l.c.) vorgeschlagenen Emendation von 2.2 *Ḫi-iš-ni-i* LUGAL(sic) KUR [URU]*Ka*[*r-ga-miš*] in: *Ḫi-iš-ni-i* DUMU.LUGAL KUR [URU]*Ka*[*r-ga-miš*] etwa an folgende Korrektur zu denken: *Ḫi-iš-ni-i*-LUGAL-*ma (=Ḫišni-Šarruma)* LUGAL KUR [URU]*Ka*[*r-ga-miš*], wobei ein Name in dieser Form bislang nicht belegt wäre; vgl. hiergegen die diversen Ergänzungsvorschläge des Namens des in KBo 4.4. III 11 genannten Königs von Karkemiš (X-)Šarma bei Klengel, *Geschichte Syriens,* 57 mit Anm. 33 u. 77" (2002, 373 n. 75).

331. Read so! Not [URU]*Ka*[*r-ga-miš*] (Mora and Giorgieri 2004, 100).

332. A clause division must occur at this point (*pace* Hagenbuchner 1989b, 8–9), since *kāšma* must occur in clause-initial position (see *GrHL* §7.21).

333. For "prepositional" *iwar* see Hoffner 1993a, 47 and *GrHL* §16.60.

334. Houwink ten Cate: "recognized him legally."

335. Houwink ten Cate: "launched."

336. Houwink ten Cate's translation "would have been successful," being a preterite, would have required S[IG$_5$-*in e-šu-un*], since the verb *eš-* can be omitted only in the presente tense (see *GrHL* §16.6). Even the restoration S[IG$_5$ ...] is highly conjectural, based on the sign trace.

337. Houwink ten Cate reads: *ú-wa-m*[*i*] "I should come."

338. Houwink ten Cate: *i*[*š-du-wa-a-ri*] "be[come known]."

339. Torri subsequently incorporated these ideas in her paper delivered at the International Congress of Hittitology in Çorum, Turkey, August 25–31, 2008. It was Torri's idea that this was a school tablet, and my idea that the model was a real letter, not some other type of text.

340. Analyze as *weš=šta,* see CHD sub *šanḫ-* 7 "to scour," which requires *-kan* or *-(a)šta*

341. CHD *peš(š)iya/e-* mngs. 3b or 4c.

342. *:za-mu-ra-nu-un* from *zammurai-*.

343. About 8 signs missing here.

344. About 6 signs missing here.

345. Hagenbuchner reads *-k*[*i*$^{!}$*-nu-un*].

346. Hittite *ḫarga-* from the verbal root *ḫark-* "to perish, be destroyed or lost," could mean either "defeat" or "death." But in this context Singer (1983b), Gurney (1993, 25 n. 37), and Cotticelli-Kurras (1995, 91) take it in the latter sense, as does the CHD sub *maḫḫan.* But sub *namma* 2 c the CHD translates "critical condition."

347. Emended following Hagenbuchner.

348. Singer restores: [*ú-e-mi-i*]*š-kán-za,* and claims a meaning "met (by you)."

349. In Akkadian the first ("I") and third person ("he") singular form of this verb is the same, *īde* (GAG §106 q). In the present context "I" seems to fit better.

350. The space on the tablet between *-at* and the KÁN sign is considerable, while that between the latter and the ZU sign is minimal. It is therefore impossible to read [*n*]*a-at-kán ZU-TAM e-eš-ša*, nor would this latter make better sense. *KÁN-ZU-TAM* must be an Akkadogram, but what word is represented? The noun *kanšūtu* "submissiveness" is so far found only in Neo-Babylonian, although the underlying adjective *kanšu* "submissive" occurs in much earlier periods. But I fail to see a good translation arising from this. Reading the KÁN sign here as *QA*$^{?!}$ (i.e., *KA*$_4$) would not yield a grammatical form of the adjective *kaṣû* (fem. *kaṣītu*) "cold."

351. For this reading, see Beal 1993, 248.

352. Or: "It [*presages*$^{??}$] the matter of illness of my lord." See van den Hout 1998, 88 n. 54. And see lines 12′ ([^{m}*T*]*u-ud-ḫa-li-ya-an-na*) and 16′ (GIG *iš*[*-tar-ak-*...]) below in the present letter.

353. A *-za* was first written by the scribe, and then erased, when he saw his mistake. Hagenbuchner (1989a, 152–53) understands that the *-za* was a mistake, but fails to mention that the scribe actually attempted to erase it. The erasure is visible both in the hand copy and in the online photo at Konk.

354. Hagenbuchner's (1989a, 152–53) reading *A-BI-YA* as an Akkadogram serving as a vocative "Mein Vater" violates the rules of direct address in Hittite (*GrHL* §16.11–17). True vocative forms constitute complete clauses. *A-BI-YA* clearly does not, since *=war=at=mu=kan ... wakkari* completes its clause. Appositional direct address requires that *ABI=YA* fit into the syntax of the enclosing clause showing the appropriate case. The

addressed party functions within the clause as acting or acted upon. Since *ABI=YA* does not perform any such function, the signs must be read *a-pí-ya*, to form the adverb *apiya* "there, then."

355. HGG read *ke-e-el* KUR-*e*-[*aš*] "of these lands."

356. Hagenbuchner 1989b reads *na-at-mu-kán TAL-SÀ AŠ-PUR* ZI *UL* "You have called it out to me, (but) I have not written my frame of mind." Because of the use of RI.ZA (or RI-*za*) elsewhere in this text, Hagenbuchner's solution (2 sg. pret. of Akk. *šasû*) is not credible (see rev. 25′). And, while right dislocation of a final negative *UL* is paralleled elsewhere, the sequence VERB + DIRECT OBJECT + NEGATIVE is not. Therefore, despite the difficulty of first person *AŠPUR* as logogram to a third person present form in -*zi*, I prefer reading *AŠ-PUR-zi* as a verb form (*ḫatraizzi*).

357. Hagenbuchner 1989b reads -⸢*ma*⸣ instead of -[*ká*]*n*.

358. Connecting these two clauses asyndetically may indicate that they say the same thing in different words. See examples and explanation in Hoffner 2007 and *GrHL* §29.49. This grammatical rule provides the basis for interpreting the less clear first clause in the light of the clearer second one.

359. Hagenbuchner 1989b reads *i*[-*y*]*a-an* instead of *m*[*a*]-*a-an*.

360. For the force of *akk-* "to die" combined with the particle -*kan* and a dative of disadvantage see *GrHL* §28.76.

361. Literally: "The male in-law of (i.e., by) a deceased (wife) …"

362. :*purpurriyaman* was not treated in CHD P. CLL 180 gives the provisional translation "obligation," following Starke 1990, 255 ("Bindung"), who understands that the person obliged was not the queen, but Tattamaru. The German translation *Bindung* is also used in translating this line by Haas 2006, 310. Van den Hout, however, translates it here as " family relationship" (German *Verwandtschaft*).

363. See discussion of this word in comments on text 55. For the Emar legal phraseology denoting such appeals against unjust rulings—Hittite *arkuwai-* or *arkuwar iya-*; Akkadian *maḫāru*—see D'Alfonso 2005b, 124–25.

364. "Nella missiva Laroche l, parallela di ETJ 32, all' itt. *arkuwai-* si sostituisce il quasi omofono *aruwai-*, inginocchiarsi. Si potrebbe pensare a un errore scribale, se non fosse che l'alternanza tra i due verbi compare in altri contesti. La spiegazione quindi un'altra: durante l'esposizione della lamentela, almeno al cospetto del Gran re, chi aveva richiesto udienza probabilmente parlava stando in ginocchio" (2005a, 126). There is a consistent spelling contrast in the 3rd sg.: arwāit and arwāizzi versus arkuwait and arkuwaizzi.

365. The figure arrived at for an Old Babylonian itinerary by W. W. Hallo and cited by Astour in *CANE* 3, 1403. Bryce 2003b, 73 employs the figures 27–37 km (17–23 miles) per day, quoting Oller in *CANE* 3, 1467. Hagenbuchner cites Kühne 1973, 105–24 for a considerably higher rate of travel from Ḫatti to Egypt, using light two-wheeled chariots: 52–63 km/day, and 20–35 km more, if relay stations for change of horses were used. But this would prevent traveling under the protection of a caravan, which would move more slowly. It is doubtful that such long distances would be covered in a *chariot*. And if more goods than the birds were being brought to the king, the light two-wheeled chariot could not be used (see also Hagenbuchner 1989a, 26). Bryce adds: "The logistical problems of transportation increased significantly when the gifts included human beings and livestock. The dowry accompanying the Hittite princess sent to Egypt to marry Ramesses II included horses, cattle and sheep, and a number of prisoners taken by the Hittites in their wars with the Kaska people from Anatolia's Pontic region" (Bryce 2003b, 104). And Liverani

writes: "Completely different is the problem of safety for messengers who carry gifts and other merchandise, or for merchants to whom the king entrusts official letters (a practice known to be followed by Babylon and Alashiya). In these cases the risk of robberies is too high … and the messenger cannot travel alone. He needs various chariots and an escort—in short, a small caravan. However, the bigger the caravan, the bigger the risk of attack, the bigger in consequence the escort needed—and the slower the journey. It is for this reason that the Amarna letters distinguish couriers (*kallû*), who travel alone and as fast as possible, from caravans, which have to follow their own slow rhythm" (2001, 73–74). About the much later Neo-Assyrian system, Parpola writes: "At regular intervals (*mardētu* 'stage', lit. 'day's march', a distance of ca. 30 km) on this highway were garrisoned road stations (*bēt mardēti*) serving as resting places for the royal army and as relay points for imperial messengers. Each station was to keep in readiness a fresh team (*urû*) of mules plus a chariot and a driver, which the messenger passing through would exchange for his tired team, thus being able to continue the journey at full speed and without interruption. The technical term for this service was *kalliu*, a word literally meaning 'reserved/held back' and hence referring primarily to the relay team, but mostly used in the extended sense of 'express service' (in adverbial usage 'by express, post-haste')" (1987, xiv).

366. KUB 30.32 rev. 12: 682 MUŠEN.ḪI.A *ŠĀBULU* 680 MUŠEN.ḪI.A *ḫuelpiš* 304 KU_6.ḪI[.A *ŠĀBULU* … KU_6.ḪI.A *ḫuelpiš*] "682 dried birds, 680 fresh birds, 304 [dried] fishes, [… fresh fishes]."

367. Or: *i-y*[*a-an-na-aḫ-ḫi*] or *i-y*[*a-an-ni-ya-mi*]; see *GrHL* §13.18 for the paradigm. Probably not *i-y*[*a-mi*] "[I will] d[o] (it)" (German *werde (ich es) t*[*un*]) (*pace* Hagenbuchner 1989b, 387), since then *na-at i-y*[*a-mi*] would be required.

Concordances

Text Number	Copy
1	Salvini 1994
2	KUB 31.79
3	KBo 15.28
4	KBo 12.62
5	KBo 18.14
6	KBo 18.95
7	HKM 1
8	HKM 2
9	HKM 3
10	HKM 4
11	HKM 5
12	HKM 6
13	HKM 7
14	HKM 8
15	HKM 9
16	HKM 10
17	HKM 12
18	HKM 13
19	HKM 14
20	HKM 15
21	HKM 16
22	HKM 17
23	HKM 18
24	HKM 19
25	HKM 20
26	HKM 21
27	HKM 22
28	HKM 23
29	HKM 24
30	HKM 25
31	HKM 26
32	HKM 27
33	HKM 28
34	HKM 29
35	HKM 36
36	HKM 30
37	HKM 31
38	HKM 32
39	HKM 33
40	HKM 34
41	HKM 35
42	HKM 37
43	HKM 38
44	HKM 39
45	HKM 43
46	HKM 44
47	HKM 45
48	HKM 46
49	ABoT 60
50	HKM 47
51	HKM 48
52	HKM 49
53	HKM 50
54	HKM 51
55	HKM 52
56	HKM 53
57	HKM 54
58	HKM 55
59	HKM 56
60	HKM 57
61	HKM 58
62	HKM 59
63	HKM 60
64	HKM 61
65	HKM 62
66	HKM 63
67	HKM 64
68	HKM 65

69	HKM 66
70	HKM 67
71	HKM 68
72	HKM 70
73	HKM 71
74	HKM 72
75	HKM 73
76	HKM 74
77	HKM 75
78	HKM 79
79	HKM 80
80	HKM 81
81	ABoT 65
82	HKM 82
83	HKM 84
84	HKM 88
85	HKM 89
86	Süel 1992: 491 (Or 90/1400)
87	HHCTO 4
88	StBoT 45: 671–72
89	Süel 2002b (Or 90/800)
90	HHCTO 1
91	HHCTO 3
92	KuT 50
93	KuT 49
94	*VBoT* 2 (= EA 32)
95	*VBoT* 1 (= EA 31)
96	EA 41
97	EA 44
98	KUB 21.38
99	KUB 26.91
100	KUB 19.5 +
100	KBo 19.79 +
101	KUB 14.3
102	KUB 19.55 +
102	KUB 48.90 +
103	KBo 18.15
104	KUB 23.102
105 (A)	KUB 23.103 rev. 8–29
105 (B)	KUB 23.92 rev. 9–21
105 (C)	KUB 40.77
106	KBo 18.2
107	Güterbock 1979: 142–44
108	KBo 18.4
109	KBo 18.48
110	KBo 13.62
111	KBo 18.54
112	KBo 18.29
113	KUB 57.123
114	KUB 19.23
115	KBo 9.82
116	KBo 2.11 rev. 11-17
117	KBo 18.79
118	KUB 57.1
119	KUB 40.1
120	Klengel 1974: 171ff (Bo 2810)
121	KUB 23.85
122	VS 28.129
123	Meskene 73.1097
124	BLMJ-C37
125	AT 125
126	ATT 35

Copy	**Text Number**
Güterbock 1979: 142-44}	107
Klengel 1974: 171–73 (Bo 2810)	120
Salvini 1994	1
Süel 1992: 491 (Or 90/1400)	86
Süel 2002b} (Or 90/800)	89
ABoT 60	49
ABoT 65	81
AT 125	125
ATT 35	126
BLMJ-C37	124
EA 41	96
EA 44	97
HHCTO 1	90
HHCTO 3	91
HHCTO 4	87
HKM 1	7
HKM 10	16
HKM 12	17
HKM 13	18
HKM 14	19
HKM 15	20
HKM 16	21

HKM 17	22	HKM 62	65
HKM 18	23	HKM 63	66
HKM 19	24	HKM 64	67
HKM 2	8	HKM 65	68
HKM 20	25	HKM 66	69
HKM 21	26	HKM 67	70
HKM 22	27	HKM 68	71
HKM 23	28	HKM 7	13
HKM 24	29	HKM 70	72
HKM 25	30	HKM 71	73
HKM 26	31	HKM 72	74
HKM 27	32	HKM 73	75
HKM 28	33	HKM 74	76
HKM 29	34	HKM 75	77
HKM 3	9	HKM 79	78
HKM 30	36	HKM 8	14
HKM 31	37	HKM 80	79
HKM 32	38	HKM 81	80
HKM 33	39	HKM 82	82
HKM 34	40	HKM 84	83
HKM 35	41	HKM 88	84
HKM 36	35	HKM 89	85
HKM 37	42	HKM 9	15
HKM 38	43	KBo 12.62	4
HKM 39	44	KBo 13.62	110
HKM 4	10	KBo 15.28	3
HKM 43	45	KBo 18.14	5
HKM 44	46	KBo 18.15	103
HKM 45	47	KBo 18.2	106
HKM 46	48	KBo 18.29	112
HKM 47	50	KBo 18.4	108
HKM 48	51	KBo 18.48	109
HKM 49	52	KBo 18.54	111
HKM 5	11	KBo 18.79	117
HKM 50	53	KBo 18.95	6
HKM 51	54	KBo 19.79 +	100
HKM 52	55	KBo 2.11 rev. 11–17	116
HKM 53	56	KBo 9.82	115
HKM 54	57	KUB 14.3	101
HKM 55	58	KUB 19.23	114
HKM 56	59	KUB 19.5 +	100
HKM 57	60	KUB 19.55 +	102
HKM 58	61	KUB 21.38	98
HKM 59	62	KUB 23.102	104
HKM 6	12	KUB 23.103 rev. 8–29	105 (A)
HKM 60	63	KUB 23.85	121
HKM 61	64	KUB 23.92 rev. 9–21;	105 (B)

KUB 26.91	99	KuT 49	93
KUB 31.79	2	KuT 50	92
KUB 40.1	119	Meskene 73.1097	123
KUB 40.77	105 (C)	StBoT 45: 671–72	88
KUB 48.90 +	102	*VBoT* 1 (= EA 31)	95
KUB 57.1	118	*VBoT* 2 (= EA 32)	94
KUB 57.123	113	VS 28.129	122

Glossary

Akkadian. The principal language spoken in ancient Iraq in the period ca. 2300–300 B.C.E., and written both there and, as a diplomatic, commercial, and literary language, all over the ancient Near East. The Hittites composed entire documents of a diplomatic and literary character in this language and used individual words from it as **logograms** within texts written in their native language, Hittite.

Akkadogram. A logogram consisting of an Akkadian word.

Alalakh. An ancient city and its associated city-state of the Amuq river valley located in the Hatay region of southern Turkey near the city of Antakya (ancient Antioch), and now represented by an extensive city mound known as Tell Atchana. Its kings included Yarîm-Lîm, Ammitakum, and Ḫammurabi in the OB period, and Idrimi, Niqmepa II, and Ilim-ilim-ma II in the MB period. In the mid-fourteenth century, the Hittite Šuppiluliuma I defeated king Tušratta of Mitanni and assumed control of northern Syria, including Alalakh, which he incorporated into the Hittite Empire. A tablet records his grant of much of Mukiš' land (that is, Alalakh's) to Ugarit after the king of Ugarit alerted the Hittite king to a revolt by the kingdoms of Mukiš, Nuḫašše, and Niye. Alalakh was probably destroyed by the Peoples of the Sea in the twelvth century, as were many other cities of coastal Anatolia and the Levant.

Aleppo (cuneiform Ḫalab, or Ḫalpa). Modern Ḥalab. City in northern Syria; capital of the kingdom Yamḫad, whose kings included Sûmu-epuḫ, Yarîm-Lîm, and Ḫammurabi. The Old Hittite kings Ḫattušili I and Muršili I put an end to this powerful kingdom, and thereafter its role in the power politics of Syria was a minor one. During the fourteenth century, after the Syrian campaigns of the Hittite king Šuppiluliuma I, Aleppo came under Hittite control, eventually ruled directly by a cadet branch of the Hittite royal family, but subordinate to the other such branch ruling at Carchemish (cuneiform Kargamiš).

alphabetic script. A writing system each of whose component signs represents a single vowel or consonant. Such a system is contrasted with a syllabic system, in which the individual signs represent syllables.

Amarna Age. A term commonly used to denote a period, the nucleus of which was the span of time during which the Egyptian capital was at (el-)Amarna (ca. 1350–1330 B.C.E.), and consequently the period covered by the famous Amarna tablets. In Egyptian terms, this would comprise the latter part of the 19th Dynasty, the pharaohs Amunḥotep III and IV (Akhenaten) and Tutankhamun, and in Hittite terms, the reigns of Tudḫaliya II/III and Šuppiluliuma I.

Amenophis. The Greek writing of the Egyptian royal name Amunḥotep.

Amunḥotep (=Amenophis) III. Pharaoh of Egypt (ca. 1391–1353 B.C.E.); husband of Tadu-ḫeba, daughter of the Hurrian king Tušratta.

Amunḥotep (=Amenophis) IV (also known as Akhenaten). Pharaoh of Egypt (ca. 1353–1336 B.C.E.). Moved the Egyptian capital from Thebes to Amarna, where his international correspondence—the Amarna tablets—was found. His chief wife was the famous Nefertiti. He corresponded with the Hittite king Šuppiluliuma I.

***arnuwala-* (NAM.RA).** A term denoting groups of foreigners captured in battle and employed by the king (or state) as laborers and farmers. The Hittite term derives from the verm *arnu-* "to transport, relocate," and since these groups were moved about as needed to work land in thinly populated areas, the English terms "transportees" and "relocated persons" can be used as translations. Other English expressions that have been used are "deportees," "civilian captives," and "transplantees."

Arzawa. An important kingdom in southwestern Asia Minor during the age of the Hittites. Hittite textual sources give the most information for the period of the early New Kingdom (i.e., reigns of Hittite kings Muršili II through Ḫattušili III). Arzawa proper was only one of several countries comprising the "Arzawa Lands," which also included Mira/Kuwaliya, the Šeḫa River Land, Ḫapalla, and Wiluša. Named rulers of Arzawa proper are Tarḫunta-radu, Anzapaḫḫaddu, Uḫḫa-ziti, and his sons SUM-LAMMA and Tapalazunawali.

Aššur. Modern Qal'at aš-Širqāṭ. Political capital of Assyria from Aššur-uballiṭ I (fourteenth century) through Aššurnaṣirpal II (ninth century); after that religious capital of Assyria and center of worship of Aššur, the supreme god of Assyria.

Babylon. Modern Babil. Ancient capital of Babylonia, site of the Esagil temple for Marduk and seat of the Hammurabi dynasty; destroyed by Sennacherib in 689 and rebuilt by Esarhaddon and Aššurbanipal in the 670s and 660s.

Benjaminite. As used in the discussion of the Mari tablets, "Benjaminites" (literally, "sons of the righthand[-bank]") refers to tribal groups living on the right (i.e., southern) side of the Euphrates River.

Bronze Tablet. Large bronze replica of a clay tablet, on which the Hittite king Tudḫaliya IV had engraved in cuneiform characters the text of a treaty with Kurunt(iy)a, son of Muwattalli II, king of Tarḫuntašša. Tarḫuntašša was a city and small kingdom to the south of the Hittite heartland, located principally in the present-day Konya Plain but extending south to the Mediterranean coast and bounded on the east by Cilicia and on the west by present-day Antalya.

Carchemish (cuneiform Kargamiš). Ancient city-state located in what is now southeastern Turkey, along the border with Syria. Carchemish lay on the west bank of the Euphrates River near the modern north Syrian town of Jerabulus (from Greek Hierapolis), and 61 kilometers southeast of Gaziantep, Turkey. It commanded a strategic crossing of the Euphrates River for caravans engaged in Syrian, Mesopotamian, and Anatolian trade. In the Old Babylonian era (eighteenth century) its kings included Aplaḫanda, Yatar-Ami, and Yaḫdun-Lîm. In the mid-fourteenth century the Hittite king Šuppiluliuma I established his son Šarri-Kušuḫ (also known as Piyaššili) as viceroy in the city, which he used as a buffer state against Assyria, Mitanni, and Egypt. Three more viceroys succeded to the throne until the fall of the Hittite empire ca. 1200 B.C.E.. From 1200–717 B.C.E. Carchemish was a small "Neo-Hittite" kingdom, whose kings bore names of a Luwian or Hurrian type, and who decorated their palaces with reliefs bearing inscriptions in hieroglyphic Luwian.

colophon. The traditional term within cuneiform studies for the closing lines of a document, usually set off from what precedes by a single or double horzontal line, containing information about the contents of the tablet and the name(s) of its scribe(s).

cuneiform. A writing style and system of writing that employed as characters "signs" composed of configurations of wedge-shaped depressions in clay (or less often, in metal).

Emar (modern Meskene). The ancient Near Eastern town of Emar/Imar was situated on the middle Euphrates in northwest Syria, about 100 kilometers east of Aleppo. Due to its geographical situation connecting Mesopotamia with the Mediterranean coast and with Anatolia, the town had a strategic function. Already the earliest mentionings in writing, namely in the palace archives of Ebla, ca. 2500 B.C.E., and especially in the Mari texts from the eighteenth century B.C.E., point to the town's importance as traffic junction and contact zone between the Assyro-Babylonian and the Syro-Anatolian cultural spheres. For the thirteenth and the early-twelfth centuries B.C.E. (the Late Bronze Age), there is written documentation from Emar itself and also references in contemporaneous texts from Boğazköy/Ḫattuša, Ras Shamra/Ugarit, and from Assyria. At that time, the town was part of the Hittite Empire, situated close to the frontier of the rivaling state of Assyria. Emar was subject to the king of Carchemish, who represented the Hittite ruler in Syria and was a member of the Hittite royal family. In Hittite texts Emar is referred to as part of the land of Aštata. South of Carchemish, and west of what is sometimes referred to as the "big bend" in the Euphrates, was situated the kingdom of Aštata.

envelope. The term for a thin layer of dried or baked clay enclosing an inscribed clay tablet, and bearing its own inscription. Such clay envelopes provided security and privacy for the enclosed tablet, and authentication by means of impressions of the sender's seal. Sometimes the general location of the addressee was inscribed on the envelope as well.

greeting formula (also known as **wish formula** or **blessing**). A fixed feature of all ancient Near Eastern letters. It followed immediately the address formula and expressed the sender's well-wishes to the addressee. See discussion in §§1.1.9.2 and 1.2.17.

greeting gift. A special gift exchanged between allied kings in the Amarna Age and the Hittite empire. Its Akkadian designation was *šulmānu* and its Hittite equivalent *aššul.*

Ḫapalla. One of the "Arzawa Lands" (see "**Arzawa**") of western Asia Minor in Hittite times. Named rulers are Targašnalli and Ura-Ḫattuša.

Ḫattuša. The name of both the capital city and the kingdom of the Hittites. The city was located near the present-day Turkish town of Boğazkale (earlier name Boğazköy), 87 kilometers from the city of Çorum, in the province (*vilayet*) of Çorum.

-ḫepa. As a component in Hurrian names (Puduḫepa, Taduḫepa), this stands for the divine name Ḫebat.

hieroglyphic. A writing style and system of writing that employed stylized drawings as its characters. The principal systems known in Hittite times were the Egyptian and the Hittite-Luwian. The word denotes the script, not the language it was employed to write.

Ḫimmuili. A high-ranking provincial officer at Tapikka/Maşat.

His Majesty, Your Majesty. English circumlocutions, the choice between which depends on whether the person so entitled is directly addressed or only referred to. The written form ᵈUTU-*ŠI*, standing for Akkadian *Šamšī* "my sun god," and probably pronounced *Ištanui=mi*, is the most important title of the Hittite emperor. In Hittite letters he is addressed or referred to with this term, followed by "my lord," and not with the term "king" (LUGAL).

Ištar. Mesopotamian goddess of fertility and war. Her chief Assyrian shrine was in Arbela. As a logogram in Hittite texts, *IŠTAR* often represents the Hurrian goddess Ša(w)uska.

Kaššū. A high-ranking provincial officer at Tapikka/Maşat, whose duties lay principally in the military area.

l.p.h. Egyptologists' abbreviation of the courtesy formula "(may he enjoy) Life, Prosperity and Health" that regulary follows the mention of the pharaoh's name.

letter carrier or courier. The Sumerogram LÚKAŠ.E (Akkadian *lāsimu* "runner, courier") in Hittite texts denotes the letter carrier, whose duties were simple transport. See also "**LÚ *ṬĒMI*.**"

letter-prayer. Mesopotamian letters *to* a god, also called "letter-prayers," were literary compositions studied by scribes (see §1.1.1).

logogram, logographic(ally). As this term is used within the discipline of Hittitology, a logogram is a complex of one or more cuneiform or hieroglyphic signs that stand for and evoke in the reader's mind an entire word in the Hittite or Luwian language, but does not itself indicate the phonetic components of that word. A sample Hittite word *uttar,* meaning "word" or "thing," can be written syllabically (or phonetically) with the signs *ut-tar.* The same word *uttar* can be represented logographically either with the Sumerian word INIM (a single cuneiform sign), or with a form of the Akkadian word *AWATUM* (expressed by several signs: *A-WA-TUM*).

Lower City. The northwestern quarter of the Hittite capital city Ḫattuša, which contained among other buildings the great Temple I.

LÚ *ṬĒMI* (Akkadian *awīl ṭēmi* "man of a message/report," Hittite *ḫalugatalla-*)**.** The official messenger (or envoy), who both carried the mail and read it aloud and interpreted it at the destination. Although his functions overlap with the simple letter carrier or courier (LÚKAŠ.E), his functions were broader and required both literacy and an understanding of the intentions of the sender of the letter. Envoys of international diplomatic letters were virtual diplomats in their own right.

mār šipri. Akkadian functional equivalent to the **LÚ *ṬĒMI*.**

Marešrē. A Hittite official and scribe during the reign of Tudḫaliya II/III (ca. 1430–1400 B.C.E.). His name is Akkadian (*mār ešrē*), meaning "son born on the 20th day of the month," a day on which a significant religious festival occurred. Compare Christian names such as Natalie.

Mari. Modern Tell Ḥariri. City and kingdom that in the second half of the third and first half of the second millennium (ca. 2500–1500 B.C.E.) occupied large areas on the Middle Euphrates and the River Ḫabur; center of worship of Dagan and site of one of the biggest royal archives excavated in the ancient Near East.

Maşat Höyük. See **Tapikka.**

Messenger. The English term can be used for both the **LÚ *ṬĒMI*** and the simple courier or letter-carrier.

Millawanda, Milawata. An ancient city on the Aegean coast of Asia Minor, during the Hittite New Kingdom a center of activity by the Aḫḫiyawans. See texts 99, 100, 102 and 103.

Miletus. See **Millawanda, Milawata.**

Mira/Kuwaliya. One of the "**Arzawa** Lands" of western Asia Minor in Hittite times. Named rulers of Mira/Kuwaliya are: Mašḫuiluwa and Kupanta-LAMMA (Kupanta-Kurunt(iy)a?).

Mitanni. Empire of the Hurrians in the fifteenth/fourteenth century: the principal rival of Egypt controlling large areas in Assyria, Syria, and Cilicia.

monumental inscription. An inscription intended for public display. A famous example is the stela on which Hammurabi's Code was written. No letter ever constituted a monumental inscription or formed a part of one.

NAM.RA. See ***arnuwala-* (NAM.RA).**

Nerik. A city in north central Asia Minor along the lower course of the Maraššanta River (= Turkish Kizilirmak). It was a major cult center for the Storm God, and was cut off from Hittite control for many years and recovered by Ḫattušili III.

Ninurta. Babylonian and Assyrian god. Son of Enlil and Mullissu/Ninḫursag; the heavenly crown prince, warrior, and farmer. The center of his worship in the Neo-Assyrian period was Calah.

ostracon, (plural **ostraca).** Potsherd used in antiquity, especially by the ancient Egyptians and Hebrews, as a surface for drawings, or as an alternative to papyrus or leather for writing.

paragraph marker. The horizontal line that divides ancient cuneiform documents into sections. On Hittite tablets a letter might contain several such lines, dividing the content into the formal components of address, well-wishing, and letter body, and—in longer letters—subdividing the letter body itself into the subjects treated.

Piyama-radu. An Aḫḫiyawan nobleman who during the reigns of the Hittite king Ḫattušili III and his immediate predecessor and successor challenged Hittite political control in western Asia Minor. His base of operations was the ancient city of Milawata (= Classical Miletus). He figures principally in the Tawagalawa Letter (text 101), but also in the Manapa-Tarḫunta letter (text 100).

Puduḫepa. Hittite queen, wife of Ḫattušili III.

Šamaš. Babylonian and Assyrian Sun God and the god of justice and truth, "Lord of Heaven and Earth," invoked in extispicy rituals.

***šaḫḫan* and *luzzi*.** Two kinds of obligation (corvée work and/or taxes) imposed by the Hittite state or crown upon certain classes of Hittite citizens.

Sammeltafel. This German term denotes a large clay tablet on which several compositions have been copied, separated by two horizontal lines. The compositions kept on such "anthologies" are of related subject matter and text genre. A significant example in the letter genre is the "Aššur Dossier," containing copies of correspondence between the Hittite and Assyrian courts.

Šamši-Adad. King of Assyria (ca. 1835/30–1777 B.C.E.); seized control of Mari after Yaḫdun-Līm, installed his sons Yasmaḫ-Addu at Mari and Išme-Dagan at Ekallatum.

Šanda. A Hittite personal name borne by an official at Tapikka/Maşat, derived from the name of a god.

Šauška. The main goddess of the Hurrians, also worshiped by the Hittites; the Hurrrian equivalent of Ištar of Nineveh.

scribe. A man (no female scribe is known among the Hittites) trained in the art of reading and writing for others, especially for the king, the state, or the temple. If private scribes existed among the Hittites, i.e., those would hired their services to the general public for a fee, we know nothing of them. The scribe (Sumerogram ^{LÚ}DUB.SAR, Hittite *tuppa(l)la-*) known from Hittite texts was a state employee, who took dictation, drafted documents, and recopied old ones in the archives of the king. For more on his activities see §1.1.5.1, §1.2.13 and van den Hout forthcoming.

seal. A carved semi-precious stone employed as a device for impressing an identifying mark of ownership and attestation on the soft surface of a clay tablet. Kings, queens, and higher officials all possessed seals.

seal impression. Surviving impressions of ancient seals found on the surfaces of clay tablets, clay envelopes, or bullae.

Šeḫa River Land. One of the "Arzawa Lands" (see "**Arzawa**") of western Asia Minor in Hittite times. Named rulers are: Muwa-UR.MAḪ (Muwawalwi?), Ura-Tarḫunta, Manapa-Tarḫunta, and Mašturi.

social distance. A significant difference in social standing, requiring special rules of behavior.

Sumerogram. A **logogram** consisting of a Sumerian word.

Tabarna. Originally a personal name, this term came to be a title or designation of all Hittite emperors. The practice is similar to the Roman use of Caesar.

tablet. The Hittite word *tuppi* (borrowed from Akkadian *ṭuppu*) denotes a clay tablet, used for writing in the cuneiform script.

Tapikka. An ancient Hittite provincial capital, believed by many to be the ruins excavated at Maşat Höyük.

Tawagalawa. An Aḫḫiyawan nobleman, perhaps the brother of the king, who is mentioned in the Tawagalawa Letter, and is a contemporary of king Ḫattušili III. His activities took him at least some of the time to the western coast of Asia Minor, specifically to the city of **Milawanda** (= Classical Miletus).

Teššub. The Hurrian name of the supreme Storm God. Reigning king of the gods according to Hurrian theology. Son of Anu. His consort is Ḫebat (= Sun Goddess of Arinna). His sons are Šarruma and the Storm God of Nerik. His vizier is Tašmi(šu). His two divine bulls are Šeri(šu) and Ḫurri (or Tella). His principal cult center and "home" is Kummiya in northern Mesopotamia.

Thousand Gods. A standard way of referring to the entire Hittite state pantheon, see §1.2.17.

Tikunan(i). See "**Tunip-Teššub**" and text 1.

Tunip-Teššub (= Tuniya). A king of the country Tikunan(i) in North Syria during the reign of the Old Hittite king Ḫattušili I (ca. 1650–1620 B.C.E.).

Tušratta. King of Mitanni, the Hurrian Empire (ca. 1365–1335/22 B.C.E.).

Ugarit. The name of an ancient city and the kingdom of which it was the capital. Its excavated ruins stand at the modern site Ras Shamra. Ugarit was situated on the Mediterranean coast of northern Syria a few kilometers north of the modern city of Latakia.

Uzzū. A scribe in the service of Kaššū, a high-ranking military officer at Tapikka/Maşat (see Alp 1991a: 104).

Wiluša. One of the "Arzawa Lands" (see "**Arzawa**") of western Asia Minor in Hittite times. Named rulers are: Kukkunni, Alakšandu, and Walmu.

wood scribe. The Sumerogram LÚDUB.SAR.GIŠ "wood scribe" designated Hittite scribes trained to write on wax-covered writing boards.

writing board. Wax-covered writing boards (Akkadogram GIŠ*LE'U*) served the Hittites as a medium on which to write documents of an impermanent nature. It is possible, but not proven, that they were exclusively used for writing in the hieroglyphic script.

Yaḫdun-Līm. King of Mari (ca. 1810–1795 B.C.E.), father of Zimri-Līm.

Yasmaḫ-Adad (= Yasmaḫ-Addu). King of Mari (ca. 1793–1775 B.C.E.), son of Šamši-Adad, king of Assyria, and brother of Išme-Dagan, king of Ekallatum (Assyria).

Zimri-Līm. King of Mari (ca. 1775–1761 B.C.E.), son of Yaḫdun-Līm.

Bibliography

Akdoğan, Rukiye. 2007. "'inan' ile ilgili yeni bir hititçe tablet parçası." Pages 1–12 in *Tabularia Hethaeorum: Hethitologische Beiträge Silvin Košak zum 65. Geburtstag.* Edited by D. Groddek and M. Zorman. DBH 25. Wiesbaden: Harrassowitz.

Akurgal, Ekrem. 1962. *The Art of the Hittites*. London: Thames and Hudson.

Albright, William F. 1937. "The Egyptian Correspondence of Abimilki, Prince of Tyre." *JEA* 23: 195–99.

Alp, Sedat. 1950–1951. "Die Soziale Klasse der NAM.RA-Leute und ihre hethitische Bezeichnung." *JKF* 1: 113–35.

———. 1977. "Maşat-Höyükte keşfedilen Hitit tabletlerinin ışığı altında yukarı yeşilırmak bölgesinin coğrafyası hakkında." *Belleten* 41: 637–47.

———. 1979. "Remarques sur la géographie de la region du Haut-Yeşilırmak d'après les tablettes de Maşat-Höyük." Pages 29–35 in *Florilegium Anatolicum: Mélanges offerts à Emmanuel Laroche*. Edited by E. Masson. Paris: Boccard.

———. 1980. "Die hethitischen Tontafelentdeckungen auf dem Maşat-Höyük. Vorläufiger Bericht." *Belleten* 44 (173): 25–59, pl. 1–4.

———. 1990. "Die Verpflichtungen *šaḫḫan* und *luzzi* in einem Maşat-Brief." *Or* 59: 107–13.

———. 1991a. *Hethitische Briefe aus Maşat-Höyük*. TTKY VI/35. Ankara: Türk Tarih Kurumu Basımevi.

———. 1991b. *Hethitische Keilschrifttafeln aus Maşat-Höyük*. TTKY VI/34. Ankara: Türk Tarih Kurumu Basımevi.

———. Alparslan, Metin. 2005. "Einige Überlegungen zur Ahhiyawa-Frage." Pages 33–41 in *Acts of the Vth International Congress of Hittitology. Çorum, September 02–08, 2002*. Edited by A. Süel. Ankara: Basım Tarihi.

Altman, Amnon. 2004. *The Historical Prologue of the Hittite Vassal Treaties: An Inquiry into the Concepts of Hittite Interstate Law*. Ramat-Gan: Bar-Ilan University Press.

Archi, Alfonso. 1973. "L'organizzazione amministrativa ittita e il regime delle offerte cultuali." *OA* 12: 209–26.

———. 1975. "L' ornitomanzia ittita." *SMEA* 16: 119–80.

———. 1988. "Société des hommes et société des animaux." Pages 25–37 in *Studi di Storia e di Filologia Anatolica dedicati a Giovanni Pugliese Carratelli*, vol. Edited by F. Imparati. Eothen 1. Firenze: ELITE.

———. 2003. "Middle Hittite—'Middle Kingdom.'" Pages 1–12 in *Hittite Studies in Honor of Harry A. Hoffner, Jr. on the Occasion of His 65th Birthday*. Edited by G. M. Beckman, R. H. Beal, and J. G. McMahon. Winona Lake, Ind.: Eisenbrauns.

———. 2007. "Transmission of Recitative Literature by the Hittites." *AoF* 34: 185–203.

Arıkan, Yasemin. 2006. "The Blind in Hittite Documents." *AoF* 33: 144–54.

Bachvarova, Mary R. 2002. From Hittite to Homer: The Role of the Anatolians in the Transmission of Epic and Prayer Motifs from the Near East to the Greeks. Ph.D. diss., University of Chicago.

Bawanypeck, Daliah. 2005. *Die Rituale der Auguren.* THeth 25. Heidelberg: Winter.

Beal, Richard H. 1986. The Organization of the Hittite Army. Ph.D. diss., University of Chicago.

———. 1992. *The Organisation of the Hittite Military.* THeth 20. Heidelberg: Carl Winter.

———. 1993. Review of A. Hagenbuchner, *Die Korrespondenz der Hethiter. JAOS* 113: 245–50.

———. 1995. "Hittite Military Organization." Pages 545–54 in *Civilizations of the Ancient Near East*, vol. 1. Edited by J. M. Sasson. New York: Scribner's.

———. 1998. Review of Jan Puhvel, *Hittite Etymological Dictionary*, Vol. 3: *Words Beginning with H. JAOS* 118: 84–86.

———. 1999. "Seeking Divine Approval for Campaign Strategy: KUB 5.1 + KUB 52.65." *Ktema* 24: 41–54.

———. 2002a. "Hittite Oracles." Pages 57–81 in *Magic and Divination in the Ancient World.* Edited by L. Ciraolo and J. Seidel. Ancient Magic and Divination 2. Leiden: Brill.

———. 2002b. "Le strutture militari ittite di attacco e di difesa." Pages 109–21 in *La battaglia di Qadesh. Ramesse II contro gli Ittiti per la conquista della Siria*. Edited by M. C. Guidotti and F. Pecchioli Daddi. Livorno: Sillabe.

Beaulieux, Paul-Alain. 2007. "Late Babylonian Intellectual Life." Pages 473–84 in *The Babylonian World.* Edited by G. Leick. New York: Routledge.

Beckman, Gary M. 1983a. *Hittite Birth Rituals.* StBoT 29. Wiesbaden: Harrassowitz.

———. 1983b. "Mesopotamians and Mesopotamian Learning at Hattusa." *JCS* 35: 97–114.

———. 1991. Review of Friedrich J.-Kammenhuber A., *Hethitisches Wörterbuch.* Band I: A. *BiOr* 48: 210–15.

———. 1995a. "Hittite Provincial Administration in Anatolia and Syria: The View from Maşat and Emar." Pages 19–37 in *Atti del II Congresso Internazionale di Hittitologia.* Edited by O. Carruba, M. Giorgieri, and C. Mora. StMed 9. Pavia: Gianni Iuculano.

———. 1995b. "The Siege of Uršu Text (CTH 7) and Old Hittite Historiography." *JCS* 47: 23–34.

———. 1996. *Texts from the Vicinity of Emar in the Collection of Jonathan Rosen.* HANE/M 2. Padova.

———. 1999a. *Hittite Diplomatic Texts.* 2nd ed. WAW 7. Atlanta: Scholars Press.

———. 1999b. "The City and the Country in Hatti." Pages 161–70 in *Landwirtschaft im Alten Orient. Ausgewählte Vorträge der XLI. Rencontre Assyriologique Internationale, Berlin, 4.–8.7.1994.* Edited by H. Klengel and J. Renger. Berliner Beiträge zum Vorderen Orient 18. Berlin: Dietrich Reimer.

———. 2006. "Hittite Treaties and the Development of the Cuneiform Treaty Tradition." Pages 279–301 in *Die deuteronomistischen Geschichtswerke Redaktions- und religionsgeschichtliche Perspektiven zur "Deuteronomismus"-Diskussion in Tora und Vorderen Propheten.* Edited by M. S. Witte, Konrad Prechel, Doris Gertz, Jan Christian. Berlin: de Gruyter.

Benveniste, Émile. 1962. *Hittite et Indo-Européen: Études comparatives*. Paris: Maisonneuve.

Bernabé, Alberto and Juan Antonio Álvarez-Pedrosa. 2000. *Historia y Leyes de los Hititas. Textos del Imperio Antiguo. El Código*. AKAL/Oriente 3. Madrid: Akal.

———. 2004. *Historia y Leyes de los Hititas. Textos del Reino Medio y del Imperio Nuevo*. AKAL/Oriente 8. Madrid: Akal.

Bilabel, Friedrich and Adolf Grohmann. 1927. *Geschichte Vorderasiens und Ägyptens vom 16. Jahrhundert v. Chr. bis auf die Neuzeit*. Heidelberg: Winter.

Bittel, Kurt. 1937. "Vorläufiger Bericht über die Ausgrabungen in Boğazköy 1936." *MDOG* 75: 32–33.

Bittel, Kurt and Peter Neve. 1966. "Vorläufiger Bericht über die Ergebnisse der Ausgrabungen in Boğazköy in den Jahren 1964 und 1965." *MDOG* 97: 3–72.

Boley, Jacqueline. 2000. *Dynamics of Transformation in Hittite. The Hittite Particles -kan, -asta and -san*. IBS 97. Innsbruck: Institut für Sprachwissenschaft der Universität Innsbruck.

———. 2001. "An Intransitive *ḫark-*." Pages 40–50 in *Akten des IV. Internationalen Kongresses für Hethitologie. Würzburg, 4.–8. Oktober, 1999*. Edited by G. Wilhelm. StBoT 45. Wiesbaden: Harrassowitz.

Bossert, Helmuth Th. 1952. "GIŠ.ḪUR." *BiOr* 9: 172–73.

Boysan-Dietrich, Nilüfer. 1987. *Das hethitische Lehmhaus aus der Sicht der Keilschriftquellen*. THeth 12. Heidelberg: Carl Winter.

Bryce, Trevor R. 1979. "Some Reflections on the Historical Significance of the Tawagalawas Letter (KUB XIV 3)." *Or* 48: 91–96.

———. 1981. "Hattusili I and the Problems of the Royal Succession in the Hittite Kingdom." *AnSt* 31: 9–17.

———. 1985a. "A Reinterpretation of the Milawata Letter in the Light of the New Join Piece." *AnSt* 35: 13–23.

———. 1985b. "A Suggested Sequence of Historical Developments in Anatolia during the Assyrian Colony Period." *AoF* 12: 259–68.

———. 1990. "The Death of Niphururiya and its Aftermath." *JEA* 76: 97–105.

———. 1998. *The Kingdom of the Hittites*. Oxford: Clarendon.

———. 2002a. *Life and Society in the Hittite World*. Oxford: Oxford University Press.

———. 2002b. "The Trojan War: Is There Truth behind the Legend?" *NEA* 65: 182–95.

———. 2003a. "Chapter Two: History." Pages 27–127 in *The Luwians*. Edited by H. C. Melchert. HbOr 68. Leiden: Brill.

———. 2003b. *Letters of the Great Kings of the Ancient Near East. The Royal Correspondence of the Late Bronze Age*. New York: Routledge.

———. 2003c. "Relations between Hatti and Ahhiyawa in the Last Decades of the Bronze Age." Pages 59–72 in *Hittite Studies in Honor of Harry A. Hoffner, Jr. on the Occasion of His 65th Birthday*. Edited by G. M. Beckman, R. H. Beal, and J. G. McMahon. Winona Lake, Ind.: Eisenbrauns.

———. 2006. *The Trojans and Their Neighbors*. London and New York: Routledge.

Carruba, Onofrio. 2001. "Anitta res gestae: paralipomena I." Pages 51–72 in *Akten des IV. Internationalen Kongresses für Hethitologie. Würzburg, 4.–8. Oktober, 1999*. Edited by G. Wilhelm. StBoT 45. Wiesbaden: Harrassowitz.

Catsanicos, Jean. 1986. "A propos des adjectifs hitt. *su-hmili-* et véd. *su-máya-*: quelques remarques sur le traitement du groupe *V-Hx-C* à la jointure des composés." *Bulletin de la Société de Linguistique de Paris* 81: 121–80.

Charpin, Dominique. 2007. "The Writing, Sending and Reading of Letters in the Amorite World." Pages 400–17 in *The Babylonian World*. Edited by G. Leick. New York: Routledge.

Chavalas, Mark W., ed. 2006. *The Ancient Near East: Historical Sources in Translation*. Oxford—Malden MA: Blackwell.

Cohen, Yoram. 2001. "The 'Unwritten Laws' of the Hittites: The Case of the *natta ara* Expression." Pages 73–82 in *Akten des IV. Internationalen Kongresses für Hethitologie. Würzburg, 4.–8. Oktober, 1999*. Edited by G. Wilhelm. StBoT 45. Wiesbaden: Harrassowitz.

———. 2002. *Taboos and Prohibitions in Hittite Society: A Study of the Hittite Expression natta āra ("not right")*. THeth 24. Heidelberg: Winter.

———. 2005. "A Family Plot: the Zu-Bala Family of Diviners and Hittite Administration in the Land of Astata." Pages 213–24 in *Acts of the Vth International Congress of Hittitology. Çorum, September 02–08, 2002*. Edited by A. Süel. Ankara: Basım Tarihi.

———. forthcoming. *The Scribes and Scholars of the City of Emar in the Late Bronze Age*. Winona Lake, Ind.: Eisenbrauns.

Cohen, Yoram and Lorenzo d'Alfonso. 2008. "The Duration of the Emar Archives and the Relative and Absolute Chronology of the City." Pages 3–25 (of 29) in *The City of Emar among the Late Bronze Age Empires: History, Landscape, and Society. Proceedings of the Konstanz Emar Conference, 25.–26.04.2006*. Edited by L. d'Alfonso, Y. Cohen, and D. Sürenhagen. AOAT 349. Münster: Ugarit-Verlag.

Collins, Billie Jean. 1998. "Hattušili I, The Lion King." *JCS* 50: 15–20.

———. 2002a. *A History of the Animal World in the Ancient Near East*. Handbook of Oriental Studies, Section I: The Near and Middle East 64. Leiden: Brill.

———. 2002b. "Animals in Hittite Literature." Pages 237–50 in *A History of the Animal World in the Ancient Near East*. Edited by B. J. Collins. Handbook of Oriental Studies. Section I: The Near and Middle East 64. Leiden: Brill.

———. 2003. "On the Trail of the Deer; Hittite *kūrala-*." Pages 73–82 in *Hittite Studies in Honor of Harry A. Hoffner, Jr. on the Occasion of His 65th Birthday*. Edited by G. M. Beckman, R. H. Beal, and J. G. McMahon. Winona Lake, Ind.: Eisenbrauns.

———. 2007. *The Hittites and Their World*. Atlanta: Society of Biblical Literature.

Cornelius, Friedrich. 1958. "Geographie des Hethiterreiches." *Or* 27: 225–51, 373–98.

Cotticelli-Kurras, Paola. 1992. "Die hethitischen Nominalsätze." Pages 99–136 in *Per una grammatica ittita: Towards a Hittite Grammar*. Edited by O. Carruba. StMed 7. Pavia: Gianni Iuculano.

———. 1995. "Hethitische Konstruktionen mit *verba dicendi* und *sentiendi*." Pages 87–100 in *Atti del II Congresso Internazionale di Hittitologia*. Edited by O. Carruba, M. Giorgieri, and C. Mora. StMed 9. Pavia: Gianni Iuculano.

———. 2007. "Versuch einer Fehlertypologie in der hethitischen Keilschrift." Pages 175–202 in *Tabularia Hethaeorum: Hethitologische Beiträge Silvin Košak zum 65. Geburtstag*. Edited by D. Groddek and M. Zorman. DBH 25. Wiesbaden: Harrassowitz.

Cunchillos, Jesús-Luis. 1989. *Estudios de epistolografía Ugarítica*. Fuentes de la ciencia bíblica. Valencia: Institución San Jerónimo.

D'Alfonso, Lorenzo. 2005a. "Free, Servant and Servant of the King: Conflict and Change in the Social Organisation at Emar after the Hittite Conquest " Pages 19–38 in *Moti-*

vation und Mechanismen des Kulturkontaktes in der späten Bronzezeit. Edited by D. Prechel. Eothen 13. Firenze: LoGisma.

———. 2005b. *Le procedure giudiziarie ittite in Siria (XIII sec. a. C.)*. 1st ed. StMed 17. Pavia: Italian University Press.

Dalley, Stephanie. 1973. "Old Babylonian Greeting Formulae and Iltani's Archive from Rimah." *JCS* 25: 79–88.

de Martino, Stefano. 1991. "Himuili, Kantuzili e la pesa del potere da parte di Tuthaliya." Pages 5–21 in *Quattro Studi Ittiti*. Edited by F. Imparati. Eothen 4. Firenze: Edizione Librarie Italiane Estere (ELITE).

———. 1996. *L'Anatolia occidentale nel Medio Regno Ittita*. Eothen 5. Firenze: Il Vantaggio.

———. 2002. "The Military Exploits of the Hittite King Ḫattušili I in Lands Situated between the Upper Euphrates and the Upper Tigris." Pages 77–86 in *Silva Anatolica: Anatolian Studies Presented to Maciej Popko on the Occasion of His 65th Birthday*. Edited by P. Taracha. Warsaw: Agade.

———. 2003. *Annali e res gestae antico ittiti*. StMed 12. Pavia: Italian University Press.

———. 2004. "Purità dei sacerdoti de dei luoghi di culto nell' Anatolia ittita." *Or* 73: 348–62.

———. 2005a. Review of A. Altman, *The Historical Prologue of the Hittite Vassal Treaties*. *BiOr* 62: 553–56.

———. 2005b. "Hittite Letters from the Time of Tutḫaliya I/II, Arnuwanda I and Tutḫaliya III." *AoF* 32: 291–321.

———. 2006. "Troia e le 'guerre di Troia' nelle fonti ittite." Pages 167–77 in *Δύνασθαι διδάκειν: Studi in onore de Filippo Càssola*. Edited by M. Faraguna and V. Vedaldi Isasbez. Trieste.

——— and Fiorella Imparati. 1995. "Aspects of Hittite Correspondence: Problems of Form and Content." Pages 103–15 in *Atti del II Congresso Internazionale di Hittitologia*. Edited by O. Carruba, M. Giorgieri, and C. Mora. StMed 9. Pavia: Gianni Iuculano.

———. 2001. "Observations on Hittite International Treaties." Pages 347–63 in *Akten des IV. Internationalen Kongresses für Hethitologie. Würzburg, 4.–8. Oktober, 1999*. Edited by G. Wilhelm. StBoT 45. Wiesbaden: Harrassowitz.

———. 2004. "La 'mano' nelle più significative espressioni idiomatiche ittite." Pages 787–802 in *Studi sulla società e sulla religione degli hittiti*. Edited by F. Imparati. Firenze: LoGisma.

de Roos, Johan. 2005. "Die Hethiter und das Ausland." Pages 39–58 in *Motivation und Mechanismen des Kulturkontaktes in der späten Bronzezeit*. Edited by D. Prechel. Eothen 13. Firenze: LoGisma.

———. 2006. "Materials for a Biography: The Correspondence of Puduḫepa with Egypt and Ugarit." Pages 17–26 in *The Life and Times of Ḫattušili III and Tutḫaliya IV. Proceedings of a Symposium Held in Honour of J. de Roos, Leiden December 12–13, 2003*. Edited by T. P. J. van den Hout. Publications de l'Institut Historique et Archéologique Néerlandais de Stamboul 103. Leiden: Nederlands Historisch-Archaeologisch Instituut te Istanbul.

del Monte, Giuseppe F. 1975a. "I testimoni del trattato con Aleppo (KBo 1 6)." *RSO* 49: 1–10.

———. 1975b. "La fame dei morti." *AION* 35: 319–46.

———. 1992. *Répertoire Géographique des Textes Cunéiformes. Band 6/2: Die Orts- und Gewässernamen der hethitischen Texte, Supplement*. Beihefte zum Tübinger Atlas des Vorderen Orients. Reihe B Nr. 7/6. Wiesbaden: Reichert.

———. 1993. *L'annalistica ittita*. TVOA 4/2. Brescia: Paideia Editrice.

———. 1995. "I testi amministrativi da Maşat Höyük/Tapika." *Orientis Antiqui Miscellanea* 2: 89–138.

———. 2005. "The Hittite Herem." Pages 21–45 in *Memoriae Igor M. Diakonoff. Babel und Bibel 2, Annual of Ancient Near Eastern, Old Testament, and Semitic Studies*. Edited by L. Kogan, N. Koslova, S. Loesov, and S. Tschenko. Orientalia et Classica. Papers of the Institute of Oriental and Classical Studies 8. Winona Lake, Ind.: Eisenbrauns.

———. del Monte, Giuseppe F. and Johann Tischler. 1978. *Répertoire Géographique des Textes Cunéiformes. Band 6: Die Orts- und Gewässernamen der hethitischen Texte*. Beihefte zum Tübinger Atlas des Vorderen Orients. Reihe B Nr. 7. Wiesbaden: Reichert.

Devecchi, Elena. 2005. *Gli annali di Ḫattušili I nella versione accadica*. StMed 16. Pavia: Italian University Press.

Dinçol, Ali M. 1998a. "The Rock Monument of the Great King Kurunta and Its Hieroglyphic Inscription." Pages 159–66 in *Acts of the IIIrd International Congress of Hittitology. Çorum, September 16–22, 1996*. Edited by S. Alp and A. Süel. Ankara: Grafik, Teknik Hazırlık Uyum Ajans.

Dinçol, Belkıs. 1998b. "Der Titel GAL.GEŠTIN auf den hethitischen Hieroglyphensiegeln." *AoF* 25: 163–67.

Durand, Jean-Marie and Dominique Charpin. 2006. "La lettre de Labarna au roi de Tigunânum, un réexamen." Pages 219–27 in *Šapal tibnim mû illakū: Studies Presented to Joaquin Sanmartin on the Occasion of his 65th Birthday*. Edited by J.-M. Durand. Aula Orientalis Supplementa 22. Sabadell, Spain: s.n.

Easton, Donald F., J. David Hawkins, A. G. Sherratt, and E. S. Sherratt. 2002. "Troy in Recent Perspective." *AnSt* 52: 75–109.

Edel, Elmar. 1994. *Die ägyptisch-hethitische Korrespondenz aus Boghazköi in babylonischer und hethitischer Sprache*. Abhandlungen der Rheinisch-Westfälischen Akademie der Wissenschaften 77. Opladen: Westdeutscher Verlag.

Edzard, Dietz Otto. 1980. "Karawane." Pages 414–22 in *Reallexikon der Assyriologie*. Band 5. Edited by E. Ebeling, B. Meissner, E. Weidner, W. von Soden, and D. O. Edzard. Berlin: de Gruyter.

Ehelolf, Hans. 1939a. "Zu Amarna KNUDTZON Nr. 29,184 und 41,39ff." *ZA* 45: 70–73.

———. 1939b. "Zu dem in Atchana gefundenen hethitischen Briefe." *ZA* 45: 73–75.

Eichner, Heiner. 1992. "Anatolian." Pages 29–96 in *Indo-European Numerals*. Edited by J. Gvozdanovic. Berlin: de Gruyter.

Ellis, Maria deJong. 1987. "The Goddess Kititum Speaks to King Ibalpiel: Oracle Texts from Ishchali." *M.A.R.I.: Annales de recherches interdisciplinaires* 5: 235–66.

Fairbairn, Andrew S. and Sachihiro Omura. 2005. "Archaeological Identification and Significance of ÉSAG (Agricultural Storage Pits) at Kaman-Kalehöyük, Central Anatolia." *AnSt* 55: 15–24.

Forlanini, Massimo. 1977. "L'Anatolia nordoccidentale nell'impero eteo." *SMEA* 18: 197–225.

———. 1980. "La prima lista di VBoT 68 e la provincia di Arinna." *SMEA* 22: 71–80.

———. 1983. "Gašipura e Gazziura." *Hethitica* 5: 11–19.

———. 1990. "Uda, un cas probable d'homonymie." *Hethitica* 10: 109–27.

———. 1997. "La ricostruzione della geografia storica del Ponto nella tarda età del bronzo e la continuità della toponomastica indigena fino all'età romana." *Istituto Lombardo Accademia di Scienze e Lettere—Rendiconti Classe di Lettere e Scienzi Morali e Storiche* 131: 397–422.

———. 1998. "L'Anatolia occidentale e gli Hittiti: appunti su alcune recenti scoperte e le loro conseguenze per la geografia storica." *SMEA* 40: 219–53.

———. 2002. "Tapikka: una marca di frontiera. Note sulla struttura territoriale ed economica." Pages 255–76 in *Anatolia Antica: Studi in memoria di Fiorella Imparati*. Edited by S. de Martino and F. Pecchioli Daddi. Firenze: LoGisma.

———. 2007. "Happurija, eine Hauptstadt von Arzawa?" Pages 285–98 in *Belkıs Dinçol ve Ali Dinçol'a Armağan VITA (Festschrift in Honor of Belkıs Dinçol and Ali Dinçol)*. Edited by M. Doğan-Alparslan, M. Alparslan, and H. Peker. Istanbul: Ege Publishing.

Forrer, Emil. 1924. "Vorhomerische Griechen in den Keilschrifttexten von Boghazköi." *MDOG* 63: 1–22.

———. 1926. *Forschungen*. 1. Band, 1. Heft. Berlin: Selbstverlag.

———. 1929. *Forschungen*. 1. Band, 2. Heft. Berlin: Selbstverlag.

Foster, Benjamin R. 1993. *Before the Muses. An Anthology of Akkadian Literature*. Bethesda, Md.: CDL.

Francia, Rita. 1996. "Funzioni sintattiche nei testi dell' antico hittita: il locativo di meta e scopo e l'accusativo di direzione." *Incontri Linguistici* 19: 137–53.

———. 2002. *Le funzioni sintattiche degli elementi avverbiali di luogo ittiti anda(n), āppa(n), katta(n), katti-, peran, parā, šer, šarā*. Rome: Herder.

———. 2006. "Scelte di linguaggio e anomalie nell'ufficio dello scriba ittita." *L'ufficio e il documento: I luoghi, i modi, gli strumenti dell'amministrazione in Egitto e nel Vicino Oriente antico*. Edited by C. P. Mora, Patrizia. Quaderni di Acme 83. Milan: Acme.

Franz-Szabó, Gabriella. 1976–1980. "'Itinierare' bei den Hethitern." Pages 220 in *Reallexikon der Assyriologie*. Band 5. Edited by E. Ebeling, B. Meissner, E. Weidner, W. von Soden, and D. O. Edzard. Berlin: de Gruyter.

Freu, Jacques. 1980. "Luwiya. Géographie historique des provinces méridionales de l'Empire hittite: Kizzuwatna, Arzawa, Lukka, Milawatta." Pages 179–352 in *Centre de Recherches Comparaties sur les Langues de la Méditerrané Ancienne, Doc. no. 6, Tome 2*. Nice.

———. 1983. *Les archives de Maşat Höyük, l'histoire du moyen empire hittite et la géographie du pays Gasga*. Centre de recherches comparatives sur le langues de la méditerranée ancienne 8.

———. 1992. "Les guerres syriennes de Suppiluliuma et la fin de l'ère amarnienne." *Hethitica* 11: 39–101.

———. 2002. "La chronologie du règne de Suppiluliuma: essai de mise au point." Pages 87–108 in *Silva Anatolica: Anatolian Studies Presented to Maciej Popko on the Occasion of His 65th Birthday*. Edited by P. Taracha. Warsaw: Agade.

———. 2004a. "Les iles de la mer Egee, Lazpa, le pays d'Ahhiyawa et les Hittites." *RAnt* 1: 275–324.

———. 2004b. *Šuppiluliuma et la veuve du Pharaon. Histoire d'un mariage manqué. Essai sur les relations égypto-hittites*. Collection Kubaba. Série Antiquité 5. Paris: Harmattan.

———. 2006. *Histoire politique du royaume d'Ugarit*. Collection Kubaba. Série Antiquité 11. Paris: Association Kubaba: Harmattan.

———. 2007. "La bataille de Niḫriya, RS 34.165, KBo 4.14 et la corresponance assyro-hittite." Pages 271–92 in *Tabularia Hethaeorum: Hethitologische Beiträge Silvin Košak zum 65. Geburtstag*. Edited by D. Groddek and M. Zorman. DBH 25. Wiesbaden: Harrassowitz.

Freu, Jacques and Michel Mazoyer. 2007. *Les débuts du nouvel empire. Les Hittites et leur histoire*. Collection Kubaba, Série Antiquité 12. Paris: L'Harmattan.

Freu, Jacques, Michel Mazoyer, and Isabelle Klock-Fontanille. 2007. *Dès origines à la fin de l'ancien royaume hittite. Les Hittites et leur histoire*. Collection Kubaba, Série Antiquité 7. Paris: L'Harmattan.

Friedrich, Johannes. 1939. "Ein hethitischer Brief aus Tell Atchana." *Or* 8: 310–16.

Garrett, Andrew. 1990. "The Origin of NP Split Ergativity." *Lg* 66: 261–96.

Garstang, John and Oliver R. Gurney. 1959. *The Geography of the Hittite Empire*. London: British Institute of Archaeology at Ankara.

Gelb, Ignace J., Thorkild Jacobsen, Benno Landsberger, A. Leo Oppenheim, Erica Reiner, Miguel Civil, and Martha T. Roth, eds. 1956–2005. *The Assyrian Dictionary of The Oriental Institute of The University of Chicago*. Chicago: The Oriental Institute of the University of Chicago.

Gesenius, W., E. Kautsch, and A. E. Cowley. 1910. *Gesenius' Hebrew Grammar*. 2nd ed. Oxford: Clarendon.

Giorgadze, Gregor G. 2005. ""Feind" und "Ansiedeln" in den hethitischen Texten aus Maşat-Höyük." Pages 371–76 in *Acts of the Vth International Congress of Hittitology. Çorum, September 02–08, 2002*. Edited by A. Süel. Ankara: Basım Tarihi.

Giorgieri, Mauro. 2001. "Der Löwe und der Fuchs in dem Brief KBo 1.14." *Or* 70: 89–96.

Goedegebuure, Petra M. 2002. "KBo 17.17+: Remarks on an Old Hittite Royal Substitution Ritual." *JANER* 2: 61–73.

———. 2002–2003. "The Hittite Distal Demonstrative *aši* (*uni, eni,* etc.)." *Die Sprache* 43 (1): 1–32.

———. 2003. Reference, Deixis and Focus in Hittite: The demonstratives *ka-* "this", *apa-* "that" and *asi* "yon". Ph.D. diss., University of Amsterdam.

Goetze, Albrecht. 1925. *Ḫattušiliš. Der Bericht über seine Thronbesteigung nebst den Paralleltexten*. MVAeG 29. Leipzig: Hinrichs.

———. 1927. *Madduwattaš*. MVAeG 32. Leipzig: Hinrichs.

———. 1930. *Verstreute Boghazköi-Texte*. Marburg a. d. Lahn: Im Selbstverlag de Herausgebers.

———. 1933. *Die Annalen des Muršiliš*. MVAeG 38. Leipzig: Hinrichs.

———. 1957. *Kleinasien*. 2nd rev. ed. Handbuch der Altertumswissenschaft. Kulturgeschichte des Alten Orients. Munich: Beck.

———. 1969. "Hittite Instructions." Pages 207–11 in *Ancient Near Eastern Texts Relating to the Old Testament*. Edited by J. B. Pritchard. Princeton: Princeton University Press.

Goren, Yuval, Israel Finkelstein, and Nadav Na'aman. 2004. *Inscribed in Clay. Prove-*

nance Study of the Amarna Tablets and Other Ancient Near Eastern Texts. Tel Aviv: Emery and Claire Yass Publications in Archaeology.

Gorny, Ronald L. 1989. "Environment, Archaeology, and History in Hittite Anatolia." *BA* 52: 78–96.

———. 1995. "Viticulture and Ancient Anatolia." Pages 133–74 in *The Origins and Ancient History of Wine*. Edited by P. E. McGovern, S. J. Fleming, and S. H. Katz. Food and Nutrition in History and Anthropology Series 11. Newark: Gordon and Breach.

Greenberg, Moshe. 1955. *The Hab/piru*. AOS 39. New Haven: American Oriental Society.

Groddek, Detlev. 2004. Review of G. Wilhelm (ed.), *Akten des IV. Internationalen Kongresses für Hethitologie, Würzburg, 4.–8. Oktober 1999*, StBoT 45. *WO* 34: 214–18.

Gruber, Mayer I. 1980. *Aspects of Nonverbal Communication in the Ancient Near East*. Studia Pohl 12. Roma.

Guilmot, Max. 1966. "Lettres aux morts dans l'Egypte ancienne." *RHR* 170: 1–27.

Gurney, Oliver R. 1983. "The Hittite Title *tuḫkanti*." *AnSt* 33: 97–101.

———. 1992. "Hittite Geography: Thirty Years On." Pages 213–22 in *Hittite and Other Anatolian and Near Eastern Studies in Honour of Sedat Alp*. Edited by H. Otten, E. Akurgal, H. Ertem, and A. Süel. Anadolu Medeniyetlerini Araştırma ve Tanıtma Vakfı Yayınları 1. Ankara: Türk Tarih Kurumu Basımevi.

———. 1993. "The Treaty with Ulmi-Tešub." *AnSt* 43: 13–28.

———. 2002. "The Authorship of the Tawagalawas Letter." Pages 133–41 in *Silva Anatolica: Anatolian Studies Presented to Maciej Popko on the Occasion of His 65th Birthday*. Edited by P. Taracha. Warsaw: Agade.

———. 2003. "The Upper Land (*mātum elītum*)." Pages 119–26 in *Hittite Studies in Honor of Harry A. Hoffner, Jr. on the Occasion of His 65th Birthday*. Edited by G. M. Beckman, R. H. Beal, and J. G. McMahon. Winona Lake, Ind.: Eisenbrauns.

Güterbock, Hans Gustav. 1939. "Das Siegeln bei den Hethitern." Pages 26–36 in *Symbolae ad iura Orientis Antiqui pertinentes Paulo Koschaker dedicatae*. Edited by T. Folkers, J. Friedrich, J. G. Lautner, and J. Miles. Studia et Documenta ad Iura Orientis Antiqui Pertinentia 2. Leiden: Brill.

———. 1944. "Ein hethitischer Brief aus Maşat bei Zile." *AnDergi* 2 (3): 399–405.

———. 1956a. Review of *Boğazköy-Ḫattuša. Ergebnisse der Ausgrabungen des Deutschen Archäologischen Instituts und der Deutschen Orient-Gesellschaft in den Jahren 1931–1939, I: Architektur, Topographie, Landeskunde und Siedlungsgeschichte* by Kurt Bittel and Rudolf Naumann; *Keilschrifttexte aus Boghazköi. Siebentes Heft* by Heinrich Otten; *Keilschrifttexte aus Boghazköi. Achtes Heft* by Heinrich Otten; *Keilschrifturkunden aus Boghazköi, Heft XXXV: Luvische und Palāische Texte* by Heinrich Otten; *Keilschrifturkunden aus Boghazköi, Heft XXXVI: Vorwiegend Mythen, Epen, Gebete und Texte in althethitischer Sprache* by Heinrich Otten; *Keilschrifturkunden aus Boghazköi, Heft XXXVII: Literarische Texte in akkadischer Sprache*, von Franz Köcher; *Luvische Texte in Umschrift* by Heinrich Otten; *Zur grammatikalischen und lexikalischen Bestimmung des Luvischen* by Heinrich Otten. *Oriens* 9: 299–303.

———. 1956b. "The Deeds of Suppiluliuma I as Told by His Son, Muršili II." *JCS* 10: 41–68, 75–98, 107–30.

———. 1967a. "Lexicographical Notes III." *RHA* XXV (81): 141–50.

———. 1967b. "The Hittite Conquest of Cyprus Reconsidered." *JNES* 26: 73–81.
———. 1971. *Keilschrifttexte aus Boghazköi. Achtzehntes Heft (Hethitische Briefe, Inventare und verwandte Texte)*. Berlin: Gebr. Mann.
———. 1975. "The Hittite Temple According to Written Sources." Pages 125–32 in *Le temple et le culte. Compte rendu de la 20ième Rencontre Assyriologique Internationale, Leiden, 1972*. Edited by E. Van Donzel. PIHANS 37. Leiden: Nederlands Historisch Archeologisch Instituut te Istanbul.
———. 1979. "Some Stray Bogazköy Tablets." Pages 137–44 in *Florilegium Anatolicum: Mélanges offerts à Emmanuel Laroche*. Edited by E. Masson. Paris: Éditions E. de Boccard.
———. 1983. "The Hittites and the Aegean World: 1. The Ahhiyawa Problem Reconsidered." *AJA* 87: 133–38.
———. 1984. "Hittites and Akhaeans: A New Look." *PAPS* 128: 114–22.
———. 1990. "Wer war Tawagalawa?" *Or* 59 (2): 157–65.
———. 1992. "A New Look at One Ahhiyawa Text." Pages 235–44 in *Hittite and Other Anatolian and Near Eastern Studies in Honour of Sedat Alp*. Edited by H. Otten, E. Akurgal, H. Ertem, and A. Süel. Anadolu Medeniyetlerini Araştırma ve Tanıtma Vakfı Yayınları 1. Ankara: Türk Tarih Kurumu Basımevi.
Güterbock, Hans Gustav, Harry A. Hoffner, Jr., and Theo P. J. van den Hout. 1989–. *The Hittite Dictionary of the Oriental Institute of the University of Chicago*. Chicago: The Oriental Institute of the University of Chicago.
Güterbock, Hans Gustav, and Timothy Kendall. 1995. "A Hittite Silver Vessel in the Form of a Fist." Pages 45–60 in *The Ages of Homer. A Tribute to Emily Townsend Vermeule*. Edited by J. B. Carter, and S. P. Morris. Austin: University of Texas Press.
Haas, Volkert. 1970. *Der Kult von Nerik*. Studia Pohl 4. Roma: Pontificium Institutum Biblicum.
———. 1985. "Betrachtungen zur Dynastie von Hattusa im Mittleren Reich (ca. 1450–1380)." *AoF* 12: 269–77.
———. 1994. *Geschichte der hethitischen Religion*. HbOr 1. Abteilung. 15. Band. Leiden: Brill.
———. 1995. Review of H. G. Güterbock and H. A. Hoffner, eds., *The Hittite Dictionary of the Oriental Instiute P*. *OLZ* 90: 514–17.
———. 1996. "Marginalien zu hethitischen Orakelprotokollen." *AoF* 23: 76–94.
———. 2002. Review of J. Tischler, *Hethitisches Handwörterbuch. Mit dem Wortschatz der Nachbarsprachen*, IBS 102. *OLZ* 97: 499–511.
———. 2006. *Die hethitische Literatur: Texte, Stilistik, Motive*. Berlin: de Gruyter.
Haas, Volkert and Ilse Wegner. 1999. "Betrachtungen zu den Ḫabiru." Pages 197–200 in *Munuscula Mesopotamica. Festschrift für Johannes Renger*. Edited by B. Börk, E. Cancik-Kirschbaum, and T. Richter. AOAT 267. Münster: Ugarit-Verlag.
Hagenbuchner, Albertine. 1989a. *Die Korrespondenz der Hethiter. 1. Teil*. THeth 15. Heidelberg: Carl Winter.
———. 1989b. *Die Korrespondenz der Hethiter. 2. Teil*. THeth 16. Heidelberg: Carl Winter.
Hagenbuchner-Dresel, Albertine. 1999. "Bemerkungen zu kürzlich edierten Briefen." *ZA* 89: 50–64.
———. 2002. *Massangaben bei hethitischen Backwaren*. DBH 1. Dresden: Technische Universität Dresden.

Hajnal, Ivo. 2003. *Troia aus sprachwissenschaftlicher Sicht: Die Struktur einer Argumentation*. IBS 109. Innsbruck.

Hallo, William W. 1968. "Individual Prayer in Sumerian: the Continuity of a Tradition." *JAOS* 88: 71–89.

Hallo, William W., and K. Lawson Younger, eds. 1997. *Canonical Compositions from the Biblical World*. Vol. 1 of *The Context of Scripture*. Leiden: Brill.

———, eds. 2000. *Monumental Inscriptions from the Biblical World*. Vol. 2 of *The Context of Scripture*. Leiden: Brill.

Harrak, Amir. 1987. *Assyria and Hanigalbat: A Historical Reconstruction of Bilateral Relations from the Middle of the Fourteenth to the End of the Twelfth Centuries B.C.* Texte und Studien zur Orientalistik 4. Hildesheim: Olms.

Hart, Gillian R. 1971. "The Hittite Particle *-PAT*." *TPS*: 94–162.

Hawkins, J. David. 1998a. "Hattusa: Home to the Thousand Gods of Hatti." Pages 65–72 in *Capital Cities: Urban Planning and Spiritual Dimensions. Proceedings of the Symposium Held on May 27–29, 1996, Jerusalem, Israel*. Edited by J. G. Westenholz. Bible Lands Museum Jerusalem Publications No. 2. Jerusalem: Bible Lands Museum.

———. 1998b. "Tarkasnawa King of Mira 'Tarkondemos', Boğazköy Sealings and Karabel." *AnSt* 48: 1–31.

———. 2000. *Corpus of Hieroglyphic Luwian Inscriptions*. Berlin: de Gruyter.

———. 2002. "Eunuchs among the Hittites." Pages 217–33 in *Assyria 1995: Proceedings of the 10th Anniversary Symposium of the Neo-Assyrian Text Corpus Project, Helsinki, September 7–11, 1995*. Edited by S. Parpola, and R. M. Whiting. Helsinki.

———. 2006. "Tudḫaliya the Hunter." Pages 49–76 in *The Life and Times of Ḫattušili III and Tutḫaliya IV: Proceedings of a Symposium Held in Honour of J. de Roos, Leiden December 12–13, 2003*. Edited by T. P. J. van den Hout. PIHANS 103. Leiden: Nederlands Historisch-Archaeologisch Instituut te Istanbul.

Hawley, Robert. 2003. Studies in Ugaritic Epistolography. Ph.D. diss., University of Chicago.

Heinhold-Krahmer, Susanne. 1977. *Arzawa: Untersuchungen zu seiner Geschichte nach den hethitischen Quellen*. THeth 8. Heidelberg: Carl Winter.

———. 1983. "Untersuchungen zu Piyamaradu (Teil I)." *Or* 52: 81–97.

———. 1986. "Untersuchungen zu Piyamaradu (Teil II)." *Or* 55: 47–62.

———. 1991–1992. "Zur Bronzetafel aus Boğazköy und ihrem historischen Inhalt." *AfO* 38–39: 138–58.

———. 1999. "Bedřich Hrozný und die Aḫḫijaṷa-Frage." *ArOr* 67: 567–84.

———. 2001. "Zur Diskussion um einen zweiten Namen Tutḫaliyas IV." Pages 180–98 in *Akten des IV. Internationalen Kongresses für Hethitologie. Würzburg, 4.–8. Oktober, 1999*. Edited by G. Wilhelm. StBoT 45. Wiesbaden: Harrassowitz.

———. 2002. "Zur Erwähnung Šaḫurunuwas im 'Tawagalawa-Brief.'" Pages 359–75 in *Anatolia Antica: Studi in memoria di Fiorella Imparati*. Edited by S. de Martino and F. Pecchioli Daddi. Firenze: LoGisma.

———. 2004. "Ist die Identität von Ilios mit Wiluša endgültig erwiesen?" *SMEA* 46: 29–57.

———. 2007a. "Drei Fragmente aus Berichten über die Taten Šuppiluliumas I.?" Pages 367–83 in *Tabularia Hethaeorum: Hethitologische Beiträge Silvin Kosak zum 65. Geburtstag*. Edited by D. Groddek and M. Zorman. DBH 25. Wiesbaden: Harrassowitz.

———. 2007b. "Zu diplomatischen Kontakten zwischen dem Hethiterreich und dem Land Aḫḫiyawa." *Keimelion. Elitenbildung und elitärer Konsum von der mykenischen Palastzeit bis zur homerischen Epoche. Akten des Internationalen Kongresses vom 3. bis 5. Februar 2005 in Salzburg*. Edited by E. Alram-Stern, and G. Nightingale. Österreichische Akademie der Wissenschaften, Philosophisch-historische Klasse, Denkschriften 350. Wien: Österreichische Akademie der Wissenschaften.

Heinhold-Krahmer, Susanne, Inge Hoffmann, Annelies Kammenhuber, and Gerlinde Mauer. 1979. *Probleme der Textdatierung in der Hethitologie*. THeth 9. Heidelberg: Winter.

Helck, Wolfgang. 1962. *Die Beziehungen Ägyptens zu Vorderasien im 3. und 2. Jahrtausend v. Chr.* Wiesbaden: Harrassowitz.

———. 1963. "Urhi-Tešup in Ägypten." *JCS* 17: 87–97.

Herbordt, Suzanne. 2005. *Die Prinzen- und Beamtensiegel der hethitischen Großreichszeit auf Tonbullen aus dem Nişantepe-Archiv in Hattusa, mit Kommentaren zu den Siegelinschriften und Hieroglyphen von J. David Hawkins*. Boğazköy-Ḫattuša 19. Mainz: von Zabern.

Hess, Richard S. 1993. *Amarna Personal Names*. Winona Lake, Ind.: Eisenbrauns.

Hoffmann, Inge. 1992. "Das hethitische Wort für 'Sohn.'" Pages 289–93 in *Hittite and Other Anatolian and Near Eastern Studies in Honour of Sedat Alp*. Edited by H. Otten, E. Akurgal, H. Ertem, and A. Süel. Anadolu Medeniyetlerini Araştırma ve Tanıtma Vakfı Yayınları 1. Ankara: Türk Tarih Kurumu Basımevi.

Hoffner, Harry A., Jr. 1968. Review of O. Carruba, *Das Beschörungsritual für di Göttin Wišurijanza*, StBoT 2. *JAOS* 88: 531–34.

———. 1972. Review of Ph. Houwink ten Cate, *Records of the Early Hittite Empire (C. 1450–1380 B.C.)*. *JNES* 31: 29–35.

———. 1973. "The Hittite Particle *-PAT*." Pages 99–118 in *Festschrift Heinrich Otten*. Edited by E. Neu and C. Rüster. Wiesbaden: Harrassowitz.

———. 1974a. *Alimenta Hethaeorum: Food Production in Hittite Asia Minor*. American Oriental Series 55. New Haven: American Oriental Society.

———. 1974b. "The *Arzana* House." Pages 113–22 in *Anatolian Studies Presented to Hans Gustav Güterbock on the Occasion of his 65th Birthday*. Edited by K. Bittel, P. H. J. Houwink ten Cate, and E. Reiner. Uitgaven van het Nederlands Historisch-Archaeologisch Instituut te Istanbul 35. Istanbul: Nederlands Historisch-Archaeologisch Institut in Het Nabije Oosten.

———. 1977a. Review of Liane Jakob-Rost, *Hethitische Rituale und Festbeschreibungen*, KUB 46. *BiOr* 34: 74–75.

———. 1977b. Review of E. Neu, *Der Anitta Text* [StBoT 18] (Wiesbaden 1974). *BASOR* 1977: 78–79.

———. 1977c. "Studies in Hittite Vocabulary, Syntax and Style. Hommage à M. Emmanuel Laroche." *JCS* 29: 151–56.

———. 1979. "The Hittite Word for 'Tribe.'" Pages 261–66 in *Studia Mediterranea Piero Meriggi dicata*. Edited by O. Carruba. StMed 1. Pavia: Aurora Edizioni.

———. 1980. "Histories and Historians of the Ancient Near East: The Hittites." *Or* 49: 283–332.

———. 1982a. "Hittite *mān* and *nūman*." Pages 38–45 in *Investigationes Philologicae et Comparativae: Gedenkschrift für Heinz Kronasser*. Edited by E. Neu. Wiesbaden: Harrassowitz.

———. 1982b. "The Milawata Letter Augmented and Reinterpreted." *AfO* Beih. 19: 130–37.

———. 1983. "A Prayer of Muršili II about his Stepmother." *JAOS* 103: 187–92.

———. 1993a. "Hittite *iwar* and Related Modes of Expressing Comparison." *IM* 43: 39–51.

———. 1993b. "Milch(produkte). B. Bei den Hethitern." Pages 702–06 in *Reallexikon der Assyriologie.* Band 8. Edited by E. Ebeling, B. Meissner, E. Weidner, W. von Soden, and D. O. Edzard. Berlin: de Gruyter.

———. 1995a. "About Questions." Pages 87–104 in *Studio Historiae Ardens: Ancient Near Eastern Studies Presented to Philo H. J. Houwink ten Cate on the Occasion of His 65th Birthday.* Edited by T. P. J. Van den Hout and J. de Roos. Publications de l'Institut historique et archéologique néerlandais de Stamboul 74. Istanbul: Institut historique et archéologique néerlandais de Stamboul.

———. 1995b. "Legal and Social Institutions of Hittite Anatolia." Pages 555–70 in *Civilizations of the Ancient Near East*, vol. 1. Edited by J. M. Sasson, K. Rubinson, J. Baines, and G. M. Beckman. New York: Scribner's.

———. 1995c. "Oil in Hittite Texts." *BA* 58: 108–14.

———. 1997a. "Mühle, bei den Hethitern." Pages 400–401 in *Reallexikon der Assyriologie.* Band 8. Edited by E. Ebeling, B. Meissner, E. Weidner, W. von Soden, and D. O. Edzard. Berlin: de Gruyter.

———. 1997b. "On Safari in Hittite Anatolia." Pages 5–21 in *Studies in Honor of Jaan Puhvel: Part One. Ancient Languages and Philology.* Edited by D. Disterheft, M. Huld, and J. A. C. Greppin. Journal of Indo-European Studies Monograph 20. Washington, D.C.: Institute for the Study of Man.

———. 1997c. "On the Hittite Use of Sumerian BAL in the Expression BAL-*nu*-." *ArAn* 3: 191–98.

———. 1997d. "Proclamation of Anitta of Kuššar." Pages 182–84 in *The Context of Scripture. Volume One: Canonical Compositions from the Biblical World.* Edited by W. W. Hallo and K. L. Younger, Jr. Leiden: Brill.

———. 1997e. "The Hittite Conquest of Cyprus: Two Inscriptions of Suppiluliuma II." Pages 192–93 in *Canonical Compositions from the Biblical World.* Vol. 1 of *The Context of Scripture.* Edited by W. W. Hallo and K. L. Younger, Jr. Leiden: Brill.

———. 1997f. "The Hittite Laws." Pages 211–47 in *Law Collections from Mesopotamia and Asia Minor.* 2nd ed. Edited by M. T. Roth. WAW 6. Atlanta: Scholars Press.

———. 1997g. *The Laws of the Hittites. A Critical Edition.* DMOA 23. Leiden: Brill.

———, ed. 1997h. *Perspectives on Hittite Civilization: Selected Writings of Hans Gustav Güterbock.* Assyriological Studies 26. Chicago: Oriental Institute.

———. 1998. "Name, Namengebung. C. Bei den Hethitern." Pages 116–21 in *Reallexikon der Assyriologie.* Band 9. Edited by E. Ebeling, B. Meissner, E. Weidner, W. von Soden, and D. O. Edzard. Berlin: de Gruyter.

———. 2000. "Hittite Laws (2.19)." Pages 106–19 in *Monumental Inscriptions from the Biblical World.* Vol. 2 of *The Context of Scripture.* Edited by W. W. Y. Hallo, K. Lawson, Jr. Leiden: Brill.

———. 2001. "*Alimenta* Revisited." Pages 199–212 in *Akten des IV. Internationalen Kongresses für Hethitologie. Würzburg, 4.–8. Oktober, 1999.* Edited by G. Wilhelm. StBoT 45. Wiesbaden: Harrassowitz.

———. 2002a. "Before and After: Space, Time, Rank and Causality." Pages 163–71 in

Silva Anatolica: Anatolian Studies Presented to Maciej Popko on the Occasion of His 65th Birthday. Edited by P. Taracha. Warszawa: AGADE.

———. 2002b. "Hittite Letters." Pages 43–53 in *Archival Documents from the Biblical World.* Vol. 3 of *The Context of Scripture*. Edited by W. W. Hallo and K. L. Younger. Leiden: Brill.

———. 2002c. "The Treatment and Long-Term Use of Persons Captured in Battle according to the Maşat Texts." Pages 61–71 in *Recent Developments in Hittite Archaeology and History*. Edited by K. A. Yener and H. A. Hoffner, Jr. Winona Lake, Ind.: Eisenbrauns.

———. 2003a. "Daily Life among the Hittites." Pages 95–118 in *Life and Culture in the Ancient Near East*. Edited by R. Averbeck, M. W. Chavalas, and D. B. Weisberg. Bethesda, Md.: CDL.

———. 2003b. "The Disabled and Infirm in Hittite Society." Pages 84*–90* in *Hayim and Miriam Tadmor Volume*. Edited by I. Ephal, A. Ben-Tor, and P. Machinist. Eretz-Israel. Archaeological, Historical and Geographical Studies 27. Jerusalem: The Israel Exploration Society.

———. 2004. "Ancient Israel's Literary Heritage Compared with Hittite Textual Data." Pages 176–92 in *The Future of Biblical Archaeology: Reassessing Methodologies and Assumptions*. Edited by J. K. Hoffmeier and A. R. Millard. Grand Rapids, Mich.: Eerdmans.

———. 2007. "Asyndeton in Hittite." Pages 385–99 in *Tabularia Hethaeorum: Hethitologische Beiträge Silvin Košak zum 65. Geburtstag*. Edited by D. Groddek and M. Zorman. DBH 25. Wiesbaden: Harrassowitz.

———. forthcoming. "A Grammatical Profile of the Middle Hittite Maşat Texts." In *Investigationes Anatolicae: Gedenkschrift für Erich Neu*, edited by J. Klinger, and E. Rieken. StBoT 52. Wiesbaden: Harrassowitz.

Hoffner, Harry A., Jr., and H. Craig Melchert.

———. 2002. "A Practical Approach to Verbal Aspect in Hittite." Pages 377–90 in *Anatolia antica: Studi in memoria di Fiorella Imparati*. Edited by S. de Martino and F. Pecchioli Daddi. Firenze: LoGisma.

———. 2008. *A Grammar of the Hittite Language*. LANE 1. Winona Lake, Ind.: Eisenbrauns.

Hornung, Erik, Rolf Krauss, and David Warburton. 2006. *Ancient Egyptian Chronology*. HbOr I/83. Leiden: Brill.

Hout, Theo P. J. van den. 1991. "A Tale of Tissaruli(ya): A Dramatic Interlude in the Hittite KI.LAM Festival?" *JNES* 50: 193–202.

———. 1993. "Der Falke und das Küken: KUB 19.20 + KBo 12.23." *ZA* 84: 60–88.

———. 1995. *Der Ulmitešub-Vertrag, Eine prosopographische Untersuchung*. StBoT 38. Wiesbaden: Harrassowitz.

———. 1998. *The Purity of Kingship: An Edition of CTH 569 and Related Hittite Oracle Inquiries of Tuthaliya IV*. DMOA 25. Leiden: Brill.

———. 2001a. "Bemerkungen zu älteren hethitischen Orakeltexten." Pages 423–40 in *Kulturgeschichten. Altorientalistische Studien für Volkert Haas zum 65. Geburtstag*. Edited by T. Richter, D. Prechel, and J. Klinger. Saarbrücken: Saarbrücker Druckerei und Verlag.

———. 2001b. "Neuter Plural Subjects and Nominal Predicates in Anatolian." Pages 167–92 in *Anatolisch und Indogermanisch/Anatolico e Indoeuropeo: Akten des Kol-*

loquiums der Indogermanischen Gesellschaft Pavia 22.–25. September 1998. Edited by O. Carruba and W. Meid. Innsbruck: Institut für Sprachwissenschaft der Universität Innsbruck.

———. 2001c. "Zur Geschichte des jüngeren hethitischen Reiches." Pages 213–23 in *Akten des IV. Internationalen Kongresses für Hethitologie. Würzburg, 4.–8. Oktober, 1999*. Edited by G. Wilhelm. StBoT 45. Wiesbaden: Harrassowitz.

———. 2002. "Another View of Hittite Literature." Pages 857–78 in *Anatolia Antica: Studi in memoria di Fiorella Imparati*. Edited by S. de Martino and F. Pecchioli Daddi. Firenze: LoGisma.

———. 2003a. "De affaire Tarhunmija. Brieven van een hettitische hofschrijver." Pages 145–53 in *Zij schreven geschiedenis. Historische documenten uit het Oude Nabije Oosten (2500–100 v. Chr.)*. Edited by R. J. Demarée and K. R. Veenhof. Leiden: Ex Oriente Lux.

———. 2003b. "Studies in the Hittite Phraseological Construction. I. Its Syntactic and Semantic Properties." Pages 177–204 in *Hittite Studies in Honor of Harry A. Hoffner, Jr. on the Occasion of his 65th Birthday*. Edited by G. M. Beckman, R. H. Beal, and J. G. McMahon. Winona Lake, Ind.: Eisenbrauns.

———. 2004a. "Geweten in nood: rampen en onheil bij de Hettieten." *Phoenix* 50: 83–92.

———. 2004b. "Pacht, D. Bei den Hethitern." Pages 183–86 in *Reallexikon der Assyriologie*. Band 10. Edited by D. O. Edzard. Berlin: de Gruyter.

———. 2006. "Institutions, Vernaculars, Publics: The Case of Second-Millennium Anatolia." Pages 221–62 in *Margins of Writing, Origins of Cultures*. Edited by S. L. Sanders. OIS 2. Chicago: The Oriental Institute of the University of Chicago.

———. 2007a. "Prayers in the Haus am Hang." Pages 401–9 in *Tabularia Hethaeorum: Hethitologische Beiträge Silvin Kosak zum 65. Geburtstag*. Edited by D. Groddek and M. Zorman. DBH 25. Wiesbaden: Harrassowitz.

———. 2007b. "Some Observations on the Tablet Collection from Maşat Höyük." Pages 387–98 in *VI. Congresso Internazionale di Ittitologia Roma, 5–9 settembre 2005*. Edited by A. Archi and R. Francia. Studi Micenei ed Egeo-Anatolici 49. Rome: CNR - Istituto de Studi sulle Ceviltà del'Egeo e del Vicino Oriente.

———. forthcoming. "Schreiber. Bei den Hethiter" in *Reallexikon der Assyriologie*. Band 12.

Houwink ten Cate, Philo H. J. 1963. "The Date of the Kurustama Treaty." *BiOr* 20: 175–276.

———. 1983–1984. "Sidelights on the Ahhiyawa Question from Hittite Vassal and Royal Correspondence." *Jaarbericht van het Vooraziatisch-Egyptisch Genootschap "Ex Oriente Lux"* 28: 33–79.

———. 1992. "The Hittite Storm God: His Role and His Rule According to Hittite Sources." Pages 83–147 in *Natural Phenomena, Their Meaning, Depiction and Description in the Ancient Near East*. Edited by D. J. W. Meijer. Amsterdam: Royal Netherlands Academy of Arts and Sciences.

———. 1995. "Ethnic Diversity and Population Movement in Anatolia." Pages 259–70 in *Civilizations of the Ancient Near East*, vol. 1. Edited by J. M. Sasson. New York: Scribner's.

———. 1996. "The Hittite Dynastic Marriages of the Period between ca. 1258 and 1244 B.C." *AoF* 23: 40–75.

———. 1998. "The Scribes of the Maşat Letters and the GAL.DUB.SAR(.MEŠ) of the Hittite Capital during the Final Phase of the Early Empire Period." Pages 157–78 in *dubsar anta-men: Studien zur Altorientalistik. Festschrift für Willem H. Ph. Römer zur Vollendung seines 70. Lebensjahres mit Beiträgen von Freunden, Schülern und Kollegen*. Edited by T. E. Balke, M. Dietrich, and O. Loretz. AOAT 253. Münster: Ugarit-Verlag.

———. 2006. "The Apparently Delayed Homecoming of Tudḫaliyaš IV to his Capital Ḫattuša." Pages 107–16 in *The Life and Times of Ḫattušili III and Tutḫaliya IV. Proceedings of a Symposium Held in Honour of J. de Roos, Leiden December 12–13, 2003*. Edited by T. P. J. van den Hout. Publications de l'Institut Historique et Archéologique Néerlandais de Stamboul 103. Leiden: Nederlands Historisch-Archaeologisch Instituut te Istanbul.

Hrozný, Bedrich. 1931. "La deuxième lettre d'Arzawa et le vrai nom des Hittites indo-européens." *Journal Asiatique* 218: 307–20.

Huxley, G. L. 1960. *Achaeans and Hittites*. Oxford.

Imparati, Fiorella. 1974. "Una concessione de terre da parte di Tudhaliya IV." *RHA* XXXII: 1–209.

———. 1983. "Aspects de l'organisation de l'état hittite dans les documents juridiques et administratifs." *JESHO* 25: 225–67.

———. 1985. "Auguri e scribi nella società ittita." Pages 255–69 in *Studi in onore di Edda Bresciani*. Edited by S. F. Bondí, S. Pernigotti, F. Serra, and A. Vivian. Pisa: Giardini.

———. 1997. "Observations on a Letter from Maşat-Höyük." *ArAn* 3: 199–214.

———. 2002. "Palaces and Local Communities in Some Hittite Provincial Seats." Pages 93–100 in *Recent Developments in Hittite Archaeology and History*. Edited by K. A. Yener, and H. A. Hoffner, Jr. Winona Lake, Ind.: Eisenbrauns.

———. 2003. "Significato politico dell'investitura sacerdotale nel regno di Hatti e in alcuni paesi vicino orientali ad esso soggetti." Pages 230–42 in *Semitic and Assyriological Studies Presented to Pelio Fronzaroli by Pupils and Colleagues*. Wiesbaden: Harrassowitz.

Imparati, Fiorella and Stefano de Martino. 2004. "La 'mano' nelle piú significative espressioni idiomatiche ittite." Pages 787–802 in *Studi sulla società e sulla religione degli ittiti*. Edited by F. Imparati. Eothen 12. Firenze: LoGisma.

Jakob, Stefan. 2006. "Pharaoh and His Brothers." *BMSAES* 6: 12–30.

Janowski, Bernd and Gernot Wilhelm, eds. 2006. *Briefe*. TUAT Neue Folge 3. Gütersloh: Gütersloher Verlagshaus.

Jasink, Anna Margherita. 2003. "Il ruolo di Tarhuntašša da Muwatalli II a Šuppiluliuma II." Pages 269–85 in *Semitic and Assyriological Studies Presented to Pelio Fronzaroli by Pupils and Colleagues*. Wiesbaden: Harrassowitz.

———. 2005. "Micenei e Vicino Oriente." Pages 209–24 in *Narrare gli eventi. Atti del convegno degli egittologi e degli orientalisti italiani in margine alla mostra 'La battaglia di Qadesh'*. Edited by F. Pecchioli Daddi, and M. C. Guidotti. Studia Asiana 3. Roma: Herder.

Joannès, Francis and Cécile Michel, eds. 2001. *Dictionnaire de la civilisation mésopotamienne*. Paris: R. Laffont.

Karasu, Cem. 2002. "Some Observations on the Women in the Hittite Texts." Pages 419–24 in *Anatolia Antica: Studi in memoria di Fiorella Imparati*. Edited by S. de Martino and F. Pecchioli Daddi. Firenze: LoGisma.

———. 2003. "Why Did the Hittites Have a Thousand Deities?" Pages 221–36 in *Hittite Studies in Honor of Harry A. Hoffner, Jr. on the Occasion of His 65th Birthday*. Edited by G. M. Beckman, R. H. Beal, and J. G. McMahon. Winona Lake, Ind.: Eisenbrauns.

Kempinski, Aharon. 1993. "Suppiluliuma I: The Early Years of His Career." Pages 81–91 in *Kinattūtu ša dārâti: Raphael Kutscher Memorial Volume*. Edited by A. F. Rainey, A. Kempinski, M. Sigrist, and D. Ussishkin. Tel Aviv: Institute of Archaeology.

Klengel, Horst. 1963. "Der Schiedsspruch des Mursili II. hinsichtlich Barga und seine Übereinkunft mit Duppi-Tesub von Amurru (KBo III 3)." *Or* 32: 32–55.

———. 1965. "Die Rolle der 'Ältesten' (LÚ.MEŠ ŠU.GI) im Kleinasien der Hethiterzeit." *ZA* 57: 223–36.

———. 1974. ""Hungerjahre" in Hatti." *AoF* 1: 165–74.

———. 2006. "Studien zur hethitischen Wirtschaft, 2: Feld- und Gartenbau." *AoF* 33: 3–21.

———. 1999. *Geschichte des hethitischen Reiches*. HbOr 1. Abt., 34. Bd. Leiden: Brill.

Klinger, Jörg. 1995a. "Das Corpus der Maşat-Briefe und seine Beziehungen zu den Texten aus Ḫattuša." *ZA* 85: 74–108.

———. 1995b. "Synchronismen in der Epoche vor Suppiluliuma I.: Einige Anmerkungen zur Chronologie der mittelhethitischen Geschichte." Pages 235–48 in *Atti del II Congresso Internazionale di Hittitologia*. Edited by O. Carruba, M. Giorgieri, and C. Mora. StMed 9. Pavia: Gianni Iuculano.

———. 1996. *Untersuchungen zur Rekonstruktion der hattischen Kultschicht*. StBoT 37. Wiesbaden: Harrassowitz.

———. 2001a. "Briefe aus hethitischen Archiven: 1. Ein akkadischsprachiger Brief Hattusilis I.; 2. Aus der innerhethitischen Verwaltungskorrespondenz; 3. Ein Beispiel für diplomatische Korrespondenz in hethitischer Sprache." Pages 65–69 in *Texte aus der Umwelt des Alten Testaments. Ergänzungslieferung*. Gütersloh: Gütersloher Verlagshaus.

———. 2001b. "Die hurritische Tradition in Hattusa und das Corpus hurritischer Texte." Pages 197–208 in *Kulturgeschichten. Altorientalistische Studien für Volkert Haas zum 65. Geburtstag*. Edited by T. Richter, D. Prechel, and J. Klinger. Saarbrücken: Saarbrücker Druckerei.

———. 2003. "Zur Paläographie akkadischsprachiger Texte aus Hattusa." Pages 237–48 in *Hittite Studies in Honor of Harry A. Hoffner, Jr. on the Occasion of His 65th Birthday*. Edited by G. M. Beckman, R. H. Beal, and J. G. McMahon. Winona Lake, Ind.: Eisenbrauns.

———. 2006. "Hethitische Texte. Briefe aus hethitischen Archiven." Pages 191–95 in *Briefe*. Edited by B. Janowski, and G. Wilhelm. TUAT Neue Folge 3. Gütersloh: Gütersloher Verlagshaus.

Klock-Fontanille, Isabelle. 1996. "Le testament politique de Ḫattušili Ier ou les conditions d'exercise de la royauté dans l'ancien royaume hittite." *AnAn* 4: 33–66.

Knudtzon, Jürgen Alexander. 1902. *Die zwei Arzawa-Briefe, die ältesten Urkunden in indogermanischer Sprache*. Leipzig: Hinrichs.

———. 1964. *Die El-Amarna-Tafeln; mit Einleitung und Erläuterungen*. Aalen: O. Zeller.

Korolëv, A. A. 1999. "Hittite Texts: New Readings, Joins, and Duplicates." *Studia Linguarum* 2: 281–90.

Kristensen, A. L. 1977. "Ugaritic Epistolary Formulas: A Comparative Study of the Ugaritic Epistolary Formulas in the Context of the Contemporary Akkadian Formulas in the Letters from Ugarit and Amarna." *UF* 9: 143–58.

Kühne, Cord. 1973. *Die Chronologie der internationalen Korrespondenz von El-Amarna.* AOAT 17. Neukirchen-Vluyn: Kevelaer.

———. 1993. "Zu einer Übersetzung der Amarnabriefe." Review of W. L. Moran, *Les lettres d'El-Amarna: Correspondance diplomatique du pharaon. Or* 62: 410–22.

Kümmel, Hans Martin. 1967. *Ersatzrituale für den hethitischen König.* StBoT 3. Wiesbaden: Harrassowitz.

———. 1985. "Hethitische historisch-chronologische Texte." Pages 455–95 in *Rechts- und Wirtschaftsurkunden. Historisch-chronologische Texte.* Edited by O. Kaiser. TUAT I/5. Gütersloh: Gütersloher Verlagshaus.

Lackenbacher, Sylvie. 1982. "Nouveaux documents d'Ugarit. I. Une lettre royale." *RA* 76: 141–56.

Laroche, Emmanuel. 1960a. *Les Hiéroglyphes Hittites, I.* Paris: CNRS.

———. 1960b. "Lettre d'un préfet au roi hittite." *RHA* XVIII (67): 81–86.

———. 1966. *Les noms des Hittites.* Paris: Klincksieck.

———. 1982. "Documents hittites et hourrites." Pages 53–60 in *Meskéné-Emar. Dix ans de travaux 1972–1982.* Edited by D. Beyer. Paris.

Lebrun, René. 1976. *Samuha, foyer religieux de l'empire hittite.* Publications de l'institut orientaliste de Louvain 11. Louvain-la-Neuve: Université Catholique de Louvain: Institut Orientaliste.

———. 2002. "Propos relatifs à Oinoanda, Pinara, Xanthos et Arnéai." *Hethitica* 15: 163–72.

Lemche, Niels Peter. 1995. "The History of Ancient Syria and Palestine: An Overview." Pages 1195–218 in *Civilizations of the Ancient Near East,* vol. 2. Edited by J. M. Sasson. New York: Scribner's Sons.

Lesko, Leonard. 2001. "Literacy." Pages 2: 297–99 in *The Oxford Encyclopedia of Ancient Egypt.* Edited by D. B. Redford. Oxford: Oxford University Press.

Lindenberger, James M. 1994. *Ancient Aramaic and Hebrew Letters.* WAW. Atlanta: Scholars Press.

Liverani, Mario. 1998. *Le lettere di el-Amarna.* TVOA 3. Brescia: Paideia.

———. 2001. *International Relations in the Ancient Near East, 1600–1100 B.C.* Houndmills, Basingstoke, Hampshire/New York: Palgrave.

Loretz, Oswald. 1984. *Habiru-Hebräer: Eine sozio-linguistische Studie über die Herkunft des Gentiliziums *ibrî vom Appellativum *habiru.* BZAW. Berlin: de Gruyter.

Lucas, Christopher J. 1979. "The Scribal Tablet-House in Ancient Mesopotamia." *History of Education Quarterly* 19: 305–32.

Lühr, Rosemarie. 2001. "Relativsätze im Hethitischen." Pages 333–46 in *Akten des IV. Internationalen Kongresses für Hethitologie. Würzburg, 4.–8. Oktober, 1999.* Edited by G. Wilhelm. StBoT 45. Wiesbaden: Harrassowitz.

Macqueen, James G. 1968. "Geography and History in Western Asia Minor in the Second Millennium B.C." *AnSt* 18: 169–85.

———. 1986. *The Hittites and their Contemporaries in Asia Minor.* 2nd ed. London: Thames and Hudson.

Marizza, Marco. 2007a. *Dignitari ittiti del tempo di Tuthaliya I/II, Arnuwanda I, Tuthaliya III.* Eothen 15. Firenze: LoGisma.

———. 2007b. "The Office of GAL GEŠTIN in the Hittite Kingdom." *KASKAL* 4: 153–80.

Mascheroni, Lorenza M. 1988. "A proposito delle cosiddette Sammeltafeln etee." Pages 131–47 in *Studi di Storia e di Filologia Anatolica dedicati a Giovanni Pugliese Carratelli*. Edited by F. Imparati. Eothen 1. Firenze: Edizione Librarie Italiane Estere (ELITE).

Meier, Samuel A. 1988. *The Messenger in the Ancient Semitic World*. HSM 45. Atlanta: Scholars Press.

Melchert, H. Craig. 1977. Ablative and Instrumental in Hittite. Ph.D. diss., Harvard University.

———. 1993. *Cuneiform Luvian Lexicon*. Lexica Anatolica 2. Chapel Hill, N.C.: Self-published.

———. 1994. *Anatolian Historical Phonology*. Leiden Studies in Indo-European 3. Amsterdam-Atlanta: Rodopi.

———. 1998. "Hittite *arku-* 'chant, intone' vs. *arkuwa(i)-* 'make a plea'." *JCS* 50: 45–51.

———. 1999. "Hittite *tuk(kan)zi-* 'cultivation, breeding.'" *Ktema* 24: 17–23.

———. 2005a. "Latin *insolesco,* Hittite *šulle(šš)-* and PIE Statives in *-ē-*." Pages 90–98 in *Hrdā mánasā: Studies Presented to Professor Leonard G. Herzenberg on the Occasion of his 70th Birthday*. Edited by N. N. Kazansky, E. R. Kryuchkova, A. S. Nikolaev, and A. V. Shatskov. Saint Petersburg: Nauka.

———. 2005b. "The Problem of Luvian Influence on Hittite: When and How Much?" Pages 445–60 in *Sprachkontakt und Sprachwandel: Akten der XI. Fachtagung der indogermanische Gesellschaft, 17.–23. September 2000, Halle an der Saale*. Edited by G. Meiser, and O. Hackstein. Wiesbaden: Reichert.

———. 2008. "Hittite *duwān* (*parā*)." Pages 201–9 in *Morphology and Language History in Honour of Harold Koch*. Edited by C. Bowern, B. Evans, and L. Micelli. Philadelphia: John Benjamins.

Meriggi, Piero. 1935–36. "Die Bleibriefe in hethitischen Hieroglyphen." *AfO* 10: 113–33, 251–67.

Meyer, Eduard. 1925. *Geschichte des Altertums*. 5th ed. Stuttgart: J. G. Cotta.

Michalowski, Piotr. 1993. *Letters from Early Mesopotamia*. WAW 3. Atlanta, Ga.: Scholars Press.

Miller, Jared L. 2001. "Hattusili I's Expansion into Northern Syria in Light of the Tikunani Letter." Pages 410–29 in *Akten des IV. Internationalen Kongresses für Hethitologie. Würzburg, 4.–8. Oktober, 1999*. Edited by G. Wilhelm. StBoT 45. Wiesbaden: Harrassowitz.

———. 2005. Review of G. Beckman, R. Beal, and G. McMahon, eds., *Hittite Studies in Honor of Harry A. Hoffner, Jr. on the Occasion of his 65th Birthday*. *JAOS* 125: 283–88.

———. 2006. "Hethitische Texte. Briefe aus hethitischen Archiven." Pages 240–47 in *Briefe*. Edited by B. Janowski, and G. Wilhelm. TUAT Neue Folge 3. Gütersloh: Gütersloher Verlagshaus.

———. 2007. "Amarna Age Chronology and the Identity of Nibḫururiya in the Light of a Newly Reconstructed Hittite Text." *AoF* 34: 252–93.

Miller, Naomi F. 1997. "Viticulture." Pages 304–6 in *The Oxford Encyclopedia of Archaeology in the Near East*, vol. 5. Oxford: Oxford University Press.

Mineck, Kathleen R., Theo P. J. van den Hout, and Harry A. Hoffner, Jr. 2006. "Hittite Historical Texts II." Pages 253–79 in *The Ancient Near East. Historical Sources in Translation*. Edited by M. W. Chavalas. Oxford: Blackwell.

Mora, Clelia. 1987. *La glittica anatolica del II millennio A.C. Classificazione tipologica*. StMed 6. Pavia: Aurora Edizioni.

———. 1995. "I Luvi e la scrittura geroglifica anatolica." Pages 275–82 in *Atti del II Congresso Internazionale di Hittitologia*. Edited by O. Carruba, M. Giorgieri, and C. Mora. StMed 9. Pavia: Gianni Iuculano.

———. 2004. "Sigilli e sigillature di Karkemiš in età imperiale ittita, I. I re, i dignitari, il (mio) Sole." *Or* 73: 427–50.

———. 2005. "Grands rois, petits rois, gouvernants de second rang." *RAnt* 2: 309–14.

Mora, Clelia and Mauro Giorgieri. 2004. *Le lettere tra i re ittiti e i re assiri ritrovate a Ḫattuša*. HANE/M 7. Padova: S.A.R.G.O.N.

Moran, William L. 1992. *The Amarna Letters*. Baltimore: The Johns Hopkins University Press.

Mori, Lucia. 2007. "Land and Land Use: The Middle Euphrates Valley." Pages 39–53 in *The Babylonian World*. Edited by G. Leick. New York: Routledge.

Morris, Ellen F. 2006. "Bowing and Scraping in the Ancient Near East: An Investigation into Obsequiousness in the Amarna Letters." *JNES* 65: 179–95.

Mountjoy, Penelope. 1998. "The East Aegean-West Anatolian Interface in the Late Bronze Age: Mycenaeans and the Kingdom of Ahhiyawa." *AnSt* 48: 33–67.

Mouton, Alice. 2007. "Au sujet du compte rendu oraculaire hittite KBo 18.142." Pages 551–55 in *Tabularia Hethaeorum: Hethitologische Beiträge Silvin Košak zum 65. Geburtstag*. Edited by D. Groddek and M. Zorman. DBH 25. Wiesbaden: Harrassowitz.

Murnane, William J. 1995. *Texts from the Amarna Period in Egypt*. WAW 5. Atlanta: Scholars Press.

Naaman, Nadav. 2000. "Habiru-Like Bands in the Assyrian Empire and Bands in Biblical Historiography." *JAOS* 120: 621–24.

Neef, Reinder. 2001. "Getreide im Silokomplex an der Poternenmauer (Boğazköy)—Erste Aussagen zur Landwirtschaft." *AA* 2001.

Neu, Erich. 1968. *Interpretation der hethitischen mediopassiven Verbalformen*. StBoT 5. Wiesbaden: Harrassowitz.

———. 1974. *Der Anitta-Text*. StBoT 18. Wiesbaden: Harrassowitz.

———. 1976. Review of J. Friedrich and A. Kammenhuber, *Hethitisches Wörterbuch*^{2} I/1 (*a-annari*). *IF* 81: 298–305.

———. 1983. *Glossar zu den althethitischen Ritualtexten*. StBoT 26. Wiesbaden: Harrassowitz.

———. 1993. "Zu den hethitischen Ortspartikeln." *Linguistica* 33: 137–52.

———. 1996. *Das hurritische Epos der Freilassung I: Untersuchungen zu einem hurritisch-hethitischen Textensemble aus Ḫattuša*. StBoT 32. Wiesbaden: Harrassowitz.

———. 1997. "Zu einigen Pronominalformen des Hethitischen." Pages 139–69 in *Studies in Honor of Jaan Puhvel*. Part One: *Ancient Languages and Philology*. Edited by D. Disterheft, M. Huld, and J. A. C. Greppin. Journal of Indo-European Studies Monograph 20. Washington, D.C.: Institute for the Study of Man.

Niedorf, Christian F. 2002. "Ein hethitisches Brieffragment aus Alalaḫ." Pages 517–26 in *Ex Mesopotamia et Syria lux: Festschrift für Manfried Dietrich zu seinem 65.*

Geburtstag. Edited by O. Loretz, K. A. Metzler, and H. Schaudig. AOAT 281. Münster: Ugarit-Verlag.

Niehr, Herbert. 2006. "Briefe in ugaritischer Sprache." Pages 264–72 in *Briefe*. Edited by B. Janowski and G. Wilhelm. TUAT Neue Folge 3. Gütersloh: Gütersloher Verlagshaus.

Niehr, Herbert and Daniel Schwemer. 2006. "Briefe aus den Archiven von Ugarit." Pages 248–72 in *Briefe*. Edited by B. Janowski and G. Wilhelm. TUAT Neue Folge 3. Gütersloh: Gütersloher Verlagshaus.

Oettinger, Norbert. 1976. *Die militärischen Eide der Hethiter*. StBoT 22. Wiesbaden: Harrassowitz.

———. 1979. *Die Stammbildung des hethitischen Verbums*. Erlanger Beiträge zur Sprach- und Kunstwissenschaft 64. Nuremberg: Hans Carl.

———. 1981. Review of J. Tischler, *Hethitisches Etymologisches Glossar Teil 1, A–K*, IBS 20. *ZDMG* 131: 286–88.

———. 1989/1990. "Die 'dunkle Erde' im Hethitischen und Griechischen." *WO* 20/21: 83–98.

———. 1994. "Etymologisch unerwarteter Nasal im Hethitischen." Pages 307–30 in *In honorem Holger Pedersen. Kolloquium der Indogermanischen Gesellschaft vom 26. bis 28. März 1993 in Kopenhagen*. Edited by J. E. Rasmussen and B. Nielsen. Wiesbaden: Reichert.

———. 2001. "Varia Hethitica." *HS* 114: 80–89.

Ofitsch, Michaela. 2001. "'Ackern' und 'pflügen' im Hethitischen—Bemerkungen zum semantischen Wandel." Pages 317–40 in *Anatolisch und Indogermanisch/Anatolico e Indoeuropeo. Akten des Kolloquiums der Indogermanischen Gesellschaft Pavia 22.–25. September 1998*. Edited by O. Carruba and W. Meid. Innsbruck: Institut für Sprachwissenschaft der Universität Innsbruck.

Oppenheim, A. Leo. 1967. *Letters from Mesopotamia*. Chicago: University of Chicago Press.

Otten, Heinrich. 1955. "Inschriftliche Funde der Ausgrabung in Boğazköy 1953." *MDOG* 87: 13–25.

———. 1956. "Hethitische Schreiber in ihren Briefen." *MIO* 4: 179–89.

———. 1959–1960. "Ein Brief aus Ḫattuša an Babu-aḫu-iddina." *AfO* 19: 39–46.

———. 1960. "Die Eidesleistung des Ašḫapala." *RHA* XVIII (67): 121–27.

———. 1967. "Ein hethitischer Vertrag aus dem 15./14. Jahrhundert v. Chr. (KBo XVI 47)." *IM* 17: 55–62.

———. 1969. *Sprachliche Stellung und Datierung des Madduwatta-Textes*. StBoT 11. Wiesbaden: Harrassowitz.

———. 1979. "Original oder Abschrift—Zur Datierung von CTH 258." Pages 273–76 in *Florilegium Anatolicum: Mélanges offerts à Emmanuel Laroche*. Edited by E. Masson. Paris: Éditions E. de Boccard.

———. 1981. *Die Apologie Hattusilis III.: Das Bild der Überlieferung*. StBoT 24. Wiesbaden: Harrassowitz.

———. 1988. *Die Bronzetafel aus Boğazköy: Ein Staatsvertrag Tuthalijas IV.* StBoT Beih. 1. Wiesbaden: Harrassowitz.

Page, Denys Lionel. 1959. *History and the Homeric Iliad*. Sather Classical Lectures 31. Berkeley and Los Angeles: University of California Press.

Pardee, Dennis. 2002. "Hebrew Letters." Pages 77–87 in *Archival Documents from the*

Biblical World. Vol. 3 of *The Context of Scripture*. Edited by W. W. Hallo and K. L. Younger, Jr. Leiden: Brill.

Pardee, Dennis and S. David Sperling. 1982. *Handbook of Ancient Hebrew Letters: A Study Edition*. SBL Sources for Biblical Study 15. Chico, Calif.: Scholars Press.

Pardee, Dennis and Robert M. Whiting. 1987. "Aspects of Epistolary Verbal Usage in Ugaritic and Akkadian." *BSOAS* 50: 1–31.

Parker, Victor. 1999. "Zum Text des Tawagalawaš-Briefes: Aḫḫiyawa-Frage und Textkritik." *Or* 68: 61–83.

Parpola, Simo. 1987. *The Correspondence of Sargon II, Part I: Letters from Assyria and the West*. SAA 1. Helsinki, Finland: Helsinki University Press.

Pecchioli Daddi, Franca. 1977. "Il LÚ Kartappu nel regno ittita." *SCO* 27: 169–90.

———. 1978–1979. "Kaššu, un antoponimo ittita." *Mesopotamia* 13–14: 201–12.

———. 1982. *Mestieri, professioni e dignità nell'Anatolia ittita*. Incunabula Graeca 69. Roma: Edizioni dell'Ateneo.

———. 2003a. *Il vincolo per i governatori de provincia*. StMed 14. Pavia: Italian University Press.

———. 2003b. "Le cariche d'oro." Pages 83–92 in *Hittite Studies in Honor of Harry A. Hoffner, Jr. on the Occasion of His 65th Birthday*. Edited by G. M. Beckman, R. H. Beal, and J. G. McMahon. Winona Lake, Ind.: Eisenbrauns.

Polvani, Anna Maria. 1988. *La terminologia dei minerali nei testi ittiti. Parte prima*. Eothen 3. Firenze: Edizione Librarie Italiane Estere (ELITE).

Popko, Maciej. 1984. "Zur Datierung des Tawagalawa-Briefes." *AoF* 11: 199–203.

Prechel, Doris. 2005. *Motivation und Mechanismen des Kulturkontaktes in der späten Bronzezeit*. Eothen 13. Firenze: LoGisma.

Pritchard, James B., ed. 1969. *Ancient Near Eastern Texts Relating to the Old Testament*. 3rd ed. Princeton, N.J.: Princeton University Press.

Pruzsinsky, Regine and Hermann Hunger, eds. 2004. *Mesopotamian Dark Age Revisited*. Wien: Verlag der österreichischen Akademie der Wissenschaften.

Puhvel, Jaan. 1984–. *Hittite Etymological Dictionary*. Berlin-New York-Amsterdam: Mouton.

———. 1993. "A Hittite Calque in the Iliad." *ZvS* 106: 36–38.

Rainey, Anson F. 2008. "Shasu of Habiru. Who Were the Early Israelites?" *BAR* 34: 51–55.

Reichardt, K. M. 1998. Linguistic Structures of Hittite and Luvian Curse Formulae. Ph.D. diss., University of Michigan.

Rieken, Elisabeth. 1999. *Untersuchungen zur nominalen Stammbildung des Hethitischen*. StBoT 44. Wiesbaden: Harrassowitz.

———. 2004. "Merkwürdige Kasusformen im Hethitischen." Pages 533–43 in *Šarnikzel: Hethitologische Studien zum Gedenken an Emil Orgetorix Forrer*. Edited by D. Groddek and S. Rößle. DBH 10. Dresden: Technische Universität Dresden.

Rosenkranz, Bernhard. 1973. Review of H. G. Güterbock, *Hethitische Briefe, Inventare und verwandte Texte*, KBo 18. *BiOr* 30: 73–75.

Rosi, Susanna. 1983. "La posizione di alcuni dignitari ittiti a corte e nell'esercito." *Studi e Ricerche* 2: 39–53.

Rost, Liane. 1956. "Die ausserhalb von Boğazköy gefundenen hethitischen Briefe." *MIO* 4: 328–50.

Roth, Martha T. and Harry A. Hoffner Jr. 1997. *Law Collections from Mesopotamia and Asia Minor*. 2 ed. Atlanta: Scholars Press.

Roth, Silke. 2005. "'In schönem Frieden befriedet und in schöner Bruderschaft verbrüdert': Zu Motivation und Mechanismen der ägyptisch-hethitischen diplomatischen Kontakte in der Zeit Ramses' II." Pages 179–226 in *Motivation und Mechanismen des Kulturkontaktes in der späten Bronzezeit*. Edited by D. Prechel. Eothen 13. Firenze: LoGisma.

Rutherford, Ian. 2006. "Preface." *JANER* 6: 1–8.

Salvini, Mirjo. 1994. "Una lettera di Hattušili I relativa alla spedizione contra Hahhum." *SMEA* 34: 61–80, pl. I–IV.

———. 1996. *The Ḫabiru Prism of King Tunip-Teššup of Tikunani*. Documenta Asiana, 3. Roma: Istituti Editoriali e Poligrafici Internazionali.

Salvini, Mirjo and Marie-Claude Trémouille. 2003. "Les textes hittites de Meskéné/Emar." *SMEA* 45: 225–71.

Sasson, Jack M., ed. 1995. *Civilizations of the Ancient Near East*. 4 vols. New York: Scribner's.

Schroeder, Otto. 1915. *Die Tontafeln von el-Amarna*. Vorderasiatische Schriftdenkmäler 11–12. Leipzig: Hinrichs.

Schwemer, Daniel. 2001. *Die Wettergottgestalten Mesopotamiens und Nordsyriens im Zeitalter der Keilschriftkulturen. Materialien und Studien nach den schriftlichen Quellen*. Wiesbaden: Harrassowitz.

———. 2006. "Briefe aus dem Archiv von el-Amarna." Pages 173–229 in *Briefe*. Edited by B. Janowski and G. Wilhelm. TUAT Neue Folge 3. Gütersloh: Gütersloher Verlagshaus.

Seeher, Jürgen. 1998. "Neue Befunde zur Endzeit von Ḫattuša: Ausgrabungen auf Büyükkaya in Boğazköy." Pages 515–24 in *Acts of the IIIrd International Congress of Hittitology. Çorum, September 16–22, 1996*. Edited by S. Alp and A. Süel. Ankara: Grafik, Teknik Hazırlık Uyum Ajans. 2000a. "Finden Sie denn auch was?" *ALTER ORIENT aktuell*, Juni, 14–18.

———. 2000b. "Getreidelagerung in unterirdischen Großspeichern: Zur Methode und ihrer Anwendung im 2. Jahrtausend v. Chr. am Beispiel der Befunde in Ḫattuša." *SMEA* 42: 261–301.

———. 2001. "Die Ausgrabungen in Boğazköy-Ḫattuša 2000." *AA* 2000.

———. 2002. *Hattusha Guide: A Day in the Hittite Capital*. 2nd ed. Ancient Anatolian towns 2. Istanbul: Ege Yayınları.

Selz, Gebhard J. 2007. "Power, Economy and Social Organisation in Babylonia." Pages 276–87 in *The Babylonian World*. Edited by G. Leick. London: Routledge.

Serbat, Guy, Jean Taillardat, and Gilbert Lazard. 1984. E. *Benveniste aujourd'hui: Actes du colloque international du C.N.R.S., Université François Rabelais, Tours, 28–30 septembre 1983*. Bibliothèque de l'information grammaticale. Paris: Société pour l'information grammaticale

Sidel'tsev, Andrej. 2007. "An Overlooked Case of Inversion in Middle Hittite." Pages 613–30 in *Tabularia Hethaeorum: Hethitologische Beiträge Silvin Košak zum 65. Geburtstag*. Edited by D. Groddek and M. Zorman. DBH 25. Wiesbaden: Harrassowitz.

Siegelová, Jana. 1986. *Hethitische Verwaltungspraxis im Lichte der Wirtschafts- und Inventardokumente*. Praha: Národní Muzeum v Praze.

———. 2002. "Blendung als Strafe." Pages 735–37 in *Anatolia Antica: Studi in Memoria di Fiorella Imparati*. Edited by S. de Martino and F. Pecchioli Daddi. Eothen 11. Firenze: LoGisma.

Singer, Itamar. 1983a. "Takuhlinu and Haya: Two Governors in the Ugarit Letter from Tel Aphek." *Tel Aviv* 10: 3–25.

———. 1983b. "Western Anatolia in the Thirteenth Century B.C. according to the Hittite Sources." *AnSt* 33: 205–17.

———. 1985. "The Battle of Nihriya and the End of the Hittite Empire." *ZA* 75: 100–123.

———. 1994. "'The Thousand Gods of Hatti': the Limits of an Expanding Pantheon." Pages 81–102 in *Concepts of the Other in Near Eastern Religions*. Edited by I. Alon, I. Gruenwald, and I. Singer. Israel Oriental Studies 14. Leiden: Brill.

———. 1996. "Great Kings of Tarhuntassa." *SMEA* 38: 63–71.

———. 1998. "From Ḫattuša to Tarḫuntašša: Some Thoughts on Muwatalli's Reign." Pages 535–42 in *Acts of the IIIrd International Congress of Hittitology. Çorum, September 16–22, 1996*. Edited by S. Alp and A. Süel. Ankara: Grafik, Teknik Hazırlık Uyum Ajans.

———. 1999a. "A New Hittite Letter from Emar." Pages 65–72 in *Landscapes. Territories, Frontiers and Horizons in the Ancient Near East. Papers Presented to the XLIV Rencontre Assyriologique Internationale, Venezia, 7–11 July 1997. Volume II. Geography and Cultural Landscapes*. Edited by L. Milano, S. de Martino, M. F. Fales, and G. B. Lanfranchi. History of the Ancient Near East Monographs III/2. Padova: Sargon.

———. 1999b. "A Political History of Ugarit." Pages 603–733 in *Handbook of Ugaritic Studies*, Der Nahe und Mittlere Osten: Bd. 39. Edited by W. G. E. Watson, and N. Wyatt. HbOr Abt. 1, Der Nahe und Mittlere Osten: Bd. 39. Leiden: Brill.

———. 2002. *Hittite Prayers*. WAW 11. Atlanta: Society of Biblical Literature.

———. 2005. "The 100th Anniversary of Knudtzon's Identification of Hittite as an Indo-European Language." Pages 651–60 in *Acts of the Vth International Congress of Hittitology. Çorum, September 02–08, 2002*. Edited by A. Süel. Ankara: Basım Tarihi.

———. 2006. "Ships Bound for Lukka: A New Interpretation of the Companion Letters RS 94.2530 and RS 94. 2523." *AoF* 33: 242–62.

———. 2007. "Who Were the Kaška?" *Phasis* 10: 166–81.

———. 2008a. "A Hittite-Assyrian Diplomatic Exchange in the Late 13th Century BCE." Pages 713–20 in *VI Congresso Internazionale di Ittitologia Roma, 5–9 settembre 2005*. Edited by A. Archi and R. Francia. Studi Micenei ed Egeo-Anatolici 49. Rome: CNR - Istituto de Studi sulle Civiltà dell'Egeo e del Vicino Oriente.

———. 2008b. "Purple-Dyers in Lazpa." Pp. 21–43 in *Anatolian Interfaces: Hittites, Greeks and Their Neighbors. Proceedings of an International Conference on Cross-Cultural Interaction, September 17–19, 2004, Emory University, Atlanta, GA*. Edited by B. J. Collins, M. R. Bachvarova, and I. Rutherford. Oxford: Oxbow.

Skaist, Aaron Jacob. 1998. "The Chronology of the Legal Texts from Emar." *ZA* 88: 45–71.

———. 2005. "When Did Ini-Tešub Succeed to the Throne of Carchemish?" *UF* 37: 609–19.

Sommer, Ferdinand. 1932. *Die Ahhijava-Urkunden*. ABAW 6. München: Verlag der Bayerischen Akademie der Wissenschaften.

Sommer, Ferdinand and A. Falkenstein. 1938. *Die hethitisch-akkadische Bilingue des Hattusili I. (Labarna II.)*. ABAW 16. München: Verlag der Bayerischen Akademie der Wissenschaften.

Soysal, Oğuz. 2004. *Hattischer Wortschatz in hethitischer Textüberlieferung*. HbOr 1/74. Leiden: Brill.

———. 2006. Review of J. Puhvel, *Hittite Etymological Dictionary*. Vol. 6: *Words Beginning with M*. *BiOr* 63: 560–72.

Starke, Frank. 1981a. "Die keilschrift-luwischen Wörter für Insel und Lampe." *ZvS* 95: 141–55.

———. 1981b. "Zur Deutung der Arzawa-Briefstelle VBoT 1, 25–27." *ZA* 71: 221–31.

———. 1982. "Ein Amarna-Beleg für *nbw nfr* 'gutes Gold.'" *Göttinger Miscellen* 53: 55–61.

———. 1990. *Untersuchung zur Stammbildung des keilschrift-luwischen Nomens*. StBoT 31. Wiesbaden: Harrassowitz.

———. 1992. Review of A. Hagenbuchner, *Die Korrespondenz der Hethiter*. *BiOr* 49: 804–15.

———. 1996. "Zur 'Regierung' des hethitischen Staates." *ZABR* 2: 140–82.

———. 1997. "Troia im Kontext des historisch-politischen und sprachlichen Umfeldes Kleinasiens im 2. Jahrtausend." *Studia Troica* 7: 447–87.

Stefanini, Ruggero. 1964. "Una lettera della regina Puduhepa al re di Alasija (KUB XXI 38)." *Annuaire de l'Institut de Philologie et d'Histoire Orientales et Slaves* 29: 3–69.

Stol, Marten. 1995. "Old Babylonian Corvée (*tupšikkum*)." Pages 293–309 in *Studio historiae ardens: Ancient Near Eastern Studies Presented to Philo H.J. Houwink ten Cate on the Occasion of his 65th Birthday*. Edited by T. van den Hout and J. de Roos. Leiden: Nederlands Historisch-Archaeologisch Instituut te Istanbul.

Süel, Aygül. 1992. "Ortaköy: Eine hethitische Stadt mit hethitischen und hurritischen Tontafelentdeckungen." Pages 487–92 in *Hittite and Other Anatolian and Near Eastern Studies in Honour of Sedat Alp*. Edited by H. Otten, E. Akurgal, H. Ertem, and A. Süel. Anadolu Medeniyetlerini Araştırma ve Tanıtma Vakfı Yayınları 1. Ankara: Türk Tarih Kurumu Basımevi.

———. 1995. "Ortaköy'ün Hitit çağındaki adı." *Belleten* 59: 271–83.

———. 1998a. "Ortaköy-Şapinuwa Bir Hitit Merkezi." *Turkish Academy of Sciences Journal of Archaeology* 1: 37–61.

———. 1998b. "Ortaköy-Šapinuwa tabletlerinin tarihlendirilmesi." Pages 551–58 in *Acts of the IIIrd International Congress of Hittitology. Çorum, September 16–22, 1996*. Edited by S. Alp and A. Süel. Ankara: Grafik, Teknik Hazırlık Uyum Ajans.

———. 2001. "Ortaköy tabletleri ışığına batı Anadolu ile ilgili bazı konular üzerine." Pages 670–78 in *Akten des IV. Internationalen Kongresses für Hethitologie. Würzburg, 4.–8. Oktober, 1999*. Edited by G. Wilhelm. StBoT 45. Wiesbaden: Harrassowitz.

———. 2002a. "Ortaköy-Šapinuwa." Pages 157–66 in *Recent Developments in Hittite Archaeology and History: Papers in Memory of Hans G. Güterbock*. Edited by K. A. Yener and H. A. Hoffner, Jr. Winona Lake, Ind.: Eisenbrauns.

———. 2002b. "Šapinuwa'daki kraliče hakkında." Pages 819–26 in *Anatolia Antica: Studi in memoria di Fiorella Imparati*. Edited by S. de Martino and F. Pecchioli Daddi. Firenze: LoGisma.

Symington, Dorit. 1991. "Late Bronze Age Writing-Boards and Their Uses: Textual Evidence from Anatolia and Syria." *AnSt* 41: 111–23.

Szabó, Gabriella. 1972–1975. "Herrscher … bei den Hethitern." Pages 342–45 in *Real-*

lexikon der Assyriologie. Band 4. Edited by E. Ebeling, B. Meissner, E. Weidner, W. von Soden, and D. O. Edzard. Berlin: de Gruyter.

Tadmor, Hayim. 1979. "The Decline of Empires in Westem Asia ca. 1200 B.C.E." *Symposia Celebrating the Seventy-Fifth Anniversary of the Founding of the American Schools of Oriental Research (1900–1975)*. Edited by F. M. Cross. Cambridge, Mass.: American Schools of Oriental Research.

Taggar-Cohen, Ada. 2002. "THE EZEN *pulaš*—A Hittite Installation Rite of a New Priest." *JANER* 2: 127–59.

———. 2006. *Hittite Priesthood*. THeth 26. Heidelberg: Winter.

Tani, Nicoletta. 2001. "More about the 'Hešni Conspiracy.'" *AoF* 28: 154–64.

Taracha, Piotr. 2000. *Ersetzen und Entsühnen. Das mittelhethitische Ersatzritual für den Großkönig Tuthalija (CTH *448.4) und verwandte Texte*. Leiden: Brill.

———. 2001. "Mycenaeans, Ahhiyawa and Hittite Imperial Policy in the West: A Note on KUB 26.91." Pages 417–22 in *Kulturgeschichten: Altorientalistische Studien für Volkert Haas zum 65. Geburtstag*. Edited by T. Richter, D. Prechel, and J. Klinger. Saarbrücken: Saarbrücker Druckerei.

Torri, Giulia. 2008. "The Scribes of the House on the Slope." Pages 771–82 in *VI. Congresso Internazionale di Ittitologia Roma, 5–9 settembre 2005*. Edited by A. Archi and R. Francia. SMEA 49. Rome: CNR - Istituto de Studi sulle Civiltà dell'Egeo e del Vicino Oriente.

Trémouille, Marie-Claude. 1997. *dḪebat*. Eothen 7. Florence: LoGisma.

Ünal, Ahmet. 1973. *Hattušili III: Hattušili bis zu seiner Thronbesteigung. Band II: Quellen*. THeth 4. Heidelberg: Carl Winter.

———. 1977. "Naturkatastrophen in Anatolien im 2. Jahrtausende v. Chr." *Belleten* 41 (163): 447–72.

———. 1978. *Ein Orakeltext über die Intrigen am hethitischen Hof (KUB XXII 70 = Bo 2011)*. THeth 6. Heidelberg: Carl Winter.

———. 1984. "Nochmals zur Geschichte und Lage der hethitischen Stadt Ankuwa." *SMEA* 24: 87–107.

———. 1989. "Drawings, Graffiti and Squiggles on the Hittite Tablets. Art in Scribal Circles." Pages 505–13 in *Anatolia and the Ancient Near East: Studies in Honor of Tahsin Özgüç*. Edited by K. Emre, B. Hrouda, M. Mellink, and N. Özgüç. Ankara: Türk Tarih Kurumu Basımevi.

———. 1991. "Two Peoples on Both Sides of the Aegean Sea: Did the Achaeans and the Hittites Know Each Other?" *BMECCJ* 4: 16–44.

———. 1998. *Hittite and Hurrian Cuneiform Tablets from Ortaköy (Çorum), Central Turkey*. Istanbul: Simurg.

van Gessel, Ben H. L. 1998–2001. *Onomasticon of the Hittite Pantheon. Parts 1–3*. HbOr 1. Abt., v. 33: 1–3. Leiden: Brill.

von Schuler, Einar. 1965. *Die Kaškäer*. Untersuchungen zur Assyriologie u. vorderasiatischen Archäologie. Ergänzungsbände zur Zeitschrift für Assyriologie 3. Berlin: de Gruyter.

Weidner, Ernst. 1923. *Politische Dokumente aus Kleinasien: Die Staatsverträge in akkadischer Sprache aus dem Archiv von Boghazköi*. Boghazköi-Studien 8. Leipzig: Hinrichs.

Wente, Edward. 1990. *Letters from Ancient Egypt*. WAW 1. Atlanta: Scholars Press.

Westenholz, Joan Goodnick and Jun Ikeda. 2000. *Cuneiform Inscriptions in the Collection of the Bible Lands Museum Jerusalem: The Emar Tablets*. Cuneiform Monographs 13. Groningen: Styx.

Wilhelm, Gernot. 1970. "ta/erdennu, ta/urtannu, ta/urtānu." *UF* 2: 277–82.

———. 1982. *Grundzüge der Geschichte und Kultur der Hurriter*. Darmstadt: Wissenschaftliche Buchgesellschaft.

———. 1998. "Zwei mittelhethitische Briefe aus dem Gebäude C in Kuşaklı." *MDOG* 130: 175–87.

———. 2002. "Noch einmal zur Lage von Šamuḫa." Pages 885–90 in *Anatolia Antica: Studi in memoria di Fiorella Imparati*. Edited by S. de Martino and F. Pecchioli Daddi. Firenze: LoGisma.

Wilhelm, Gernot and Johannes Boese. 1987. "Absolute Chronologie und die hethitische Geschichte des 15. und 14. Jahrhunderts vor Christus." Pages 74–117 in *High, Middle or Low?*. Edited by P. Åström. Studies in Mediterranean Archaeology and Literature. Pocket-book 56. Gothenburg, Sweden: Åströms.

Winckler, Hugo and Ludwig Abel. 1889. *Der Thontafelfund von El-Amarna*. Berlin: W. Spemann.

Wiseman, Donald J. 1953. *The Alalakh Tablets*. London: British Institute of Archaeology at Ankara.

Woolley, C. Leonard. 1939. "Excavations at Atchana-Alalakh." *Antiquaries' Journal* 19: 1–37.

Wouters, Werner. 1989. "Urḫi-Teššub and the Ramses-Letters from Boghazköy." *JCS* 41: 226–34.

Yakar, Jak. 1980. "Recent Contributions to the Historical Geography of the Hittite Empire." *MDOG* 112: 75–94.

———. 2000. *Ethnoarchaeology of Anatolia: Rural Socio-Economy in the Bronze and Iron Ages*. Institute of Archaeology Monography Series 17. Tel Aviv: Institute of Archaeology.

Yamada, Masamichi. 1998. "The Family of Zū-Ba'la the Diviner and the Hittites." Pages 323–34 in *Past Links: Studies in the Languages and Cultures of the Ancient Near East Dedicated to Professor Anson F. Rainey*. Edited by Shlomo Izre'el, Itamar Singer, and R. Zadok. IOS 18. Winona Lake, Ind.: Eisenbrauns.

———. 2006. "The Hittite Administration in Emar: The Aspect of Direct Control." *ZA* 96: 222–34.

Yoshida, Kazuhiko. 1991. "Reconstruction of Anatolian Verbal Endings: The Third Person Plural Preterites." *JIES* 19: 357–74.

Ziegler, Nele. 2001. "Correspondance." Pages 202–5 in *Dictionnaire de la civilisation mésopotamienne*. Edited by F. Joannès and C. Michel. Paris: R. Laffont.

Index of Names

Deities

^{d}É.A 61, 99, 100–102, 272, 387
^{d}Ḫalmaššuit 266
^{d}Ḫebat 234, 287, 404, 408
^{d}*IŠTAR* 287, 383
^{d}*IŠTAR* ^{URU}Šamuḫa 72
Šamaš 29, 107
^{d}Telipinu 9
^{d}U 77, 283, 287, 291–92, 295, 303, 318, 408
^{d}U ^{URU}Nerikka 72, 406
^{d}U AN-*E* 289
^{d}UD.SIG$_{5}$ 318
^{d}UTU 206, 283, 312
^{d}UTU AN-*E* 317
^{d}UTU ^{URU}TÚL-na 287, 360–61, 386

Persons

Adad-bēlī 45–46, 53, 91–92, 95, 173–74, 207, 209, 217–22
Adad-nirari I 16
Adad-šar-ilī 55
Aḫaltena 55
Akhenaten 17, 32, 55, 62, 277, 402
Alalimi 55
Alantalli 314, 316
Aliziti 55
Alziya-muwa 367–73
Amunḥotep 17, 34, 55, 61, 256, 268–69, 270–71, 273, 277, 387, 402
Amurru-ašarēd 325
Amutaru 55
Ari-Teššub 330
Arma-ziti 55, 242–43, 247, 261
Arnuwanda I 40–41, 89, 102, 119, 141, 160, 175, 179, 181, 186, 189, 270, 322
Aruḫipa 338
Arwašši 55
Ašduwarrae 208
Aššur-reṣuwa 23
Aššur-uballiṭ 62, 402
Atiuna 136, 138, 185–87, 243
Atpā 291, 293–96, 300–301, 304–7, 316, 391–92
Attaršiya 256
Awawa 84

Bēl-qarrad 55
Bentešina 15
Bulliṭ-adi 78, 80

Duddumi 86
Dūrī-Aššur 18

Ebina'e 55
Ellil-bēl-nišê 55
EN-tarawa 103–4, 238
Enlil-bēl-nišē 288, 290

GUR.$^{(d)}$LUGAL-*ma* 53

Ḫalpa-ziti 262–63
Ḫani 55
Ḫapiri 181–83
Ḫašammili 53, 56, 92, 95, 125–27, 131, 151–55
Ḫašduili 361
Ḫattuša-ziti 54
Ḫattušili (palace official) 262–63

Ḫattušili (scribe) 21, 33, 56, 73, 93–94, 115–17, 144, 145, 147, 190–94, 196–97, 230, 239–40, 243–45, 365–66
Ḫattušili I 56–57, 75–77, 79–80, 222, 401, 408
Ḫattušili III 9, 17, 25, 48, 71–72, 181, 256, 271, 282, 284, 289, 296, 298, 300, 314, 327, 331, 336, 349, 352–53, 364, 368, 386, 389, 392, 402, 406–8
Ḫešni 53, 68, 332
Ḫilanni 55, 84
Ḫimmuili 73, 92–95, 99, 102–3, 111, 115–17, 135, 141–42, 144–48, 151–58, 168, 190–206, 210, 214–17, 221, 225, 238, 378, 404
Ḫuilli 94, 201–5, 207, 210–11, 237, 248
Ḫūliya-zalmanu 257
Ḫulla 94–95, 122–25, 138, 140, 213–14, 219–20, 222, 226–27
Huziya 334

Ilali 204–5, 207
Ilī-kakkab 91
Ilī-tukultī 91, 207, 209
Iltaḫmu 55
Ini-Teššub 16
Iršappa 55
Iya 266–67

Kadašman-Enlil 15, 17, 25, 181
Kalbaya 55, 269–71
Kallu 130–32
Kašilti 204–5, 207
Kaškanu 113
Kašša 205
Kaššū 56, 63, 93–112, 115–23, 125, 127–32, 135–36, 138, 176, 198–200, 202, 216, 223–27, 230–32, 234–35, 237, 295, 340–42, 377, 380, 385, 388
Kaštanda 204–7
Kašturraḫšeli 189–90
Kuikuišanduwa 253–54
Kikarša 207
Kukuli 55
Kulana-ziti 316, 319–20
Kula-ziti 54
Kuliziya 55
Kunni 55
Kupanta-Kuruntiya 256–57
Kupanta-zalma 257
Kupapa 86
Kurkalli 55
Kurunt(iy)a 7, 305, 392
Kurunt(iy)a-ziti 82–84

Labarna II. *See* Ḫattušili I
Laḫurzi 300–301, 303
Lariya 7
Lilawanta 68
Lullu 221
Lupakki 53
Lušiwali 211–12

Madduwatta 44, 431
Manapa-Tarḫunta 291, 293–94, 316, 407
Manni 212–13
Marakui 170–71
Mār-ešrē 45–46, 53, 73, 91–92, 96, 135, 157–58, 197, 245
Mariya 181–83
Marruwa 64, 118–20
Mār-Šeruwa 53
Maša-muwa 15–16, 55
Mašḫuiluwa 88–89, 314, 321–22, 406
Mašturi 257, 407 Mar-ešrē 134, 160, 197–98, 233, 245
Mitanna-muwa 9
Mizra-muwa 55
Mizri-muwa 8
Muršili II 9, 88–89, 106, 197, 293, 299–300, 314, 321, 329, 336, 356–57, 368, 386, 389–91, 393, 402
Muršili III 300, 314, 322–23, 368
Muwattalli II 291, 293, 298, 300, 314, 322, 403
Muwatti 314, 321

Nananza 53, 365–66
Našadda 221
Nerikkaili 54–55, 176–77, 389–90
NU.GIŠ.SAR 53
NU.^{GIŠ}KIRI$_6$ 84–85
Nunnuta 67

Pallā 53, 96, 242–44
Pallanna 212–13, 224–25, 240, 242
Pazzanna 67
Pazzu 88–89, 321–22
Pigaššilta 358
Piḫašdu 55
Piḫapzuppi 113
Piḫinakki 111–13
Pikašti 54
Pipappa 95–96, 131–32, 162, 204
Pipitaḫi 124
Pirwannu 373
Pišeni 56, 95–96, 128–29, 135–41
Piššunupašši 207–8
Pittalaḫ 190
Pittalaḫša 189
Pittanipi 88
Pittaruru 168–69
Piyama-radu 256–57, 291, 293–95, 297, 300–311, 316, 318, 390–92, 406
Piyama-Tarḫu(nta) 95–96
Piyama-Tarḫunta 215–16, 330
Pizzumaki 96, 124–25
Puduḫepa 46, 48, 273, 281–82, 289–90, 327, 346–47, 364, 390, 407, 415
Pulli 4, 56, 66, 73, 95–96, 127–30, 132–34, 200, 202, 217, 380

Ramses II 16, 46, 48, 55, 273, 281, 390
Reamašši 55

Šalmaneser I 16
Samson 121, 209
Šamuḫa-ziti 346
Šanda 4, 45–46, 53, 56, 93, 96, 132–34, 203, 361, 407
Sargon II 23, 432
Šarla-LAMMA 96, 98, 178–80
Šarpa 50, 96, 193–94, 208, 210–11, 212–13, 388
Šarri-Kušuḫ 69, 403
Šaušga-muwa 55, 315
Šaušga-ziti 53, 337
Ṣillī-Aššur 55, 325
SUM-^{d}U 215–16
Šuppiluliuma 34, 40, 70, 88–89, 93, 164, 223, 256, 270, 273, 275, 277, 280, 314, 321, 340, 349, 390, 392, 401–3
Šuriḫili 53, 56, 91–92, 96, 99–100, 101, 238

Taduḫepa 17, 102, 404
Taḫazzili 94, 96, 207, 213, 221, 377
Taki-Šarruma 332, 345
Takuḫli 55
Tapala-Tarḫunta 301, 307
Tapalazunawali 402
Tarḫumimma 96, 138, 185, 218
Tarḫu-muwa 96, 204–6
Tarḫuni 210
Tarḫunmiya 8, 45, 49, 51, 53, 95–97, 111, 117–18, 141, 144, 146, 148, 190, 193–95, 204, 211–14, 218, 227, 229–30, 238–42
Tarḫunta-radu 61, 256–57, 270–71, 273, 275, 315, 402
Tarkašnatalana 335–37
Tarkašnawa 313–16
Taruppišni 361
Taškuwanni 84
Tatta 68, 94, 138, 140
Tawagalawa 46, 52, 296–97, 299–302, 305, 307, 315, 353, 389–90, 392, 407–8
Tazzukuli 99
Telipinu (king) 7, 77
Tiglath-pileser III 18
Tiḫi-Teššub 55
Tili-Teššub 55
Tippurrui 190
Tudḫaliya 374
Tudḫaliya I/II 290, 292
Tudḫaliya III 34, 40, 64, 88–89, 102, 119, 256, 322
Tudḫaliya IV 7, 60, 313–16, 323–25, 327, 331–32, 347, 353, 364, 392
Tukulti-Ninurta I 16, 323–24
Tumna-ziti 85
Tumnī 85
Tunip-Teššub (Tuniya) 75, 80, 408
Tuttuwaili 85
Tuwā 88–89
Tuwazzi 218

Uḫḫa-muwa 49, 255–56

Uḫḫa-waranu 257
Uḫḫa-ziti 314
Urapa-^{d}U 55
Ura-Tarḫunta 331
Urḫi-Teššub 71–72, 283, 300, 314, 322, 368
^{md}U-SIG$_5$ 84
Uzzū 4, 51, 53, 56, 96–97, 99, 100–102, 116, 126–27, 131, 133–35, 154–55, 157–58, 160, 168, 196–98, 229–30, 233, 238, 240, 242

Walmu 316, 319, 408
Walwanu 53
Wandapa-ziti 55

Yarappiya 211–12

Zaldumanni/Zardumanni 160–61, 210–11, 224, 382
Zidašdu 82–84
Zilapiya 94–95, 97, 120–23, 125–26, 169–70, 225, 237
Zimri-Līm 5, 16, 28, 408–9
Zinupi 55
Ziti 86, 376
Zitwalla 55
Zu-Baʿla 367–72
Zuwa 53, 55, 258
Zuwanna 221
Zuzu 55

Places

Aḫḫiyawa 46, 48, 71, 290–92, 296–301, 304–5, 308, 310, 315, 352–53, 389–90, 392
Alabanda 390
Alalakh 39, 42, 63, 179, 372–74
Aleppo 16, 76
Amarna 15, 20, 22, 29–30, 34–35, 37, 39, 42, 46, 48, 57, 62–63, 255, 268–69, 273, 351, 396
Amurru 15, 55, 286, 288, 315, 427
Ankuwa 86, 347–48, 376
Anziliya 159, 187, 199–200
Appawiya 391
Arinna 315–16, 320
Aruḫipa 338
Arzawa 21, 42, 55, 256, 268–75, 293, 300, 314, 352–53, 387
Arziya 81, 83
Aššaranda 344
Aššur 19, 50, 55, 59
Aššuwa 290, 292
Assyria 2, 16, 19–20, 34–35, 48, 64, 283, 315, 322–24, 332, 350–52, 392, 402–9, 421, 432
Aštata 367, 369, 404
Ašuwa 256
Atriya 303, 316, 318, 320
Attarimma 69, 256, 300, 302, 313, 389
Awarna 320
Awina 256

Cappadocia 19, 271, 275
Carchemish 16, 23, 55, 63, 71, 332–34, 367–68, 371–73, 401, 403–4
Ceyhan River 76

Dankuwa 68, 366

Egypt 1–4, 6, 13, 17, 19–24, 26, 31–32, 35–37, 42, 46, 54–55, 65, 70, 181, 268–70, 272, 275, 278, 280–82, 288–90, 315, 338, 352–54, 388, 390, 392, 395–96, 402–3, 406, 415, 428, 430, 436
Emar 30, 39, 42–43, 53, 179, 193, 367–69, 403
Euphrates 76, 81, 323, 403–4, 406

Ḫaḫḫum 76, 78–80
Ḫaninkawa 199
Ḫanikkawa 201
Ḫanziwa 259–61
Ḫapara 105, 138, 171
Ḫappuriya 256–57
Ḫariya 199, 201, 214
Ḫaššarpanda 204–5
Ḫaššum 76
Ḫatti 8, 15, 20–22, 24–25, 30, 41, 59, 70, 76–77, 189, 228, 274, 280, 282, 286–87, 289, 291, 293–94, 302, 305–8, 310–11, 316–17, 321–24,

335, 352–53, 357–58, 368, 387, 392, 395
Ḫattuša 1, 8, 39, 41–44, 46, 48–49, 53, 58, 73, 80–81, 85–86, 92–97, 100, 110, 117, 121–23, 125, 131, 133–35, 144, 152–54, 166, 190, 203, 222, 227, 230, 242–45, 253, 261, 268–69, 276, 281, 291, 321, 332, 336, 340, 345–46, 352–53, 356–58, 362, 364–65, 371, 387, 392, 404–5
Ḫawalta 233
Ḫimmuwa 93, 118–19
Ḫupišna 187
Ḫuršanašša 69

Išaš 381
Išḫupitta 112–15, 128–29, 132, 149–50, 228, 236–37
Išteruwa 173–74
Išuwa 331
Iyalanda (Alinda) 301–4, 391

Kakattuwa 120
Kalzana 139–40, 190
Kammamma 67
Kammammanda 94, 213
Kapapaḫšuwa 124–25
Kappazuwa 348
Kappušiya 109
Karaḫna 124–25, 228, 250
Kašaša 40, 97–98, 103, 145, 156, 163, 179–80
Kašepura 40, 103, 105, 130, 137–40, 150, 156, 171–72, 198, 200, 217, 381
Kaška, Kaškaeans 64, 82, 91, 94–95, 98, 104, 107, 109–15, 119–21, 125, 130, 136–37, 143, 149, 164, 169, 173–74, 176, 198, 220–21, 223, 227, 276, 357, 377
Kikarša 207
Kizzuwatna 52, 58, 234–36, 284
Kummaḫa 256
Kummanni 346
Kuršamma 256
Kurupaššiya 136
Kušaklı 36, 39, 42–43, 265. *See also* Šarišša
Kušpišša 84
Kuwaliya 256, 314, 321, 402, 406. *See also* Mira

Lalanda 256, 348–49
Lašti[…] 362–63
Lawanta 256
Lazpa 291, 293–94
Lišipra 111–15, 121, 378
Lukka Lands 300
Lycia 300

Malazziya 105, 179–80, 217
Maraša 255–57
Maraššantiya 243
Marišta 124–25, 137, 139–40, 355
Mari 5–7, 16, 18, 20–21, 24–25, 28, 43–44, 52, 54, 61, 66–67, 189–90, 255, 385, 402–3, 405, 407–9
Maša 256, 310–11, 314, 350
Maşat Höyük 1, 7, 36, 39–40, 42, 53, 91, 97, 168, 252, 272, 387. *See also* Tapikka
Millawanda 291–93, 299–301, 304–5, 308, 311, 313, 315–16, 319–20, 390–92, 406
Mira 89, 299, 313–16, 321, 377, 402, 406. *See also* Kuwaliya
Mittanni 24, 34, 71
Mt. Ammana 323
Mt. Arinnanda 69
Mt. Ḫaluna 253–55
Mt. Šaktunuwa 173, 228

Nerik 72
Niḫriya 76, 78, 80
Ninišankuwa 228

Ortaköy 36, 42–43, 49, 91, 191, 243, 252–57, 259, 262, 300. *See also* Šapinuwa

Panāta 142, 179–80, 219, 221, 223
Papanḫi 324–26
Partuwata 256
Paštuwatuwa 221
Pina 320
Pišatenitišša 179–80

Pitašša 257
Pittalaḫšuwa 189–90
Pitteyariga 81–83
Puranta 69

Šaḫurunuwa 7, 95–96, 223–24, 250, 309, 364
Šaktunuwa (Mt.) 228
Šallapa 256, 300, 302
Šamuḫa 72, 81–83, 346, 348
Šanaḫuitta 139
Šapinuwa 1, 36, 43, 49, 91, 100, 117, 122, 132, 177, 191, 193, 198, 207–8, 210–11, 215, 252–54, 259, 261, 340, 386. *See also* Ortaköy
Šarišša 1, 36, 42, 185, 262. *See also* Kuşaklı
Šeḫa River Land 291, 293, 314–16, 402, 407
Šipišaši 179–80
Šuppiluliya 213
Šuruta 69

Taḫara River Land 358
Taḫašara 200
Taḫazzimuna 98, 138, 145, 152, 171
Takkašta 105–7, 125, 179–81
Takša 137
Talmaliya 249, 356, 386
Tankuwa. *See* Dankuwa
Tapallazunawalli 402
Taparukka 351
Tapašpa 68
Tapḫallu 176–77
Tapikka 1, 7, 19, 47–49, 56, 58, 62–64, 66, 72, 91–98, 102, 110–12, 116–17, 119, 121–22, 125, 131–35, 138, 143, 146, 150, 159–60, 164, 173, 175, 179–80, 184, 188, 190–91, 193, 198–200, 203, 207, 215, 219–21, 230, 235, 243–46, 248, 252, 261, 270, 340, 380, 404–8. *See also* Maşat Höyük
Tarḫuntašša 7, 60, 283, 314, 349, 389, 392, 403
Tarḫuntišša 93, 242–43
Tattašša 354
Tawaštiya 358
Tikunani 75–76, 78–80, 408
Tiwara 251
Tumanta 256

Uda 86, 271, 350
Ugarit 16, 21–22, 26, 28–30, 34, 39, 55–56, 60, 332, 352, 363, 381, 389, 393, 401, 404, 408
Ukuduipuna 107
Ura 362–63
Urišta 205
Uršapikannuwa 139
Uršum 76–77
Ušša 361
Utima 316, 318, 320

Waliwanda 301–2
Wiluša 293–94, 298, 300, 311, 314, 316, 319, 402

Yazılıkaya 61

Zalpa 78, 80, 189
Zaruna 256
Zikkašta 234–35
Zikkatta 114–15
Zimmala 255
Zišpa 173–74
Zulabi 283
Zuliya River 173

Index of Subjects

A

Abduction (of a slave) 204, 206
Agriculture 66, 200. *See also* Crops; Famine; Food shortages; Plowing; Seed; Seed grain; Silos; Sowing; Vineyards
Akkadian 3, 9, 11, 13–14, 21, 25–26, 29–30, 34, 36–39, 42, 44, 46, 48, 50, 52, 53, 56–57, 60–62, 66–67, 75–77, 91–92, 160–61, 164, 182, 194, 199, 206–207, 209, 219, 222, 230–32, 268–69, 272–73, 340, 352, 369, 372, 377, 382, 387, 389, 393–95, 401, 404–5, 408
Allative case 108
Ambassadors 14, 16, 290
  as intelligence agents 15
Ancestral gods 321–22
Animal metaphors 77
  birds 77
  snake 77
Anointing 274, 329
Appeals to the king 194
Arrest warrants 118
Aruwai- 30, 371, 395
Arzawa Letters 268–69
Aššur dossier 49
Augurs 84–85, 179–80, 263, 265–66
Augury 84, 263. *See also* Birds of agitation; Divination

B

Behind the city 385–86
Birds
  as food 373, 396
  of agitation 184, 263–64. *See also* Augury
Blessing formulas 61
Blinding, blind persons 119–21, 123, 150–51, 161, 208, 210, 247, 378–79
  as punishment for treason 119
Blood relationship 117, 129, 271, 299
Boats, flat-bottomed
  transporting goods in shallow rivers 81
Booty 64, 79–80, 164, 188
Border crossings 63–64
Bridge building 231
Briefing documents 46, 48, 297
Bulls 77–78, 325–26

C

Captives 64
Casualties 64
Cattle 64, 66, 68, 95, 102–4, 114–15, 124, 175, 177, 198–200, 283–84, 396
Chariots, Charioteers 171, 284, 301, 307–8
Climate 65
Colophons 9–11, 44–45, 52, 298, 312, 389, 403
Correspondence. *See* Letters; Oral correspondence
Correspondents 20
  identified only by title 58
  relative social status or rank 20, 57, 273
Couriers 14, 16, 24, 53–54, 135, 321, 366, 396
Courts, regional 117

Crops 64–66, 91, 94–95, 103, 109–10, 125, 128, 130, 133, 140, 180, 187, 196, 221–22, 249–50
Crown prince 64, 301–2, 305, 389–90, 392, 406

D

Dating of texts 39, 61, 80–81, 84, 86, 89, 138, 141, 175, 179, 181, 185–86, 189, 270, 298
Dead 291
  letters to 3
  spirits of 259–60
Deeds of Šuppiluliuma I 81, 419
Diplomatic passports 392. *See also* Letters of safe conduct
Diplomats. *See* Ambassadors; Messengers
Divination 3, 24, 48, 179. *See also* Augurs; Augury; Oracular inquiries
Dogs 77–78, 271
Double-saying formula 57
Dowry 282–83, 290, 396
Dreams 24, 262–63
Drought 65–66
Ductus 39, 75, 89, 95, 347, 373

E

Edomite letter 57
Envelopes, tablet 10, 34–35, 46–47
Epictetus 375
Erasures 34, 84, 107–8, 165, 315
Eunuchs 64, 281, 284
Extradition 314
Enemy activity 64–65

F

Family relationship terms 10, 20, 58–59
  Father 10, 20, 27, 40, 53, 58, 71, 89, 151–52, 159, 212–14, 240, 241, 242, 244–45, 256, 270, 277–81, 286, 305, 316–18, 320, 324–25, 331, 368
  Mother 20, 27, 59–60, 213, 240–42, 293, 324, 327–28, 347
Famine 65, 108, 137, 139, 188, 340, 363
Favors 73, 202, 236, 272, 299, 323, 334, 384, 390
Food shortages. *See* famine
Foxes 77, 79, 375
Fugitives 88, 95, 110–11, 120, 137–38, 164, 176, 214, 256–57, 309, 318, 393

G

Gift giving 353
Governmental structure of the kingdom, three-tiered 117
Great King 18, 71, 77, 179, 273–75, 282, 286, 291, 299, 303, 305–6, 309, 312, 315, 323–24, 359, 390–92
Greeting gifts 16, 278–80, 352–54

H

Ḫalkueššar 81–82
Ḫapirū 76, 182
Historical texts 69–72
Hittite language 21, 36, 42, 48, 63, 232, 269, 352
Horn 78, 80
Horse hairs 78
Horses 17, 34, 73, 78, 94, 99, 111, 130, 145, 147, 168, 172, 175–76, 217–21, 223, 247–48, 344, 352, 395
  chariot 111
Hospitality 32, 392
Hostages 93, 114, 119, 121, 150–51, 177–78, 219, 221, 251, 256, 301, 316, 320, 392
Humor 63

I

Ice 19, 63, 65, 355
Illness 6, 9, 89, 108, 243, 245, 265, 294, 321, 338, 347, 355
Information gathering 15, 255
International correspondence 10–11, 14, 21–22, 34, 273, 402
  intercepted 25

languages used in 21
uninterrupted 16
Irony 62, 121
Islands 290–91, 293–94, 298–99, 301

J

Judging 205, 207

K

Karabel inscription 314

L

Letter carriers. *See* Couriers
Letter corpora
Egypt 35
El-Amarna 34
Ugarit 34–35
Letter-prayers 3
Letters. *See also* Correspondence
above-the-line additions 34
address line 25, 272
body of 61–63
censoring of 21
change of subject in 25
cover letters 20, 253–54
dating of 39–41
definition of 2
drafts 10, 21, 36, 48–49, 58, 297, 322, 324, 362
duplicates 48–49
envelopes 10, 34, 46–47
find spots 8, 39, 41, 44
format of 25, 44–48, 56, 61
formulas 26, 30–34, 50, 57, 61–63
address 25–27, 56–59, 79, 91, 273, 321, 331, 347, 404
blessing 61
greeting 25, 28–29, 56, 59–61, 245
gestures 29–30
humor and hyperbole in 62–63
intercepted 25
language of 3–4, 21
materials used 6–7
model 11
multiple addressees in 58
multiple topics in 33
outward appearance of 44
period of retention 6
piggyback 11, 20–21, 36, 52, 56–57, 66, 72–73, 85, 93, 95–96, 99–102, 111, 115–16, 125–29, 131, 133, 135, 144–48, 151–54, 157, 160, 166, 168, 194, 197, 204, 207, 209, 212, 214, 218, 227, 229, 231, 233, 240, 242, 245, 248, 258, 261, 272, 328–30, 244, 362, 374, 380
postscripts 72
preliminary drafts or notes 10, 21
private 13, 20
proofreading of 34
quoting previous letters 33, 67
reading aloud 50–51
rebukes in 62
requests in 4, 72–73, 130, 135, 145, 153, 158, 341
of safe conduct 24, 46
sarcasm in 62, 104, 123, 202, 227
size of 6, 46
subjects of 63–66
terminology for 49–50
to/from a god 3, 24
to the dead 3
types of 21–25
Lions 75, 77–78, 375
Literacy 4–5
Israelite 51
Livestock 66, 94–96, 103, 165, 175–76, 188, 396
Locusts 65–66, 130
Logograms 14, 38, 401
Lukka people 302
Luwian language 36, 50, 54, 59, 86, 184, 232, 268, 272, 274, 280–81, 336, 384
Luzzi 93–94, 146, 164, 192–95, 211, 239, 367–70, 372

M

Marriage 269–75, 281, 284–86, 289–90, 314, 321, 323, 364–65, 388

Mār šipri 14, 53, 405
Maşat correspondence 38, 48, 50, 58, 62–64, 66, 91–93, 105, 108, 114, 122–23, 129, 179, 225, 243, 245, 252, 270, 378, 381
  chronology of 40
Mayor 265–66
Messages
  inaccurate or false 5
  oral 5
  secure 5
Messengers 1, 2, 14–18, 22, 25, 27, 35–36, 53–55, 93, 146, 195, 199–202, 221, 223, 271, 278, 280, 282–86, 288, 299, 333, 388, 396
  duration of service 15
  international 15
  merchants as 24
  pairs 15
  required character traits 15
  risks and dangers 16
  traveling 16
Mill houses 208

N

NAM.RA-people 68–69, 76, 112, 114, 121, 139–40, 164–65, 235, 283–84, 304, 309–10, 383, 391, 402, 406, 411

O

Oaths 114, 208, 379
Oracle birds 84
Oracular inquiries 18–19, 263. *See also* Divination
  countercheck 263, 265
Oral correspondence 4–5
  accuracy of 5, 52
  greetings 4
Orphans 206
Oxen 78–79, 91, 109, 150, 259–60

P

Pain 61, 257
  backache 258
  headache 258
Palace 7, 20, 25, 43, 85, 116–17, 137, 139, 164, 190–92, 195–96, 198–99, 201, 208, 215, 235–36, 241, 250, 252, 263–64, 299, 321, 330, 340, 346, 366, 386, 403
  regional 117
Paleography 75, 298
Peace 54, 64, 111–14, 227, 249, 274, 311, 386
Personnel. *See* Couriers; Messengers; Scribes; Royal secretary
Pidgin language 54
Plague 130, 185, 187–88, 197, 358
Plowing 199
Political Testament 77
Postal system 13
Prisoners 164, 208, 301, 315, 396
Prosopography 39
Punishments
  beheading 52
  blinding 119
  for falsification 52
Purification ritual 259, 261

Q

Quivers 197–98, 203. *See also* Weapons
Quote within a quote 82, 125, 176

R

Ransom 120–21, 208
Refugees 111
Rhyta 40, 353
River traffic 81
Roads 18–19, 124, 177, 227, 259–60, 379
Routes of travel 19, 76, 176
Royal secretary 20–21, 190

S

Sacrilege 259–60
Safe conduct 301, 305, 307, 308. *See also* Diplomatic passports
  letters guaranteeing 24, 46

Šaḫḫan 93–94, 146, 164, 190–95, 211, 239, 367–72
Sammeltafel 12, 49
Sarcasm. *See* Letters, sarcasm in
Scouts, scouting 64, 105, 107, 366
Scribes 3–10, 13, 16, 21, 35–36, 42, 44–45, 49, 52–63, 72, 75, 93, 100, 116, 192–93, 209, 243, 269, 272–73, 299, 337, 351, 365, 373, 405, 408
  administrators and generals as 5, 7
  family or social background 7
  hierarchy 10
  noms de plume 209
  novice 10
  patron deity of 61
  supervisor 44
  titles of 7, 10
  training of 8, 12, 242, 335
  translation by 11
  traveling 8, 11
  writing-board 7
Seal impressions 40, 47, 102, 119
Seals, sealings 6, 8, 10, 16, 40, 46, 64, 102, 392, 404
Seed 87, 96, 128–29, 139, 165, 172, 198–200, 202, 214, 239
Sexual offence 260
Sheepfolds 124–25, 149–50
Ships 82–83, 315, 362–63, 375
Siege 104
Silos, underground 128
Snow 18–19, 65, 355
Sorcery 261
Sowing 94, 199, 201
Stylus, tablet 229–30

T

Tablets 44–48
  baskets for transport of 55
  envelopes of 46
  pillow-shaped 46
  reading aloud 9
  storage of 8
TARTENU 389–90
Tawagalawa Letter 256, 296, 315, 392, 407–8
Tax collectors 193
Tax records 193
Telipinu Proclamation 80
Thousand Gods 60, 212–13, 240–41, 327, 408
Threats of punishment 118–20, 123
Trade 14, 19, 59, 81, 277, 299, 315, 403
Travel, Traveling 8, 11, 16, 18, 24, 43, 125, 143, 395. *See also* Routes of travel
  conveying perishables 373
  itineraries 19, 85, 256, 395
  by the king 49
  protection during 17
  by sea 299
  Tapikka to Ḫattuša 125
Treason 119–21
  punishment for 119
Tribes. *See* Kaška, Kaškaeans
Tribute 22
Tuḫkanti- 389–90

U

Ur III period 9
dUTU-*ŠI* (royal title) 28, 57, 60, 68, 88, 97–98, 100, 102–3, 105–7, 110, 112–13, 116–23, 127–28, 130, 132, 134–35, 137–38, 140, 144, 149, 154, 156, 158, 161, 163, 167, 174–75, 177–78, 180, 183, 185–87, 190, 201, 208, 212, 216, 218, 223, 225, 243, 253–54, 256–58, 262, 272, 275, 277, 284, 294–95, 302, 316–20, 322, 325, 327, 329, 331–34, 338–39, 342, 344–46, 349–51, 357–62, 372, 374, 383, 405

V

Vassals 16, 28, 35, 75–77, 79, 291, 293, 299–300, 302, 314–16, 319, 323
Vineyards 66, 94, 98, 102, 156, 161, 163, 166

W

Warrants for arrest 118
Weapons 197, 203. *See also* Quivers
Weather conditions 65
Widows 206
Winter 18, 66, 124, 165, 284
Writing boards 2, 6, 8, 10, 50, 68, 283, 319, 408
Writing direction 44
Writing materials 6–8

www.ingramcontent.com/pod-product-compliance
Lightning Source LLC
Chambersburg PA
CBHW021113300426
44113CB00006B/137
9781589832121